Coasts and seas of the United Kingdom

Region 11 The Western Approaches: Falmouth Bay to Kenfig

edited by
J.H. Barne, C.F. Robson, S.S. Kaznowska, J.P. Doody,
N.C. Davidson & A.L. Buck

Joint Nature Conservation Committee
Monkstone House, City Road
Peterborough PE1 1JY
UK

This volume has been produced by the Coastal Directories Project of the JNCC
on behalf of the project Steering Group and
supported by WWF-UK.

JNCC Coastal Directories Project Team

Project directors	Dr J.P. Doody, Dr N.C. Davidson
Project management and co-ordination	J.H. Barne, C.F. Robson
Editing and publication	S.S. Kaznowska, J.C. Brooksbank, A.L. Buck
Administration & editorial assistance	C.A. Smith, R. Keddie, J. Plaza, S. Palasiuk, N.M. Stevenson

The project receives guidance from a Steering Group which has more than 200 members. More detailed information and advice came from the members of the Core Steering Group, which is composed as follows:

Dr J.M. Baxter	*Scottish Natural Heritage*
R.J. Bleakley	*Department of the Environment, Northern Ireland*
R. Bradley	*The Association of Sea Fisheries Committees of England and Wales*
Dr J.P. Doody	*Joint Nature Conservation Committee*
B. Empson	*Environment Agency*
Dr K. Hiscock	*Joint Nature Conservation Committee*
C. Gilbert	*Kent County Council & National Coasts and Estuaries Advisory Group*
Prof. S.J. Lockwood	*MAFF Directorate of Fisheries Research*
C.R. Macduff-Duncan	*Esso UK (on behalf of the UK Offshore Operators Association)*
Dr D.J. Murison	*Scottish Office Agriculture, Environment & Fisheries Department*
Dr H.J. Prosser	*Welsh Office*
Dr J.S. Pullen	*WWF-UK (World Wide Fund for Nature)*
N. Hailey	*English Nature*
Dr P.C. Reid	*Plymouth Marine Laboratory*
Dr M.J. Roberts	*Water Resources and Marine, Department of the Environment*
S.L. Soffe	*Countryside Council for Wales*
M.L. Tasker	*Joint Nature Conservation Committee*
R.G. Woolmore	*Countryside Commission*

Recommended citation for this volume:

Barne, J.H., Robson, C.F., Kaznowska, S.S., Doody, J.P., Davidson, N.C., & Buck, A.L., *eds*. 1996. *Coasts and seas of the United Kingdom. Region 11 The Western Approaches: Falmouth Bay to Kenfig*. Peterborough, Joint Nature Conservation Committee. (Coastal Directories Series.)

Recommended citation for a chapter in this volume (example):

Davidson, N.C. 1996. Chapter 4.1 Estuaries. *In: Coasts and seas of the United Kingdom. Region 11 The Western Approaches: Falmouth Bay to Kenfig*, ed. by J.H. Barne, C.F. Robson, S.S. Kaznowska, J.P. Doody, N.C. Davidson & A.L. Buck, 63-67. Peterborough, Joint Nature Conservation Committee. (Coastal Directories Series.)

Region 1: ISBN 1 873701 75 6
Region 2: ISBN 1 873701 76 4
Region 3: ISBN 1 873701 77 2
Region 4: ISBN 1 873701 78 0
Region 5: ISBN 1 873701 79 9
Region 6: ISBN 1 873701 80 2
Region 7: ISBN 1 873701 81 0
Region 8: ISBN 1 873701 82 9
Region 9: ISBN 1 873701 83 7
Region 10: ISBN 1 873701 84 5
Region 11: ISBN 1 873701 85 3
Region 12: ISBN 1 873701 86 1
Region 13: ISBN 1 873701 87 x
Region 14: ISBN 1 873701 88 8
Regions 15 & 16: ISBN 1 873701 89 6
Region 17: ISBN 1 873701 92 6

Set of 17 regions: ISBN 1 873701 91 8

Contents

Foreword

Information is vital for sound policy formulation. Decision makers at national and local level need to know more than just the scale, location and importance of natural resources that are of value to humans. They have to understand how human activities affect the value of those resources and how to conduct those activities in an environmentally sustainable way. This is true for virtually every activity that impinges on the natural environment. In the coastal zone the complexity of the relationships between the physical and biological systems adds another dimension to the problems of formulating management policy.

I am pleased, therefore, to be introducing the *Coasts and seas of the United Kingdom* series. The Coastal Directories project, of which this series of seventeen regional reports, covering the whole of the UK coast, is an important product, has brought together an encyclopaedic range of information on our coastal resources and the human activities that are associated with them. Amongst the topics covered are the basic geology of the coasts around the United Kingdom and measures taken for coast defence and sea protection, the distribution and importance of the wildlife and habitats of our coasts and seas, including fish and fisheries, and the climate and sea level changes to which they all are subject.

In addition to the value of the information itself, the way the project has been run and the data collected has made an important contribution to the quality of the product. A wide range of individuals and organisations concerned with the conservation and use of the coastal margin have collaborated in collating the information, their variety reflecting the extent of the interplay between the coastal environment and human activities. These organisations included the Ministry of Agriculture, Fisheries and Food, the Scottish Office, the Department of the Environment (Northern Ireland), the National Rivers Authority (now the Environment Agency), the Countryside Commission, the Welsh Office, the Department of the Environment, the Sea Fisheries Committees, English Nature, Scottish Natural Heritage and the Countryside Council for Wales, together with local authorities, voluntary conservation organisations and private companies (notably those in the oil industry, through the UK Offshore Operators Association). I am also pleased to be able to acknowledge the contribution made by the staff of the Joint Nature Conservation Committee. As the work has evolved since the first meetings of the Steering Group in 1990, the value of involving such a broad span of interests has been highlighted by the extent to which it has allowed new approaches and information sources to be identified.

The regional reports will be of value to all who live and work in the maritime areas of the UK, where informed management is the key to the sustainable use of resources. The reports should become indispensable reference sources for organisations shouldering new or expanded responsibilities for the management of Special Areas of Conservation under the EC Habitats Directive. In addition, the reports will make an important contribution to the implementation of the UK Biodiversity Action Plan.

Selborne

The Earl of Selborne
Chairman, Joint Nature Conservation Committee

How to use this book

These notes provide some general guidance about finding and interpreting the information in this book.

Structure

The book is divided into ten chapters, each split into sections containing summary data on the topics shown in the Contents list. Chapter 2 provides a general physical background to the region. Sections in Chapters 3, 4 and 5 have been compiled to the following standard format:

- **Introduction**: presents the important features of the topic as it relates to the region and sets the region in a national context.
- **Important locations and species**: gives more detail on the region's features in relation to the topic.
- **Human activities**: describes management and other activities that can have an effect on the resource in the region.
- **Information sources used**: describes the sources of information, including surveys, on which the section is based, and notes any limitations on their use or interpretation.
- **Acknowledgements**
- **Further sources of information**: lists references cited, recommended further reading, and names, addresses and telephone numbers of contacts able to give more detailed information.

Sections in the remaining chapters all have the last three subsections and follow the other elements as closely as practicable, given their subject nature.

At the end of the book there is a list of the addresses and telephone numbers of organisations most frequently cited as contacts, as well as a core reading list of books that cover the region or the subject matter particularly well. Finally there is a full list of authors' names and addresses.

Definitions and contexts

The word 'region' (as in 'Region 11') is used throughout this book to refer to the coastal and nearshore zone, broadly defined, between the two points given in the title of this book. The area covered varies between chapter sections, depending on the form in which data are available. Coverage is usually either coastal 10 km squares, sites within one kilometre of Mean High Water Mark, or an offshore area that may extend out to the median line between the UK and neighbouring states. Inland areas of the counties concerned are not included unless specifically stated. Information is presented in the context of the local authority units existing before April 1996, except where data are very recent, making reference to the new local authority units possible.

'Britain' here means Great Britain, i.e. including only England, Scotland and Wales. 'United Kingdom' also includes Northern Ireland.

The term 'North Sea Coast', as used here, means the coast of Britain covered by *The directory of the North Sea coastal margin* (Doody, Johnston & Smith 1993): that is, from Cape Wrath (longitude 5°W) along the east and south coasts of Britain to Falmouth (again longitude 5°W), and including Orkney and Shetland.

The 'West Coast', as used here, normally includes the coast and seas from Falmouth to Cape Wrath along the west coast of Britain. Only where explicitly stated have data for the Isle of Man and / or Northern Ireland been included in West Coast descriptions.

Sites within each chapter section are described in clockwise order around the coast, incorporating islands within the sequence. Maps and tables are numbered sequentially within their chapter section; for example in section 5.4, Map 5.4.1 is the first map referred to and Table 5.4.2 is the second table.

Throughout the book, the information given is a summary of the best available knowledge. The sites mentioned as important, the numbers and distributions of species, archaeological features discovered and information on all the other elements of the natural and man-made environment are as known at December 1994, unless otherwise stated. The fact that no information is presented about a topic in relation to a locality should not be taken to mean that there are no features of interest there, and fuller details should be sought from the further sources of information listed at the end of each section. Note, however, that under the Environmental Information Regulations (1992; Statutory Instrument No. 3240) you may be asked to pay for information provided by organisations.

Acknowledgements

This regional report is one of a series of products from the Coastal Directories Project of the JNCC. The compilation and publication of the series has been made possible by generous contributions from the members of the Coastal Directories Funding Consortium, listed below:

Arco British Ltd[1]
Ards District Council
Avon County Council
Banff and Buchan District Council
BHP Petroleum Ltd[1]
Ceredigion District Council
Cheshire County Council
Chevron UK Ltd[1]
Cleveland County Council
Clwyd County Council
Clyde River Purification Board
Colwyn Borough Council
Copeland Borough Council
Countryside Commission
Countryside Council For Wales
Cumbria County Council
Cunninghame District Council
Delyn Borough Council
Department of the Environment (DoE)
DoE (Northern Ireland) Environment & Heritage Service
DoE (Northern Ireland) Water Service
Derry City Council
Devon County Council
Dorset County Council
Down District Council
Dumfries and Galloway Regional Council
Dyfed County Council
Eastbourne Borough Council
English Nature
Essex County Council
Fife Regional Council
Forest of Dean District Council
Gwynedd County Council
Hampshire County Council
Highland River Purification Board
Humber Forum
Isle of Man Government, Department of Industry
Isle of Man Government, Department of Local Government and the Environment
Isle of Man Government, Department of Transport
Kyle and Carrick District Council
Lancashire County Council
Lincolnshire County Council
Marathon Oil UK Ltd[1]
Ministry of Agriculture, Fisheries and Food Directorate of Fisheries Research
National Rivers Authority
Neath Borough Council
Newry and Mourne District Council
Newtownabbey Borough Council
Norfolk County Council
North Cornwall District Council
North East Fife District Council
Nuclear Electric plc
Preseli Pembrokeshire District Council
Restormel Borough Council
Samara Consulting
SCOPAC (Standing Conference on Problems Associated with the Coastline)
Scottish Natural Heritage
Scottish Office Agriculture, Environment and Fisheries Department
Scottish Salmon Growers Association Ltd
Sefton Borough Council
Shepway District Council
Solway River Purification Board
Somerset County Council
South Pembrokeshire District Council
Standing Conference on Regional Policy In South Wales
Stroud District Council
Tayside Regional Council
Torridge District Council
UK Offshore Operators Association[2]
Vale of Glamorgan Borough Council
Water Services Association
Welsh Office
World Wide Fund For Nature (UK)

Notes

[1]Funding from these companies was given to the Cardigan Bay Forum to fund the supply of information to the Project.

[2]The UK Offshore Operators Association is the representative organisation for the British offshore oil and gas industry. Its 34 members are the companies licensed by HM Government to explore for and produce oil and gas in UK waters.

This collaborative project involves many other branches of JNCC in addition to the project team listed on page 2. These are: Marine Conservation Branch (Keith Hiscock, Tim Hill, Bill Sanderson), Vertebrate Ecology and Conservation Branch (Deirdre Craddock, David Stroud, Alan Law, Becci May, Steve Gibson), Species Conservation Branch (Nick Hodgetts, Deborah Procter, Martin Wigginton), and Seabirds and Cetaceans Branch (Mark Tasker, Andy Webb). We thank them all for their help and support.

The project has also received widespread support from the country conservation agencies: Countryside Council for Wales, English Nature, Scottish Natural Heritage and the Department of the Environment (Northern Ireland). We are grateful to the many regional and headquarters staff listed below as well as the representatives on the Core Steering Group.

Special thanks for consultation on this volume go to Sam Davies of English Nature and Joan Edwards and Mike Camplin of the Devon Wildlife Trust. The editors would also like to thank the many people who have provided information for the project or gave their time to comment on drafts, as well as those who gave editorial assistance:

Miran Aprahamian, EA; Tricia Bradley, RSPB; Alastair Burn, EN; Peter Cranswick, The Wildfowl and Wetlands Trust; Kaja Curry, Project Explore Manager; Ben Ferrari, National Monuments Records Centre; Tony Gent, EN; David George, Natural History Museum; Wells Grogan, Marathon Oil; Paul Harding, Institute of Terrestrial Ecology; Duncan Huggett, RSPB; Graham King, National Coasts and Estuaries Advisory Group; Colin Macduff-Duncan, ESSO; Tony Murray, The Crown Estate; Frank Parrish, The Crown Estate; Pauline Simpson, Institute of Oceanographic Sciences; Chris Stroud, Whale and Dolphin Conservation Society; Chris Vivian, MAFF; Jeremy Williams, Dodman-Fal Estuary Countryside Service; and Sarah Welton, Marine Conservation Society.

Where appropriate, individual acknowledgements are given also at the end of each section.

The island of Steepholm continues the line of the Mendips, a chain of hills that meets the coast at Brean Down, Somerset. Eastwards, the shores of the Severn Estuary are dominated by tidal flats, saltmarshes and the extensive wet grasslands of the Gwent and Somerset Levels; to the west, cliffs characterise much of the coast. The whole estuary is of the highest importance for wildlife, especially waterfowl, reflected in its protection under numerous national and international conservation provisions. Photo: Peter Wakely, English Nature.

Chapter 1 Overview

1.1 The Coastal Directories Project

Dr J.P. Doody

1.1.1 Introduction

Developing sound policies for coastal environmental management depends on wide ranging contextual information being available. Collecting such information is always time-consuming and difficult, especially ensuring that all relevant aspects are covered.

This problem is widely recognised. Nevertheless the solution - amassing the encyclopaedic knowledge required, collating it in useable form and disseminating it to potential users while the information is still current - has until recently been too daunting a project for any single organisation to tackle. However, with the help of sponsorship from a large number of organisations and support and practical help from many bodies, ranging from government departments to voluntary organisations, and using numerous experts as writers and consultees, the Joint Nature Conservation Committee has undertaken to prepare such a compendium of information for the coast of the whole United Kingdom.

This undertaking - the Coastal Directories Project - collates existing information on the United Kingdom and Isle of Man coastal zone to provide national and regional overviews of its natural resources and human activities, and indexes more detailed sources of information. The project uses a broad definition of the coastal margin that encompasses all the main habitats from offshore waters through to dry land, including any habitat forming part of the functioning coastal system; in addition areas of former tidal land now enclosed from the sea and lowland wet grassland alongside tidal rivers are included. At times it can be either unhelpful or impossible to set precise limits on the geographic areas that need to be covered, for example in the marine environment, such as when discussing fisheries or sources of contamination. However, where possible, coverage is of coastal 10 km squares, or sites within one kilometre of Mean High Water Mark, or (for marine topics) from the landward limit of high tides out to the median line between the UK and neighbouring states. Areas inland of these limits are not included unless specifically stated.

The relationships between the many and varied components of the coastal zone, that is, between the physical functioning of the zone, its biological components and the human activities that take place there, are complex. With this in mind, a wide-ranging approach to collating coastal information has been adopted in the project; information has been drawn from many sources, from national databases and nation-wide published surveys to the personal observations of field specialists and the newsletters of amateur societies. The approach has also served to highlight the interactions and interdependence between the environmental components (and between the various bodies and individuals) involved. This should help to ensure that users of the information develop policies and adopt strategies that secure the integrated, sustainable use and management of the coastal zone while maintaining biological diversity - a key element of Agenda 21 of the Rio Earth Summit in 1992.

1.1.2 Origins and early development of the project

The concept of providing integrated coastal information took a long time to evolve into the Coastal Directories Project. As early as 1984, the need for such data was acknowledged at the first International Conference on the Protection of the North Sea. In 1987, recognising the significant gaps that existed in the scientific understanding of the North Sea, the Second International Conference on the Protection of the North Sea established the North Sea Task Force (NSTF). Under the guidance of the International Council for the Exploration of the Sea (ICES) and the Oslo and Paris Commissions, the NSTF organised a programme of study with the primary aim of producing a (mainly marine) assessment of the North Sea (the *North Sea Quality Status Report* (QSR)) by 1993.

In 1989 at the second meeting of the NSTF the UK suggested that the North Sea QSR should include consideration of terrestrial habitats and species. This was to involve the collection of information dealing with the coastal margin of the North Sea (defined as being east of longitude 5° West - i.e. from Cape Wrath in northern Scotland around the North Sea and the English Channel coasts to the Fal Estuary in Cornwall) and the collation of this information into book form. A project was set up by the Nature Conservancy Council (NCC) and, after 1991, the Joint Nature Conservation Committee (JNCC), to produce this information, with part funding from the Department of the Environment (DoE). A small group was invited to steer the project and to help identify information sources, including the DoE, the Ministry of Agriculture, Fisheries and Food (MAFF), the National Rivers Authority (NRA) (now the Environment Agency (EA)), the Countryside Commission (CC), the Scottish Office (SO), the Welsh Office (WO) and the country conservation agencies (English Nature, Scottish Natural Heritage, Countryside Council for Wales). With its help, a draft text was prepared in 1990-91; the resulting *Directory of the North Sea coastal margin* - the first product of the Coastal Directories Project, as it was to become - was presented to Ministers at the Intermediate Ministerial Meeting on the North Sea held in Denmark in December 1993 (Doody *et al.* 1993).

The principal aims of the *Directory* were to produce "a comprehensive description of the North Sea coastal margin, its habitats, species and human activities, as an example to other North Sea states" (North Sea Task Force 1993), and thus to help to ensure that terrestrial habitats and species were considered in the QSR. In this it succeeded, and the QSR, also published in 1993, included descriptions of terrestrial habitats and species in several of the sub-regional reports, together with comments on the human impacts on the ecosystems.

The North Sea Task Force was wound up in December 1993, following completion of the *North Sea QSR*, and its work is now carried on by a new Assessment and Monitoring Committee (ASMO), under the 1992 Convention for the Protection of the Marine Environment of the North East Atlantic (the OSPAR Convention). This convention requires that assessments similar to the North Sea QSR be produced for all the constituent parts of the north-east Atlantic, and for that area as a whole, by the year 2000. The Celtic Seas, including the Irish Sea and the west coast of Britain, are one of the first areas to be subject to assessment.

In the UK during the period 1990 - 1993 there was a considerable upsurge of interest in the principles of coastal management. For example, between November 1991 and February 1992 the House of Commons Environment Committee examined the issues for England; their report on *Coastal zone protection and planning* was published in March 1992 (House of Commons Environment Committee 1992). This report, together with initiatives at UK and European levels, encouraged a more integrated, local approach to management issues. At the same time, as the work on the *Directory of the North Sea coastal margin* proceeded, the emphasis of the approach changed. The main aim had been the collection of information, but gradually the process of working with people to gather the data threw the spotlight more on the benefits of a partnership approach and its value for promoting coastal zone management, with which the Coastal Directories Project became more directly linked.

1.1.3 Recent developments

These developments in coastal management fostered interest in the Coastal Directories Project and increased demand for information at a regional level, as well as at the level of whole seaboards (the approach adopted for the *Directory of the North Sea coastal margin*). In 1992, therefore, it was proposed to produce a *West Coast Directory* to cover the remainder of the coast of Great Britain, the Isle of Man and, by later agreement, Northern Ireland, as well as a series of regional volumes to cover the whole coast of the UK. Regions were defined, wherever possible, by the current local or national government coastal boundaries that most closely approximated to the limits of major coastal process cells (see section 2.4), to ensure that pragmatic management requirements were matched by an ecologically coherent information base. Volumes covering seventeen regions have been or are now being prepared: the areas that they cover are shown in Map 1.1.1. Regions 1 - 10 cover the area of the *Directory of the North Sea coastal margin*; Regions 11 - 17 deal with the west coast of the United Kingdom and the Isle of Man. These regional volumes provide a more detailed level of information than the *Directory of the North Sea coastal margin*, to help set each region in a national context and

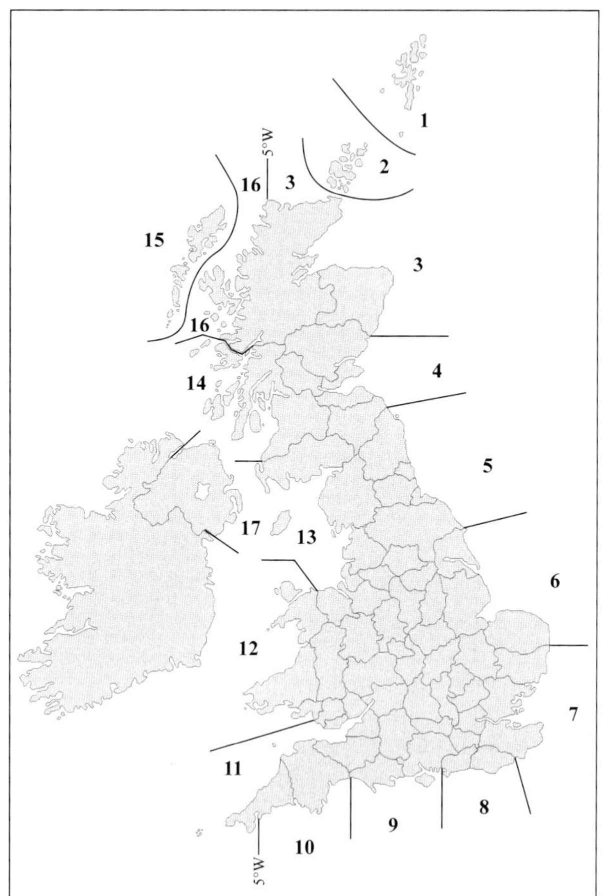

Map 1.1.1 Regions in the series. Region names are given in Table 1.1.2.

facilitate the preparation of regional plans. Discussions in the main steering group (see below) in February 1996 resulted in a decision to make the completion of the regional volumes the priority, rather than the production of the overview *West Coast Directory*.

Whereas work for the *Directory of the North Sea coastal margin* was funded principally by the DoE and the NCC/JNCC, it was decided to seek funding for the extended project from a consortium of private organisations and public bodies, including the original steering group members, as well as coastal local authorities (see page 7). In the event more than 200 organisations, from government departments and oil, water and power companies to nature conservation organisations, both statutory and voluntary, have contributed either money or information or both to the project; further participants are still coming forward. Those organisations that contributed money - the funding consortium - and a number of others comprise the main steering group, and from this group a smaller number were identified to form the core steering group (Table 1.1.1).

Interest in the project has been reflected in the level of sponsorship that the project has received and in the commitment shown by members of the steering groups, which meet regularly. The main steering group meets annually for a seminar: so far it has considered the *Role of the Directories in the development of coastal zone management* (January 1994), the *Use of electronic storage and retrieval mechanisms for data publication* (February 1995) and *The tide turns for coastal zone management: Coastal Directories users report back on their experiences* (February 1996). In addition the core steering group also meets at least annually.

Table 1.1.1 Coastal Directories project management structure

Group	*Role*	*Undertaken by*
JNCC Coastal Conservation Branch (CCB)	Day to day management	Head of CCB, project coordinators
Project management board	Liaison & executive decisions	Country conservation agencies (English Nature, Scottish Natural Heritage, Countryside Council for Wales), JNCC Coastal Conservation Branch, Department of the Environment (Northern Ireland)
Core steering group	Steer work, provide information and support	See page 2
Main steering group (includes, amongst others, all funding consortium members)	Review progress, consider new developments, provide expert advice and act as consultees	All members, through an annual steering group seminar and individually

1.1.4 The contribution of the project to coastal management

At the outset it was agreed that the work should involve as many as possible of the individuals and organisations concerned with the use of the coastal margin, to reflect the complex nature of the habitats and species and the wide-ranging influence of human activities. As the project evolved, the value of this approach has been highlighted by the extent to which new approaches and information sources have been identified. The dialogue between the Coastal Directories Project funding consortium members has confirmed the importance of the project in providing basic resource information to support new approaches to coastal management.

Increasingly, the regional volumes are seen as providing essential information to inform the development of coastal zone management policy at a national level. They provide information that complements the approach currently being promoted by a range of government reports. These include PPG 20: *Planning Policy Guidelines: coastal planning* (DoE/Welsh Office 1992), the *Policy guidelines for the coast* (DoE 1995) and the two consultation documents that followed up the House of Commons Environment Committee report: *Development below low water mark* (DoE/Welsh Office 1993a) and *Managing the coast* (DoE/Welsh Office 1993b) (note that these reports do not cover Scotland, Northern Ireland or the Isle of Man). MAFF too has promoted the setting up of flood and coastal defence 'coastal cell groups', to encourage sustainable shoreline management.

It has also been recognised that the summary information in the regional volumes is valuable in preparing and assessing applications for oil and gas licensing around the coastal margin. An injection of funds from the United Kingdom Offshore Operators Association (UKOOA) made possible the early production of draft regional reports for most of the potential licensing areas in the 16th Offshore Oil and Gas Licensing Round in 1994.

1.1.5 Outputs

The regional volumes are being published as hardback books. In addition a first release of coastal conservation data, covering national surveys of terrestrial habitats and coastal Sites of Special Scientific Interest (SSSIs), and a second release of marine conservation data, covering marine

Table 1.1.2 (Provisional) titles and publication dates of products of the Coastal Directories Project

Product	*Publication date*
Book editions	
Directory of the North Sea coastal margin	1993
Region 1. Shetland	Due 1997
Region 2. Orkney	Due 1997
Region 3. North-east Scotland: Cape Wrath to St. Cyrus	1996
Region 4. South-east Scotland: Montrose to Eyemouth	Due 1997
Region 5. North-east England: Berwick-on-Tweed to Filey Bay	1995
Region 6. Eastern England: Flamborough Head to Great Yarmouth	1995
Region 7. South-east England: Lowestoft to Dungeness	Due 1997
Region 8. Sussex: Rye Bay to Chichester Harbour	Due 1997
Region 9. Southern England: Hayling Island to Lyme Regis	1996
Region 10. South-west England: Seaton to the Roseland Peninsula	1996
Region 11. The Western Approaches: Falmouth Bay to Kenfig	1996
Region 12. Wales: Margam to Little Orme	1995
Region 13. Northern Irish Sea: Colwyn Bay to Stranraer including the Isle of Man	1996
Region 14. South-west Scotland: Ballantrae to Mull	Due 1997
Regions 15 & 16. North-west Scotland: the Western Isles and west Highland	Due 1997
Region 17. Northern Ireland	Due 1997
Electronic editions	
Coastal and marine UKDMAP datasets: Version 1	1994
Regions 3, 5, 6, 9, 10, 11, 12, 13	1996
Other regions	Following book publication

benthic surveys, have been published in electronic format (Barne *et al.* 1994) compatible with UKDMAP, the electronic atlas developed by the British Oceanographic Data Centre, Birkenhead (BODC 1992). Other forms of electronic publication are now being evaluated, and electronic editions of the published Regions 3, 5, 6, 9, 10, 11, 12 and 13 are now available. The current position on the publication of book and electronic editions is shown in Table 1.1.2.

1.1.6 Further sources of information

A. References cited

Barne, J., Davidson, N.C., Hill, T.O., & Jones, M. 1994. *Coastal and marine UKDMAP datasets: a user manual.* Peterborough, Joint Nature Conservation Committee.

British Oceanographic Data Centre. 1992. *United Kingdom digital marine atlas. User guide. Version 2.0.* Birkenhead, Natural Environment Research Council, British Oceanographic Data Centre.

Department of the Environment. 1995. *Policy guidelines for the coast.* London, HMSO.

DoE / Welsh Office. 1992. *Planning policy guidance - coastal planning.* London, HMSO. (PPG 20.)

DoE / Welsh Office. 1993a. *Development below Low Water Mark - a review of regulation in England and Wales.* London, HMSO.

DoE / Welsh Office. 1993b. *Managing the coast: a review of coastal management plans in England and Wales and the powers supporting them.* London, HMSO.

Doody, J.P., Johnson, C., & Smith, B. 1993. *Directory of the North Sea coastal margin.* Peterborough, Joint Nature Conservation Committee.

House of Commons Environment Committee. 1992. *Coastal zone protection and planning. Second Report.* 2 volumes. London, HMSO.

North Sea Task Force. 1993. *North Sea quality status report.* London, Oslo and Paris Commissions.

B. Further reading

Bird, E.C.F. 1984. *Coasts - an introduction to coastal geomorphology.* 3rd ed. Oxford, Blackwell.

C. Contact names and addresses

Type of information	*Contact address and telephone no.*
Information about the Coastal Directories project and UKDMAP version; sales of electronic editions of the regional volumes	*Project Co-ordinator, Coastal Conservation Branch, JNCC, Peterborough, tel: 01733 62626
Sales outlet for book editions of the regional volumes, the Directory of the North Sea coastal margin, and other JNCC publications	Natural History Book Service Ltd, 2-3 Wills Road, Totnes, Devon TQ9 5XN, tel: 01803 865913

*Starred contact addresses are given in full in the Appendix.

1.2 Introduction to the region

Dr J.P. Doody

1.2.1 Introduction

This section gives a brief introduction to the character of the region, its wildlife and the extent of its human use and development, synthesising information presented in Chapters 2-10. The main coastal locations are shown on Map 1.2.1. Map 1.2.2 shows the coastal 10 km squares in the region.

Region 11 covers the the major part of the coast of Cornwall, the north coast of Devon, the shores of the Bristol Channel and the Severn Estuary. The coast is 1,205.5 km long (JNCC Coastal Resources Database), which is 6.4% of the total coastline of Great Britain and includes 18.8% of the coast of England and 10.8% of that of Wales. It has a varied geology but can be characterised in two broad sections - the cliffed coasts of Cornwall, north Devon and parts of Somerset, which have a rugged and open character and are popular tourist destinations, and the low-lying coast of south Wales and the Severn Estuary, where sedimentary coastal plain estuarine shores predominate.

The prevailing wind is from the south-west, and much of the north coasts of Cornwall and Devon are exposed to its full force. The Isles of Scilly, for example, experience 25 days of gales per year. This compares with the more sheltered inner Bristol Channel and Severn Estuary, where figures as low as three days of gales are recorded, at Cardiff for example. Owing to the funneling effect of the Bristol Channel the tidal range of the Severn Estuary is one of the highest in the world, second only to the Bay of Fundy in Canada: it reaches as much as 12.3 m at Avonmouth. This high tidal range increases the threat of flooding to the low-lying areas around the Severn Estuary, especially as water levels may be raised by up to 1.5 m during a storm surge. Relative regional sea level is rising at an estimated rate of approximately 2 mm per year, despite the rise in absolute land level (at a rate of about 0.7 mm per year) as a result of the removal of the last ice sheets some 10,000 years ago.

Relatively low-intensity agriculture is a major land use, with stock farming predominating in the south-west and on the south coast of Wales. Around the Severn and the coastal lowlands of south Wales, crops are grown more intensively, while the wet grasslands, such as on the Somerset and Gwent levels, continue to be used for livestock. These grasslands are important landscape and conservation features. Avonmouth and Cardiff are major industrial locations built on formerly intertidal land, but over much of the rest of the region intensive agriculture or industrial development is the exception rather than the rule. Fishing activity centres on the two major ports of Newlyn (one of the biggest fishing ports in England and Wales) and Falmouth, both on the south coast, where there are more diverse fish stocks and numerous sheltered harbours. The majority of the coastal area is relatively free from human infrastructure development, and along much of the coasts of north Cornwall, north Devon and Somerset, access by road is not easy. However, the principal cities of Bristol, Newport and Cardiff and their associated ports have good road links with the rest of mainland Britain. Elsewhere, Newquay in the extreme south-west, Bude, Weston-super-Mare and, in Wales, Barry Island are traditional destinations for family holidays, and the whole of the South-West Peninsula is an important tourist destination.

1.2.2 Structure and landscape

The solid geology of the region changes from the extreme south-west to the north and east, at a broad scale being composed of progressively 'younger' rocks. Most of the harder rocks of the south-west, including Cornwall, Devon and the westernmost part of Somerset, are of Carboniferous or Devonian age (more than 360 million years old). Land's End and the Isles of Scilly are composed of granite, while the peninsula of the Lizard has an unusual and complex geology, with ultrabasic igneous rocks that are unique in southern Britain. Northwards as far as Minehead the nature of the predominantly rocky cliffed coast is determined by the combination of resistant rocks forming headlands or steep cliffs, within which the softer rocks, typically shales and slates, erode to form bays or coves.

North and east of Minehead, stretching into Bridgwater Bay and the Severn Estuary, Triassic (248-213 million years ago) and Jurassic (213-144 million years ago) rocks are exposed along the shore. The relative softness of these rocks, together with the extreme heights of the tides in the Bristol Channel, have combined to create a wide rocky intertidal area along stretches of the coast. Elsewhere within the inner Bristol Channel and the Severn Estuary the shore is defined by tidal flats, which are extensive in places, and fringing saltmarsh, backed by sea walls. The sea walls enclose extensive areas of formerly tidal land, including the coastal levels around Bridgwater (the Somerset Levels) and around Cardiff/Newport (the Wentlooge Levels).

Unlike much of the rest of the UK, the land surface of the region is thought to have been virtually free from ice for most of the Pleistocene glacial period, although offshore there is evidence for the intrusion of a tongue of ice, which may have extended to the Isles of Scilly.

1.2.3 The natural environment

The sea and sea bed

The seas in this region are greatly influenced by the Atlantic, particularly the Gulf Stream, and support important fisheries. Mackerel are amongst the most abundant fish spawning along the edge of the continental shelf to the south-west. Herring are locally plentiful, spawning in Cornish estuaries. Cod is one of the most important exploited fish, and there appears to be a pronounced aggregation of spawning fish off the north Cornish coast between March and April. The inshore area has exploited populations of sea-bed crustacea, notably lobsters. Offshore there are extensive scallop and edible crab grounds of national and international significance. Basking sharks also occur in the coastal waters off this region.

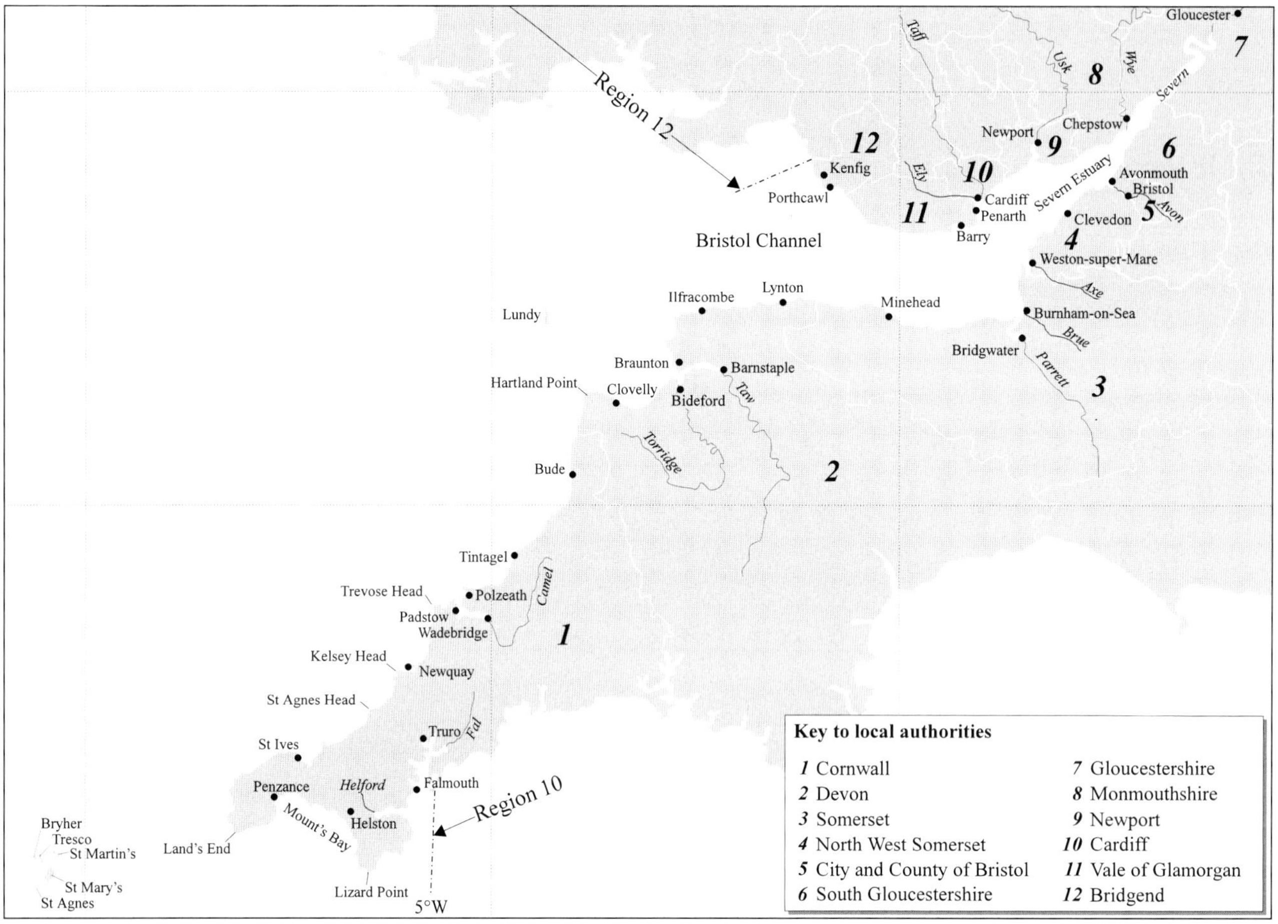

Key to local authorities

1 Cornwall	*7* Gloucestershire
2 Devon	*8* Monmouthshire
3 Somerset	*9* Newport
4 North West Somerset	*10* Cardiff
5 City and County of Bristol	*11* Vale of Glamorgan
6 South Gloucestershire	*12* Bridgend

Map 1.2.1 Rivers, major towns and other coastal locations in the region

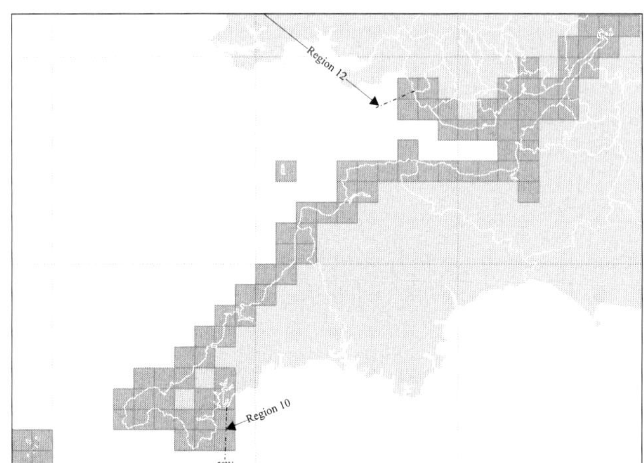

Map 1.2.2 National grid 10 km x 10 km squares included as 'coastal' for this region

Close to the shore the sea bed shelves steeply to about 60 m and then slopes gently to the edge of the Continental shelf. The sea bed is covered with a thin veneer of mobile sediments, except in a few deeper 'valleys', which have become infilled with recent (Holocene) sediments. The most important of these valleys is in the Severn and is obliterated by sand banks in its upper reaches but remains a distinct feature westwards to the south-west of Gower. Region 11 supports one of the most diverse ranges of communities of sea-bed plants and animals in Great Britain. This is a reflection of the range and type of substratum, the degree of variation in exposure, particularly around islands (especially the Isles of Scilly and Lundy Island), and the warming influence of the Gulf Stream. Many of the rarer species are Mediterranean-Atlantic in their distribution and include sea fans, cup corals and soft corals that in Great Britain are confined to the south-west. The coastal nearshore area around the region is among the most diverse such areas in Europe and includes 39 rare and 31 scarce marine benthic species. The coastal waters also have some of the richest and most diverse populations of non-exploited fish, with 111 of the 336 species found around the UK recorded in the Severn Estuary alone, an above average regional total and much higher than the 48 found along England's North Sea coast.

Grey seals are the only seal species present in the area; whilst not numerous, they produce 0.5% of the pups born in Great Britain. The Isles of Scilly and Lundy are the major sites, with small colonies scattered along the Cornish coast. Elsewhere in the region they are virtually absent. Leatherback *Dermochelys coriacea* and loggerhead *Caretta caretta* turtles have been recorded relatively frequently in this region. Most leatherbacks are sighted swimming at sea west of Land's End, and the loggerheads recorded were found stranded in Mount's Bay, Cornwall. The south-west approaches to the English Channel are richer in cetaceans than any other part of southern Britain, with seventeen species recorded, nine of them either present throughout the year or recorded annually as seasonal visitors to the region. Cetacean species richness and abundance declines markedly from west to east in the Bristol Channel.

The Isles of Scilly, Lundy and to a lesser extent Flat Holm and Steep Holm in the Bristol Channel include a wide variety of rare plants and animals, on the islands, in the surrounding sea and on the near-shore sea-bed. Some species or sub-species, such as the Lundy cabbage *Coincya wrightii*, are extremely rare or unique to the islands. This combination of terrestrial species and offshore marine conservation interest represents an extremely rich environment.

Estuarine shores

The estuaries in the region represent more than 12% of the British resource and include one of the ten most extensive estuary systems in the UK: the inner Bristol Channel, the Severn Estuary and its several tributary rivers including the Taff/Ely. Taken together with Bridgwater Bay, the complex is important at a European scale. The whole of the Severn Estuary is a Special Protection Area and Ramsar Site and has been identified as a candidate Special Area of Conservation (SAC) under the EC Habitats & Species Directive. The Severn Estuary and Bridgwater Bay (also a Ramsar Site) together hold around 3.5% of the British wintering waterfowl population, a highly significant proportion for a single estuarine complex. The area is also important because it usually remains frost free during the winter, and in periods of hard weather elsewhere in the UK it may increase in importance to waterfowl, with major influxes of species such as teal and wigeon. Extensive (up to 6 km wide at low spring tides) tidal mudflats also occur at Bridgwater Bay. The region also includes Falmouth Bay (south Cornwall), one of Britain's best and largest examples of a ria, an estuary type well represented further east on the south coast, particularly in Region 10. The River Camel is the only significant example of a ria on the north coast.

There has been extensive enclosure for agriculture since Roman times around all the main estuaries, particularly those associated with the Severn. Despite the extent of saltmarsh lost to enclosure in the Severn Estuary, which Pye & French (1993) estimate to have been 84,000 ha, there is still a significant area (1,400 ha including Bridgwater Bay) remaining - nearly 4% of the Great Britain resource. Although more than 40% of the marsh is dominated by common cord-grass *Spartina anglica,* there is an extensive sequence of more mature marshes, including upper marsh and transitions to brackish swamp with common reed *Phragmites australis*. Some of these upper marshes include a number of coastal species typically confined to salt or brackish marshes covered infrequently by the tides, such as the rare slender hare's ear *Bupleurum tenuissimum* and sea barley *Hordeum marinum*. Where it is found elsewhere in south-east England it occurs uncharacteristically on sea walls and coastal grazing marsh.

In several areas of former saltmarsh and swamp, secondary habitats, managed for low-intensity agriculture over many hundreds of years, have developed their own man-modified wildlife habitats. These include two of the most extensive areas of coastal wet grassland in Great Britain, the Somerset Levels, and the Caldicot and Wentlooge Levels in south Wales, which are derived from former tidal lands (enclosed from Roman times onwards). Their landscape consists of small meadows interspersed with narrow drainage ditches, and large areas of the Somerset Levels may be flooded in winter. Having remained largely free from intensive agricultural use in recent years, they have maintained considerable conservation interest. Of special note are wintering waterfowl, and breeding waders, for which the Somerset Levels support one of the five biggest populations on lowland grassland in southern Britain. Some of the unimproved grasslands and the drainage ditches have a rich variety of plants and notable invertebrate animals, and where there are gradations from fresh to brackish water these assemblages may be particularly rich.

Non-estuarine shores

Sea cliffs abound in the region, making up a high proportion of the region's coastline and 10% of the British resource in terms of its length. From the south-west to the north-east they occur as progressively younger and softer rocks, with Minehead providing a geographical divide between the more rugged coasts of Cornwall, north Devon and Somerset and those adjacent to the Bristol Channel and the Severn Estuary. The region's cliffs are generally 50-100 m high, rising to more than 100 m around the coast of Lundy Island and in parts of Cornwall, and to 150 m at Embury Beacon south of Hartland Point. Steeper rugged sections of cliff occupy the majority of the coast of south and north Cornwall to Somerset. These include the Lizard, Land's End and the north-west facing cliffs of north Cornwall, north Devon and the west facing section of Somerset including the coast of the Exmoor National Park, which adjoins the coast near Lynton. Generally the geological strata are a (sometimes very complex) mixture of calcareous and non-calcareous rocks. Superimposed on the effects of the underlying geology, slope and aspect is the influence of exposure and salt spray, which helps to create an almost complete sequence of sea-cliff plant communities. These include extensive exposed maritime communities, including spray zone crevice communities with golden samphire *Inula crithmoides,* grassland and heath, the latter with examples of vegetation dominated by the rare Cornish heath *Erica vagans*, calcareous cliff and cliff-top vegetation and coastal woodlands in the valleys. Occasionally on the exposed Cornish coast, where the effects of wind and salt spray are extreme (such as at the Dizzard), there may be stunted woodlands in which the height of individual trees - even mature oaks - is restricted to a few metres. There are significant stretches of soft cliffs, with communities ranging from tall grassland/scrub through to open ephemeral communities on unstable ground, though these are much less frequent than on the coasts of Regions 9 and 10 to the east. Some of the best examples of the Atlantic cliff vegetation type identified in the EC Habitats & Species Directive, representing the southern element of the community type, occur in this region. In addition to the Lizard, an extensive stretch of coast between Tintagel, Marsland and Clovelly is a candidate SAC.

On this region's cliffs occur six of the nine nationally rare (e.g. wild asparagus *Asparagus officinalis* subsp. *prostratus*) and three of the four nationally scarce (e.g. thyme broomrape *Orobanche alba*) plants that are virtually restricted to sea cliffs in Great Britain. These and the other rare species occurring on cliffs (although not restricted to them) in the region (e.g. wild leek *Allium ampeloprasum*) make the cliff sections of this region's coast amongst the most significant in Great Britain. Pride of place from a botanical point of view goes to the Lizard. Here, not only are many of the rarities present in good populations, but the cliff-tops and surrounding land also support some of the best examples of the rare Cornish heath, at sites such as Goonhilly Downs.

The invertebrate fauna of many of the region's cliffs is outstanding, with many scarce and threatened species occurring, including several that depend on the associated warm and bare or sparsely vegetated ground. The cliffs also provide habitat for sizeable populations of some of the more widespread reptiles, including adders, slow worms and lizards, and they are also of national significance for bats. Thirteen of the fourteen British species occur in the region, and the disused mines on the coast provide hibernating sites for significant populations of the rare greater and lesser horseshoe bats (*Rhinolophus ferrumequinum* and *R. hipposideros*). These species rely on semi-natural pastures and ancient woodland respectively for foraging, both habitats that occur relatively extensively throughout the region.

The cliffs are also notable for animal species that have been lost but which are now being reintroduced, including the large blue butterfly, which formerly had strongholds on the cliff tops of the region. Exposure to wind and salt spray, coupled with grazing, used to minimise the growth of coarse grasses and scrub and maintain the open, close-cropped grassland thought to be important for this species. The move away from livestock farming may well have helped in its demise, although collecting may also have had an adverse impact.

There are three large sand dune systems in the region, each with in excess of 500 ha of blown sand: Penhale Dunes, Braunton Burrows and Kenfig in south Wales. All three are candidate SACs and together with the more than 40 other smaller dune sites represent 6% of the Great Britain sand dune resource. The sites are scattered throughout the region on exposed, generally west-facing coasts, where the prevailing winds blow the sand onshore to form hindshore dunes. Occasionally, as at Penhale and Merthyr Mawr in south Wales, sand is blown over a cliff to form climbing dunes. Other physical types of dune are less well represented. The dunes at Kenfig and Penhale are within National Nature Reserves, and parts of them are used by the MoD for training. Despite the presence of a golf course at Kenfig this site remains one of the most intact dune systems in Great Britain and has a number of rare species including sea stock *Mathiola sinuata*. The dunes at Penhale include tourist developments with a caravan park and erosional pressures above the beach, which resulted in the need for extensive erosion control including marram planting. By contrast, Braunton Burrows and Kenfig Dunes, which are less heavily used, have different management problems, the most important of which are caused by the growth of scrub and the loss of open, species-rich dune grassland. At the former site the introduction of Soay sheep and an extensive mowing regime are being used in an attempt to control the problem and reverse the encroachment of scrub. Both Braunton and Kenfig also have large areas of dune slack, a rich habitat that is well represented in the western and wetter parts of Great Britain.

Other sedimentary habitats are small but have an important influence on the nature of the landscape. Shingle shores are restricted in the region because of the absence of suitable material along the hard rock cliffs of Cornwall and Devon. Nevertheless there are several shingle areas in the region which, though small in area in a national context, show a considerable variation in their structure and vegetation. These include Porlock, which has a shingle ridge enclosing an area of traditional farmland, Loe Bar, enclosing a large freshwater lake, and the Aberthaw system, which comprises a small series of shingle spits enclosing saltmarsh.

The region is not of particular significance in terms of the total numbers of seabirds present or the species it holds, although it is close to the southern limit of the breeding range of several species. The Isles of Scilly have the most significant breeding colonies, with all but one of the six nationally important and three internationally important species present in the region occurring there.

1.2.4 Landscape and nature conservation

The value of the region for landscape and nature conservation is shown by the number and combined extent of sites afforded official protection, especially designations reflecting national or international importance. These include 157 Sites of Special Scientific Interest (SSSIs) and five National Nature Reserves (NNRs). There are two Special Protection Areas (the Severn Estuary and Walmore Common) and three designated Ramsar sites (the Severn Estuary, Walmore Common and Bridgwater Bay), a relatively small number when compared with most other regions, though reflecting the predominantly cliffed nature of a high proportion of the coast. The region also includes twelve sites proposed as SACs for their coastal/marine biological interest. The total number of sites and total areas of the main designations are given in Table 1.2.1.

There are also many sites owned and managed by non-governmental organisations, including the RSPB, National Trust and Wildlife Trusts. Nearly a quarter of the region's coast is owned or leased by the National Trust - around a third of its coastal holdings in Great Britain. The presence of thirteen out of 35 Heritage Coasts and the extent of the coast designated as Areas of Outstanding Natural Beauty (AONB) - 27% by length of that in England and Wales - is indicative of the great conservation importance of this region. The area includes the only statutory Marine Nature Reserve in England, and there are also seven Sensitive Marine Areas identified by English Nature as being of national importance.

1.2.5 Human activities, past and present

In this region, because the land was never covered by ice sheets, considerable evidence survives of some of the earliest human settlements in Britain. These have been dated to 450,000 years ago: in one cave on the edge of the Somerset Levels, flint axes have been found in association with the bones of animals that became extinct at around that time. Hunter-gatherers continued to use the region in the post-glacial period, and from about 4,000 - 3,500 years ago cultivation and animal husbandry were practised, associated with small settlements. Widespread use of the region continued up to the Roman occupation, though their presence appears to have left no lasting impression on the more remote parts. However, on land fringing the estuaries

Table 1.2.1 Main landscape and nature conservation designations in Region 11

Designation	*No. of sites in region*	*Total area in this region (ha)*	*% of GB coast total in region*
Biosphere Reserves	1	604	2.2
Ramsar sites	3	27,412	9.9
Special Protection Areas (SPAs)	2	24,709	8.5
Environmentally Sensitive Areas (ESAs)	2	87,900	6.3
Biogenetic Reserves	1	1,300	34.4
National Nature Reserves (NNRs)	5	5,406	6.2
Sites of Special Scientific Interest (SSSIs)	157	56,005	8.0
Marine Nature Reserve (MNR)	1	1,390	48.1
National Parks	1	69,300	9.3
Local Nature Reserves (LNRs)	9	692	5.2
National Trust sites	149	14,363	22.8
RSPB reserves	3	235	0.6
Wildfowl and Wetlands Trust sites	1	305	19.2
Wildlife Trust sites	20	227	1.0

Source: JNCC. Note: any site that is wholly or partly intertidal, and any terrestrial site at least partly within 1 km of the Mean High Water Mark, or any tidal channel as depicted on 1:50,000 Ordnance Survey maps, is included as 'coastal'.

the influence of the Romans is more obvious, and their enclosure of wetlands on what has become the Somerset Levels and elsewhere is thought to have been extensive (Pye & French 1993). Many of these areas may now lie outside the current line of sea defence, suggesting erosion of the shoreline since the original land claim.

Maritime trade continued throughout the Dark Ages and subsequently, and fishing became a significant commercial activity from about the 1300s, when one of the main species caught was the pilchard. Today Newlyn (one of the biggest ports in England and Wales) and Falmouth are the two main fishing ports. Demersal fish form the biggest landings, with 4% of the total for Britain; landings of conger eel represent 45% of the British total and landings of megrim, hake and pollack all exceed 30%. The many small fishing ports around the region rely heavily on potting for crustacea, including lobsters and edible crabs; total shellfish landings represent about 2% of the total catch landed in Britain. The three diadromous fish species widespread in British waters, the Atlantic salmon, sea trout and eel, are all fished for in this region. Elvers are particularly important and support a major traditional fishery both below Bridgwater and in the Severn.

Tin mining in Cornwall may have begun as early as the 5th century BC. The industry continued through many ups and downs until the collapse of the tin market in 1985 resulted in its almost total demise (one tin mine, not on the coast, remains active in the county). From 18th century onwards significant commercial activity was based largely on the exchange of raw materials, with coal from south Wales being exported across the Bristol Channel for a variety of industrial and domestic purposes. At the same time copper from Cornwall was taken to the foundries of south Wales, where the coal fields provided the power for smelting. Today, Newport, Cardiff and Avonmouth are the main centres of industrial activity, but population density in the region in general is much lower than on the coast of south-east England. The degree of exposure of the region to westerly gales and the high tidal range of the Severn Estuary have highlighted the area's potential for renewable forms of power generation. Four years' research into the feasibility of a tidal energy barrage across the Severn suggested that it could produce up to 6% of the UK's electricity needs, although its potential cost has not so far been considered justified. Wind power generation occurs on a small scale in the region, where there are five wind farms.

Local intertidal land claim, including significant loss of tidal habitats in Cardiff Bay and around Avonmouth for port and industrial development, has reduced the area of tidal land, continuing the process started by the Romans. Change continues to occur and the building of a barrage on the Taff/Ely Estuary where it enters Cardiff Bay will result in another major loss of intertidal land, to be submerged by a lake. The objective is to revitalise the now run-down area and create an exciting coastal city. The existing Severn road bridge has been augmented by a second river crossing, opened in 1996, which will greatly speed up economic development in the area. A relatively small proportion - 4.3% - of the region's coastline has man-made protection against erosion or flooding. Apart from small structures around some of the urban locations in the south-west, sea defences are concentrated around the shores of the Severn Estuary and inner Bristol Channel. Much of this area is low-lying and substantial areas of the Somerset, Caldicot and Wentlooge levels are at risk from flooding.

The fact that a considerable part of the coastal hinterland, particularly in the south-west, remains in pastoral use has had a important part to play in its continuing landscape value. Much of the coastline is characterised by semi-natural habitats such as cliff-top pasture, meadows and woodland. Some coastal heaths and pastures have been ploughed, but recent changes in agricultural support have made this a less attractive option and the implementation of a variety of schemes such as Environmentally Sensitive Areas and set-aside are reducing the impact of intensification and even contributing to the restoration of some sites.

With its attractive landscape and many facilities the south-west has been a major centre for tourism for many years. There are several large holiday centres, including the older traditional family resorts of Newquay, Weston-super-Mare and Barry Island. The construction of the M5, and improvements to the A30, which reaches into the heart of south Cornwall, means that the whole of the south-west has been opened to mass tourism. The traditional beach-based holiday is catered for around the whole of the Mount's Bay area on the south coast, and at St. Ives and Newquay on the north Cornish coast, Minehead and Burnham on the Somerset coast and Penarth, Barry and Porthcawl in Wales. Elsewhere also a wide range of facilities exist, including golf courses, theme parks and marinas, and activities such as rock climbing (for example at Land's End), walking, sand yachting (the Severn) and natural history study are popular. Offshore the variety is equally diverse, with beach and sea angling, water skiing, jet skiing, canoeing and yachting, and the region has some of the best surfing beaches in Britain.

The importance of this region for the conservation of the natural environment and the archaeological heritage, coupled with present-day human use and enjoyment, make coastal management an important issue. Many initiatives in the region are addressing the need for integrated management, including the South West Regional Planning Conference, the various Heritage Coast Services and the Standing Conference of Severnside Local Authorities (SCOSLA).

1.2.6 Further sources of information

A. References cited

Pye, K., & French, P.W. 1993. *Erosion and accretion processes on British saltmarshes.* London, Ministry of Agriculture, Fisheries and Food.

B. Further reading

Davidson, N.C., Laffoley, D.d'A., Doody, J.P., Way, L.S., Gordon, J., Key, R., Drake, C.M., Pienkowski, M.W., Mitchell, R.M., & Duff, K.L. 1991. *Nature conservation and estuaries in Great Britain.* Peterborough, Nature Conservancy Council.

Robinson, A., & Millward, R. 1983. *The Shell book of the British coast.* Newton Abbot, David and Charles.

Steers, J.A. 1973. *The coastline of England and Wales.* Cambridge, Cambridge University Press.

The geology of the Lizard is unique in southern Britain. Originally part of an ancient ocean floor, the rocks of which it was formed were thrust to the surface more than 400 million years ago. These rocks have eroded at different rates, creating a coast of great complexity and savage beauty. The thin, ultra-basic soils of the peninsula harbour some of the country's rarest flowering plants. Photo: Pat Doody, JNCC.

Chapter 2 Geology and physical environment

2.1 Coastal geology

British Geological Survey

2.1.1 Introduction

The region covers the south-westernmost tip of Cornwall, the whole of the southern coast of the Bristol Channel and much of the inner channel's northern coast. The north-western coast of Devon and Cornwall in particular abounds with localities of great geological interest. From the southernmost coast of Cornwall to Minehead the coast is composed of a range of Devonian and Carboniferous rocks arranged in a structurally complex assemblage of folds, and intruded by dykes, sills and granite domes. The structural 'grain' of the region, reflected in the orientation of the major and minor folds, is east-west, although the folds are cut by NW-SE faults which had a history of movement until at least the mid-Tertiary. The main granite body of Devon and Cornwall forms an almost unbroken batholith at depth, extending from Dartmoor to the Isles of Scilly and reaching the surface in several places. East and north of Minehead, structurally simpler and younger Triassic and Jurassic rocks are exposed along the coast, with local outcrops of Carboniferous and older rocks seen in anticlinal cores (the eroded tops of folds) (Map 2.1.1; Table 2.1.1).

Mesozoic sedimentary basins lie offshore (see also section 2.2.3), but these sediments reach land only along the inner Bristol Channel.

Much of the detailed geomorphology of the coast is determined by the resistance of the rocks to marine erosion. The softer shales and slates form bays, coves or clefts according to the scale of their exposure, while the more massive rocks form pronounced headlands or steep cliffs. Intrusion of the granites has locally altered the rocks surrounding them and given rise to mineralised veins. Tin is an important economic mineral in the region, and in places the rocks contain a diverse suite of unusual minerals.

The region lay to the south of the late Devensian ice sheet, though a tongue of ice extended south from the Celtic Sea to reach the Isles of Scilly. Glacial deposits are therefore almost absent from the coast, although isolated erratics and

Table 2.1.1 Geological column

Era	*Period*	*Epoch*	*Age of start (million yrs)*	*Stratigraphic units mentioned in the text*	*Significant geological events*
Cenozoic	Quaternary	Holocene	0.01		
		Pleistocene	1.6		Periglacial conditions, fluctuating sea-levels
	Tertiary (Neogene)	Pliocene	5.1	St. Erth Beds	
		Miocene	25		
	Tertiary (Palaeogene)	Oligocene	38		
		Eocene	55		
		Palaeocene	65		Emplacement of Lundy granite
Mesozoic	Cretaceous		144		
	Jurassic		213	Lias	Marine deposition
	Triassic		248	Rhaetic	
				Mercia Mudstone	Deposition of non-marine 'continental' sediments
Palaeozoic (Upper)	Permian		286		Deposition of non-marine 'continental' sediments
	Carboniferous		360		Emplacement of granites, Variscan Orogeny
	Devonian		408	Mylor Slates, Meadfoot Beds	Variscan Orogeny, marine deposition
Palaeozoic (Lower)	Silurian		438		
	Ordovician		505		
	Cambrian		590		
	Precambrian				

Note: shaded boxes show ages of rocks with important or extensive exposures in the region.

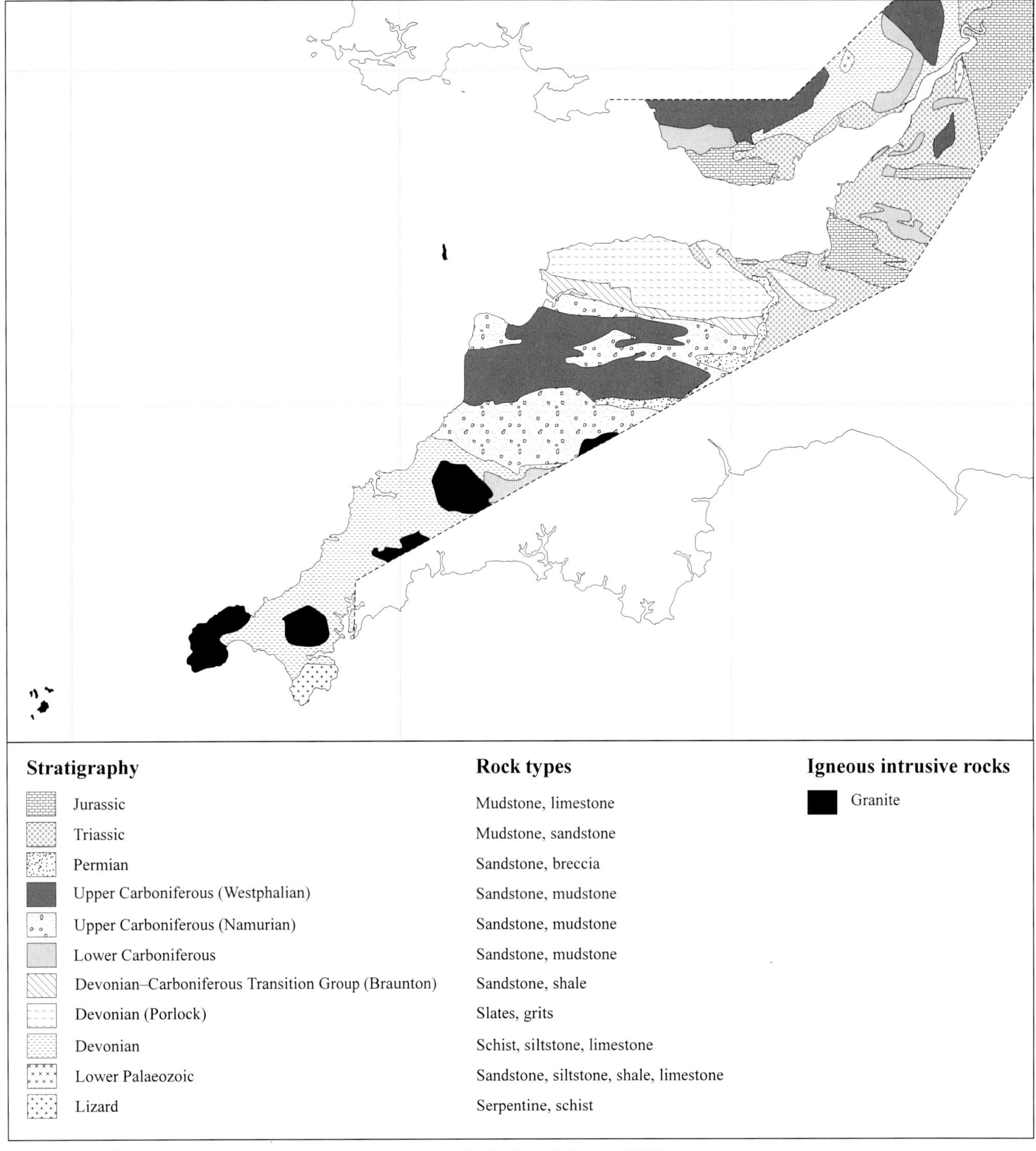

Map 2.1.1 Onshore coastal geology of the region. Source: British Geological Survey (1991).

small exposures of possible till have been recorded, attributed to an Anglian or Wolstonian ice sheet that occupied the Celtic Sea.

2.1.2 Stratigraphy

Falmouth - Porlock

Thick, alternating sandstone and mudstone sequences of Middle and Upper Devonian age are seen at the coast around Falmouth Bay and the south-eastern end of Mount's Bay. They originated in a deep-water basin to the south and were transported northwards in late Devonian times within thick thrust sheets (nappes), onto shallow shelf deposits. At Falmouth and at Loe Bar in Mount's Bay they rest upon younger Upper Devonian mudstones and siltstones, which are visible along the west side of Carrick Roads and around Mount's Bay to just south of Penzance.

The rocks forming the Lizard peninsula are part of a Devonian ocean plate thrust over contemporaneous sedimentary rocks during the late Devonian closure of the so-called Rheic Ocean. The rocks of Lizard Point itself originated as mudstones, sandstones and lavas on the deep basin floor and were then recrystallised under high temperature and pressure to form schists. The complex of igneous rocks forming most of the rest of the Lizard peninsula typifies the rocks forming the earth's crust beneath the oceans and is thought to be a fragment of a Devonian ocean basin floor thrust upwards, together with basin sedimentary rocks, during the Variscan deformation. Together they form a complex association of schists, granulite and serpentinite intruded by gabbro dykes and granite that is unique in southern Britain. The serpentinite is relatively soft, and the shores of the plateau that forms the peninsula have been eroded into steep cliffs.

The sweep of Mount's Bay to the west is largely eroded into Devonian Mylor Slates, although more resistant metamorphosed dolerites and granites are seen in places and often form minor headlands and islands.

The granites of south-west England were intruded soon after the Variscan deformation. They form a minor part of the coast just north of Porthleven in Mount's Bay, as well as the rugged, cliffed coast between Mousehole and Land's End. Some of the granites are traversed by mineralised veins, and that forming the south side of St. Michael's Mount contains greisen (a mineralised rock containing mica and quartz) veins in which have been found unusual minerals such as topaz, wolframite and cassiterite. The Land's End peninsula from Mousehole almost to St. Ives is formed of granite, though metamorphosed slate, commonly intruded by dykes and mineralised veins, forms a narrow strip along the coast north of Cape Cornwall. St. Ives Bay, the most westerly bay on the northern coast, is incised into softer Mylor Slates.

The Isles of Scilly are low, flat-topped islands formed of granite, with the metamorphosed sediment (killas) that surrounds the granite being exposed only on White Island, off St. Martin. Most of the sand on the beaches and between the islands is derived from erosion of the granite.

Western Cornwall is formed of a series of plateau surfaces, at heights of roughly 228 m, 183 m and 131 m above sea level. Lower terraces also occur and are associated with raised beach deposits. Isolated outliers of Pliocene deposits (the most extensive are the St. Erth Beds) are associated with the 131 m level. The general form of the area suggests a mature landscape, formed during the Tertiary, that has suffered some uplift since the Pliocene. The uplift has led to erosion of the coastal fringes, which continues today.

The largely cliffed coast northwards to Hartland Point cuts across the east-west trend of the geological structures to produce a generally straight coastline, broken only by major valleys at Padstow and Bude. In the south around Portreath the coast is formed of Devonian turbidites (impure sandstones) with interbedded grey slate. A small inlier of granite with many bands of greisen forms Cligga Head, and from Perran Bay to Newquay the coast is formed of the grey calcareous slates and thin limestones of the Meadfoot Beds. A major anticlinal structure exposed at the coast in Watergate Bay, north of Newquay, has a core of purple and green slates rich in fish remains. Devonian slates, with local intrusions of metamorphosed dolerite, form the coast from Newquay to Padstow Bay. At Tintagel the sequence passes up into folded and faulted Carboniferous sandstones and shales, which are associated with locally sheared lava and tuff. The same strata, but without the lavas, form the coast northwards to Hartland Point and the southern half of Bideford Bay. Cascades of large, recumbent folds occur in the cliffs at Cambeak, between Boscastle and Widemouth Bay. At Instow a bed of fish remains is exposed on the foreshore. Devonian rocks, comprising red-brown sandstones and shales along with grey slates, reappear north of the sand dunes at Braunton Burrows and form the spectacular, steeply cliffed coast north to Morte Point. A fine exposure of fossiliferous Devonian sandstones and siltstones is visible at Baggy Point.

Lundy is a steeply cliffed, flat-topped island formed largely of early Tertiary granite that is locally intruded by dykes. Devonian slates form the south-western corner of the island. The granite is the most southerly intrusion of the Tertiary Igneous Province in Britain; the nearest major body of the same age forms the mountains of Mourne in Northern Ireland.

The north coast of Devon from Morte Point to Porlock displays steep cliffs where the high, rounded inland hills meet the coast. Narrow linear valleys, some of which are located along fault lines, reach the coast at Coombe Martin and Lynmouth, for example. The cliffs are formed of Devonian slates and grits with subtle variations in form related to the structure or chemistry of the rocks.

Porlock - Kenfig

The form of the coast changes dramatically east of Minehead, where steep cliffs of Devonian rocks are replaced by lower cliffs of Triassic and Jurassic sandstones, shales and mudstones. The large tidal range in the Bristol Channel and the rapid erosion of the cliffs has produced a wide rocky foreshore along parts of this coast. The axis of a major east-west syncline passes westwards into the Bristol Channel from Brent Knoll near Burnham-on-Sea. Lower Jurassic rocks (primarily Lias) occupy the core of the syncline, with Triassic and Carboniferous sediments on the flanks.

Triassic rocks forming the southern flank of the syncline are well exposed at Blue Anchor Bay, and the Rhaetic (part of the upper Triassic containing an interesting range of lithologies) is exposed on the foreshore near Watchet. Local faulting and folding of these units has produced a foreshore of great geological complexity.

The inner Bristol Channel, east of a line from Bridgwater to Cardiff, is flanked largely by wide estuarine flats of Holocene age underlain by softer Triassic or Jurassic strata. The Somerset Levels on the south coast and the Wentlooge Levels on the north coast are the most extensive of these flats, which are now mostly land-claimed for agricultural use. Rising above the levels, and locally forming the coast, are the steep-sided hills forming Brean Down, Middle Hope and the area between Portishead and Clevedon. The islands of Steep Holm and Flat Holm form similar features. Most of these hills or islands occupy anticlinal cores, where Carboniferous Limestone or Devonian grits, which are more resistant to erosion than the overlying rocks, reach the surface.

Along the northern coast of the inner Bristol Channel there are no bedrock exposures from Sudbrook westwards to Cardiff except for the small hill at Goldcliff. However, bedrock is rarely far below the surface and isolated exposures are visible in the intertidal zone.

The coast south and west of the mouth of the River Taff at Cardiff is formed mainly of steep, low cliffs composed of the gently dipping, well-bedded Mercia Mudstone Group, consisting of Rhaetic (Triassic) and Liassic (Jurassic) sediments. Isolated inliers of Carboniferous rocks are exposed on the coast at Barry. Steep cliffs of Liassic limestones and shales, locally fossiliferous, form the almost continuously cliffed coastline west of Barry to Nash Point and northwards to Ogmore-by-Sea. These well-bedded sediments are spectacularly exposed on the wide, sloping foreshore of this coast. Some minor valleys, such as at Nash Point, are abruptly truncated at the coast.

The Triassic and underlying Carboniferous rocks on the northern flanks of the Bristol Channel syncline reappear at Porthcawl, but the bedrock is concealed along much of the eastern side of Swansea Bay by extensive sand dunes.

2.1.3 Further sources of information

A. Maps

British Geological Survey. 1982. *Scilly. Sheet 49°N-08°W. Sea bed sediments.* 1:250,000 series. Keyworth, British Geological Survey.

British Geological Survey. 1982. *Scilly. Sheet 49°N-08°W. Solid geology.* 1:250,000 series. Keyworth, British Geological Survey.

British Geological Survey. 1983. *Lizard. Sheet 49°N-06°W. Sea bed sediments.* 1:250,000 series. Keyworth, British Geological Survey.

British Geological Survey. 1983. *Lizard. Sheet 49°N-06°W. Solid geology.* 1:250,000 series. Keyworth, British Geological Survey.

British Geological Survey. 1983. *Lundy. Sheet 51°N - 06°W. Sea bed sediments.* 1:250,000 series. Keyworth, British Geological Survey.

British Geological Survey. 1983. *Lundy. Sheet 51°N - 06°W. Solid geology.* 1:250,000 series. Keyworth, British Geological Survey.

British Geological Survey. 1985. *Land's End. Sheet 50°N - 06°W. Solid geology.* 1:250,000 series. Keyworth, British Geological Survey.

British Geological Survey. 1986. *Bristol Channel. Sheet 51°N - 04°W. Sea bed sediments and Quaternary geology.* 1:250,000 series. Keyworth, British Geological Survey.

British Geological Survey. 1987. *Land's End. Sheet 50°N - 06°W. Sea bed sediments and Quaternary geology.* 1:250 000 series. Keyworth, British Geological Survey.

British Geological Survey. 1988. *Bristol Channel. Sheet 51°N - 04°W. Solid geology.* 1:250,000 series. Keyworth, British Geological Survey.

British Geological Survey. 1991. *Geology of the United Kingdom, Ireland and the adjacent continental shelf (south sheet).* 1:1,000,000 scale. Keyworth, British Geological Survey.

Geological Survey of Great Britain (England and Wales). 1977. *Bideford and Lundy Island (sheet 292 and parts of 275,276,291 and 308). Solid and drift edition.* 1:50,000 scale. Keyworth, British Geological Survey.

B. Further reading

Section 7.4 lists the Geological Conservation Review (GCR) sites occurring in the region. Detailed descriptions of GCR sites in the region can be found in volumes of the Geological Conservation Review series.

Campbell, S., & Bowen, D.Q. 1989. *Quaternary of Wales.* Peterborough, Joint Nature Conservation Committee. (Geological Conservation Review series, No. 2.)

Campbell, S., *ed.* In prep. *Quaternary of south-west England.* London, Chapman and Hall. (Geological Conservation Review series, No. 14.)

Cleal, C.J., & Thomas, B.A. 1996. *British upper Carboniferous stratigraphy.* London, Chapman and Hall. (Geological Conservation Review series, No. 11.)

Edmonds, E.A., McKeown, M.C., & Williams, M. 1975. *British regional geology: south-west England.* London, HMSO for Institute of Geological Sciences.

Ellis, N.V. (*ed.*), Bowen, D.Q., Campbell, S., Knill, J.L., McKirdy, A.P., Prosser, C.D., Vincent, M.A., & Wilson, R.C.L. 1995. *An introduction to the Geological Conservation Review.* Peterborough, Joint Nature Conservation Committee. (Geological Conservation Review series, No. 1.)

Evans, C.D.R. 1991. *The geology of the western English Channel and its western approaches.* London, HMSO. (British Geological Survey, United Kingdom Offshore Regional Report.)

Flett, J.S., & Hill, J.B. 1946. Geology of the Lizard and Meneage. *Memoir of the Geological Survey of Great Britain,* Sheet 359 (England and Wales).

Floyd, P.A., Exley, C.S., & Styles, M.T. 1993. *Igneous rocks of south-west England.* London, Chapman and Hall. (Geological Conservation Review series, No. 5.)

George, T.N. 1970. *British regional geology: South Wales.* London, HMSO for Institute of Geological Sciences.

Goode, A.J.J., & Taylor, R.T. 1988. Geology of the country around Penzance. *Memoir of the British Geological Survey,* Sheets 351 and 358 (England and Wales).

Gregory, K.J., *ed.* In prep. *Fluvial geomorphology of Great Britain.* London, Chapman and Hall. (Geological Conservation Review series, No. 13.)

Green, G.W. 1992. *British regional geology: Bristol and Gloucester region.* Keyworth, British Geological Survey.

Leveridge, B.E., Holder, M.T., & Goode, A.J.J. 1990. Geology of the country around Falmouth. *Memoir of the British Geological Survey,* Sheet 352 (England and Wales).

Steers, J.A. 1969. *The coastline of England and Wales.* Cambridge, Cambridge University Press.

Tappin, D.R., Chadwick, R.A., Jackson, A., Wingfield., R.T.R., & Smith, N.J.P. 1994. *The geology of Cardigan Bay and the Bristol Channel.* London, HMSO, for the British Geological Survey. (United Kingdom Offshore Regional Report.)

C. Contact names and addresses

Type of information	*Contact address and telephone no.*
Geological information for region and the whole of Britain, including geological maps at 1:50,000 scale	Coastal Geology Group, British Geological Survey, Keyworth, Nottingham NG12 5GG, tel: 0115 936 3100
Geological Conservation Review sites, Devon & Cornwall	*English Nature Devon and Cornwall Team, Okehampton, tel: 01837 55045
Geological Conservation Review sites, Somerset & Avon	*English Nature Somerset and Avon Team, Taunton, tel: 01823 283211
Geological Conservation Review sites, Gwent, Mid Glamorgan & S. Glamorgan	*Countryside Council for Wales, Cardiff, tel: 01222 772400
Geological Conservation Review	*JNCC, Peterborough, tel: 01733 62626

*Starred contact addresses are given in full in the Appendix.

2.2 Offshore geology

British Geological Survey

This section deals briefly with the geology of the rocks and sediments at and below the sea bed. The bulk of the information is shown on the maps, with some additional explanation provided by the text.

2.2.1 Holocene sea-bed sediments

Sea-bed sediments across the region have been deposited in very different environments and as a result vary considerably between south Cornwall and the Severn Estuary. In the south-west of the region the bulk of the sediments are sands or thin spreads of gravel, generally less than one metre thick. Extensive areas of bedrock are exposed at sea bed near the coast, particularly off the Lizard, Land's End, the Isles of Scilly and Padstow Bay (Map 2.2.1). The coarse nature of the sediments suggests that finer material has been borne away by wave or tidal action.

An extensive area north-west of Lundy and south of Dyfed is covered by a major sand wave field. Individual sand waves, orientated NNW-SSE, rise to over 20 m above the level of the surrounding sea bed. Their asymmetry indicates that net sediment transport is towards the west, where finer-grained sediments are found in the Celtic Deep.

The distribution of sediments to the east of Lundy is complex. Detailed sediment distributions and bedforms within the inner Bristol Channel and the Severn Estuary are related to a series of circulation cells generated by tidal currents. Generally the thickness of the sea-bed sediment decreases eastwards as tidal current speeds increase. Much of the inner Bristol Channel has bare rock at the sea bed, with mobile sediment restricted to isolated linear banks near the coast. The location to the north of Nash Sand and the other sand banks is due to the change in tidal current velocities as the channel opens out to the west of Nash Point. The sand banks are active features, changing form in response to storm conditions.

Bridgwater Bay is underlain by an extensive mud sheet locally over 20 m thick and displaying a sharp seaward termination; the mud passes landward into a sandy upper beach. Similar mud flats are found seaward of the Wentlooge Levels between Newport and Cardiff, but the mud here is generally only a few metres thick. The upper part of the Severn Estuary is infilled with sand banks traversed by two major linear channels, the Bristol Deep and Newport Deep.

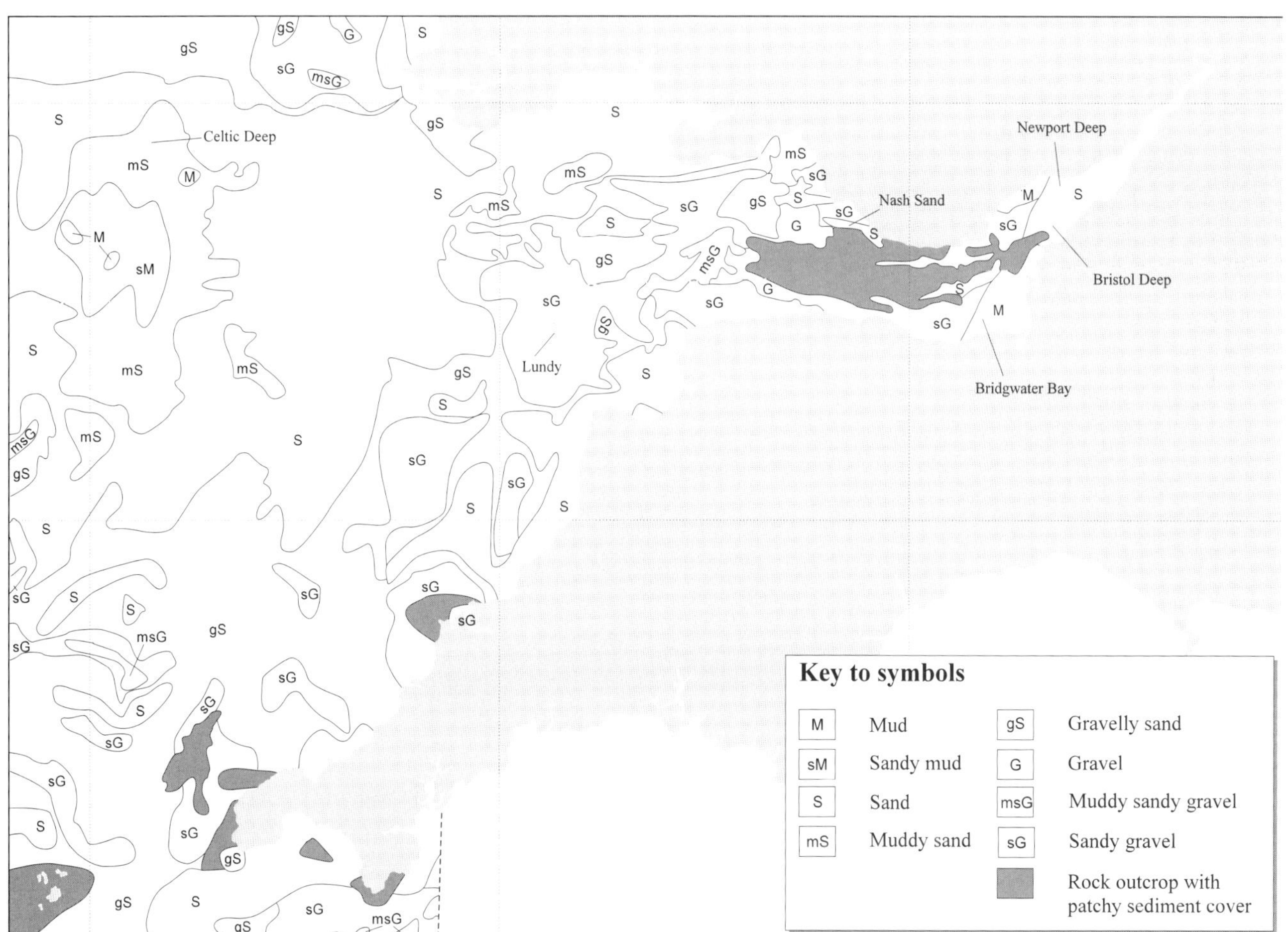

Map 2.2.1 Sea-bed sediments. Source: British Geological Survey (1991); sediment classification modified after Folk (1954).

2.2.2 Pleistocene geology

Determining the extent of the major Pleistocene ice sheets across the region is problematic. The last major ice sheet, which formed during the late Devensian, covered most of south Wales but reached the coast only at Swansea Bay. Until offshore investigations commenced some twenty years ago the southern limit of this icesheet, and thus of Pleistocene deposits, was drawn from Dyfed across to southern Ireland. However, seismic and drilling evidence indicates that a tongue of the icesheet extended southwards into the Celtic Sea to reach the Isles of Scilly (Scourse *et al.* 1990). This ice sheet, which was probably about 100 m thick, did not reach the west coast of Devon and Cornwall.

A Quaternary basin in the Celtic Sea south-west of Dyfed contains a sequence of tills and sediments over 200 m thick (Map 2.2.2). Narrow linear deposits of sediment infill between the basin and the coast are probably related to erosion at the base of an ice sheet. Three channel sequences are recognised within the basin, suggesting that three major ice sheets traversed the area, the youngest being during the late Devensian.

Isolated erratics of lithologies uncommon to the area suggest that an earlier ice sheet may have reached the coast of Devon or Cornwall. One of the best examples is the 'giant' boulder of garnetiferous gneiss at Porthleven in Mount's Bay, which rests on a rock platform with cemented beach gravels. Few definite basal ice-sheet deposits have been identified along the coast, although outwash gravels, periglacial deposits and possible interglacial clays have been found. The till underlain by beach gravels at Fremington was probably laid down by an ice sheet, but its age is uncertain.

Non-glacial Pleistocene deposits in the English Channel tend to be limited to palaeovalley infills beneath Holocene sea-bed sediments. These valleys, now infilled with sand, clay and gravel, have little topographic expression. A deposit of peat recovered from a buried valley in Mount's Bay at a depth of 32 m yielded a radiocarbon age of 12,070 years BP.

2.2.3 Solid (pre-Quaternary) geology

The South-West Peninsula is a basement massif bounded by Mesozoic sedimentary basins to the south (English Channel Basin), the west (Celtic Sea Basin) and the north (the Bristol Channel Basin). Mesozoic strata approach the shore along the south coast of Devon and Cornwall (Region 10), but within this region they are seen onshore only along the coast of the inner Bristol Channel.

The Mesozoic basins were formed during early Permo-Triassic times, when thick red marl and sandstone sequences accumulated in fault-controlled basins. Later, Jurassic limestones, shales and clays were deposited more extensively across the basins and on their flanks.

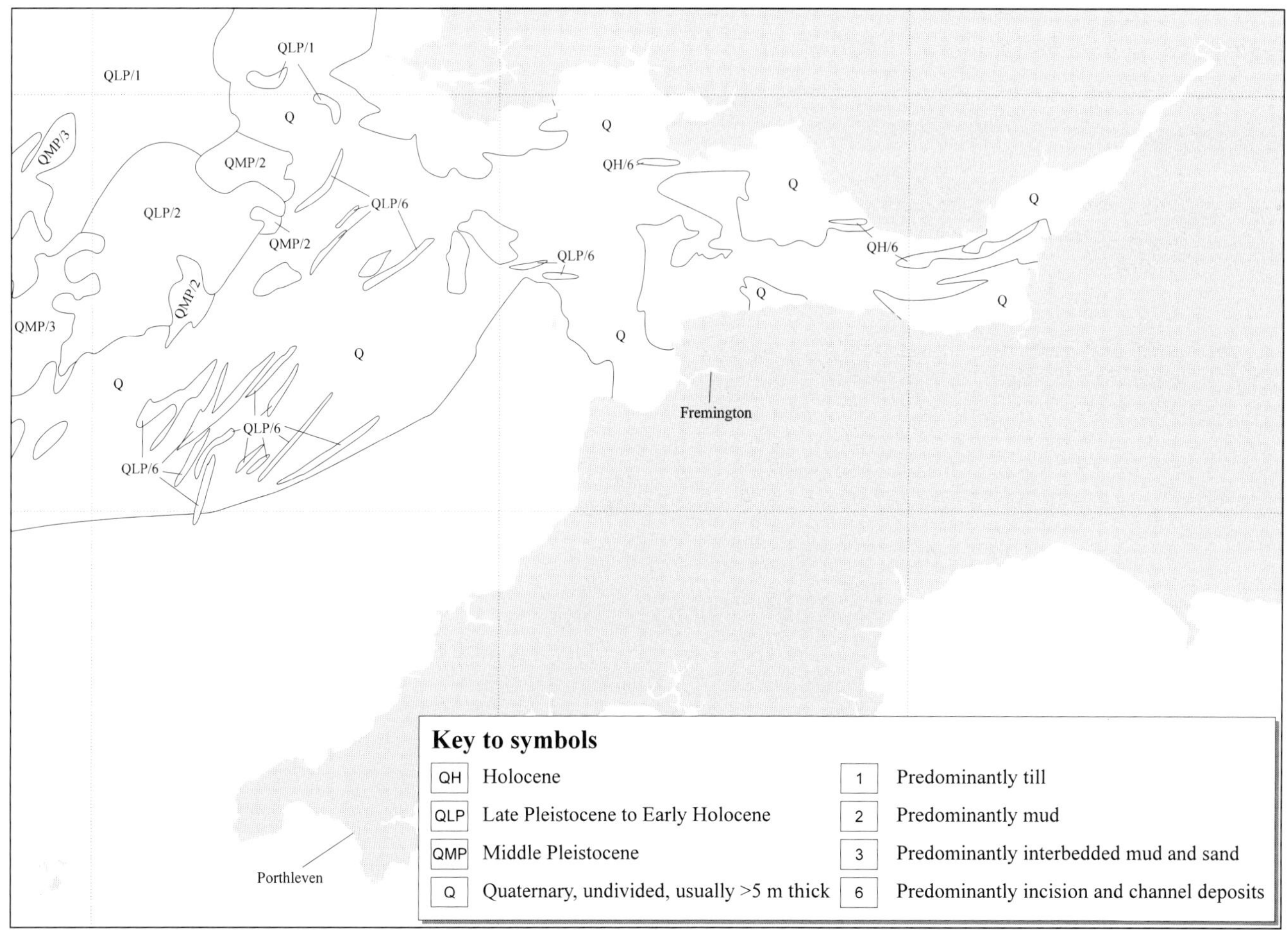

Map 2.2.2 Offshore Pleistocene deposits. Source: British Geological Survey (1994).

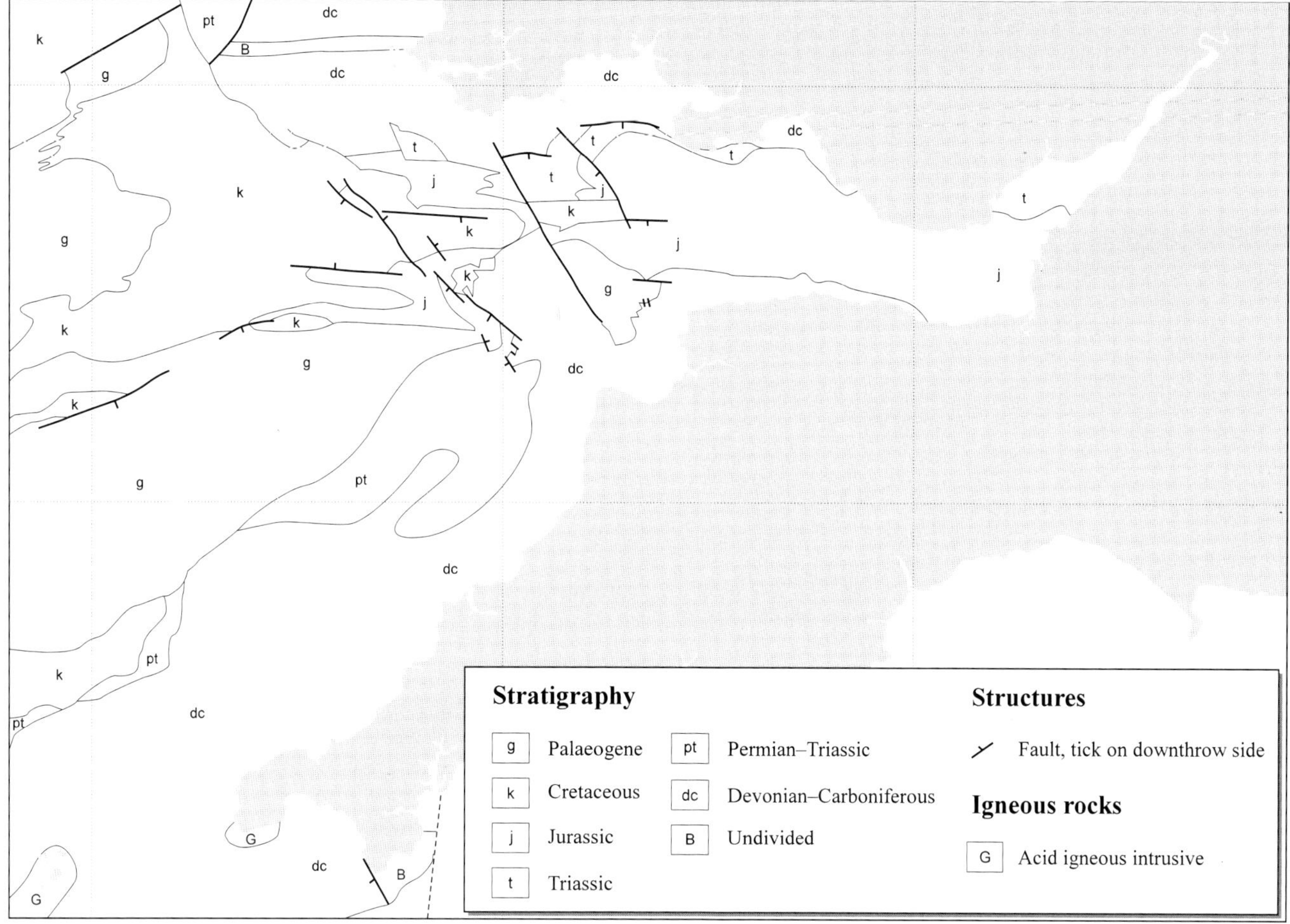

Map 2.2.3 Offshore solid (pre-Quaternary) geology. Source: British Geological Survey (1991).

Subsequent uplift led to the removal, in the English Channel and elsewhere, of much of the Jurassic sequence, and the accumulation of thick Lower Cretaceous sediments. An overlying blanket of chalk (Upper Cretaceous) covers much of the complex structure of the buried early Mesozoic sequences (Map 2.2.3).

The removal of much of the Jurassic sediment from the English Channel Basin has greatly reduced its potential as a hydrocarbons province. The Celtic Sea Basin, which has salt structures in the Jurassic sediments and a thick Cretaceous cover, has greater potential. The hydrocarbons potential of the Bristol Channel is highest in the west, where the thick and relatively complete Jurassic and Lower Cretaceous succession is overlain by a thick Upper Cretaceous and Tertiary blanket.

Tertiary (Palaeogene) sediments preserved in the Celtic Sea Basin are largely of Oligocene or Eocene age. Of interest is the Stanley Bank Basin to the east of Lundy. This basin, containing sediments of Oligocene age, is formed along the Sticklepath Fault, which is traceable north-westwards into Dyfed and south-eastwards into Devon.

The rocks making up the Lizard (see section 2.1.2) extend a short distance offshore, before becoming concealed beneath Devonian and Permo-Triassic rocks. At Land's End, Devonian rocks were intruded by a granite batholith during the early Permian, and the coarse granite outcrops on the sea bed.

2.2.4 Further sources of information

A. Maps

British Geological Survey. 1982. *Scilly. Sheet 49°N-08°W. Sea-bed sediments.* 1:250,000 series. Keyworth, British Geological Survey.

British Geological Survey. 1982. *Scilly. Sheet 49°N-08°W. Solid geology.* 1:250,000 series. Keyworth, British Geological Survey.

British Geological Survey. 1983. *Land's End. Sheet 50°N-06°W. Solid geology.* 1:250,000 series. Keyworth, British Geological Survey.

British Geological Survey. 1983. *Lizard. Sheet 49°N-06°W. Sea-bed sediments.* 1:250,000 series. Keyworth, British Geological Survey.

British Geological Survey. 1983. *Lizard. Sheet 49°N-06°W. Solid geology.* 1:250,000 series. Keyworth, British Geological Survey.

British Geological Survey. 1983. *Lundy. Sheet 51°N-06°W. Sea-bed sediments.* 1:250,000 series. Keyworth, British Geological Survey.

British Geological Survey. 1983. *Lundy. Sheet 51°N-06°W. Solid geology.* 1:250,000 series. Keyworth, British Geological Survey.

British Geological Survey. 1985. *Land's End. Sheet 50°N-06°W. Sea-bed sediments.* 1:250,000 series. Keyworth, British Geological Survey.

British Geological Survey. 1986. *Bristol Channel. Sheet 51°N-04°W. Sea-bed sediments and Quaternary geology.* 1:250,000 series. Keyworth, British Geological Survey.

British Geological Survey. 1986. *Haig Fras. Sheet 50°N - 08°W. Sea bed sediments.* 1:250,000 series. Keyworth, British Geological Survey.

British Geological Survey. 1987. *Haig Fras. Sheet 50°N - 08°W. Solid geology.* 1:250,000 series. Keyworth, British Geological Survey.

British Geological Survey. 1988. *Bristol Channel. Sheet 51°N-04°W. Solid geology.* 1:250,000 series. Keyworth, British Geological Survey.

British Geological Survey. 1991. *North Celtic Sea sheet, Quaternary geology.* 1:250,000 series. Keyworth, British Geological Survey.

B. References cited

British Geological Survey. 1991. *Geology of the United Kingdom, Ireland and the adjacent continental shelf.* 1:1,000,000 scale. Keyworth, British Geological Survey.

British Geological Survey. 1994. *Quaternary geology around the United Kingdom (north & south sheets).* Keyworth, British Geological Survey.

Folk, R.L. 1954. The distinction between grain-size and mineral composition in sedimentary rock nomenclature. *Journal of Geology, 62:* 344-359.

Scourse, J.D., Bateman, R.M., Catt, J.A., Evans, C.D.R., Robinson, J.E., & Young, J.R. 1990. Sedimentology and micropalaeontology of glacimarine sediments from the central and south-western Celtic Sea. *In: Glacimarine sediments: processes and sediments,* ed. by J.A. Dowdeswell & J.D. Scourse, 329-347. London, Geological Society. (Special Publication No. 53.)

C. Further reading

Evans, C.D.R. 1991. *The geology of the western English Channel and its western approaches.* London, HMSO, for the British Geological Survey. (United Kingdom Offshore Regional Report.)

Hamblin, R.J.O., Crosby, A., Balson, P.S., Jones, S.M., Chadwick, R.A., Penn, I.E., & Arthur, M.J. 1992. *The geology of the English Channel.* London, HMSO, for the British Geological Survey. (United Kingdom Offshore Regional Report.)

Pantin, H.M. 1991. *The sea bed sediments around the United Kingdom: their bathymetric and physical environment, grain size, mineral composition and associated bedforms.* Keyworth, British Geological Survey. (BGS Research Report SB/90/1.)

Tappin, D.R., Chadwick, R.A., Jackson, A., Wingfield., R.T.R., & Smith, N.J.P. 1994. *The geology of Cardigan Bay and the Bristol Channel.* London, HMSO, for the British Geological Survey. (United Kingdom Offshore Regional Report.)

Taylor, R.T., & Goode, A.J.J. 1987. Late Pleistocene and Holocene radiocarbon dates from the Penzance District, Cornwall. *Proceedings of the Ussher Society, 6:* 559.

D. Contact names and addresses

Type of information	*Contact address and telephone no.*
Geological information for region and the whole of Britain	Coastal Geology Group, British Geological Survey, Keyworth, Nottingham NG12 5GG, tel: 0115 936 3100
UKDMAP 1992. Version 2. United Kingdom digital marine atlas. Oceanographic maps	*BODC, Birkenhead, tel: 0151 652 3950

2.3 Wind and water

British Geological Survey

The offshore part of the region may be divided into two environments: the main part, off the Cornwall and Devon coast northwards to about Minehead, and in south Wales a short stretch of coast north of Nash Point, is open to the influence of the Atlantic Ocean. The inner Bristol Channel and Severn Estuary are more sheltered.

2.3.1 Wind

The wind rose data (Figure 2.3.1) for the Isles of Scilly shows winds predominantly from a westerly direction, with an average of 25 days of gales per year, most of which occur in the winter months (Hydrographic Department 1960). The wind rose for Cardiff shows a similar westerly predominance, but the low percentage of winds from northerly and southerly directions may be due to local topographic effects. Gales at the Cardiff station averaged three days a year.

Much of the coast of the region is fully exposed to the prevailing winds. Maps 2.3.1 and 2.3.2 show that the maximum wind speeds occur across western Cornwall and the Isles of Scilly. Wind speeds decrease eastwards in the Bristol Channel. Meteorological Office data show that the mean wind speeds along the exposed coasts of this region are similar to those across the west coast of Wales but slightly less than those across the west coast of Scotland.

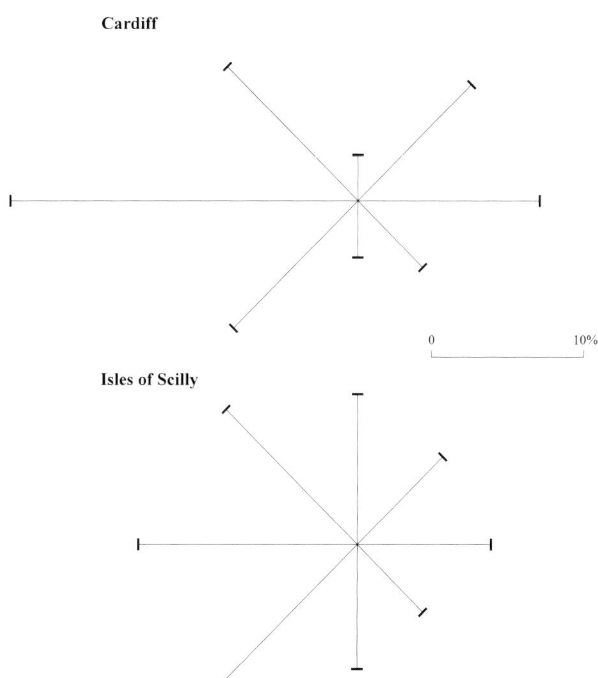

Figure 2.3.1 Wind directions at Cardiff and on the Isles of Scilly shown as % of observations during the years 1916 - 1950. Flat calm (% of observations) = Cardiff (13.5%); Isles of Scilly (18%). Source: Hydrographic Department (1960).

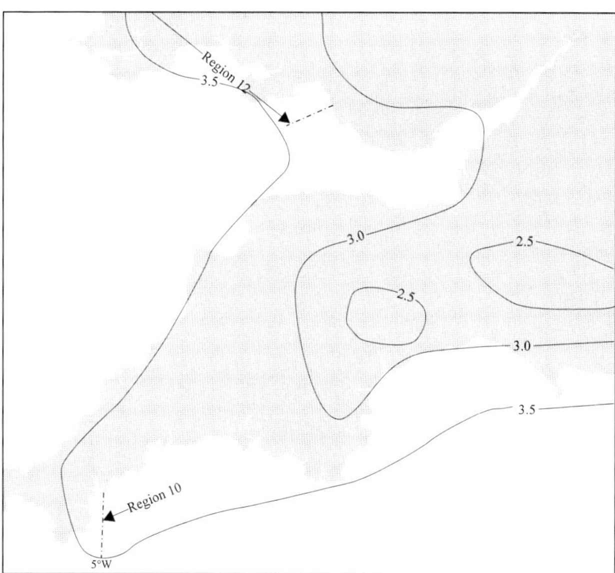

Map 2.3.1 Hourly mean windspeed (in m/s) exceeded for 75% of the time. Source: Caton (1976).

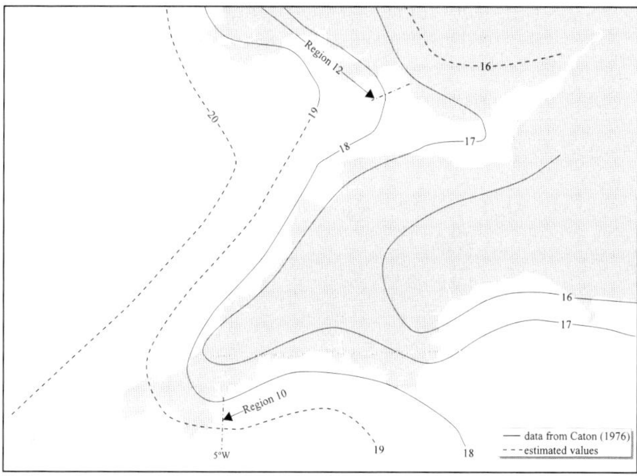

Map 2.3.2 Hourly mean windspeed (in m/s) exceeded for 0.1% of the time. Source: Caton (1976).

2.3.2 Water depth

The morphology of the sea bed is influenced by the nature of its bedrock, the exposure of the area to wave attack and the supply of mobile sediment. The sea bed of most of this region slopes steeply and regularly down to a depth of about 60 m, levelling out onto the westward-sloping continental shelf (Map 2.3.3). Much of it is covered in thin, mobile sediments and thus reflects the shape of the bedrock surface. This surface was modelled during the late Tertiary and Quaternary, and changes to the coast since the last glaciation 10,000 years ago have probably been minimal, except for the infilling of some areas in the upper part of the Bristol Channel.

Detailed analysis of the bathymetry around the coast of Cornwall and the Isles of Scilly reveals a number of submerged cliffs down to a depth of about 70 m. Locally the

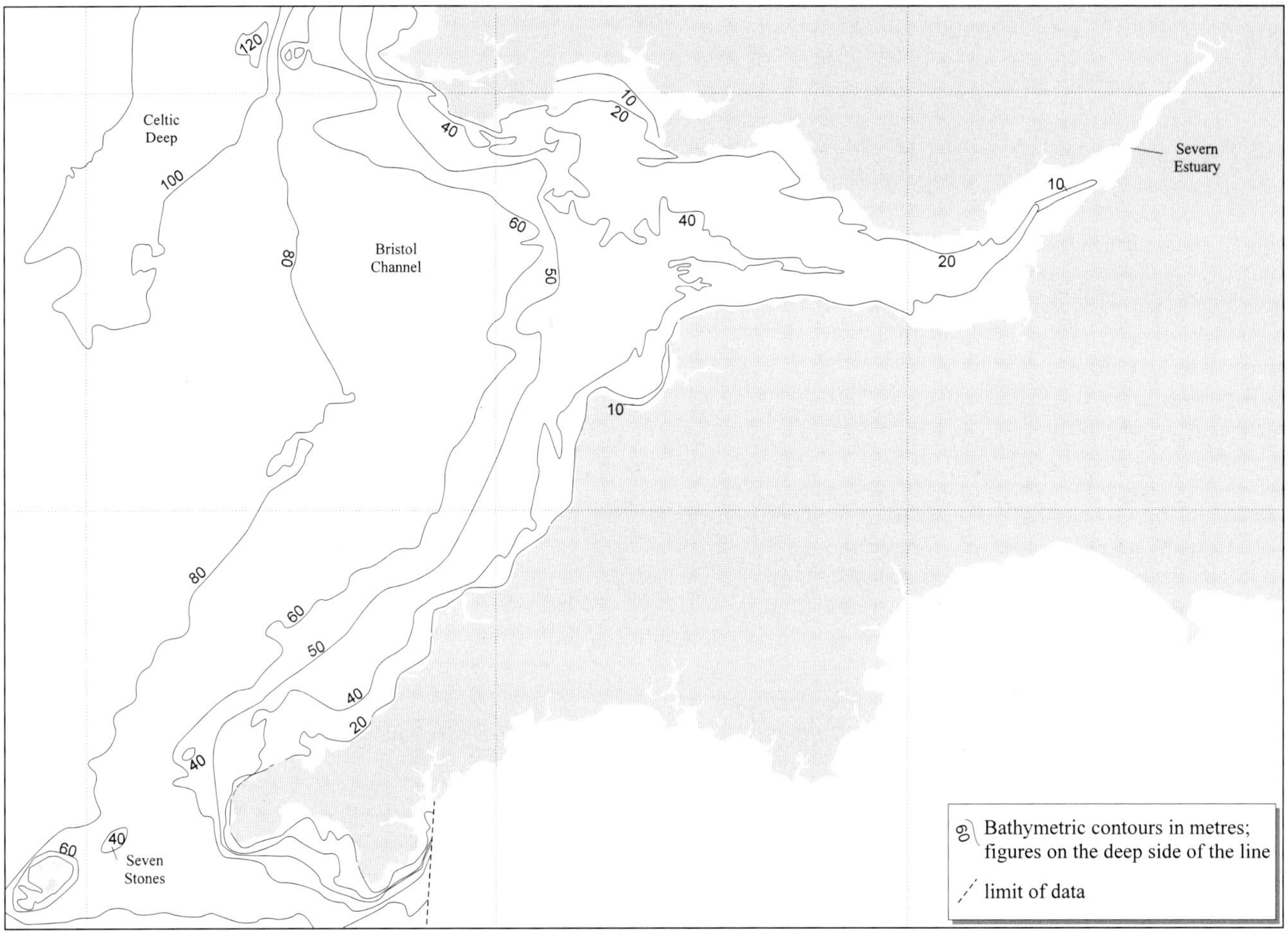

Map 2.3.3 Bathymetry. Source: British Geological Survey (1987).

cliffs are breached by valleys incised during periods of lower sea level and now infilled with Holocene sediment. The best-developed incised valley in the region is that of the Severn: in the upper part of the estuary, sand banks infill and obliterate the valley, but from about Weston-super-Mare it is a well-developed bathymetric feature, stretching westwards for some 100 km.

2.3.3 Tidal currents

Along the coast of Cornwall the maximum tidal currents exceed 2 knots only near headlands and in the channel between the Isles of Scilly and the mainland (Map 2.3.4). However, going eastwards into the Bristol Channel, speeds increase progressively, and within the Severn Estuary maximum currents locally exceed 7 knots (Lee & Ramster 1981). Admiralty Charts, which are thought to give a more accurate reflection of currents in restricted embayments such as the Severn Estuary, show a maximum surface ebb current of 4.6 knots off Foreland Point and a maximum flood current of 4.2 knots off Weston-super-Mare.

Computer modelling of the tides in the area by Uncles (1983) has shown that the tidal currents are mostly orientated parallel to the medial axis of the Bristol Channel but locally point into bays. This helps to explain why sand and mud accumulate in Barnstaple, Bridgwater and Swansea Bays.

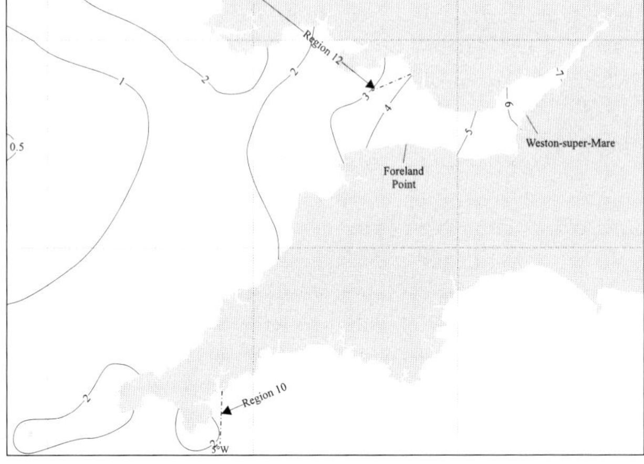

Map 2.3.4 Maximum tidal current speed (in m/s) at mean spring tides. Source: Sager & Sammler (1968).

2.3.4 Tidal range

The mean tidal range at spring tides along the coast of the region shows a steady increase north-eastwards from 5 m at Land's End to 12.3 m at Avonmouth (Map 2.3.5). This increase is due to the amplification of the tidal movement as it is funnelled eastwards up the Bristol Channel. Storm surges may increase this value by more than 1.5 m in the inner Bristol Channel and Severn Estuary.

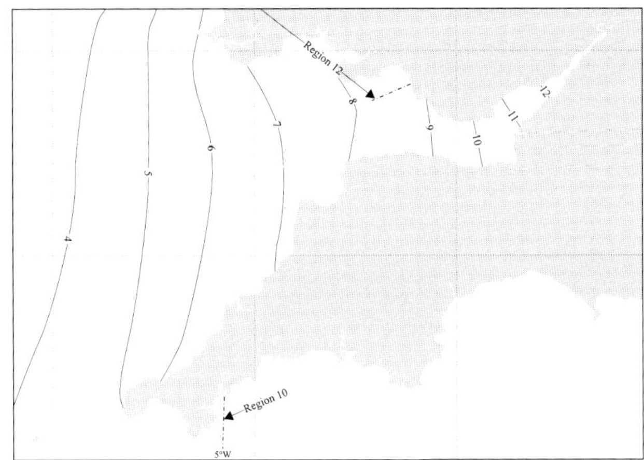

Map 2.3.5 Tidal range (m) at mean spring tides. Source: Lee & Ramster (1981). © Crown copyright.

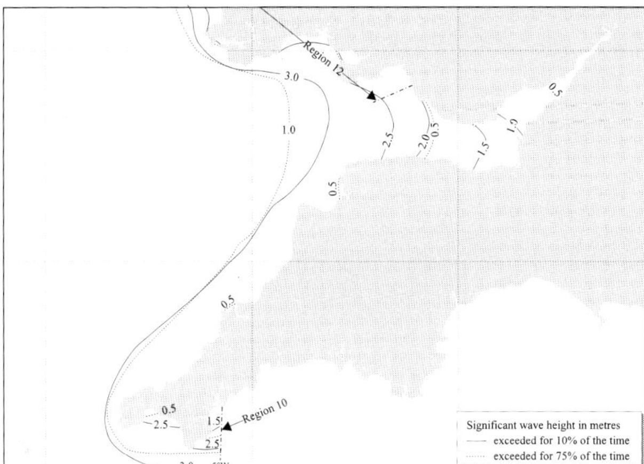

Map 2.3.6 Significant wave height (m) exceeded for 10% and 75% of the year. Source: Draper (1991).

The tidal range of the Severn Estuary is the largest in the UK and the second largest in the world. Under certain conditions spring tides cause the formation of a tidal wave known as the 'Severn Bore', which can reach as far upstream as Gloucester.

2.3.5 Wave exposure and sea state

There is a long 'fetch' across the Atlantic Ocean and the prevailing westerly winds generate large waves on the coasts of Cornwall and parts of Devon. In addition the relatively steep nearshore bathymetric gradient results in high waves approaching close to the coast. Significant wave heights during the winter exceed 4 m for 10% of the time offshore and at Land's End, and exceed 3 m for 10% of the time along much of the Cornish coast (Map 2.3.6). Wave conditions as severe as this are found elsewhere in Britain only off the coast of north-west Scotland.

The wave height predicted to occur once in fifty years is 20 m along the south-west Cornwall coast, decreasing to about 18 m at the mouth of the Bristol Channel. This compares with a predicted height of over 30 m along the north-west coast of Scotland.

Wave data from the Seven Stones Lightship west of Land's End provide evidence that significant wave heights have increased progressively between 1962 and 1984, indicating a gradual increase in storminess in the North Atlantic during this time.

2.3.6 Water characteristics

Water temperature

The mean sea surface temperatures for summer and winter are shown on Map 2.3.7. The data are for August and February, which are the months of, respectively, highest and lowest values. In February the open waters in the south-west of the region have a temperature of about 9.0-9.5°C, compared with 10.5°C for the waters at the edge of the continental shelf some 200 km to the south-west of Land's End. Water temperatures decrease in the shallower waters to the north-east, and the mean in the inner Severn Estuary is less than 6°C. By August temperatures are at a maximum for the year, attaining approximately 16°C throughout the region.

Stratification of the water column occurs when the effects of the warming of the surface water outweigh those of mixing by winds and tides (see also section 4.3). Layers of water develop whose temperature and density vary with depth. Stratification develops in the Celtic Sea by late spring and spreads eastwards along the north Cornwall coast. The turbid waters of the Bristol Channel remain well-mixed throughout the year. By early winter the coastal waters of the region have become fully mixed again, leaving only an offshore tongue of stratified water in the Celtic Sea (Pingree 1980).

Salinity

The waters of the southern part of the region are open to the influence of the Atlantic Ocean, so their mean surface salinity, at 35 g/kg or more, is typical of oceanic water (Map 2.3.8). Salinity decreases north-eastwards into the Bristol Channel as the influence of freshwater input increases. Variations in the salinity of the Severn Estuary and inner Bristol Channel follow changes in the riverine flow, with generally lower salinities in winter (when river flows are greater) than in summer. Salinity values in the upper estuary in winter may be as low as 20 g/kg (Collins & Williams 1981).

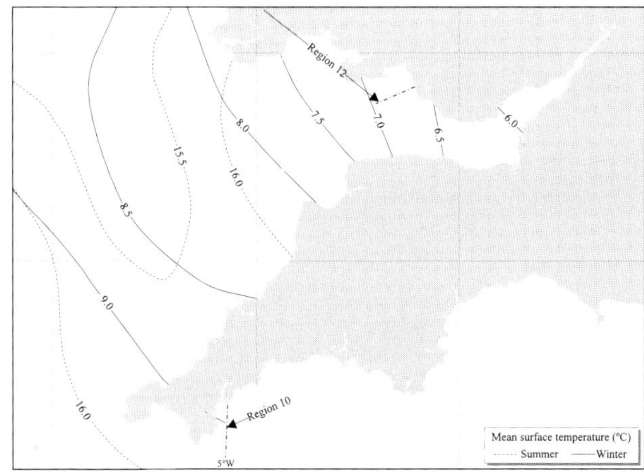

Map 2.3.7 Mean surface water temperature in summer and winter (°C). Source: Lee & Ramster (1981). © Crown copyright.

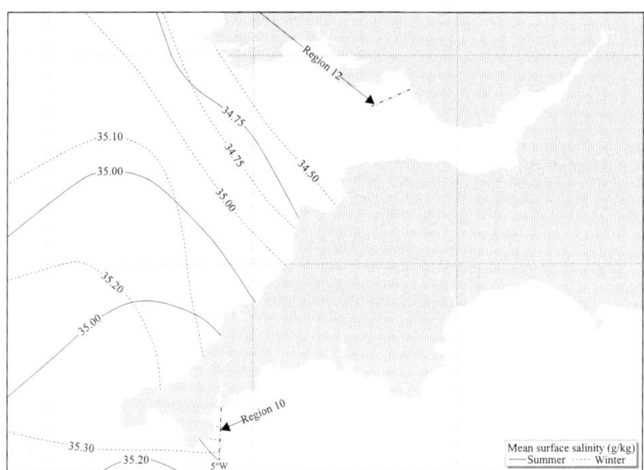

Map 2.3.8 Mean surface salinity of seawater in summer and winter in g/kg of total dissolved salt. Source: Lee & Ramster (1981). © Crown copyright.

Water turbidity

The waters off the South-West Peninsula are derived from the Atlantic Ocean and contain virtually no terrestrially-derived suspended sediments. Nearshore, the rivers carry suspended sediment into the sea, especially after high rainfall. Such plumes of suspended sediment are quickly mixed in by waves and tides.

The situation is very different in the inner Bristol Channel and Severn Estuary, where the water is highly turbid. This has been determined using satellite imagery (Collins 1983) as well as by analysis of the water column. Estimates have been made that the estuary carries 10 million tonnes of suspended sediments at spring tides (Buck 1993). The area of highest turbidity is in water depths of less than 30 m, but the boundary moves seaward during spring tides as strong currents cause resuspension of mud from the sea bed. Higher turbidity water tends to move west along the northern shores of the inner Bristol Channel, while lower turbidity water is found along the southern shores. The observed pattern is of an overall westerly transport of suspended sediment within the inner Bristol Channel. The average turbidity within the Severn Estuary is highest between Avonmouth and the outer part of Bridgwater Bay, where the surface water contains 0.5-1.0 g/l of suspended solids, while at the sea bed the concentration may be three to six times this value.

2.3.7 Further sources of information

A. *References cited*

British Geological Survey. 1987. *Map of seabed sediment around the United Kingdom.* 1:1,000,000 scale. Keyworth, British Geological Survey.

Buck, A.L. 1993. *An inventory of UK estuaries. Volume 2. South-west Britain.* Peterborough, Joint Nature Conservation Committee.

Caton, P.G. 1976. *Maps of hourly wind speed over the UK 1965-73.* Bracknell, Meteorological Office. (Climatological Memorandum No. 79.)

Collins, M. 1983. Supply, distribution and transport of suspended sediment in a macrotidal environment: Bristol Channel, UK. *Canadian Journal of Fisheries and Aquatic Sciences, 40*(1): 44-59.

Collins, N.R., & Williams, R. 1981. Zooplankton of the Bristol Channel and Severn Estuary. The distribution of four copepods in relation to salinity. *Marine Biology, 64:* 273-283.

Draper, L. 1991. *Wave climate atlas of the British Isles.* London, HMSO.

Hydrographic Department. 1960. *West coast of England pilot.* London, Hydrographic Department.

Lee, A.J., & Ramster, J.W. 1981. *Atlas of the seas around the British Isles.* Lowestoft, Ministry of Agriculture, Fisheries and Food.

Pingree, R.D. 1980. Physical oceanography of the Celtic Sea and English Channel. *In: The north-west European shelf seas: the sea bed and the sea in motion. Vol. 2. Physical and chemical oceanography and physical resources,* ed. by F.T. Banner, M.B. Collins & K.S. Massie, 415-465. Amsterdam, Elsevier. (Oceanography Series.)

Sager, G., & Sammler, R. 1968. *Atlas der Gezeitenströme für die Nordsee, den Kanal und die Irische See.* Rostock, Seehydrographischer Dienst der DDR.

Uncles, R. 1983. Hydrodynamics of the Bristol Channel. *Marine Pollution Bulletin, 15*(2): 47-53.

B. *Further reading*

Banner, F.T., Collins, M.B, & Massie, K.S., *eds.* 1980. *The north-west European shelf seas: the sea bed and the sea in motion. Vol. 2. Physical and chemical oceanography, and physical resources.* Amsterdam, Elsevier. (Oceanography Series.)

Barne, J., Davidson, N.C., Hill, T.O., & Jones, M. 1994. *Coastal and marine UKDMAP datasets: a user manual.* Peterborough, Joint Nature Conservation Committee.

British Geological Survey. 1994. *Quaternary geology around the United Kingdom (North and South Sheets).* 1:1,000,000 scale. Keyworth, British Geological Survey.

British Oceanographic Data Centre. 1992. *United Kingdom digital marine atlas user guide. Version 2.* Birkenhead, Natural Environment Research Council.

Department of the Environment. 1992. *Digest of environmental protection and water statistics.* London, Government Statistical Service, HMSO.

Dyer, K.R. 1984. Sedimentation processes in the Bristol Channel/Severn Estuary. *Marine Pollution Bulletin, 15*(2): 53-57.

Graff, J. 1981. An investigation of the frequency distributions of annual sea level maxima at ports around Great Britain. *Estuarine, Coastal and Shelf Science, 12:* 389-449.

Hydrographic Department. 1970. *Underwater handbook, western approaches to the British Isles.* London, Hydrographic Office.

Hydrographic Department. 1984. *Channel Pilot. Isles of Scilly and south coast of England, from Cape Cornwall to Bognor Regis. NP 27.* London, Hydrographic Office.

Hydrographic Office. 1993. *Admiralty Tide Tables, Vol. 1: European waters.* London, Hydrographic Office.

C. *Contact names and addresses*

Type of information	*Contact address and telephone no.*
UKDMAP (United Kingdom digital marine atlas) Version 2. Oceanographic maps	*BODC, Birkenhead, tel: 0151 652 3950
Monthly, seasonal and annual windroses	J. Hammond, Meteorological Office Marine Enquiry Service, Johnstone House, London Road, Bracknell RG12 2SY, tel: 01344 854979

*Starred contact addresses are given in full in the Appendix.

2.4 Sediment transport

British Geological Survey

2.4.1 Introduction

Currents produced by waves and tides are the dominant mechanism of sediment transport, and both are important in the coastal zone of the region. Most of the northern coast of Cornwall and Devon is open to the prevailing westerly winds, and the resulting waves are agents of sediment transport down to greater depths than along most British coasts. Within the Bristol Channel tides become the more important mechanism for sediment transport but waves remain important in the littoral zone.

The dominant sediment transport direction between Land's End and Bridgwater Bay is northwards and then eastwards, but the pattern of small inlets and headlands that characterises the coast, coupled with the low volume of available mobile sediment, limits littoral drift along the coast. Motyka & Brampton (1993) suggest that there is only limited evidence for northward drift along the west Cornwall and Devon coast, though wave action may cause strong seasonal onshore / offshore movement of sediment. South and west of Barnstaple Bay tides are generally weak, and storm waves are responsible for transport of sea-bed sediment near the coast.

Bridgwater Bay and the Severn Estuary (defined here as being east of a line from Brean Down to Lavernock Point) have a complex pattern of sediment transport. Detailed sediment distributions and bedforms within the inner Bristol Channel and the Severn Estuary are related to a series of circulation cells generated by tidal currents. A number of methods have been employed to identify these cells and deduce the direction and volume of transport, including computer modelling, analysis of the asymmetry of ripples and sand waves at the sea bed, and tracking changes in sediment grain sizes. The results show that mud, sand and gravel display different transport paths.

Gravel transport is dominated by the wave climate along the high water mark, sand is transported as bed load, and mud is transported as suspended sediment. Because of their different modes of transport, sand and mud are deposited in different areas. Sand transport is particularly complex, with each major sand bank (e.g. Culver Sand or Cardiff Grounds) displaying its own circulation cell. Ebb-dominated westward transport tends to occur in the mid-channel, with flood-dominated eastward transport restricted to narrow coastal boundary zones (Harris & Collins 1988). Over the past few thousand years the net movement of sand has been eastwards from the Celtic Sea into the estuary. The major sand banks infilling the central estuary and the isolated sandbanks found in the inner Bristol Channel are probably derived from a western, marine, rather than an eastern, alluvial, source.

Coastal erosion across the region is generally limited in scale compared with that taking place along the south and east coasts of England. Many of the coastal dune systems along the west coast of the peninsula are undergoing erosion. Cliff erosion is taking place in Mount's Bay and at Porthleven and beach erosion is taking place at Perran Sands. The hanging valleys and waterfalls of the rocky coast of Devon and Cornwall are an indication that the cliffs have been eroded, but the current rate of retreat is generally so slow as to be difficult to measure. The Carboniferous rocks forming the cliffs along the north coast of Devon are retreating at a negligible rate, and cliffs formed of Devonian rocks are thought to be retreating at about 4 cm / year (Williams *et al.* 1991). This erosion must also have been taking place through much of the late Tertiary and Quaternary. The cliffs of soft Mesozoic rock along the Somerset coast are undergoing erosion at a rate of about 20 cm / year, with higher values locally. Much of the coast of the Severn Estuary is protected by man-made structures and is not retreating, but erosion is taking place on the foreshore, which is becoming steeper.

2.4.2 Description

Sediment transport is described within the context of coastal cells and sub-cells. These divide the coastline into sections within which sediment erosion and accretion are inter-related and largely independent of other cells. Cells are separated by either littoral drift divides or sediment sinks.

Motyka & Brampton (1993) describe the coast of the region as being part of three coastal cells, which are further divided into eight coastal sub-cells. The sub-cells are described below and are shown on Map 2.4.1. Note that the sediment transport shown is of sand and gravel 'bed load', not suspended sediments. The Isles of Scilly were not included in Motyka & Brampton's study.

Sub-cell 6d: Rame Head - Lizard Point

Only the westernmost portion of this sub-cell lies within the region. There is virtually no net drift within this sub-cell. Drowned river valleys such as Carrick Roads and Helford River interrupt sediment movement. Beaches are of sand or pebbles, generally confined within individual coves. There is local cliff erosion.

Sub-cell 6e: Lizard Point - Land's End

There is very low eastward drift of sand in Mount's Bay and seasonal alongshore movements along Loe Bar but no apparent net drift. Wave action is dominant and can cause significant onshore and offshore beach movements. There is little evidence of recent accretion. Cliff and beach erosion is known to occur in Mount's Bay.

Sub-cell 7a: Land's End - Trevose Head

There are extensive stretches of sand along this coast, separated by areas of rocky foreshore. There is little evidence of littoral drift in this sub-cell, but waves cause strong seasonal onshore and offshore movements. There is dune erosion at a number of places and cliff erosion at Newquay.

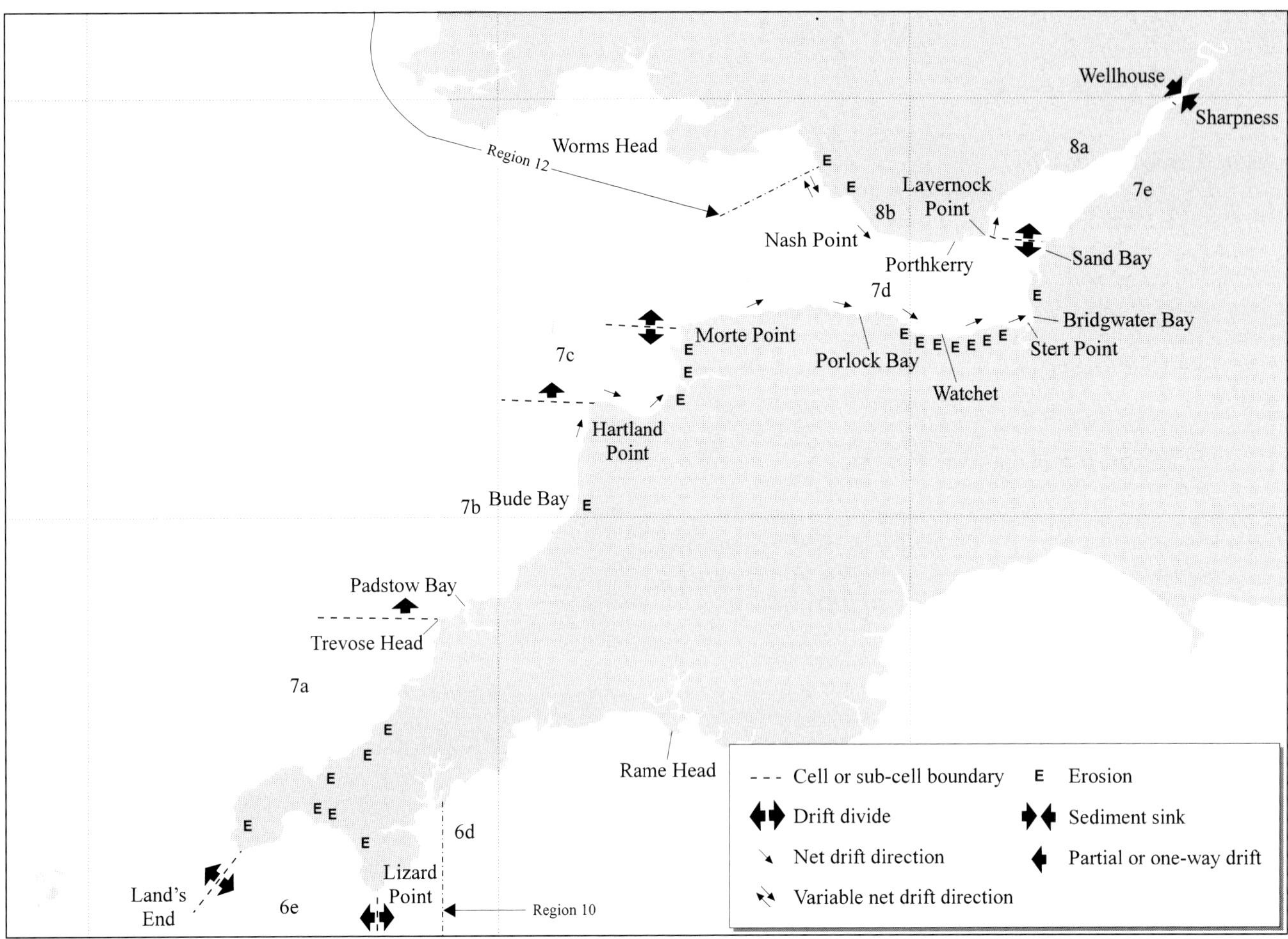

Map 2.4.1 Sediment transport and coastal cells. Source: Motyka & Brampton (1993). Adapted with permission from MAFF Flood and Coastal Defence Division.

Sub-cell 7b: Trevose Head - Hartland Point

This part of the coastline is characterised by long stretches of boulder-strewn beach separated by beaches of fine sand. There is low northward littoral drift, but waves have a stronger influence upon sediment movement. There is dune erosion in Padstow Bay and Bude Bay and erosion of boulder clay overburden in Bude Bay.

Sub-cell 7c: Hartland Point - Morte Point

The Barnstaple Bay sub-cell shows littoral drift into a sediment sink in the south-eastern corner of the bay, with low eastward drift of sediment from Hartland Point to Westward Ho! Both waves and tides affect sediments in the mouth of the Taw-Torridge Estuary. There is erosion at a number of places, including the Westward Ho! shingle ridge, as well as at Braunton Burrows, Putsborough and Woolacombe. Croyde and Morte Bays have sediment movement that is independent of that in Barnstaple Bay.

Sub-cell 7d: Morte Point - Sand Bay

Morte Point is a littoral-drift divide, and sediments east of the point move eastwards towards Bridgwater Bay, which is a sediment sink. Beach sediment ranges from boulders, pebbles and shingle in Porlock Bay and between Watchet and Stert Point, through sand to mud. Erosion occurs in many places along the relatively low, soft cliffs between Minehead and Hinkley Point, and there is dune erosion at Brean. Tidal currents and wind affect the sediment regime in Bridgwater Bay as far as Sand Bay.

Sub-cell 7e: Sand Bay - Sharpness

The coastline of this sub-cell is alluvial, dominated by mudflats and saltmarshes. There is no appreciable drift and little wave action, although serious erosion can occur when high tidal levels coincide with storms.

Sub-cell 8a: Wellhouse - Lavernock Point

There is little drift in this sub-cell, other than a weak drift of pebbles northwards from Lavernock Point towards Penarth. The coastline is alluvial, dominated by mudflats and saltmarshes.

Sub-cell 8b: Lavernock Point - Worms Head

The rocky foreshore as far as Nash Point gives way to sandy beaches further west. Littoral drift, including of the shingle along the high tide line at Porthkerry, is low to moderate and predominantly eastwards. The low cliffs between Barry and Southerndown are suffering erosion, as are the beaches and dunes around Porthcawl and Kenfig. Short-term (annual) sediment changes are minimal between Cardiff and

Merthyr Mawr: drawdown of the beaches occurs as a result of storms but much of the sediment is reinstated on the beaches during subsequent calmer intervals.

Estimates of cliff recession rates along the South Glamorgan coast have been made using historic maps, evidence from the positions of Iron Age forts and measurements of cliff-top retreat over an eight-year period (Williams & Davies 1987). The results show considerable variation, with Nash Point estimated to be retreating at around 2-11 cm/year. On average, retreat along this coast is estimated at roughly 1-8 cm/year, occurring as a series of discrete cliffs falls: local rates, measured over a short time, may be much greater.

2.4.3 Further sources of information

A. References cited

Harris, P.T., & Collins, M. 1988. Estimation of annual bedload flux in a macrotidal estuary: Bristol Channel, UK. *Marine Geology, 83:* 237-252.

Motyka, J.M., & Brampton, A.H. 1993. *Coastal management - mapping of littoral cells.* Oxford, HR Wallingford. (Report SR 328.)

Williams, A.T., & Davies, P. 1987. *Rates and mechanisms of coastal cliff erosion in Lower Lias rocks. Proceedings of a speciality conference on advances in understanding of coastal sediment processes New Orleans, Louisiana May 12-14, 1987.* New York, American Society of Civil Engineers. (Coastal Zone 87, Vol. II.)

Williams, A.T., Morgan, N.R., & Davies, P. 1991. *Coastal Zone 91, Vol. 3: Proceedings of the Seventh Symposium on coastal and ocean management, Long Beach California, July 8-12, 1991.* New York, American Society of Civil Engineers.

B. Further reading

Allen, J.R.L., & Rea, J.E. 1987. Late Flandrian shoreline oscillations in the Severn Estuary: a geomorphological and stratigraphical reconnaissance. *Philosophical Transactions of the Royal Society of London, 315*: 185-230.

Coastal Research Group, Glasgow University Department of Geography and Topographic Science. 1994. *Coastal processes and conservation. Taw Torridge.* Peterborough, unpublished report to English Nature.

Institute of Estuarine and Coastal Studies, University of Hull. 1995. *Coastal processes and conservation: the Fal.* Peterborough, unpublished report to English Nature.

Mouchell, L.G., & Parners Ltd. 1995. *Shoreline Management Plan for coastal sediment sub-cell 6e: Lizard to Land's End.* Bristol, NRA/Penwith District Council.

Rendel Geotechnics. 1995. *Coastal planning and management: a review of earth science information needs.* London, HMSO.

C. Contact names and addresses

Type of information	*Contact address and telephone no.*
Coast protection policy and sediment cells: England; Shoreline Management Plans for sub-cells in the region (see also section 10.2.7)	*Ministry of Agriculture, Fisheries and Food (MAFF), Flood and Coastal Defence Division, London, tel: 0171 238 3000/0171 238 6855
Coast protection policy and sediment cells: Wales	*Welsh Office Environment Division, Cardiff, tel: 01222 825111
Sediment cells	HR Wallingford Ltd, Howbury Park, Wallingford, Oxfordshire OX10 8BA, tel: 01491 835381
Review of erosion, deposition and flooding in Great Britain (maps and database)	Minerals Division, Room C15/19, Department of the Environment, 2 Marsham Street, London SW1P 3EB, tel: 0171 276 0900
North Sea Project data set CD ROM	*BODC, Birkenhead, tel: 0151 652 3950

*Starred contact addresses are given in full in the Appendix.

2.5 Sea-level rise and flooding

British Geological Survey

2.5.1 Sea-level changes in the region

Apparent sea-level rise is the combined effect of local crustal movements (owing to the removal of the weight of ice since the last glacial period, Scotland is rising whereas south-eastern England is sinking) and global rises in sea level, estimated as rising between 1.5 and 2 mm/year (Woodworth 1987). Reviews which attempt to estimate future changes in apparent sea level (e.g. Woodworth 1987) cite the regional and temporal variability shown by tide gauge data as major causes of uncertainty. In this region, sea level trends between 1917 and 1981, measured on a tide gauge at Newlyn, show an average annual rise in relative sea level of 0-3 mm/year (Map 2.5.1) (Emery & Aubrey 1985). This value includes both the global rise and the uplift in the land level, the rate of which is calculated to be 0.7 mm/year.

Holocene sea-level changes in south-west England and Wales, inferred from radiocarbon dates of peat deposits, have been summarised by Heyworth & Kidson (1982). Such peats are exposed in the intertidal zone in Mount's Bay, Barnstaple Bay (Westward Ho!) and Bridgwater Bay, as well as at depth within the Somerset Levels. Results suggest that sea level has risen steadily by 5 m over the last 5,000 years. The results from the English Channel, Bristol Channel and Somerset Levels were in general agreement, confirming that there has been little vertical movement of these areas relative to each other.

2.5.2 Flooding risk

There are extensive areas of low-lying land in the region that are susceptible to flooding. The main areas at risk are within the Severn Estuary and along the coast of Bridgwater Bay (Map 2.5.1). Parts of the coast at Mount's Bay, Portreath, Perranporth, Porlock and south of Porthcawl are susceptible to local flooding. Long stretches of the coast of the Somerset Levels and the shores of the Severn Estuary are protected from flooding by man-made defences (see also section 8.4).

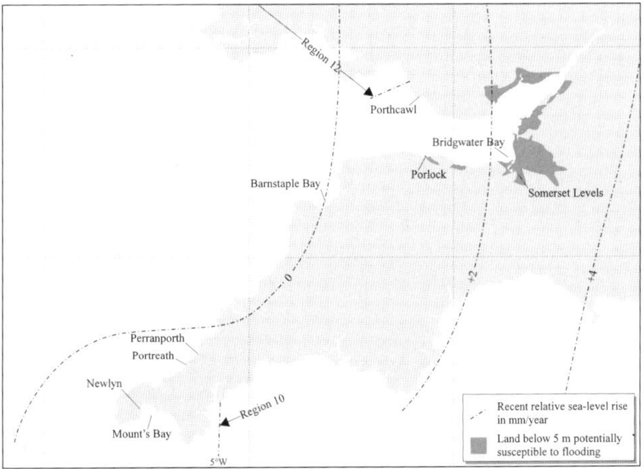

Map 2.5.1 Estimated rates of recent relative sea-level rise (mm/yr), low-lying areas susceptible to flooding and locations mentioned in the text. Source: after Emery & Aubrey (1985).

2.5.3 Further sources of information

A. References cited

Emery, K.O., & Aubrey, D.G. 1985. *Sea levels, land levels, and tide gauges.* New York, Springer-Verlag.

Heyworth, A., & Kidson, C. 1982. Sea-level changes in south-west England and Wales. *Proceedings of the Geological Association, 93:* 91-111.

Woodworth, P.L. 1987. Trends in UK mean sea level. *Marine Geodesy, 11:* 57-58.

B. Further reading

Anon. 1992. *The Irish Sea Forum: global warming and climatic change - seminar report.* Liverpool, University of Liverpool Press.

Boorman, L.A., Goss-Custard, J.D., & McGrorty, S. 1989. *Climatic change, rising sea level and the British coast.* London, HMSO/Natural Environment Research Council. (Institute of Terrestrial Ecology Research Publication No. 1.)

Burd, F., & Doody, P. 1990. *Sea level rise and nature conservation. A review of NCC experience.* Peterborough, Nature Conservancy Council. (Coastal Ecology Branch, Coastal Habitat Network Paper No. 3.)

Climate Change Impacts Review Group. 1991. *The potential effects of climate change in the United Kingdom. Report 1.* London, HMSO. (Department of the Environment.)

Department of the Environment. 1988. *Possible impacts of climate change on the natural environment in the United Kingdom.* London, HMSO.

Department of the Environment. 1992. *The UK environment: coast erosion, flooding and sea level change.* London, HMSO.

Department of the Environment/Meteorological Office. 1990. *Global climate change.* London, HMSO.

Doornkamp, J.C., *ed.* 1990. *The greenhouse effect and rising sea levels in the UK.* Nottingham, M1 Press.

Motyka, J.M., & Brampton, A.H. 1993. *Coastal management: mapping of littoral cells.* Oxford, HR Wallingford. (Report SR 328.)

Posford Duvivier Environment. 1991. *Environmental opportunities in low lying coastal areas under a scenario of climate change.* Peterborough, Report to National Rivers Authority, Department of Environment, Nature Conservancy Council and Countryside Commission.

Rendel Geotechnics. 1995. *Coastal planning and management: a review of earth science information needs.* London, HMSO.

Shennan, I. 1989. Holocene crustal movements and sea-level changes in Great Britain. *Journal of Quaternary Science, 4:* 77-89.

Shennan, I. 1993. Sea-level changes and the threat of coastal inundation. *The Geographical Journal, 159*(2): 148-156.

Shennan, I., & Woodworth, P.L. 1992. A comparison of late Holocene and twentieth-century sea-level trends from the UK and North Sea region. *Geophysical Journal International, 109:* 96-105.

Tooley, M.J., & Shennan, I., *eds.* 1987. *Sea level changes.* Oxford, Basil Blackwell. (Institute of British Geographers Special Publication Series, No. 20.)

Woodworth, P. 1990. Measuring and predicting long term sea level changes. *NERC News, 15:* 22-25. Swindon, NERC.

C. Contact names and addresses

Type of information	*Contact address and telephone no.*
Coast protection policy and sediment cells: England	*Ministry of Agriculture, Fisheries and Food (MAFF), Flood and Coastal Defence Division, London, tel: 0171 238 3000
Coast protection policy and sediment cells: Wales	*Welsh Office Environment Division, Cardiff, tel: 01222 825111
Flood defence - South-west England	*Environment Agency - South West Region, Exeter, tel: 01392 444000
Flood defence - Somerset and Avon	*Environment Agency - South West Region, Bridgwater, tel: 01278 457333
Flood defence - Severn Estuary	*Environment Agency - Severn-Trent Region, Solihull, tel: 0121 711 2324
Flood defence - Wales	*Environment Agency - Welsh Region, Cardiff, tel: 01222 770088
Sediment cells	HR Wallingford Ltd, Howbury Park, Wallingford, Oxfordshire OX10 8BA, tel: 01491 835381
Review of erosion, deposition and flooding in Great Britain (maps and database)	Minerals Division, Room C15/19, Department of the Environment, 2 Marsham Street, London SW1P 3EB, tel: 0171 276 0900
North Sea Project data set CD ROM; tide gauge data	*BODC, Birkenhead, tel: 0151 652 3950

*Starred contact addresses are given in full in the Appendix.

2.6 Coastal landforms

British Geological Survey

2.6.1 Description

The coasts of this region display a great diversity of landforms, ranging from the almost continuous cliffs of Devon and Cornwall to the low-lying muddy coasts of the Severn Estuary. Much of the diversity results from variations in the strength and lithology of the rocks forming the coast.

Falmouth Bay - Minehead

Along the coast of Devon and Cornwall, shales and slates form embayments whilst the more massive igneous rocks and sandstones form projecting coastal features. The tectonic complexity of the coasts of Devon and Cornwall introduces numerous variations in lithology, resulting in a diversity in the form of the coast at both local and regional scales. The many hanging valleys testify to the erosional nature of the coast, but the rate of erosion is so slow that an accurate assessment of the rate of erosion is difficult (see also section 2.4.1).

Geological evidence suggests that the high plateau land surfaces of Devon and Cornwall were incised during periods of high sea level during the Tertiary. Lengthy periods of static sea level produced widespread planation surfaces, some of which are now backed by 'fossil' cliff lines. Along much of the south Cornish section there are early Pleistocene cliff and bench features up to 35 m above Ordnance Datum (OD). The lowest, at 2-5 m OD, is a raised beach platform backed by a prominent cliff, the latter overlain in places by drift deposits, including a periglacial deposit known as 'head', up to 30 m thick.

The Fal Estuary (Carrick Roads) and Helford River are typical drowned river valleys ('rias') and form two of the few breaks in the cliffed coastline of south Cornwall. The cliffs along the eastern coast of the Lizard peninsula are less steep than those on the western side. Raised beaches are found 1-8 m above present beach levels. In contrast, the cliffs along the western coast of the Lizard are imposing: they abruptly truncate the inland plateau surface and are associated with deep narrow coves and small offshore islands. At Church Cove sand blown over the cliff has partly buried the church tower (Steers 1969).

Most of the shoreline in Mount's Bay is rocky, with narrow, sandy pocket beaches. However, Loe Bar in the eastern part of the bay is a shingle and sand bar, kept intact by the action of waves, which throw material onto its crest. It confines a freshwater lake which extends 1.8 km up the valley towards Helston. The low-lying area of alluvium between Marazion and Penzance is fronted by sand dunes; at the entrance to Penzance Dock a submerged forest bed is exposed at low water.

Granite forms most of the cliffs from Mount's Bay to Cape Cornwall; their character is determined by the orientation and spacing of joints within the rock. At Land's End the cliffs have a castellated aspect but elsewhere they are less severe and slope gently towards the sea. Many of the small valleys terminate in small bays at the coast, in many of which remnants of raised beaches are preserved.

The low-lying Isles of Scilly are formed of granite traversed by mineralised veins and joints. Marine erosion has accentuated these planes of weakness to give a rectilinear aspect to sections of the coast. Small outcrops of raised beach and glacial and head deposits are preserved; these are of great importance in understanding the late Pleistocene history of southern Britain. The beaches are formed of white sand, resulting from marine erosion of the granite, and carbonate shell sand; locally the sand has been blown onshore to form dunes.

From Cape Cornwall to St. Ives Bay the coast is steeply cliffed. The lower reaches of the River Hayle, which enters the sea here, are infilled with alluvium. The coast to the north-east of the river mouth is covered with a broad expanse of sand dunes.

The coast from the northern end of St. Ives Bay to Cligga Head is predominantly cliffed, broken only by narrow linear valleys. Further north the rocky headlands are interspersed with sandy beaches. Holywell and Perran Bays south of Newquay are backed by an extensive stretch of deep sand dunes. Dunes connect Trevose Head to the mainland and sand dune systems have developed on the sheltered shores of the Camel Estuary. Landslips are common along the coast between Boscastle and Widemouth and produce a complex, tumbled aspect to the cliffs. The material forming the sandy beaches and dunes around Bude is probably derived from erosion of the exposed cliffs and foreshore. Northwards towards Hartland Point there are magnificent, almost unbroken, flat-topped cliffs with a narrow boulder beach at their foot. Coastal waterfalls at the seaward end of hanging valleys are a feature of this coastline and give a clear indication of the rapid rate of marine erosion, compared with the slower down-cutting erosion of the streams. The steeply-cliffed coast with a wide rocky foreshore extends along the southern part of Bideford Bay to the Taw-Torridge Estuary at Westward Ho!. Many of these cliffs display long and heavily wooded seaward slopes and much of the coast is landslipped.

The mouth of the Rivers Taw and Torridge forms a wide estuary, infilled with Holocene alluvium in its upper part. A narrow shingle ridge lies seaward of the dunes at Northam Burrows, between Westward Ho! and the south side of the estuary mouth. Wave action is moving the shingle ridge landward over the sand dunes. North of the estuary lie the extensive dunes of Braunton Burrows, which extend locally up to 2 km inland and are up to 30 m high. Wide tidal sand-flats lie to seaward. Morte Bay to the north has a fringe of sand dunes at the foot of steeply rising ground.

The cliffs from Bull Point to Minehead are broken only by small, narrow valleys with villages such as Coombe Martin and Lynmouth at their seaward termination. A mass of boulders in a delta-like formation occupies the foreshore at Lynmouth. The cliffs along this coast are of the 'hog's back' type, initially cut by marine erosion but having a series of bevels due to degradation by several stages of subaerial activity (Arber 1911).

Porlock Bay west of Minehead is fringed by a shingle ridge broken only at Porlock Wear, near its western limit. Littoral drift moves the shingle from west to east along the

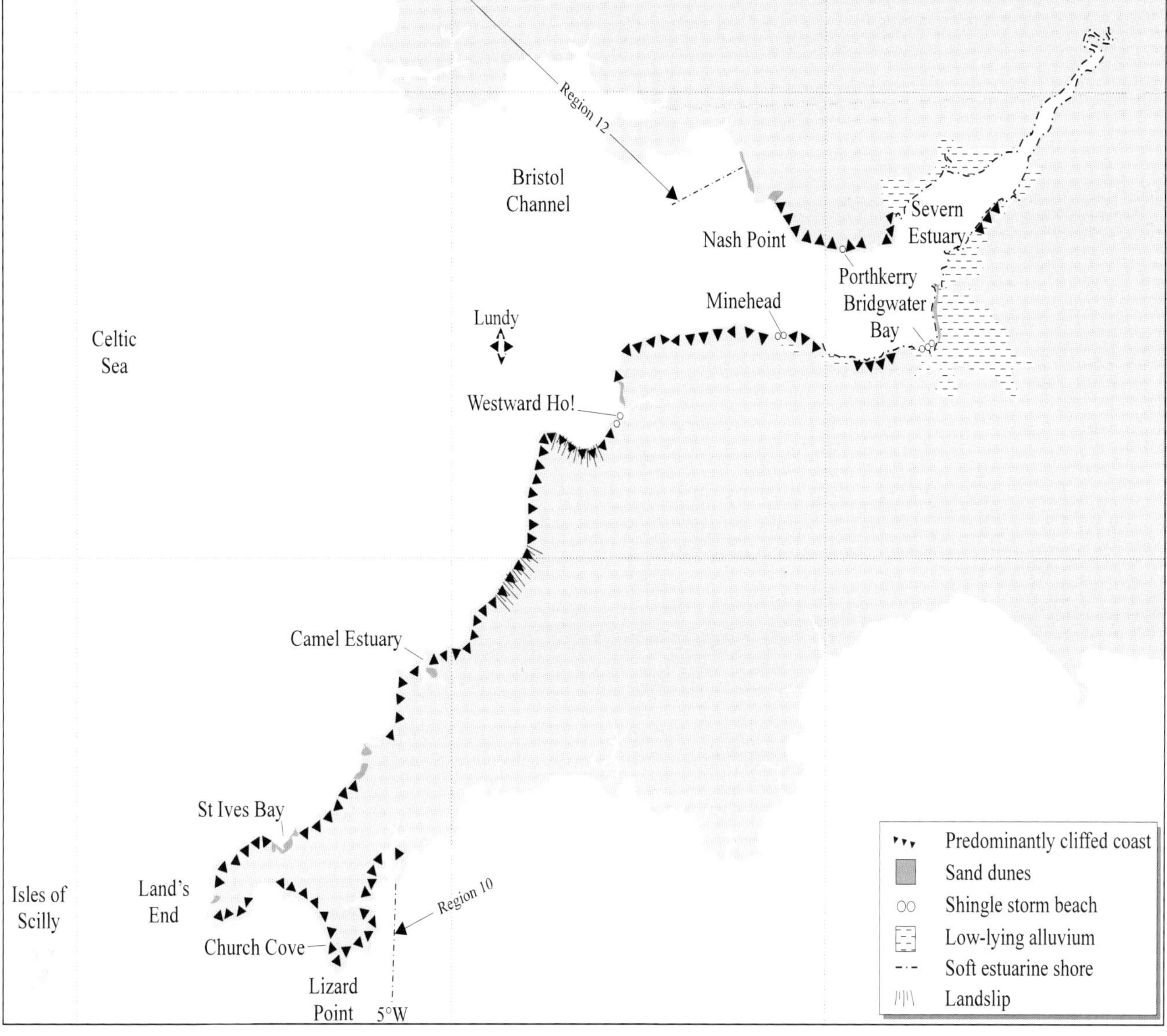

Map 2.6.1 Major coastal landforms

ridge, and the pebbles increase in roundness eastwards. At present natural and man-made changes threaten to breach the ridge near its centre. The large tidal range and high wave energy in the bay has resulted in the exceptional height of the eastern part of the ridge.

Minehead - the Severn

At Minehead a large area of intertidal mud and shingle stretches for almost 9 km along the shore. Eastwards, the form of the coast changes abruptly to low, steep cliffs, fronted by a wide foreshore covered with sand, shingle, mud or bedrock platform. Landslips are common where the red marls of the Mercia Mudstone Group form cliffs. Groynes are common along stretches of this coast and their infill shows that littoral drift of the shingle is consistently eastward. The occurrence of damaged groynes within some lower shingle beaches indicates that coastal erosion is locally a major problem.

The coast fringing Bridgwater Bay, from Hinkley Point north-eastwards to Brean Down, marks the seaward limit of the low-lying Somerset Levels, an area of Holocene sediments up to 25 m thick. The intertidal flats along the shore here are up to 6 km wide at low spring tides. Along the south coast of the bay the flats are covered with mud and bordered by a narrow but continuous shingle ridge which terminates at Stert Point near the mouth of the River Parrett. Along the eastern coast of the bay the mud flats (Berrow Flats) pass landward into a flat sandy upper beach. Sand dune systems have developed along the coast of the three westward-facing bays from the mouth of the Parrett northward to Middle Hope. Saltmarsh development along some of this coast indicates coastal accretion, but much of the dune system is retreating. In Sand Bay beach replenishment has been used to protect the man-made sea walls in front of the dunes.

The southern coast of the Severn Estuary, from Middle Hope to Clevedon and from Portishead to north of Avonmouth, is formed of low, predominantly muddy Holocene estuarine deposits, protected by a low sea wall. Along the upland area from Clevedon to Portishead the wooded interior slopes gently down to the steep, rocky foreshore.

The estuary has one of the highest tidal ranges in the world (see also section 2.3.4), resulting in a wide intertidal zone.

The Severn - Kenfig

Muddy Holocene sediments mark the coast along the northern shore of the Severn Estuary as far west as Cardiff, with a sea wall protecting the low ground of the Caldicot and Wentlooge Levels, which are separated by the estuary of the River Usk. Areas of saltmarsh front the sea walls. These shores have a long history of accretion and erosion, documented by changes in the level of the saltmarsh and the dates of artifacts found associated with each level (Allen & Rea 1987). Erosion continues in places on the foreshore but is limited by the sea walls. Peat deposits, which locally contain tree-trunks, are exposed on the foreshore above the early Holocene muds.

South and west of Cardiff the coastline is mostly cliffed as far as Ogmore-by-Sea. Typically, steep cliffs are fronted by a wide rock-cut platform. There are minor pocket beaches, for example at Whitmore Bay on Barry Island, and a fine shingle storm beach fronts the cliffs at Porthkerry. The cliffs are broken by the valley of the River Thaw at Aberthaw, where a highly dynamic shingle spit dominates the shore. Between Aberthaw and Ogmore-by-Sea several small valleys reach the coast, but landward retreat of the coast has left them abruptly truncated, as at Nash Point.

Extensive sand dunes occur to the north of the Ogmore River at Merthyr Mawr Warren and at Kenfig Burrows north of Porthcawl. Dune erosion is a problem along parts of this coast (Carr & Blackley 1977).

2.6.2 Further sources of information

A. *References cited*

Allen, J.R.L., & Rea, J.E. 1987. Late Flandrian shoreline oscillations in the Severn estuary: a geomorphological and stratigraphical reconnaissance. *Philosophical Transactions of the Royal Society of London, 315:* 185-230.

Arber, E.A.N. 1911. *The coast scenery of north Devon.* London, Dent.

Carr, A.P., & Blackley, M.W.L. 1977. Topic report : Swansea Bay (SKER) Project. *Institute of Oceanographic Sciences Report,* No. 42.

Steers, J.A. 1969. *The coastline of England and Wales.* Cambridge University Press.

B. *Further reading*

Edmonds, E.A., McKeown, M.C., & Williams, M. 1975. *British regional geology: south-west England.* London, HMSO for Institute of Geological Sciences.

Kidson, C. 1960. The shingle complexes of Bridgwater Bay. *Transactions of the Institution of British Geographers, 28:* 75-87.

Kidson, C. 1977. The coast of south-west England. *In: The Quaternary history of the Irish Sea,* ed. by C. Kidson & M.J. Tooley. *Geological Journal (Special Issue), 7:* 257-298.

C. *Contact names and addresses*

Type of information	*Contact address and telephone no.*
Coast protection: England	*Ministry of Agriculture, Fisheries and Food, Flood and Coastal Defence Division, London, tel: 0171 238 3000
Coast protection: Wales	*Welsh Office Environment Division, Cardiff, tel: 01222 825111
Geomorphological information for region; 1:50,000 scale maps	Coastal Geology Group, British Geological Survey, Keyworth, Nottingham NG12 5GG, tel: 0115 936 3100

*Starred contact addresses are given in full in the Appendix.

Chapter 3 Terrestrial coastal habitats

This chapter covers terrestrial habitats that are maritime influenced, i.e. are distinctive because of their association with the coast and coastal processes. Adjacent to some parts of the coast there are other semi-natural habitats of importance that are not directly influenced by the sea, including in this region principally heaths, ancient semi-natural woodland, mines and quarries and their spoil heaps, and islands.

The island nature of the Isles of Scilly and Lundy results in the occurrence there of both maritime and non-maritime species and subspecies that are endemic to the islands or have very limited UK distributions. For example a subspecies of the speckled wood butterfly, *Pararge aegeria insula,* occurs only on the Isles of Scilly, and the Isles are also notable as one of the few sites in the UK for the lesser white-toothed shrew *Crocidura suaveolens.* Lundy is the only known site in the world for the beetle *Psylliodes luridipennis,* which feeds on Lundy cabbage *Coincya wrightii,* which is endemic to the island. The Isles of Scilly are a candidate Special Area of Conservation (SAC) under the EC Habitats & Species Directive as the location of a number of rare coastal habitats and the shore dock *Rumex rupestris,* Europe's most endangered dock species (see also sections 5.2 and 7.2.4).

The Lizard peninsula, one of only five Biogenetic Reserves on the coast of Great Britain (see section 7.2.6) and a candidate SAC, is the location of a number of habitat types that are extremely rare in a European context. A priority habitat under the EC Habitats & Species Directive, Mediterranean temporary ponds, is found in this country only on the Lizard and in the New Forest (Region 9), and the serpentinite type of this habitat is confined to the Lizard. Another habitat, dry coastal heathland with Cornish heath *Erica vagans* and gorse *Ulex europaeus* (see also section 5.2), occurs in Europe only here, in the Basque country (France/Spain) and at one site in Brittany. On the Lizard this habitat is of a unique variant dominated by Cornish heath *Erica vagans* and black bog-rush *Schoenus nigricans,* reflecting the underlying ultrabasic serpentinite rocks. Areas of another priority habitat under the Directive - Northern Atlantic wet heaths with heather *Erica tetralix* - are also included in the candidate SAC. In exposed locations the Lizard heaths, influenced by the strong south-westerly prevailing winds, take on a characteristic 'waved' surface appearance. Of the other types of heath present on the region's coast, North Exmoor (Exmoor Coastal Heaths SSSI), Somerset, comprises the best preserved and most extensive upland dry heath in south-west England. Coastal heaths in the region support large numbers of common lizards, adders and slow-worms, all three species protected under the Wildlife & Countryside Act 1981 and the Bern Convention (see also section 5.6).

The mild climate of the region as a whole, and the Lizard and Isles of Scilly in particular, coupled with low summer rainfall, results in growing conditions that are characteristic of southern Europe. The diverse higher plant flora of the Lizard is world famous and includes a large number of species that are rare or scarce in the UK. The Lizard peninsula is also part of one of the richest stretches of coastline for lichens and bryophytes (see also section 5.1), and for terrestrial and freshwater invertebrates (see also section 5.3).

The centuries of mining and quarrying activity in the region have created a wealth of distinctive and uncommon habitats that augment the region's resource of semi-natural habitats. Tin, lead, igneous rock and china clay workings in Cornwall, coal mines in the Forest of Dean (Gloucestershire), slate quarries in the Welsh counties and limestone quarries throughout the region (except Cornwall) (see also section 9.3) provide niches for a number of rare and scarce plant and animal species. Old mine workings and china clay quarries are a characteristically Cornish landscape feature supporting a unique and specialised lower plant flora. Some bryophytes and lichens are specialists of soils that are rich in heavy metals and may be virtually confined in the UK to spoil tips of old lead and copper mines. The liverwort western rustwort *Marsupella profunda,* a priority species under the Habitats & Species Directive, is confined in Britain to a single former china clay site in Cornwall. Mines and quarries in the region are also of interest for their rare and scarce higher plants, and the wet habitats they often contain are important for amphibians, as at former brick pits in Bridgwater Bay and derelict mining areas in Glamorgan and the Forest of Dean. These and other derelict industrial sites along some of the developed or degraded parts of this coastline, for instance in Mid and South Glamorgan, are also important for reptiles such as common lizards and slow-worms (see also section 5.6).

The region contains thirteen of the fourteen bat species found in the UK, and several species make use of the region's caves and mines (see also section 5.13). For example, greater and lesser horseshoe bats (*Rhinolophus ferrumequinum* and *R. hipposideros*) occur in large numbers in the Wye Valley/Forest of Dean. The location, a candidate SAC, contains by far the largest concentration of the lesser horseshoe bats in the UK (26% of the total population) and a significant proportion (6%) of the UK's greater horseshoe bats, in breeding colonies and hibernacula in disused coal mines. Their location in an extensive ancient woodland with its rich supplies of invertebrate food contributes to the bats' abundance.

Coastal woodlands in the region, especially on the fringes of Exmoor and in sheltered ravines in Cornwall and Devon, contain a distinctive range of oceanic (i.e. warmth- and moisture-loving) lower plant species, particularly slime moulds. Many oceanic species (most notably some small liverworts) are confined to coastal woodlands, which in this region support more oceanic species than sites further north. In addition, trees in some parklands in the region support a good epiphytic lichen flora, and a number of woodlands in the region are known to be important sites for lower plants. Invertebrates find conditions in the undisturbed woodlands of the ria valleys in Cornwall and Devon particularly favourable (see also section 5.3). These woods are the only known British location for the threatened weevil *Anchonidium unguiculare,* which lives in leaf litter. Other scarce species occurring in the region's coastal woodlands include moths whose larvae feed on epiphytic lichens on trees: the dotted carpet moth *Alcis jubata* is one example.

Wooded combes in Devon and Somerset linked to sheltered areas of heath or bracken provide habitat for two threatened butterflies: the high brown fritillary *Argynnis adippe* and the heath fritillary *Mellicta athalia*. The region's woodlands are also important for a number of the UK's rarest mammals (see also section 5.13), including the dormouse *Muscardinus avellanarius*, which occurs in coastal coombe valley woodland along the north Cornwall, north Devon, Somerset and Avon coasts. The red squirrel *Sciurus vulgaris* is rare and declining in England and Wales; in this region it occurs in woodlands in Cornwall and Gwent.

Avon Gorge National Nature Reserve is a candidate SAC as it represents a habitat type (ravine forest) rare in Europe. The Wye Valley Woodlands are a candidate SAC as an example of a varied beech forest.

The Valley of the Rocks, on the Exmoor coast, Devon, is typical of the vegetated cliffs of the western part of the region. Region 11 is the most important in the UK for rare cliff-growing plants. Although the cliffs are exposed to strong winds and heavy salt spray, the frequent rain and year-round mild temperatures allow many uncommon flowers to flourish, including some, such as the wild asparagus and peony, more at home in the Mediterranean. Photo: Peter Wakely, English Nature.

3.1 Cliffs and cliff-top vegetation

Dr T.C.D. Dargie

3.1.1 Introduction

Geology and geological structure, together with past environmental history (marine erosion and glacial processes) determine cliff form (Jones & Lee 1994; Lee 1995). The most distinctive cliff types are consolidated (hard cliffs developed from resistant bedrock) and unconsolidated (soft cliffs developed in easily-eroded materials). Soft cliffs are rare in this region, where hard cliffs predominate (Table 3.1.1).

The region has a total cliff length of 407.5 km (Table 3.1.1; Map 3.1.1), which represents much of the region's coast and 10% of the British resource; the region's cliffs are therefore of great importance in the national context. There are also very fine extents of cliff-top habitat (Table 3.1.1). A total of 753 ha of maritime grassland is recorded for the English coast in the region (40% of the total extent in England (Table 3.1.1)).

Cliffs in the region exhibit good diversity in form (Table 3.1.2).

The soils and vegetation of cliffs and cliff-tops are closely related to slope angle, soil type and salt spray deposition, with much local variability possible with changing exposure around headlands. The major natural and semi-natural cliff and cliff-top habitats in Great Britain are bare ground, spray-zone lichen-covered rock, rock crevice, cliff-ledge, seabird colony, perched saltmarsh, maritime grassland and maritime heath. Very sheltered cliffs and cliff-top sectors that receive little salt spray input are not here treated as coastal habitats. Soft cliffs on sheltered coasts can develop undercliff vegetation of woodland, scrub, tall herb and rank grassland, often very close to the sea. The full extent of cliff-top habitat in the region has not been surveyed but the exposure of the coast to very strong winds and heavy spray deposition probably allows mainly maritime grassland to develop, with most of this restricted to hard cliffs.

The scenic contribution of cliffs within the region is outstanding, with tall and lengthy hard cliffs cut in varied sedimentary, igneous and metamorphic rocks. This scenic value is recognised by 326 km of largely cliffed coast fronting Areas of Outstanding Natural Beauty in the Isles of Scilly, Cornwall, north Devon and Somerset (Quantock Hills) and 38 km fronting Exmoor National Park, with further recognition of 259 km as lengths of Heritage Coast (Gubbay 1988; Heritage Coast Forum 1993). Large stretches of cliff, especially in Cornwall and Devon, are also designated as Sites of Special Scientific Interest (SSSIs).

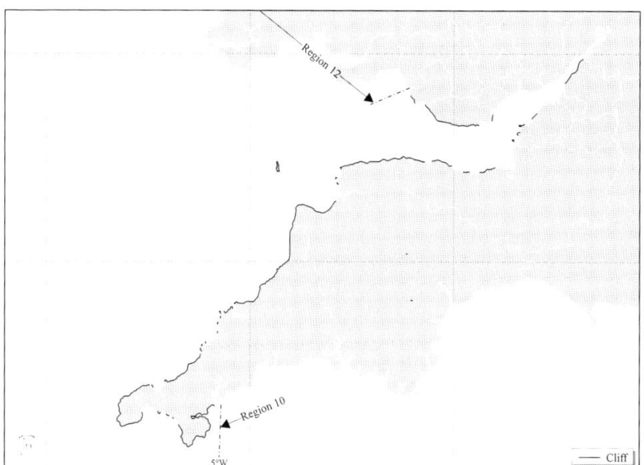

Map 3.1.1 Sea cliffs. Source: JNCC Coastal Database and OS Landranger maps. © Crown copyright.

3.1.2 Important locations and species

Soft cliffs are rare in the region and are restricted to very short sectors in Cornwall, north Devon, Somerset and Avon. Hard cliffs are much more extensive, with especially fine lengths of tall (50-100 m) near-vertical cliffs with relatively flat tops developed in Cornwall in igneous and metamorphic rocks, including the famous headlands of the Lizard, Land's End and Cape Cornwall. Taller, stepped cliffs are developed in sedimentary rocks between Boscastle and Wanson in Cornwall, up to 160 m height and descending from up to 400 m inland. A notable additional feature of cliffs in Cornwall is a gradation to climbing sand

Table 3.1.1 Cliff and maritime cliff grassland resource[a] in context

Area	*Soft cliffs* Total length (km)	*Soft cliffs* % of total in Region 11	*All cliffs* Total length (km)	*All cliffs* % of total in Region 11	*Maritime cliff grassland* Area (ha)	*Maritime cliff grassland* % of total in Region 11
Isles of Scilly	-	-	29	7	70	?
Cornwall	2	?	199	49	502	?
Devon	2	?	95	23	137	?
Somerset	1	?	29	7	17	?
Avon	1	?	20	5	9	?
Gloucestershire	-	-	8	2	18	?
Mid-Glamorgan	?	?	9	2	?	?
South Glamorgan	?	?	21	5	?	?
Region 11	?	-	*408*	-	?	?
England	256	2	1,165	32	1,895	40
Wales	?	?	523	6	?	?
West Coast*	?	?	2,272	18	?	?
GB*	?	?	4,059	10	?	?

Source: Pye & French (1993). Key: *excluding the Isle of Man; [a]all figures have been rounded to the nearest whole number; ? = unknown.

Table 3.1.2 Lengths (km)[a] of cliff types

	Vertical >20 m high		*Vertical <20 m high*		*Non-vertical >20 m high*		*Non-vertical <20 m high*	
	Length (km)	*% of total length in Region 11*	*Length (km)*	*% of total length in Region 11*	*Length (km)*	*% of total length in Region 11*	*Length (km)*	*% of total length in Region 11*
Isles of Scilly	0	0	1	4	1	1	27	69
Cornwall	93	57	3	12	101	55	3	8
Devon	30	19	1	4	60	33	5	13
Somerset	10	6	2	8	16	9	1	3
Avon	5	3	11	44	4	2	1	3
Gloucestershire	2	1	1	4	1	1	4	12
Mid Glamorgan	5	3	4	16	-	-	-	-
South Glamorgan	18	11	3	12	-	-	-	-
Region 11	***162***	***100***	***25***	***100***	***182***	***100***	***39***	***100***
England	320	43	49	38	629	29	167	23
Wales	329	4	46	14	110	-	39	-
West Coast*	725	22	439	6	813	22	284	14
Great Britain*	1,325	12	818	3	1,371	13	545	7

Source: JNCC Coastal Resources Database (cliff height and angle categories). Key: *excluding the Isle of Man; [a]all figures have been rounded to the nearest whole km/ha/% point; - = <0.5 km/<0.5%.

dunes, which have been blown against and over cliffs at Mexico Towans, Gwithian Towans, Godrevy Towans and Penhale Sands. Sedimentary rocks dominate cliffs in north Devon and Somerset, with considerable lengths exceeding 100 m in height, rising to 157 m at Embury Beacon, south of Hartland Point. The entire coast of Lundy Island is cliffed, most to a height in excess of 100 m. Sheltered stepped cliffs in north Devon around Clovelly are notable for mature woodland. The cliffed coastline of Exmoor has perhaps the finest examples of hogsback cliff in Britain, with a low active cliffline at the base topped by steep convex slopes rising to 300 m height, probably representing fossil cliffs developed during periods of higher sea level. High cliffs are rare east of Exmoor and are restricted to the Carboniferous limestone headlands of Brean Down and Middle Hope and the island of Steep Holm.

Of the twelve National Vegetation Classification (NVC) maritime cliff vegetation communities in the UK (Rodwell in prep.), ten are recorded from England, the remaining two being confined to Scotland. Although no detailed map information is available for cliff habitats in the region, except at the Lizard and Cape Cornwall, a zonation is recognised on the hard limestone cliffs of southern Britain (Mitchley & Malloch 1991), ranging from high spray and exposure conditions (NVC communities MC1 rock samphire *Crithmum maritimum* - rock sea-spurrey *Spergularia rupicola* rock-crevice, MC4 wild cabbage *Brassica oleracea* cliff ledge, MC8 red fescue *Festuca rubra* - thrift *Armeria maritima* maritime grassland) to more sheltered cliff-top conditions (MC11 red fescue *Festuca rubra* - wild carrot *Daucus carota* maritime grassland and CG2 sheep's-fescue *Festuca ovina* - meadow oat-grass *Avenula pratensis* calcicolous grassland, which is probably common on Carboniferous limestone cliff-tops).

In Great Britain nine nationally rare and four nationally scarce species or subspecies of higher plant are found mainly or exclusively on cliffs. Most are restricted to the south and west of Britain, and six such nationally rare cliff species (wild asparagus *Asparagus officinalis* subsp. *prostratus*, goldilocks aster *Aster linosyris*, white rock-rose *Helianthemum apenninum*, Somerset hair-grass *Koeleria vallesiana*, peony *Paeonia mascula* (an old introduction), Lundy cabbage *Coincya wrightii*) and three nationally scarce species (maidenhair fern *Adiantum capillus-veneris*, thyme broomrape *Orobanche alba* and yellow vetch *Vicia lutea*) are present in Region 11.

Other nationally rare and scarce species more typical of other habitats also occur on cliffs, and several such nationally rare non-cliff species are present in the region: hairy greenweed *Genista pilosa*, fringed rupturewort *Herniaria ciliolata*, smaller tree-mallow *Lavatera cretica*, slender bird's-foot-trefoil *Lotus angustissimus*, sea stock *Matthiola sinuata*, orange bird's-foot *Ornithopus pinnatus*, four-leaved allseed *Polycarpon tetraphyllum*, shore dock *Rumex rupestris* and honewort *Trinia glauca*. Nationally scarce non-cliff species present on cliffs in the region are Babington's leek *Allium ampeloprasum* var. *babingtonii*, wild cabbage *Brassica oleracea*, golden samphire *Inula crithmoides*, hairy bird's-foot-trefoil *Lotus subbiflorus*, spring sandwort *Minuartia verna*, curved hard-grass *Parapholis incurva*, bulbous meadow-grass *Poa bulbosa*, early meadow-grass *P. infirma*, autumnal squill *Scilla autumnalis*, western clover *Trifolium occidentale* and suffocated clover *Trifolium suffocatum*. This large assemblage of rare and scarce species makes this region the most significant in Britain for notable species on cliffs.

Maritime heath is a nationally important feature of cliff-top habitat and is present on the more acidic rocks in Devon and Cornwall and on limestone at Brean Down in Somerset. The lichen flora of such heath at Castle Down to Kettle Point (Isles of Scilly), the Lizard (Cornwall) and Brean Down is rated of national importance, with lichens of regional interest at Hartland Point (Devon) (Fletcher *et al.* 1984).

Two cliff sites, the Isles of Scilly and the Severn Estuary, have important seabird colonies (Stroud *et al.* 1990), and smaller seabird populations occur on cliffs elsewhere in the region. No systematic survey of invertebrates in cliff and cliff-top habitats has been carried out, but these environments have a rich habitat diversity and thus support large numbers of species (Mitchley & Malloch 1991). Several cliffs in the region have excellent or good invertebrate lists, with some notable and rare (Red Data Book) species; the Lizard, Lundy, Kynance Cove, Steeple Point to Black Church, Boscastle to Widemouth, Godrevy Point to St. Agnes Head, Steeple Point to Marsland Moor, Sennen Cove, West Exmoor

Coast, Tintagel Cliffs, Mullion Cliffs to Predannack, Brean Down, and Saunton to Baggy Point are regionally important cliff locations on the Invertebrate Site Register.

Localised recession problems occur along the hard rock cliffs that dominate much of the Cornish and North Devon coasts at sites such as Marazion, Towan Beach (Newquay), Bude Bay and Hartland Point. In Bridgwater Bay, the soft cliffs developed in interbedded clays, marls and limestones are prone to debris slides and rockfalls. At Blue Anchor Bay, for example, erosion has threatened the coast road, which now has coast protection. The limestone and shale cliffs of the Glamorgan coast are particularly prone to large rockfalls, topples and rock slides, with average rates of recession of 0.3 m to 0.7 m / year. In 1983 a large rockfall at Nash Point involved some 20,000 m^3 of material.

3.1.3 Human activities

Cliffs are among the least modified of terrestrial habitats, although the cliff-top zone, especially its inner sectors, has been affected by a variety of human impacts, sometimes leading to major habitat loss. At a national scale the most extensive influences on hard cliff vegetation are grazing and burning, the major management techniques for cliff-top habitat (Mitchley & Malloch 1991). In this region, residential development has caused only low to moderate habitat loss and vegetation disturbance. Outside the coastal settlements catering for coastal visitors, much of the cliffed coast is undeveloped, and in general, visitor erosion has caused relatively little damage to habitats. However, fire and visitor trampling in maritime heath at the Lizard in Cornwall are threats to the strong lichen interest of the area (Fletcher *et al.* 1984). Car parks are common in places commanding fine views from cliffs and headlands. Footpaths have heavy usage in some parts of the region, and erosion is present along parts of the South West Coast Path, for example. Very large coastal tracts are in the ownership of the National Trust and much attention is paid to careful visitor management, especially along long-distance footpaths. Cliff climbing is locally a problem and has necessitated habitat restoration. Arable agricultural land often reaches close to the cliff edge, and targets for re-creating maritime cliff grassland from such arable or improved pasture are discussed by Pye & French (1993). Invasive *Rhododendron ponticum* is a problem on the cliffs of the Exmoor coast and poses a threat to coastal heath vegetation and woodland in that area.

The very slow retreat of the predominantly hard cliffs of the region has necessitated only little coast protection of property, as has the absence of residential development on soft cliff sectors (see also section 8.4). However, over the next five decades it is anticipated that coast protection will be required for property adjacent to soft cliffs at Porthmeor, Cornwall (Pye & French 1993). These defences will probably alter local patterns of sediment input to the coast because slumped material is a sediment source for beaches downdrift (see also section 2.4).

3.1.4 Information sources used

Detailed NVC survey of cliff vegetation in the region is confined to two studies: the Lizard and Cape Cornwall (Cooper 1988a, b). This work was part of a pilot study involving thirteen surveys to assess the feasibility of mapping all cliff habitat in Britain. These surveys, all carried out in the summer of 1987, use a consistent methodology. The data provide a sound baseline for future cliff vegetation studies and local management of the cliff resource. The plant ecology of cliffs of the Lizard is perhaps the best-studied in Britain in terms of relationships with salt spray effects, management and historical ecology; all studies are reviewed by Mitchley & Malloch (1991). No other detailed surveys of cliff vegetation in the region have been carried out. Existing information is insufficient to detail the regional extent of individual cliff and cliff-top habitats, apart from maritime cliff grassland.

3.1.5 Acknowledgements

Assistance with sources was kindly provided by the Species Conservation Branch of the Joint Nature Conservation Committee. Thanks also go to Rendel Geotechnics for information on landsliding and cliff erosion.

3.1.6 Further sources of information

A. *References cited*

Cooper, E.A. 1988a. *Survey of sea-cliff vegetation of Great Britain. 2. Cape Cornwall.* Peterborough, Nature Conservancy Council.

Cooper, E.A. 1988b. *Survey of sea-cliff vegetation of Great Britain. 3. The Lizard.* Peterborough, Nature Conservancy Council.

Fletcher, A., Coppins, B.J., Gilbert, O.L., James, P.W., & Lambley, P.W. 1984. Survey and assessment of lowland heathland lichen habitats. *Nature Conservancy Council, CSD Report,* No. 522.

Gubbay, S. 1988. *Coastal directory for marine nature conservation.* Ross-on-Wye, Marine Conservation Society.

Heritage Coast Forum. 1993. *Heritage coasts in England and Wales: a gazetteer.* Manchester, Manchester Metropolitan University.

Jones, D.K.C., & Lee, E.M. 1994. *Landsliding in Great Britain.* London, HMSO.

Lee, E.M. 1995. Coastal cliff recession in Great Britain: the significance for sustainable coastal management. *In: Directions in European coastal management,* ed. by M.G. Healey & J.P. Doody, 185-193. Cardigan, Samara Publishing.

Mitchley, J., & Malloch, A.J.C. 1991. *Sea-cliff management handbook for Great Britain.* Lancaster, University of Lancaster.

Pye, K., & French, P.W. 1993. *Targets for coastal habitat re-creation.* Peterborough, English Nature. (English Nature Science, No. 13.)

Rodwell, J.S., *ed.* In prep. *British plant communities. Volume 5: maritime and weed communities.* Cambridge, Cambridge University Press.

Stroud, D.A., Mudge, G.P., & Pienkowski, M.W. 1990. *Protecting internationally important bird sites.* Peterborough, Nature Conservancy Council.

B. *Further reading*

Further details of coastal habitat sites, including cliffs, are available on the *Coastal & marine UKDMAP datasets* module disseminated by JNCC Coastal Conservation Branch, Peterborough.

Barne, J., Davidson, N.C., Hill, T.O., & Jones, M. 1994. *Coastal & marine UKDMAP datasets: a user manual.* Peterborough, Joint Nature Conservation Committee.

British Oceanographic Data Centre. 1992. *United Kingdom digital marine atlas. User guide. Version 2.0.* Birkenhead, Natural Environment Research Council, British Oceanographic Data Centre.

Davidson, N.C., Laffoley, D.d'A., Doody, J.P., Way, L.S., Gordon, J., Key, R., Drake, C.M., Pienkowski, M.W., Mitchell, R.M., & Duff, K.L. 1991. *Nature conservation and estuaries in Great Britain.* Peterborough, Nature Conservancy Council.

Mitchley, J. 1989. *A sea-cliff bibliography.* Peterborough, Nature Conservancy Council. (Research & survey in nature conservation, No. 18.)

Steers, J.A. 1964. *The coastline of England and Wales.* Cambridge, Cambridge University Press.

C. Contact names and addresses

Type of information	*Contact address and telephone no.*
Flora, fauna, habitat information, location of site reports, site management - England	*Coastal Ecologist, Maritime Team, English Nature, Peterborough, tel: 01733 340345
Flora, fauna, habitat information, location of site reports, site management - Wales	*Coastal Ecologist, CCW HQ, Bangor, tel: 01248 370444
National and international policy and advice on cliff conservation	*Coastal Conservation Branch, JNCC, Peterborough, tel: 01733 62626
Cliffs in Cornwall	*Cornwall Wildlife Trust, Truro, tel: 01872 273939
Cliffs in Devon	*Conservation Data Manager, Devon Wildlife Trust, Exeter, tel: 01392 79244
National Landslide Databank	Rendel Geotechnics, Norfolk House, Smallbrook Queensway, Birmingham B5 4LJ, tel: 0121 627 1777
Invertebrate fauna of cliffs	*Invertebrate Site Register, Species Conservation Branch, JNCC, Peterborough, tel: 01733 62626

*Starred contact addresses are given in full in the Appendix.

At more than 600 hectares, Kenfig Dunes National Nature Reserve is the largest sand dune system in a region notable for its many extensive dune sites. Although backed by heavy industry, the dunes themselves are remarkably unaltered by human use; in the slacks – wet depressions, as pictured here – they have the largest areas in Wales of two rare plant communities. Photo: Pat Doody, JNCC.

3.2 Sand dunes

Dr T.C.D. Dargie

3.2.1 Introduction

The region's coast contains a large number of sand dune systems associated with bays, estuaries and hard cliffs. The English dunes in this region represent nearly one quarter of the total English dune area and 6% of the British resource (Table 3.2.1). The region is therefore nationally important. There are no vegetated sand dunes in Gloucestershire, Gwent or South Glamorgan.

Table 3.2.1 Region 11 vegetated dune resource in context

	Total area (ha)[a]	*% of total in Region 11*
Cornwall	1,258	-
Devon	713	-
Somerset	160	-
Avon	6	-
Mid-Glamorgan	990	-
Region 11	*3,229*	
England	9,282	24
Wales	8,483	12
West Coast	31,308	10
GB	50,200	6

Sources: Dargie (1993), Dargie (1995), DAFF (1995), Radley (1994), JNCC Coastal Resources Database. Key: [a]all figures have been rounded to the nearest whole hectare. Note: survey data for Scotland are incomplete and therefore totals for the West Coast and for Great Britain are provisional estimates.

The region has a high proportion of the GB resource of certain dune vegetation types, in particular mobile and semi-fixed dunes, neutral/calcareous fixed dune grassland and dune slack (Table 3.2.2). The large extent and diverse range of habitats (some very rare) make the sand dunes of the region of great interest.

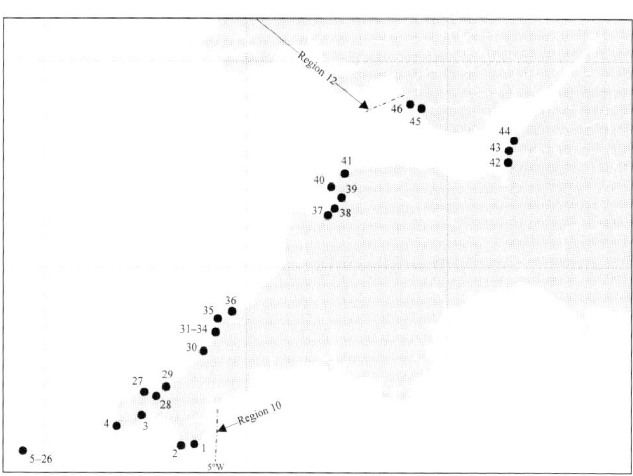

Map 3.2.1 Sand dune sites. Numbers refer to Table 3.2.3. Source: JNCC Coastal Database.

3.2.2 Important locations and species

The region has a total of 46 dune sites (Table 3.2.3 and Map 3.2.1) containing 3,229 ha of vegetated sand and other land cover. Their importance is reflected in the range of nature conservation designations applied to them: 23 are Sites of Special Scientific Interest (SSSIs), two are National Nature Reserves, one falls within a Biosphere Reserve and one is a county wildlife trust reserve; dunes also occur in the region in Areas of Outstanding Natural Beauty, a Heritage Coast and property owned by the National Trust (Table 3.2.3).

The largest dunes are hindshore types (e.g. Gwithian to Mexico Towans, Penhale Sands, Braunton Burrows, Merthyr Mawr, Kenfig Dunes), developed above beaches with a good sand supply and an onshore prevailing wind, which drives sand inland as a series of dune ridges or mobile parabolic dunes. These are found in the most exposed sectors of the Bristol Channel coast. Ness/foreland dunes develop on shores with sand supply from two directions and gradually extend seawards; the only example in the region is a small dune system in the Isles of Scilly (Bar Point, St. Mary's). Spit dunes (e.g. Northam Burrows, The Neck of

Table 3.2.2 Areas (ha[a]) of dune vegetation types

	Strand and embryo dune	*Mobile and semi-fixed dune*	*Acidic fixed dune grassland*	*Neutral and calcareous fixed dune grassland*	*Dune heath and bracken*	*Dune slack*	*Other dune wetland*	*Dune woodland and scrub*	*Transitions to saltmarsh*	*Transitions to maritime cliff*	*Other land cover*
Cornwall	10	15	2	831	26	9	<1	194	0	29	142
Devon	3	404	1	92	0	128	0	18	0	0	67
Somerset	3	13	1	34	0	<1	15	58	<1	0	36
Avon	1	1	<1	<1	0	0	0	3	<1	0	<1
Mid Glam.	4	263	11	387	1	139	3	103	3	6	70
Region 11	***21***	***696***	***15***	***1,343***	***27***	***277***	***18***	***375***	***3***	***35***	***315***
England	179	2,484	671	2,710	197	487	150	1,189	141	30	1,044
Wales	136	1,961	162	2,034	136	614	221	2,364	59	21	775
Great Britain	340	8,504	4,953	15,228	2,615	2,175	4,114	8,965	836	64	2,406

Sources: Radley (1994), Dargie (1995), JNCC Coastal Resources Database, Dargie (1993). Key: [a] all figures have been rounded to the nearest whole hectare. Note: survey data for Scotland are incomplete and therefore totals for Great Britain are provisional estimates.

Table 3.2.3 Sand dune sites in Region 11

Site no.	Name	Grid ref.	Area (ha)[a]	Dune type	Conservation status
	Cornwall				
1	Kennack Sands	SW737166	7	Bay	
2	Church and Poldhu Coves, Gunwalloe	SW662202	55	Bay	
3	Marazion	SW499309	1	Bay	
4	Whitesand Bay	SW360270	26	Bay	
5	Wingleton Down	SV884075	4	Bay	SSSI
6	Burnt Island	SV878086	7	Bay	SSSI
7	Porth Conger	SV887084	3	Bay	SSSI
8	Porth Hellick Pool	SV923108	5	Bay	SSSI
9	Porth Loo and Portmelon	SV908114	3	Bay	
10	Pelistry Bay	SV928119	7	Bay	
11	Bar Point, St. Mary's	SV916128	7	Ness/foreland	
12	Samson Flats	SV872131	35	Bay, climbing	SSSI
13	Appletree Banks	SV893137	39	Bay	SSSI
14	Rushy Bay Dunes	SV876145	12	Bay	SSSI
15	Popplestone Banks	SV875152	<1	Bay	SSSI
16	East Bryher Coast	SV880154	<1	Bay	
17	Pentle Bay, Isles of Scilly	SV901146	17	Bay	
18	Old Grimsby	SV894155	6	Bay	
19	Gimble Porth	SV888159	4	Bay	
20	Norwethel	SV896164	<1	Bay	SSSI
21	St. Helen's South Coast	SV901168	<1	Bay	SSSI
22	Tean	SV906166	30	Bay	SSSI
23	Lower Town Dunes	SV917160	8	Bay	
24	Great Bay Dunes	SV924172	13	Bay, climbing	SSSI
25	Higher Town Dunes	SV934153	6	Bay	
26	Eastern Isles, including Little Arthur	SV938142	5	Bay	SSSI
27	Lelant	SW544383	9	Hindshore	
28	Gwithian to Mexico Towans	SW573395	282	Hindshore, climbing	SSSI, AONB, CWT
29	Godrevy Towans	SW584417	43	Hindshore, climbing	
30	Porthtowan Dunes	SW692481	<1	Bay	
31	Penhale Sands	SW769567	508	Hindshore, climbing	SSSI
32	Holywell Dunes	SW767593	56	Bay, climbing	SSSI
33	Crantock Dunes	SW785609	20	Bay	NT
34	Fistral Dunes	SW799618	40	Bay	
35	Constantine Bay	SW860747	15	Bay, climbing	
36	Padstow Bay, Rock Dunes	SW926767	89	Bay	SSSI, SPA, HC
	Devon				
37	Northam Burrows	SS445305	53	Spit	
38	Instow Sands	SS479316	26	Bay	
39	Braunton Burrows	SS454352	597	Hindshore/spit	SSSI, AONB, BR
40	Croyde Bay	SS437392	11	Bay	
41	Woolacombe Bay Rock Dunes	SS454425	26	Climbing	
	Somerset				
42	Berrow Dunes	ST293544	160	Bay	SSSI, Ramsar site
	Avon				
43	Weston Dunes	ST315599	3	Bay	SSSI
44	Sand Bay	ST331655	3	Bay	SSSI
	Mid Glamorgan				
45	Merthyr Mawr	SS860786	369	Hindshore, climbing	HC, SSSI
46	Kenfig Dunes	SS788815	621	Hindshore	SSSI, NNR

Source: Dargie (1993, 1995), Radley (1994). Key: [a]all figures have been rounded to the nearest whole hectare; AONB = Area of Outstanding Natural Beauty; CWT = County Wildlife Trust reserve; HC = Heritage Coast; NNR = National Nature Reserve; SPA = Special Protection Area; SSSI = Site of Special Scientific Interest; BR = Biosphere Reserve. Note: site no. refers to Map 3.2.1.

Braunton Burrows) develop at the mouths of estuaries and depend strongly on river sediment for their sand supply. Bay dunes (e.g. Whitesand Bay) are the most common type of dune site in the region and develop on sand trapped within the shelter of rock headlands. Climbing dunes (e.g. Gwithian to Mexico Towans, Woolacombe Bay, Merthyr Mawr) occur when sand is blown up on to terrain inland of the main dune system, in some cases covering large areas of steep cliff. The sand often forms only a thin veneer and the vegetation reflects a strong influence from the underlying geology. The larger dune systems in the region develop a fresh (or, rarely, brackish) watertable, which influences the vegetation of depressions, forming a distinctive type of wetland termed dune slack. This habitat is common on hindshore dunes but is rare or absent from other dune types. Permanent open water is a rare dune habitat, present at Kenfig Pool.

Ninety National Vegetation Classification communities are recorded for all English and Welsh dunes, with a total of 156 types for communities and sub-communities combined, not all of them exclusive to dunes. Kenfig is particularly notable in having the largest areas in Wales of two rare dune slack communities (SD13 creeping willow *Salix repens* - moss *Bryum pseudotriquetrum* slack and SD14 creeping willow *Salix repens* - moss *Campylium stellatum* slack), with Braunton Burrows having the largest areas of the SD14 type in England.

In Great Britain, four nationally rare and thirteen nationally scarce higher plants are found mainly or exclusively on dunes. Of the nationally rare dune plants, water germander *Teucrium scordium* is present in the region (see also Tables 5.2.2, 5.2.3 and 5.2.4). Variegated horsetail *Equisetum variegatum*, Portland spurge *Euphorbia portlandica,* sea buckthorn *Hippophae rhamnoides* and dune fescue *Vulpia fasciculata* are nationally scarce dune plants found in the region. Nationally rare and scarce species more typical of other habitats also occur on dunes in the region, including shore dock *Rumex rupestris*, dwarf pansy *Viola kitaibeliana*, sea stock *Matthiola sinuata*, wild leek *Allium ampeloprasum* var. *ampeloprasum*, balm-leaved figwort *Scrophularia scorodonia*, fen orchid *Liparis loeselii* subsp. *ovata*, early meadow-grass *Poa infirma*, orange bird's-foot *Ornithopus pinnatus*, sharp rush *Juncus acutus*, ivy broomrape *Orobanche hederae* and sea-heath *Frankenia laevis.* Rare and scarce bryophytes (e.g. *Southbya nigrella, Petalophyllum ralfsii, Pleurochaete squarrosa*) and lichens (e.g. *Fulgensia fulgens, Toninia caeruleonigricans*) also occur. Most dune site reports contain details of some of the notable species present.

Many sites have long lists of recorded invertebrates, with many notable and rare (Red Data Book) species. Outstanding dune locations in the JNCC's Invertebrate Site Register include Braunton Burrows, Merthyr Mawr, Kenfig, Berrow, Penhale Dunes, Kennack Sands and Gwithian to Mexico Towans (see also section 5.3).

3.2.3 Human activities

In general, sand dunes are among the least heavily modified of terrestrial habitats. However, the inner edge of many sand dune sites in the region has been strongly affected by a variety of human impacts, sometimes leading to habitat loss (Doody 1989) or conversion to other, common, vegetation types. Residential and recreational development has encroached on many sites because of their high recreational amenity value. Damage from recreational use is controlled by the provision of car parking space and hardened paths and boardwalks to reduce path erosion. Many sites show the effects of heavy visitor pressure, with small areas of trampling erosion present in the majority of sites and severe, widespread trampling damage at Whitesand Bay, Porthtowan and Penhale Dunes. Moderate to severe vehicle damage is recorded for Gunwalloe and Porthtowan Dunes. Nine sites are recorded as having golf courses on part of their area, with associated modification of dune habitats. Leisure activities and leisure-related development such as caravan and camp sites are also common on the edge of many sites. Military use is present on a few sand dune sites but the total area of impact and damage is slight. Dunes at Bar Point (St. Mary's, Isles of Scilly) have been proposed as a landfill site (Dargie 1990).

Many sites are covered by one or more conservation designations or forms of planning control (Table 3.2.3) (Dargie 1993, 1995; Radley 1994). Conservation is a major aim in these and other locations, and positive conservation management is common. Natural succession to creeping willow scrub in slacks and to rank grassland and scrub on dry dunes is a considerable problem, reducing the extent of bare sand and open young slacks. Several sites have required scrub removal, notably of sea buckthorn *Hippophae rhamnoides,* which has been eradicated from Braunton Burrows but threatens to replace much open dune habitat at Merthyr Mawr (Dargie 1992). Grazing is a traditional form of management which has been re-introduced to several sites, or has been replaced by mowing for small areas of flat dune. Most sites still support rabbit populations, which are important in maintaining high species diversity in fixed dune grassland. Most sites adjacent to population centres and fronting low-lying land have some form of coastal protection against erosion, but many large sites remain unprotected and hence reflect the natural balance between erosion and accretion at the outer dune edge. Coastal erosion is not a serious problem at most sites although locally it may be a serious issue. There is evidence from surveys within the last decade of a recent net loss of habitat for the region (Radley 1994).

3.2.4 Information sources used

All areas of vegetated sand dune in the region have been surveyed in recent years using the National Vegetation Classification (Rodwell 1991a, b, 1992, 1995, in prep.). This work was part of the sand dune survey of Great Britain initiated by the Nature Conservancy Council in 1987 and continued after 1991 by the JNCC on behalf of country conservation agencies. NVC surveys use a reliable, consistent methodology yielding very detailed information (Rodwell in prep.). The vegetation is mapped and described, and information on coastal erosion and accretion, atypical vegetation and adjoining land use is also recorded. The data represent a sound baseline for future dune vegetation studies and both strategic and local management of the dune resource. Individual site reports and national reports for England (Radley 1994) and Wales (Dargie 1995) are available from the JNCC. Most data discussed here are derived from the national reports.

Survey of dunes in Scotland is still in progress; the lack of full survey data for Scotland prevents calculation of precise figures on the extent of the sand dune resource for either the West Coast or Great Britain. An estimate of dune habitats for Scotland is used here, based on a sample set of sites (Dargie 1993), to allow some form of British context to be made.

There are no detailed ecological studies on animal populations of the dunes in the region, but the invertebrate fauna is well studied. Details are recorded on the JNCC's Invertebrate Site Register.

3.2.5 Acknowledgements

Assistance with sources was kindly provided by the Species Conservation Branch, JNCC.

3.2.6 Further sources of information

A. References cited

Dargie, T.C.D. 1990. Isles of Scilly dune vegetation survey 1990. *Nature Conservancy Council, CSD Reports*, No. 1,179.

Dargie, T.C.D. 1992. *Historical extent, potential threat, and control of sea buckthorn* Hippophae rhamnoides *L. at Merthyr Mawr Warren, South Wales.* Cardiff, Countryside Council for Wales. (Unpublished report.)

Dargie, T.C.D. 1993. *Sand dune vegetation survey of Great Britain. Part 2 - Scotland.* Peterborough, Joint Nature Conservation Committee.

Dargie, T.C.D. 1995. *Sand dune vegetation survey of Great Britain. Part 3 - Wales.* Peterborough, Joint Nature Conservation Committee.

Doody, J.P. 1989. Conservation and development of the coastal dunes in Great Britain. *In: Perspectives in coastal dune management*, ed. by F. van der Meulen, P.D. Jungerius & J. Visser, 53-67. The Hague, SPB Academic Publishing.

Radley, G.P. 1994. *Sand dune vegetation survey of Great Britain. Part 1 - England.* Peterborough, Joint Nature Conservation Committee.

Rodwell, J.S., *ed.* 1991a. *British plant communities. Volume 1: woodlands and scrub.* Cambridge, Cambridge University Press.

Rodwell, J.S., *ed.* 1991b. *British plant communities. Volume 2: mires and heaths.* Cambridge, Cambridge University Press.

Rodwell, J.S., *ed.* 1992. *British plant communities. Volume 3: grasslands and montane vegetation.* Cambridge, Cambridge University Press.

Rodwell, J.S., *ed.* 1995. *British plant communities. Volume 4: aquatic communities, swamps and tall herb fens.* Cambridge, Cambridge University Press.

Rodwell, J.S., *ed.* In prep. *British plant communities. Volume 5: maritime and weed communities.* Cambridge, Cambridge University Press.

B. Further reading

Further details of coastal habitat sites, including sand dunes, are available on the *Coastal & marine UKDMAP datasets* module disseminated by JNCC Coastal Conservation Branch, Peterborough.

Barne, J., Davidson, N.C., Hill, T.O., & Jones, M. 1994. *Coastal & marine UKDMAP datasets: a user manual.* Peterborough, Joint Nature Conservation Committee.

British Oceanographic Data Centre. 1992. *United Kingdom digital marine atlas. User guide. Version 2.0.* Birkenhead, Natural Environment Research Council, British Oceanographic Data Centre.

Brooks, A., & Agate, E. 1986. *Sand dunes: a practical conservation handbook.* Wallingford, British Trust for Conservation Volunteers.

Davidson, N.C., Laffoley, D.d'A., Doody, J.P., Way, L.S., Gordon, J., Key, R., Drake, C.M., Pienkowski, M.W., Mitchell, R.M., & Duff, K.L. 1991. *Nature conservation and estuaries in Great Britain.* Peterborough, Nature Conservancy Council.

Doody, J.P., *ed.* 1985. *Sand dunes and their management.* Peterborough, Nature Conservancy Council. (Focus on nature conservation, No. 13.)

Doody, J.P., *ed.* 1991. *Sand dune inventory of Europe.* Peterborough, Joint Nature Conservation Committee.

Fletcher, A., Coppins, B.J., Gilbert, O.L., James, P.W., & Lambley, P.W. 1984. Survey and assessment of lowland heathland lichen habitats. *Nature Conservancy Council, CSD Report*, No. 522.

Nature Conservancy Council. 1990. *On course conservation: managing golf's natural heritage.* Peterborough, Nature Conservancy Council.

Radley, G.P., & Woolven, S.C. 1990. *A sand dune bibliography.* Peterborough, Nature Conservancy Council. (Contract Surveys, No. 122.)

Ranwell, D.S. 1972. *Ecology of salt marshes and sand dunes.* London, Chapman and Hall.

Ranwell, D.S., & Boar, R. 1986. *Coast dune management guide.* Huntingdon, Institute of Terrestrial Ecology.

Williams, A.T., & Randerson, P.F. 1989. Nexus: ecology, recreation and management of a dune system in South Wales. *In: Perspectives in coastal dune management*, ed. by F. van der Meulen, P.D. Jungerius & J. Visser, 217-227. The Hague, SPB Academic Publishing.

C. Contact names and addresses

Type of information	*Contact address and telephone no.*
Sand dune flora, fauna, habitat information, site management - England	*Maritime Team Leader, English Nature, Peterborough, tel: 01733 340345
Sand dune flora, fauna, habitat information, site management - Wales	*Coastal Ecologist, CCW HQ, Bangor, tel: 01248 370444
Advice on national and international policy and dune conservation	*Coastal Conservation Branch, JNCC, Peterborough, tel: 01733 62626
Invertebrate data	*Invertebrate Site Register, Species Conservation Branch, JNCC, Peterborough, tel: 01733 62626

*Starred contact addresses are given in full in the Appendix.

3.3 Vegetated shingle structures and shorelines

Dr R.E. Randall

3.3.1 Introduction

Shingle means sediments larger than sand but smaller than boulders: that is, between 2-200 mm in diameter. Where the coast features shingle, it is often mixed with large amounts of sand, or else sand dunes (see section 3.2) have developed on it. Shingle sites include both simple fringing beaches and also more complex structures where the shingle is vegetated yet not buried by more than 20 cm of sand (e.g. at Braunton Burrows). Shingle plant communities around Britain are distinctive (Sneddon & Randall 1993a), with some communities being widespread and others limited to a particular region or substrate.

This region contains only a small amount of the British shingle resource, but four sites (the Isles of Scilly, Porlock, Bridgwater and East Aberthaw) extend to over 10 ha. Indeed, the largest quantities of shingle in the south-west occur on the Isles of Scilly, where a series of bars, raised beaches and shingle spreads occur throughout several of the islands. Pure shingle is uncommon in western Britain: Scilly, Appledore and Porthkerry are important in this respect. Much of the shingle in this region occurs in very high energy environments and suffers considerable storm movement.

The region as a whole has a wide representation of shingle vegetation communities. Several sites in the region are significant in having representative western and south-western communities. According to Sneddon (1992), the Isles of Scilly shingle structures rate very highly in Britain based on floristics, size and lack of disturbance. The sites at Bridgwater Bay and East Aberthaw are significant for showing the saline influence of adjacent saltmarsh on shingle vegetation, and Loe Bar and some of the Scilly bars are good examples of the influence of sand matrix on the shingle flora. At the Western Rocks shingle on Scilly the presence of birds and seals has influenced the nature of the vegetation.

Table 3.3.1 Area of vegetated shingle structures in Region 11

	Area (ha)
Cornwall	0
Isles of Scilly	10.0
North Devon	0
Somerset	53.3
Avon	0
Gloucestershire	0
Gwent	0
Mid Glamorgan	0
South Glamorgan	12.3
Region 11	***75.6***
West Coast	656.8
England	4,353.1
Wales	103.4
Great Britain	5,129.1
% West Coast total in region	11.5
% England total in region (English counties only)	1.7
% GB total in region	1.5

Source: Sneddon & Randall (1994), JNCC Coastal Database

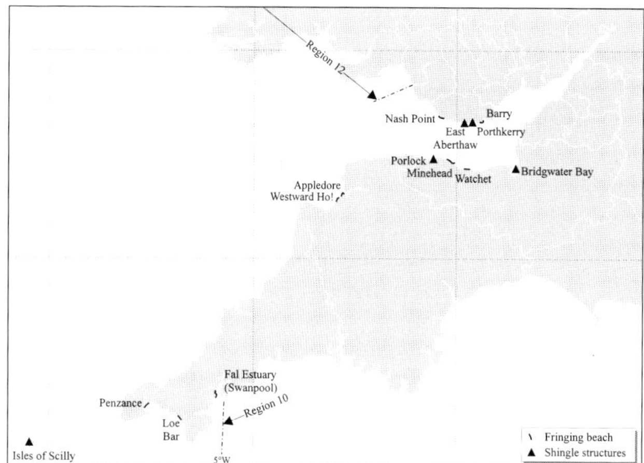

Map 3.3.1 Vegetated shingle structures and fringing shingle beaches. Source: Sneddon & Randall (1993a).

3.3.2 Important locations and species

The major shingle sites in the region are shown on Map 3.3.1. Surveyed shingle sites are listed in Table 3.3.2 and fringing shingle beaches in Table 3.3.3.

Much of the coastline of Cornwall and north Devon is cliffed, and shingle is only present at the few sites where deposition can occur (Steers 1964). Shingle is present in the Fal Estuary at Swanpool (Dorey *et al.* 1973). A series of bars, raised beaches and shingle spreads are present on several of the Isles of Scilly, and a flint shingle bar encloses Loe Pool just west of the Lizard; Milner (1922) suggests that these sediments (along with flints on Scilly) may have come from the north-east, carried by a river that once traversed the St. Erth channel. A fringing beach of sandy shingle occurs on the west side of Mount's Bay along the back of the beach near Penzance.

Between Croyde and Westward Ho! in Barnstaple Bay, sand dunes and shingle occur in the Taw-Torridge Estuary. At Westward Ho! (Stuart & Hookway 1954) and along the more sheltered pebble ridge at Appledore (Parkinson 1980) the shingle is mobile. In contrast, much of the south coast of the Bristol Channel from Porlock to the mouth of the Parrett is bordered by shingle being carried eastward from Liassic rock outcrops (Kidson 1960). The major formations are at Porlock and Steart in Bridgwater Bay, with significant fringing beaches at Minehead and Watchet. In South Glamorgan, on the north shore of the Bristol Channel, there are further coarse shingle spreads and some sand, which has travelled from the west from Liassic and Carboniferous limestone outcrops and been deposited at Barry, Porthkerry pebble ridge, East Aberthaw and Nash Point.

A common pioneer vegetation community on shingle sites in the region is dominated by sea beet *Beta vulgaris* subsp. *maritimum* with red fescue *Festuca rubra* and sea mayweed *Tripleurospermum maritimum*. In some locations curled dock *Rumex crispus* and sea kale *Crambe maritima* are important species in this assemblage, and on the Isles of Scilly the nationally rare shore dock *Rumex rupestris* occurs. An unusual southern variant includes bittersweet *Solanum*

Table 3.3.2 Surveyed shingle structures

Site name	*Grid ref.*	*Area surveyed (approx. ha)*	*Site type*	*Conservation status*	*Activities/management/disturbances*
Isles of Scilly	SV900100	10	Shingle bars and raised beaches	SSSI	Some trampling, light rabbit grazing, seabird enrichment
Porlock Beach	SS890484	28	Storm beach and shingle	NT	Localized trampling, tidal damage, stabilisation measures
Bridgwater Bay	ST239457	25	Multiple ridge with thin alluvial cover	SSSI, NNR	Grazing, vehicular damage, past gravel extraction, natural reworking
Porthkerry	ST091670	2	Limestone shingle bar	None	Light trampling
East Aberthaw	SS033657	10	Sandy and silty shingle spit	SSSI	Groyne stabilisation

Source: after Sneddon & Randall (1994). Key: NT = National Trust, NNR = National Nature Reserve; SSSI = Site of Special Scientific Interest.

dulcamara, and in the most south-westerly sites tree mallow *Lavatera arborea* becomes a major component of the community. Where there is a high silt content in the shingle matrix, common scurvygrass *Cochlearia officinalis* and grass-leaved orache *Atriplex littoralis* are sometimes associated with the sea beet. Unique to the Isle of Scilly is a sea beet community with a large number of associate species, the commonest of which are sea carrot *Daucus carota* subsp. *gummifer* and rock samphire *Crithmum maritimum*. On sites where sand is the major component of the matrix, sea sandwort *Honkenya peploides* is typical, often with sea campion *Silene maritima*, sea-holly *Eryngium maritimum*, sea spurge *Euphorbia paralias* and occasionally marram *Ammophila arenaria*. Secondary pioneer communities frequently contain curled dock, yellow horned-poppy *Glaucium flavum*, common ragwort *Senecio jacobaea*, sticky groundsel *S. viscosus* and biting stonecrop *Sedum acre* or English stonecrop *S. anglicum*.

Further inland on more stable shingle structures, fescue grasslands develop. Where there is a silt matrix, for example in Bridgwater Bay, red fescue dominates, with buck's-horn plantain *Plantago coronopus*, spear-leaved orache *Atriplex prostrata* and greater sea-spurrey *Spergularia media*. In the Isles of Scilly and at other south coast sites, thrift *Armeria maritima,* sea beet and sea mayweed are the main associates. More widespread and away from saltmarsh, red fescue has common bird's-foot-trefoil *Lotus corniculatus*, ribwort plantain *Plantago lanceolata* and mosses *Dicranum scoparium* and *Hypnum cupressiforme* as major associates. On sandy matrix sites marram and sand sedge *Carex arenaria* are the main associate species.

Heath communities are not present on shingle structures in this region, but the most inland parts of Porlock beach are stable enough to allow a gorse *Ulex europaeus* - bramble *Rubus fruticosus* scrub, or bramble - false oat-grass *Arrhenatherum elatius* scrub to develop. The most sheltered sites on Scilly contain an open bracken *Pteridium aquilinum* - bramble community rich in grass species, and at the base of the lee slope of the Bridgwater Bay ridges there is a western blackthorn *Prunus spinosa* - bramble scrub, with ivy *Hedera helix*, burnet rose *Rosa pimpinellifolia* and bittersweet.

There are good populations of sea kale on the south Cornwall sites and the Isles of Scilly. Sea knotgrass *Polygonum maritimum* and purple spurge *Euphorbia peplis* had their last strongholds on fine shingle in this region but have not been recorded in recent years. Ray's knotgrass *P. oxyspermum* is, however, still present though declining (Margetts & David 1981). The tree mallow, though present elsewhere in the south-west, reaches its greatest vigour in this region, as does the sea radish *Raphanus maritimus*.

Table 3.3.3 Fringing shingle beaches

Site name	*Grid ref.*	*Length of structure (km*)*	*Site type*
Fal Estuary (Swanpool)	SW8031	0.5	Sandy shingle
Loe Bar	SW6425	1.0	Flint shingle with coarse sand
Penzance	SW4629	1.0	Sandy shingle
Westward Ho!	SS4329	1.0	Mobile sandy shingle
Appledore	SS4532	0.5	Pebble bank
Minehead	SS9847	2.0	Semi-mobile shingle with sand matrix
Watchet	ST0744	0.5	Mud and sand matrix in shingle
Barry	ST1267	1.0	Sandy coarse shingle
Nash Point	SS9169	0.5	Coarse shingle and boulders

Source: Randall (unpublished survey, early 1980s). Key: *to nearest 0.5 km.

Shore dock is a rare Celtic fringe species that has its best development in the Isles of Scilly (see also section 5.2).

The invertebrate fauna of shingle sites in this region has not been well studied, but Loe Bar is the only known site for the Cornish sandhill rustic moth *Luperina nickerlii leechi* (see also section 5.3). The shingle sites of the Western Rocks and the Eastern Isles, Scilly, are important roosting and nesting locations for shag, guillemot, storm petrel and manx shearwaters (see sections 5.10, 5.11 and 5.12) as well as being haul-out sites for seals (see section 5.14).

3.3.3 Human activities

Many of this region's shingle sites are subject to recreational pressure. Bridgwater Bay has vehicular access, and gravel has been extracted in the past. Portlock Beach and East Aberthaw have both been groyned and graded. The more distant islands of the Isles of Scilly are subject to landing restrictions during the bird breeding season. None of the fringing shingle beaches of this region is grazed.

3.3.4 Information sources used

Not all shingle sites are vegetated, especially not those on exposed high-energy coasts or where disturbance is great. Unvegetated sites have not been surveyed. The major vegetated shingle structures of the region were surveyed during the NCC's 1989 national shingle structure survey, which used the National Vegetation Classification (NVC) framework (Sneddon & Randall 1993a, b, 1994). Not all shingle sites fall into the category of shingle structures. Many of the region's fringing shingle beaches were examined by the author in the early 1980s as part of a survey sponsored by British Petroleum. These sites were only examined qualitatively and target notes were used to describe physical and biological features of interest. This information became the basis of the geographical variation data published in Randall (1989).

Loe Bar has been surveyed over many years by the Biological Records Centre of the Cornwall Naturalists' Trust (Turk 1964; Murphy 1986), the Nature Conservancy (Haynes 1972) and the National Trust (1983). The coast of Bridgwater Bay is particularly well documented in Warren (1956).

3.3.5 Further sources of information

A. References cited

Dorey, A.E., Little, C., & Barnes, R.S.K. 1973. An ecological study of the Swanpool, Falmouth. ii. Hydrology and its relation to animal distributions. *Estuarine and Coastal Marine Sciences, 1:* 153-176.

Haynes, C.J. 1972. *Report on Loe Bar, Cornwall.* London, Nature Conservancy (unpublished report).

Kidson, C. 1960. The shingle complexes of Bridgwater Bay. *Transactions of the Institute of British Geographers, 28:* 75-87.

Margetts, L.J., & David, R.W. 1981. *Review of the Cornish flora, 1980.* Truro, Institute of Cornish Studies.

Milner, H.B. 1922. Origin of the Pliocene deposits of Cornwall. *Quarterly Journal of the Geological Society, 78:* 348-363.

Murphy, R.J. 1986. A study of Loe Bar. *Cornish Studies, 14:* 23-33.

National Trust. 1983. *Biological survey - Loe Bar and Pool.* Cheltenham, National Trust (unpublished report).

Parkinson, M. 1980. *Coastlines of Devon.* Exeter, Devon County Council.

Randall, R.E. 1989. Geographical variation in British shingle vegetation. *Botanical Journal of the Linnean Society, 101:* 3-18.

Sneddon, P. 1992. *Variations in shingle vegetation around the British coastline.* PhD thesis, University of Cambridge.

Sneddon, P., & Randall, R.E. 1993a. *Coastal vegetated shingle structures of Great Britain: main report.* Peterborough, Joint Nature Conservation Committee.

Sneddon, P., & Randall, R.E. 1993b. *Coastal vegetated shingle structures of Great Britain: Appendix 1. Wales.* Peterborough, Joint Nature Conservation Committee.

Sneddon, P., & Randall, R.E. 1994. *Coastal vegetated shingle structures of Great Britain: Appendix 3. England.* Peterborough, Joint Nature Conservation Committee.

Steers, J.A. 1964. *The coastline of England and Wales.* London, Cambridge University Press.

Stuart, A., & Hookway, R.J.S. 1954. *Coastal erosion at Westward Ho!.* Unpublished report to the Coastal Protection Committee of Devon County Council.

Turk, S.M. 1964. *Report on Loe Bar and Loe Pool.* Unpublished report, Monks Wood, Biological Records Centre.

Warren, A. 1956. *The coast of Bridgwater Bay.* PhD thesis, Fitzwilliam House, University of Cambridge.

B. Further reading

Further details of coastal habitat sites, including shingle structures and shorelines, are available on the *Coastal & marine UKDMAP datasets* module disseminated by JNCC Coastal Conservation Branch, Peterborough.

Barne, J., Davidson, N.C., Hill, T.O., & Jones, M. 1994. *Coastal and marine UKDMAP datasets: a user manual.* Peterborough, Joint Nature Conservation Committee.

British Oceanographic Data Centre. 1992. *United Kingdom digital marine atlas. User guide. Version 2.0.* Birkenhead, Natural Environment Research Council, British Oceanographic Data Centre.

Chapman, V.J. 1976. *Coastal vegetation.* Oxford, Pergamon Press.

Davey, F.H. 1909. *Flora of Cornwall.* Penryn, F. Chegwidden.

Ferry B., Lodge, N., & Waters, S. 1990. *Dungeness: a vegetation survey of a shingle beach.* Peterborough, Nature Conservancy Council. (Research & survey in nature conservation, No. 26.)

Fuller, R.M. 1987. Vegetation establishment on shingle beaches. *Journal of Ecology, 75:* 1077-1089.

Howarth, W.O. 1920. Notes on the habitats and ecological characters of three sub-varieties of *Festuca rubra. Journal of Ecology, 8:* 216-231.

Nature Conservancy Council. 1982. *Bridgwater Bay National Nature Reserve - the effects of Hinkley Point Nuclear Power Station.* Peterborough, unpublished report to Central Electricity Generating Board.

Oliver, F.W. 1912. The shingle beach as a plant habitat. *New Phytologist, 11:* 73-99.

Paton, J.A. 1970. *Flowers of the Cornish coast.* Truro, B. Barton.

Ratcliffe, D.A., *ed.* 1977. *A nature conservation review.* London, Cambridge University Press.

Scott, G.A.M. 1963. The ecology of shingle beach plants. *Journal of Ecology, 51:* 517-527.

Sneddon, P., & Randall, R.E. 1989. *Vegetated shingle structures survey of Great Britain: bibliography.* Peterborough, Nature Conservancy Council. (Research & survey in nature conservation, No. 20.)

C. Contact names and addresses

Type of information	*Contact address and telephone no.*
Braunton Burrows	Site Manager, Braunton Burrows, Braunton, Devon EX33 2NQ, tel: 01271 812552
Shingle on the Devon coast	*English Nature Devon and Cornwall Team, Okehampton, tel: 01837 55045
Appledore and Westward Ho! shingle habitats	The Warden, The Burrows Centre, Northam Burrows Country Park, Northam, Bideford EX39 1LY, tel: 01237 479708
Somerset and Avon coast	*English Nature Somerset and Avon Team, Taunton, tel: 01823 283211
Shingle on the Cornwall coast	*English Nature Devon and Cornwall Team, Truro, tel: 01872 262550
Shingle on the Isles of Scilly	*Isles of Scilly Environmental Trust, St. Mary's, tel: 01720 22156
Biological records for Cornwall coast shingle	*Conservation Officer, Cornwall Wildlife Trust, Allet, tel: 01872 73939
Biological records for Devon coast shingle	*Conservation Officer, Devon Wildlife Trust, Exeter, tel: 01392 279244
Gwent, Mid Glamorgan & S. Glamorgan coast shingle	*CCW Cardiff, tel: 01222 772400

*Starred contact addresses are given in full in the Appendix.

3.4 Coastal lagoons

Dr R.N.Bamber & Dr R.S.K.Barnes

3.4.1 Introduction

The term coastal lagoons is used here to include true lagoons, i.e. those wholly or partially separated from the sea by a natural sedimentary barrier, and also artificial brackish ponds and coastal pools, of a similarly restricted tidal range and often containing comparable lagoonal wildlife. Lagoons are commonly shallow, often with a varying salinity ranging from above to below normal sea-water levels (35 g/kg). Freshwater systems are not considered here, nor are fully flushed tidal pools.

The contribution of the region's lagoons to the size of the British resource as a whole is shown in Table 3.4.1. The five true lagoons of the region total 8.5 ha, amounting to just over 1% of Britain's total natural lagoonal resource (or 4% of that resource excluding The Fleet, Dorset, which is by far Britain's largest lagoon, comprising nearly 70% of the total resource) and 6% of the lagoonal resource that was regarded by Barnes (1989) as being 'especially noteworthy in the national context', again excluding The Fleet. The region is therefore of low significance nationally, although the Swanpool Lagoon, Falmouth, Cornwall, is important in the national context. Throughout the region there are also a number of small pools retained behind sea walls and coastal sluices, generally less than 1 ha in size and of low salinity (e.g. Tresemple, and Dennis Cove Pool, Cornwall).

Table 3.4.1 Lagoonal areas for region in context

Region	*Lagoonal area (ha)**	*Overall % of GB total*	*% of GB total excl. The Fleet*
Cornwall (part)	6	<1	1
Somerset	1	<1	<1
Avon	0	0	0
Gloucester	0	0	0
Gwent	0	0	0
S. Glamorgan	2	<1	<1
Mid Glamorgan	0	0	0
Region 11	***9***	***1***	***1***
West Coast	98	8	.13
Great Britain	1,261		

Sources: Seaward (1986), Sheader & Sheader (1987, 1989). Key: *areas rounded to the nearest whole hectare.

Table 3.4.2 Lagoons surveyed

Name	*Grid ref.*	*Area (ha*)*	*Type*
Cornwall			
Tresemple	SW855446	<1	Sluiced pond
Swanpool	SW802315	4	Natural, estuarine
Maenporth	SW788297	0.5	Natural, estuarine
The Pool, Bryher, Isles of Scilly	SV874149	1.5	Natural, uncertain
Dennis Cove Pool	SW921744	<1	Sluiced pond
Somerset			
Catsford Common	ST248451	1	Natural, percolation
S. Glamorgan			
Aberthaw Lagoon	ST036602	1.5	Estuarine

Source: Barnes (1988, 1989). Key: *to the nearest 0.5 ha.

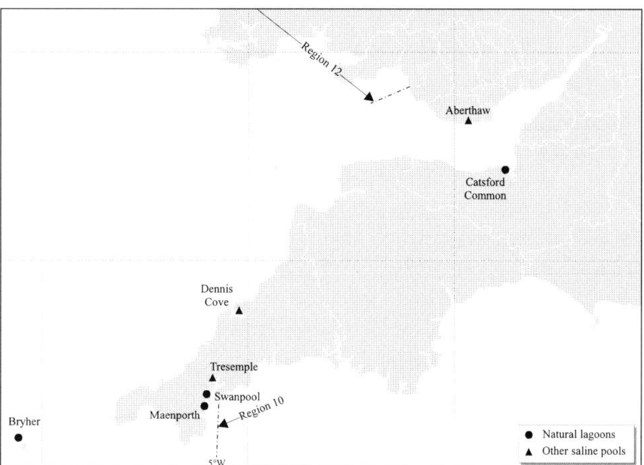

Map 3.4.1 Coastal lagoons and lagoon-like habitat

3.4.2 Important locations and species

Map 3.4.1 shows the locations of the lagoonal and other saline pools mentioned; Table 3.4.2 gives details of their areas and physiography.

True lagoons support only three types of aquatic vegetation, namely stands of green algae (*Chaetomorpha* spp., *Ulva* spp. and *Enteromorpha* spp.), of sea-grasses and similar plants (predominantly tasselweeds *Ruppia* spp.) and, much more rarely, of stoneworts (especially *Lamprothamnium*). Much of the area of their beds, however, is bare sediment, devoid of vegetation cover. Fringing stands of reeds *Phragmites* spp., saltmarsh plants and/or sea club-rush *Scirpus maritimus* are usual. All these communities, with the exception of the stoneworts, occur in the region.

Lagoons possess a characteristic aquatic invertebrate fauna that shows little regional variation, even within Europe. In Britain, several of these species are very rare and are protected under the Wildlife & Countryside Act 1981. One of these protected species, the trembling sea mat *Victorella pavida*, has its only UK occurrence in this region, in Swanpool. Swanpool is also one of the very few British localities for the copepod *Ergasilus lizae*, which is parasitic on grey mullet. Other notable lagoonal species are the brackish-water sand-shrimp *Gammarus chevreuxi* (in three lagoons: Swanpool, Maenporth and Bryher), the lagoonal mud snail *Hydrobia ventrosa* (at Catsford Common, Somerset), and the lagoonal shrimp *Corophium insidiosum* and lagoonal cockle *Cerastoderma glaucum* (in dense populations in Aberthaw Lagoon). The lagoonal prawn *Palaemonetes varians* is common in the lagoons and small saline pools of the region.

3.4.3 Human activities

Little active management is applied to the coastal lagoons themselves, although the surrounding land is often intensively managed. Aberthaw Lagoon has been much reduced in area as a result of waste fuel ash dumping from Aberthaw Power Station, which owns the land. Following advice, a policy was instigated in 1991 to maintain the water conditions for the benefit of the lagoonal invertebrates (see Bamber *et al.* 1993). Algicide is occasionally used in Swanpool to control summer blooms of potentially toxic blue-green algae.

3.4.4 Information sources used

All likely lagoons in the region were surveyed as part of the Nature Conservancy Council's national lagoon survey in 1980-1988 (Little 1985; Seaward 1986; Sheader & Sheader 1987; Barnes 1989). Detailed reports are available, including maps of the habitats and species lists. The data are summarised by Barnes (1989), Sheader & Sheader (1989) and Smith & Laffoley (1992), from which the data in this section were derived.

Surveys of the smaller ponds in Cornwall were generally brief (single visits), with little intensive sampling. However, extensive data exist for both the Aberthaw and Swanpool Lagoons, as a result of their histories of study, including seasonal and longer-term variations. Swanpool Lagoon has been the subject of intensive study since the late 1960s by a research team based in the University of Bristol (see Crawford *et al.* 1979 for descriptive literature). The Aberthaw Lagoon, South Glamorgan, has been studied by Cardiff University, principally for its fish population (see e.g. Creech 1990), and by Fawley Aquatic Research Laboratories in 1990-91, who also revisited some of the Cornish sites (Bamber *et al.* 1993).

3.4.5 Further sources of information

A. References cited

Bamber, R.N., Batten, S.D., & Bridgwater, N.D. 1993. Design criteria for the creation of brackish lagoons. *Biodiversity and Conservation, 2*: 127-137.

Barnes, R.S.K. 1988. The coastal lagoons of Britain: an overview. *Nature Conservancy Council, CSD Report,* No. 933.

Barnes, R.S.K. 1989. The coastal lagoons of Britain: an overview and conservation appraisal. *Biological Conservation, 49*: 295-313.

Crawford, R.M., Dorey, A.E., Little, C., & Barnes, R.S.K. 1979. Ecology of Swanpool, Falmouth. V. Phytoplankton and nutrients. *Estuarine and Coastal Marine Science, 9*: 135-160.

Creech, S. 1990. *The ecology and taxonomy of two European atherinids (Teleostei: Atherinidae).* PhD Thesis, University College of Wales, Cardiff.

Little, C. 1985. Coastal saline lagoons in Cornwall. *Nature Conservancy Council, CSD Report,* No. 601.

Seaward, D.R. 1986. Survey of coastal saline lagoons. Somerset and north Devon. *Nature Conservancy Council, CSD Report,* No. 754.

Sheader, M., & Sheader, A. 1987. *Lagoon survey of Avon and Gloucestershire (Weston-super-Mare to Gloucester), July 1987.* Peterborough, Nature Conservancy Council.

Sheader, M., & Sheader, A. 1989. *The coastal saline ponds of England and Wales: an overview.* Peterborough, Nature Conservancy Council. (Contract Surveys, No. 1009.)

Smith, B.P., & Laffoley, D. 1992. *A directory of saline lagoons and lagoon like habitats in England.* Peterborough, English Nature.

B. Further reading

Further details of coastal habitat sites are available on the *Coastal & marine UKDMAP datasets* module disseminated by the JNCC (Barne *et al.* 1994). Further details of lagoons and quasi-lagoonal features are available on the *UKDMAP datasets* module disseminated by the British Oceanographic Data Centre (BODC 1992).

Al-Suwailem, A.M. 1992. *The ecology of a saline lagoon in southern England.* PhD Thesis, Department of Oceanography, University of Southampton.

Bamber, R.N., Batten, S.D., & Bridgwater, N.D. 1992. On the ecology of brackish water lagoons in Great Britain. *Aquatic Conservation: Marine and Freshwater Ecosystems, 2*: 65-94.

Barne, J., Davidson, N.C., Hill, T.O., & Jones, M. 1994. *Coastal and marine UKDMAP datasets: a user manual.* Peterborough, Joint Nature Conservation Committee.

British Oceanographic Data Centre. 1992. *United Kingdom digital marine atlas. User guide. Version 2.0.* Birkenhead, Natural Environment Research Council, British Oceanographic Data Centre.

Little, C. 1986. Lagoon types in Cornwall. *Porcupine Newsletter, 3*: 166-169.

Seaward, D. 1986. NCC survey of coastal saline lagoons in Dorset, Devon and Somerset. *Porcupine Newsletter, 3*: 164-165.

C. Contact names and addresses

Type of information	*Contact address and telephone no.*
Brackish lagoons of the region	Dr R.S.K. Barnes, St. Catharine's College, University of Cambridge, Cambridge CB2 1RL, tel: 01223 333296
Brackish lagoons	Dr M. Sheader, Department of Oceanography, University of Southampton, Southampton SO9 5NH, tel: 01703 595000
Lagoons in England	*Maritime Team, English Nature HQ, Peterborough, tel: 01733 340345
Lagoonal species in Cornwall	Cornish Biological Records Unit (CBRU), Trevithick Centre, Trevenson Road, Pool, Redruth, Cornwall TR15 3PL, tel: 01209 710424
Lagoonal species in Devon	*M. Camplin, Devon Wildlife Trust, Exeter, tel: 01392 79244

*Starred contact addresses are given in full in the Appendix.

3.5 Wet grassland

Dr H.T. Gee

3.5.1 Introduction

Wet grassland includes both coastal grazing marsh subject to maritime influence and lowland wet grassland adjacent to tidal reaches of estuaries. No national survey exists of wet grassland as here defined, or indeed of coastal grazing marsh or lowland wet grassland separately, so detailed inter-region comparisons are not possible.

Coastal grazing marsh is a distinctive habitat consisting of low-lying grassland drained by a series of ditches that may be either brackish or freshwater. Much grazing marsh was formed by the enclosure of saltmarsh behind sea walls. Smaller areas of freshwater grazing marsh have been created landward of natural barriers such as sand dunes or shingle beaches. Wet grassland sites may remain wet throughout the year and may be managed for stock grazing and/or as hay meadow.

The steep, rocky character of the coasts of Devon and Cornwall has precluded the development of wet grassland along much of the western part of the region. However, adjacent to the Severn Estuary there are extensive areas of wet grassland, including two of the most important areas of wet grassland in the British Isles - the Somerset Levels on the south bank and the Gwent Levels on the north. These levels are nationally important areas of wet grassland for their extent, the proportion of the national resource they represent and the rare birds, plants and invertebrates that they support. This national importance is recognised by the designation of seven SSSIs on the Somerset Levels and six SSSIs on the Gwent Levels, the latter covering more than 4,500 ha. The Somerset Levels and Moors Environmentally Sensitive Area (ESA) represents some 27,000 ha of lowland grassland contiguous with coastal wet grassland. There are also areas of wet grassland on the shores of the upper Severn Estuary in Avon and Gloucestershire and small areas associated with the Taw-Torridge Estuary in north Devon.

Dargie (1993) estimated that there was a total of 63,499 ha of lowland wet grassland in south-west England, of which an estimated 41,275 ha were in Somerset and 11,122 ha in Avon. The lowland wet grassland of these two counties (most of which is grazing marsh) therefore comprises approximately 80% of the lowland wet grassland resource of south-west England, and approximately one quarter of that in England. The Gwent Levels represent over half the lowland wet grassland in Wales. The lowland wet grassland resource of Region 11 is therefore important in the national context.

3.5.2 Important locations and species

Table 3.5.1 lists the locations of wet grassland sites in the region, shown on Map 3.5.1.

Despite similarities, the levels of Somerset and Gwent on either side of the Severn Estuary have distinct differences. Much of the Somerset Levels remains under pasture, with some fields retaining grasslands of conservation value. By contrast, the Gwent Levels have experienced considerable agricultural improvement, with much of the land turned

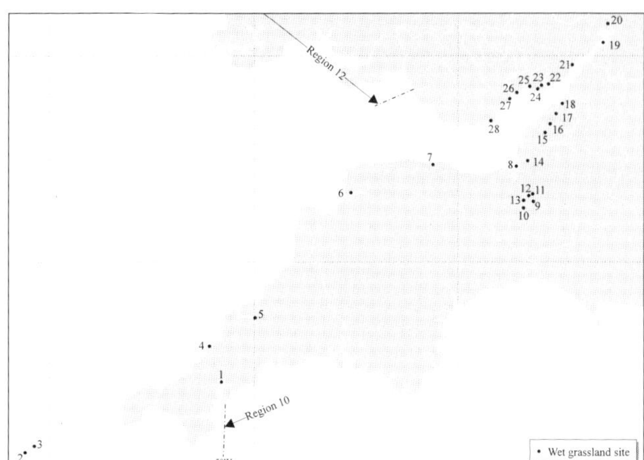

Map 3.5.1 Wet grassland sites (numbers refer to Table 3.5.1) in the region. Source: Dargie *et al.* (1994).

over to improved pasture or arable use. Patches of semi-improved grassland of higher conservation value do however, remain, often comprising areas of National Vegetation Classification (NVC - Rodwell (1995)) community MG5 crested dog's-tail *Cynosurus cristatus* - common knapweed *Centaurea nigra* grassland, which is typical of the habitat. These include grass communities containing the nationally scarce saltmarsh grass species bulbous foxtail *Alopecurus bulbosus*.

Some parts of the Somerset Levels, particularly those near the shoreline, such as Catsford Common, Wall Common, Pawlett Hams and the Huntspill Level, show a distinct maritime influence. Pawlett, Wickmore and Northmore all have brackish back ditches, and Wall Common experiences occasional inundation by the sea, which has led to the development of unusual plant communities in the soaks and gutters of the remnant tidal creek system. In the Somerset Moors and the Gordano Levels (Avon), further inland, the wet grassland overlies peat; most of the grassland here developed from freshwater marsh. The Gordano Levels also experience considerable calcareous influence, which gives rise to vegetation communities different from those found on the Somerset Moors. At Pennsylvania Fields, Gloucestershire, inundation on spring tides has led to the development of communities of a saltmarsh character containing saltmarsh rush *Juncus gerardi* and sea arrowgrass *Triglochin maritima* and brackish ditches supporting brackish water-crowfoot *Ranunculus baudotii*. The Gordano Levels have retained grasslands of significant conservation value, including areas of mesotrophic grassland and fen-mire communities.

The ditch communities of the region's wet grasslands are of considerable regional and national significance. Nationally rare species found on the Somerset Levels include brown beak-sedge *Rhynchospora fusca*, brown galingale *Cyperus fuscus*, short-leaved water-starwort *Callitriche truncata* and cut-grass *Leersia oryzoides*. The nationally notable fen pondweed *Potamogeton coloratus* and whorled water-milfoil *Myriophyllum verticillatum* are both present on the Gordano Levels. The Avon Levels between Weston-super-Mare and Clevedon are designated as SSSIs

Table 3.5.1 Wet grassland sites identified in Region 11

No. (see Map 3.5.1)	*Location*	*Grid ref.*	*Conservation status*	*Notes*
	Cornwall south coast			
1	Fal Estuary	SW835429	Adjacent to SSSI	Agriculturally improved pasture
	Isles of Scilly			
2	Big Pool	SV879087	SSSI	Pool and wet maritime grassland
3	Lower Moors	SV912106	SSSI	10 ha maritime wet meadows and fen
	Cornwall north coast			
4	Kelsey Head	SW775600	SSSI	Brackish marsh
5	Amble Marshes	SW994746	SSSI	57 ha grazing marsh
	Devon			
6	Braunton Marshes	SS475345	Undesignated; adjacent to two SSSIs	Grazing marsh
	Somerset			
7	Porlock Marsh	SS880479	SSSI	Swamp and brackish ditch habitats
8	Bridgwater Bay	ST290480	SSSI	Grazing marsh with brackish and freshwater ditches
9	Southlake Moor	ST370300	SSSI	196 ha grazing marsh (part of Somerset Levels and Moors)
10	Curry and Hay Moors	ST323273	SSSI	472 ha grazing marsh (part of Somerset Levels and Moors)
11	Langmead Level	ST365335	SSSI	≃ 84 ha grazing marsh (part of Somerset Levels and Moors)
12	Weston Level	ST353330	SSSI	≃ 84 ha grazing marsh (part of Somerset Levels and Moors)
13	North Moor	ST325305	SSSI	676 ha grazing marsh (part of Somerset Levels and Moors)
14	Berrow Marsh	ST293520	SSSI	
	Avon			
15	Puxton Moor	ST4263	SSSI	Part of Avon Levels. Drainage ditch interest.
16	Biddle Street Triangle	ST4265	SSSI	Part of Avon Levels. Drainage ditch interest.
17	Tickenham, Nailsea and Kenn Moors	ST4369	SSSI	Part of Avon Levels. Drainage ditch interest.
18	Gordano Levels	ST4573	NNR, SSSI	126 ha wet grassland
	Gloucestershire			
19	Upper Severn Estuary	SO720060	SSSI	Saltmarsh and pasture next to estuary
20	Walmore Common	SO740155	SSSI	57 ha grassland with ditches, flooded in winter
21	Pennsylvania Fields	ST565953	SSSI	Grazing marsh/saltmarsh transition
	Gwent			
22	Magor and Undy	ST440860	SSSI	586 ha wet pasture (part of Gwent Levels)
23	Redwick and Llandevenny	ST410855	SSSI	940 ha wet pasture (part of Gwent Levels)
24	Whitson	ST390840	SSSI	938 ha wet pasture (part of Gwent Levels)
25	Nash and Goldcliff	ST350850	SSSI	954 ha wet pasture (part of Gwent Levels)
26	St. Brides	ST290825	SSSI	1,322 ha wet pasture (part of Gwent Levels)
27	Rhymney and Peterstone	ST250800	SSSI	972 ha wet pasture (part of Gwent Levels)
	South Glamorgan			
28	Cog Moor	ST159694	Undesignated	Wet grassland

Source: Dargie *et al.* (1994). Key: SSSI = Site of Special Scientific Interest; NNR = National Nature Reserve. Note: areas have been rounded to the nearest whole hectare.

solely for the biological interest of the ditches. Designation only extends 6 m from the edge of the ditches and does not include the ploughed and reseeded fields. In Wales plant species such as narrow-leaved water-plantain *Alisma lanceolatum,* frogbit *Hydrocharis morsus-ranae,* flowering-rush *Butomus umbellatus* and whorl-grass *Catabrosa aquatica* are chiefly restricted to the Gwent Levels.

The importance of the region's wet grasslands for birds (see also sections 5.11 and 5.12) is indicated by the current designation of the Somerset Levels and Moors as an SPA/ Ramsar Site, which although not coastal by the definition used in Chapter 7 abuts areas of coastal wet grassland. The RSPB manage 526 ha of the Somerset Levels at Sedgemoor as a reserve, notable for breeding waders, including the nationally rare black-tailed godwit *Limosa limosa,* and also quail *Coturnix coturnix.* The reserve is also important for passage and wintering birds, including whimbrel *Numenius phaeopus* and Bewick's swan *Cygnus bewickii,* both of which are protected under Schedule 1 of the Wildlife & Countryside Act. Areas of wet grassland in the Wildfowl & Wetlands Trust's Slimbridge Reserve adjacent to the upper Severn Estuary regularly hold internationally important numbers of wintering Bewick's swan *Cygnus columbianus bewickii* and gadwall *Anas strepera,* as well as nationally important populations of other duck and wader species. Also adjacent to the Upper Severn is Walmore Common, which supports internationally important numbers of wintering Bewick's swan and nationally important numbers of several other wildfowl and wader species, notably wigeon *Anas penelope,* gadwall, shoveler *Anas clypeata* and pochard *Aythya ferina.*

The Somerset and Gwent Levels are of national

importance for the assemblage of invertebrate species they support, including many rare and notable beetle, bug and fly species (see also section 5.3). Drake *et al.* (1984) identified a total of eighteen nationally rare Red Data Book (RDB) and 124 nationally notable invertebrate species on the Somerset Levels, and Drake (1986) found 21 RDB species and 97 notable species on the Gwent Levels. Although the conservation status of some of these species has subsequently been downgraded, the wealth of the invertebrate fauna of both these areas is unquestionably of national importance. Important species found in both areas include the great silver water beetle *Hydrophilus piceus*, the diving beetle *Hydaticus tranversalis* and the soldier fly *Odontomyia ornata.*

3.5.3 Human activities

The Braunton Marshes former SSSI next to the Taw-Torridge Estuary was denotified in 1987 as a result of significant reduction of its conservation interest. Although this area is identified as having considerable potential, its conservation interest was thought to have been reduced by the change from hay meadow management to all-year round grazing, and possibly by pollution of the ditches. Braunton Marshes are currently considered as a high priority for water level management.

The Somerset Levels and the Gwent Levels have been subject to agriculture and management, including land claim, since the Roman occupation and have a rich archaeological heritage associated with man's use of the Severn Estuary and its marshes since prehistoric times (see also Chapter 6). Much of the low-lying land now occupied by wet grassland was claimed from the intertidal area or the fringing freshwater marshes of the estuary. The Levels have suffered severe damage due to intensification of farming and increased land drainage. This has led to the conversion of much floristically rich pasture to species-poor improved pasture and arable land, which are also of much less value for breeding wading birds. Similarly, improved drainage and the use of fertilisers have resulted in the ecological impoverishment of many of the ditch systems as a result of nutrient enrichment, reduced water flows and unsympathetic ditch management. An additional threat on the Somerset Moors is the habitat destruction caused by peat cutting. Peat shrinkage due to excessive drainage and consequent drying out and oxidation is a further source of concern as it leads to irreparable damage to the soils and thus changes in the habitats they support. There is also considerable concern about damage to archaeological remains as a result of excess drying of the peat moors. Mountford & Sheail (1984) concluded from the historical record that "it is clear that many species have experienced a decline rather than an increase", which they attributed largely to peat cutting and agricultural improvement. They also noted that the ditch communities of the Somerset Levels have remained much less altered than those of the Moors and pastures, a view supported by the results of the Somerset Wetlands Project, an extensive survey of the flora carried out by the Nature Conservancy Council in 1976-78.

Water level management schemes are being developed for wet grasslands throughout the region. In response to concern over the long-term future of the Somerset Levels, the Water Level Management Steering Committee (WLMSC) was set up in 1988, and the (then) National Rivers Authority (NRA - now the Environment Agency) have since developed a water level management and nature conservation strategy (NRA Wessex Region 1992). The WLMSC have set up trial areas for raising water levels, the ecological effects of which are being monitored by MAFF, English Nature and the Environment Agency. Further conservation management by SSSI landowners is encouraged on the Somerset Levels in order to maximise diversity. This may include provision of pools for foraging waders, manure fertilisation to increase invertebrate density, and predator control and bank reprofiling. The wet grassland of the Gordano Levels NNR is managed through controlled summer grazing, mostly by cattle.

The development pressures that have already resulted in the loss of much wet grassland to the west of the Gwent Levels and around Cardiff and Newport remain a threat. The landfall, toll plaza and approach roads for the Second Severn Crossing, commercial developments (including the Europark development at Llandevenny), and an extension to the landfill site at Lamby Way have all contributed to the loss of wet grassland in the region. There is also a proposal for an M4 relief road that would affect the Gwent Levels. Pressures from such developments are particularly strong in south Wales, where development of these areas to create employment is an economic priority.

3.5.4 Information sources used

The effects of changing agricultural practices on the terrestrial flora of the Somerset Moors and Levels is comparatively well documented (Mountford & Sheail 1984) and can be assessed here much more accurately than for many other regions of the UK. Mountford & Sheail (1984) also undertook extensive analysis of their survey results to identify the effect that different factors such as ditch depth, bank gradient, cattle trampling and shade had on the aquatic flora.

Both the Somerset Levels and Gwent Levels are well surveyed, compared with many other areas of wet grassland in Britain. Recently, surveys of the ditch flora have been carried out on the Gwent Levels by Glading (1984), Mountford & Sheail (1984) and Winder *et al.* (1991), and the Countryside Council for Wales (CCW) hold Phase II survey data for areas of the Gwent Levels and Cog Moor in South Glamorgan. Invertebrate fauna surveys were carried out by the Nature Conservancy Council on the Somerset Levels (Drake *et al.* 1984) and the Gwent Levels (McLean 1982; Drake 1986), and these provide many data on the conservation value of these habitats. CCW hold a body of information on the Gwent Levels as part of the Severn Estuary Coastal Cell database, and considerable ecological information has been collected to monitor the effects of the construction of the Severn Crossing on the Caldicot Level and the Avon Levels (Environmental Advisory Unit 1991; SGS Environment 1995). Surveys have also been carried out as part of the Environmental Assessment of other proposed schemes, including extension of the Lamby Way Landfill (Environmental Advisory Unit 1993).

Much of the work on water level management schemes in the region was pioneered by the RSPB and is discussed in Burgess & Hirons (1990) with reference to work carried out managing water levels on a number of sites, including West Sedgemoor.

3.5.5 Acknowledgements

Thanks are due to the staff of English Nature's Local Teams and the Countryside Council for Wales for providing information on wet grassland sites.

3.5.6 Further sources of information

A. *References cited*

Burgess, N.D., & Hirons, G.J.M. 1990. *Techniques of hydrological management at coastal lagoons and lowland wet grasslands on RSPB Reserves.* Sandy, Royal Society for the Protection of Birds.

Dargie, T.C. 1993. *The distribution of lowland wet grassland in England.* Peterborough, English Nature. (English Nature Research Reports, No. 49.)

Dargie, T., Dargie, M., & Tantram, D. 1994. *Lowland wet grassland in England - module 2. Resource distribution & biota reference inventory.* Peterborough, English Nature.

Drake, C.M. 1986. *A survey of the invertebrates of the Gwent Levels 1985.* Peterborough, Nature Conservancy Council.

Drake, C.M., Foster, A.P., & Palmer, M.A. 1984. *A survey of the invertebrates of the Somerset Levels and Moors.* Peterborough, Nature Conservancy Council.

Environmental Advisory Unit. 1991. *The ecology of the Gwent and Avon Levels. Study report 3: Severn Bridges Bill Environmental Statement, supporting documents.* Cardiff, Cardiff City Council.

Environmental Advisory Unit. 1993. *Lamby Way Landfill, eastern extension.* Cardiff, Cardiff City Council.

Glading, P.R. 1984. *A survey of the flora of the reens (drainage ditches) of the Gwent Levels, 1982-83.* Peterborough, Nature Conservancy Council.

McLean, I.F.G. 1982. *The Gwent Levels: a report on the terrestrial invertebrates recorded in July 1981.* Peterborough, Nature Conservancy Council.

Mountford, J.O., & Sheail, J. 1984. *Plant life and the watercourses of the Somerset Levels and Moors.* Peterborough, Nature Conservancy Council.

National Rivers Authority Wessex Region. 1992. *Somerset Levels water level management and nature conservation strategy.* Almondsbury, NRA.

Rodwell, J.S., *ed.* 1995. *British plant communities. Volume 4: aquatic communities, swamps & tall-herb fens.* Cambridge, Cambridge University Press.

SGS Environment. 1995. *Gwent Levels monitoring programme - annual report 1994.* Cardiff, SGS Environment (Report to Laing-GTM/Second Severn Crossing Group).

Winder, J., Spencer, J., & Wood, A. 1991. *A botanical survey of the reens on the Gwent Levels.* Bangor, Countryside Council for Wales.

B. *Further reading*

Bratton, J.H., *ed.* 1991. *British Red Data Books: 3. Invertebrates other than insects.* Peterborough, Joint Nature Conservation Committee.

Cooter, J., Cropper, R., Heckford, R., McLean, I.F.G., Palmer, M., & Stubbs, A. 1979. A survey of the invertebrates of the Somerset Levels. *Nature Conservancy Council, CSD Report,* No. 324.

Davidson, N.C. 1991. Breeding waders on British estuarine grasslands. *Wader Study Group Bulletin, 61, Supplement*: 36-41.

Davidson, N.C., Laffoley, D.d'A., Doody, J.P., Way, L.S., Gordon, J., Key, R., Drake, C.M., Pienkowski, M.W., Mitchell, R., & Duff, K.L. 1991. *Nature conservation and estuaries in Great Britain.* Peterborough, Nature Conservancy Council.

Gibbs, D.J. 1991. *A quantitative baseline survey of the invertebrates of the Gwent Levels, 1991.* Bangor, CCW.

Green, R.E. 1986. *The management of lowland wet grassland for breeding waders.* Sandy, RSPB. (Unpublished.)

National Rivers Authority Welsh Region. 1991. *NRA sea defences, Wentlooge and Caldicot Levels Environmental Statement.* Almondsbury, NRA.

Pye, K., & French, P.W. 1993. *Erosion and accretion processes on British saltmarshes.* London, Ministry of Agriculture, Fisheries and Food.

Raine, P. 1980. *The flora of drainage ditches, an ecological study of part of the Somerset Levels.* MSc Thesis, University College London.

Robins, M., Davies, S.G.F., & Buisson, R.S.K. 1991. *An internationally important wetland in crisis: The Somerset Levels and Moors: a case history of wetland destruction.* Sandy, RSPB.

Sheppard, D.A. 1985. *A survey of the aquatic invertebrates from selected ditches in the Somerset Levels.* Peterborough, Nature Conservancy Council.

C. *Contact names and addresses*

Type of information	*Contact address and telephone no.*
Wet grassland - Cornwall	*English Nature, Devon & Cornwall Local Team, Truro, tel: 01872 262550
Wet grassland- Devon	*English Nature, Devon & Cornwall Local Team, Okehampton, tel: 01837 55045
Braunton Burrows	English Nature Site Manager, Broadford Farm, Heddon Mill, Braunton, Devon EX33 2NQ, tel: 01271 812552
Wet grassland - Somerset & Avon	*English Nature Somerset & Avon Local Team, Taunton, tel: 01823 283211
Gordano Valley NNR	English Nature Site Manager, 1 Rangers Cottage, Valley Road, Leigh Woods, Bristol BS8 3PZ, tel: 0117 973 1645
Wet grassland - Gwent and Glamorgan	*CCW, Cardiff, tel: 01222 772400
Grassland ecology	*Grassland Ecologist, Lowlands Team, English Nature HQ, Peterborough, tel: 01733 340345

*Starred contact addresses are given in full in the Appendix.

3.6 Saltmarsh

Dr M.I. Hill

3.6.1 Introduction

There are 1,870 ha of saltmarsh in Region 11, representing approximately 8% of the resource on the West Coast and 4% of that in Britain (Table 3.6.1). Of this, more than 1,400 ha is found in the Severn Estuary and Bridgwater Bay. Elsewhere in the region, only the Fal complex and Taw-Torridge Estuary contain more than 50 ha of saltmarsh. Approximately 28% of the coastlines of Avon, Gloucestershire and Gwent support saltmarsh, compared to 12% in Somerset, 9% in South Glamorgan and 10% in the whole of Devon and Cornwall (the southern parts of the coastline of these two counties being in Region 10). In Mid Glamorgan only 6% of the coastline is fronted by saltmarsh.

Table 3.6.1 shows the areas of saltmarsh vegetation recorded in the national survey (Burd 1989 a-d). More than 40% of the saltmarsh area in the region was cord-grass *Spartina* spp. marsh, a much greater proportion than on the west coast or in Britain as a whole (15-16%). Whilst *Spartina* still forms an important pioneer saltmarsh community in the region, this figure for the proportion of *Spartina* marsh is now an over-estimate, as the species has certainly decreased in area since the date of the survey (see section 3.6.4).

3.6.2 Important locations and species

Saltmarsh sites surveyed during the national survey (Burd 1989a-d) are listed in Table 3.6.2 and shown on Map 3.6.1. This survey did not include the Isles of Scilly; however, there are no significant areas of saltmarsh vegetation on the islands (J.P. Doody pers. comm.). In Devon and Cornwall, the high energy coastline means that there are only small saltmarshes, restricted to sheltered sites. Most of the saltmarshes in the region are of the estuarine fringing type, but ria head (Fal and Helford River), open embayment (Bridgwater Bay) and back-barrier (Berrow/Bridgwater Bay and Taw-Torridge) types are also found (Pye & French 1993). At Porlock, there is saltmarsh behind the shingle beach, maintained by seawater percolation through the ridge. In the Severn Estuary, substantial areas of saltmarsh have been subject to land-claim since Roman times, leaving a narrow discontinuous saltmarsh fringe.

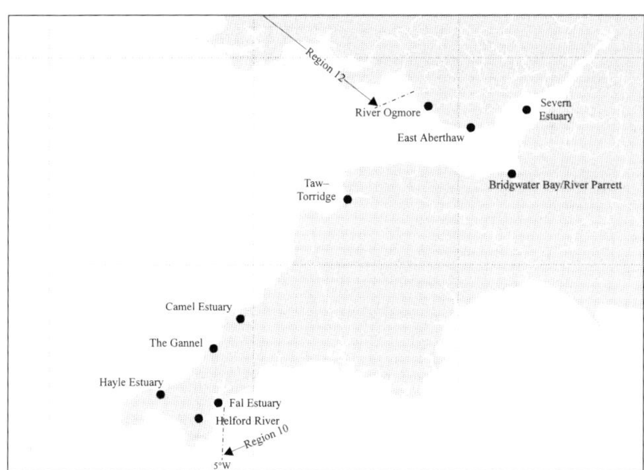

Map 3.6.1 Saltmarsh sites surveyed in National Saltmarsh Survey (see Table 3.6.2). Source: JNCC Coastal Database.

Sites of Special Scientific Interest (SSSIs) containing saltmarsh in the region are listed in Table 3.6.3 (see also Chapter 7).

There is no saltmarsh zonation that can be said to be characteristic of the region, as the marshes vary greatly in structure, age, sediment type and management. Common cord-grass *Spartina anglica* is the main pioneer species and the low-mid marsh is most usually of common saltmarsh-grass *Puccinellia maritima*. Mid to upper marsh vegetation is frequently dominated by common saltmarsh-grass, red fescue *Festuca rubra*, saltmarsh rush *Juncus gerardi* and creeping bent *Agrostis stolonifera*. Upper marsh swamps of sea club-rush *Scirpus maritimus* and common reed *Phragmites australis* are spreading at the landward edge of ungrazed or less heavily grazed marshes. At Bridgwater Bay, for example, a new saltmarsh was formed when *Spartina* became established in 1929, but since the 1950s the

Table 3.6.1 Areas (ha) of saltmarsh communities in context

	Spartina	*Pioneer*	*Low-mid*	*Mid-upper*	*Drift-line*	*Upper swamp*	*Transition*	*Wet depression*	*Total*	*% of total in region*
Cornwall (part)	14	28	38	70	2	19	15	0	187	10
Devon (part)	48	51	95	32	9	4	0	0	240	13
Somerset	340	6	8	123	6	16	0	0	499	27
Avon	159	0	32	108	14	0	0	0	314	17
Gloucestershire	28	1	20	196	12	1	0	0	258	14
Gwent	155	0	28	55	28	0	0	0	267	14
South Glamorgan	36	0	7	44	0	0	4	0	91	5
Mid Glamorgan	0	0	5	10	0	0	1	0	15	1
Region 11	***781***	***85***	***234***	***638***	***71***	***41***	***19***	***0***	***1,870***	***100***
England	5,166	2,641	10,299	9,948	1,493	686	833	0	31,533	-
Wales	1,681	468	1,555	2486	267	202	89	0	6,748	-
West Coast of GB	3,487	1,340	4,159	11,270	473	410	1,327	1	22,582	8
Great Britain	6,948	3,470	12,353	16,042	1,824	1,475	1,670	2	44,370	4

Source: National Saltmarsh Survey (Burd 1989a-d). Key: - = % not calculated. Note: areas have been rounded to the nearest whole hectare; percentages have been rounded up to whole numbers.

Table 3.6.2 Saltmarsh sites surveyed

Name	*Grid ref.*	*Area (ha)**
Cornwall		
Fal Estuary complex	SW850405	93
Helford River	SW720258	4
Hayle Estuary	SW555375	19
The Gannel	SW809607	20
Camel Estuary	SW945739	50
Devon		
Taw - Torridge	SS470310	240
Somerset		
Bridgwater Bay / River Parrett	ST281485 & ST294521	487
Avon & Gloucestershire		
Severn Estuary[a] (England)	ST400800	583
Gwent		
Severn Estuary[b] (Wales)	ST400800	349
South Glamorgan		
East Aberthaw	ST042660	8
Mid Glamorgan		
River Ogmore	SS870761	15

Source: National Saltmarsh Survey (Burd 1989a-d). Note: for large sites the grid reference given is a reasonably central point. Key: [a]20 separate sites; [b]9 separate sites; *areas have been rounded to the nearest whole hectare.

Table 3.6.3 SSSIs containing saltmarsh in Region 11

Site name	*Grid ref.*	*Other designations*
Fal / Ruan Estuary	SW850410	pSAC
Hayle Estuary and Carrack Gladden	SW550370	-
Taw-Torridge Estuary	SS470310	-
Porlock Marsh	SS880479	-
Bridgwater Bay	ST290480	NNR
Berrow Dunes	ST293520	LNR
Severn Estuary	ST480830	Ramsar, SPA, pSAC
Upper Severn Estuary	SO720060	Ramsar, SPA
Taff / Ely Estuary	ST185735	-
Cwm Cydfin, Leckwith	ST165739	-
East Aberthaw Coast	ST042658	-
Merthyr Mawr Warren	SS861768	-
Kenfig	SS790820	pSAC, NNR, LNR

Source: JNCC integrated coastal database. Key: pSAC = possible Special Area of Conservation; NNR = National Nature Reserve; LNR = Local Nature Reserve; Ramsar = Ramsar site (wetland of international importance); SPA = Special Protection Area for birds.

Spartina has gradually been replaced by sea club-rush, common reed and bulrush *Typha latifolia* (Ranwell 1964a, b). A similar pattern has been documented on the east side of Bridgwater Bay at Berrow (Willis 1990), although in this case a common saltmarsh-grass and glasswort *Salicornia* spp. marsh pre-dated the establishment of *Spartina*. The highest saltmarsh around the driftline is usually dominated by sea couch *Elymus pycnanthus*, with spear-leaved orache *Atriplex prostrata*. Saline pans on the upper marsh support a vegetation of reflexed saltmarsh-grass *Puccinellia distans* and lesser sea-spurrey *Spergularia marina*. Because of substantial land-claim of saltmarsh in the past, transitions to other habitats are not widespread. However, transitions to dune are present at Berrow and Merthyr Mawr, and to woodland in the Fal / Ruan Estuary.

Upper levels of grazed saltmarshes of the Severn Estuary support an unusual and distinctive plant community. This is a type of *Festuca* saltmarsh and contains the nationally scarce species bulbous foxtail *Alopecurus bulbosus*, slender hare's-ear *Bupleurum tenuissimum* and sea barley *Hordeum marinum*. Meadow barley *Hordeum secalinum* is present in this vegetation in the inner Severn (Rodwell in prep.). The full extent of this vegetation type is not known.

The three British species of eelgrasses *Zostera* spp., all nationally scarce, are present in intertidal and subtidal zones in the region. The Welsh shore of the inner Severn Estuary contains an unusual eelgrass bed that is reputed to contain all three *Zostera* species. Other nationally scarce plants found on saltmarshes in the region are: curved hard-grass *Parapholis incurva*, marsh-mallow *Althaea officinalis*, long-stalked orache *Atriplex longipes* and sea clover *Trifolium squamosum*. Such scarce species are mostly found at the upper levels of the saltmarshes and in transitions to other habitats. Sea heath *Frankenia laevis*, a species of sand or shingle margins of saltmarshes on the south and east coasts of England, has been recorded at Merthyr Mawr saltmarsh in the Ogmore Estuary. This is one of only two records for this species in Wales.

Saltmarshes in the region provide roosting sites for shorebirds and food for wildfowl. The redshank *Tringa totanus* breeding on saltmarshes on the north shore of the Severn Estuary form a significant proportion of the Welsh population. The Severn also supports a significant breeding population of shelduck *Tadorna tadorna*, which use the upper levels of saltmarshes as nesting sites (Fox & Salmon 1988) (see also section 5.11).

Saltmarshes in the Severn Estuary and Bridgwater Bay are subject to erosion of the marsh edge, but many continue to accrete vertically. Elsewhere, the erosion or accretion status of the marshes varies. Some sites, such as the Hayle, Camel, Taw-Torridge and Ogmore, have new saltmarsh development (both lateral and vertical accretion) and others such as the Fal and Gannel have erosion of the marsh edges (lateral erosion and vertical accretion) (Pye & French 1993). In many places the Severn saltmarshes are made up of a series of terraced surfaces, separated by erosion cliffs. These represent periods of new saltmarsh formation, followed by erosion. Lateral erosion of the marshes, due to sea level rise, has affected marshes of the outer and middle estuary since at least mediaeval times. More recently, since the 1970s, erosion appears to have accelerated. This is thought to have been caused by an increase in the frequency of storm events. Various methods have been used to try to slow the rate of erosion of the marshes in the Severn, including the construction of groynes and armouring of the seaward face.

3.6.3 Human activities

Enclosure and drainage of saltmarsh in the Severn Estuary since Roman times has created the extensive wet grasslands of the coastal levels (see also section 3.5). Pye & French (1993) estimate that 84,000 ha of saltmarsh has been enclosed in the Severn Estuary. Saltmarsh in the Taff / Ely Estuary will be lost during construction of the Cardiff Bay Barrage.

Grazing is probably the oldest form of saltmarsh management; in this region many of the saltmarshes are grazed, including most in Bridgwater Bay and the Severn Estuary. Figures for stocking densities range from one to six animals per hectare, with grazing usually taking place from May to September.

Spartina was planted in the Severn from 1913 onwards and spread rapidly, particularly in the 1950s and 1960s. However, since the 1970s the extent of *Spartina* marsh has declined, owing to both erosion of the low marsh and replacement by other species (Dent 1987; Ranwell 1961, 1964a, b; Willis 1990). The spread of *Spartina*, therefore, caused only a temporary aberration in the long-term trend of saltmarsh loss in the Severn.

3.6.4 Information sources used

Saltmarshes in Devon, Cornwall and River Ogmore were surveyed in 1982 as part of the NCC's national saltmarsh survey; detailed reports are available and the results are summarised in Burd (1989a-d). Data presented here are derived from that database. The national saltmarsh survey provided an intermediate level of detail between Phase 1 habitat survey and the National Vegetation Classification (NVC: Rodwell in prep.). It did not include all areas of transition to other habitats such as sand dune, shingle and freshwater marsh. Saltmarsh vegetation in non-tidal marshes or behind permeable barriers, as at Porlock Marsh, and areas of eelgrass were not recorded. Some small sites, such as the River Kenfig and the Isles of Scilly, were not covered by the national survey.

For the Severn (including Bridgwater Bay and East Aberthaw), the national survey used the results of earlier work by Smith (1979). As the Severn data are now quite old and there were some difficulties in fitting them into the categories used by the national survey, they must be treated with more caution than data for other parts of the coastline.

The history and development of the Severn saltmarshes have been studied in detail by Allen (summarised in Allen (1992)). Several vegetation surveys of saltmarshes in the Severn Estuary were carried out as part of feasibility studies for barrages. The study by Dent (1987) provides vegetation descriptions and maps for the saltmarshes between Cardiff and Newport and includes a comparison of recent and historic maps and aerial photographs. Teverson (1981) gives an account of the Severn saltmarshes as a whole, plus detailed descriptions, histories and marsh profiles for four case study sites. Gray *et al.* (1989) used levelled line transects (including several sites in the Severn) to draw conclusions about the niche of *Spartina*.

Saltmarsh surveys have also been carried out for other development proposals and are reported in the Environmental Statements, as for example, for the Severn at Caldicot (Environmental Advisory Unit 1991) and at Rhymney (SGS Environment 1995). The extent and vigour of the *Zostera* bed in the Severn Estuary are being monitored in connection with the construction of the second Severn crossing.

Studies of saltmarsh succession in Bridgwater Bay are reported by Ranwell (1961, 1964a, b) and Willis (1990). The history and extent of *Spartina anglica* in the Severn is summarised by Martin (1990) and the distribution of *Spartina* species, including the infertile hybrid *Spartina townsendii*, by Holland (1981). An account of the invertebrate fauna of a saltmarsh in the Severn is provided by Little (1990).

3.6.5 Acknowledgements

Staff of English Nature and the Countryside Council for Wales kindly provided information and reference material.

3.6.6 Further sources of information

A. References cited

Allen, J.R.L. 1992. Tidally influenced marshes in the Severn Estuary, southwest Britain. *In: Saltmarshes: morphodynamics, conservation and engineering significance*, ed. by J.R.L. Allen & K. Pye, 123-147. Cambridge, Cambridge University Press.

Burd, F. 1989a. *The saltmarsh survey of Great Britain.* Peterborough, Nature Conservancy Council. (Research & survey in nature conservation, No. 17.)

Burd, F. 1989b. *Saltmarsh survey of Great Britain. Regional Supplement No. 2. West Midlands.* Peterborough, Nature Conservancy Council.

Burd, F. 1989c. *Saltmarsh survey of Great Britain. Regional Supplement No. 3. South West England.* Peterborough, Nature Conservancy Council.

Burd, F. 1989d. *Saltmarsh survey of Great Britain. Regional Supplement No. 11. South Wales.* Peterborough, Nature Conservancy Council.

Dent, S. 1987. *The current status and recent history of* Spartina anglica *in the Severn Estuary between Newport and Cardiff.* Peterborough, Nature Conservancy Council.

Environmental Advisory Unit. 1991. *The Second Severn Crossing - effects on estuary ecology and fisheries.* London, Severn Bridges Bill Parliamentary Session 1990/91. Study report SR4.

Fox, A.D., & Salmon, D.G. 1988. *Shelducks on the Severn Estuary.* Report to the Department of Energy. (Severn Tidal Power Report No. SBP 40.)

Gray, A.J., Clarke, R.T., Warman, E.A., & Johnson, P.J. 1989. Spartina *niche model. Prediction of marginal vegetation in a post-barrage environment.* Harwell, ETSU. (Energy Technology Research Unit Report ETSU-TID-4070.)

Holland, S.C. 1981. *Spartina* of the Severn Estuary. *Gloucestershire Naturalists' Society Journal, 32(3) Supplement*: 1-8.

Little, C.M. 1990. Animals of the Severn Estuary saltmarshes. *Proceedings of the Bristol Naturalists' Society, 50*: 83-94.

Martin, M.H. 1990. A history of *Spartina* on the Avon coast. *Proceedings of the Bristol Naturalists' Society, 50*: 47-56.

Pye, K., & French, P.W. 1993. *Erosion and accretion processes on British saltmarshes.* London, Ministry of Agriculture, Fisheries and Food.

Ranwell, D.S. 1961. *Spartina* marshes in southern England. I. The effects of sheep grazing at the upper limits of *Spartina* marsh in Bridgwater Bay. *Journal of Ecology, 49*: 325-340.

Ranwell, D.S. 1964a. *Spartina* marshes in southern England. II. Rate and seasonal pattern of sediment accretion. *Journal of Ecology, 52*: 79-95.

Ranwell, D.S. 1964b. *Spartina* marshes in southern England. III. Rates of establishment, succession and nutrient supply at Bridgwater Bay, Somerset. *Journal of Ecology, 52*: 95-105.

Rodwell, J.S., *ed.* In prep. *British plant communities. Volume 5: Maritime and weed communities.* Cambridge, Cambridge University Press.

SGS Environment. 1995. *Lamby Way proposed landfill development. Environmental statement.* Cardiff, City of Cardiff.

Smith, L.P. 1979. A survey of salt marshes in the Severn Estuary. Volumes 1 and 2. *Nature Conservancy Council, CSD Report,* No. 265.

Teverson, R. 1981. *Saltmarsh ecology in the Severn Estuary.* Report to the Department of Energy. (Severn Tidal Power Report No. STP51.)

Willis, A.J. 1990. The development and vegetational history of Berrow saltmarsh. *Proceedings of the Bristol Naturalists' Society, 50*: 57-73.

B. Further reading

Further details of coastal habitat sites, including saltmarshes, are available on the *Coastal & marine UKDMAP datasets* module disseminated by JNCC Coastal Conservation Branch, Peterborough.

Adam, P. 1978. Geographical variation in British saltmarsh vegetation. *Journal of Ecology, 66*: 339-366.

Barne, J., Davidson, N.C., Hill, T.O., & Jones, M. 1994. *Coastal and marine UKDMAP datasets: a user manual.* Peterborough, Joint Nature Conservation Committee.

British Oceanographic Data Centre. 1992. *United Kingdom digital marine atlas. User guide. Version 2.0.* Birkenhead, Natural Environment Research Council, British Oceanographic Data Centre.

Halcrow & Partners. 1994. *A guide to the understanding and management of saltmarshes.* Bristol, National Rivers Authority. (R & D Note No. 324.)

C. Contact names and addresses

Type of information	*Contact address and telephone no.*
Data from National Saltmarsh Survey	*Coastal Conservation Branch, JNCC, Peterborough, tel: 01733 62626
Saltmarsh sites in England	*Coastal Ecologist, English Nature HQ, Peterborough, tel: 01733 340345
Saltmarsh sites in Cornwall	*English Nature Devon & Cornwall Local Team, Truro, tel: 01872 262550
Saltmarsh sites in Devon	*English Nature Devon & Cornwall Local Team, Okehampton, tel: 01837 55045
Saltmarsh sites in Somerset and Avon	*English Nature Somerset & Avon Local Team, Taunton, tel: 01823 283211
Saltmarsh sites in Gloucestershire	*English Nature Three Counties Team, Malvern Wells, tel: 01684 560616
Saltmarsh sites in Gwent and Glamorgan	*Coastal Ecologist, CCW, Cardiff, tel: 01222 772400
Wildlife Trust sites in Cornwall	*Cornwall Wildlife Trust, Truro, tel: 01872 273939
Wildlife Trust sites in Devon	*Devon Wildlife Trust, Exeter, tel: 01392 79244
Wildlife Trust sites in Somerset	*Somerset Wildlife Trust, tel: 01823 451587
Wildlife Trust sites in Avon	*The Wildlife Trust for Bristol, Bath & Avon, Bristol, tel: 0117 926 8018
Wildlife Trust sites in Gloucestershire	*Gloucestershire Wildlife Trust, Gloucester, tel: 01452 383333
Wildlife Trust sites in Gwent	*Gwent Wildlife Trust, Monmouth, tel: 01600 715501
Wildlife Trust sites in Glamorgan	*Glamorgan Wildlife Trust, Bridgend, tel: 01656 724100

*Starred contact addresses are given in full in the Appendix.

Some of the country's richest areas of marine life are concentrated within the region. The rocky coast from Ilfracombe to Combe Martin supports a number of rare or little-known marine species, including corals and sponges. The huge range of species reflects the warmth of the waters, the wide variety of substrates and the different degrees of exposure to currents and wave action. This stretch of coast has been identified by English Nature as a Sensitive Marine Area and is safeguarded as a Voluntary Marine Wildlife Reserve. Photo: Peter Wakley, English Nature.

Chapter 4 Marine and estuarine environments

4.1 Estuaries

Dr N.C. Davidson

4.1.1 Introduction

Estuaries are "partially enclosed tidal areas at least partly composed of soft tidal shores, open to saline water from the sea, and receiving fresh water from rivers, land run-off or seepage" (Davidson *et al.* 1991). They comprise both aquatic (marine and freshwater) and terrestrial habitats including adjacent sand dunes, coastal grasslands and maritime heaths. All the estuaries discussed here are covered by the NCC's Estuaries Review (Davidson *et al.* 1991), with a minimum size for selection being 2 km of tidal channel or 2 km of shoreline over 0.5 km wide at low tide, either now or historically. This section gives an overview of the main features of the estuarine resource in Region 11; for further details of habitats, species and human uses refer to relevant sections in Chapters 3, 5 and 9 respectively.

The contribution of Region 11 estuaries to the wider resource is summarised in Table 4.1.1. The region makes a substantial contribution to the UK's estuarine resource and has a varied and important suite of estuaries. There are almost 70,000 ha of estuarine habitat in Region 11, which represents nearly 4% of the estuarine habitat of north-west Europe. Overall, the eleven estuaries in the region (Map 4.1.1) form 12% by area of the total UK estuarine resource and over 21% of the west coast resource. The estuarine resource of the region is dominated by the large coastal-plain type Severn Estuary, alone comprising 80% of the total regional estuarine area and almost 90% taken together with contiguous Bridgwater Bay to the south. At over 55,000 ha the Severn Estuary is the second largest estuary in the UK. Elsewhere in the region only Bridgwater Bay exceeds 5,000 ha and seven of the region's eleven estuaries are each under 1,000 ha in total area. Five of the region's estuaries are on the Cornish coast, and at least part of an estuary lies in each of the other counties in the region, with the Severn Estuary spanning five counties. Several of the estuaries have considerable geomorphological, wildlife and nature conservation importance, reflected in many national and international designations. These estuaries have important sea-bed communities, and rare plant and animal species, including internationally important bird populations.

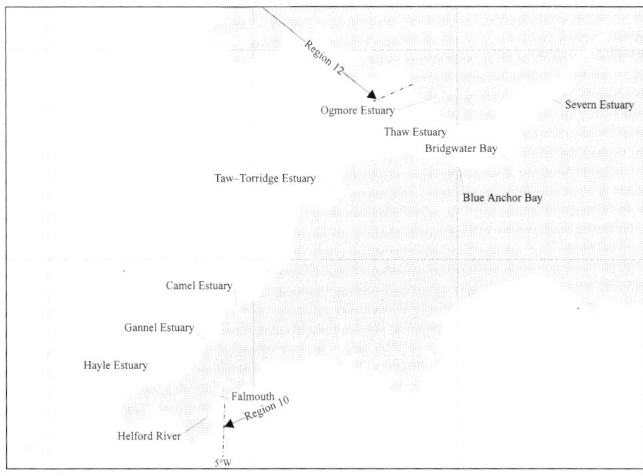

Map 4.1.1 Estuaries. Source: JNCC Coastal Database.

Large tidal ranges, especially from north Devon eastwards around the Severn Estuary, mean that much of the intertidal sediment is mobile sandflats, with mudflats and saltmarshes restricted to the more sheltered side-arms, bays and upper reaches. Many of the estuaries are predominantly sediment-filled, with large proportions of only the Fal, Helford River and Severn Estuary remaining water-filled at low water. There are extensive areas of saltmarshes in the Taw-Torridge Estuary, Bridgwater Bay and the Severn Estuary, with saltmarsh in the region overall forming 9% of the West Coast resource (see also section 3.6). Additional interest comes from the natural shoreline transitions from saltmarsh, tidal flats and rocky shores to fringing woodland in some of the rias, especially the Helford River, and the substantial areas of wet grasslands

Table 4.1.1 Contribution of the region's estuaries to the national resource

Resource	*Regional total (ha/km)*	*West Coast total (ha/km)*	*% West Coast*	*GB total (ha/km)*	*% GB*	*UK total (ha/km)*	*% UK*
Intertidal area	26,690	195,770	13.6	321,050	8.3	332,350	8.0
Saltmarsh area	1,870	20,710	9.0	48,380	4.5	*	*
Total estuarine area	69,740	323,180	21.6	525,650	13.1	581,290	12.0
Shoreline length	815	14,546	5.6	9,054	4.2	9,727	4.0
Longest channel lengths	229	1,335	17.1	2,461	8.7	2,640	8.1

Sources: Buck (1993; in prep.); Davidson & Buck (in prep). Key: *areas of saltmarsh were not available for Northern Ireland and so estuarine saltmarsh area comparisons are not made for the UK. Note: areas rounded to the nearest 10 ha; lengths rounded to the nearest 1 km.

around the coastal plain estuaries, notably the Somerset Levels, which stretch inland from Bridgwater Bay, and the Gwent Levels along the northern shore of the Severn Estuary.

4.1.2 Important locations and species

Map 4.1.1 shows the estuaries in the region and Table 4.1.2 summarises their main physical characteristics. Estuaries in the west of the region are mostly rias - non-glaciated river valleys submerged by rising sea-levels; in the lower-lying landscape further east are embayments and coastal plain estuaries. All the region's estuaries are macrotidal (i.e. have a spring tidal range >4 m). Tidal range increases from west to east in the region, in Cornwall being between 4.7 m (Helford River) and 6.4 m (Gannel Estuary). The Severn Estuary, with a spring tidal range of over 12 m, has the second largest tidal range in the world.

On the south coast of Cornwall, on the rocky shores around their mouths and in the sheltered soft sediments further upstream, the rias of Falmouth and the Helford River support important and diverse sea-bed communities, including maerl and *Zostera* spp. (eelgrass) beds. These narrow, sinuous estuaries are predominantly subtidal, with narrow strips of fringing tidal flats and saltmarshes, especially in their upper reaches; much of the Helford River is fringed by ancient woodlands. On the north Cornwall coast the small Hayle Estuary has formed behind sand spits and has been much modified by human uses; further east, the rias of the Gannel and Camel Estuaries have formed in an otherwise cliffed and rocky coast. Both Gannel and Camel are shallow and predominantly sandy, but with rocky areas near their mouths. In north Devon the confluent Taw-Torridge Estuary has formed behind the two sand spits of Northam and Braunton Burrows, the latter in particular being of major nature conservation importance as one of the largest dune systems in Britain, with an extensive matrix of grasslands and dune slacks.

On the Somerset coast Blue Anchor Bay is a broad area of intertidal flats and shingle forming part of a series of broad shore platforms, unusual in a macrotidal environment. Further east, the River Parrett discharges across the broad tidal flats of Bridgwater Bay, a system developed partly in the shelter of Brean Down and which includes vegetated shingle banks and sand dunes with a particularly rich flora. The upper tidal reaches of the River Parrett stretch into part of the extensive meadows and marshes of the Somerset Levels; both the Levels and Bridgwater Bay are internationally important for their wintering waterfowl populations, and the Levels are important also for breeding waterfowl.

North from Bridgwater Bay the vast coastal plain estuary of the River Severn is of great importance for a wide variety of features. With its very large tidal range the Severn Estuary provides an extreme example of a highly turbid system. Much of the outer part is subtidal, and in the main estuary the intertidal flats are mostly highly mobile sand; only in the shelter of side bays and estuaries such as the Avon, Wye, Usk and Taff/Ely are there more stable muds. The estuary supports very diverse sea-bed communities, especially on soft substrates but also on intertidal rock platforms. Large areas of mostly grazed saltmarsh fringe the estuary and there are important wet grassland areas around Slimbridge (Gloucestershire) and on the Gwent Levels, the latter supporting a range of rare aquatic invertebrates. The Severn supports more species of migratory fish (seven), including the allis and twaite shad *Alosa alosa* and *A. fallax*, than any other UK estuary. There are large wintering waterfowl populations on the estuary, including five species each occurring in internationally important numbers.

Table 4.1.2 Physical characteristics of Region 11 estuaries

Estuary	*Centre grid ref.*	*Geomorph-ological type*	*Total area (ha[a])*	*Inter-tidal (ha[a])*	*Salt-marsh (ha[a])*	*Shoreline length (km[a])*	*Main channel (km[a])*	*Spring tidal range (m)*	*Sub-tidal %*
Cornwall									
154. Falmouth	SW8334	Ria	2,482	746	93	127	18	5.3	69.9
155. Helford River	SW7626	Ria	568	186	5	44	9	4.7	67.3
1. Hayle Estuary	SW5538	Bar-built	358	321	19	20	2	5.0	10.3
2. Gannel Estuary	SW8061	Ria	122	85	20	9	4	6.4	30.3
3. Camel Estuary	SW9375	Ria	839	610	50	43	15	5.9	27.3
Devon									
4. Taw-Torridge Estuary	SS4631	Bar-built	2,463	2,018	240	88	21	7.3	18.1
Somerset									
5. Blue Anchor Bay	ST0244	Embayment	350	350	0	9	0	9.7	0.0
6. Bridgwater Bay	ST2947	Embayment	6,529	5,147	487	109	46	11.1	21.2
Somerset, Avon, Glos., Gwent, S. Glamorgan									
7. Severn Estuary	ST4080	Coastal plain	55,684	16,890	933	353	111	12.3	69.7
S. Glamorgan									
8. Thaw Estuary	ST0366	Coastal plain	160	160	8	5	0	10.5	0.0
Mid Glamorgan									
9. Ogmore Estuary	SS8776	Coastal plain	187	173	15	8	2	8.9	7.5

Sources: Buck (1993; in prep.); JNCC Integrated Coastal Database. Key: [a]areas/lengths rounded to the nearest whole hectare/kilometre. Notes: estuary numbers are those used in Davidson *et al.* (1991). 'Geomorphological type' relates to nine estuary categories, described further in Chapter 5.7 of Davidson *et al.* (1991) and Chapter 4.5 of Davidson & Buck (in prep). 'Spring tidal ranges' are for the monitoring station closest to the mouth of the estuary.

West along the northern Bristol Channel shore the inner shores of the small Thaw Estuary were almost entirely converted from intertidal to dry land in the 1960s, but on the outer, coastal, shores there remain small but diverse patches of coastal habitats including vegetated shingle, saltmarsh, sand dune and rocky shores. The narrow Ogmore Estuary borders Merthyr Mawr, an accreting sand dune system, one of the last remaining major areas of sand dune on this coastline.

Many of the region's estuaries have one or more nationally rare plants associated with them (see section 5.2), and there are nationally rare terrestrial or marine invertebrates associated with the Fal, Helford, Hayle, Taw-Torridge, Bridgwater Bay, Severn, Thaw and Ogmore Estuaries (see also section 5.3). The Fal, Helford, Camel and Taw-Torridge are sea bass nursery areas (see also section 5.7).

4.1.3 Human activities

Throughout the region estuaries are predominantly rural, although most have towns associated with them. In the south-west of the region towns and villages are predominantly either holiday resorts and/or harbours for fishing and leisure craft. There are major urban and industrial developments, including docks at the mouth of the Fal. The Hayle has a long history of industrialisation and most of the inner estuary shore is urban or industrial. There are several harbours and boat-building yards in the Taw-Torridge. The Severn Estuary is the most extensively developed and industrialised estuary in the region: over one million people live in the towns and major cities on its shores, notably Bristol, Cardiff, Gloucester and Newport (see also section 8.3). There are major port and industrial complexes at Avonmouth and around Newport and Cardiff, and it is from these areas that most waste, including heavy metals, is discharged into the estuary (see also section 9.6). The former inner estuary of the Thaw is now mostly occupied by a power station.

Estuarine water quality is generally good in the region, but in parts of the Fal Estuary, Bridgwater Bay and Severn Estuary it is classified as poor (Table 4.1.3) (Buck in prep.).

Land claim has affected several of the region's estuaries, chiefly those in the lower-lying and more populous east of the region. Some of the historic land claim was for ports, harbours and associated developments, such as in the Hayle, Taw-Torridge and in Cardiff Bay (Severn Estuary). Other areas of former tidal marshes of the Taw-Torridge, Bridgwater Bay and the Severn Estuary are now lowland wet grasslands behind sea walls. In several places in the Fal Estuary there are pools created from tidal arms of the estuary, one of which is the only surviving tidal mill pond in Cornwall, and on the Severn Estuary the forthcoming amenity barrage will remove Cardiff Bay from the tidal estuary. A proposal for a similar barrage at Newport was rejected.

There is extensive general recreational use of the region's estuaries, with sailing and water sports widespread, especially in the sheltered inlets of the Fal, Helford River, Camel and Taw-Torridge, and general use of beaches in the outer parts of many estuaries, especially in Devon, Cornwall and Somerset. Natural resource exploitation, chiefly shellfisheries, fisheries and bait-collecting, is widespread, being an important use of all but the smaller estuaries, and wildfowling occurs on parts of the larger estuaries, especially in many places around the Severn Estuary (see also section 9.7).

4.1.4 Information sources used

This section is summarised chiefly from JNCC's *An inventory of UK estuaries,* being published in six regional volumes along with an introductory and methods volume. Most estuaries in Region 11 are included in *Volume 2. South-west Britain* (Buck 1993), with Falmouth and Helford River in

Table 4.1.3 Human uses and water quality on Region 11 estuaries

Estuary	*Centre grid ref.*	*Human use type* urban	industrial	rural*	recreational	*Water quality*
Cornwall						
154. Falmouth	SW8334	○	○	●	●	A, (B)
155. Helford River	SW7626			●	●	A
1. Hayle Estuary	SW5538	●	●	○	●	A
2. Gannel Estuary	SW8061	●	○	●	●	A
3. Camel Estuary	SW9375	○	○	●	●	A
Devon						
4. Taw-Torridge Estuary	SS4631	●	○	●	●	A
Somerset						
5. Blue Anchor Bay	ST0244			●	●	n/a
6. Bridgwater Bay	ST2947	○	○	●	●	A, B
Somerset, Avon, Glos., Gwent, S. Glamorgan						
7. Severn Estuary	ST4080	●	●	●	●	B, A
S. Glamorgan						
8. Thaw Estuary	ST0366		●		○	A
Mid Glamorgan						
9. Ogmore Estuary	SS8776			●	○	A

Sources: Davidson & Buck (in prep.), National Rivers Authority (1991). Key: *includes natural resource exploitation. ● = major human use; ○ = minor human use; n/a = water quality assessment not available. Notes: multiple water quality codes are in downstream sequence; brackets indicate a water quality found in only a small part of the estuary.

Volume 6. Southern England (Buck in prep.). Data presented in the inventory are drawn largely from material collected during 1989-1990 (updated to 1994 where appropriate) for the Nature Conservancy Council's Estuaries Review (Davidson *et al.* 1991). Saltmarsh data come originally from Burd (1989a, b, c), whose surveys covered mostly saltmarshes of >0.5 ha.

Hydrological data, e.g. catchment areas and river flows, are available for some but not all estuaries as defined here from sources including National Rivers Authority (now the Environment Agency) Catchment Management Plans (now known as Local Environment Action Plans (LEAPs) - see section 10.2.8). Chapter 10 gives further information on Estuary Management Plans (section 10.2.4). Catchment areas and river flows are summarised in a five-year catalogue of river flow gauging stations (Marsh & Lees 1993), but note that for whole estuary data further interpretation is usually necessary.

4.1.5 Acknowledgements

Thanks are due to Dr Pat Doody and John Barne (JNCC) for helpful comments on draft texts.

4.1.6 Further sources of information

A. References cited

Buck, A.L. 1993. *An inventory of UK estuaries. 2. South-west Britain.* Peterborough, Joint Nature Conservation Committee.

Buck, A.L. In prep. *An inventory of UK estuaries. 6. Southern England.* Peterborough, Joint Nature Conservation Committee.

Burd, F. 1989a. *The saltmarsh survey of Great Britain.* Peterborough, Nature Conservancy Council. (Research & survey in nature conservation, No. 17.)

Burd, F. 1989b. *Saltmarsh survey of Great Britain. Regional supplement No. 3. South-west England.* Peterborough, Nature Conservancy Council.

Burd, F. 1989c. *Saltmarsh survey of Great Britain. Regional supplement No. 11. South Wales.* Peterborough, Nature Conservancy Council.

Davidson, N.C., & Buck, A.L. In prep. *An inventory of UK estuaries. 1. Introduction and methods.* Peterborough, Joint Nature Conservation Committee.

Davidson, N.C., Laffoley, D.d'A., Doody, J.P., Way, L.S., Gordon, J., Key, R., Drake, C.M., Pienkowski, M.W., Mitchell, R.M., & Duff, K.L. 1991. *Nature conservation and estuaries in Great Britain.* Peterborough, Nature Conservancy Council.

Marsh, T.J., & Lees, M.L., *eds.* 1993. *Hydrometric register and statistics 1986-90.* Wallingford, Institute of Hydrology.

National Rivers Authority. 1991. *The quality of rivers, canals and estuaries in England and Wales.* Bristol, National Rivers Authority. (Water Quality Series, No. 4.)

B. Further reading

Further details of estuaries are in the *Coastal & marine UKDMAP datasets* module (Barne *et al.* 1994), available from JNCC Coastal Conservation Branch, Peterborough. A list of selected further reading for each estuary discussed in section 4.1 is given in Buck (1993; in prep.) (section 4.1.6 A above).

Barne, J., Davidson, N.C., Hill, T.O., & Jones, M. 1994. *Coastal & marine UKDMAP datasets: a user manual.* Peterborough, Joint Nature Conservation Committee.

British Oceanographic Data Centre. 1992. *United Kingdom digital marine atlas. User guide. Version 2.0.* Birkenhead, Natural Environment Research Council, British Oceanographic Data Centre.

Crothers, J.H., Little, C., & Mettam, C., *eds.* 1994. Evolution and change in the Bristol Channel and Severn Estuary. *Biological Journal of the Linnean Society, 51*(1 & 2).

Davidson, N.C. 1991. *Estuaries, wildlife and man.* Peterborough, Nature Conservancy Council.

Noble, L., *ed.* 1995. *Estuaries and coastal waters of the British Isles. An annual bibliography of recent scientific papers. Number 19.* Plymouth, Plymouth Marine Laboratory and Marine Biological Association.

Peck, K. 1993. Estuaries inventory - research towards a better understanding of the interactions between birds and human activities on UK estuaries. *RSPB Conservation Review, 7:* 42-46.

Smith, J., & Moore, J. In prep. Marine nature conservation review. The marine biology of marine inlets in south-west Britain: area summaries (MNCR Sectors 8-9). *JNCC Report.*

C. Contact names and addresses

Type of information	Contact address and telephone no.
Integrated Coastal Database: national database of estuaries; coastal habitats; statutory & non-statutory protected sites. Summary data available also in Coastal Directories UKDMAP display version.	*Coastal Conservation Branch, JNCC, Peterborough, tel: 01733 62626
Statutory protected sites; detailed wildlife site information; coastal geomorphology for England. Estuaries Initiative & estuary management plans. Numerical and some digitised data.	*Estuarine Ecologist / Estuaries Initiative Officer / Marine Ecologist, English Nature HQ, Peterborough, tel: 01733 340345
Statutory protected sites; detailed wildlife site information; coastal geomorphology for Wales	*Coastal Ecologist, CCW HQ, Bangor, tel: 01248 370444
RSPB Estuaries Inventory: mapped and numerical information on land use and selected human activities for 57 major UK estuaries. In Region 11 the inventory covers the following estuaries: Fal, Camel, Taw-Torridge, and Severn.	*Estuaries Inventory Project Officer, RSPB, Sandy, tel: 01767 680551
National River Flow Archive: catchments and river flows from upstream gauging stations; interpreted analyses for whole estuaries	National Water Archive Manager, Institute of Hydrology, Maclean Building, Crowmarsh Gifford, Wallingford, Oxfordshire OX10 8BB, tel: 01491 838800
Water quality information: south-west England	*Environment Agency (EA) South-Western Region, Exeter, tel: 01392 444000
Water quality information: Gloucestershire	*EA Midlands Region, Solihull, tel: 0121 711 2324
Water quality information: Wales	*EA Welsh Region, Cardiff, tel: 01222 770088

*Starred contact addresses are given in full in the Appendix.

4.2 The sea bed

R.A. Irving

4.2.1 Introduction

This section covers the occurrence and distribution of sea-bed habitats and of groups of species that live on the sea bed (benthic communities, collectively called the benthos), both in the intertidal zone and subtidally; the distribution and occurrence of individually rare and scarce species is covered in section 5.4.

There are a great variety of marine habitats and communities present along the coastline of this region. At the western tip of Cornwall are very exposed rocky shores, high cliffs and exposed sandy beaches; in the upper Bristol Channel there are extensive sandflats and mudflats subject to variable salinity and a huge tidal range (12.3 m during spring tides at Avonmouth - the second largest range in the world). In the sublittoral there is a wide range of habitats, and communities associated with these are often particularly rich in species. The influence of the relatively warm waters of the Gulf Stream, which bathe the South-West Peninsula, and to a lesser extent of a Lusitanian current from the south give a distinctive character to many communities. Many of the Mediterranean-Atlantic species that occur, such as sea fans, cup corals and soft corals, are of high nature conservation importance largely as a result of their rarity in the UK, confined as they are to the south-west. In addition, they are often very colourful, thereby adding to the aesthetic appeal of many sites.

Some of the country's richest areas of marine life are concentrated within the region. Many of these are now recognised by various designations (see also Chapter 7). England's first (and at present only) statutory Marine Nature Reserve exists around the island of Lundy in the Bristol Channel. There are also five Voluntary Marine Nature Reserves in the region: at Roseland, on the Fal River (established 1982, although currently inactive), the Helford River Voluntary Marine Conservation Area (1987); around the Isles of Scilly (1989); Polzeath Voluntary Marine Wildlife Area (Cornwall) (1995) and the north Devon coast from Morte Point to Combe Martin (1994). English Nature has identified seven Sensitive Marine Areas (SMAs) within this region (English Nature 1994a) (see Map 7.4.1). SMA is a non-statutory designation that highlights areas of particular conservation interest. In addition there are four possible Special Areas of Conservation (SACs) qualifying for their marine interest. These are the Fal and Helford, the Isles of Scilly, Lundy Island and the Severn Estuary.

A number of wrecks (ships, aircraft and other solid material) occur off the coast of this region, as elsewhere (see also section 6.4). These objects offer hard substrate in areas that may be largely sedimentary, thus providing discrete new habitats for opportunistic colonising species that otherwise would not be present.

4.2.2 Important locations and species

Table 4.2.1 lists locations of marine biological importance mentioned in the text (Map 4.2.1). There are likely to be other areas of importance for which there is currently insufficient information on which to base an assessment.

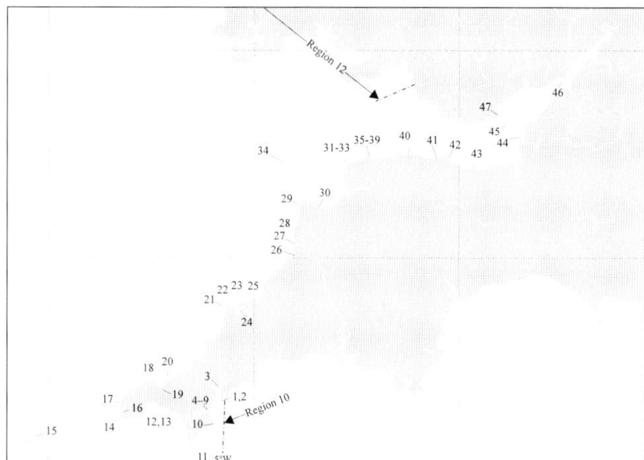

Map 4.2.1 Locations of marine biological interest described in the text (see Table 4.2.1).

Falmouth to Land's End

Falmouth and the Helford River together form one of the best ria (drowned river valley) systems in Britain. It is of major nature conservation interest and has been put forward as a possible Special Area of Conservation (SAC) for its sublittoral sandbanks, intertidal mudflats and sandflats and large shallow inlets and bays. Its interest is also recognised by the identification of the stretch from Dodman Point (Region 10) to the Lizard as a Sensitive Marine Area (SMA) (English Nature 1994a) (see also section 7.4.4). The Fal Estuary has a high diversity of marine habitats, communities and species. Slow tidal streams and a high rate of siltation have resulted in the presence of extensive sediment banks (Davies in prep. b). A number of sites within the Fal Estuary are of particular importance. Place Cove, including the adjacent Amsterdam Point, near the mouth of the Percuil River, is a sheltered sediment cove with nationally important rich communities of burrowing species (Powell *et al.* 1978). Patches of sublittoral rock, an uncommon habitat within marine inlets, provide a substratum for a rich sponge and sea squirt community (Davies in prep. b). The St. Mawes Bank to the west of the Roseland peninsula is also of national importance for its extensive (approximately 150 ha) bed of living maerl, an unusual calcareous alga. This is the best developed maerl bed outside Scotland. Two species are present: *Phymatolithon calcareum* and *Lithothamnion coralloides*. The maerl nodules form a lattice structure which supports a wealth of animal and algal species, including the rare Couch's goby *Gobius couchi* and two nationally important species of red alga. Further inshore, the coarse sediment is colonised by eelgrass *Zostera marina*, which also has a rich and distinctive community associated with it. Further north, at Turnaware Point, the tide-swept stony sediment has a diverse array of species of regional importance (Rostron 1987).

The Helford River is a shallow estuary, with rocky shores and moderate tidal streams in the lower reaches, leading to the development of interesting marine communities. Powell *et al.* (1978) described the whole

Table 4.2.1 Locations of marine importance mentioned in the text

No. on Map 4.2.1	*Location*	*Grid ref.*
Cornwall		
1	Place Cove	SW8532
2	St. Mawes Bank	SW8432
3	Turnaware Point	SW8338
4	Prisk Cove	SW7927
5	Helford River	SW7826
6	Passage Cove	SW7626
7	Treath	SW7626
8	The Gew	SW7826
9	Nare Point	SW8025
10	The Manacles	SW8121
11	Lizard Point	SW7011
12	Mount's Bay	SW5230
13	St. Michael's Mount	SW5130
14	Land's End	SW3425
15	Isles of Scilly	SV80, SV81, SV90, SV91
16	Sennen Cove	SW3526
17	Cape Cornwall	SW3431
18	St. Ives Bay	SW5541
19	Hayle Estuary	SW5537
20	Godrevy Point	SW5743
21	Trevose Head	SW8576
22	Trevone	SW8876
23	Trebetherick	SW9278
24	Rock	SW9375
25	Kellan Head	SW9781
26	Widemouth	SS1902
27	Bude	SS2006
28	Duckpool	SS2011
	Devon	
29	Hartland Quay	SS2224
30	Clovelly	SS3124
31	Morte Point	SS4445
32	Rockham Bay	SS4546
33	Bull Point	SS4646
34	Lundy Island	SS1346
35	Rillage Point	SS5448
36	Smallmouth	SS5647
37	Sandy Bay	SS5747
38	Wild Pear Beach	SS5847
39	Combe Martin	SS5848
40	Foreland Point	SS7551
	Somerset	
41	Porlock Bay	SS8849
42	Greenaleigh Point	SS9548
43	Watchet	ST0744
44	Brean Down	ST2759
	Somerset, Gloucester, Avon, Gwent, Mid Glam., S. Glam.	
45	Severn Estuary	ST26
	Gwent	
46	Sudbrook	ST5087
	S. Glam.	
47	Lavernock Point	ST1868

estuary as being a site of national marine biological importance. Three areas within the estuary are of particular interest (Rostron 1987): Prisk Cove has extensive rockpools and overhang communities of national importance; the shore and sea bed between Treath and The Gew have an array of plant communities of regional or even national importance; and Passage Cove is of regional importance for the burrowing animals within the sediment, particularly the large numbers of polychaete worms *Myxicola infundibulum* and *Branchiomma bombyx*. A number of surveys have been undertaken within the Helford Voluntary Marine Conservation Area since 1986. These have shown a total loss of intertidal eelgrass *Zostera marina* beds at Treath and Helford Passage between 1986-1988 and an overall increase in populations of the barnacle *Elminius modestus* and the peacock worm *Sabella pavonina* (Tompsett 1994).

The east coast of the Lizard Peninsula, from Nare Point to Lizard Point, was considered a site of primary marine biological importance by Powell *et al.* (1978). The cliff-backed secluded rocky shores are relatively sheltered compared with the peninsula's west coast and have communities representative of these habitats. Around the Manacles, a small group of rocks about 2 km offshore, strong tidal currents encourage dense growths of sponges, hydroids and sea squirts in the sublittoral. The spectacular underwater scenery here attracts many SCUBA divers. Beyond Lizard Point, the shores are described as very exposed; indeed, they are often cited as classic examples of this shore type (Davies in prep. b). The rocky reefs provide overhangs and crevices for rich populations of sponges, anemones and sea squirts. Mount's Bay is relatively sheltered and provides a variety of shore habitats including extensive stretches of sand and rocky reefs, the area being considered a site of primary marine biological importance by Powell *et al.* (1978). The boulder shore on the north-west corner of St. Michael's Mount has rich communities associated with it (Powell *et al.* 1978). A local fishery for sea urchins *Echinus esculentus* is centred on Penzance, with large numbers being found amongst the dense kelp forests present below low water mark around the bay. Deeper water is characterised by anemones, particularly jewel anemones *Corynactis viridis*. Further west, Land's End has some of the finest examples of very exposed rocky shore communities in Britain and as such is considered as another site of primary marine biological importance (Powell *et al.* 1978). Upper shores are dominated by the barnacles *Chthamalus montagui* and *C. stellatus*, limpets and winkles. In the sublittoral fringe, the pink coralline alga *Corallina officinalis* is common, overlain by the kelp *Alaria esculenta*, typically found at exposed sites.

The Isles of Scilly

The Isles of Scilly, situated 45 km west of Land's End, are the only Lusitanian oceanic archipelago in Britain. They have been proposed as a possible SAC for their sublittoral sandbanks and their intertidal mudflats and sandflats. The diversity of habitats, communities and species found on the shores and in the sublittoral around the islands and rock outcrops is very high and of international marine biological importance (Powell *et al.* 1978). The range of substrata and the varying exposure to prevailing wave action (from extremely exposed to very sheltered) give rise to a great diversity in community types. Following extensive work by the Nature Conservancy Council in the 1980s, in 1988 the Isles of Scilly Environmental Trust established a Marine Park in recognition of the importance of the area. The archipelago has recently been identified as a Sensitive Marine Area by English Nature (1994a). There is also a strong southern influence on the biota of the islands, owing to their south-westerly position and the warmth of the sea water (0.5-1.0°C higher than at adjacent mainland sites during winter). Many marine species recorded within the islands are unrecorded on the mainland, and some species considered common on the mainland are rare in the islands. The exceptionally clear water allows algae to grow at greater depths than in mainland coastal waters; the kelp *Laminaria ochroleuca* for instance has been recorded at depths of up to 30 m.

Areas of intertidal sediment consist of a coarse-grained granite sand with rich communities characterised by polychaetes, bivalves and the burrowing heart urchins *Echinocardium cordatum* and *E. pennatifidum*. Well-developed sheltered beds of eelgrass *Zostera marina*, amongst the best in Britain, are present between several of the islands, with an associated diverse community including rare red algae, anemones, stalked jellyfish, polychaetes, molluscs and echinoderms (English Nature 1994a). The communities on rocky shores vary with the degree of exposure, from the very exposed shores of the Western Rocks, where only the hardiest of species survive, to the relative shelter of enclosed shores, where boulders have rich under-boulder communities. Algal communities in particular are important because of their high species diversity and the presence of many rarities.

In the subtidal below the algae-dominated zone, vertical rock surfaces are dominated by colourful anemones, soft corals and encrusting sponges. Deeper still, on the sheltered east-facing coast of St. Mary's, several south-western species are found, including the zoanthid anemone *Parazoanthus axinellae*, the rare hard corals *Leptopsammia pruvoti* and *Hoplangia durotrix* and the sea fan *Eunicella verrucosa*. A survey in 1983 identified eighteen sublittoral rock habitats and six sublittoral sediment habitats within the archipelago, together with a number of other 'restricted' habitats such as caves, overhangs, crevices and under-boulders (Hiscock 1984). Most communities identified had a strong southern element. Tide-swept cobble habitats had rich algal communities, considered to be of national importance.

The Marine Park is bounded by the 50 m depth contour, encompassing all of the islands and rocks. A number of Special Areas have been identified within the Park as being particularly vulnerable to damage, including the intertidal sandflats between Samson, Tresco and St. Martin's; areas of deep sheltered bedrock off the east coast of St. Mary's; the boulder shores and rockpools of St. Agnes; sublittoral pebbles and cobbles in Smith Sound and St. Mary's Road; and the exposed Western Rocks. Monitoring work within the Marine Park over the past ten years has revealed marked changes in the populations of the Devonshire cup coral *Caryophyllia smithii* (Fowler & Pilley 1992) and the re-appearance in 1991 of the *Zostera* 'wasting disease' (caused by a slime mould of the genus *Labyrinthula*), which decimated the eelgrass beds in the 1930s and 1940s (Raines *et al.* 1993).

Land's End to Hartland Point

This section of coast has some of the most dramatic coastal scenery in England, with its rugged cliffs and extensive sandy bays. At the southern end of Sennen Cove just north of Land's End there are large granite boulders sitting on bedrock with dense growths of thongweed *Himanthalia elongata* on the low shore amongst a luxuriant covering of red algae. From Cape Cornwall to St. Ives, the exposed rocky shores have a typical covering of barnacles, limpets and fucoid algae. Within rockpools on the lower shore, the south-western brown alga *Bifurcaria bifurcata* and the limpet *Patella aspersa* are unusually abundant (Powell *et al.* 1978). Extensive bedrock platforms occur in the sublittoral, with the kelp forest, dominated by the southern species *Laminaria ochroleuca*, extending to over 20 m below chart datum (Hiscock 1981). Below this, a bryozoan/hydroid turf covers rock surfaces, with encrusting sponges, barnacles, the soft coral *Alcyonium digitatum*, jewel anemones *Corynactis viridis* and the white anemone *Actinothoë sphyrodeta*.

St. Ives Bay and the Hayle Estuary have been declared a Sensitive Marine Area by English Nature (1994a), largely on account of their overwintering bird populations. The marine life is not particularly outstanding, being typical of that associated with mud and sand, though of note are the large numbers of the sponges *Leucosolenia* spp. and *Sycon ciliatum*, and the anemones *Anemonia sulcata* and *Corynactis viridis*, attached to hard substrata. Published marine biological information is sparse for the stretch of coast north from Godrevy Point to Trevose Head. The most extensive rocky shores on the north Cornwall coast are found close to Padstow, at Trevone and Trebetherick. These were considered by Powell *et al.* (1978) to be of primary marine biological importance because of their rich intertidal flora and fauna. Besides the midshore mussel/limpet/barnacle-dominated zone, unusual features include a low-shore zone of the brown peacock weed *Cystoseira tamariscifolia* at Trevone and the rare Celtic sea-slug *Onchidella celtica* at Trebetherick Point. Sublittoral communities found at The Bull near Trevose Head were distinctly different from those further north, being dominated by mussels *Mytilus edulis* and the small red sea squirt *Dendrodoa grossularia* (Hiscock 1981). Within the Camel Estuary, sandy sediments have rich populations of the lugworm *Arenicola marina* and dense beds of the cockle *Cerastoderma edule*. At Rock, the common mussel *Mytilus edulis* and the Mediterranean mussel *Mytilus galloprovincinalis* have populations alongside each other - an unusual occurrence. At the mouth of the estuary, rock habitats are subject to strong tidal streams and support dense growths of sponges, sea squirts, hydroids and anemones. The small sea squirt *Pycnoclavella aurilucens* nears the northern limit of its distribution here.

Below low water on the open coast, much of the sea bed consists of a flat or gently-sloping sand plain with rock outcrops and broken reefs. Sand is clearly an important influence on the structure of communities in the area, except around headlands (Hiscock 1981). The restricted depth limits of algal species (for instance kelp only extends to 3 m below chart datum) are attributed to the presence of suspended sediment in the water column, limiting light penetration. Characterising species on bedrock deeper than 15 m include the bryozoan *Pentapora foliacea*, the sea squirt *Stolonica socialis* and the sea fan *Eunicella verrucosa*. The south-west Britain sublittoral survey (Hiscock 1981) found species richness for benthic communities to be generally low, with the richest and most representative site for the area being at Kellan Head. The whole of the area from Trevose Head to Boscastle, including the Camel Estuary, falls within English Nature's North Cornwall SMA (English Nature 1994a), and is notable for the variety of habitats and exposure conditions present. At Boscastle, rock extends a considerable distance offshore and is dominated to depths in excess of 20 m by algae, there being little sand along this section of coast.

From Boscastle north to Hartland Point, the shore is mostly of rock with occasional small sandy coves, larger expanses of sand occurring at Widemouth and north of Bude. At Duckpool near the Devon border, the lower shore has exceptionally fine colonies of the reef-building honeycomb tube-worm *Sabellaria alveolata*. These colonies are considered to be the finest in Britain (Cunningham *et al.* 1984), the area being considered by Powell *et al.* (1978) to be of primary marine biological importance. The sea bed in this area consists of gently sloping bedrock with boulders at some sites, rock surfaces having an even covering of sand (Hiscock 1981). In depths down to 26 m, these habitats are dominated by algae, particularly the brown seaweeds *Dictyota dichotoma* and *Dictyopteris membranacea* and various foliose red species. Vertical and upward-facing rock surfaces are dominated by bryozoans, sea squirts and sponges, with erect sponges such as *Raspailia hispida* being common.

Hartland Point to Foreland Point (including Lundy)

The coastline of north Devon comprises high cliffs punctuated by the broad, sandy beaches of Bideford Bay. Little published information is available for many areas within this section, though it was the seashore life of north Devon that enthused the well-known nineteenth century naturalists Philip Henry Gosse and Charles Kingsley. Sublittoral communities dominated by mussels *Mytilus edulis* are present in the Clovelly area and also at Morte Point. These communities appear to be different from those of north-east Cornwall or the north Devon coast east of Bull Point (Hiscock 1981), which may indicate the presence of a biogeographical boundary. The Taw-Torridge Estuary complex is a broad sedimentary estuary extending some distance inland. Marine habitats and communities within the estuary have been surveyed for the Nature Conservancy Council (Little 1989, in Davies in prep. a), though communities found had a low species richness and abundance.

The island of Lundy lies 18 km off the north Devon coast and measures just 5 km by 1.25 km, with a 15 km coastline ranging from very exposed to very sheltered from wave action. It has been proposed as a possible SAC for its reefs. Most of the island is formed of granite, with inaccessible shores at the base of steep cliffs, though the south-east corner is of more friable slate, which supports rich intertidal communities. The island is of great marine biological importance: it became Britain's first Voluntary Marine Nature Reserve in 1973 and the country's first statutory Marine Nature Reserve in 1986. The waters around the island now constitute a Sensitive Marine Area (English Nature 1994a), on account of the outstanding variety of its nearshore habitats and communities (Table 4.2.2). Owing to the influence of a number of physical conditions (e.g. strong tidal currents, variable wave exposure, juxtaposition of various coastal and oceanic water masses), several of these are habitats and communities that are rarely encountered elsewhere in Great Britain. West-facing shores are classified as being very exposed, with rich lichen communities, below

Table 4.2.2 Marine subtidal communities of international/national importance around Lundy

Importance	*Notes*
International	
Mostly unbroken rock	Within each ecological depth zone, widely different communities are present at different locations around the island. The community type is related to the degree of exposure to wave action and tidal streams, and to other environmental factors, such as siltation, influenced by exposure. Many of the animal communities, particularly on the east coast, include colourful Mediterranean-Atlantic species in abundance and are of high aesthetic appeal. The range of communities, their richness and the presence of many Mediterranean-Atlantic species are outstanding in the context of north-east Atlantic sublittoral ecosystems.
National	
Stable boulders	Algal communities on sublittoral boulders are often distinctly different from those of nearby rock, although it is not clear whether this results from the habitat or natural variability. Animal communities on boulders are distinctly different from those of nearby rock and are comparatively impoverished. The areas of boulder substratum around Lundy are very extensive and include wave-sheltered areas where distinctive communities not observed or rarely observed elsewhere in south-west Britain are present.
Muddy gravel	The extensive areas off the east coast are colonised by a distinctive fauna rarely encountered elsewhere nearshore in south-west Britain. The communities correspond to the 'Boreal offshore muddy-gravel association' described by Holme (1966) for areas off Plymouth. Their assessment as being of national importance here is made because this type of community was not described by Jones (1950) and therefore appears to be unusual, and because of the convenience for study in shallow water at Lundy.
Mud and muddy sand	These extensive areas nearshore off the east coast support a rich community characterised by several conspicuous species including *Amphiura filiformis*, *Goneplax rhomboides* and *Cepola rubescens*. The community has been assigned to the *Amphiura filiformis* community of Thorson (1957) and is probably similar to the 'Boreal offshore muddy-sand association' described by Holme (1966) for the English Channel. This appears to be an unusual habitat for the Bristol Channel, and is particularly interesting because of the presence of *Cepola rubescens*, which upgrades the rating to one of national importance.
Cliffs	The extensive sublittoral cliffs present at Gannets Rock Pinnacle and Seals Rock provide good examples of semi-exposed and exposed cliff faunas respectively. Smaller areas of sublittoral cliffs are present on other parts of the coasts and include communities different from those of surrounding upward-facing or broken rock.
Wrecks	The community present on the wreck of the M.V. *Robert* is extremely well-developed as a distinctly different community from those of rocks in similar conditions and can be considered a 'classic' wreck community. The *Robert* is one of very few intact wrecks present around the coast and should remain intact for several years, although it must be considered a transitory feature. Other wrecks around Lundy are mostly broken-up and the communities present differ little from adjacent rock communities.

Sources: Hiscock (1983); English Nature (1994b)

which limpets and barnacles dominate. Sheltered shores have a greater dominance of algae, particularly the knotted wrack *Ascophyllum nodosum*, which provides shelter for the anemone *Actinia equina*, winkles and small crustacea.

The Lundy marine algal flora is very rich and totals 316 species, many of which are southern in origin. The sublittoral fringe is characterised by the kelps *Alaria esculenta* and *Laminaria digitata*, the rock surface being almost entirely covered by pink encrusting calcareous algae. Below this, a kelp forest of *Laminaria hyperborea* extends to 8 m depth below chart datum, with foliose algae continuing to 22 m. The richest animal communities occur below the zone of algal domination, with erect and encrusting sponges, sea anemones, soft corals and sea fans in amongst a turf of hydroids and bryozoans. On vertical and overhanging rock surfaces off the sheltered east coast are communities of great scientific interest, which include the rare cup corals *Caryophyllia inornatus, Hoplangia durotrix, Leptopsammia pruvoti* and the soft coral *Parerythropodium coralloides* (see also section 5.4). Other colourful Mediterranean-Atlantic species that thrive in similar conditions include the anemone *Parazoanthus axinellae*, the sea fan *Eunicella verrucosa* and the soft coral *Alcyonium glomeratum*. Monitoring studies over a number of years have found many of these species to be very long-lived and slow-growing and to have a poor capacity for recovery because they replace their numbers slowly at the margins of their distribution. The mixed sediments of gravel, mud and muddy-sand off the east coast of Lundy are colonised by distinctive communities, several of which are rarely found elsewhere in Britain. Burrowing species of particular interest include the angular crab *Goneplax rhomboides*, the anemones *Mesacmaea mitchellii* and *Halcampoides purpurea*, and the eel-like red band fish *Cepola rubescens*. Table 4.2.2 summarises the importance of the marine communities of high scientific interest around Lundy.

From Morte Point eastwards, the coastline resumes a north-facing aspect, with rocky shores interspersed with small sandy coves backed by high cliffs. Many species reach the eastern limit of their distribution here, as a transition occurs between the open coast and the Bristol Channel. The area from Morte Point to Combe Martin has been identified by English Nature (1994a) as a Sensitive Marine Area (extending 2-3 km offshore) and in 1994 was also declared a Voluntary Marine Conservation Area. The rocky shores are moderately exposed to wave action and contain a variety of habitats. At Rockham Bay, boulder-filled gullies, abundant rockpools and overhanging surfaces add to the overall interest of the site. Further east at Smallmouth, overhanging and vertical rock surfaces support rich communities. A number of rare species have been recorded from the coast between Ilfracombe and Combe Martin, including the cup corals *Balanophyllia regia* and *Hoplangia durotrix* and the colonial anemone *Isozoanthus sulcatus* (see also section 5.4). In addition, several species rarely recorded on the shore are present, such as the Devonshire cup coral *Caryophyllia smithii* and the sponges *Polymastia mammilaris* and *Tethya aurantium* (English Nature 1994a). Sublittoral habitats and communities for this section of coast are best represented in the area from Rillage Point to Sandy Bay (Hiscock 1981). To the east of Combe Martin, Wild Pear Beach was considered by Powell *et al.* (1978) to be of marine biological importance. The bladderless form of bladderwrack *Fucus vesiculosus* var. *evesiculosus* was noted at more exposed locations, and two other species of particular interest were the strawberry anemone *Actinia fragacea* and the honeycomb worm *Sabellaria alveolata*. Beyond Combe Martin, the shores of Exmoor are predominantly of boulders with occasional rocky reefs and some stretches of sand, backed by steep cliffs.

The Inner Bristol Channel: Foreland Point to Nash Point

Foreland Point marks the western limit of a transition zone to the inner Bristol Channel/Severn Estuary biota, with a strong boundary being present a little further to the east in Porlock Bay (Hiscock 1981). A similar boundary is found on the northern side of the Bristol Channel in Swansea Bay. The Severn Estuary has been proposed as a possible SAC for its sublittoral sandbanks, intertidal mudflats and sandflats and estuarine habitats. The physical conditions that exist within the estuary have a direct effect on the marine communities present. Besides the inflow from the River Severn itself, the estuary receives a large volume of fresh water from five other rivers: the Parrett and Avon on the south shore and the Wye, Usk and Taff on the north shore. This leads to a gradual reduction in salinity the further east one goes. It also introduces a considerable load of silt to the estuary, kept in suspension by strong tidal streams resulting from the particularly large tidal range. The scouring action of this silt-laden water reduces larval settlement on the few rocky outcrops present. Shallow areas sheltered from these streams may consist largely of 'liquid mud', providing very poor conditions for colonisation by benthic species.

The estuary contains a variety of intertidal habitats, which makes it one of the largest and most important intertidal zones in Britain. Thirteen community types have been identified from areas of littoral sediment within the Severn Estuary (Severn Tidal Power Group 1989). Their distribution appears to be determined primarily by sediment type and the level of consolidation, with salinity being of lesser importance. Communities within sediments are characterised by polychaete worms (the most dominant species being ragworms *Nereis* spp. and *Neanthes* spp. and the lugworm *Arenicola marina*) and amphipod *crustacea* (*Corophium* spp. and *Bathyporeia* spp.); those on top of the sediment are characterised by gastropod molluscs (in particular the spire shell *Hydrobia ulvae*). The rich invertebrate biomass present within these extensive intertidal sediment flats supports internationally important numbers of wading birds. Limited patches of eelgrass are present on some sheltered mudflats and sandbanks. All three species of *Zostera* occur, with the most common, *Z. marina*, extending to 4 m depth below chart datum (English Nature 1994a). Dives were undertaken off Porlock Bay, Greenaleigh Point and Watchet as part of the South-west Britain sublittoral survey (Hiscock 1981). All of these sites had a low species richness compared with open coast sites further west. Algae were recorded only above chart datum level. Stable hard substratum was characterised by the reef-building polychaetes *Sabellaria alveolata* and *Sabellaria spinulosa*, with the sea squirt *Dendrodoa grossularia*, mussels *Mytilus edulis* and the polychaete *Polydora ciliata* common at some sites.

In the sublittoral, the Severn Tidal Power Group (1989) identified ten species associations within the Severn Estuary from grab samples, the associations again being determined largely by sediment type and exposure to tidal currents.

Coarse sediments of consolidated gravel, pebbles and cobbles were dominated by the reef-building polychaete *Sabellaria* (mainly *S. alveolata*, although some *S. spinulosa* was also recorded). These *Sabellaria* reefs may cover extensive areas of the sea bed, particularly where there are tide-swept hard substrata affected by turbid water - a feature rarely found in other UK estuaries. Indeed, the richest association of species within the estuary (up to 25 species per sample) was associated with these reefs. Areas of medium/fine sand in shallower water close to both north and south coasts were characterised by a mix of bivalves, amphipods and polychaetes. Dives undertaken off Porlock Bay, Greenaleigh Point and Watchet as part of the South-west Britain Sublittoral Survey (Hiscock 1981) revealed a low species richness compared with open sites further west. Algae were recorded only above chart datum level. Stable hard substrata were also found to have both species of *Sabellaria*, with the sea squirt *Dendrodoa grossularia*, mussels *Mytilus edulis* and the polychaete *Polydora ciliata* common at some sites. The Severn Estuary SMA has as its seaward boundary a line from Brean Down to Lavernock Point (English Nature 1994a).

There is little difference between the intertidal and subtidal habitats found along the northern shoreline of the Severn Estuary and those on the southern shoreline: both consist largely of mud and sand mixtures with varying amounts of gravel and occasional exposures of rock. A survey of soft sediment macroinvertebrates between Sudbrook and Lavernock Point on the Welsh coast revealed three main invertebrate groupings from a total of 62 taxa (Jones & Davies 1983, in Davies in prep. a). These were dominated by polychaete worms, bivalve molluscs and amphipod crustaceans. Rocky shores predominate between Lavernock Point and Nash Point. It appears that Nash Point marks the eastern edge of a biogeographical transition zone, which extends westwards into Swansea Bay. For instance, the gastropod *Littorina neritoides* and the kelp *Laminaria digitata* are rarely found to the east of the headland (Davies 1995a).

Offshore (defined as beyond 3 km or 50 m depth)

There is little offshore information available for the Cornish coast of this region but the sublittoral habitats and communities of the Bristol Channel and the Severn Estuary have been well studied. Here, grab and dredge sampling on a grid of 155 stations in 1972/3 provided information on the composition and distribution of communities within the system (Warwick & Davies 1977). These were divided into five main community types (Table 4.2.3).

4.2.3 Human activities

The effects of fisheries and mariculture on sea-bed habitats and communities in the region are described in sections 5.5.3, 9.1.3 and 9.2.3. Other human activities that disturb the sea bed include the extraction of marine aggregates and navigational dredging (section 9.4) and maerl dredging (section 5.5). Water quality is affected by the discharge of industrial and sewage effluent (section 9.6).

4.2.4 Information sources used

The information used is predominantly that gathered for the JNCC's Marine Nature Conservation Review (MNCR). The MNCR team (and their contractors) use a standard recording methodology for both littoral and sublittoral surveys, which includes descriptions of both habitats and their associated communities (see Connor & Hiscock 1996). Survey information from other sources may vary considerably in its methodology and coverage. Table 4.2.4 shows the number of sites in the region with marine benthic (sea-bed and sea-shore) habitat and species information held on the MNCR database. Maps 4.2.2 and 4.2.3 show the locations of all littoral and all near-shore sublittoral surveys on the MNCR database. This information is not fully comprehensive. Records additional to those cited here may exist in sources that were not consulted. The shores of Devon and Cornwall were investigated by the Nature Conservancy Council-commissioned *Intertidal survey of Great Britain* (Powell *et al.* 1978). A considerable amount of published and unpublished information on Cornish shores is held at the Cornish Biological Records Unit, and on Devon's shores by the Devon Wildlife Trust. The Institute for Marine and Environmental Research, Plymouth, undertook a survey of sea-bed habitats and communities in the Bristol Channel in 1972/73, taking grab and dredge samples; the distribution of the main community types is mapped in Warwick & Davies (1977). Nearshore sublittoral habitats and

Table 4.2.3 Sublittoral communities present in the Bristol Channel and the Severn Estuary

	Community	*Habitat description*	*Notes/associated species*
I	Bivalve *Venus* community	Sands, especially in the outer Bristol Channel	A bivalve *Tellina* community on hard-packed sand, and a bivalve *Spisula* community on loose sands.
II	Bivalve *Abra* community	On silty or mixed bottoms in the outer Channel	The bivalve *Abra alba*, the polychaetes *Scalibregma inflatum* and *Lagis koreni*, and others
III	Horse mussel *Modiolus* community	On hard substrate, mostly in the central Channel	The hermit crab *Pagurus bernhardus*, the scaleworm *Lepidonotus squamatus*, the brittlestar *Ophiothrix fragilis*, and others
IV	Reduced species diversity hard substrate community	On rocky substrate subjected to strong tidal scour, mostly in the inner part of the Channel	The polychaetes *Typosyllis armillaris*, *Eulalia tripunctata*, *Sabellaria alveolata*, *Sabellaria spinulosa* and others
V	Reduced species diversity soft substrate community	In fluid muds of the inner Channel	The polychaetes *Tharyx marioni*, *Nephtys hombergii* and *Peloscolex* spp.

Source: after Warwick & Davies (1977)

Table 4.2.4 Number of sites with marine benthic habitat and species information held on the MNCR database

Littoral	Near-shore sublittoral	Offshore	Total
449	831	0	1258

Source: MNCR Database 1994. Note: these records are not comprehensive: additional records may exist in sources that were not consulted.

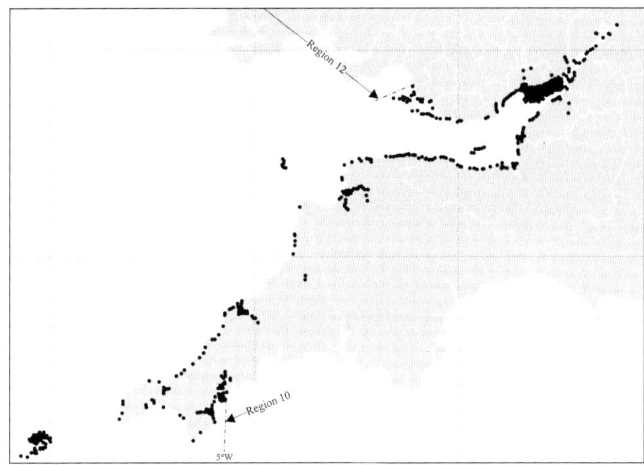

Map 4.2.2 Littoral surveys recorded on the MNCR database. Source: JNCC.

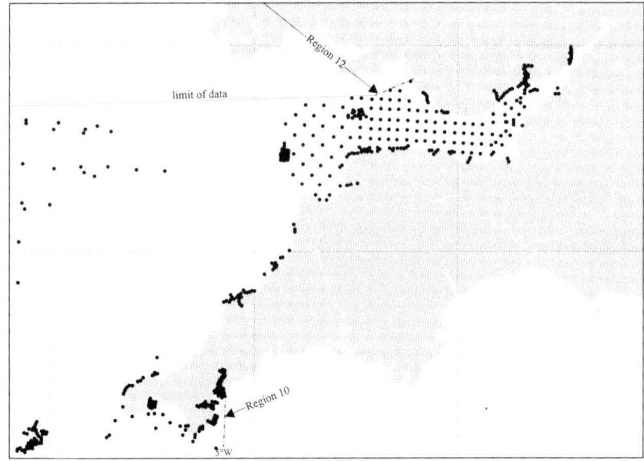

Map 4.2.3 Near-shore sublittoral surveys recorded on the MNCR database. Source: JNCC.

communities were surveyed during the *South-west Britain sublittoral survey* (Hiscock 1981), which included much of the coast within this region. A further NCC-commissioned survey undertaken during the 1980s of *Harbours, rias and estuaries in southern Britain*, covered the following estuaries: Hayle (Gill 1989); Camel (Gill & Mercer 1989); Taw-Torridge (Little 1989); and Taf, Twyi and Gwendraeth (Mercer 1989) - all referenced in Davies (in prep a, b). Part of the near-shore sea bed off the Lizard peninsula was surveyed by the BioMar team on behalf of English Nature during 1994, using analysis of echo soundings and drop-down video. Lundy has been most comprehensively described in Hiscock (in press.). A considerable amount of information on the inner Bristol Channel/Severn Estuary is available from studies undertaken by the Severn Tidal Power Group (e.g. Severn Tidal Power Group 1989).

4.2.5 Acknowledgements

The author acknowledges the help of JNCC's Marine Nature Conservation Review team (particularly Dr Tim Hill) in compiling and presenting the information given here.

4.2.6 Further sources of information

A. References cited

Connor, D.W., & Hiscock, K. 1996. Data collection methods. *In: Marine Nature Conservation Review: rationale and methods*, ed. by K. Hiscock, 51-65 & Appendices 5-10. Peterborough, JNCC. (Coasts and seas of the United Kingdom. MNCR Series.)

Cunningham, P.N., Hawkins, S.J., Jones, H.D., & Burrows, M.T. 1984. The geographical distribution of *Sabellaria alveolata* (L.) in England, Wales and Scotland, with investigations into the community structure of, and the effects of trampling on, *Sabellaria alveolata* colonies. *Nature Conservancy Council, CSD Report*, No. 535.

Davies, J. In prep. a. Bristol Channel and Approaches (MNCR Sector 9). *In: Benthic marine ecosystems: a review of current knowledge for Great Britain and the north-east Atlantic*, ed. by K. Hiscock, Chapter 10. Peterborough, Joint Nature Conservation Committee. (Coasts and seas of the United Kingdom. MNCR Series.)

Davies, J. In prep. b. Western Channel (Durlston Head to Cape Cornwall, including the Isles of Scilly) (MNCR Sector 8). *In: Benthic marine ecosystems: a review of current knowledge for Great Britain and the north-east Atlantic*, ed. by K. Hiscock, Chapter 9. Peterborough, Joint Nature Conservation Committee. (Coasts and seas of the United Kingdom. MNCR Series.)

English Nature. 1994a. *Important areas for marine wildlife around England*. Peterborough, English Nature.

English Nature. 1994b. *Managing Lundy's wildlife: a management plan for the Marine Nature Reserve and Site of Special Scientific Interest*. Okehampton, English Nature.

Fowler, S.L., & Pilley, G.M. 1992. *Report on the Lundy and Isles of Scilly marine monitoring programmes, 1984-1991*. Peterborough, English Nature. (English Nature Research Reports, No. 10.) (Contractor: Nature Conservation Bureau Ltd., Newbury.)

Hiscock, K. In press. Marine biological research at Lundy. *In: Island studies - 50 years of the Lundy Field Society*, ed. by R.A. Irving, A.J. Schofield & C.J. Webster. Appledore, Westwell Publications.

Hiscock, K. 1981. South-west Britain sublittoral survey. Final report. *Nature Conservancy Council, CSD Report*, No. 327.

Hiscock, K. 1983. *Lundy Marine Nature Reserve management plan draft*. Huntingdon, Nature Conservancy Council.

Hiscock, K. 1984. Sublittoral survey of the Isles of Scilly. July 2nd to 16th, 1983. *Nature Conservancy Council, CSD Report*, No. 529.

Holme, N.A. 1966. The bottom fauna of the English Channel. II. *Journal of the Marine Biological Association of the United Kingdom, 46*: 401-493.

Jones, N.S. 1950. Marine bottom communities. *Biological Reviews, 25*: 283-313.

Powell, H.T., Holme, N.A., Knight, S.J.T., & Harvey, R. 1978. Survey of the littoral zone of the coast of Great Britain: report of the shores of Devon and Cornwall. *Nature Conservancy Council, CSD Report*, No. 209.

Raines, P., Nunny R., & Cleator, B. 1993. *Coral Cay Conservation Sub-Aqua Club Isles of Scilly Expedition 1992*. Edinburgh, Cleator Associates (unpublished report).

Rostron, D. 1987. Survey of harbours, rias and estuaries in southern Britain: the Helford River. *Nature Conservancy Council, CSD Report*, No. 850.

Severn Tidal Power Group. 1989. *Severn Barrage Project: detailed report, Vol. IV: Ecological studies, landscape and nature conservation*. London, HMSO for Severn Tidal Power Group / Department of Energy.

Thorson, G. 1957. Bottom communities (sublittoral or shallow shelf). *Memoirs of the Geological Society of America, 67*: 461-534.

Tompsett, P.E. 1994. *Helford River survey: monitoring report No. 4 for 1993*. Helford Voluntary Marine Conservation Area Advisory Group (unpublished report).

Warwick, R.M., & Davies, J.R. 1977. The distribution of sublittoral macrofauna communities in the Bristol Channel in relation to the substrate. *Estuarine and Coastal Marine Science, 5*: 267-288.

B. Further reading

Bolt, S.R.L., Mitchell, R., Williams, P.F., McKirdy, A.P., Ninnes, R., Coney, B., Bennett, T.L., Burgoyne, C., Baldock, B., Davies, J., & Hiscock, K. 1989. Severn barrage development project: nature conservation. *Nature Conservancy Council, CSD Report*, No. 1,156. (Severn Tidal Power Group Report.)

Foster-Smith, R.L. 1991. A boulder survey in the Isles of Scilly, September 5th to 9th, 1990. *Nature Conservancy Council, CSD Report*, No. 1,226.

Groves, M. 1988. *Exploring underwater: the Isles of Scilly*. St. Agnes, Cornwall, Porth Books.

Gubbay, S. 1988. *Coastal directory for marine nature conservation*. Ross-on-Wye, Marine Conservation Society.

Hiscock, K. 1984a. Rocky shore surveys of the Isles of Scilly. March 27th to April 1st and July 7th to 15th 1983. *Nature Conservancy Council, CSD Report*, No. 509.

Hiscock, K. 1984b. Sublittoral survey of the Isles of Scilly. July 2nd to 16th, 1983. *Nature Conservancy Council, CSD Report*, No. 529.

Holbrook, A. 1991. *The Severn Barrage: a bibliography, 1909-1990*. 1st ed. Bath, University of Bath, University Library.

Mills, D.J.L., Hill, T.O., Thorpe, K., & Connor, D.W. 1993. Atlas of marine biological surveys in Britain. *Joint Nature Conservation Committee Report*, No. 167. (Marine Nature Conservation Review Report MNCR/OR/17.)

Nichols, D., & Harris, T. 1982. A survey of the low tide flats of the Isles of Scilly. *Nature Conservancy Council, CSD Report*, No. 413.

Rostron, D.M. 1989. Animal communities from sublittoral sediments in the Isles of Scilly. September 1988. *Nature Conservancy Council, CSD Report*, No. 918.

Stone, V., & Deeble, M. 1984. *Exploring underwater in a Cornish estuary (the Fal)*. St. Agnes, Cornwall, Porth Books.

Tompsett, P. 1996. *Marine life between Dodman Point and Lizard Point*. Redruth, Cornish Biological Records Unit.

Wood, E., *ed*. 1988. *Sea life of Britain and Ireland*. London, Immel. (Marine Conservation Society.)

C. Contact names and addresses

Type of information	*Contact address and telephone no.*
Marine nature conservation issues in England	*Maritime Team, English Nature, Peterborough, tel: 01733 340345
Marine nature conservation issues in Wales	*Countryside Council for Wales, Bangor, tel: 01248 370444
Published and unpublished marine studies of the Cornish coast	Dr Stella Turk, Cornish Biological Records Unit, Trevithick Centre, Trevenson Road, Pool, Redruth, Cornwall TR15 3PL, tel: 01209 710424
Studies of the Hayle, Gannel and Camel Estuaries	Plymouth Marine Laboratory, Prospect Place, West Hoe, Plymouth PL1 3DH, tel: 01752 633100
The Isles of Scilly Marine Park: interest and management	The Director, The Isles of Scilly Environmental Trust, Carn Thomas, Hugh Town, St. Mary's, Isles of Scilly TR21 0PT, tel: 01720 422153
Surveys of Isles of Scilly *Zostera* beds since 1992	Coral Cay Conservation Sub-Aqua Club, c/o 154 Clapham Park Road, London SW4 7DE, tel: 0171 498 6248
Littoral studies in the Isles of Scilly	Dr Tegwyn Harris, Department of Biological Sciences, University of Exeter Hatherley Labs., Prince of Wales Road, Exeter, Devon EX4 4PS, tel: 01392 263263
Marine nature conservation issues in Devon	Marine Conservation Officer, Devon Wildlife Trust, 188 Sidwell Street, Exeter, Devon EX4 6RD, tel: 01392 79244
Polzeath Voluntary Marine Wildlife Area	*North Cornwall Heritage Coast and Countryside Service, North Cornwall District Council, tel: 01208 74121 ext. 239
Marine studies within the Lundy MNR	Robert Irving, Secretary, Lundy Marine Nature Reserve Advisory Group, 14 Brookland Way, Coldwaltham, Pulborough, West Sussex RH20 1LT, tel: 01798 873581
North Devon Voluntary Marine Conservation Area	Marine Ranger, North Devon Heritage Coast Service, Council Offices, Northfield Road, Ilfracombe, Devon EX34 8AL, tel: 01271 867496

*Starred contact addresses are given in full in the Appendix.

4.3 Plankton

M. Edwards & A.W.G. John

4.3.1 Introduction

Plankton include the bacteria (bacterio-), plant (phyto-) and animal (zoo-) plankton. In temperate continental shelf seas, as in this region, the phytoplankton assemblage is dominated by diatoms and dinoflagellates, and the zooplankton, although containing representatives of most marine animal phyla at some stage, is dominated by crustaceans, principally copepods. The plankton's abundance is strongly influenced by factors such as depth, tidal mixing and temperature stratification, which determine the vertical stability of the water column. The distribution of species, here and elsewhere, is influenced directly by salinity and temperature, by water flows into the area and by the presence of local benthic (bottom-dwelling) and littoral (shoreline) communities. Many of the species of these communities, including commercially important fish and shellfish (see sections 5.5 and 5.7), have temporary planktonic larval forms (meroplankton). Tidal fronts (boundary zones between stratified and well mixed water masses) in this region are likely to be of significant biological importance, since they are usually rich in plankton, which attracts other marine life. Phytoplankton blooms (transient, unsustainable growths, usually of a single species and often associated with a visible discolouration of the water) are a normal feature in the seasonal development of plankton. Some blooms may reach exceptional proportions (>10^6 cells/l) or contain species (principally dinoflagellates) that can be toxic to humans and possibly have an important economic impact on mariculture, fisheries and tourism.

In Region 11, as elsewhere, the plankton has a fundamental role in the food chain of both benthic (sea-bed) organisms (see sections 4.2, 5.4 and 5.5) and fish (see sections 5.7 - 5.9). For both ecosystems, the availability of food and nutrients, larval survival, maintaining populations and timing of egg production are highly dependent on the amount of phyto/zooplankton available. Any environmental stress imposed on the plankton will have consequences throughout the food chain and may affect the amount of food available to fish, birds, marine mammals etc. In coastal management, plankton can also give early warning of adverse human impacts (for example the effects of eutrophication) and highlight different water masses.

Section 2.3 describes the physical environment of the seas in Region 11. In the Celtic Sea, thermal stratification becomes well established by late spring and spreads eastward along the north Cornish coast, establishing frontal boundaries at Land's End and the eastern part of the Celtic Sea (Map 4.3.1). In the Bristol Channel, however, vertical mixing is sufficient to maintain vertical homogeneity of the water column throughout the year.

Owing to high levels of turbidity in the inner Bristol Channel, estimated annual primary production is low (6.8 g C m^{-2}) compared with the outer channel (164.9 g C m^{-2}) and the Celtic Sea (Joint & Pomroy 1981). Figure 4.3.1 shows the seasonal cycles of phytoplankton production for Region 11, based on a visual estimate of chlorophyll and the numbers of copepods per sample (Warner & Hays 1994).

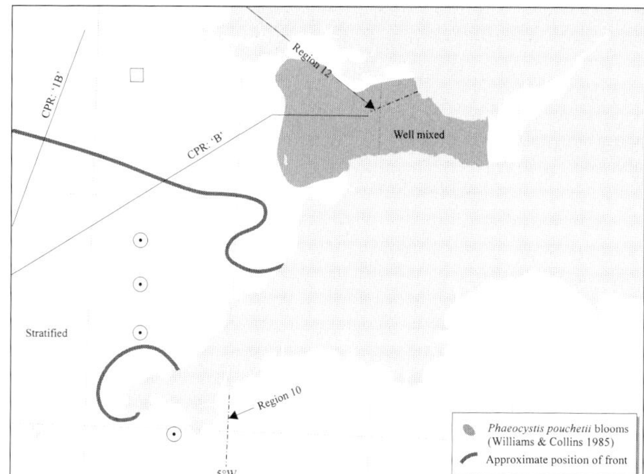

Map 4.3.1 Plankton surveys, 'fronts' and areas of well mixed and transitional water. See Table 4.3.1 for symbols and details of surveys. Source: Sir Alister Hardy Foundation for Ocean Science (SAHFOS).

4.3.2 Important locations and species

Evidence from the Continuous Plankton Recorder (CPR) and other surveys indicates that the phytoplankton of this region is fairly typical of shallow and enclosed waters around the British Isles. The dominant phytoplankton associated with the spring bloom in the Celtic Sea are *Skeletonema costatum* and *Thalassiosira* spp., while in the Bristol Channel diatoms such as *Rhizosolenia hebetata* and *Coscinodiscus* spp. dominate. The onset of the spring bloom is associated with the development of the thermocline (a

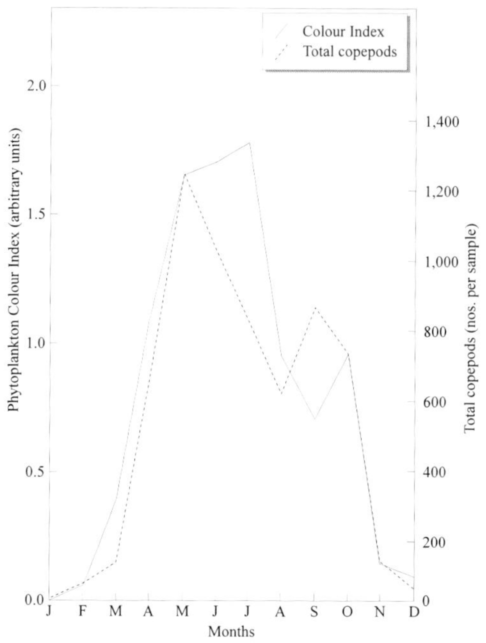

Figure 4.3.1 Average seasonal cycles of an index of phytoplankton colour (a visual estimate of chlorophyll) and the numbers of copepods per sample (approximately 3 m^3 of water filtered), derived from Continuous Plankton Recorder data for 1958-1992. Source: SAHFOS.

temperature gradient), which usually begins in the Celtic Sea and spreads eastward. By summer the highest levels of chlorophyll *a* are found along frontal boundaries on the stratified side, reaching 8 mg m^{-3} (Pingree *et al.* 1976). High levels of chlorophyll *a* may persist along frontal boundaries right through the summer until late September, until the thermocline disintegrates. Although the Bristol Channel has higher levels of nutrients than the Celtic Sea, phytoplankton development is delayed and chlorophyll *a* levels are low (1-2 mg m^{-3}) because of the high levels of turbidity encountered in the Channel (Joint & Pomroy 1981). The zooplankton of this region is typically dominated by copepods such as *Acartia clausi*, *Pseudocalanus elongatus* and *Temora longicornis*. Studies by Collins & Williams (1981) found that seasonal variations in distribution and abundance of the most numerically dominant copepods found in the Bristol Channel - *Eurytemora affinis*, *Acartia bifilosa* and *Centropages hamatus* - are related to different salinity regimes (<30 g/kg, 27-33.5 g/kg and 31-35 g/kg respectively). The copepod *Calanus helgolandicus* (important food for fish), more commonly found in the Celtic Sea, penetrates into the Bristol Channel when higher salinities (>33 g/kg) intrude up the channel. Copepod abundance begins to increase in March and reaches maximum densities in July in the Bristol Channel (nearly 100 times winter levels). Other commonly found zooplankton include small hydromedusae, amphipods and meroplanktonic larvae of echinoderms, polychaetes, decapods, molluscs and cirripeds. Studies by Collins & Williams (1981) and Southward (1962) have shown that the biodiversity of zooplankton in the Bristol Channel is relatively low compared with other shelf seas.

4.3.3 Human activities

In June 1974 a bloom of *Phaeocystis pouchetii* was observed in the central Bristol Channel, producing high levels of chlorophyll *a* (see Map 4.3.1). These blooms occur in most years in the Bristol Channel and make a considerable contribution to the phytoplankton standing crop (Williams & Collins 1985). However, it is not known why *Phaeocystis* blooms develop in some years and not in others (for a comparison of chlorophyll *a* concentrations for a bloom year and a non-bloom year, see Joint & Pomroy (1981)). These blooms are of importance to the coastal manager because in Dutch coastal waters they have been associated with eutrophication, and once they collapse they may result in the accumulation on beaches of large banks of foam, which look and smell unpleasant.

A bloom of *Alexandrium tamarense* in the Fal Estuary in July 1995 caused the first recorded instance of Paralytic Shellfish Poisoning (PSP) in the UK south of the Humber (Reid *et al.* 1995) (see also section 5.5).

4.3.4 Information sources used

During the 1970s and early 1980s the planktonic assemblage of the Bristol Channel was extensively studied (Table 4.3.1). Details of zooplankton distributions and a taxonomic list of phytoplankton and zooplankton can be found in Williams & Collins (1985). Joint & Pomroy (1981, 1982) studied levels of primary production within the Bristol Channel between 1973-1977, and the importance of bacterioplankton within the estuary. Apart from the CPR survey, which includes long-term data, studies of the eastern Celtic Sea tend to be limited to occasional surveys (Southward 1962; Pingree *et al.* 1976).

Table 4.3.1 Details of surveys

Identification in Map 4.3.1	*Frequency*	*Period*	*Reference*
CPR: 'B' route	Monthly	1967-1993	Warner & Hays 1994
CPR: 'IB' route	Monthly	1986-present	Warner & Hays 1994
Bristol Channel	Monthly	1973-1975	Williams & Collins 1985
Bristol Channel	Various	1975-1978	Joint & Pomroy 1982
Bristol Channel	Monthly	1973-1977	Joint & Pomroy 1981
Bristol Channel	Seasonal	1977-1978	Burkill & Kendall 1982
Celtic Sea	Occasional	1975	Pingree *et al.* 1976
Celtic Sea	Occasional	1958-1960	Southward 1962
Coastal regions	Occasional	1970-1985	Riley *et al.* 1986
PS (□)	Occasional	1980-1982	Williams *et al.* 1987
PS (○)	Occasional	1976	Holligan *et al.* 1980

Key: CPR: Continuous Plankton Recorder; PS: Plankton samples.

4.3.5 Further sources of information

A. References cited

Burkill, P.H., & Kendall, T.F. 1982. Production of the copepod *Eurytemora affinis* in the Bristol Channel. *Marine Ecology Progress Series, 7*: 21-31.

Collins, N.R., & Williams, R. 1981. Zooplankton of the Bristol Channel and Severn Estuary. The distribution of four copepods in relation to salinity. *Marine Biology, 64*: 273-283.

Holligan, P.M., Maddock, L., & Dodge, J.D. 1980. The distribution of dinoflagellates around the British Isles in July 1977: a multivariate analysis. *Journal of the Marine Biological Association of the United Kingdom, 60*: 851-867.

Joint, I.R., & Pomroy, A.J. 1981. Primary production in a turbid estuary. *Estuarine, Coastal and Shelf Science, 13*: 303-316.

Joint, I.R., & Pomroy, A.J. 1982. Aspects of microbial heterotrophic production in a highly turbid estuary. *Journal of Experimental Marine Biology and Ecology, 58*: 33-46.

Pingree, R.D., Holligan, P.M., Mardell, G.T., & Head, R.N. 1976. The influence of physical stability on spring, summer and autumn phytoplankton blooms in the Celtic Sea. *Journal of the Marine Biological Association of the United Kingdom, 56*: 845-873.

Reid, P.C., Pratt, S., & Harbour, D. 1995. *A red tide event in the Fal Estuary*. Plymouth, Sir Alister Hardy Foundation for Ocean Science. (Unpublished report for NRA.)

Riley, J.D., Symonds, D.J., & Woolner, L.E. 1986. Determination of the distribution of the planktonic and small demersal stages of fish in the coastal waters of England, Wales and the adjacent area between 1970 and 1984. *MAFF Fisheries Research Technical Report, 84*: 1-23.

Southward, A.J. 1962. The distribution of some plankton animals in the English Channel and approaches. II. Surveys with the Gulf III high speed sampler, 1958-1960. *Journal of the Marine Biological Association of the United Kingdom, 42*: 275-375.

Warner, A.J., & Hays, G.C. 1994. Sampling by the Continuous Plankton Recorder survey. *Progress in Oceanography, 34*: 237-256.

Williams, R., & Collins, N.R. 1985. *Zooplankton atlas of the Bristol Channel and Severn Estuary*. Plymouth, Institute for Marine Environmental Research.

B. Further reading

Bottrell, H.H., & Robins, D.B. 1984. Seasonal variations in length, dry weight, carbon and nitrogen of *Calanus helgolandicus* from the Celtic Sea. *Marine Ecology Progress Series, 14*: 259-268.

Collins, N.R., & Williams, R. 1982. Zooplankton communities in the Bristol Channel and Severn Estuary. *Marine Ecology Progress Series, 9*: 1-11.

Head, P.C. 1975. Bibliography of estuarine research. *The Natural Environment Research Council Publication Series C,* No. 17.

Joint, I.R. 1984. The microbial ecology of the Bristol Channel. *Marine Pollution Bulletin, 15*: 62-66.

Pingree, R.D., & Griffiths, D.K. 1978. Tidal fronts on the shelf seas around the British Isles. *Journal of Geophysical Research, 83*: 4,615-4,622.

Simpson, J.H. 1976. A boundary front in the summer regime of the Celtic Sea. *Estuarine, Coastal and Marine Science, 4*: 71-81.

Williams, R. 1984. Zooplankton of the Bristol Channel and Severn Estuary. *Marine Pollution Bulletin, 15*: 66-70.

Williams, R., & Collins, N.R. 1984. Distribution and variability in abundance of *Schistomysis spiritus* (Crustacea: Mysidacea) in the Bristol Channel in relation to environmental variables, with comments on other mysids. *Marine Biology, 80*: 197-206.

Williams, R., & Collins, N.R. 1985. Chaetognaths and ctenophores in the holoplankton of the Bristol Channel. *Marine Biology, 85*: 97-105.

Williams, R., & Conway, D.V.P. 1980. Vertical distribution of *Calanus finmarchicus* and *C. helgolandicus* (Crustacea: Copepoda). *Marine Biology, 60*: 57-61.

Williams, R., & Fragopoulu, N. 1985. Vertical distribution and nocturnal migrations of *Nyctiphanes couchi* (Crustacea: Euphausiacea) in relation to the summer thermocline in the Celtic Sea. *Marine Biology, 89*: 257-262.

C. Contact names and addresses

Type of information	*Contact address and telephone no.*
Continuous Plankton Recorder (CPR) survey data	Director, Sir Alister Hardy Foundation for Ocean Science, The Laboratory, Citadel Hill, Plymouth PL1 2PB, tel: 01752 633100
Plankton research	Head of Department, Department of Oceanography, Southampton University, University Road, Southampton SO9 5NH, tel: 01703 595000 ext. 3642
Bristol Channel data	Director, Plymouth Marine Laboratory, Prospect Place, The Hoe, Plymouth PL1 3DH, tel: 01752 633130
Ichthyoplankton	*MAFF DFR, Fisheries Laboratory, Lowestoft, tel: 01502 562244
Lundy plankton	The Warden, Lundy, Bristol Channel, via Bideford, Devon EX39 2LY, tel: 01237 431831

*Starred contact addresses are given in full in the Appendix.

Woods in Region 11 resemble a subtropical rainforest in the lushness of their vegetation. Because of the mild, moist climate and unpolluted atmosphere, they host a rich array of bryophytes, lichens and other lower plants, including slime moulds. Some parkland trees are swathed in warmth-loving epiphytic lichens, such as those pictured here at the Dizzard, Cornwall. Photo: Pat Doody, JNCC.

Chapter 5 Important species

5.1 Terrestrial lower plants

N.G. Hodgetts

5.1.1 Introduction

This section covers lichens, bryophytes (mosses and liverworts), stoneworts (a group of freshwater and brackish algae - the latter are covered in section 5.4) and fungi occurring in the coastal 10 km squares of the region. This region is of considerable importance for lower plants, especially those that have an oceanic, Lusitanian or Mediterranean-Atlantic distribution pattern. Many of the lower plants found in the region are not known elsewhere in Britain, being at the northern limit of their European range, and many also have a very restricted international distribution. About 51% of the British bryophyte flora and about 48% of the stonewort flora occur in the region. Similar figures are not available for other groups, but a high percentage of the lichen and fungus floras can be expected, because of the oceanic climate and the great variety of habitats.

A number of the region's habitats are particularly favoured by lower plants. The Cornish coast, especially on the Lizard peninsula, is one of the richest stretches of cliff and cliff-top coastline in Britain for lichens and bryophytes. In addition the region's dune systems are particularly rich in liverworts and fungi. Coastal ravine woodlands in the region contain a distinctive range of oceanic species, particularly slime moulds. The Isles of Scilly form a unique lower plant locality and an outpost for many Lusitanian species at the edge of their range.

5.1.2 Important locations and species

Table 5.1.1 lists all the sites in the region that are known to be important for lower plants and that have had at least some degree of survey work. Many are large, in which case the grid reference given refers to a reasonably central point. Most of the sites were selected for conservation on the basis of their bryophyte and lichen interest. Many of the sites contain rare and scarce species and qualify for Site of Special Scientific Interest (SSSI) status on the basis of their lower plant flora (Hodgetts 1992). There are notably few important sites for lower plants in the south Wales part of the region. Locations are shown on Map 5.1.1.

Like higher plants, lower plant species tend to occur in characteristic assemblages that are found in particular habitats. Lichens are particularly well represented on cliff rocks, while skeletal soils on cliff-tops harbour unique bryophyte communities. Coastal hard rock cliffs and cliff-top grassland and heath, for example, support some of the most distinctive south-western species assemblages. In particular, the Lizard peninsula, where the substrate rock is serpentinite, is of great importance, with several species

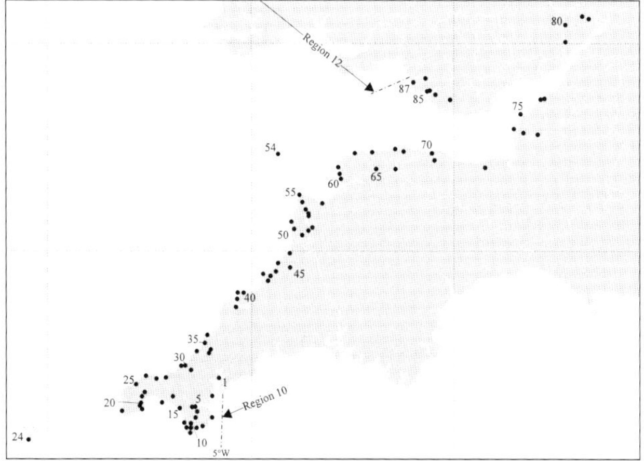

Map 5.1.1 Sites (in coastal 10 km squares) known to be important for lower plants. Site numbers refer to those in Table 5.1.1. Source: JNCC Red Data Book database.

having their only British occurrences here. More unstable cliffs can also be important for lower plants, as at Saunton Down in Devon. There is a distinctive, and threatened, community of both lower and higher plants that occurs only in wheel ruts and other bare hollows on heathland on the Lizard. There are also important dune systems in Devon and Cornwall, although they are relatively small. Some dune sites support good populations of the liverwort *Petalophyllum ralfsii* and the lichen *Fulgensia fulgens*, along with several other species virtually restricted to this habitat. Braunton Burrows in particular is rich in fungi, with 141 species recorded. Many of the fungi on sand dunes are mycorrhizal with (depend on a close association with the root systems of) higher plants, with willow and marram grass apparently being important associates.

Old mine workings and china clay quarries are a characteristically Cornish landscape feature supporting a unique and specialised lower plant flora. Some bryophytes and lichens are specialists of soils that are rich in heavy metals, and these species may be virtually confined to spoil tips of old lead and copper mines. Woodland on the fringes of Exmoor and sheltered wooded ravines in Cornwall and Devon are important for their oceanic bryophytes, lichens and fungi, particularly myxomycetes (slime moulds). Many oceanic species (most notably small liverworts of the family Lejeuneaceae) are confined to this habitat. Fungi are important as wood decomposers. The species composition of woods in the region tends to be slightly different from that of woods further north, with a greater preponderance of warmth-loving species. The trees in some parklands in the region support a good epiphytic lichen flora.

There are several lower plant species that occur only on the Isles of Scilly, apart from on the Lizard. Important

Table 5.1.1 Lower plant sites in coastal 10 km squares

Site no.	*Site name*	*Grid ref.*	*Protected status*
	Cornwall		
1	Trelissick Park	SW8339	Part NT
2	Pennance Point	SW8030	Not protected
3	Gweek Wood	SW7025	Not protected
4	Coverack to Porthoustock	SW8020	SSSI, part NT
5	Mawgan, Trelowarren Mills	SW7125	Not protected
6	Trelowarren Wood	SW7223	Not protected
7	Kennack to Coverack	SW7516	SSSI, part NT
8	Goonhilly Downs	SW7120	SSSI, part NNR
9	Caerthillian to Kennack	SW7215	SSSI, part NT
10	Hayle Kimbro Pool	SW6917	SSSI
11	Kynance Cove	SW6913	SSSI, part NNR, part NT
12	West Lizard	SW6715	SSSI, part NNR, part NT
13	Ruan Pool	SW6915	SSSI
14	Mullion Cliffs to Predannack Cliff	SW6617	SSSI, part NNR
15	Loe Pool	SW6425	SSSI
16	Tregonning Hill	SW6030	SSSI
17	Cudden Point to Prussia Cove	SW5527	SSSI
18	Trevaylor Valley	SW4632	Not protected
19	Castle Horneck	SW4530	Not protected
20	Chyenhal Moor	SW4427	SSSI
21	Trevelloe	SW4425	Not protected
22	Lamorna Cove	SW4524	Not protected
23	Porthgwarra to Pordenack Point	SW3523	SSSI
24	Isles of Scilly	SV9010	Part SSSI
25	Carn Galver & Hannibal's Carn	SW4236	Part NT
26	Cape Cornwall to Clodgy Point	SW4740	SSSI
27	Carbis Bay to Porthminster Point	SW5239	Part NT
28	Gwithian to Mexico Towans	SW5739	SSSI
29	Godrevy Head to St. Agnes	SW6445	SSSI, part NT
30	Nance Wood	SW6645	SSSI
31	Gilbert's Combe	SW6943	Not protected
32	Cligga Head	SW7252	SSSI
33	Goonhavern	SW7953	Part CWT
34	Ventongimps Moor	SW7851	SSSI
35	Penhale Sands	SW7656	Part SSSI
36	Kelsey Head	SW7760	SSSI
37	Dennis Hill, Padstow	SW9274	Not protected
38	Rock Dunes	SW9277	Not protected
39	Pentire Peninsula	SW9280	SSSI
40	Portquin Bay	SW9580	Part NT
41	Trewarmett quarries	SX0786	Not protected
42	Tintagel Cliffs	SX0589	SSSI, part NT
43	St. Nectan's Glen	SX0888	SSSI
44	Peter's Wood	SX1190	Not protected
45	Kernick & Ottery Meadows	SX1892	SSSI
46	Boscastle to Widemouth	SX1294	SSSI, part NT
47	Millook Woods	SX1899	Not protected
	Cornwall (continued)		
48	Norton Wood	SS2408	Not protected
49	Tamar Lake	SS2911	Not protected
50	Coombe Valley	SS2111	Not protected
51	Lymsworthy Meadows	SS2710	SSSI
52	Steeple Point to Marsland Mouth	SS1914	SSSI
53	Meddon Moor	SS2717	SSSI
	Devon		
54	Lundy	SS1346	SSSI
55	Marsland to Clovelly Coast	SS2327	SSSI
56	Deptford Farm Pastures	SS2718	SSSI
57	Bursdon Moor	SS2620	SSSI
58	Hartland Vale	SS2424	Not protected
59	Hobby to Peppercombe	SS3423	SSSI
60	Braunton Burrows	SS4335	SSSI; part NNR
61	Saunton Down	SS4338	Not protected
62	Saunton to Baggy Point Coast	SS4241	SSSI
63	Torrs Walk, Ilfracombe	SS5047	Not protected
64	Wild Pear Beach & Little Hangman	SS5848	Not protected
65	Arlington	SS6040	SSSI
66	West Exmoor Coast & Woods	SS7049	SSSI
67	Watersmeet	SS7448	SSSI
68	North Exmoor (part)	SS7040	SSSI
	Somerset		
69	North Exmoor (part)	SS8944	SSSI
70	Porlock Marsh	SS8847	SSSI
71	The Quantocks: Hodder's Combe	ST1440	SSSI
72	Crook Peak to Shute Shelve Hill	ST4056	SSSI
73	Brean Down	ST2959	SSSI
	Avon		
74	Purn Hill	ST3357	SSSI
75	Middle Hope	ST3266	SSSI
76	Walton Common	ST4273	SSSI
77	Gordano Valley	ST4373	NNR
	Gloucestershire		
78	Soudley Ponds	SO6611	SSSI
79	Speech House Oaks	SO6212	SSSI
80	Astridge Wood	SO5408	SSSI
81	Shorn Cliff & Caswell Wood	SO5400	SSSI
	South Glamorgan		
82	New Breach Fields	SS9773	Not protected
83	Candleston Castle	SS8777	Not protected
	Mid Glamorgan		
84	Afon Alun Valley	SS9075	Not protected
85	Merthyr Mawr Warren	SS8677	SSSI
86	Cefn Cribwr Meadows	SS8583	SSSI
87	Kenfig Pool & Dunes	SS7981	NNR

Sources: references listed in section 5.1.5 A and JNCC protected sites database. Key: NNR = National Nature Reserve; SSSI = Site of Special Scientific Interest; NT = National Trust; CWT = Cornwall Wildlife Trust. Note: site numbers refer to Map 5.1.1.

habitats include hard rock coast, coastal heath and grassland, bulb fields and, on Tresco, an excellent epiphytic lichen community (although this has been much reduced recently by unusually hard frosts).

Calcareous grassland is often rich in lower plants, including rare and threatened species, and good examples of this habitat, such as at Brean Down, occur near the coast in Somerset and Avon. Some specialist aquatic or semi-aquatic species of all groups occur where there are streams or rivers. Reservoir and pool margins support important specialist bryophyte communities of bare mud that is exposed in drought years. Small coastal bogs and areas of wet heath are rich in bryophytes, particularly *Sphagnum* spp., and also support some specialist fungi. Stonewort communities occur in some open waters, ditches (e.g. in the Somerset Levels) and temporary pools (particularly on the Lizard).

The region contains a number of threatened species, some of which are given special protection under national and international legislation. Table 5.1.2 lists the Red Data

Table 5.1.2 Red Data Book lower plants found in the region

Species	*Locations/habitat*
Liverwort	
Cephaloziella dentata	In shallow depressions and old tracks, Ruan Pool, Cornwall
Cephaloziella massalongi	Moist, copper-rich waste in old mine workings, most notably near Redruth and Gwennap, Cornwall
Cephaloziella turneri	Crumbling acid soil, several sites in Cornwall and one in Gloucestershire
Marsupella profunda[a, b]	Crumbling granite in old china clay workings west of Helston
Petalophyllum ralfsii[a, b]	Short, damp turf in sand dunes, Penhale Sands, Cornwall, Braunton Burrows, Devon, and Kenfig, Mid Glamorgan
Riccia bifurca[b]	Damp hollows on heathy tracks, the Lizard, Cornwall
Riccia crystallina	Bulb fields and paths in the Isles of Scilly, Cornwall
Riccia huebeneriana	On mud at reservoir margin, Tamar Lake, Cornwall
Sphaerocarpos texanus	Bulb fields in the Isles of Scilly, Cornwall
Telaranea nematodes	Peaty soil, Trevelloe, south-west of Penzance, Cornwall
Mosses	
Barbula cordata (Didymodon cordatus)[b]	Crumbling sandstone soil, Saunton Down, Devon
Bryum warneum	Dune slacks, Braunton Burrows, Devon
Bryum gemmiparum	Rock crevices in streams, Welcombe Mouth and Malmesmead, Devon
Fissidens serrulatus	Riverside rocks and gravel, Castle Horneck, Cornwall
Habrodon perpusillus	Epiphytic, Candleston Castle, Glamorgan
Tortula cuneifolia	Bare soil at scattered coastal localities from Cornwall to Avon
Weissia levieri	Thin calcareous soil, Brean Down, Somerset
Weissia multicapsularis	Moist, non-calcareous soil, near Wadebridge and Pentire Point, Cornwall
Stoneworts	
Chara baltica	Slightly saline pools, the Lizard, Cornwall, and Braunton Burrows, Devon
Chara fragifera	Clear, shallow moorland pools and vehicle ruts, the Lizard, Cornwall
Tolypella intricata	Alkaline water in ditch, Gordano Valley, Avon
Lichens	
Acarospora subrufula	Exposed granite rocks, Isles of Scilly
Arthonia anglica	On bark in ancient woodland, Millook Valley, Cornwall, and Peppercombe, Devon
Bacidia incompta	On tree trunks, the Lizard, Cornwall, Valley of Rocks, Devon, and New Breach Fields, Glamorgan
Caloplaca aractina	Coastal rocks, Kynance Cove, the Lizard, Cornwall
Caloplaca luteoalba[b]	Epiphytic; unlocalised records, Devon, Somerset and Glamorgan
Caloplaca virescens	Epiphytic; unlocalised record, the Lizard, Cornwall
Cladonia convoluta	Sunny calcareous coastal slopes, Crook Peak, Somerset, Purn Hill, Avon, and an unlocalised record from north Devon
Cladonia mediterranea	Calcareous soil, Kynance Cove, the Lizard, Cornwall
Collema latzeli	Sunny coastal rocks, several sites on the Lizard, Cornwall
Cryptolechia carneolutea	Epiphytic, Landewednack and Coverack, Cornwall, and Hartland Vale, Devon
Endocarpon pusillum	Calcareous soil in railway cutting, Afon Alun Valley, Glamorgan
Heterodermia isidiophora	On mosses, Kynance Cove, the Lizard, Cornwall
Heterodermia leucomelos[b]	Exposed coastal rocks and turf, several localities in the Isles of Scilly and mainland Cornwall
Heterodermia propagulifera[b]	Exposed peaty soil, Tresco, Isles of Scilly
Lecanactis amylacea	On ancient oak bark, Trelissick, Cornwall
Lecanora strobilina	Unlocalised record, Isles of Scilly
Lecidea sarcogynoides	On exposed granite; unlocalised record, Isles of Scilly
Opegrapha subelevata	On slate, Torrs Walk, Ilfracombe, Devon
Parmelia minarum[b]	On bark of oak near Fal Estuary, Trelissick, Cornwall
Parmelia quercina	On walnut, Horner Valley, Somerset, and on elm and several unlocalised records from Devon
Parmelia tinctina	On rocks, Kynance Cove, the Lizard, Cornwall
Physcia tribacioides[b]	On nutrient-enriched tree bark and boulders, Kynance Cove and the Lizard, Cornwall
Porina sudetica	On heavy metal-rich soil and rocks near mine workings, Botallack and Porthglaze Cove, Cornwall
Pseudocyphellaria aurata	Heather stems in coastal heath, Wingletang Down, St. Agnes, Isle of Scilly
Ramalina chondrina	On soil and shaded rocks, Land's End, Cornwall
Schismatomma graphidioides	On ash trees, Horner Combe, Somerset
Solenopsora liparina[b]	On serpentinite rocks, Kynance Cove, the Lizard, Cornwall
Sticta canariensis	On rocks and trees (unlocalised records, Devon and Cornwall)
Teloschistes flavicans[b]	Nutrient-rich rocks, bark, soil etc. at scattered coastal localities throughout the region

Source: JNCC lower plants database. Key: [a]protected under Annex II of the EC Habitats & Species Directive and Appendix I of the Bern Convention; [b]protected under Schedule 8 of the Wildlife & Countryside Act.

Book (RDB - i.e. nationally rare) species found in the region (out of a total of 137 bryophytes, twelve stoneworts and 179 lichens on the British Red Lists), excluding extinct species. The moss *Ditrichum cornubicum* is endemic to Cornwall (i.e. occurs nowhere else) and is confined to a single site. The liverwort *Marsupella profunda* is the only British plant listed in the EC Habitats & Species Directive as a 'priority species', for which Special Areas of Conservation must be selected. One additional bryophyte, the liverwort *Cephaloziella nicholsonii,* is endemic to Great Britain. In addition, the region contains 97 out of 313 nationally scarce bryophytes and four of the nine nationally scarce stoneworts (figures for nationally scarce species are provisional). There is currently not enough information to provide even provisional regional lists of nationally scarce lichens and fungi.

5.1.3 Human activities

Current issues that may have a bearing on the lower plant flora of the region include urban expansion, road construction programmes, holiday and leisure developments, marine pollution and acid rain. Lowering of the water table may have an effect on wetland sites, particularly bogs and wet heath. Wet heaths are vulnerable to scrub encroachment and eventual drying out, often the result of insufficient or no grazing. Overgrazing in woodlands has an effect on the lower plant communities in the long term, as the average age of the trees increases. Most of the old derelict mine sites rich in heavy metals are potential targets for redevelopment. Cliff-top grassland and heathland are subject to erosion in some places, particularly close to conurbations: the fragile mosaics of thin vegetation are prone to replacement with coarse grassy swards when enriched with manure or fertiliser. A close species-rich sward with bare soil should be maintained at important coastal grassland sites: a certain amount of instability and a low level of nutrient input is often desirable to achieve this. Pollution is a general problem but may be aggravated in some areas by new power stations, oil spillages etc. Many of the larger and more important sites in the region are National Nature Reserves (NNRs) or SSSIs and therefore nature conservation is taken into account in their management.

5.1.4 Information sources used

Data are generally good for bryophytes and the larger lichens but are less complete for fungi, algae and the smaller lichens. In general, Cornwall has better survey coverage than Devon, although a smaller proportion of the sites have protected status.

The computerised database at the Biological Records Centre (BRC), Monks Wood, and the Red Data Book database at JNCC include recent records collected over decades by expert bryologists as well as important historical records. Some important, or potentially important, coastal lichen sites have been identified in recent surveys (Fletcher 1984; James & Wolseley 1991), but as relatively few have been comprehensively surveyed, there may be more sites of importance for lichens than are shown in Tables 5.1.1 and 5.1.2. All British Mycological Society foray data are currently being put onto a computer database at the International Mycological Institute under a JNCC contract. Computerised stonewort data are held at BRC and JNCC.

5.1.5 Further sources of information

A. References cited

Fletcher, A., *ed.* 1984. Survey and assessment of lowland lichen heath habitats. *Nature Conservancy Council, CSD Report,* No. 522.

Hodgetts, N.G. 1992. *Guidelines for selection of biological SSSIs: non-vascular plants.* Peterborough, Joint Nature Conservation Committee.

James, P.W., & Wolseley, P.A. 1991. *A preliminary report of coastal lichen sites in England, Wales and Scotland.* Peterborough, unpublished report to the Nature Conservancy Council.

B. Further reading

British Lichen Society Woodland Lichens Working Party. 1993. Revised assessment of epiphytic lichen habitats - 1993. *Joint Nature Conservation Committee Report,* No. 170.

Fletcher, A., *ed.* 1982. Survey and assessment of epiphytic lichen habitats. *Nature Conservancy Council, CSD Report,* No. 384.

Hawksworth, D.L. 1972. The natural history of Slapton Ley Nature Reserve. IV. Lichens. *Field Studies, 3*: 535-578.

Hill, M.O., Preston, C.D., & Smith, A.J.E. 1991. *Atlas of the bryophytes of Britain and Ireland. Volume 1. Liverworts.* Colchester, Harley Books.

Hill, M.O., Preston, C.D., & Smith, A.J.E. 1992. *Atlas of the bryophytes of Britain and Ireland. Volume 2. Mosses (except Diplolepideae).* Colchester, Harley Books.

Hill, M.O., Preston, C.D., & Smith, A.J.E. 1994. *Atlas of the bryophytes of Britain and Ireland. Volume 3. Mosses (Diplolepideae).* Colchester, Harley Books.

Ing, B. 1992. A provisional red data list of British fungi. *The Mycologist, 6*(3): 124-128.

Paton, J.A. 1969. A bryophyte flora of Cornwall. *Transactions of the British Bryological Society, 5*: 669-756.

Ratcliffe, D.A., *ed.* 1977. *A nature conservation review.* Cambridge, Cambridge University Press.

Rotheroe, M. 1992. A survey of the mycoflora of British sand dunes 1991-92. *Joint Nature Conservation Committee Report,* No. 60.

C. Contact names and addresses

Type of information	Contact address and telephone no.
Lichens (hard rock coasts)	T. Duke, Sandrock, The Compa, Kinver, Staffs. DY7 6HS, tel: 01384 872798
Lichens (general coastal)	P.W. James, c/o Department of Botany, The Natural History Museum, Cromwell Road, London SW7 5BD, tel: 0171 938 9123
Lichens (woodland, coastal and general: British Lichen Society database)	Dr A. Fletcher, Leicestershire Ecology Centre, Holly Hayes, 216 Birstall Road, Birstall, Leicester LE4 4DG, tel: 0116 267 1950
Fungi (general and sand dune)	M. Rotheroe, Fern Cottage, Falcondale, Lampeter, Dyfed SA48 7RX, tel: 01570 422041
Fungi (British Mycological Society database)	Dr P. Cannon, International Institute of Mycology, Bakeham Lane, Englefield Green, Egham, Surrey TW20 9TY, tel: 01784 470111
Bryophytes (BRC database)	*C.D. Preston, Biological Records Centre, Institute of Terrestrial Ecology, Monks Wood, tel: 01487 773381
Freshwater stoneworts	Director, Institute of Freshwater Ecology - Head Office, Windermere Laboratory, Far Sawrey, Ambleside, Cumbria LA21 0LP, tel: 015394 42468
Bryophytes (British Bryological Society herbarium)	A.R. Perry, Department of Botany, National Museum of Wales, Cardiff CF1 3NP, tel: 01222 397951
Lower plants (species status; Red Data Book Database; site register etc.)	*N.G. Hodgetts, JNCC, Peterborough, tel: 01733 62626

*Starred contact addresses are given in full in the Appendix.

Nearly a quarter of all the UK's rare and half its scarce flowering plants and ferns occur in the region, and several are found nowhere else in the country. Although not uncommon nationally (unlike the rare autumn squill, which also grows in the region), the delicate lavender blooms of spring squill (pictured) make a characteristic and colourful contribution to the region's grassland flora. Photo: Pat Doody, JNCC.

5.2 Flowering plants and ferns

V.M. Morgan

5.2.1 Introduction

This section describes the importance of the region for vascular plants (i.e. flowering plants and ferns), particularly species that are rare or scarce in Great Britain, occurring in the region's coastal 10 km national grid squares, whether or not they are regarded as 'coastal' species. Region 11 is of international importance for its many rare and scarce higher plant species (Table 5.2.1).

Table 5.2.1 Numbers of rare and scarce higher plant species in coastal 10 km squares of the region*

	Protected species	*Other Red Data Book species*	*Scarce species*
Cornwall	8	25	55
Isles of Scilly	2	7	24
Devon	7	8	39
Somerset	3	14	50
Avon	5	15	54
Gloucestershire	1	3	42
Gwent	1	5	36
South Glamorgan	1	5	23
Mid Glamorgan	1	5	24
Region 11	***22***	***51***	***112***

Source: JNCC rare plants database; Stewart *et al.* (1994); BRC database. Key: *excludes known introductions and records from before 1970.

Classic British botanical localities include the Lizard peninsula, the Isles of Scilly, Braunton Burrows and the Avon Gorge. The interest of the region derives in part from the climate, which is characterised by mild winters: snow is very rare in the Isles of Scilly and uncommon in the rest of the region. Rainfall is moderate, but slightly higher in parts of north Cornwall and Devon that are exposed to the westerly Atlantic gales and lower in more sheltered areas such as the Taw-Torridge Estuary (Keble Martin & Fraser 1939). A number of different geographic elements are found in the flora as a result of the climatic history of the last 25,000 years; for example 42% of the British species that are of 'Mediterranean' character are found in the Isles of Scilly. Several taxa rely on the mild winters, which allow continuous growth, for example Babington's leek *Allium ampeloprasum* var. *babingtonii* and Italian lords-and-ladies *Arum italicum* subsp. *neglectum* (Lousley 1971).

Rare and scarce plants grow in a wide range of habitats, but of particular importance in the region are heaths, including 'waved' heaths formed in extremely exposed conditions and the unique heaths of the Lizard peninsula, calcareous grassland, cliffs, beaches and sand dunes. In addition to the key localities shown on Map 5.2.1, which are noted for rarities, there are a number of moderately species-rich sites throughout the region. Centres of plant biodiversity such as those in Map 5.2.1 result from a combination of geology, climate and history. The world-famous flora of the Lizard peninsula grows on ultra-basic rocks, and seven of the other key localities contain lime-rich rocks or sand, which typically support a diverse flora.

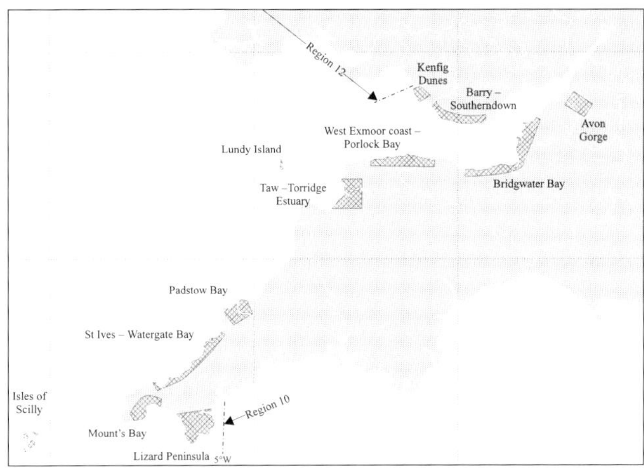

Map 5.2.1 Key localities for rare and scarce higher plants. Sites are listed in Table 5.2.2. Source: JNCC Rare Plants Database.

5.2.2 Important locations and species

Some of Europe and Britain's most threatened species are present in the region, including four that are listed on Annexes IIb and IVb of the EC Habitats & Species Directive. The Killarney fern *Trichomanes speciosum* is listed on the EC Habitats & Species Directive and the Bern Convention. It has two forms: the larger, vascular form is extremely rare and is found at one location in the region. The tiny, non-vascular form resembles a liverwort and has recently been discovered to be relatively widespread, being known from over eighty 10 km squares in Great Britain, of which five are in the region. It is expected that more sites will be found (F. Rumsey pers. comm.). The shore dock *Rumex rupestris* is Europe's most endangered dock and the total British population of around 250-300 plants (L. McDonnell pers. comm.) is of international importance. 22 species in the region are among the 107 vascular plants listed on Schedule 8 of the Wildife & Countryside Act (1981). There are 73 species in the region defined as nationally rare or 'Red Data Book' (RDB) species (out of 317 in Great Britain according to Perring & Farrell 1983).

Of the 254 scarce species in Great Britain (i.e. known from between sixteen and one hundred 10 km squares), 112 occur in this region (Stewart *et al.* 1994). Two of these, Vigur's eyebright *Euphrasia vigursii* and early gentian *Gentianella anglica*, are endemic (confined) to England, the latter being represented in the region by the subspecies *cornubiensis*, which is itself found only on the north coasts of Cornwall and Devon. Western ramping-fumitory *Fumaria occidentalis* is endemic to Cornwall and the Isles of Scilly, and Lundy cabbage *Coincya wrightii* is endemic to Lundy Island. Fourteen other species are not known elsewhere in Britain. Areas with important populations of protected species and/or five or more rare species are listed in Table 5.2.2 and shown on Map 5.2.1. Tables 5.2.3 and 5.2.4 list protected and other rare species in the region.

Table 5.2.2 Key localities for nationally rare (RDB) and scarce plants (records post 1970)

Locality	*Status*	*Species*
Lizard Peninsula	Part NNR, part SSSI, part undesignated	RDB species: Cornish heath *Erica vagans*, Dorset heath *Erica ciliaris*, dwarf rush *Juncus capitatus*, four-leaved allseed *Polycarpon tetraphyllum*, fringed rupturewort *Herniaria ciliolata*, hairy greenweed *Genista pilosa*, land quillwort *Isoetes histrix*, long-headed clover *Trifolium incarnatum* subsp. *molineri*, nit-grass *Gastridium ventricosum*, pennyroyal *Mentha pulegium*, pigmy rush *Juncus pygmaeus*, prostrate toadflax *Linaria supina*, sea knotgrass *Polygonum maritimum*, shore dock *Rumex rupestris*, slender bird's-foot-trefoil *Lotus angustissimus*, spotted cat's-ear *Hypochoeris maculata*, three-lobed crowfoot *Ranunculus tripartitus*, twin-headed clover *Trifolium bocconei*, upright clover *Trifolium strictum*, Vigur's eyebright *Euphrasia vigursii*, western ramping-fumitory *Fumaria occidentalis*, wild asparagus *Asparagus officinalis* subsp. *prostratus*
Mount's Bay	Part SSSI, part undesignated	RDB species: Bermuda-grass *Cynodon dactylon*, Dorset heath, Greek sea-spurrey *Spergularia bocconii*, shore dock, three-lobed crowfoot, western ramping-fumitory
Isles of Scilly	part SSSI, part undesignated	RDB species: dwarf pansy *Viola kitaibeliana*, four-leaved allseed, Greek sea-spurrey, least adder's-tongue *Ophioglossum lusitanicum*, orange bird's-foot *Ornithopus pinnatus*, purple viper's-bugloss *Echium plantagineum*, shore dock, smaller tree-mallow *Lavatera cretica*, western ramping-fumitory
St. Ives to Watergate Bay	Part SSSI, part undesignated	RDB species: Bermuda-grass, Cornish heath, Dorset heath, early gentian *Gentianella anglica*, hairy-fruited cornsalad *Valerianella eriocarpa*, hairy greenweed, Irish spurge *Euphorbia hyberna*, little-Robin *Geranium purpureum*, pennyroyal, shore dock, slender bird's-foot-trefoil, spotted cat's-ear, Vigur's eyebright, western ramping-fumitory, wild asparagus
Padstow Bay	Part SSSI, part undesignated	RDB species: field eryngo *Eryngium campestre*, hairy-fruited cornsalad, little-Robin, slender bird's-foot-trefoil, western ramping-fumitory, wild asparagus
Lundy Island	SSSI	RDB species: Lundy cabbage *Coincya wrightii*
Taw-Torridge Estuary	Part NNR, part SSSI	RDB species: early gentian, fen orchid *Liparis loeselii*, hairy-fruited cornsalad, pennyroyal, sea stock, round-headed club-rush *Holoschoenus vulgaris*, sea stock *Matthiola sinuata*, slender bird's-foot-trefoil, water germander *Teucrium scordium*
West Exmoor coast to Porlock Bay	Part SSSI, part undesignated	RDB species: Irish spurge, May lily *Maianthemum bifolium*, whitebeams *Sorbus anglica*, *S. subcuneata*, *S. vexans*
Bridgwater Bay	Part NNR, part SSSI, part undesignated	RDB species: Bermuda-grass, branched horsetail *Equisetum ramosissimum*, Cheddar pink *Dianthus gratianopolitanus*, compact brome *Bromus madritensis*, goldilocks aster *Aster linosyris*, honewort *Trinia glauca*, lizard orchid *Himantoglossum hircinum*, nit-grass, purple gromwell *Lithospermum purpurocaeruleum*, rough marsh-mallow *Althaea hirsuta*, round-headed club-rush, Somerset hair-grass *Koeleria vallesiana*, smooth rupture-wort *Herniaria glabra*, wall germander *Teucrium chamaedrys*, white rock-rose *Helianthemum apenninum*
Avon Gorge	Part SSSI, part undesignated	RDB species: Bristol rock-cress *Arabis stricta*, compact brome, honewort, little-Robin, nit-grass, round-headed leek *Allium sphaerocephalon*, whitebeams *Sorbus anglica*, *S. bristoliensis*, *S. eminens*, *S. wilmottiana*
Barry to Southerndown	Part SSSI, part undesignated	RDB species: compact brome, hoary stock *Matthiola incana*, nit-grass, purple gromwell, tuberous thistle *Cirsium tuberosum*
Kenfig Dunes	SSSI, LNR, NNR	RDB species: fen orchid, sea stock

Sources: JNCC rare plants database; Stewart *et al.* (1994); SSSI citation sheets; BRC database. Key: SSSI - Site of Special Scientific Interest; NNR - National Nature Reserve; LNR - Local Nature Reserve.

5.2.3 Human activities

In the past, some species have been threatened by collecting, particularly in the era of botanical exchange clubs around the end of the last century, when herbarium specimens were swapped amongst botanists. Problems of collecting have now passed, but the precise localities of potentially collectable species such as Plymouth pear are still kept strictly confidential, to prevent unwelcome attention.

Many of the rare species depend on the maintenance of open vegetation and cannot compete if vigorous or weedy species dominate. Species such as four-leaved allseed and sea knotgrass depend on trampling. Changes in land use, such as afforestation and agricultural intensification, can also affect rare species. Agricultural changes including intensification and reduced grazing have affected many species, including pennyroyal, western ramping-fumitory and least adder's-tongue (R. FitzGerald & R. Parslow pers. comm.). Attempts to stabilise dunes by planting sea buckthorn *Hippophae rhamnoides* have damaged some communities (Gillham 1987). Any rises in sea-level as a result of climate change would affect species of shorelines, especially shore dock.

Construction projects such as sea defences, culverting of streams and tourist developments can lead to loss of habitats and have affected such species as shore dock. As most of the important sites for rare species have been designated as Sites of Special Scientific Interest (SSSI), these factors now affect scarce species more than rare ones; examples of affected scarce species include early gentian (Morgan & Palmer 1991).

5.2.4 Information sources used

All the counties in the region were covered by rare plant surveys between 1982 and 1989, and a series of detailed confidential reports was produced, now in the care of the Countryside Council for Wales (CCW), English Nature and

Table 5.2.3 Recorded occurrence of protected species since 1970, excluding known introductions and extinctions

Species	*Recorded occurrence in:* total no. of 10 km squares in GB	no. of coastal 10 km squares in region	no. of sites in region (approx)	Key localities	Habitat
Round-headed leek *Allium sphaerocephalon**	1	1	1	Avon Gorge	Limestone rocks
Rough marsh-mallow *Althaea hirsuta**	4	1	1	Watchet (ST04)	Dry, open limestone turf
Bristol rock-cress *Arabis stricta*[1]*	2	2	3	Cannington Park (ST24); Avon Gorge	Limestone rocks
Lundy cabbage *Coincya wrightii**	1	1	1	Lundy Island	Cliffs and slopes on granite and slate
Brown galingale *Cyperus fuscus**	7	1	1	Gordano Valley (ST47)	Poached ditches
Cheddar pink *Dianthus gratianopolitanus*[2]*	4	1	1	Bridgwater Bay	Limestone
Branched horsetail *Equisetum ramosissimum*[2]*	2	1	1	Bridgwater Bay	Town park
Field eryngo *Eryngium campestre**	10	1	1	Padstow Bay	Dry grassland
Martin's ramping-fumitory *Fumaria martinii**	2	1	1	Tresamble (SW73)	Cultivated ground
Early gentian *Gentianella anglica***	62	3	Not known	St. Ives to Watergate Bay; Taw-Torridge Estuary	Cliff-tops and dunes
Lizard orchid *Himantoglossum hircinum**	18	2	2	Bridgwater Bay	Calcareous grassland
Fen orchid *Liparis loeselii***	7	2	2	Taw-Torridge Estuary; Kenfig Dunes	Dunes
Grass-poly *Lythrum hyssopifolia**	5	1	1	Slimbridge (SO70)	Shores of muddy lake
Pennyroyal *Mentha pulegium**	15	5	Not known	Lizard Peninsula; St. Ives to Watergate Bay; Taw-Torridge Estuary	Damp places
Least adder's-tongue *Ophioglossum lusitanicum**	1	1	1	Isles of Scilly	Short-grazed heath
Childing pink *Petrorhagia nanteuilii*[2]*	3	1	1	Cardiff (ST27)	Sandy and gravelly grassland
Sea knotgrass *Polygonum maritimum**	4	1	1	Lizard Peninsula	Sandy beaches
Plymouth pear *Pyrus cordata**	3	2	4	Truro area	Hedgerows and green lanes
Shore dock *Rumex rupestris***	13	5	7	Lizard Peninsula; Mount's Bay; Isles of Scilly; St. Ives to Watergate Bay	Damp raised beaches and dune slacks
Meadow clary *Salvia pratensis**	25	1	1	Rogiet (ST48)	Pasture
Water germander *Teucrium scordium**	3	1	2	Taw-Torridge Estuary	Dune slacks
Killarney fern *Trichomanes speciosum***[3]	5	1	1	(Location confidential)	Damp, shady places

Source: JNCC rare plants database and rare plant survey reports. Key: *listed for special protection on schedule 8 of the Wildlife & Countryside Act 1981; **listed on schedule 8 of the Wildlife & Countryside Act 1981 and on annexes IIb & IVb of EC Habitats Directive; [1]at its Somerset sites the Bristol rock-cress was introduced; [2]thought to have been introduced into the region; [3]only the occurrence of the vascular (sporophyte) form of the Killarney fern is noted in the table; the species is also present in the region in its non-vascular (gametophye) form. Notes: grid references are given for non-confidential localities not shown on Map 5.2.1; spiked speedwell *Veronica spicata* is listed on schedule 8 of the Wildlife & Countryside Act 1981 but it has been excluded from this table as the sub-species found in the region, *V. spicata* subsp. *hybrida*, is scarce rather than nationally rare.

the Joint Nature Conservation Committee (JNCC). Further work has been carried out by CCW and English Nature as part of their programme of monitoring. Records of Red Data Book species are maintained in JNCC's rare plants database. Members of the Botanical Society of the British Isles (BSBI) have recently collected up-to-date records of scarce species; these data are held at the Biological Records Centre and have been summarised in *Scarce plants in Britain* (Stewart *et al.* 1994). A Red Data Book for Cornwall is being prepared by the Institute of Cornish Studies.

5.2.5 Acknowledgements

Thanks go to J. Barne, D. Bolton, R. FitzGerald, I. Jamieson, L. McDonnell, R.J. Murphy, R.E. Parslow, K. Turvey, I. Carl, M. Wigginton and staff at the Biological Records Centre.

Table 5.2.4 Recorded occurrence of other RDB species since 1970, excluding known introductions and extinctions

Species	Recorded occurrence in: *total no. of 10 km squares in GB*	*no. of coastal 10 km squares in region*	*no. of sites in region (approx.)*
Wild asparagus *Asparagus officinalis* subsp. *prostratus*	9	6	8
Goldilocks aster *Aster linosyris*	7	2	2
Compact brome *Bromus madritensis*[1]	18	8	11
Tuberous thistle *Cirsium tuberosum*	14	3	5
Bermuda-grass *Cynodon dactylon*[1]	16	5	8
Purple viper's-bugloss *Echium plantagineum*[1]	2	2	2
Dorset heath *Erica ciliaris*	11	4	5
Cornish heath *Erica vagans*	5	5	19
Irish spurge *Euphorbia hyberna*	2	2	4
Upright spurge *Euphorbia serrulata*	11	4	11
Vigur's eye-bright *Euphrasia vigursii*	19	7	15
Blue fescue *Festuca longifolia*[1]	5	1	1
Western ramping-fumitory *Fumaria occidentalis*[2]	*c.* 28	21	*c.* 60
Nit-grass *Gastridium ventricosum*	20	6	12
Hairy greenweed *Genista pilosa*	12	4	11
Little-Robin *Geranium purpureum*	15	4	14
White rock-rose *Helianthemum apenninum*	6	3	4
Fringed rupturewort *Herniaria ciliolata*	3	3	10
Smooth rupturewort *Herniaria glabra*	12	1	1
Round-headed club-rush *Holoschoenus vulgaris*	6	4	4
Spotted cat's-ear *Hypochoeris maculata*	9	2	2
Land quillwort *Isoetes histrix*	2	2	6
Dwarf rush *Juncus capitatus*	3	4	9
Pigmy rush *Juncus pygmaeus*	3	3	9
Somerset hair-grass *Koeleria vallesiana*	5	3	9
Smaller tree-mallow *Lavatera cretica*[1]	8	4	4
Cut-grass *Leersia oryzoides*	8	1	1
Prostrate toadflax *Linaria supina*[1]	7	3	3
Purple gromwell *Lithospermum purpurocaeruleum*	13	4	8
Slender bird's-foot-trefoil *Lotus angustissimus*	24	10	9
May lily *Maianthemum bifolium*[1]	8	1	1
Hoary stock *Matthiola incana*	12	2	2
Sea stock *Matthiola sinuata*	5	2	6
Orange bird's-foot *Ornithopus pinnatus*	3	3	6
Four-leaved allseed *Polycarpon tetraphyllum*	13	4	5
Three-lobed crowfoot *Ranunculus tripartitus*	19	5	13
A whitebeam *Sorbus anglica*	13	4	6
A whitebeam *Sorbus bristoliensis*	1	1	2
A whitebeam *Sorbus domestica*	1	1	1
A whitebeam *Sorbus eminens*	4	2	2
A whitebeam *Sorbus subcuneata*	4	4	9
A whitebeam *Sorbus vexans*	3	3	7
A whitebeam *Sorbus wilmottiana*	1	1	2
Greek sea-spurrey *Spergularia bocconii*[1]	4	3	3
Wall germander *Teucrium chamaedrys*	7	1	1
Twin-headed clover *Trifolium bocconei*	2	2	4
Long-headed clover *Trifolium incarnatum* subsp. *molinerii*	2	2	4
Upright clover *Trifolium strictum*	3	2	7
Honewort *Trinia glauca*	6	3	11
Hairy-fruited cornsalad *Valerianella eriocarpa*	6	3	4
Dwarf pansy *Viola kitaibeliana*	2	2	5

Source: JNCC rare plants database, rare plant survey reports and Stewart *et al.* (1994). Key: [1]may be introduced. [2]records since 1970; now probably fewer locations.

5.2.6 Further sources of information

A. References cited

Gillham, M. 1987. *Sand dunes*. Bridgend, Glamorgan Wildlife Trust. (Glamorgan Heritage Coast Wildlife Series, Vol. 1.)

Keble Martin, W., & Fraser, G.T., *eds*. 1939. *Flora of Devon*. Arbroath, T. Buncle & Co. Ltd.

Lousley, J.E. 1971. *Flora of the Isles of Scilly*. Newton Abbot, David & Charles.

Morgan, H.W., & Palmer, M. 1991. *Second quinquennial review of Schedules 5 and 8, Wildlife and Countryside Act, 1981*. Peterborough, Joint Nature Conservation Committee. (Confidential report JNCC P91/8.)

Perring, F.H., & Farrell, L. 1983. *British Red Data Books: 1. Vascular plants*. Nettleham, Royal Society for Nature Conservation.

Stewart, A., Pearman, D.A., & Preston, C.D. 1994. *Scarce plants in Britain*. Peterborough, Joint Nature Conservation Committee/Institute of Terrestrial Ecology/Botanical Society of the British Isles.

B. Further reading

Davey, F.H. 1909. *Flora of Cornwall.* Penryn, F. Chegwidden.
Ellis, R.G. 1983. *Flowering plants of Wales.* Cardiff, National Museum of Wales.
Farrell, L. 1983. *Isles of Scilly rare plants survey.* Peterborough, Nature Conservancy Council. (Unpublished confidential report.)
FitzGerald, R. 1990. Rare plant survey of south-west England. Volume 2: Devon. *Nature Conservancy Council, CSD Report,* No. 1,059. (Unpublished confidential report.)
FitzGerald, R. 1990. Rare plant survey of south-west England. Volume 3: Cornwall. *Nature Conservancy Council, CSD Report,* No. 1,060. (Unpublished confidential report.)
French, C.N., *ed.* 1994. *Checklist of the flowering plants and ferns of Cornwall and the Isles of Scilly.* Redruth, Institute of Cornish Studies/University of Exeter/Cornwall County Council.
Frost, L.C., Hughes, M.G.B., Nichols, C., & Lawman, J.M. 1982. *A total population estimate of the land quillwort* (Isoetes histrix) *at the Lizard district and recommendations for its conservation.* Bristol, University of Bristol. (Lizard Project Report No. 4.)
Gillham, M. 1993. *Coastal downs: Ogmore and Dunraven.* Bridgend, Glamorgan Wildlife Trust. (Glamorgan Heritage Coast Wildlife Series Vol. 4.)
Heath, J., & Wills, G. 1987. *Devon's wildlife, a guide to nature conservation in Devon.* Exeter, Devon Books.
Hutchinson, G., & Thomas, B.A. 1992. Distribution of Pteridophyta in Wales. *Watsonia, 19*(1): 1-19.
Ivimey-Cook, R.B. 1985. *Atlas of the Devon flora: flowering plants and ferns.* Exeter, Devon Association for the Advancement of Science, Literature and Art.
King, M.P 1989. *An investigation into the current status of the shore dock* Rumex rupestris *in Devon and Cornwall.* University College, London, MSc thesis.
Lawman, J. 1994. *A natural history of the Lizard peninsula.* Redruth, Institute of Cornish Studies/Dyllansow Truranc.
Margetts, L.J. 1988. *The difficult and critical plants of the Lizard district of Cornwall.* Bristol, Grenfell Publications.
Margetts, L.J., & David, R.W. 1981. *A review of the Cornish flora.* Redruth, Institute of Cornish Studies.
Margetts, L.J., & Spurgin, K.L. 1990. *The Cornish flora supplement.* St. Ives, Trendrine Press.
Matthews, J.R. 1955. *Origin and distribution of the British flora.* London, Hutchinson's University Library.
McDonnell, L. 1994. *The current status of* Rumex rupestris *in Britain.* Furzebrook, unpublished report to Institute of Terrestrial Ecology.
Morgan, V.M. 1989. Rare plant survey of Wales (South Wales region): Gwent. *Nature Conservancy Council, CSD Report,* No. 963. (Unpublished confidential report.)
Morgan, V.M. 1989. Rare plant survey of Wales (South Wales region): Mid & South Glamorgan. *Nature Conservancy Council, CSD Report,* No. 961. (Unpublished confidential report.)
Parslow, R.E. 1994. *The current status of* Rumex rupestris *in the Isles of Scilly.* Furzebrook, unpublished report to Institute of Terrestrial Ecology.
Perring F.H., & Walters, S.M. 1990. *Atlas of the British flora.* London, Botanical Society of the British Isles.
Roe, R.G.B. 1981. *Flora of Somerset.* Taunton, Somerset Archaeology and Natural History Society.
Stace, C. 1991. *New flora of the British Isles.* Cambridge, Cambridge University Press.
Taylor, I. 1990. Rare plant survey of South-west England. Volume 5, Avon. *Nature Conservancy Council, CSD Report,* No. 1,062. (Unpublished confidential report.)
Turpin, P.G. 1982. *The heathers of the Lizard district of Cornwall.* Bristol, University of Bristol. (Lizard Project Report, No. 2.)
Wade, A.E., Kay, Q.O.N., & Ellis, R.G. 1994. *Flora of Glamorgan.* Cardiff, Natural History Museum/HMSO.
Wilson, P.J. 1984. *Rare plant species survey. East Cornwall.* Peterborough, Nature Conservancy Council. (Unpublished report.)

C. Contact names and addresses

Type of information	*Contact*
Species on SSSIs and NNRs, other protected areas, rare and scarce species, rare plant surveys, licensing and protected species - England	*Coastal Ecologist, Maritime Team, EN HQ, Peterborough, tel: 01733 340345
Species on SSSIs and NNRs, other protected areas - Wales	*Group Leader, Statutory Protection & Monitoring Group, CCW HQ, Bangor, tel: 01248 370444
Rare and scarce species, rare plant surveys, licensing and protected species - Wales	*Group Leader, Natural Science Group, CCW HQ, Bangor, tel: 01248 370444
Database of rare and protected species	*Species Conservation Branch, JNCC, Peterborough, tel: 01733 62626
Distribution and history of plants in Wales, herbarium records, local floras and archives	Department of Botany, National Museum of Wales, Cardiff CF1 3NP, tel: 01222 397951
Local records of vascular plants - Cornwall	Institute of Cornish Studies, Trevithick Centre, Trevenson Road, Pool, Redruth TR15 3PL, tel: 01209 710424
Local records of vascular plants - Devon	*Conservation Data Manager, Devon Wildlife Trust, Exeter, tel: 01392 79244
Local records of vascular plants - Somerset	The Director, Somerset Environmental Records Centre, Pickney, Kingston St. Mary, Taunton TA2 8AS, tel: 01823 451778
Local records of vascular plants - Avon	Bristol Regional Environmental Records Centre, Ashton Court Visitor Centre, Ashton Court Estate, Long Ashton, Bristol BS18 9JW, tel: 0117 953 2140
Local records of vascular plants - Gloucestershire	Data Manager, Gloucestershire Environmental Data Unit, Church House, Standish, Stonehouse, Gloucestershire GL10 3EU, tel: 01453 822761
Local BSBI vice-county recorders' records - England	*C.D. Preston, ITE, Monk's Wood, Huntingdon, tel: 01487 773381
Local BSBI vice-county recorders' records - Wales	Hon. Secretary, Welsh Committee, Botanical Society of the British Isles, c/o National Museum of Wales, Cardiff CF1 3NP, tel: 01222 397951

*Starred contact addresses are given in full in the Appendix.

5.3 Land and freshwater invertebrates

A.P. Foster & M.S. Parsons

5.3.1 Introduction

There are over 28,000 species in the better known invertebrate groups in Great Britain (Kirby 1992). This section deals with most insect orders, though not all families, together with a wide range of non-insect invertebrates, known from sites within the coastal 10 km Ordnance Survey grid squares of the region. Lagoonal species are covered in section 5.4.

The region is internationally significant for its land and freshwater invertebrates, on a number of counts. Eleven species of terrestrial and freshwater invertebrate listed on international directives or conventions or on Schedule 5 of the Wildlife & Countryside Act have been recorded within the region (Table 5.3.1), although five of these have not been recorded recently. The region is also nationally important for the conservation of many invertebrate species, including some known in the UK in recent times only from this region. Among these are the thyme lacebug *Lasiacantha capucina*, the micro-moth *Nothris congressariella*, the scarce blackneck moth *Lygephila craccae* and the spider *Gnaphosa occidentalis*.

Of the 358 Red Data Book (RDB) and 455 nationally scarce species listed by Kirby (1994a, b) as known to be associated with coastal habitats astonishing numbers, 74 and 207 respectively, are recorded in this region. These totals include recent (since 1969) records for twelve RDB beetles and thirteen RDB solitary bees and wasps. Other species of equivalent rank, but not covered by Kirby, also occur. Map 5.3.1 shows the numbers of all nationally rare (RDB) invertebrate species (including Kirby's 'coastal' species and all others) recorded in coastal 10 km squares in the region. Endemic species include the beetle *Psylliodes luridipennis*, whose only world site is Lundy Island, and the weevil *Cathormiocerus britannicus* which is unknown outside Cornwall. Certain subspecies are also confined to this region: one threatened example, the sandhill rustic moth *Luperina nickerlii leechi*, is unique to one sand bar in west Cornwall, while other subspecies are more widespread in the region although unknown outside it. *Pararge aegeria insula*, for

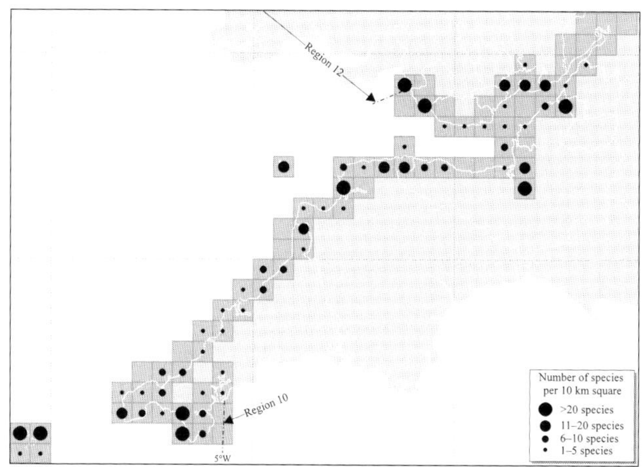

Map 5.3.1 Numbers of nationally rare (i.e. RDB) species of invertebrates recorded in coastal 10 km squares (all dates). Distribution may reflect differences in recording effort. Source: Invertebrate Site Register, JNCC.

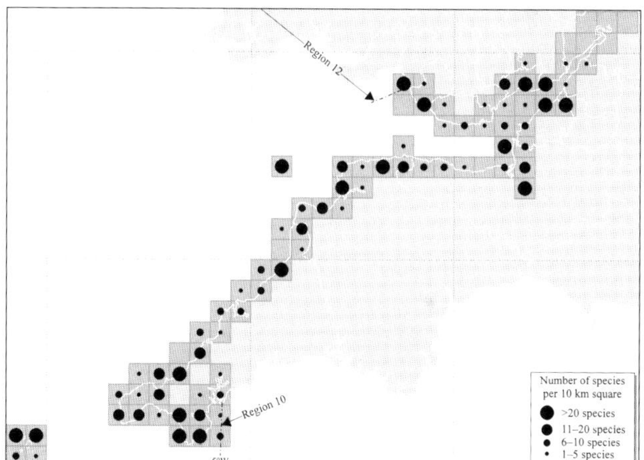

Map 5.3.2 Numbers of nationally scarce species of invertebrates recorded in coastal 10 km squares (all dates). Distribution may reflect differences in recording effort. Source: Invertebrate Site Register, JNCC.

Table 5.3.1 Protected invertebrate species in the region

Species	*Protected status*	*Locations*
Sandbowl snail *Catinella arenaria*	1	Devon
Desmoulin's whorl snail *Vertigo moulinsiana*	2	Devon (last recorded in 1933)
Fairy shrimp *Chirocephalus diaphanus*	1*	Cornwall, Devon, Somerset, Avon (last record pre-1970)
Atlantic stream crayfish *Austropotamobius pallipes*	1**, 2, 4, 6	Gloucestershire, Gwent
Stag beetle *Lucanus cervus*	4, 6	Cornwall, Gwent (last record pre-1970)
Large blue butterfly *Maculinea arion*	1, 3, 5	Cornwall, Devon (reintroduced; native populations extinct)
High brown fritillary butterfly *Argynnis adippe*	1***	Cornwall, Devon, Somerset, Gloucestershire
Marsh fritillary butterfly *Eurodryas aurinia*	2, 5	Cornwall, Devon, Somerset, Avon, Glamorgan
Heath fritillary butterfly *Mellicata athalia*	1	Somerset
Ladybird spider *Eresus niger*	1	Cornwall - unconfirmed sighting 1932
Medicinal leech *Hirudo medicinalis*	1*, 4, 6, 7	Glamorgan

Key to protected status codes: 1 = Wildlife & Countryside Act 1981 (excluding Schedule 5 section 9(5), sale only); *Variation of Schedules Order 1988; **Variation of Schedule Order 1988, but only in respect of section 9(1) taking and sale only; ***Variation of Schedules 5 & 8 Order 1992; 2 = Annex II, EC Habitats & Species Directive; 3 = Annex IV, EC Habitats & Species Directive; 4 = Annex V, EC Habitats & Species Directive; 5 = Annex II, Bern Convention; 6 = Annex III, Bern Convention; 7 = CITES (the Convention on International Trade in Endangered Species of Wild Fauna and Flora).

example, a subspecies of the speckled wood butterfly, occurs only on the Isles of Scilly. Map 5.3.2 maps the recorded distribution of all nationally scarce invertebrates in the region. Note that survey effort has not been equal throughout the region, so actual occurrence may differ from recorded distributions. Also represented are scarce and threatened species that are not strictly coastal in terms of their national distribution but which have populations on coastal sites. Many scarce and threatened invertebrates that are confined to south-western maritime habitats within Great Britain have substantial proportions of their known distribution along this section of coast. These include the hoary footman moth *Eilema caniola*, the Devonshire wainscot moth *Mythimna putrescens*, the click beetle *Cardiophorus erichsoni* and the weevil *Cathormiocerus attaphilus*.

5.3.2 Important locations and species

Table 5.3.2 lists coastal terrestrial or freshwater RDB species as defined by Kirby (1994a, b) that have been recently recorded from the region.

Table 5.3.2 Coastal Red Data Book (RDB) species in region

Species	*Description and notes on recorded occurrence in the region*
RDB1	
Aegialia rufa	3.5-4.5 mm long globular red beetle living among plant litter in sand dunes. Very rare. Known from a small number of dunes on the Welsh and Lancashire/Merseyside coasts. Merthyr Mawr Warren, 1981.
Cathormiocerus attaphilus	*Small (3 mm) globular weevil, eats many plant species but appears to favour buck's-horn plantain *Plantago coronopus*. Maritime cliff grassland; internationally rare with the main centres of distribution in south-west Britain. The Lizard, 1932.
Cathormiocerus britannicus	Endemic weevil, favours ribwort plantain *Plantago lanceolata*. Gunwalloe Fishing Cove, 1985; Kynance, 1979; Penrose Estate, 1958; Porthleven, 1984; The Lizard, 1981; Tintagel area, old record.
Catinella arenaria	Very rare snail, currently known from only two sites in Great Britain. Largest colony is at Braunton Burrows. Smaller population by an upland calcareous flush in Cumbria. A third population, in Glamorganshire, is believed to be extinct. Only reliably distinguished from *Succinea oblonga* by dissection. Braunton Burrows, 1990.
Epitriptus arthriticus	*Large robber fly recorded from Breckland heath and a sand dune. Life history unknown, though the larvae are probably soil-dwelling predators. Only three British records, two in Norfolk and one in Somerset. Berrow Dunes, 1955.
Formica rufibarbis	Large reddish predatory ant found in open sunny situations such as grassy banks. Nest is built underground, often a foot below the surface and with no visible earthworks. 1979 atlas shows records only from Surrey and the Isles of Scilly. The Surrey colonies are possibly now extinct. St. Martin's, 1980.
Geotomus punctulatus	Ground-dwelling shieldbug of coastal sand dunes, confined in Britain to a single Cornish locality. Sennen Cove, 1987.
Gnaphosa occidentalis	*Hunting spider known from two sites in Cornwall early this century. Habitat unknown. Cadgwith Cove, old record; Kynance Cove, 1935.
Halictus maculatus	*Mining bee that nests in light soils, probably in aggregations. Recorded from seven localities in southern England. Porth Kidney Sands, 1968.
Sandhill rustic moth *Luperina nickerlii leechi*	Extremely local subspecies confined to a small shingle beach in Cornwall, the larvae feeding in the stem bases and root crown of sand couch *Elymus farctus*. Loe Pool SSSI, 1989; Penrose Estate (Loe part of the site), 1979.
pRDB1	
Nothris congressariella	Small moth. Larva feeds on the leaves or shoots of balm-leaved figwort *Scrophularia scorodonia*. Bryher, 1993; Gannel Estuary, 1988; Lundy, 1994; St. Martin's, 1989; St. Mary's, 1989; Tresco, 1989.
Panagaeus cruxmajor	*7.5-9 mm long red and black ground beetle, lives only in moist places, occurring at the margins of standing or slow-flowing water amongst rich vegetation. Known recently from only a single coastal site in S. Wales. Merthyr Mawr Warren, 1915.
Paralister obscurus	*6-8 mm shiny black carrion beetle living in dung and preying on other invertebrates. Very rare, with scattered records north to Lancashire. Opportunist species not attached to particular site or habitat. Braunton Burrows, 1949.
RDB2	
Anchonidium unguiculare	Weevil occurring in sessile oak woodland and on sea cliffs. In leaf litter, moss and at the roots of various plants. Known only from Cornwall and south Devon. Gweek Woods, 1984; Merthen Wood, 1984; Tremayne Woods, 1984.
Andrena rosae	Mining bee known from a variety of habitats, including coastal landslips, soft-rock cliffs and rough cliff tops. Nesting habits are poorly known, but burrows probably dug in sparsely vegetated, sunny areas on light soils. Extremely scarce throughout its range; has apparently declined considerably. Post-1970 records are known from only a handful of sites in E. Cornwall, N. Devon, W. Kent and Pembrokeshire. Boscastle, 1956; Goonhilly Downs, 1928; Sandy Mouth, Duckpool and Coombe Valley, 1991; Treen Cliff SSSI, 1954.
Andrena simillima	Mining bee typically recorded from coastal sites. Probably needs patches of bare ground in warm, sunny situations for nesting. Carbis Bay, pre-1970; Cross Coombe, nr. Perranporth, pre-1970; Gunwalloe Fishing Cove, 1972; Gunwalloe Marsh, 1972; Kelligerran Head, 1991; Loe Pool SSSI, 1991; Pentire Peninsula SSSI, 1860; Porthleven, 1991; Rock Dunes SSSI, 1939; Tintagel Cliffs SSSI, 1984; Trebarwith area, 1962.
Ceutorhynchus pilosellus	Weevil associated with lesser dandelion *Taraxacum laevigatum*. Larvae probably feed in the flowerheads. Holywell Bay, 1984; Merthyr Mawr Warren, 1992.

Table 5.3.2 Coastal Red Data Book (RDB) species in region (continued)

Species	*Description and notes on recorded occurrence in the region*
RDB2 (continued)	
Cryptocheilus notatus	Spider-hunting wasp, known from only about a dozen counties in southern England. Always considered rare. Nests in burrows of small mammals, especially moles. Prey includes spiders of the genera *Agelena, Trochusa, Tegenaria* and *Drassodes*. Chapel Porth, 1954; Church Cove, 1991; Gurnard's Head and Treen Cove, 1954; Loe Pool SSSI, 1931; Sennen Cove, 1969; The Lizard, 1890-1899, Treen Cliff SSSI, 1954.
White spot moth *Hadena albimacula*	*On shingle beaches and chalk or limestone cliffs. Larvae on Nottingham catchfly *Silene nutans*. Very local on south coast: Kent, Hampshire, South Devon and Cornwall. Mullion Cliffs to Predannack Head SSSI, 1958.
Lejops vittata	Large hoverfly of brackish ditches. Closely associated with sea club-rush *Scirpus maritimus*, on which the adults feed on pollen. Larvae aquatic. Scattered records from the coastal marshes of southern England including the Thames Estuary, Kent, Sussex and Somerset. Pawlett Hams, 1982-1983; Southlake Moor, 1982-1983.
Odontomyia ornata	Soldier fly. Larvae develop in shallow water of ponds and rivers, the adults visiting flowers nearby. Locally frequent, though declining, in the coastal levels of Sussex, Somerset and Gwent. Known elsewhere from scattered localities as far north as Norfolk, occasionally inland. Catcott, Edington and Chilton Moors SSSI, 1982 - 1983; Gordano Valley, 1983; Gwent Levels - Redwick & Llandevenny SSSI, 1985; Gwent Levels - St. Brides, 1985; Gwent Levels - Whitson SSSI, 1985; Moorlinch, 1983; North Moor SSSI, 1982-1983; Pawlett Hams, 1982-1983; Peterstone Great Wharf, 1991; Southlake Moor, 1983; Wentlooge Level, 1985.
Pherbellia argyra	Rare snail-killing fly found at the edge of permanent ponds. Larvae have been found in the snails *Planorbis planorbis* and *Anisus vortex*. Probably several generations pass in a year. The Lizard, 1981.
Psen bicolor	Small black and red solitary wasp nesting in moist sandy soil, predatory on planthoppers. England north as far as Yorkshire, uncommon. St. Erth Pools, 1927.
Tychius quinquepunctatus	Yellowish weevil associated with vetch species. Recorded from southern Britain. Kenfig Burrows & Pool, 1992.
pRDB2	
Cardiophorus erichsoni	9 mm mottled grey click beetle living in sandy soil on the coast. Larvae (wireworms) feed on grass roots. Very rare, restricted to Devon and Lundy,with small persistent colonies. Lundy, 1985; The Lizard, 1977.
Cicindela hybrida	*12-16 mm bronze/purple tiger beetle. Hunts over open ground, particularly sand and gravel, most often though not exclusively on the coast. Widely distributed north to Cumbria in the west, Norfolk in the east. Nowhere common. Braunton Burrows, 1950; Gwithian to Mexico Towans SSSI, 1958.
Dicronychus equiseti	8-9 mm mottled grey brown click beetle living in sandy places on the coast, usually dunes and cliffs. Larvae (wireworms) feed at the base of dune vegetation. South-western species, Devon, Pembrokeshire and Glamorganshire. Braunton Burrows, 1984; Kenfig Burrows & Pool, 1992; Merthyr Mawr Warren, 1988.
Monochroa elongella	Moth apparently primarily associated with sand dunes. Larvae thought to feed on silverweed *Potentilla anserina*. Braunton Burrows, 1984.
Nephrotoma quadristriata	*Cranefly confined to the major dune systems on the west coast of England and Wales. Usually found on the backs of mobile dunes, especially near the edges of slacks. Braunton Burrows, pre 1970.
Psylliodes luridipennis	3-4 mm flea beetle feeding on Lundy cabbage *Coincya wrightii* on cliff sites on Lundy Island. Currently thought to be endemic to the island. Lundy 1990s.
RDB3	
Andrena alfkenella	Widespread but very local solitary bee occurring in sandy places on heathland and at the coast, or on chalk grassland or chalk heath. Nests probably in burrows in dry, bare soil or short turf. Rare and local, seldom numerous at a site, records confined to southern England north to Lincolnshire. Harlyn Bay, 1955; Millook Valley, 1951; Tintagel Cliffs SSSI, 1984.
Andrena proxima	*Mining bee known from coastal landslips and soft rock cliffs, and inland on heathland, the banks of country lanes and other disturbed situations. Also on chalk downland in Kent and Berkshire. Closely associated with the flowers of umbellifers. Nest burrows probably in warm, sunny ground with short turf or sparse vegetation. Extremely scarce: about 20 post-1970 sites, mostly in S. Devon, the Isle of Wight and Kent. Single records from Berkshire and E. Sussex. St. Gennys and Crackington Haven, 1951; The Lizard, 1910.
Arachnospila consobrina	5-9 mm spider-hunting wasp; burrows in sand mainly in coastal dunes. Biology unknown. Scattered sites on the south coast, the Norfolk and Suffolk coast and from south Wales north to Cheshire on the west coast. Rare. Kenfig Burrows & Pool, 1993; Merthyr Mawr Warren, 1991.
Marsh moth *Athetis pallustris*	*Marginal fenland and marshy places in sand dunes. Larvae feed on hemp agrimony *Filipendula ulmaria* and other fenland plants. Secretive; found locally in Lincolnshire, Cambridgeshire and Norfolk; old records elsewhere. Gweek Woods, old unconfirmed record.
Cathormiocerus maritimus	Weevil recorded from coastal cliffs and rough open ground near the coast. Probably varied plant diet. Often associated with buck's-horn plantain *Plantage coronopus*. Known only on the coast from South Hampshire to North Devon. Penrose Estate, 1988.
Cathormiocerus myrmecophilus	Weevil recorded from coastal cliffs and rough open ground near the coast. Probably varied plant diet. Known only on the coast from East Sussex to West Cornwall. The Lizard, 1981.
Clubiona genevensis	Spider found under stones and among low vegetation near the coast in south-west England and S. Wales. Kynance Cove SSSI, 1959-1969; The Lizard, 1977.
Coelioxys mandibularis	Cuckoo bee. Confined in Britain to coastal dunes where its probable hosts *Megachile maritima* or *M. leachella* occur, digging their nest burrows in sunny, sparsely vegetated areas. Very local, recorded from the Merseyside and Wallasey area of S. Lancashire and Cheshire; Glamorganshire, Carmarthenshire and Pembrokeshire; and W. Sussex and E. Kent. Merthyr Mawr Warren, 1980.

Table 5.3.2 Coastal Red Data Book (RDB) species in region (continued)

Species	*Description and notes on recorded occurrence in the region*
RDB3 (continued)	
Colletes cunicularius	Mining bee, confined to the sandhills of north-west England and Wales. Colonises old erosion hollows, forming dense colonies on steep inclines. Requires creeping willow *Salix repens* as a pollen source. Can be locally numerous within its range, but has a very restricted distribution. Kenfig Burrows & Pool, 1993.
Emblethis verbasci	Strictly coastal groundbug; found in a range of vegetation types within its restricted range. Known only from the Isles of Scilly, Cornwall and Kent in Britain. Bryher, 1965-1969; Gugh, 1966; Samson Group, 1965-1969; Sennen Cove, 1989; St. Agnes, 1966; St. Martin's, 1987; St. Mary's, 1899; Tean, 1965-1969; Tresco, 1987.
Haematopota bigoti	Coastal blood sucking cleg (horsefly). Larvae in soil in saltmarshes. Southern coastlands north to Humber-Mersey. Middle Hope, 1983.
Hedychrum niemelai	Ruby-tailed wasp, parasitoid of sphecid wasps of the genus *Cerceris*, which are characteristic of open sandy habitats such as heathland and dunes. Apparently locally common in southern England in the past, from W. Cornwall to W. Norfolk, but now seems to be very scarce, with post-1970 records from only a handful of sites. Porthleven, 1991; Tidna Valley, 1981; Tintagel Cliffs SSSI, 1974.
Marbled clover moth *Heliothis viriplaca*	*Breckland, waste places, shingle and sandy beaches and chalk downland; larvae feed mainly on the flowers of wasteland plants, e.g. catchflies *Silene* spp., restharrows *Ononis* spp. etc. Braunton Burrows, old record which possibly requires confirmation.
Lathys stigmatisata	*Small spider so far recorded only from Kent, East Sussex, Cornwall and Lundy Island. Coastal heath and shingle. Chapel Porth, 1960s; Kynance Cove SSSI, 1935; Lundy, 1920-1929.
Beautiful gothic moth *Leucochlaena oditis*	*Frequents grassy slopes and cliffs by the sea. Larvae feed on grasses. Very local in south-west England, Isle of Wight, Dorset and South Devon. The Lizard, 1903.
Limonia (Dicranomyia) goritiensis	Cranefly, on seepages on coastal cliffs and rock faces. Biology unknown, although larvae probably develop in damp soil or moss beside seepages. Widely scattered but very local, occurring mainly in the north and west. Cudden Point, 1989; Cwm Afon Col-Huw, 1992; East Aberthaw Coast, 1992; Godrevy Point and the Knavocks, 1990; Lundy, 1972; Morte Point, 1990; Pentire Peninsula SSSI, 1990.
Lionychus quadrillum	*3-4 mm bronze-black ground beetle. Associated with river shingle, sand or gravel, sometimes in quite dry places, but often near water or near the shore. Loe Pool SSSI, old record.
Blackneck moth *Lygephila craccae*	Scarce; frequents cliffs and rocky places by the sea; larvae feed on wood vetch *Vicia sylvatica*. North Devon, north Cornwall and a single site in N. Somerset. Babbacombe Mouth, 1965; Foreland Point, 1971; Hobby to Peppercombe, 1967; Lizard Point, 1985; St. Gennys and Crackington Haven, 1968; Steeple Point to Marsland Mouth SSSI, 1991; Steeplepoint-Black Church - 1984; Watersmeet SSSI, 1971; West Exmoor Coast & Woods, 1971.
Miarus micros	Small weevil associated with sheep's-bit *Jasione montana*. Larvae live gregariously and pupate in the flowerheads. Known only from Cornwall. Kynance Cove SSSI, 1970; The Lizard, pre-1970.
Nomada fulvicornis	Nomad bee, steals the food of *Andrena bimaculata, A. pilipes* and *A. tibialis*. In most of the habitats used by its hosts, including sandy areas on heaths, waste ground, coastal grassland and soft rock cliffs. Formerly widely distributed in southern England, but post-1970 records from only about 20 sites. About half recent records are from Kent and Sussex. Near Winford Bridge, Arlington, 1991.
Nomada hirtipes	*Rare southern cuckoo bee associated with the solitary bee *Andrena bucephala*. Durdham Down, old record.
Nomada lathburiana	Nomad bee, striped in yellow, black and red, steals the food of the bee *Andrena cineraria*. Widely distributed, especially in the south, but extremely local. Chipman Valley, 1991.
Ochthebius poweri	1 mm black water beetle. South-western species restricted to small seepages on cliff faces. Cliffs in Devon, Cornwall and Pembrokeshire; best known locality is the Red Sandstone cliffs between Exmouth and Teignmouth in south Devon. East Aberthaw Coast, 1992; Sennen Cove, 1912.
Piesma quadratum spergulariae	So far as is known, this subspecies is endemic to the Isles of Scilly, where it was discovered in 1965. Feeds on rock sea-spurrey *Spergularia rupicola* on rocky headlands. Originally described as a separate species. Cruther's Point, St. Martin's, 1987; Pelistry Bay, St. Mary's, 1987; Peninnis Head, St. Mary's, 1987.
Psen littoralis	Digger wasp, prey unknown, nesting possibly in the stems of marram *Ammophila arenaria*. Frequents marram dunes, locally common in Devon, parts of Wales and Lancashire. Braunton Burrows, 1969; Kenfig Burrows & Pool, 1993.
Solenopsis fugax	*Minute ant, nests usually constructed under deep stones and often linked with other ant species, such as *Lasius* and *Formica*. Noted on or near the coast in Cornwall, Devon, Somerset, Dorset, Isle of Wight, Kent and Essex. Brean Down, 1960; the Lizard, 1927.
Urophora spoliata	Small fly in a family of mostly picture-winged flies, though this species has mainly clear wings. Detailed biology unknown, although seemingly associated with saw wort *Serratula tinctoria*. Known only from S. Hampshire, the Isle of Wight and Cornwall. Boscastle: Willapark to Harbour, 1990; Pentargon Cliff, 1989; the Lizard, 1981.
pRDB3	
Amara strenua	8-9.5 mm bronze-black oval plant-eating ground beetle living under debris in saltmarshes. Very uncommon, recorded from southern and south eastern coasts. Dubious record from Derbyshire. Pawlett Hams, 1982-1983.
Dialineura anilis	Stiletto fly associated with sand dunes. Life history unknown though larvae probably develop in damp sand at base of vegetation. Mainly noted from the Welsh coast and the west coast of Scotland, also known from Somerset and Lancashire. Kenfig Burrows & Pool, 1992; Merthyr Mawr Warren, 1992.
Lasiacantha capucina	Lacebug; feeds on thyme *Thymus drucei*. Confined to Cornwall, and extremely localised even there. Beagles Point, 1989; Chapel Porth, 1990; Chyvarloe Cliffs, 1989; Kynance Cliff, 1989; Lizard Point, 1989; Lower Predannack Cliff, 1989; Mullion Cliffs to Predannack Head SSSI, 1989.

Table 5.3.2 Coastal Red Data Book (RDB) species in region (continued)

Species	*Description and notes on recorded occurrence in the region*
pRDB3 (continued)	
Pamponerus germanicus	Robber fly frequenting sand dunes just behind the marram belt. Larvae possibly develop in moist sand as predators of other invertebrates. On the major sand dunes of western Britain from north Devon to the north-east coast of Scotland. Occasionally reported inland. Braunton Burrows, pre-967; Kenfig Burrows & Pool, 1992; Merthyr Mawr Warren, 1990.
Pherbellia knutsoni	Widely recorded but very local snail-killing fly of southern Britain. Many records are from dry sand dunes, breck heath or chalk grassland. Kenfig Burrows & Pool, 1992.
Poecilobothrus ducalis	*Small dancefly, larvae probably semi-aquatic carnivores in mud beside saline pools and ditches. All modern records are from north Kent marshes, though old records also from Hants. and Somerset. Berrow Dunes, 1951.
Pogonus luridipennis	*6-8.5 mm metallic green and yellow ground beetle found in saltmarshes under seaweed and driftwood. S. and E. England north to Humber. Very local. Severn Beach, 1943.
Thereva fulva	Active light brown hairy fly associated with dunes and other sandy areas near the coast, apparently preferring areas of fixed sand with well established vegetation and small open areas. Most records are from north Kent and S. Wales; appears to have declined greatly this century. Merthyr Mawr Warren, 1992.
RDB I	
Scopaeus ryei	2.5 mm orange rove beetle living among shingle and gravel on the foreshore. Known only from a small number of localities in Cornwall and Devon. Helston, pre-1970; Loe Pool SSSI, 1936; Penrose Estate, 1970.
RDB K	
Atomaria scutellaris	*Small beetle found in a range of habitats usually near the coast. Tresco, 1965.
Lithobius lapidicola	Centipede only recently recorded in the wild in Britain from Sandwich Bay, Kent. Often confused with *L. borealis*. Countybridge Quarry Heath, near Mullion, 1977; the Lizard, 1980-1981.
Metatrichoniscoides celticus	Small woodlouse found under boulders embedded in turf. Discovered new to science in 1979 on the Glamorganshire coast; now also known from a limestone quarry in Carmarthenshire, St. Bees beach, Cumbria, and the Giant's Causeway, Co. Antrim. Cliffs at St. Donat's post-1970; Nash Point, 1979; Ogmore Flats, 1979; Ogmore-by-Sea Cliffs, 1979; Southerndown Coast SSSI, 1979; St. Donat's Bay to Col-huw Point, 1979.
pRDB K	
Actocharis readingi	1.5-1.7 mm yellow rove beetle living among stones and dead seaweed below the high water mark. South-West Peninsula only. Rockham Bay, Mortehoe, 1907; St. Mary's, 1970.
Bledius diota	Small rove beetle which feeds on seaweed. Builds burrows in coastal sand or the banks of saltmarsh creeks, leaving small piles of soil similar to wormcasts. Local in England; also known from Scotland but probably rarer in the north of its range. Berrow Dunes, 1978.
Halticus macrocephalus	*Bug known only from sand dunes in a small area of north Cornwall, where it feeds on lady's bedstraw *Galium verum*. Rock, near Padstow, 1957; Porth Kidney Sands, 1968.
Omalium rugulipenne	Rove beetle recorded from under dead seaweed. Local in England. Berrow Dunes, 1981.
Phytosus nigriventris	*2-2.8 mm black rove beetle with yellow legs; associated with coastal habitats. St. Martin's, pre-1970.

Source: JNCC (after Kirby 1994a, b). Key: Red Data Book categories: RDB1 = endangered; RDB2 = vulnerable; RDB3 = rare; RDB I = indeterminate; RDB K = insufficiently known; pRDB = proposed species as categorised in e.g. Hyman & Parsons (1992); pRDB K = proposed species as categorised in e.g. Hyman & Parsons (1994); *= old records in the region (before approx. 1970). For further description of RDB categories, see Shirt (1987) and Bratton (1991).

The JNCC's Invertebrate Site Register (ISR) has records from 590 sites within the region, from the Fal Estuary in Cornwall to Kenfig Dunes in Mid Glamorgan, although many of these are subsites of much larger statutory nature conservation areas. Scarce and threatened species have been recorded at many ISR sites. Table 5.3.3 lists those sites known to be of major importance for the conservation of invertebrates. Site selection was based on the range and/or scarcity of species present, the species habitat associations and the amount of available habitat. Many of these sites are National Nature Reserves (NNRs) or Sites of Special Scientific Interest (SSSIs); other under-recorded localities in the region may warrant similar status on the basis of their invertebrate interest.

Most of the scarce or threatened species occurring in the region have exacting habitat requirements in one or more stages of their life histories. They are often restricted in range and in some cases are known from only a few localities. Assemblages of species associated with rocky cliffs, coastal heaths and grasslands, foreshores, sand dunes or coastal woodlands are particularly well represented in this region.

Rocky cliffs and their associated coastal heaths and grasslands are of outstanding importance in this region, with large numbers of scarce or threatened species recorded. Many of these are thermophilous species depending on warm, bare or sparsely vegetated ground. One such example, the bug *Pterometus staphyliniformis*, is exclusive to thinly vegetated cliff-top habitat, occurring in the region in one area of Cornwall. Other scarce insects have specific associations with threatened plants; for example larvae of the micro-moths *Phyllonorycter staintonella* and *Syncopacma sueciciella* feed only on hairy greenweed *Genista pilosa* and the beetle *Psylliodes luridipennis* is exclusive to Lundy cabbage *Coincya wrightii* (see also section 5.2). Scarce herbivorous invertebrates feeding on more widespread plants within the region are perhaps restricted in distribution by climatic factors. Seepages and small trickles on cliffs are the habitat of scarce species such as the cranefly *Limonia goritiensis* and the water beetle *Ochthebius poweri*.

Table 5.3.3 Sites important for invertebrate conservation

Site	*Grid ref.*	*Status*
Cornwall		
Swanpool	SW8031	
Mawnan Glebe	SW7826	NT
Merthen Wood	SW7326	SSSI
Gweek Wood	SW7026	
Coverack Cliffs	SW7818	SSSI
Kennack Cove to Blackhead Cliffs (including Beagles Point)	SW7616	SSSI/NT (in part)
South & east Lizard	SW6911	SSSI/NT
Kynance Cove	SW6813	SSSI/NT (in part)/Wildlife Trust reserve
West Lizard	SW6616	NNR/SSSI/NT (in part)
Mullion Cliffs to Predannack Head	SW6617	SSSI/NT/Wildlife Trust reserve
Gunwalloe Church Cove and Marsh	SW6620	NT
Loe Pool	SW6424	SSSI/NT
Porthleven Cliffs	SW6324	SSSI/NT
Marazion Marsh	SW5131	SSSI
Treen Cliff	SW4022	SSSI/NT
Sennen Cove	SW3526	
Cape Cornwall to Clodgy Point	SW3531-SW5041	SSSI/NT (in part)
Gwithian to Mexico Towans	SW5740	SSSI
Godrevy Head to St. Agnes	SW5842-SW7151	SSSI/NT (in part)
Cligga Head	SW7254	SSSI
Penhale Dunes	SW7757	SSSI/NT (in part)
Kelsey Head (including Holywell Bay)	SW7660	SSSI/NT (in part)
Trevose Head and Constantine Bay	SW8575	SSSI
Pentire Peninsula	SW9280	SSSI/NT
Tintagel Cliffs	SX0487	SSSI/NT (in part)
Boscastle to Widemouth	SX0991- SS1901	SSSI/NT(in part)
Steeple Point to Marsland Mouth	SS2117-SS0211	SSSI/NT (in part)/Wildlife Trust reserve (in part)
Isles of Scilly	SV80-SV81 & SV90-SV91	Many ISR sites covering the main islands, some of them SSSI
Devon		
Marsland Mouth to Clovelly	SS2117-SS3125	SSSI/NT (in part)/Wildlife Trust reserve (in part)
Lundy Island	SS1346	SSSI/NT/Landmark Trust/Marine Nature Reserve
Hobby to Peppercombe	SS3224-SS3824	SSSI/NT
Babbacombe Mouth	SS3924	NT
Westward Ho! Cliffs	SS4026	SSSI
Northam Burrows	SS4431	LNR
Braunton Burrows	SS4635	SSSI/Biosphere Reserve
Saunton to Baggy Point	SS4438	SSSI/NT
Morte Point	SS4545	SSSI/NT
West Exmoor coast and woods	SS6654	SSSI/NT
Watersmeet	SS7448	SSSI/NT
Foreland Point	SS7551	NT
Somerset		
Porlock Marsh	SS8747	SSSI/NT
Berrow Dunes	ST2952	SSSI/LNR
Brean Down	ST2959	SSSI/NT
Severn Estuary	ST2859-ST1968	SSSI
Avon		
Steep Holm	ST2260	SSSI
Middle Hope	ST3265	SSSI/NT/Wildlife Trust reserve
Gwent		
Gwent Levels (includes Caldicot, Magor & Wentlooge Levels)	ST28, ST38	SSSI/Wildlife Trust reserve
Mid-Glamorgan		
Methyr Mawr dunes	SS8477	SSSI
Kenfig Pool & dunes	SS7980	SSSI/NNR

Source: JNCC ISR. Key: NNR = National Nature Reserve; SSSI = Site of Special Scientific Interest; NT = National Trust; LNR = Local Nature Reserve.

Sand dune systems have many scarce species, including some restricted to south-western coasts, for example the bugs *Geotomus punctulatus* and *Halticus macrocephalus,* both of which feed on lady's bedstraw *Galium verum* at just a few dunes in Cornwall. The damp dune slacks at Braunton Burrows are one of only two localities in Britain for the sandbowl snail *Catinella arenaria.* The click beetle *Dicronychus equiseti* is known only from marram dunes in Devon and south Wales, and the ground beetle *Nebria complanata* has a similarly restricted distribution, inhabiting strandline habitats along sandy foreshores.

Coastal wet grasslands (see section 3.5) support a number of scarce and threatened species associated, in one or more stages of their life histories, with the water-filled rhyns (ditches). The best examples of these habitats occur in Somerset and Gwent, where the great silver water beetle *Hydrophilus piceus,* the diving beetle *Hydaticus transversalis* and the soldier fly *Odontomyia ornata* abound.

Two species afforded statutory protection (Table 5.3.1) are recorded from water bodies in the region - the medicinal leech *Hirudo medicinalis,* from a large dune pool, and the fairy shrimp *Chirocephalus diaphanus,* from temporary pools. A further rarity associated with temporary pools is the mud snail *Lymnaea glabra.*

Wooded ria valleys in Cornwall are home to the threatened weevil *Anchonidium unguiculare,* which lives in leaf litter. Other scarce species occurring in these woodlands include moths whose larvae feed on epiphytic lichens on trees: the dotted carpet *Alcis jubata* is one example. Wooded combes in Devon and Somerset linked to sheltered areas of heath or bracken provide habitat for two threatened butterflies: the high brown fritillary *Argynnis adippe* and the heath fritillary *Mellicta athalia.*

5.3.3 Human activities

As with other nature conservation interests, the main threats to invertebrate communities in the region include inappropriate management of sites and direct habitat loss or degradation, such as by construction of stabilising sea defences or the clearing away of organic strandline debris. Appropriate site management is vital for maintaining invertebrate interest, since invertebrates occur in the full range of coastal habitats and many require particular microhabitats in a suitable condition, often using subtle features of vegetation structure or areas of bare ground. As invertebrates generally have annual life cycles, the habitat features they utilise must be present in the right condition in each and every year. This is compounded by the fact that many scarce species have poor powers of dispersal and are thus unable to colonise suitable habitat from afar. Site management often overlooks many features that are of importance to invertebrates, many species surviving by default. Grazing has the potential to both create and destroy or damage invertebrate habitat. Appropriate levels of grazing maintain the varied ground conditions and heights of sward that favour a variety of invertebrates. However, too heavy grazing reduces the value of, for example, maritime grassland for invertebrates, by increasing nutrient levels in the soil and altering soil structure, thus changing the plant species that occur and restricting the height of the vegetation. Along flushes, where ground water emerges along slopes, heavy poaching can be particularly damaging, as the trampling crushes the soft plants and cuts through the sward, leading to soil erosion and muddying of the water. On some sites insufficient or no grazing allows vegetation to become rank and dense, reducing the range of species that it can support and favouring commoner species. The fundamentals of managing coastal habitats for invertebrates are covered by Kirby (1992).

5.3.4 Information sources used

The data used here come from the ISR, a computerised GB-wide database based on literature searches of entomological journals and those of local naturalist societies, collation of data from local biological record centres and the Biological Records Centre, Monks Wood, and consultation with invertebrate specialists and non-governmental organisations.

The level of recording around the region varies considerably, although a few areas have been studied in considerable detail. Most of the better known invertebrate groups have been recorded in the region, although some much more so than others. The Hemiptera (true bugs), Lepidoptera (butterflies and moths), Coleoptera (beetles) and Hymenoptera (solitary bees and wasps) are among the best studied groups. Some areas, for example the Lizard peninsula in Cornwall, have been extensively recorded in both historic and modern times. Even so, new discoveries are still made; examples include the discovery of micro-moth species new to science (Heckford & Langmaid 1988) or previously unknown from Great Britain (Heckford 1986) and of a new subspecies, *Lupernia nickerlii leechi,* of the sandhill rustic moth (Goater 1976).

Several modern publications review the occurrence of invertebrates within the region, with Fowles (1994) providing an overview of the most important sites and species in Wales. On a county basis, Duff (1993) covers the beetles of Somerset and Horton (1994) the butterflies and moths of Monmouthshire. In addition, other publications have mapped the distribution of certain groups on a county basis: for example Bristow *et al.* (1993) deals with the butterflies of Devon and Randolph (1992) the dragonflies in counties around Bristol. Extensive invertebrate surveys have been undertaken, concentrating on particular habitat types: Drake (1986) covers many of the groups occurring in wet grasslands on the Gwent Levels. In addition, there are numerous publications in entomological journals relating to this region: for invertebrates of the Isles of Scilly and Lundy Island, bibliographies for certain groups or areas are provided by Smith & Smith (1983); Chalmers-Hunt (1989) lists publications for Lepidoptera. Colvin & Reavey (1993) provides a more comprehensive list of addresses for societies, individuals and national and local recording schemes.

5.3.5 Acknowledgements

Thanks are due to D. Procter and Dr S. Ball (JNCC) for providing raw data from the ISR (Table 5.3.1) and for assistance in producing maps.

5.3.6 Further sources of information

A. References cited

Bratton, J.H., *ed.* 1991. *British Red Data Books: 3. Invertebrates other than insects.* Peterborough, Joint Nature Conservation Committee.

Bristow, C.R. Mitchell, S.H., & Bolton, D.E. 1993. *Devon butterflies.* Tiverton, Devon Books.

Chalmers-Hunt, J.M. 1989. *Local lists of Lepidoptera.* Uffington, Hedera Press.

Colvin, M., & Reavey, D. 1993. *A directory for entomologists.* 2nd ed. Middlesex, Amateur Entomologist's Society. (Pamphlet No. 14.)

Drake, C.M. 1986. *A survey of the invertebrates of the Gwent levels, 1985.* Peterborough, Nature Conservancy Council. (Unpublished.)

Duff, A. 1993. *Beetles of Somerset: their status and distribution.* Taunton, Somerset Archaeological & Natural History Society.

Fowles, A.P. 1994. *Invertebrates of Wales: a review of important sites and species.* Peterborough, Joint Nature Conservation Committee.

Goater, B. 1976. A new subspecies of *Luperina nickerlii* (Freyer) (Lep. Noctuidae) from Cornwall. *Entomologist's Gazette, 27:* 141-143.

Heckford, R.J. 1986. *Syncopacma suecicella* (Wolff) (Lepidoptera: Gelechiidae) new to the British Isles. *Entomologist's Gazette, 37:* 87-89.

Heckford, R.J., & Langmaid, J.R. 1988. *Eulamprotes phaeella* sp. n. (Lepidoptera: Gelechiidae) in the British Isles. *Entomologist's Gazette, 39:* 1-11.

Horton, G.A.N. 1994. *Monmouthshire Lepidoptera. The butterflies and moths of Gwent.* Malvern, Comma International Biological Systems.

Hyman, P.S., & Parsons, M.S. 1992. *A review of the scarce and threatened Coleoptera of Great Britain. Part 1.* Peterborough, Joint Nature Conservation Committee. (UK Nature Conservation, No. 3.)

Hyman, P.S., & Parsons, M.S. 1994. *A review of the scarce and threatened Coleoptera of Great Britain. Part 2.* Peterborough, Joint Nature Conservation Committee. (UK Nature Conservation, No. 12.)

Kirby, P. 1992. *Habitat management for invertebrates: a practical handbook.* Peterborough, Joint Nature Conservation Committee.

Kirby, P. 1994a. *Habitat fragmentation; species at risk.* Peterborough, English Nature. (English Nature Research Reports, No. 89.)

Kirby, P. 1994b. *Habitat tabulations for rare and scarce invertebrates: Coleoptera (part); Dolichopodidae & Empididae; macro-moths; Ethmiinae, Stathmopodinae and Gelechiidae.* Peterborough, Joint Nature Conservation Committee (unpublished report).

Randolph, S. 1992. *Dragonflies of the Bristol region.* Bristol, City of Bristol Museums and Art Gallery / Avon Regional Environmental Records Centre.

Shirt, D.B. 1987. *British Red Data Books: 2. Insects.* Peterborough, Nature Conservancy Council.

Smith, K.G.V., & Smith V. 1983. *A bibliography of the entomology of the smaller British offshore islands.* Faringdon, Classey.

B. Further reading

Agassiz, D.J.L. 1981. *A revised list of the Lepidoptera of the Isles of Scilly.* Isles of Scilly Museum Association.

Davidson, N.C., Laffoley, D.d'A., Doody, J.P., Way, L.S., Gordon, J., Key, R., Drake, C.M., Pienkowski, M.W., Mitchell, R., & Duff, K.L. 1991. *Nature conservation and estuaries in Great Britain.* Peterborough, Nature Conservancy Council.

Drake, C.M., Foster, A.P., & Palmer, M.A. 1984. *A survey of the invertebrates of the Somerset Levels and Moors.* Peterborough, Nature Conservancy Council.

Falk, S. 1991. *A review of the scarce and threatened bees, wasps and ants of Great Britain.* Peterborough, English Nature. (Research & survey in nature conservation, No. 35.)

Falk, S. 1991. *A review of the scarce and threatened flies of Great Britain (part 1).* Peterborough, English Nature. (Research & survey in nature conservation, No. 39.)

Haes, E.C.M. 1990. *Grasshoppers and related insects in Cornwall.* Redruth, Cornish Biological Records Centre / Institute of Cornish Studies.

Harding, P.T., & Sutton, S.L. 1985. *Woodlice in Britain and Ireland: distribution and habitat.* Huntingdon, Natural Environmental Research Council, Institute of Terrestrial Ecology.

Heath, J., & Emmet, A.M., *eds.* 1991. *The moths and butterflies of Great Britain and Ireland. Volume 7, part 2.* Colchester, Harley Books.

Kerney, M.P., *ed.* 1976. *Atlas of non-marine mollusca of the British Isles.* Huntingdon, Conchological Society of Great Britain and Ireland / Biological Records Centre, Institute of Terrestrial Ecology.

Kirby, P. 1992. *A review of the scarce and threatened Hemiptera of Great Britain.* Peterborough, Joint Nature Conservation Committee. (UK Nature Conservation, No. 2.)

Mendel, H. 1988. *Provisional atlas of the click beetles (Coleoptera: Elateroidea) of the British Isles.* Huntingdon, Biological Records Centre.

Merrett, P. 1990. *A review of the nationally notable spiders of Great Britain.* Peterborough, Nature Conservancy Council. (Contract surveys, No. 127.)

Parsons, M.S. 1993. *A review of the scarce and threatened pyralid moths of Great Britain.* Peterborough, Joint Nature Conservation Committee. (UK Nature Conservation, No. 11.)

Parsons, M.S. 1995. *A review of the scarce and threatened ethmiid, stathmopodid and gelechiid moths of Great Britain.* Peterborough, Joint Nature Conservation Committee. (UK Nature Conservation, No. 16.)

Robbins, J. 1990. *The moths and butterflies of Exmoor National Park.* Minehead, Exmoor Natural History Society.

Spalding, A. 1992. *Cornwall's butterfly and moth heritage.* Truro, Twelveheads Press.

Wallace, I.D. 1991. *A review of the Trichoptera of Great Britain.* Peterborough, Nature Conservancy Council. (Research & survey in nature conservation, No. 32.)

C. Contact names and addresses

Type of information	Contact address and telephone no.
Occurrence of invertebrates in the region	*Biological Records Centre, Institute of Terrestrial Ecology, Monks Wood, tel: 01487 773381
Invertebrate site and species information - England	*Dr R.S. Key, Dr C.M. Drake and Dr D.A. Sheppard, Invertebrate Zoologists, Lowlands Team, English Nature HQ, Peterborough, tel: 01733 340345
Invertebrate site and species information - south Wales	*A.P. Fowles, Countryside Council for Wales HQ, Bangor, tel: 01248 370444
Invertebrate Site Register (ISR) (computerised national inventory of sites of significance to invertebrate conservation; contains records of local, scarce and threatened species of all groups of invertebrates)	*Invertebrate Site Register, JNCC, Peterborough, tel: 01733 62626
Conservation of butterflies and moths - Cornwall	G. Pilkington, Butterfly Conservation, Chapel Cottage, Gooseham Mill, Morwenstow, Cornwall EX23 9PQ
Conservation of butterflies and moths - Devon	D. Bastow, British Butterfly Conservation Society, 19 Ashmill Court, Bradley Valley, Newton Abbot, Devon TQ12 1SQ
Conservation of butterflies and moths - Avon	Dr H. Cole, Butterfly Conservation, 2 Manor Cottages, Stoke Street, Rodney Stoke, Cheddar, Somerset BS27 3UN
Conservation of butterflies and moths - Gloucestershire	S. Glover, Butterfly Conservation Society, Brook Cottage, Two Bridges, Blakeney, Gloucestershire GL15 4AF
Conservation of butterflies and moths - Glamorgan	R. Smith, Butterfly Conservation Society, 28 Llanmaes Road, Llantwit Major, South Glamorgan CF6 9XF
Invertebrates in Cornwall	Cornwall Biological Records Unit, Trevithick Centre, Trevenson Road, Pool, Redruth, Cornwall TR15 3PL, tel: 01209 710424
Invertebrates in Devon	D. Bolton, Exeter Biological Records Centre, Royal Albert Memorial Museum, Queen Street, Exeter EX4 3RX, tel: 01392 265858
Invertebrates in Exmoor National Park	D. Boyce, Entomologist/Ecologist, Exmoor National Park, Exmoor House, Dulverton, Somerset TA22 9HL, tel: 01398 323665
Invertebrates in Somerset	Somerset Environmental Records Centre, Hestercombe House, Cheddon Fitzpaine, Taunton, Somerset TA2 8LQ, tel: 01823 33410
Invertebrates in Avon	Avon Environmental Records Centre, Bristol Museums & Art Gallery, Queen's Road, Bristol BS8 1RL, tel: 0117 922 3571
Invertebrates in Gwent	Gwent Biological Records Centre, Newport Museum & Art Gallery, John Frost Square, Newport, Gwent NP9 1HZ, tel: 01633 840 063
Dragonflies in Glamorgan	S.J. Moon, Recorder, Glamorgan Group of British Dragonfly Survey, c/o Kenfig NNR, Ton Kenfig, Pyle, Mid Glamorgan CF33 4PT, tel: 01656 743 386
Moths in Glamorgan	S. Moon (Mid Glamorgan) or J. Gilmore (South Glamorgan), Glamorgan Moth Recording Group, c/o Kenfig NNR, Ton Kenfig, Pyle, Mid Glamorgan CF33 4PT, tel: 01656 743 386
Recording schemes for key invertebrate sites in Gloucestershire	Gloucestershire Invertebrate Group, Gloucestershire Wildlife Trust, The Dulverton Building, Robins Wood Hill Country Park, Reservoir Road, Gloucester GL4 6SX, tel: 01452 383 333

*Starred contact addresses are given in full in the Appendix.

5.4 Rare sea-bed species

Dr W.G. Sanderson

5.4.1 Introduction

This section considers rare and scarce marine benthic (sea-bed) species, excluding fish. The occurrence and distribution of benthic communities is discussed in section 4.2. 'Nationally rare' marine benthic species in this section are those native organisms that occur in eight or fewer of the 10 km squares (of the Ordnance Survey national grid) containing sea within the three-mile territorial limit for Great Britain. 'Nationally scarce' are those that occur in nine to 55 such squares. This methodology and these criteria are analogous to those used for other groups of organisms in British Red Data Books (e.g. Bratton 1991) and by the International Union for Conservation of Nature and Natural Resources (IUCN) (see IUCN Species Survival Commission 1995). The development of the current criteria and the choice of study area for rarity assessment in the marine benthos of Great Britain are discussed in detail by Sanderson (1996). Species considered in this chapter are those that are conspicuous and readily identifiable in the field by the Marine Nature Conservation Review (MNCR) and similar techniques or for which taxonomic or biogeographic experts consider that sufficient data exist on a national basis to warrant their inclusion. Species at the limit of their global distribution (e.g. 'southern' or 'northern' species) may be rare only within Great Britain's territorial seas. Indeed, the majority of the species listed from this region are southern species near or at the northern margins of their range in Region 11. A species described here as 'nationally rare' or 'nationally scarce' is therefore not necessarily endangered, and although without doubt of national interest (and perhaps important to national biodiversity), the conservation importance of species listed here needs to be carefully considered. The analysis in this section represents the first attempt to quantify the rarity of marine benthic species and to summarise the known occurrence of rare and scarce species in Great Britain. As either more data become available or populations change, the status of species listed in this chapter will require re-evaluation.

Other regions in south-west Britain (9, 10 and 12) appear to be comparatively rich in nationally rare and scarce species. Region 11 is, however, the richest: there are 39 rare and 31 scarce marine benthic species recorded from this region. Maps 5.4.1 and 5.4.2 summarise their current known occurrence in recent times. Areas around the Fal Estuary, Helford River, the Lizard, Isles of Scilly and Lundy apparently contain more rare and scarce marine benthic species than other areas. These appearances may be somewhat misleading, however, since survey effort in this region is not uniform. Some of the rare and scarce species found in Region 11 are currently protected under the Wildlife and Countryside Act 1981 or listed under the EC Habitats and Species Directive.

5.4.2 Important locations and species

Table 5.4.1 lists the rare and scarce marine benthic species that have been recorded in Region 11, together with their known areas of occurrence and other key information. Species names are after Howson (1987).

Some nationally rare and scarce species described here are restricted to very specific habitat types in Great Britain that are themselves rare, scarce or in some cases threatened. Such species may therefore be of nature conservation importance. Species confined to saline lagoons, maerl or seagrass beds have been so considered (see e.g. Anon. 1995).

Within this region of Great Britain many species may also be 'nationally rare' or 'scarce' because they are Mediterranean-Atlantic species at the margins of their distribution in Great Britain. It has been argued that populations of many sessile (non-mobile) southern species have a poor capacity for recovery and recruit (≈ reproduce) slowly at the margins of their distribution and are therefore particularly vulnerable to even the most minor, infrequent impacts. Communities of southern species have therefore been considered important as reference sites for monitoring

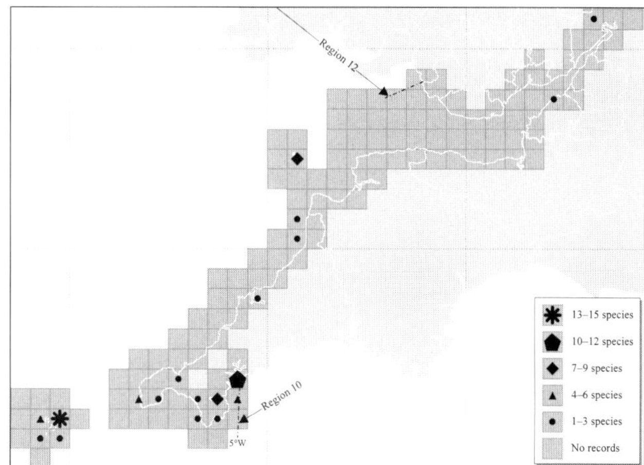

Map 5.4.1 Numbers of rare marine benthic species recorded in 10 km squares containing sea within the 3 mile limit. Apparent distribution may be influenced by differences in recording effort.

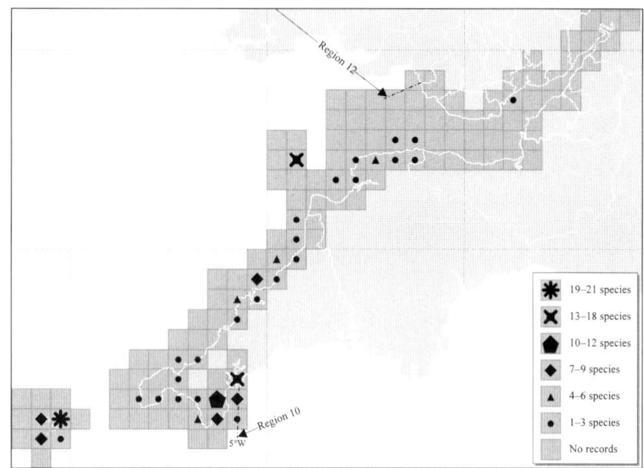

Map 5.4.2 Numbers of scarce marine benthic species recorded in 10 km squares containing sea within the 3 mile limit. Apparent distribution may be influenced by differences in recording effort.

Table 5.4.1 'Nationally rare' and 'nationally scarce' marine benthic species found in the region

Species	*Type of organism*	*Area(s) of occurrence*	*Habitat/associations*	*Comments*	*Useful reference*
Stelletta grubii	A sponge	Mullion Island	On rock, often dark or overhung, from intertidal to 135 m. Associated with epifaunal organisms.	Often obscured by associated epifauna. May be under-recorded (B.E. Picton pers. comm.).	Ackers *et al.* (1992)
Axinella damicornis	A sponge	Isles of Scilly, Lundy	On vertical & horizontal faces at sites of moderate wave action. Sometimes with some silt at sites generally below 20 m.	Southern, Mediterranean species, at northern limit of range	Ackers *et al.* (1992)
*Adreus fascicularis**	A sponge	Lundy	At sites with strong tidal streams. On rock overlain with silt or sediment. Often half buried in shelly gravel. Deeper than about 12 m.	Southern. Also Channel Islands and Spain.	Ackers *et al.* (1992), Hiscock *et al.* (1983)
Tethyspira spinosa	A sponge	Isles of Scilly, Tintagel Head, Lundy	Wave exposed coasts. Shallow subtidal rock to 60 m+.	South-western distribution in British Isles. May be somewhat under-recorded.	Ackers *et al.* (1992)
*Desmacidon fruticosum**	A sponge	Isles of Scilly	On horizontal surfaces. Wide range of substrata. Generally in oceanic water >25 m. Probably confined to same habitat as *Axinella damicornis*.	Also known from France, Spain and Ireland	Ackers *et al.* (1992)
Aglaophenia kirchenpaueri	A hydroid	Porthkerris/Pencra Head, Mullion, Lundy	Mostly exposed sites on hard substrata in shallow water. Has been recorded at 400 m.	A Mediterranean species. May occur more widely in south-west Britain than current records suggest.	Cornelius (1995)
Laomedea angulata	A hydroid	River Fal, Isles of Scilly, Blackchurch Rock (Clovelly)	Often on eel grass. Low water to 8 m.	South from the English Channel	Hayward & Ryland (1990)
Parerythropodium coralloides	Soft coral	Pendennis Point, Creggan Rocks, Isles of Scilly, Beeny Cliff Cave, Lundy	Overhangs and crevices out of light. Sheltered from strong wave action. 0-25 m.	Southern. More common in SW Europe and Mediterranean. Somewhat hard to spot but still probably scarce.	Manuel (1988)
Eunicella verrucosa#	The pink sea fan	Falmouth Bay, Manacles, Lowland Point, Staggs, Pollack Ground, Mulberry Harbours, Tater du, Longships Reef, Isles of Scilly, Cat's Cove, Newquay, Gulland Rock, N. of the Mouls, Kellan Head, Lundy	On rocky surfaces, often vertical or overhung. Especially between 20-200 m.	Cautiously regarded as scarce. Southern species. SW Europe, the Mediterranean and N. Africa. Not uncommon locally. Historically heavily collected in some places in GB. Colonies long lived and slow growing.	Manuel (1988)
Anthopleura thallia	Glaucus pimplet (an anemone)	St. Mawes, Black Head, Battery Rocks (Penzance), Isles of Scilly	Mid to lower wave exposed shores. In pools and gullies, sometimes partially buried by gravel.	Extreme south westerly species in GB. Can be locally common. Also known from Atlantic coast of France.	Manuel (1988)
Aiptasia mutabilis	Trumpet anemone	Fal Estuary, near Rosemullion Head, Porthkerris Bay, Helford River, King's Cove, Isles of Scilly, Towan Porthcothan, Haryn Bay, Kellen Head, off Penally Hill and Concleave, Lundy	Overhangs, in lower shore pools, but more often in shallow subtidal amongst the holdfasts of kelps	An extreme south-western species in GB. Found south to the Mediterranean.	Hayward & Ryland (1990)

Table 5.4.1 'Nationally rare' and 'nationally scarce' marine benthic species found in the region (continued)

Species	*Type of organism*	*Area(s) of occurrence*	*Habitat/associations*	*Comments*	*Useful reference*
Cataphellia brodricii	Latticed corklet (an anemone)	S. of Pencabe Head, Kennack, Pentreath Beach, Isles of Scilly	Lower shore and subtidal to 20 m. Under stones, in kelp holdfasts, attached to hard substrata beneath sand.	Southern species. Can be locally common in Devon & Cornwall. Elsewhere N. France.	Manuel (1988)
*Amphianthus dohrnii**	Fan anemone	Off Pencra Head (Lizard), Lundy	Found on pink sea-fan *Eunicella verrucosa*	Sporadic occurrence. Also from Scandinavia to the Mediterranean.	Manuel (1988)
*Caryophyllia inornata**	A cup coral	Isles of Scilly, Lundy, Ilfracombe	Typically in sheltered and shaded location. On rock (0-30 m).	Resembles more common relative. Edge of range in GB. Common in Mediterranean.	Manuel (1988)
*Hoplangia durotrix**	Weymouth carpet coral	Isles of Scilly, Lundy	On rocks in shaded locations. Shallow subtidal.	South-western species. Elsewhere south to Mediterranean.	Manuel (1988)
Balanophyllia regia	Gold and scarlet star coral	Falmouth, between Swanpool & Maenporth, Merope Rocks (near Padstow), Mullion Cove, Isles of Scilly, St. Michael's Mount, Cat's Cove, Dead Man's Cove, Pentire Point, Camel, Beeny Cliff Cave, Lundy, Ilfracombe	Gullies and overhangs. Occasionally low shore. More often shallow subtidal to 25 m.	Elsewhere from Brittany to Mediterranean. Appears to be long lived. Can be locally common.	Manuel (1988)
*Leptopsammia pruvoti**	Sunset coral	Lundy, Isles of Scilly	On rock. Often sheltered from strong current. 10-40 m.	Sporadic southern species. Also SW Europe and Mediterranean.	Manuel (1988)
*Mitella pollicipes**	A goose barnacle	Carn-les-boel	On hard substrata (low shore reef in this case)	Southern. Elsewhere Atlantic Europe to N. Africa. In GB also occasionally on floating debris.	Bassindale (1964)
*Apherusa clevei**	An amphipod	Helford River, Isles of Scilly	Often in association with subtidal algae	Elsewhere scattered locations in Atlantic Europe. May be somewhat under-recorded.	Hayward & Ryland (1990)
Apherusa ovalipes	An amphipod	Helford River, Isles of Scilly	Generally amongst subtidal algae	Mainly southern GB coast. Also Atlantic Europe & North Sea. May be somewhat under-recorded.	Hayward & Ryland (1990)
*Pereionotus testudo**	An amphipod	Fal Estuary, Helford River, Isles of Scilly	Among coralline algae on the low shore and shallow subtidal	Southern species. Also known south to the Mediterranean and the Red Sea.	Hayward & Ryland (1990)
Gammarus chevreuxi	An amphipod	Swanpool, Taw-Torridge Estuary, East Cardiff	From brackish waters, especially coastal marsh	Southern. May occur in a few more sites in south-west England than current records suggest.	Hayward & Ryland (1990)
*Microdeutopus stationis**	An amphipod	Fal Estuary	Often on kelp holdfasts. Found from 0-50 m.	Southern species. Atlantic Europe and south to the Mediterranean.	Lincoln (1979)
*Corophium lacustre**	An amphipod	Newhaven (upper Bristol Channel)	Builds tubes on plants and hydroids in shallow and intertidal marshy banks and ditches	Known from scattered locations in GB	Bratton (1991)
Synisoma lancifer	Sea slater	Battery Rocks, Marazion, Isles of Scilly, Trevone	Amongst algae and boulders in the subtidal fringe	A distinctive southern species. South of GB to Mediterranean.	Naylor (1972)

Table 5.4.1 'Nationally rare' and 'nationally scarce' marine benthic species found in the region (continued)

Species	*Type of organism*	*Area(s) of occurrence*	*Habitat/associations*	*Comments*	*Useful reference*
*Typton spongicola**	The sponge shrimp	Isles of Scilly	Subtidal. Living in sponges to 90 m.	Southern species. Cryptic, therefore may not be as rare as current records suggest.	Hayward & Ryland (1990)
*Clibanarius erythropus**	A hermit crab	Lizard Point (?), Porthleven (?), Marazion (?), Great Hogus Reef (?), Battery Rocks (near Penzance)	Intertidal pools and subtidal to 40 m. Seems to favour dogwelk shells.	Southern species. Formerly at scattered locations in S. Devon & Cornwall. Appears to have declined substantially. See text.	Southward & Southward (1988), Ingle (1993)
*Cestopagurus timidus**	A hermit crab	Isles of Scilly	Low shore to about 70 m	Southern. Also Mediterranean and Canary Islands. Northernmost limit appears to be SW Scotland. Therefore may not be as rare as the dearth of records suggests.	Ingle (1993)
Dromia personata	Sponge crab or sleepy crab	Off Portreath, Lundy	Rocky or stony ground from 10-30 m	Cautiously regarded as scarce. Many old, scattered records exist from southern coasts in GB (Clark 1986). Elsewhere south to W. Africa, Azores and Mediterranean.	Hayward & Ryland (1990)
Achaeus cranchii	Cranch's spider crab	Fal Estuary, Isles of Scilly, Lundy	On hydroids, bryozoans and sea squirts from about 5-70 m	Known from scattered locations from south and west GB to SW Scotland	Ingle (1993)
*Leptochiton scabridus**	A coat-of-mail (chiton)	Helford (Prisk Cove)	On stones in coarse sand. Recently from maerl bed (J.M. Baxter pers. comm. 1994).	Thought to be southern but recent record from Orkney maerl may indicate that it occurs more widely (J.M. Baxter pers. comm. 1994).	Jones & Baxter (1987)
*Jujubinus striatus**	A sea snail	Fal Estuary, Helford River, Isles of Scilly	Low water to 200 m. Often associated with weeds (*Zostera, Ulva, Codium*).	Southern species. Populations seem to have crashed early this century and appear not to have recovered (D.R. Seaward pers. comm. 1995).	Graham (1988)
Alvania cancellata	A sea snail	Helford River	Low water to 90 m Southern species.	South from English Channel.	Graham (1988)
Paludinella littorina#	A sea snail	Martinhoe	Upper shore. In shingle, caves and crevices.	Southern species. Mediterranean and from Britain to Madeira.	Killeen & Light (1994), Bratton (1991)
*Bittium simplex**	A sea snail	Isles of Scilly	Poorly known	Taxonomic confusion may have resulted in a degree of under-recording.	Graham (1988)
*Ocinebrina aciculata**	A sea snail	Porlock (Somerset)	Often with barnacles. On rocky shores from low water to 15 m.	Southern. Elsewhere south to the Mediterranean.	Graham (1988)
Tritonia nilsodhneri	The fan slug	Falmouth Bay, Manacles, off Lizard, Mount's Bay, Isles of Scilly, Newquay, Kellan Head, Lundy	Occurs and feeds on pink sea fan *Eunicella verrucosa* in GB	South-western species. Also known south to Spain. Prone to substantial population fluctuations.	Hiscock (1994), Picton & Morrow (1994)
*Okenia elegans**	Yellow skirt slug	Lundy	Feeds on the sea squirt *Polycarpa rustica*	Wide-ranging records from Devon to Scandinavia. Recent British records are from the SW.	Picton & Morrow (1994)

Table 5.4.1 'Nationally rare' and 'nationally scarce' marine benthic species found in the region (continued)

Species	*Type of organism*	*Area(s) of occurrence*	*Habitat/associations*	*Comments*	*Useful reference*
Trapania pallida	A sea slug	Isles of Scilly, Lundy	Usually found amongst bryozoans, hydroids and sponges. Rocky subtidal areas from 10-20 m.	Also W. Scotland to Atlantic France and Spain.	Picton & Morrow (1994)
*Greilada elegans**	Blue spot slug	Lundy	Associated with and feeds on the bryozoans *Bugula turbinata* and *B. flabellata*	Southern species. Populations are known to fluctuate considerably at Lundy (see Hiscock 1994).	Picton & Morrow (1994)
*Atagema gibba**	A sea slug	Porthkerris Point, Isles of Scilly	Known from steep rock between 8-15 m. Often with sponges.	Southern (?). Elsewhere from Mediterranean.	Picton & Morrow (1994)
*Tenellia adspersa** #	Lagoon sea slug	Portishead (Bristol Channel)	Intertidal & shallow subtidal. Normally brackish, feeding on a range of hydroids.	May prove to occur more widely in GB. Elsewhere globally distributed. Populations fluctuate widely in The Fleet (Region 9).	Picton & Morrow (1994)
*Caloria elegans**	A sea slug	Lundy	Found on various hydroids	Southern, also occurring south to the Mediterranean	Picton & Morrow (1994)
Atrina fragilis	Fan mussel	Helford River (also old and shell records from other parts of the region)	Point of shell down in mud, sand and gravel. Shallow subtidal to considerable depths. Sometimes gregarious.	Widely distributed in GB but rarely encountered. N. of Scotland to Iberian Peninsula. May have declined owing to sea-bed disturbance and collection (Holme 1995). Aggregations may be of importance.	Tebble (1976)
*Pteria hirundo**	Wing-shell	Between Nare Head and Dodman Point	Often on pink sea fan *Eunicella verrucosa*	Southern. Also off-shore but overall rare in British seas. Elsewhere south to Iberian Penninsula and Mediterranean.	Hayward & Ryland (1990)
*Lucinella divaricata**	A bivalve	Porthcurno	Muddy gravel sand. Intertidal.	Southern. South to the Mediterranean and the Black Sea, Madeira and the Canary Is.	Tebble (1976)
*Galeomma turtoni**	Weasel-eye shell	3/4 mile SE of Anthony Lighthouse	Low on shore to about 37 m. Sometimes attached to sea bed by byssus threads.	Southern. Elsewhere Channel Islands and south to Mediterranean, Black Sea and African coast to Senegal.	Tebble (1976)
*Acanthocardia aculeata**	Spiny cockle or red nose	Isles of Scilly (also recent fresh shells collected from Fal Estuary and Helford River)	Infaunal. Also occurs offshore but not commonly.	Southern. Also occurring S. to Mediterranean and NW Africa. Collected as food in past. Seems to have declined.	Hayward & Ryland (1990)
*Callista chione**	A bivalve	Amsterdam Point - Carricknath Point (Fal Estuary), Helford River, Isles of Scilly (old and shell records also).	In sand. Occurs offshore also (to 100 m but not known to be common off-shore).	Southern species. Elsewhere south to the Mediterranean, Canary Islands and Azores.	Hayward & Ryland (1990).
*Victorella pavida**#	Trembling sea mat	Swanpool (S. Cornwall)	Brackish water on a variety of substrata	Known in the UK only from this lagoonal site. Also known from locations between the Baltic and the Mediterranean and other scattered sites around the world.	Barnes (1992)

Table 5.4.1 'Nationally rare' and 'nationally scarce' marine benthic species found in the region (continued)

Species	*Type of organism*	*Area(s) of occurrence*	*Habitat/associations*	*Comments*	*Useful reference*
*Watersipora complanata**	A sea mat	Isles of Scilly	Intertidal. Distinctive encrustations on hard substrata.	Southern. Elsewhere widely distributed in the Mediterranean.	Hayward & Ryland (1979)
*Smittina affinis**	A sea mat	Lundy	Encrusting hard substrata from about 2-18 m	Elsewhere from Brittany	Hayward & Ryland (1990)
*Schizobrachiella sanguinea**	A sea mat	Off Helford River	Sublittoral on hard substrata from 10-50 m	Southern species. Occurs south to the western Mediterranean.	Hayward & Ryland (1979)
*Hippoporidra lusitania**	A sea mat	Lundy	Little known	Also known from Isle of Man and N. Brittany. May be relict species.	
*Turbicellepora magnicostata**	Orange peel bryozoan	Isles of Scilly	Encrusting a variety of hard substrata and algae. Occurs intertidally to 50 m.	Southern. In Great Britain known only from the Isles of Scilly. Also known south to the Mediterranean.	Hayward & Ryland (1979)
Pycnoclavella aurilucens	A sea squirt	Porthkerris Bay, Isles of Scilly, Gurley Rock (Harlyn Bay), Camel, Kellan Head, Lobber Point, Sharpnose Point, Lundy, Rillage Point, Blackstone Point, Highveer Point	Current-swept rocks at 10-30 m	Cautiously regarded as scarce. Southern Also from Brittany & perhaps south to Mediterranean.	Hayward & Ryland (1990)
Phallusia mammillata	A sea squirt	Helford River, Isles of Scilly	On hard substrata with slow to fast water movement. Lower shore to 180 m.	Southern species. In GB occurs mainly off southern Cornwall and Devon. Also Spain & Mediterranean.	Hayward & Ryland (1990)
Molgula oculata	A sea squirt	Helford River, Isles of Scilly, St. Ivels Island, Lundy	Low shore and sublittoral sediments, usually partly protruding	May occur more widely than currently known	Hayward & Ryland (1990)
*Aglaothamnion diaphanum**	A red seaweed	Isles of Scilly	On variety of substrata including other algae and bedrock. Subtidal from about 7-25 m at moderately wave-exposed sites.	Southern species. Also known south to Atlantic coast of France.	Maggs & Hommersand (1993)
*Aglaothamnion priceanum**	A red seaweed	Manacles	On other algae from about 5-30 m. Occurs on moderately exposed shores.	Occurs from Norway to NW France. Found very infrequently.	Maggs & Hommersand (1993)
*Cryptonemia lomation**	A red seaweed	Manacles, Isles of Scilly	Habitat poorly known	Southern species. These are the first authentic records outside the Mediterranean.	Maggs & Guiry (1987a)
*Gelidium sesquipedale**	A red seaweed	Sennen Cove, Gurnard's Head, Isles of Scilly	Shallow subtidal. Occurs on coasts exposed to severe wave action.	Southern species restricted in GB to Cornwall & Devon. Elsewhere south to Mediterranean & N. Africa.	Dixon & Irvine (1977)
Gelidiella calcicola##	A red seaweed	Fal Estuary, Isles of Scilly	Normally confined to maerl	Localised in restricted habitat	Maggs & Guiry (1987b)
Lithothamnion corallioides##	Maerl	Fal Estuary, Helford River	Forming maerl beds. Associated with rich assemblages of deposit and suspension feeders.	On EC Habitats & Species Directive, Annex Vb. Falmouth has the most extensive living maerl bed in England. In Helford it is the most abundant maerl species.	Irvine & Chamberlain (1994)

Table 5.4.1 'Nationally rare' and 'nationally scarce' marine benthic species found in the region (continued)

Species	*Type of organism*	*Area(s) of occurrence*	*Habitat/associations*	*Comments*	*Useful reference*
Gracilaria bursa-pastoris	A red seaweed	Helford River, Bosahan Head, Kennack Sands, Isles of Scilly	On stone in sheltered places. Upper subtidal, often with sand deposition.	Southern. Elsewhere widely distributed in warm waters.	Dixon & Irvine (1977)
Gracilaria multipartita	A red seaweed	Helford River	On stone from upper subtidal to 15 m. Tolerant of sand and silt deposition.	Southern. Probably widely distributed in warm waters.	Dixon & Irvine (1977)
Schmitzia hiscockiana	A red seaweed	Carrick North Point (Fal Estuary), Isles of Scilly, Lundy	Subtidal current-exposed cobbles	Scattered distribution in GB. Common at few sites of occurrence. Possibly endemic to the British Isles.	Maggs & Guiry (1985)
Gigartina pistillata	A red seaweed	Lizard (Kennack, Soapy Cove, Asparagus Is., Kynance Cove, Jangye-ryn), Isles of Scilly	On stone. Shallow subtidal, in pools and occasionally exposed by the tide. Tolerant of sand cover. Sheltered and slightly wave-exposed sites.	South-western species in British Isles	Dixon & Irvine (1977)
Cruoria cruoriaeformis##	A red seaweed	Fal Estuary, Isles of Scilly	Virtually confined to maerl	Southerly species in the British Isles	Maggs & Guiry (1989)
*Bornetia secundiflora**	A red seaweed	Helford River, Isles of Scilly, Booby's Bay (?)	Boulders and bedrock. Subtidal fringe to 3 m depth. Moderate to exposed sites.	Southern species. Occurring south to Morocco and Mediterranean.	Maggs & Hommersand (1993)
Pterosiphonia pennata	A red seaweed	Lizard (Cadgwith), Isles of Scilly, Greenaway Beach, Tintagel Head, Penhally Hill, off Beeny Sisters, Concleave Strand, Lower Sharpnose Point, Lundy	On muddy bedrock and pebbles and also on maerl. Moderate to very wave sheltered sites. Extreme low water to 10 m.	Southern species. SW Europe and Mediterranean. Wide distribution in Atlantic and Pacific.	Maggs & Hommersand (1993)
Zanardinia prototypus	A brown seaweed	Mother Ivey's Bay, Camel, Penally Hill, Beeny Sisters, Pentagon, Lundy, Concleave Strand, Baggy Point to Foreland Point	On hard substrata. Subtidal to 20 m. Especially on silty rock.	Subtropical to warm temperate species. Ephemeral species - probably substantial annual fluctuations in population size.	Fletcher (1987)
Choristocarpus tenellus	A brown seaweed	E. Pennally Hill, Lundy	On gravel around 20 m	Little known	
Padina pavonica	Turkey feather alga	Boscastle	On hard substrata	Southern. Ephemeral species - substantial changes in populations with time.	Price *et al.* (1979)
Carpomitra costata	A brown seaweed	Falmouth, Manacles, UCY reef, Isles of Scilly, off Penally Hill, off Beeny Sisters, Lundy	On bedrock and boulders. Subtidal to 37 m. Tolerant of sand cover.	Probably a summer annual. Southern species.	Fletcher (1987)

Species names are after Howson (1987); in the absence of a specific common name the nearest available group name has been used. Key: * = nationally rare; # = protected under the Wildlife & Countryside Act 1981; ## = maerl or in association with maerl; ? = present occurrence at this site uncertain/dubious record. Note: many of the scarce species listed here are only a little more common than the rare species listed.

the marine environment in the UK (Fowler & Laffoley 1993). It may also be possible that some out-posted populations of particular species at the limit of their range may be genetically isolated and/or divergent from core populations and important to the genetic biodiversity of the species as a whole. The importance of genetic, species and habitat biodiversity in the UK has recently been the focus of *Biodiversity: the Steering Group report* (Anon. 1995). Ecological and pragmatic arguments for the conservation of populations of species that are rare because they are at the margins of wider distributions are summarised by Hunter & Hutchinson (1994).

It has been suggested that the Isles of Scilly are important for marine species. The Isles of Scilly are the only Lusitanian, semi-oceanic archipelago in Europe (Anon. 1995). Added to this the waters around the Isles of Scilly have an unusual temperature regime, varying annually by only about 5°C - a factor that may be responsible for its rich and varied algal communities, for example (Maggs & Guiry 1987b). Many nationally rare and scarce species discussed here are found in the Isles of Scilly and Lundy. This may be to some extent a result of geographically localised survey effort. However, many small offshore islands are often habitat-rich when compared to similar areas of open coast, because they contain, within a small area, both areas exposed to and others sheltered from wave action and currents. If rarities occur in a wide range of habitat types, the likelihood that rarities will be found in a habitat-rich area may be higher. Furthermore, extreme south-western shores in the British Isles tend to bear species-rich floras and faunas (e.g. Price *et al.* 1980; Connor *et al.* 1995; Anon. 1995), probably because of varied topography and geology combined with position (in the path of the North Atlantic Drift) (Turk 1983). In biogeographic terms Cornwall has sometimes been regarded as more akin to northern France than to the rest of the British Isles (Turk 1983).

None of the species from this region is known to be a common deep-water species, and so it is unlikely that any appear rare simply because their distribution only just includes the generally shallower near-shore sea area that is the focus of this study. Some of the listed species, however, are likely to occur to some extent in the waters of Great Britain beyond the scope of this study.

5.4.3 Information sources used

The sites of intertidal and subtidal benthic survey data utilised in this analysis are mapped in section 4.2. In Region 11 some of the available data come from MNCR survey work and earlier NCC-funded surveys. There is a history of collecting associated with the Marine Biological Association in Plymouth (Marine Biological Association 1957). Data are also available from environmental impact assessments and Environment Agency (formerly the National Rivers Authority) surveys as well as from publications arising from the extensive collections of local marine biological recorders and staff at the Cornish Biological Records Centre and the Universities of Exeter and Plymouth. Additional records have been considered following personal communications with experts in many taxonomic fields. It has not been possible in this chapter to list all the available literature on which this analysis has been based, but the information reviews and recent papers listed in sections 5.4.5 and 4.2.5 should allow access to the majority of the available information.

The availability of suitable information in the subtidal zone of Region 11 shows concentrations. Coverage is generally good but some areas are more heavily surveyed. Intertidal surveys in Region 11 also show a patchy distribution, with some concentrations in estuaries and sounds.

In Region 11 records go back over many years; for example, marine molluscs were first recorded in the area as early as the mid 1700s (Turk 1983). Whereas every effort has been made to obtain biogeographic data for rarity assessment in the present study, data have not been used from reports prior to 1965. There are also, however, old records from the Isles of Scilly, the Helford River and other parts of south Cornwall and Devon of, for example, the rarely recorded sea anemone *Anemonactis mazeli*, the crabs *Bathynectes longipes* and *Eurynome spinosa*, the shrimp *Alpheus macrocheles*, the snails *Gibbula pennanti*, *Jordaniella truncatula*, *Ocinebrina aciculata* and *Paludinella littorina* and the bryozoan *Diporula verrucosa.* The warty cockle *Plagiocardium papillosum* is no longer thought to exist at its former sites of occurrence in the Helford and the Isles of Scilly, and the hermit crab *Clibanarius erythropus* has apparently disappeared from most of its known sites in south Cornwall, following either natural environmental changes or human environmental impact (Southward & Southward 1988). It would be valuable to attempt to re-confirm old records. Species that are likely to be very under-recorded or overlooked on a national scale have been avoided in the present work.

MNCR survey work uses a consistent methodology to record conspicuous species (Hiscock 1996). Not all the data available from surveys in this region are as broad in scope as MNCR surveys and they may not include less common species or those less familiar to a specialist worker. Inconsistent recording has, however, not substantially reduced the quantity of available information for rarity assessment in this region. The MNCR of Great Britain is at present incomplete but in future will substantially increase the quality and evenness of distribution of the available data. This combined with other surveys will almost certainly expand our knowledge of the 'nationally rare' and 'scarce' species in Region 11. Consequently the nationally rare and scarce status of the organisms presented here may require re-evaluation, and in future further species may be added to the list for this region. Populations of species with short life histories, such as ephemeral algae and sea slugs, may require more regular re-evaluation of their occurrence than others. Longer-term trends in the English Channel may cause range extensions and even the loss of certain species from the extreme south-west of the British Isles (see Southward & Crisp 1954; Turk 1983).

5.4.4 Acknowledgements

The author is grateful for the assistance of the JNCC Marine Conservation and Coastal Conservation Branches as well as the expert advice of Dr R.N. Bamber, Dr J.M. Baxter, Dr J. Brodie, P.F. Clark, D.W. Connor, Dr M.J. Costello, Dr R.L. Fletcher, Dr J.D. Fish, Dr P.R. Garwood, Dr J.M. Hall-Spencer, Dr T. Harris, Dr P.J. Hayward, Dr K. Hiscock, J.M. Light, I.J. Killeen, Dr G. Könnecker, Dr C.A. Maggs, Dr J.D. McKenzie, Prof. P.G. Moore, J.J. Moore, D. Moss, Prof. T.A. Norton, Dr J.D. Nunn, B.E. Picton, D.R. Seaward, Dr E.C. Southward, I. Tittley, S.M. Turk and Dr R.B. Williams. The regional expertise of M. Camplin, Dr P. Gainey and especially S.M. Turk has also been of great value, as has the general assistance and comments on drafts by Dr R.S.K Barnes, Dr J.D. George, Dr T.O. Hill and Dr A. Rogers. Access to the JNCC's Marine Nature Conservation Review Database, the NIBESRC Database at the Ulster Museum and the ERICA database run by the Cornish Biological Records Unit has been invaluable for the overall analysis.

5.4.5 Further sources of information

A. References cited

Ackers, R.G., Moss, D., & Picton, B.E. 1992. *Sponges of the British Isles ('Sponge V') - a colour guide and working document.* 5th ed. Ross-on-Wye, Marine Conservation Society.

Anon. 1995. *Biodiversity: the UK Steering Group Report.* London, HMSO, for Department of the Environment.

Barnes, R.S.K. 1992. *Brackish water fauna of north-western Europe.* Cambridge, Cambridge University Press.

Bassindale, R. 1964. *British barnacles with keys and notes for the identification of the species.* London, Linnean Society of London. (Synopses of the British Fauna, No. 14.)

Bratton, J.H., *ed.* 1991. *British Red Data Books: 3. Invertebrates other than insects.* Peterborough, Joint Nature Conservation Committee

Connor, D.W., Hill, T.O., Little, M.C., & Northen, K.O. 1995. Marine Nature Conservation Review: intertidal biotope manual. Version 6.95. *Joint Nature Conservation Committee Report,* No. 249.

Cornelius, P.F.S. 1995. North-west European thecate hydroids and their medusae, part 2. Keys and notes for the identification of the species. *In: Synopses of the British Fauna (New Series), No. 50,* ed. by R.S.K. Barnes & J.H. Crothers. Shrewsbury, Field Studies Council, for Linnean Society of London / Estuarine and Coastal Sciences Association.

Dixon, P.S., & Irvine, L.M. 1977. *Seaweeds of the British Isles. Vol. 1. Rhodophyta. Part 1. Introduction, Nemaliales, Gigartinales.* London, British Museum (Natural History).

Fletcher, R.L. 1987. *Seaweeds of the British Isles. Vol. 3: Fucophyceae (Phaeophyceae).* London, British Museum (Natural History).

Fowler, S., & Laffoley, D. 1993. Stability in Mediterranean-Atlantic sessile epifaunal communities at the northern limits of their range. *Journal of Experimental Marine Biology & Ecology, 172:* 109-127.

Graham, A. 1988. *Molluscs: Prosobranch and pyramidellid gastropods. Keys and notes for the identification of the species.* 2nd ed. Leiden, E.J. Brill / Dr W. Backhuys, for Linnean Society of London / Estuarine and Brackish-water Sciences Association. (Synopses of the British Fauna (New Series), No. 2.)

Hayward, P.J., & Ryland, J.S. 1979. *British ascophoran bryozoans. Keys and notes for the identification of the species.* London, Academic Press, for Linnean Society of London / Estuarine and Brackish-Water Sciences Association. (Synopses of the British Fauna (New Series), No. 14.)

Hayward, P.J., & Ryland, J.S., *eds.* 1990. *The marine fauna of the British Isles and north-west Europe.* 2 vols. Oxford, Clarendon Press.

Hiscock, K. 1994. Marine communities at Lundy - origins, longevity and change. *Biological Journal of the Linnean Society, 51:* 183-188.

Hiscock, K., *ed.* 1996. *Marine Nature Conservation Review of Great Britain. Volume 1: rationale and methods.* Peterborough, Joint Nature Conservation Committee. (Coasts and seas of the United Kingdom. MNCR series.)

Hiscock, K., Stone, S.M.K., & George, J.D. 1983. The marine fauna of Lundy. Porifera (Sponges): a preliminary study. *Report of the Lundy Field Society, 34:* 16-35.

Holme, N.A. 1995. Conservation of marine molluscs in the British Isles. *In: The conservation biology of molluscs,* ed. by E.A. Kay. Gland, Switzerland, IUCN.

Howson, C.M., *ed.* 1987. *Directory of the British marine fauna and flora. A coded checklist of the marine fauna and flora of the British Isles and its surrounding seas.* 1st ed. Ross-on-Wye, Marine Conservation Society.

Hunter, M.L., & Hutchinson, A. 1994. The virtues and shortcomings of parochialism: conserving species that are locally rare, but are globally common. *Conservation Biology, 8:* 1163-1165.

Ingle, R. 1993. *Hermit crabs of the north-eastern Atlantic Ocean and Mediterranean Sea. An illustrated key.* London, Chapman & Hall, for Natural History Museum Publications.

Irvine, L.M., & Chamberlain, Y.M. 1994. *Seaweeds of the British Isles. Vol. 1. Rhodophyta. Part 2B. Corallinales, Hildenbrandiales.* London, Natural History Museum.

IUCN Species Survival Commission. 1995. *IUCN Red List Categories.* Gland, Switzerland, & Cambridge, UK, IUCN.

Jones, A.M., & Baxter, J.M. 1987. *Molluscs: Caudofoveata, Solenogastres, Polyplacophora and Scaphopoda. Keys and notes for the identification of the species.* London, E.J. Brill / Dr. W. Backhuys, for Linnean Society of London / Estuarine and Brackish-Water Sciences Association. (Synopses of the British Fauna (New Series), No. 37.)

Killeen, I.J., & Light, J.M. 1994. *A survey of the prosobranch mollusc* Paludinella littorina *on the Pembrokeshire coast.* Bangor, Countryside Council for Wales. (CCW Science Report, No. 62.)

Lincoln, R.J. 1979. *British marine Amphipoda: Gammaridea.* London, British Museum (Natural History).

Maggs, C.A., & Guiry, M.D. 1985. Life history and reproduction of *Schmitzia hiscockiana* sp. nov. (Rhodophyta, Gigartinales) from the British Isles. *Phycologia, 24:* 297-310.

Maggs, C.A., & Guiry, M.D. 1987a. An Atlantic population of *Pikea californica* (Dumontiaceae, Rhodophyta). *Journal of Phycology, 23:* 170-176.

Maggs, C.A., & Guiry, M.D. 1987b. *Gelidiella calcicola* sp. nov. (Rhodophyta) from the British Isles and northern France. *British Phycological Journal, 22:* 417-434.

Maggs, C.A., & Guiry, M.D. 1989. A re-evaluation of the crustose red algal genus Cruoria and the Family Cruoriaceae. *British Phycological Journal, 24:* 253-269.

Maggs, C.A., & Hommersand, M.H. 1993. *Seaweeds of the British Isles. Volume 1: Rhodophyta. Part 3A: Ceramiales.* London, HMSO for Natural History Museum.

Manuel, R.L. 1988. *British Anthozoa (Coelenterata: Octocorallia and Hexacorallia); keys and notes for the identification of the species.* 2nd ed. Leiden, Linnean Society of London / Estuarine and Brackish Water Sciences Association.

Marine Biological Association of the United Kingdom. 1957. *Plymouth marine fauna.* 3rd ed. Plymouth, Marine Biological Association of the United Kingdom.

Picton, B.E., & Morrow, C.C. 1994. *A field guide to the nudibranchs of the British Isles.* London, Immel Publishing.

Price, J.H., Hepton, C.A., & Honey, S.I. 1980. The inshore benthic biota of the Lizard Peninsula, south west Cornwall. II. The marine algae: Rhodophyta; discussion. *Cornish Studies, 8:* 5-36.

Price, J.H., Tittley, I., & Richardson, W.D. 1979. The distribution of *Padina pavonica* (L.) Lamour. (Phaeophyta: Dictyotales) on British and adjacent European shores. *Bulletin of the British Museum (Natural History), Botany Series, 7:* 1-67.

Sanderson, W.G. 1996. Rare marine benthic flora and fauna in Great Britain: the development of criteria for assessment. *Joint Nature Conservation Committee Report,* No. 240.

Southward, A.J., & Crisp, D.J. 1954. Recent changes in the distribution of the intertidal barnacles *Chthamalus stellatus* and *Balanus balanoides* in the British Isles. *Journal of Animal Ecology, 23:* 163-177.

Southward, A.J., & Southward, E.C. 1988. The distribution and ecology of the hermit crab *Clibanarius erythropus* in the Western Channel. *Journal of the Marine Biological Association of the UK, 57:* 441-452.

Tebble, N. 1976. *British bivalve seashells. A handbook for identification.* 2nd ed. Edinburgh, HMSO for Royal Scottish Museum.

Turk, S.M. 1983. Cornish marine conchology. *Journal of Conchology, 31:* 137-151.

B. Further reading

Boyden, C.R., Crothers, J.H., Little, C., & Mettam, C. 1977. The intertidal invertebrate fauna of the Severn estuary. *Field Studies, 4:* 477-554.

Davies, J. 1994. Benthic marine ecosystems in Great Britain: a review of current knowledge. Western Channel and Bristol Channel and approaches (MNCR Coastal sectors 8 and 9). *Nature Conservancy Council, CSD Report,* No. 1173. (Marine Nature Conservation Review Report, No. MNCR/OR/9.)

Dipper, F. 1981. Sublittoral survey of the Scilly Isles and south Cornwall. *Nature Conservancy Council, CSD Report,* No. 364.

Eno, N.C. 1992. *Lundy Marine Nature Reserve littoral monitoring report, 5th - 9th October 1991.* Peterborough, English Nature. (English Nature Research Report, No. 12.)

Fowler, S.L. 1992. *Marine monitoring in the Isles of Scilly.* Peterborough, English Nature. (English Nature Research Report, No. 9.)

Gill, C., & Mercer, T. 1989. Surveys of harbours, rias and estuaries in southern Britain: the Camel estuary. *Nature Conservancy Council, CSD Report,* No. 954. (Field Studies Council Report, No. FSC/OPRU/14/88.)

Hayward, P.J. 1976. The marine fauna and flora of the Isles of Scilly: Bryozoa II. *Journal of Natural History, 10*: 319-330.

Hayward, P.J. 1976. The marine fauna of Lundy - Bryozoa. *Report of the Lundy Field Society, 27:* 16-34.

Hiscock, K. 1979. South-west Britain sublittoral survey. Field survey of sublittoral habitats and species in the upper Bristol Channel (Mid-Glamorgan, South Glamorgan and north Somerset). June 14th 1978 and July 2nd to 5th 1978. *Nature Conservancy Council, CSD Report,* No. 283.

Hiscock, K. 1981. South-west Britain sublittoral survey. Final report. *Nature Conservancy Council, CSD Report,* No. 327.

Hiscock, S., & Maggs, C.A. 1984. Notes on the distribution and ecology of some new and interesting seaweeds from south-west Britain. *British Phycological Journal, 19*: 73-87.

Little, A. 1989. Surveys of harbours, rias and estuaries in southern Britain: Taw and Torridge estuary. *Nature Conservancy Council, CSD Report,* No. 1002. (Field Studies Council Report, No. FSC/OPRU/10/88.)

Maggs, C., & Hiscock, K. 1979. South-west Britain sublittoral survey. Field survey of sublittoral habitats and species in north east Cornwall (Tintagel Head to the Devon border). *Nature Conservancy Council, CSD Report,* No. 282.

Picton, B.E. 1978. The marine fauna of Lundy: Prosobranchia. *Report of the Lundy Field Society, 29*: 38-45.

Price, J.H., Hepton, C.E.L., & Honey, S.I. 1979. The inshore benthic biota of the Lizard Peninsula, south west Cornwall. 1. The marine algae: history; Chlorophyta; Phaeophyta. *Cornish Studies, 7*: 7-37.

Rostron, D. 1985. Surveys of harbours, rias and estuaries in southern Britain: Falmouth. *Nature Conservancy Council, CSD Report,* No. 623. (Field Studies Council Report, No. FSC/OPRU/49/85.)

Smith, B.P., & Laffoley, D. 1992. *Saline lagoons and lagoon-like habitats in England.* 1st ed. Peterborough, English Nature. (English Nature Science, No. 6.)

Smith, L.P., & Little, C. 1980. Intertidal communities on rocky shores in the Severn estuary. *Proceedings of the Bristol Naturalists' Society, 38*: 61-67.

Tompsett, P.E. 1994. *Helford River survey. Monitoring report No. 4 for 1993.* Redruth, Helford Voluntary Marine Conservation Area Advisory Group (unpublished report).

Wilson, J.G. 1981. The marine fauna of Lundy - Bivalvia. *Report of the Lundy Field Society, 32*: 29-37.

C. Contact names and addresses

Type of information	*Contact address and telephone no.*
Cornish records	S.M. Turk & Dr P. Gainey, Cornish Biological Records Unit, Trevithick Centre, Trevenson Road, Pool, Redruth, Cornwall TR15 3PL, tel: 01209 710424
Helford River	P. Tompsett, Helford VMCA Working Group, c/o Cornish Biological Records Unit, Trevithick Centre, Trevenson Road, Pool, Redruth, Cornwall TR15 3PL, tel: 01209 710424
N. Devon records	*M. Camplin, Devon Wildlife Trust, Exeter, tel: 01392 79244
Saline lagoons	Dr R.S.K. Barnes, St. Catharine's College, University of Cambridge, Cambridge CB2 1RL, tel: 01223 333296
Sponges, sea slugs, hydroids	B.E. Picton, BioMar, Environmental Science Unit, University of Dublin, Trinity College, Dublin 2, Republic of Ireland, tel: 00353 16772941
Amphipods	Prof. P.G. Moore, University Marine Biological Station, Millport, Isle of Cumbrae KA28 0EG, tel: 01475 350581
Crabs	P.F. Clark, Department of Zoology, Natural History Museum, Cromwell Road, London SW7 5BD, tel: 0171 938 9123
Molluscs	J.M. Light, 88 Peperharow Road, Godalming, Surrey GU7 2PN, tel: 01483 417782
Sea squirts	*D.W. Connor, Marine Conservation Branch, JNCC, tel: 01733 62626
Bryozoans	Dr P.J. Hayward, School of Biological Sciences, University College Swansea, Singleton Park, Swansea, West Glamorgan SA2 8PP, tel: 01792 205678
Brown algae	Dr R.L. Fletcher, University of Portsmouth, Marine Laboratory, Ferry Road, Hayling Island, Hants. PO1 10DG, tel: 01705 876543
Red algae	Dr C.A. Maggs, School of Biology & Biochemistry, Queen's University of Belfast, Belfast BT7 1NN, tel: 01232 245133

*Starred contact addresses are given in full in the Appendix.

5.5 Exploited sea-bed species

Dr M.G. Pawson & C.F. Robson

5.5.1 Introduction

This section describes the distribution of large populations of species that live on, near, or in the bottom sediments of the sea bed (collectively called 'the benthos') and that are routinely exploited, mainly for human food. The exploitation itself is described in sections 9.1 and 9.2. Many of these species also provide an essential food source for other species, such as fish and birds, for example seabirds, waders and wildfowl. Most of the species discussed have planktonic larvae; the dispersal of planktonic larvae and the interrelation between populations of the same species can only be inferred from studies on movements of water masses. Their distributions are determined by factors such as water temperature (see section 2.3) and available habitat/substrate type (see also section 4.2). The species described may also be found elsewhere in the region, but in smaller numbers.

All species apart from *Nephrops* are referred to by their common names in the text. The scientific names of the species are given in Table 5.5.1.

This region is characterised by important populations of crustacea, such as lobster, spider crab and crawfish. These are prevalent around the coasts of Cornwall, Isles of Scilly and north Devon, with smaller distributions along the south Wales and Somerset coasts. There are extensive scallop and edible crab grounds, which are of national significance. Crawfish, which have a south-westerly distribution in Britain, are also very important in this region. There are relatively few sheltered estuarine areas in the region and this is reflected in the existence of few important stocks of molluscs, such as mussels and cockles.

Table 5.5.1 Species names

Common name	*Scientific name*
Lobster	*Homarus gammarus*
Edible or brown crab	*Cancer pagurus*
Spider crab	*Maja squinado*
Crawfish, spiny lobster	*Palinurus elephas*
Dublin Bay prawn, scampi, Norway lobster or langoustine	*Nephrops norvegicus*
Deep water prawn (or shrimp - referred to as both)	*Pandalus borealis*
Pink prawn (or shrimp - referred to as both)	*Pandalus montagui*
Brown shrimp	*Crangon crangon*
Cockle	*Cerastoderma edule*
Mussel	*Mytilus edulis*
Native oyster	*Ostrea edulis*
Periwinkle	*Littorina littorea*
Razor shell	*Ensis* spp.
Scallop	*Pecten maximus*
Queen scallop	*Aequipecten opercularis*
Cuttlefish	*Sepia officinalis*
Squid	*Loligo* spp.
Whelk	*Buccinum undatum*
Lugworm	*Arenicola marina*
Ragworm/king ragworm	*Neanthes virens/Hediste diversicolor*
Maerl	*Lithothamnion coralloides* & *Phymatolithon calcareum*

5.5.2 Important locations and species

Crustacea

The broad-scale distributions of lobster, crawfish and brown shrimp in the region are shown in Map 5.5.1 and those of edible crab and spider crab on Map 5.5.2. Lobsters are distributed inshore in the region, along exposed or rocky shorelines wherever there is suitable habitat, such as rocky reefs with crevices for protection. Lobsters are uncommon in the Bristol Channel east of the Devon-Somerset border, owing to a lack of suitable habitat.

Spider crabs and edible crabs are found along most of the exposed or rocky shorelines in the region, often on softer sediments - ranging from sand/gravel to rock - than lobsters. The inshore waters of Cornwall around to Hartland Point on the north Devon coast are an important nursery ground for juvenile edible crabs (Pawson 1995).

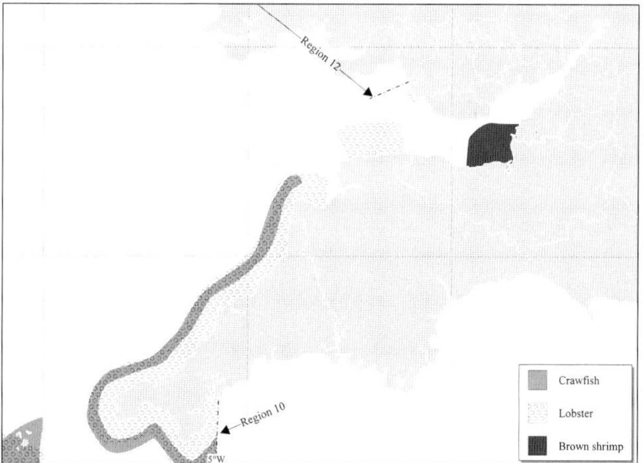

Map 5.5.1 Distribution of lobster, crawfish and brown shrimp. © MAFF.

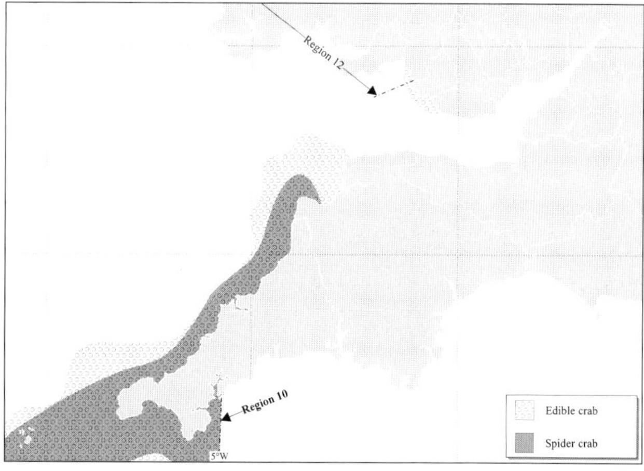

Map 5.5.2 Distribution of edible crab and spider crab. © MAFF.

Juvenile edible crabs tend to be found inshore and adults further offshore (Rees & Dare 1993).

Crawfish have a westerly distribution in the UK and are more widely distributed in this region than in some others. Compared with lobster, crawfish are less common and are found further offshore. Brown shrimp are common in sandy estuaries and are particularly numerous in Bridgwater Bay. *Nephrops*, deep-water prawns and pink prawns are not known to occur in exploitable quantities in the region.

Molluscs

The main locations where exploitable populations of cockles, mussels and native oysters are found in the region are shown on Map 5.5.3. Cockles are found in the intertidal zones of estuaries such as the Fal and in other sheltered sites in this region. There are known exploitable stocks of native oyster in the Fal Estuary and Helford River, the Camel Estuary and off Porthcawl. Mussels occur from the mid-shore to the subtidal zone in water of normal or variable salinity, and in areas exposed to water currents. They attach themselves using 'byssus threads' to bedrock, sand, gravel or pebble substrata or other mussels and empty shells and have the effect of binding the substratum. Small stocks of mussels are distributed around coastal sites in the region, such as in the Tresillian River and Ruan Creek in the Fal Estuary, off Port Navas in the Helford River, and in the Taw-Torridge Estuary. Periwinkles are present throughout the region on algae growing on rocky shorelines. Razor shells occur in the inshore areas around the region, mainly where the sea bed is clean sand.

Scallops live on sandy/gravel areas of the sea bed, and in this region they are found mainly in areas off the Cornwall and Isles of Scilly coasts. There are no known exploitable quantities of queen scallops in the region. Cuttlefish numbers are concentrated in the centre of the Western Channel during the winter and move into coastal areas during spring and summer. Spawning of cuttlefish occurs from mid-April to mid-May. Squid are found offshore seasonally throughout the region, and move inshore to spawn in the spring. Whelks are widely dispersed throughout the region. The broadscale distribution of scallops in the region is shown in Map 5.5.4.

Polychaetes

The intertidal and subtidal zones in the region's estuaries support populations of polychaetes such as lugworm and ragworm. Lugworms are common in less exposed areas where there is a higher organic content in the substratum. They occur elsewhere in a wide range of sediment types, from almost pure mud to clean sand (Davidson *et al.* 1991). Ragworms are usually found in the intertidal and sublittoral in slightly estuarine conditions. They live in burrows in muddy sediments or under rocks and stones. Both ragworm and lugworm are dug for angling bait in several parts of the region (see section 9.1.2).

Others

Maerl is a collective name given to various species of calcareous algae within the Rhodophyta (red seaweeds) that live unattached on the substratum in sheltered areas. The

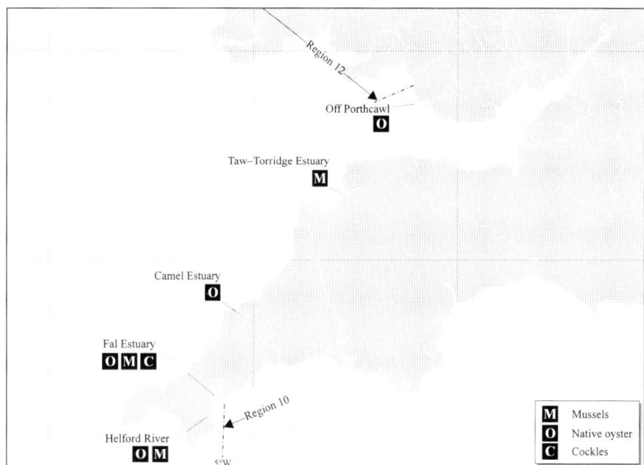

Map 5.5.3 Main inshore and estuarine locations of mussels, cockles and native oysters. © MAFF.

Map 5.5.4 Main locations of scallops. © MAFF.

two most common maerl species are both listed on Annex Vb of the EC Habitats & Species Directive (see sections 4.2 and 5.4). The most extensive known beds of living maerl in England and Wales are located in the Fal Estuary (Cordrey 1996; Farnham & Jephson 1977; Tompsett 1996), where beds are mainly located on the St. Mawes Bank (Davies & Sotheran 1995). Maerl has also been found at locations in the Helford River, but in a smaller area than in the Fal. Dead maerl is dredged from the sea bed for application to soil (see section 5.5.3). There are concentrations of dead maerl which form a wide offshore bank that extends across Falmouth Bay from Rosemullion Point to Gull Rock (Cordrey 1996). The Falmouth Bay area has been surveyed to confirm the distribution of such benthic biotopes (Davies & Sotheran 1995).

5.5.3 Human activities

The exploitation by fisheries of the species covered in this section is described in section 9.1, and by mariculture in section 9.2. Issues relating to exploited sea-bed species are commonly associated with the method by which they are exploited and the amounts taken. Restrictions are imposed by the authorities who manage the resource, and include minimum landing sizes and catch quotas. There are national statutory Minimum Landing Size (MLS) limits for edible crab, lobster, spider crab, *Nephrops*, scallops and velvet crab. The actual size limits may vary between the Sea Fisheries Committees (SFC) that apply them. In addition the Cornwall SFC sets an MLS on crawfish, the Devon SFC on periwinkles and the South Wales SFC on cockles. Other management tools, such as the zoning scheme around the Lundy Marine Nature Reserve, identify restrictions on some fishing methods, including potting in sensitive zones of special marine conservation interest - i.e. the Knoll Pins. There are fishery bylaws in the Midlands Region of the Environment Agency that prohibit the taking of brown shrimp between sunset on Saturdays and 6 am on Mondays. It is thought that overfishing has had a serious impact on stocks of migratory species, such as crawfish. Some fishermen also attribute the decline of crawfish stocks to the over-use of tangle nets.

During this century, the overfishing of native oysters has caused the traditional industry of oyster dredging to become less productive in several estuaries in the region, notably the Helford (Masters 1994). The use of antifouling paint containing tributyltin (TBT) caused problems for the native oyster fishery in the region in the 1980s. However the use of TBT in anti-fouling paint for boats over 25 m in length was banned in 1987 and the water quality appears to be improving. In a survey of the native oyster population in the Helford River, Protz (1995) found the majority of individuals were under 18 months old, a fact attributed to the effects of parasites (such as *Bonamia*), TBT pollution and illegal collection. Mussels are not currently being exploited from the Taw-Torridge Estuary, owing to reduced water quality. The effects on estuarine organisms of long-term contamination by mining waste was studied by Bryan & Gibbs (1993).

There has been concern in the region about the continuing effects on stocks of native oysters of the protozoan parasite *Bonamia* and its possible spread to other areas. For this reason the movement of native oysters is carefully controlled and the Pacific oyster, which is resistant to the parasite, is farmed in preference. Another issue of concern in the region is the introduction of other non-native species, such as the hard-shelled clam, and the effect that their subsequent exploitation has on native species and their habitat. A bloom of the phytoplankton species *Alexandrium tamarense* in the Fal Estuary in July 1995 caused the first recorded instance of Paralytic Shellfish Poisoning (PSP) in the UK south of the Humber (Reid *et al.* 1995).

Maerl is rich in calcium carbonate and dead maerl is dredged by the Cornish Calcified Seaweed Company from the sea bed in Falmouth Bay and further east for liming soil. This extraction is contentious, as live maerl, which is rare and fragile, with two species listed in the EC Habitats & Species Directive (Table 5.4.1), may also be found in the areas made up mostly of dead maerl.

Much of the region's coast has been subjected to localised navigational dredging and marine aggregate extraction licence applications, but production licences for marine aggregate extraction in the region are currently limited to the Bristol Channel (see also section 9.4). All dredging activities have short-term, localised effects, such as the removal of material and organisms, but long-term effects on, for example, shellfish stocks or morphology are much more difficult to assess, owing to the difficulty of determining which effects are the result of dredging and which the result of the many other factors operating (Doody *et al.* 1993). Short- or long-term changes in sediment deposition can result, as well as inevitable changes in the topography of the bed. A joint Welsh Office and Department of the Environment project, *Bristol Channel marine aggregate: resources and constraints,* will study the effects of marine aggregates dredging on benthic resources in the Bristol Channel.

Bait collection, especially digging for polychaetes, can have major localised effects on intertidal habitats and communities and can also cause disturbance to birds, particularly when they are concentrated in estuaries and embayments (see sections 5.11.3 and 5.12.3 and references in section 5.5.6B). Bait collection in the region is described in section 9.1.2.

5.5.4 Information sources used

The four maps in this section show schematically the known broad-scale distributions of the main species of interest, based on current knowledge from MAFF Directorate of Fisheries Research fishery officers and the Devon and Cornwall SFCs on the locations of the species and their fisheries. There is supporting information in the form of catch statistics (for commercial landings) and biological samples of crustacea, collected at the main ports and some secondary ports (see sections 9.1 and 9.2), plus intertidal surveys for molluscs in selected areas. These data provide some information about the location of spawning and nursery areas, but to establish the links between individual areas for spawning, nursery and adults would require specific research vessel investigations on the planktonic stages, the hydrography and the movement (or otherwise) of juveniles and adults. Barring substantial climate change or over-exploitation, these distributions and relationships are likely to remain stable over several decades. The seaward boundaries on the maps are only indicative, and because only large, exploitable populations are described, the species may also be found elsewhere in the region but in smaller numbers.

Maps were provided by the Shellfish Resource Group, MAFF Directorate of Fisheries Research and the Sea Fisheries Committees. Information was also used from Lee & Ramster (1981). Pawson (1995) presents information including distribution maps of selected species (scallops, cuttlefish, lobster, edible crab and spider crab) around the British Isles and has a species-specific bibliography. Masters (1994) describes the natural history of the native oyster in the Helford River and Fal Estuary.

5.5.5 Acknowledgements

The authors thank the following for their comments on draft text: R.C.A. Bannister (Shellfish Resource Group, MAFF Directorate of Fisheries Research, Lowestoft), Mike Camplin (Devon Wildlife Trust), A.S. Churchward (Environment Agency Midlands Region), Terry Allen (MAFF Wales District), Paul Knapman (English Nature), Neil Downes (Devon Sea Fisheries Committee), Phil Coates (South Wales Sea Fisheries Committee), Alan Winstone (Environment Agency Welsh Region), E.J. Derriman (Cornwall Sea Fisheries Committee) and Mark Tasker (JNCC).

5.5.6 Further sources of information

A. References cited

Bryan, G.W., & Gibbs, P.E. 1993. *Heavy metals in the Fal Estuary, Cornwall: a study of long-term contamination by mining waste and its effects on estuarine organisms.* Plymouth, Marine Biological Association of the UK.

Cordrey, L., *ed.* 1996. *The biodiversity of the south-west: an audit of the south-west biological resource.* Taunton, South West Regional Planning Conference. (Prepared by a partnership of nature conservation bodies (RSPB and the County Wildlife Trusts) and the South West Regional Planning Conference.)

Davidson, N.C., Laffoley, D.d'A., Doody, J.P., Way, L.S., Gordon, J., Key, R., Drake, C.M., Pienkowski, M.W., Mitchell, R., & Duff, K.L. 1991. *Nature conservation and estuaries in Great Britain.* Peterborough, Nature Conservancy Council.

Davies, J., & Sotheran, I. 1995. *Mapping the distribution of benthic biotopes in Falmouth Bay and the lower Fal Ruan Estuary.* Peterborough, English Nature. (English Nature Research Reports, No. 119a.)

Doody, J.P., Johnston, C., & Smith, B. 1993. *Directory of the North Sea coastal margin.* Peterborough, Joint Nature Conservation Committee.

Farnham, W.F., & Jephson, N.A. 1977. A survey of the maerl beds of Falmouth (Cornwall). *British Phycological Journal, 12*: 119.

Lee, A.J., & Ramster, J.W. 1981. *Atlas of the seas around the British Isles.* Lowestoft, MAFF.

Masters, J. 1994. *The Helford oysterage with notes on the River Fal.* Truro, Cornwall County Council. (A report to the Helford Voluntary Marine Conservation Area Advisory Group.)

Pawson, M.G. 1995. *Biogeographical identification of English Channel fish and shellfish stocks.* Lowestoft, Ministry of Agriculture, Fisheries & Food, Fisheries Laboratory. (Fisheries Research Technical Report, No. 99.)

Protz, C. 1995. *Distribution of oysters and other molluscs in the Helford River.* Redruth, Helford Voluntary Marine Conservation Area Advisory Group. (Unpublished report.)

Rees, H.L., & Dare, P.J. 1993. *Sources of mortality and associated life-cycle traits of selected benthic species: a review.* Lowestoft, MAFF Directorate of Fisheries Research. (Fisheries Research Data Report, No. 33.)

Reid, P.C., Pratt, S., & Harbour, D. 1995. *A red tide event in the Fal Estuary.* Plymouth, Sir Alister Hardy Foundation for Ocean Science. (Unpublished report for NRA.)

Tompsett, P. 1996. *Marine life between Dodman Point and Lizard Point.* Redruth, Cornish Biological Records Unit.

B. Further reading

Beaumont, A.R., & Budd, M.D. 1984. High mortality of the larvae of the common mussel at low concentrations of tributyltin. *Marine Pollution Bulletin, 15:* 402-405.

Bennett, D.B., & Brown, C.G. 1983. Crab (*Cancer pagurus*) migrations in the English Channel. *Journal of the Marine Biological Association of the UK, 63:* 371-398.

Blunden, G., Binns, W.W., & Perks, F. 1975. Commercial collection and utilisation of maerl. *Economic Botany, 29:* 140-145.

Blunden, G., Farnham, W.F., Jephson, N., Barwell, C.J., Fern, R.H., & Plumcett, B.A. 1981. The composition of maerl beds of economic interest in northern Brittany, Cornwall and Ireland. *In: 10th International Seaweed Symposium:* 651-655.

Brown, C.G., & Bennett, D.B. 1980. Population and catch structure of the edible crab (*Cancer pagurus*) in the English Channel. *Rapports et Proces-verbaux des Reunions. Conseil Permanent International pour I'Exploration de la Mer, 39*(1): 88-100.

Clark, P.F. 1986. *North-east Atlantic crabs; an atlas of distribution.* Ross-on-Wye, Marine Conservation Society.

Cleary, J.J., & Stebbing, A.R.D. 1985. Organotin and total tin in coastal waters of south-west England. *Marine Pollution Bulletin, 16:* 350-355.

Cryer, M., Whittle, G.N., & Williams, R. 1987. The impact of bait collection by anglers on marine intertidal invertebrates. *Biological Conservation, 42:* 83-93.

Dare, P.J., Darby, C.D., Durance, J.A., & Palmer, D.W. 1994. The distribution of scallops (*Pecten maximus*) in the England Channel and Celtic Sea in relation to hydrographic and substrate features affecting larval dispersal and settlement. *In: Proceedings of 9th International Pectinid Workshop, Nanaimo, B.C., Canada, April 1993,* ed. by N.F. Bourne, B.L. Bunting & L.D. Townsend. Canadian Technical Report of Fisheries and Aquatic Sciences, Volume 1.

Ebdon, L., Evans, K., & Hill, S. 1989. The accumulation of organotins in adult and seed oysters from selected estuaries prior to the intoduction of UK regulations governing the use of tributyl-based antifouling paints. *Science of the Total Environment, 83:* 63-84.

Edwards, E. 1979. *The edible crab and its fishery in British waters.* Farnham, Fishing News Books.

Eno, N.C., *ed.* 1991. *Marine conservation handbook.* 2nd ed. Peterborough, English Nature.

Farnham, W.F., & Bishop, G.M. 1985. Survey of the Fal estuary, Cornwall. *Progress in Underwater Science, 10*: 53-63.

Fowler, S.L. 1989. *Nature conservation implications of damage to the seabed by commercial fishing operations.* Peterborough, Nature Conservancy Council. (Contract surveys, No. 79.)

Franklin, A., Pickett, G.D., & Connor, P.M. 1980. *The scallop and its fishery in England and Wales.* Lowestoft, MAFF. (Directorate of Fisheries Research, Laboratory Leaflet No. 51.)

Hancock, D.A. 1971. The role of predators and parasites in a fishery for the mollusc *Cardium edule* L. *In: Dynamics of populations,* ed. by P.J. den Boer & G.R. Gradwell. Wageningen, Centre for Agricultural Publication and Documentation. (Proceedings of the Advanced Studies Institute, Oosterbeck, 1970.)

Hardiman, P.A., Rolfe, M.S., & White, I.C. 1976. Lithothamnion *studies off the south-west coast of England.* Copenhagen, International Council for the Exploration of the Sea. (ICES C.M. 1976/K:9.)

Helford Voluntary Marine Conservation Area. 1995. *The Helford River bait digging.* Truro, Cornwall County Council/WWF/ English Nature.

Helford Voluntary Marine Conservation Area. 1995. *The Helford River oysters.* Truro, Cornwall County Council/WWF/English Nature.

Henderson, P.A., & Holmes, R.H.A. 1987. On the population biology of the common shrimp *Crangon crangon* in the Severn Estuary and Bristol Channel. *Journal of the Marine Biological Association of the United Kingdom, 67*: 825-847.

Henderson, P.A., Seaby, R., & Marsh, S.J. 1990. The population zoogeography of the common shrimp (*Crangon crangon*) in British waters. *Journal of the Marine Biological Association of the United Kingdom, 70*(1): 89-97.

Huggett, D. 1992. *Foreshore fishing for shellfish and bait.* Sandy, Royal Society for the Protection of Birds.

Huggett, D. Undated. *Coastal zone management and bait digging. A review of potential conflicts with nature conservation interests, legal issues and some available regulatory mechanisms.* Sandy, Royal Society for the Protection of Birds (unpublished).

Jackson, M.J., & James, R. 1979. The influence of bait digging on cockle *Cerastoderma edule* populations in north Norfolk. *Journal of Applied Ecology, 16:* 671-679.

Jones, S., 1993. *Population study of the common cockle* (Cerastoderma edule) *in the beds at Helford Passage.* Truro, Helford Voluntary Marine Conservation Area Advisory Group. (Unpublished report.)

McLusky, D.S., Anderson, F.E., & Wolfe-Murphy, S. 1983. Distribution and population recovery of *Arenicola marina* and other benthic fauna after bait digging. *Marine Ecology Progress Series, 11:* 173-179.

Olive, P.J.W. 1993. Management of the exploitation of the lugworm *Arenicola marina* and the ragworm *Nereis virens* (Polychaeta) in conservation areas. *Aquatic Conservation: Marine and Freshwater Ecosytems, 3:* 1-24.
Seaward, D.R. 1990. *Distribution of the marine molluscs of north-west Europe.* Peterborough, Nature Conservancy Council, for Conchological Society of Great Britain and Ireland.
Seaward, D.R. 1993. Additions and amendments to the distribution of the marine molluscs of north-west Europe (1990). *Joint Nature Conservation Committee Report,* No. 165.
Southward, A.J., & Boalch, G.T. 1993. The marine resources of Devon's coastal waters. *In: The new maritime history of Devon,* ed. by M. Duffy, S. Fisher, B. Greenhill, D. Starkey & J. Youings, 51-61. London, Conway Maritime Press.
South West Regional Planning Conference. 1994. *South West Regional Planning Conference regional strategy: the landscape, coast and historic environment of the South West.* Taunton, South West Regional Planning Conference.
Thompson, B.M., & Ayers, R.A. 1987. *Preliminary crab* (Cancer pagurus L.) *larval studies in the English Channel.* Copenhagen, International Council for the Exploration of the Sea. (ICES S.C. 1987/K:48.)
Wildgoose, P.B., Blunden, G., Brain, K.R., & Williams, D.C. 1981. Effects of maerl in agriculture. *Proceedings of the International Seaweed Symposium, 8:* 754-759.
Wray, T. 1995. Cleaner brown shrimp catches - saving flatfish for the future. *Fishing News International, 34*(7): 36-38.

C. Contact names and addresses

Type of information	Contact address and telephone no.
Shellfish stocks and fisheries advice to assist with management and policy decisions for the coastal zone	*Head of Laboratory, MAFF Directorate of Fisheries Research, Fisheries Laboratory, Conwy, tel: 01492 593883
Assessment and provision of advice on the conservation of commercial fish and shellfish stocks	*Director, MAFF Directorate of Fisheries Research, Lowestoft, tel: 01502 562244
Inshore fisheries information and advice - Cornwall	Chief Fishery Officer, Cornwall Sea Fisheries Committee, The Old Bonded Warehouse, Quay Street, Penzance, Cornwall TR18 4BD, tel: 01736 69817
Inshore fisheries information and advice - Isles of Scilly	Assistant Chief Executive, Isles of Scilly Sea Fisheries Committee, Town Hall, St. Mary's, Isles of Scilly TR1 0LW, tel: 01720 422536
Inshore fisheries information and advice - Devon	Deputy Clerk & Chief Fishery Officer, Devon Sea Fisheries Committee, Forde House, Newton Abbot, Devon TQ12 3XX, tel: 01803 854648/882004
Inshore fisheries information and advice - South Wales	Director, South Wales Sea Fisheries Committee, Queens Buildings, Cambrian Place, Swansea, West Glamorgan SA1 1TW, tel: 01792 654466
Research on species	Plymouth Marine Laboratory, Prospect Place, Plymouth PL1 3DH, tel: 01752 633100
Marine conservation issues and fisheries in England	*Fisheries Liaison Officer, English Nature HQ, Peterborough, tel: 01733 340345
Marine conservation issues and fisheries in Wales	*Marine and Coastal Section, CCW HQ, Bangor, tel: 01248 370444
Benthic surveys: Marine Nature Conservation Review Database	*Marine Conservation Branch, JNCC, Peterborough, tel: 01733 62626
Marine Fisheries Task Group papers; marine conservation	*Dr. Clare Eno, Fisheries Officer, JNCC, Peterborough, tel: 01733 62626
Marine conservation issues	*Conservation Officer, RSPB, Sandy, tel: 01767 680551
Marine conservation issues	*Fisheries Officer, Marine Section, WWF-UK, Godalming, tel: 01483 426444
Marine conservation issues	*Conservation Officer, Marine Conservation Society, Ross-on-Wye, tel: 01989 566017
Marine conservation issues	Honorary Secretary, The Marine Forum for Environmental Issues, c/o University College Scarborough, Filey Road, Scarborough YO11 3AZ, tel: 01723 362392
Marine conservation issues - Cornwall	*Cornwall Wildlife Trust, Truro, tel: 01872 273939
Marine conservation issues - Devon	*Devon Wildlife Trust, Exeter, tel: 01392 79244
Marine conservation issues - Somerset	*Somerset Wildlife Trust, Bridgwater, tel: 01823 451587
Marine conservation issues - Avon	*The Wildlife Trust for Bristol, Bath & Avon, Bristol, tel: 0117 926 8018
Marine conservation issues - Gloucestershire	*Gloucestershire Wildlife Trust, Gloucester, tel: 01452 383333
Marine conservation issues - Gwent	*Gwent Wildlife Trust, Monmouth, tel: 01600 715501
Marine conservation issues - Glamorgan	*Glamorgan Wildlife Trust, Bridgend, tel: 01656 724100

*Starred contact addresses are given in full in the Appendix.

5.6 Amphibians and reptiles

Dr M.J.S. Swan

5.6.1 Introduction

This region supports all nine of the widespread species of amphibians and terrestrial reptiles native to the UK: common frog *Rana temporaria*, common toad *Bufo bufo*, smooth newt *Triturus vulgaris*, palmate newt *T. helveticus*, great crested newt *T. cristatus*, slow-worm *Anguis fragilis*, common lizard *Lacerta vivipara*, grass snake *Natrix natrix* and adder *Vipera berus*. However the smooth newt and great crested newt are virtually absent from Cornwall. There are no recent records of rare reptiles occurring naturally within the region, but several areas in the region have been proposed as introduction (or reintroduction) sites for the sand lizard *Lacerta agilis,* as part of the English Nature's Species Recovery Programme (Corbett 1994; Whitten 1990).

Marine turtles have been recorded relatively frequently in this region: since 1990, thirteen leatherback turtles *Dermochelys coriacea* and three loggerhead turtles *Caretta caretta* have been reported. Most of the leatherbacks were sighted swimming at sea west of Land's End, and the three loggerheads were found stranded in Mount's Bay, Cornwall.

The great crested newt and both the turtle species are totally protected under the Wildlife & Countryside Act 1981, although all the species listed are afforded some degree of protection under national and international legislation (Table 5.6.1).

Two sites in the region are known to be nationally important for their amphibian species assemblages: Robinswood Hill, Gloucestershire, and Park Pond, Mid Glamorgan (Swan & Oldham 1993a). However, little quantitative recording has been carried out in the southern counties of the region, and sites of equal or greater importance for amphibians may exist. Table 5.6.2 shows the numbers of amphibian and terrestrial reptile records in relation to survey effort.

Table 5.6.1 Protected status of amphibians and reptiles occurring in region

Species	*Protection (see footnote)*
Amphibians	
Common frog *Rana temporaria*	1, 2, 3
Common toad *Bufo bufo*	1, 2
Smooth newt *Triturus vulgaris*	1, 2
Palmate newt *Triturus helvetica*	1, 2
Great crested newt *Triturus cristatus*	1, 2, 3
Reptiles	
Slow worm *Anguis fragilis*	1, 2
Common lizard *Lacerta vivipara*	1, 2
Grass snake *Natrix natrix*	1, 2
Adder *Vipera berus*	1, 2
Loggerhead turtle *Caretta caretta*	1, 2, 3, 4
Leatherback turtle *Dermochelys coriacea*	1, 2, 3, 4

Key: 1 = Wildlife & Countryside Act (1981); 2 = Bern Convention (1979) ; 3 = EC Habitats & Species Directive (1992); 4 = CITES Convention.

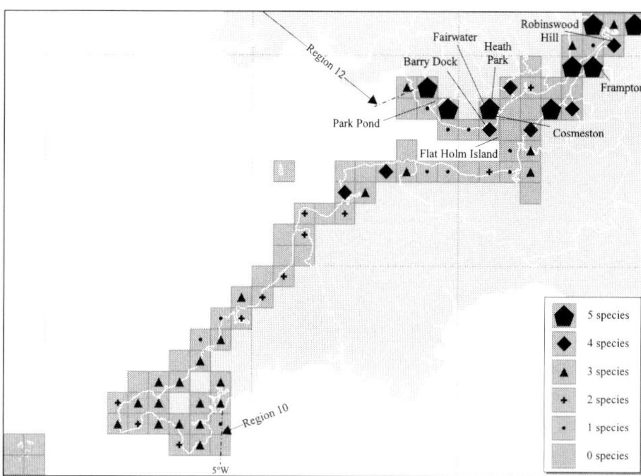

Map 5.6.1 Numbers of amphibian species recorded in coastal 10 km squares and key localities for amphibians (listed in Table 5.6.2). Distribution may reflect differences in recording effort. Source: Biological Records Centre, ITE Monks Wood. Note: not all rare species data are held by BRC and therefore some records may not be shown.

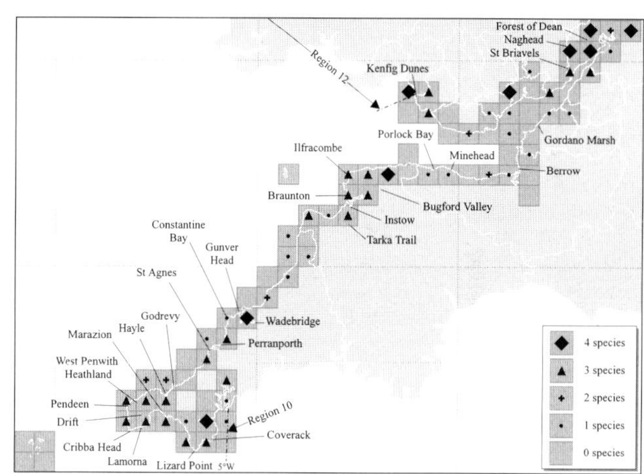

Map 5.6.2 Numbers of reptile species recorded in coastal 10 km squares and key localities for reptiles (listed in Table 5.6.2). Distribution may reflect differences in recording effort. Source: Biological Records Centre, ITE Monks Wood. Note: not all rare species data are held by BRC and therefore some records may not be shown.

The known diversity of amphibian species in the region is relatively high (Map 5.6.1): 64% of 10 km squares throughout the region support at least three species, compared with 49% for the West Coast as a whole and 22% for the whole of mainland Britain. Of particular note are Avon, Gloucestershire, Gwent and Mid Glamorgan. Reptile diversity varies between counties, but is also comparatively high overall: 53% of squares contain at least three species, compared to 44% for the West Coast and 45% for mainland Britain (Map 5.6.2). Recorded diversity is particularly high in parts of Devon and Cornwall and in Gloucestershire and Mid Glamorgan, and low in Somerset, Avon and South Glamorgan. However in the poorly recorded counties low diversity may simply reflect low recording effort.

Table 5.6.2 Records of amphibians and terrestrial reptiles related to survey effort

	*Total no. of 10 km squares**	*% 10 km squares surveyed for:*			*Total no. of individual records*		*Mean no. of individual records per surveyed 10 km square*	
		Any herp. species	*Amphibians*	*Reptiles*	*Amphibians*	*Reptiles*	*Amphibians*	*Reptiles*
Cornwall (in Region 11)	32	91	78	78	207	138	8.3	5.5
Devon (in Region 11)	12	83	58	75	47	53	6.7	5.9
Somerset	9	78	78	56	18	7	2.6	1.4
Avon	10	80	70	60	59	26	8.4	4.3
Gloucestershire	8	100	100	100	143	90	17.9	11.3
Gwent	9	78	44	67	24	22	6.0	3.7
South Glamorgan	7	100	71	57	38	10	7.6	2.5
Mid Glamorgan	5	80	80	60	39	12	9.8	4.0
Region 11	***96***	***83***	***70***	***69***	***575***	***358***	***8.6***	***5.4***
West Coast	620	63	53	49	3,383	1,536	10.2	5.1
GB coast	1,124	69	59	49	7,524	3,138	11.3	5.7
GB (coast and inland)	2,862	84	79	66	27,182	8,803	12.1	4.7

Source: Biological Records Centre, Monks Wood. Key: *total includes squares that are partly in the county, but excludes squares that are exclusively marine.

5.6.2 Important species and locations

Table 5.6.3 lists coastal 10 km squares (two digits) and coastal 1 km OS grid squares (four digits) in which rare and vulnerable species are found, and areas that support regionally or nationally important amphibian species assemblages (Swan & Oldham 1989, 1993a, b) or outstanding populations of widespread species. Sites proposed for the (re)-introduction of the sand lizard are also listed. In addition to the two nationally important sites for amphibian species assemblages noted above, six regionally important assemblages are also noted. There has been a shortage of quantitative recording in the southern counties of the region, so the table is probably far from complete.

Most amphibians in the region breed in freshwater habitats, mainly small agricultural field ponds, in the agricultural coastal hinterland. Other habitats and locations important for amphibians include mineral extraction sites, such as the brick pits at the northern end of Bridgwater Bay, derelict mining areas in Glamorgan and the Forest of Dean, and coastal marshes, such as Porlock and Minehead Marshes in Somerset. The reen (ditch) systems inland of Bridgwater Bay and the Gwent Levels are also likely to be important for amphibians. The great crested newt has been reported to be relatively abundant in the Bridgend area of South Glamorgan (Wisniewski 1984).

The relatively dry coastal habitats are important for reptiles: cliffs (with associated scree), paths, coastal heath and moorland and sand dunes support high numbers of common lizards, adders and slow worms. Reptiles are particularly abundant where extensive areas of semi-natural habitat are contiguous with the coastal strip, such as along much of the coastline of Cornwall and Devon or at the edge of Exmoor. Along some of the developed or degraded parts of this coastline mining spoil heaps and other derelict industrial sites provide important alternative reptile habitats. Grass snakes are not common in the rugged or dry coastal areas, being more frequently associated with the lusher, moister habitats of river valleys, woodland, coastal marshes and agricultural drainage systems, such as the Forest of Dean in Gloucestershire and the agricultural ditch systems of the Gwent Levels and the hinterland of Bridgwater Bay. Grass snakes are also relatively common at Slimbridge Wildfowl and Wetlands Trust Reserve (Gloucestershire). Within the Forest of Dean, reptiles have frequently been observed along the disused railway lines.

5.6.3 Human activities

Amphibians and reptiles have probably benefited from the protected status of much of the coast of the South-West Peninsula, which has limited the extent and impact of tourist developments. For reptiles in the south-western counties of the region, tourist pressure is largely confined to areas around coastal holiday towns.

Throughout the region, the encroachment of arable land and an associated loss of semi-natural or unmanaged terrain in the coastal hinterland has reduced the extent of available habitat for amphibians and reptiles; reptiles in particular are often restricted to a narrow coastal strip. Habitats may also be further threatened by the invasion of blackthorn and bracken in some areas. In Cornwall, Devon, Somerset and Gloucestershire improved field drainage has led to the drying up of many small agricultural ponds and has also reduced the extent of moist habitats suitable for amphibians during their terrestrial phase. In Somerset and Gwent much of the potential amphibian habitat in the ditch systems is reported to be affected by agricultural run-off (English Nature pers. comm.; County Wildlife Trusts pers. comm.). Proposals for 'hard' coastal defences threaten some areas of coastal habitat in Cornwall. In Gloucestershire, the expansion of tourism in the Forest of Dean, particularly the development of cycle tracks along disused railway lines, has resulted in increased levels of disturbance. To the west of Newport, habitats are being lost through industrial and recreational development, and parts of the coast of South Glamorgan are already extensively developed. The protected habitats along the coast of Mid Glamorgan are therefore increasingly important strongholds for amphibians and reptiles in South Wales.

Certain sand dune sites in Cornwall and Devon have been identified as potential (re-)introduction sites for the rare sand lizard, as part of the English Nature sand lizard Species Recovery Programme (Table 5.6.3) (Corbett 1994; Whitten 1990).

Table 5.6.3 Sites of important amphibian species assemblages, abundant widespread reptiles or proposed sand lizard introductions

Site name	*Grid ref.*	*Habitat*	*Importance of site*
Cornwall			
Lizard Point to Coverack	SW71	Grassland, heath, cliff	AWR: common lizard, slow worm, adder
Marazion	SW5230	Grassland, marsh	AWR: common lizard, slow worm, adder
West Penwith heathland hinterland	SW43	Heath	AWR: common lizard, slow worm, adder
Drift	SW4628	Reservoir	AWR: common lizard, slow worm, adder
Lamorna	SW4524	Grassland, heath	AWR: common lizard, slow worm, adder
Cribba Head to Pendeen	SW32-SS33	Grassland, heath, cliff	AWR: common lizard, slow worm, adder
Hayle to Godrevy	SW53-SS54	Sand dunes	AWR: common lizard, slow worm, adder
Wheal Charlotte Moor, Chapelporth	SW64	Heath	AWR: common lizard, slow worm, adder
St. Agnes	SW7051	Grassland, heath, cliff	AWR: common lizard, adder
Perranporth	SW7554	Grassland, heath, cliff	AWR: slow worm, grass snake
Gunver Head and Constantine Bay	SW87	Sand dune, upper shore	Proposed sand lizard introduction site. AWR: common lizard, slow worm, adder
Wadebridge	SW9973	Railway embankment	AWR: common lizard, grass snake
Devon			
Tarka Trail	SS41, SS42, SS43, SS53	Grassland, heath, woodland, scrub, railway	AWR: common lizard, slow worm, adder, grass snake
Instow Sand Dunes	SS4730-SO4731	Sand dune, grassland, scrub, railway	AWR: common lizard, slow worm
Braunton to Ilfracombe	SS4535-SS4543-SS5146	Sand dune, grassland, railway	Two proposed sand lizard introduction sites. AWR: common lizard, slow worm, adder.
Bugford Valley	SS6042	Grassland, woodland	AWR: common lizard, slow worm, grass snake
Avon			
Gordano Marsh NNR	ST47	Wetland with ditches	AWR: grass snake
Somerset			
Porlock Bay to Minehead	SS8049-SS9050	Grassland, ditch systems	AWR: common lizard, slow worm, adder, grass snake
Berrow Dunes	ST2953	Sand dunes	AWR: common lizard, slow worm, grass snake
Gloucestershire			
St. Briavels	SO5503, SO5802, SO5806	Grassland, wetland	AWR: slow worm, adder
Naghead NNR	SO5908, SO6008, SO6009	Grassland, heath, woodland, mineral extraction sites	AWR: common lizard, slow worm, adder, grass snake
Forest of Dean	SO60/61	Grassland, heath, woodland, mineral extraction sites, railway	AWR: common lizard, slow worm, adder, grass snake
Frampton	SO747078	Pond	RIA: common frog, common toad, smooth newt, great crested newt
Robinswood Hill	SO8314-SO8414	Ponds	NIA: common frog, common toad, smooth newt, palmate newt, great crested newt
South Glamorgan			
Heath Park	ST177799	Pond	RIA: smooth newt, palmate newt, great crested newt
Cosmeston	ST170690	Pond	RIA: common frog, common toad, smooth newt, great crested newt
The Dell, Fairwater	ST143777	Pond	RIA: smooth newt, palmate newt, great crested newt
Barry Dock	ST133684	Pond in dockland	RIA: common frog, common toad, smooth newt
Flatholm Island	ST222648	Grassland	AWR: common lizard, slow worm
Mid Glamorgan			
Park Pond	SS879843	Pond	NIA: common frog, common toad, smooth newt, palmate newt, great crested newt
Kenfig Dunes	SS7980-SS8081	Sand dunes	RIA: common frog, common toad, smooth newt, great crested newt. AWR: common lizard, grass snake.

Sources: Swan & Oldham (1993a, b), Cornwall Wildlife Trust, English Nature, Devon Wildlife Trust, Perrins (1991). Key: AWR = abundant widespread reptile species; NIA = nationally important amphibian species assemblage; RIA = regionally important amphibian species assemblage.

5.6.4 Information sources used

Most (83%) of the region's coastal 10 km squares have received some survey coverage for amphibians and reptiles (Table 5.6.2). The extent varies, but in most counties coverage is above the average for the West Coast and for the GB coast as a whole. The thoroughness of the recording effort (i.e. the number of records made per surveyed 10 km square) is more variable than the coverage. There are few amphibian records for Devon, Somerset and Gwent, and reptile recording has been inadequate in Somerset, Gwent and South Glamorgan. Coastal squares in Gloucestershire, on the other hand, have been comparatively well surveyed for both amphibians and reptiles.

National distribution data for the widespread amphibians and terrestrial reptiles were provided by the Biological Records Centre (BRC) at Monk's Wood (Arnold 1983, 1995). These comprise post-1970 species records held by BRC and include all the data collected during the National Amphibian and Reptile Surveys (NARS) undertaken by De Montfort University on behalf of English Nature. The NARS formed the focus of national amphibian and reptile recording during the 1980s and early 1990s (Oldham & Nicholson 1986; Swan & Oldham 1989, 1993a, b). Most of these data were collected through a volunteer, mainly amateur, recorder network.

Information on the sand lizard Species Recovery Programme came from English Nature's Lowlands Team, Corbett (1994) and Whitten (1990). Turtle data and information were supplied by the Natural History Museum and Southampton University. Information on local impacts, habitat associations and important sites was provided by the County Wildlife Trusts, Biological Record Centres, English Nature Local Teams, Countryside Council for Wales regional staff and county herpetological groups.

Marine turtle distribution data were supplied by the Natural History Museum, Southampton University and Penhallurick (1990); all sightings at sea and strandings should be reported to the Natural History Museum in London. Concise information on turtle identification, reporting of sightings, UK legislation and instructions on what to do with turtles caught in fishing gear is contained in *The turtle code* (Nature Conservancy Council 1990).

5.6.5 Acknowledgements

Thanks are due to the following people for providing information: N.V. Allen, Richard Archer, Henry Arnold, David Bolton, Philippa Burrell, Annabel Campbell, Liz Biron, Bob Corns, Keith Corbett, Jane Garner, Tony Gent, John Harper, Colin McCarthy, Andrew McDouall, Mark Nicholson, Robin Prowse, Karen Turvey, Colin Twissell, Lindi Wilkinson and Doug Woods.

5.6.6 Further sources of information

A. References cited

Arnold, H.R., *ed.* 1983. *Distribution maps of the amphibians and reptiles of the British Isles.* Huntingdon, Biological Records Centre, ITE Monks Wood.

Arnold, H.R., *ed.* 1995. *Atlas of amphibians and reptiles in Britain and Ireland.* Huntingdon, Biological Records Centre, ITE Monks Wood.

Corbett, K. 1994. *Pilot study for sand lizard UK recovery programme.* Peterborough, English Nature. (English Nature Research Report, No. 102.)

Nature Conservancy Council. 1990. *The turtle code.* Peterborough. (Advice sheet.)

Oldham, R.S., & Nicholson, M. 1986. *Status and ecology of the warty newt* Triturus cristatus. *Final Report.* Peterborough, Nature Conservancy Council. (Unpublished report.)

Penhallurick, R.D. 1990. *Turtles off Cornwall, the Isles of Scilly and Devonshire.* Truro, Dyllansow Pengwella.

Perrins, F. 1991. *A guide to Britain's conservation heritage.* London, Thorsons, Harper Collins.

Swan, M.J.S., & Oldham, R.S. 1989. *Amphibian communities. Final report.* Peterborough, Nature Conservancy Council. (Unpublished report.)

Swan, M.J.S., & Oldham, R.S. 1993a. *Herptile sites. Volume 1: national amphibian survey.* Peterborough, English Nature. (English Nature Research Report, No. 38.)

Swan, M.J.S., & Oldham, R.S. 1993b. *Herptile sites. Volume 2: national reptile survey.* Peterborough, English Nature. (English Nature Research Report, No. 39.)

Whitten, A.J. 1990. *Recovery: a proposed programme for Britain's protected species.* Peterborough, Nature Conservancy Council.

Wisniewski, P.J. 1984. Distribution of amphibians and reptiles in Glamorgan, South Wales. *British Herpetological Society Bulletin, 9:* 29-34.

B. Further reading

British Herpetological Society. 1990. *Garden ponds as amphibian sanctuaries.* London, BHS Conservation Committee.

British Herpetological Society. 1990. *Save our reptiles.* London, BHS Conservation Committee.

British Herpetological Society. 1990. *Surveying for amphibians.* London, BHS Conservation Committee.

Corbett, K.S. 1988. Conservation strategy for the sand lizard (*Lacerta agilis agilis*) in Britain. *Mertensiella, 1:* 101-109.

Corbett, K.S. 1988. Distribution and status of the sand lizard (*Lacerta agilis agilis*) in Britain. *Mertensiella, 1:* 92-100.

Corbett, K.S. 1990. *Conservation of European reptiles and amphibians.* London, Christopher Helm.

Corbett, K.S., & Tamarind, D.L. 1979. Conservation of the sand lizard *Lacerta agilis* by habitat management. *British Journal of Herpetology, 5:* 799-823.

Denton, J.S. 1991. *The terrestrial ecology of the natterjack,* Bufo calamita, *and the common toad,* Bufo bufo. PhD Thesis, University of Sussex.

Denton, J.S., & Beebee, T.J.C. 1993. Summer and winter refugia of the natterjack (*Bufo calamita*) and common toads (*Bufo bufo*) in Britain. *Herpetological Journal, 3:* 90-94.

Herpetofauna Consultants International. 1994. *Crested newt survey of selected areas in South Wales.* Cardiff, Countryside Council for Wales. (Unpublished report.)

Mallinson, J.J. 1990. Turtle rescue. *Marine Conservation,* Winter 1990/91: 8-9.

Mallinson, J.J. 1991. Stranded juvenile loggerheads in the United Kingdom. *Marine Turtle Newsletter, 54:* 14-16.

McCartney, P. 1990. *Ponds in Cornwall.* Bristol, NRA. (Unpublished report.)

Nature Conservancy Council. 1983. *The ecology and conservation of amphibian and reptile species endangered in Britain.* Peterborough.

Spellerberg, I.F. 1988. Ecology and management of *Lacerta agilis* L. populations in England. *Mertensiella, 1:* 113-121.

C. Contact names and addresses

Type of information	*Contact address and telphone no.*
Conservation and captive breeding of amphibians and reptiles, nationally	British Herpetological Society, c/o The Zoological Society of London, Regent's Park, London NW1 4RY, tel: 0181 452 9578
Conservation of threatened reptiles and amphibians in Britain; priority species in Europe	Conservation Officer, The Herpetological Conservation Trust, 655A Christchurch Road, Boscombe, Bournemouth, Dorset BH1 4AP, tel: 01202 391319
National secretariat to local amphibian and reptile groups	Common Species Coordinator, Herpetofauna Groups of Britain and Ireland, c/o HCIL, Triton House, Bramfield, Halesworth, Suffolk IP19 9AE, tel: 0198 684 518
National recording schemes and biological data from throughout UK	*Environmental Information Centre, Institute of Terrestrial Ecology, Monks Wood, Huntingdon, tel: 01487 773381
The turtle code; amphibians and reptiles in England; Species Recovery Programme	*Herpetologist, English Nature HQ, Peterborough, tel: 01733 340345
Turtles	Dr C. McCarthy, Natural History Museum, Cromwell Road, London SW7 5BD, tel: 0171 938 9123
Turtles	Dept. of Oceanography, Southampton University, Highfield, Southampton SO9 5NH, tel: 01703 595000
Reptiles and amphibians in Cornwall and Devon	*Devon and Cornwall Amphibian and Reptile Group, c/o Cornwall Wildlife Trust, Truro, tel: 01872 73939
Protected sites in Cornwall	*English Nature, Truro, tel: 01872 262550
Reptiles and amphibian sites in Devon	*Devon Wildlife Trust, Exeter, tel: 01392 279244
Reptiles and amphibian sites in Devon	Biological Records Centre, Royal Albert Memorial Museum, Queen Street, Exeter, Devon EX4 3RX, tel: 01392 265858
Protected sites in Devon	*English Nature, Okehampton, tel: 01837 55045
Reptile and amphibian sites in Somerset	*Somerset Wildlife Trust, Bridgwater, tel: 01823 451587
Protected sites in Somerset and Avon	*English Nature, Taunton, tel: 01823 283211
Amphibians and reptiles at Bridgwater Bay NNR	English Nature Site Manager, Bridgwater Bay NNR, Dowells Farm, Steart, Bridgwater, Somerset TA5 2PX, tel: 01278 652426
Amphibians and reptiles at Braunton Burrows	English Nature Site Manager, Braunton Burrows, Broadeford Farm, Heddon Mill, nr. Braunton, Devon EX33 2NQ, tel: 01271 812552
Reptile and amphibian sites in Avon	Bristol Regional Environmental Records Centre (BRERC), Ashton Court Visitor Centre, Ashton Court Estate, Long Ashton, Bristol BS18 9JN, tel: 0117 953 2140
Reptile and amphibian sites in Gloucestershire	*Gloucestershire Wildlife Trust, Gloucester, tel: 01452 383333
Reptile and amphibian sites in South Wales	*CCW South Area Office, Cardiff, tel: 01222 772400
Reptile and amphibian sites in Gwent	*Gwent Wildlife Trust, Monmouth, tel: 01600 715501
Reptile and amphibian sites in Mid and South Glamorgan	*Glamorgan Wildlife Trust, Tondu, tel: 01656 724100

*Starred contact addresses are given in full in the Appendix.

5.7 Fish: exploited sea fish

Dr M.G. Pawson & C.F. Robson

5.7.1 Introduction

This section describes the distribution of sea fish that are of interest because they are exploited by people, mainly for food. Their exploitation by fisheries is described in section 9.1. Sea fish described as pelagic are most commonly found in shoals swimming in midwater; they typically make extensive seasonal movements or migrations between sea areas. Demersal fish are those found living at or near the bottom of the sea. For this series, all sea fish that are not 'pelagic' are termed 'demersal'; thus the latter term includes bass and grey mullet. Demersal species are divided here into four groups: elasmobranchs (sharks, skates and rays), gadoids (the cod family), flatfish, and other demersal fish. Most demersal species gather in late winter or spring on persistent and recognisable spawning grounds, to release millions of minute free-floating eggs. From these hatch larvae, which feed on and move with the plankton, often for a hundred miles or more, before metamorphosing into tiny fish, which in some cases may recruit to inshore nursery grounds. Some juveniles making the transition to the adult phase may move into the Irish Sea from the Bristol Channel, or vice versa.

The distribution of exploited sea fish species can be mapped from analysis of catch data. This description of their distribution covers their occurrence at identifiable locations in the region during particular phases of their life history, and Maps 5.7.1 - 5.7.6 show the known spawning and nursery areas of key species. Barring substantial climate change or stock collapse, these distributions and relationships will remain stable over several decades.

Table 5.7.1 lists the main pelagic and demersal species occurring in the region and gives examples of protection measures in this region (see also section 5.7.3).

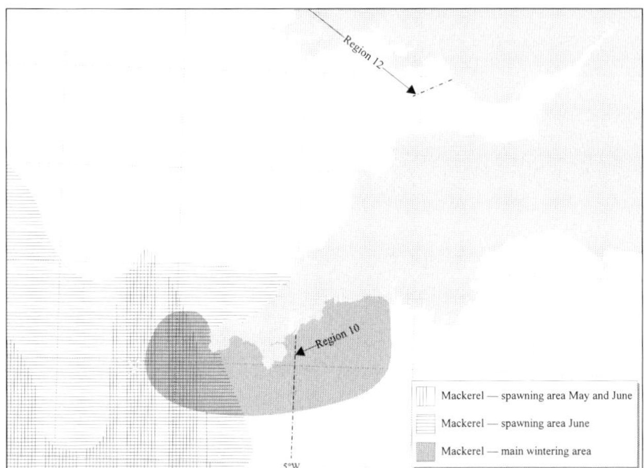

Map 5.7.1 Mackerel wintering and spawning areas. Source: Lee & Ramster (1981). © Crown copyright.

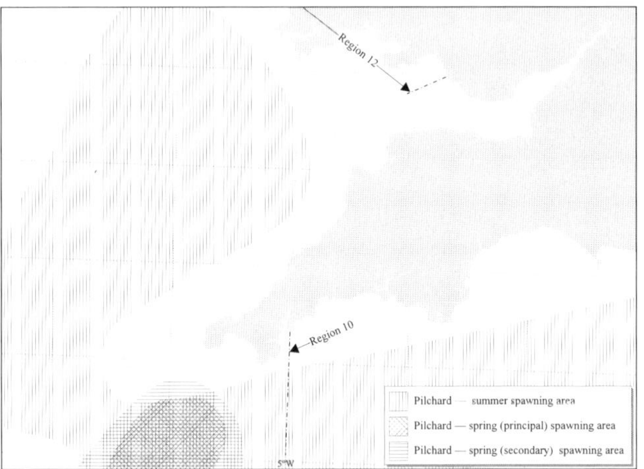

Map 5.7.2 Pilchard spawning areas. Source: Pawson (1995). © Crown copyright.

5.7.2 Important locations and species

Of the pelagic species, mackerel is the most abundant off the west coast of Britain. Mackerel spawn throughout the shelf waters of the British Isles, but most prolifically along the edge of the continental shelf and west of the South-West Peninsula in May and June (Map 5.7.1). Growing juveniles and adults migrate to coastal waters after spawning, where they remain until autumn. Overwintering concentrations are found in this region off the south coast of Cornwall (Map 5.7.1).

Herring are locally abundant and may be found around the Cornish coasts, where spawning occurs in estuaries in the spring; there are no autumn or winter coastal spawning areas in the region. The timing of spawning depends on the locality. The herring larvae drift to shallow nursery areas.

Pilchard and horse mackerel are more southerly than other pelagic species and only occur in abundance along the coast of the western English Channel. Map 5.7.2 shows the pilchard spawning areas in the region. Spawning takes place in spring in an area to the south of the Isles of Scilly and Land's End. By June and September eggs can be found in the Bristol Channel and along the southern English coast (Pawson 1995). Horse mackerel (also known as 'scad') spawn at a low density in the region in July. The main spawning areas are along the continental shelf edge.

Sprats are widely dispersed throughout the shallower areas of the region, and juveniles are often found mixed with young herring in inshore areas, when they are known as 'whitebait'. They migrate to spawning areas, which include all the region's waters, with the main area being west of Hartland point (Map 5.7.3). Spawning mainly peaks from April to June and is temperature dependent. Sprats migrate inshore to overwinter, and no clearly-defined nursery areas have been identified.

Elasmobranch species produce relatively small numbers of live young (10-100 per year, but can be fewer in big sharks), or lay large eggs on the sea bed close to their nursery areas. Several species of shark - including the basking shark (see also section 5.9) - occur at low densities off the coast during their summer migrations, but only the spurdog is found regularly in sufficient abundance to support a directed fishery. The thornback ray is also important locally, especially *en route* to its spring spawning grounds in shallow bays around the region. A number of

Table 5.7.1 Pelagic and demersal species and examples of measures for their protection

Species	*Protection measures*
Pelagic species	
Mackerel *Scomber scombrus*	MLS/QM
Horse mackerel *Trachurus trachurus*	MLS/QM
Herring *Clupea harengus*	MLS/QM
Sprat *Sprattus sprattus*	QM
Pilchard *Sardinia pilchardus*	No limitation
Demersal species	
Elasmobranchs	
Spurdog *Squalus acanthias*	No limitation
Thornback ray *Raja clavata*	No limitation
Gadoids	
Cod *Gadus morhua*	MLS/QM
Haddock *Melanogrammus aeglefinus*	MLS/QM
Whiting *Merlangius merlangus*	MLS/QM
Ling *Molva molva*	No limitation
Pollack *Pollachius pollachius*	MLS/QM
Saithe *Pollachius virens*	MLS/QM
Hake *Merluccius merluccius*	MLS/QM
Flatfish	
Plaice *Pleuronectes platessa*	MLS/QM
Dab *Limanda limanda*	MLS
Dover sole *Solea solea*	MLS/QM
Lemon sole *Microstomus kitt*	MLS
Turbot *Psetta maxima*	MLS
Brill *Scophthalmus rhombus*	MLS
Flounder *Platichthys flesus*	MLS
Megrim *Lepidorhombus whiffiagonis*	MLS/QM
Witch *Glyptocephalus cynoglossus*	MLS
Other demersal fish	
Bass *Dicentrarchus labrax*	MLS
Grey mullets *Chelon labrosus, Liza ramada* and *L. aurata*	MLS
Monkfish (angler) *Lophius piscatorius*	QM
Sandeels *Ammodytes* spp.	No limitation
Conger eel *Conger conger*	MLS
Gurnards *Triglidae* spp.	No limitation
Wrasse *Labridae* spp.	No limitation
Red sea bream *Pagellus* spp.	MLS
Red mullet *Mullus surmuletus*	MLS
John Dory *Zeus faber*	No limitation

Source: European Council (1986, 1995). Key: MLS = minimum landing size; QM = catch quota management.

other ray species are patchily distributed in the area.

Of the gadoids, cod is one of the most important exploited fish species in the North Atlantic and is widely distributed in the region. Local fishermen suggest that cod in the area migrate between deep-water wrecks and reefs in the summer and inshore areas in winter (Pawson 1995). There is a pronounced aggregation of spawning cod, which peaks between March and April, in deep water off Trevose Head, North Cornwall (Map 5.7.4). Whiting, also members of the cod family, are widely distributed around Britain and are present in the region, especially in inshore waters on the south coast of Cornwall. The whiting spawning season is prolonged - from January to July depending on the latitude - and there is an identified spawning area within that of cod, off Trevose Head (Map 5.7.4). Haddock are rare in the region and are not as widely distributed as they are further north. Spawning takes place between February and June and the main spawning areas are outside the region (Lee & Ramster 1981). Pollack and saithe are less abundant than other gadoids and more locally distributed, with saithe in particular here being close to the southern limits of its distribution. Ling spawn mainly along the continental shelf edge, and the whole region, apart from the Severn Estuary, forms part of this species' nursery area (Pawson 1995). Ling, like pollack and saithe, are commonly found in areas of stony ground, reefs and wrecks. Hake, though not a gadoid, is found in the deeper water of the Celtic Sea and the western English Channel, though the main part of its population lies outside coastal waters towards the edge of the continental shelf, where they spawn.

Plaice and dab are the most abundant flatfish species in the coastal waters of the region and occur on sandy areas of sea bed. Juvenile plaice live close to the shore in nursery areas such as Port Isaac Bay and gradually move to deeper waters as they mature. The knowledge of plaice spawning areas (Map 5.7.5) is obtained from the distribution of newly spawned eggs in spring, determined by plankton surveys (Lee & Ramster 1981). Dover sole are present throughout the region and have a similar lifestyle to plaice and dab, though they are more confined to areas with higher bottom temperatures. In the coastal waters of west England and Wales Dover sole are found in greatest abundance in the Bristol Channel and the north-east Irish Sea (Symonds & Rogers 1995). Dover sole spawn in early spring (February to April) in the region, in two large areas: off the North

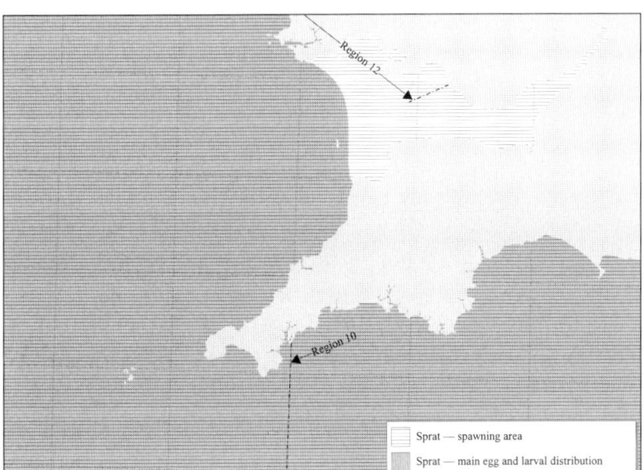

Map 5.7.3 Sprat spawning areas and main egg and larval distribution. Source: Lee & Ramster (1981). © Crown copyright.

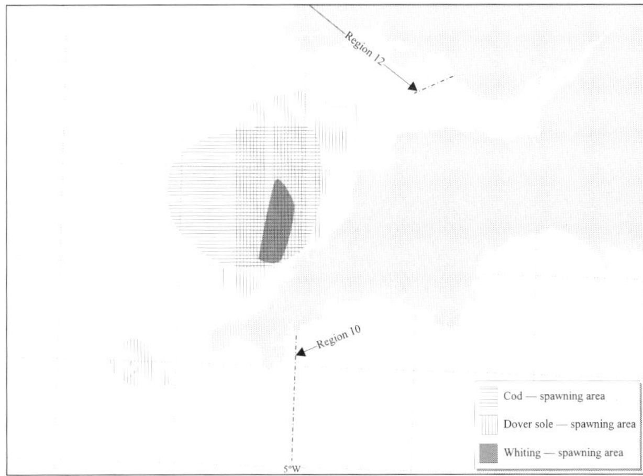

Map 5.7.4 Cod, Dover sole and whiting spawning areas. Sources: Pawson (1995), Lee & Ramster (1981). © Crown copyright.

Cornwall and Devon coasts and around the Isles of Scilly (Map 5.7.4). Their inshore nursery areas are shown on Map 5.7.6. Turbot and brill are much less abundant than plaice, dab or sole species but have a similar lifestyle. None of the flatfish species exhibits extensive migrations, though their larvae can drift for several weeks from offshore spawning grounds to inshore nursery areas. There may be some interchange, either way, between spawning stocks and nursery grounds in this and adjacent regions in, for example, the Irish Sea and the English Channel. In contrast, a more local distribution is recorded for the lemon sole, which has an apparently discrete population around the south-west English peninsula in the western Channel. It is assumed that the adults do not make extensive migrations. Flounder migrate from inshore, estuarine and even riverine nursery areas all along the coast of the region in the summer to spawn up to 20 or 30 miles offshore in late winter, and there appears to be little coastal movement other than in the egg or larval phase. At the other extreme, in this region both megrim and witch tend to be found only in deeper water.

Bass and the grey mullet are seasonally abundant inshore and in estuaries, and both species move south and west along the coast in the autumn to overwintering areas in this region. Spawning takes place offshore as the fish return north to feeding grounds in the spring, and in this region there is strong recruitment of stocks, thought to be linked to the warm sea temperatures in spring (Pawson 1992). From June onwards juvenile bass are found extensively in the region's many creeks, estuaries, backwaters and shallow bays (Kelley 1988). Areas such as these have been designated by MAFF as bass nursery areas, with angling restrictions imposed (Map 5.7.6) (see also section 5.7.3).

Monkfish (angler) spawn in deep water along the shelf edge mainly between March and June, but juveniles and non-spawning adults can be found throughout the western coastal area, even in shallow nearshore waters. Other demersal species of minor importance are conger eel and various gurnards and wrasse species. Sandeels are distributed widely throughout the region and provide an important food source for many commercial species and are a target of the bait industry. They burrow in coarse sand at night and during the winter; their distribution is thus influenced by that of coarse sand. Owing to the warmer water temperatures of the South-West Peninsula, species such as sea bream, red mullet and John Dory are at the northerly limit of their distribution in this region.

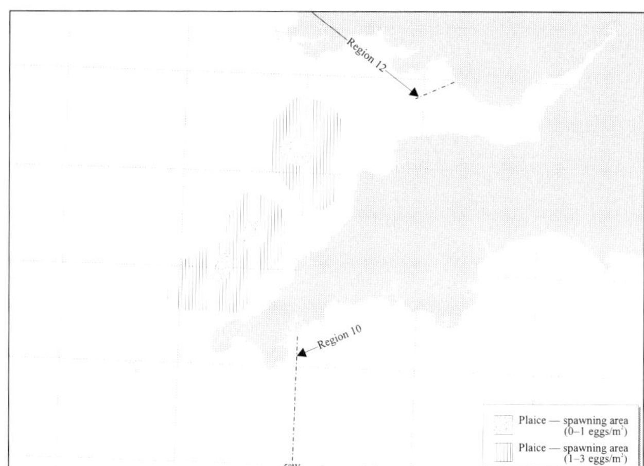

Map 5.7.5 Plaice spawning areas. Source: Lee & Ramster (1981). © Crown copyright.

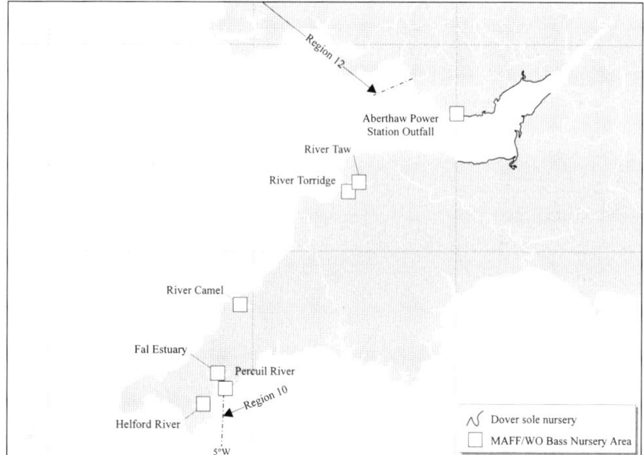

Map 5.7.6 Dover sole nursery coast and bass nursery areas. Sources: MAFF & WO (1990), Lee & Ramster (1981). © Crown copyright.

5.7.3 Human activities

A feature of all fish stocks, and the primary reason for their fluctuation, is the variability of recruitment of juvenile fish to the exploited populations. This variability, the causes of which are not fully understood, is determined by environmental conditions at the time of spawning and in the subsequent larval survival. Exploitation of fish stocks may increase the extent of these fluctuations.

Efforts are made to conserve stocks of pelagic and demersal species by implementing a variety of management measures, including: minimum landing sizes (MLS), minimum mesh size regulations, gear regulations, bycatch restrictions and quantitative controls on catches of 'pressure stock' species (through catch quota management by the setting of annual Total Allowable Catches (TACs, further explained further in section 9.1.3). Two such protection measures are shown in Table 5.7.1. Catch quota management indicates that the UK has been allocated a portion of the TAC in International Council for the Exploration of the Sea (ICES) Divisions VIIe & f (which include Region 11). Their implementation means that fish caught below MLS or for which the quota is exhausted must be discarded at sea, and this may affect stocks of exploited fish, as well as other fish, birds and species that live on the sea bed. Under the EU Common Fisheries Policy, an area offshore from the South-West Peninsula and including all the coastal waters of Region 11 has been designated the 'Mackerel Box'. This measure was introduced in order to conserve juvenile mackerel. Within the Mackerel Box there are restrictions on retaining mackerel on board; however, this does not apply to fishermen using handlines or gill nets.

In order to safeguard the bass fishery in coastal waters, 34 areas in England and Wales have been designated statutory bass nurseries (The Bass (Specified Sea Areas) (Prohibition of Fishing) Order 1990: SI 1990 No. 1156) (Ministry of Agriculture, Fisheries & Food/Welsh Office Agriculture Department 1990). Nursery areas are where juvenile bass are more abundant and are more easily caught, particularly during the summer months. The legislation prohibits fishing for bass from any vessel for the duration the closed season, and although fishing from the shore is not covered, anglers are expected to return to the sea any bass caught from within nursery areas. There are seven designated bass nursery areas in this region (Table 5.7.2; Map 5.7.6).

Table 5.7.2 MAFF/WO-designated bass nursery areas in the region

Name of area	*Duration of closed season*
Percuil River	1 May - 31 December
Fal Estuary	1 May - 31 December
Helford River	1 May - 31 December
River Camel	1 May - 30 November
River Torridge	1 May - 31 October
River Taw	1 May - 31 October
Aberthaw Power Station Outfall	All year

Source: Ministry of Agriculture, Fisheries and Food & Welsh Office Agriculture Department (1990)

The current status of bass populations in the Helford River bass nursery area was investigated in 1994 by the Helford Voluntary Marine Conservation Area Working Group (Goodwin 1995). In some areas the gill net fishery targeting bass has been restricted by netting restrictions introduced to protect salmon and sea trout. In order to protect bass stocks further, Cornwall Sea Fisheries Committee bylaws restrict the use of gill nets in the Manacles and Runnelstone areas to those with a mesh size larger than 250 mm and stipulate a 'minimum taking size' for bass of 37.5 cm.

Elasmobranch species in the region do not have any protected status. As a result of the relatively long time they take to reach reproductive maturity and the small numbers of young that they produce, they are held to be particularly vulnerable to exploitation.

Cetaceans compete with fisheries for their common food resource and are prone to accidental capture in fishing gear. The use of gill nets is widespread in the region and this can result in the accidental capture of seals, cetaceans and seabirds. The entanglement of cetaceans, particularly the harbour porpoise, is being studied by the Cornwall Wildlife Trust to establish whether observed bycatches are significant in relation to the known populations. Many seabirds used to be entangled in gill nets in St. Ives Bay, and since 1987 a voluntary code of conduct has operated in this area. This advises that, inside a line drawn from Pedn Olva Point to the northern extremity of the Black Cliffs, monofilament gill nets with a mesh size of less than 51 mm (usually used to target herring) should be used only between one hour before sunset and two hours after sunrise. The aim is to minimise the entanglement of seabirds, which do not feed during these hours.

Spawning and nursery areas may be vulnerable to other activities, such as marine aggregate extraction, sewage sludge disposal, dredging and dredge material disposal and the development of infrastructure such as barrages and pipelines. MAFF is a statutory consultee for, or licenses, activities such as these, in which the distributions of exploited fish populations and their identifiable spawning and nursery areas have to be taken into account.

Much of the region's coast has been subject to localised navigational dredging and marine aggregate extraction licence applications, but extraction licences for marine aggregates in the region are currently limited to the Bristol Channel (see section 9.4). All dredging activities have short-term, localised effects, such as the removal of material and organisms, but long-term effects on fish stocks or morphology are much more difficult to assess, owing to the difficulty of determining which effects are the result of dredging and which the result of the many other factors operating (Doody *et al.* 1993). Short- or long-term changes in sediment deposition can result, as well as inevitable changes in the topography of the bed. Disturbance of muddy material in order to access underlying aggregate can destroy feeding grounds for flatfish through the displacement of muddy sand fauna. A joint Welsh Office and Department of the Environment project entitled *Bristol Channel marine aggregate: resources and constraints* will study the effects of marine aggregates dredging on exploited fish species in the Bristol Channel.

Other activities, such as sea angling (see section 9.1.2) and seismic activity for oil and gas exploration (Turnpenny & Nedwell 1994), may also have an effect on fish populations.

5.7.4 Information sources used

Whereas the life history of the exploited crustacean and mollusc species can be observed at or near the sites at which they are harvested, the distributions of fish populations can change considerably between juvenile and adult phases and with seasonal migrations. Therefore, the information used in this section is based on the distribution and relative abundance of fish species as revealed by fisheries catch statistics obtained from recorded commercial landing figures. In addition, information is used from research vessel catch data and data from biological sampling during fishing surveys. Data from these surveys on the occurrence of spawning fish and juveniles can be used to identify spawning and nursery areas. However, this information is sometimes limited, and there may be other areas in addition to those described or shown on the maps where the species might also occur. Research surveys involving plankton sampling, hydrographic studies, fishing and tagging are required to establish the links between spawning groups and specific nursery areas, and between growing juveniles there and the adult populations to which they eventually recruit. Lee & Ramster (1981) has been used as a source for the maps, as well as Pawson (1995), which shows distribution maps of selected fish species around the north-east Atlantic and the British Isles and has a species-specific bibliography.

European Council Regulations detailing the Total Allowable Catches (TACs) and the national catch quotas for fish and shellfish species for all European countries, and certain conditions under which the species can be fished, are published in Luxembourg in the Official Journal of the European Communities. These regulations are updated annually and the regulations for 1996 are given in European Council (1995).

5.7.5 Acknowledgements

The authors thank the following for their comments on draft text: Mike Camplin (Devon Wildlife Trust), Terry Allen (MAFF Wales District), Stephanie Tyler (Gwent Wildlife

Trust), Paul Knapman (English Nature), Alan Winstone (Environment Agency Welsh Region), E.J. Derriman and R.G. Teague (Cornwall Sea Fisheries Committee), Stuart Bray (Environment Agency South-West Region) and Mark Tasker (JNCC).

5.7.6 Further sources of information

A. References cited

Doody, J.P., Johnston, C., & Smith, B. 1993. *The directory of the North Sea coastal margin.* Peterborough, JNCC.

European Council. 1986. EC Regulation No. 3094/86 (as amended). *Official Journal of the European Communities, L288 (29).*

European Council. 1995. EC Regulation No. 3074/95. *Official Journal of the European Communities, L 330* (38).

Goodwin, D.C. 1995. *Helford River survey bass project 1994.* Truro, Cornwall County Council. (Report to the Helford Voluntary Marine Conservation Area Advisory Group.)

Kelley, D.F. 1988. The importance of estuaries for sea-bass, *Dicentrarchus labrax* (L.). *Journal of Fish Biology, 33* (Supplement A): 25-33.

Lee, A.J., & Ramster, J.W. 1981. *Atlas of the seas around the British Isles.* Lowestoft, MAFF.

Ministry of Agriculture, Fisheries and Food & Welsh Office Agriculture Department. 1990. *Bass Nursery Areas and other conservation measures.* London, Ministry of Agriculture, Fisheries and Food.

Pawson, M.G. 1992. Climatic influences on the spawning success, growth and recruitment of bass (*Dicentrarchus labrax*) in British waters. *ICES Marine Science Symposium, 195:* 388-392.

Pawson, M.G. 1995. *Biogeographical identification of English Channel fish and shellfish stocks.* Lowestoft, Ministry of Agriculture, Fisheries & Food, Fisheries Laboratory. (Fisheries Research Technical Report No. 99.)

Symonds, D.J., & Rogers, S.I. 1995. The influence of spawning and nursery grounds on the distribution of sole *Solea solea* (L.) in the Irish Sea, Bristol Channel and adjacent areas. *Journal of Experimental Marine Biology and Ecology, 190*: 243-261.

Turnpenny, A.W.H., & Nedwell, J.R. 1994. *The effects on marine fish, diving mammals and birds of underwater sound generated by seismic surveys.* Southampton, Fawley Aquatic Research Laboratories Ltd.

B. Further reading

Brander, K.M. 1985. Sole survey in the Western English Channel. *Fishing Prospects, 1985,* 53-55.

Bucke, D., & Feist, S.W. 1990. *Marine fish diseases: an overview of 10 years' investigation by MAFF (UK).* Copenhagen, International Council for the Exploration of the Sea. (ICES C.M. 1990/E:12.)

Carpentier, A., Lemoine, M., & Souplet, A. 1989. *Description and first results of a new ground fish survey in the English Channel.* Copenhagen, International Council for the Exploration of the Sea. (ICES C.M. 1989/G:43.)

Earll, R.C., *ed.* 1992. *Shark, skate and ray workshop.* Ross-on-Wye, Marine Conservation Society, for Joint Nature Conservation Committee.

Eaton, D.R. 1989. Spawning-stock biomass of scad (*Trachurus trachuras L.*) to the west of the British Isles, as indicated by egg surveys. *Journal of the International Council for the Exploration of the Sea, 45*: 231-247.

Helford Voluntary Marine Conservation Area. 1995. *The Helford River fish.* Truro, Cornwall County Council/WWF/English Nature.

Henderson, P.A., & Holmes, R.H.A. 1991. On the population dynamics of dab, sole and flounder within Bridgwater Bay in the lower Severn Estuary, England. *Netherlands Journal of Sea Research, 27(3/4):* 337-344.

Horwood, J. 1993. The Bristol Channel sole (*Solea solea*): a fisheries case study. *Advances in Marine Biology, 29:* 215-367.

International Council for the Exploration of the Sea. 1993. *Atlas of North Sea fishes.* ICES Cooperative Research Report, No. 194.

Milligan, S.P. 1986. *Recent studies on the spawning of sprat (*Sprattus sprattus*) in the English Channel.* Lowestoft, Ministry of Agriculture, Fisheries & Food, Fisheries Laboratory. (Fisheries Research Technical Report, No. 83.)

Pawson, M.G., & Pickett, G.D. 1987. *The bass* Dicentrarchus labrax *and management of its fishery in England and Wales.* Lowestoft, MAFF Directorate of Fisheries Research. (Fisheries Laboratory Leaflet, No. 59.)

Rogers, S.I. 1992. Environmental factors affecting the distribution of sole (*Solea solea* (L.)) within a nursery area. *Netherlands Journal of Sea Research, 29*(1-3): 153-161.

Vas, P. 1990. The abundance of the blue shark, *Prionance glauca,* in the western English Channel. *Environmental biology of fishes, 29*(3): 209-225.

Vas, P. 1995. The status and conservation of sharks in Britain. *Aquatic Conservation: Marine and Freshwater Ecosystems, 5*: 67-79.

C. Contact names and addresses

Type of information	Contact address and telephone no.
Advice to assist with management and policy for the coastal zone	*Head of Laboratory, MAFF Directorate of Fisheries Research, Fisheries Laboratory, Conwy, tel: 01492 593883
Assessment and provision of advice on the conservation of exploited fish stocks. MAFF fish databases.	*Director, MAFF Directorate of Fisheries Research, Fisheries Laboratory, Lowestoft, tel: 01502 562244
UKDMAP software with maps showing distributions of selected sea fish species and spawning areas	*Project Manager, BODC, Birkenhead, tel: 0151 652 3950
Research on species	Plymouth Marine Laboratory, Prospect Place, Plymouth PL1 3DH, tel: 01752 633100
Marine science research	Dept. of Biological Sciences, University of Plymouth, Drake Circus, Plymouth PL4 8AA, tel: 01752 600600
Local inshore fisheries information and advice	Chief Fishery Officer, Cornwall Sea Fisheries Committee, The Old Bonded Warehouse, Quay Street, Penzance, Cornwall TR18 4BD, tel: 01736 69817
Local inshore fisheries information and advice	Assistant Chief Executive, Isles of Scilly Sea Fisheries Committee, Town Hall, St. Mary's, Isles of Scilly TR1 0LW, tel: 01720 422536
Local inshore fisheries information and advice	Deputy Clerk & Chief Fishery Officer, Devon Sea Fisheries Committee, Forde House, Newton Abbot, Devon TQ12 3XX, tel: 01803 854648 / 882004
Local inshore fisheries information and advice	Director, South Wales Sea Fisheries Committee, Queens Buildings, Cambrian Place, Swansea, West Glamorgan SA1 1TW, tel: 01792 654466
Marine conservation issues and fisheries in England	*Fisheries Liaison Officer, English Nature HQ, Peterborough, tel: 01733 340345
Marine conservation issues and fisheries in Wales	*Marine and Coastal Section, CCW HQ, Bangor, tel: 01248 370444
Marine Fisheries Task Group papers; marine conservation	*Fisheries Officer, JNCC, Peterborough, tel: 01733 62626
Marine conservation issues	*Conservation Officer, RSPB, Sandy, tel: 01767 680551
Marine conservation issues	*Fisheries Officer, Marine Section, WWF-UK, Godalming, tel: 01483 426444
Marine conservation issues	*Conservation Officer, Marine Conservation Society, Ross-on-Wye, tel: 01989 566017
Marine conservation issues	Honorary Secretary, The Marine Forum for Environmental Issues, c/o University College Scarborough, Filey Road, Scarborough YO11 3AZ, tel: 01723 362392

*Starred contact addresses are given in full in the Appendix.

5.8 Fish: salmon, sea trout and eels

Dr M. Aprahamian & C.F. Robson

5.8.1 Introduction

Diadromous fish spend part of their lives in fresh water and part at sea. The three exploited diadromous fish species covered in this section - the Atlantic salmon *Salmo salar*, sea trout *Salmo trutta* and eel *Anguilla anguilla* - are widespread in British waters and have been recorded in rivers in this region. (Twaite shad *Alosa fallax* are also diadromous but are included in section 5.9, as they are not routinely exploited.) The salmonids (salmon and sea trout) spawn in fresh water and then migrate out to sea to mature, while the eel matures in fresh water and reproduces at sea. Sea trout and brown trout are the same species, but the latter is a freshwater form and is therefore not covered in this section. Information on the life-cycles of these fish can be found in Jones (1959), Mills (1971, 1989), Moriarty (1978), Shearer (1992), Sinha & Jones (1975) and Tesch (1977).

Map 5.8.1 Salmon and sea trout rivers. Source: Environment Agency.

5.8.2 Important locations

Salmon, sea trout and eels have a widespread distribution in rivers and the coastal seas of British waters. The distribution of salmon and sea trout is controlled by natural factors, such as river levels, by man-made barriers that may limit the extent to which they can go upstream, and by pollution levels. They are present in many rivers and the coastal seas of this region (Map 5.8.1). Eels (adult silver eels and juvenile elvers) are probably found in all river systems in the region, as elsewhere in Britain, and are most common in the Severn. It is highly likely that there are diadromous fish present in the region in other rivers, small tributaries and streams that are not shown on Map 5.8.1.

5.8.3 Human activities

Under the Environment Act 1995, the functions of the NRA under the Water Resources Act 1991 were transferred to the Environment Agency (EA) on 1 April 1996. The South West, Midlands and Welsh Regions of the EA have a responsibility to regulate, protect and monitor salmon, sea trout and eel fisheries from rivers to coastal waters out to 6 nautical miles from baselines. The four Sea Fisheries Committees (SFCs) of the region have powers to support the conservation of salmonid fisheries while exercising their responsibilities towards the regulation of sea fisheries (see section 9.1). There is no SFC east of the Devon SFC boundary to the England / Wales border in the Severn Estuary; the Environment Agency (EA)'s South West Region undertakes SFC functions in this area. The EA South West Region also act as the Sea Fisheries Committee for the Taw-Torridge Estuary and all Cornish estuaries including the Fal. The EA Welsh Region undertakes SFC functions east of Cardiff (from Beachly) to the mouth of the River Rhymney (see Map 9.1.2). The EA uses a variety of techniques, such as netting, electric fishing and monitoring of angling catches, to assess stocks of salmon and sea trout. The 'Fisheries Classification Scheme' allocates fisheries to a quality class on the basis of fish and river habitat data (National Rivers Authority 1994b). 'Salmon Management Plans' are being developed by the EA for key salmon rivers (National Rivers Authority 1996). These plans will form part of the 'Local Environment Action Plans', developed from Catchment Management Plans. The EA construct fish passes around natural barriers, or make them passable by fish in other ways. The EA also undertakes physical habitat improvement by, for example, creating pools and adding spawning gravels, riffles and trees for cover.

The effects of exploitation, especially by different catch methods (rod-and-line or nets), is an issue for salmon and sea trout stocks (MAFF / SO 1991). The use of coastal fixed nets and drift nets close to the coast and in estuaries is a potential barrier to migrating salmonids. There is particular concern with regard to Irish drift nets, which take approximately 30% of grilse returning to the south-west rivers. As well as rod-and-line, a wide variety of nets are licensed for use in many of the region's rivers (see section 9.1.2), and fyke, putchers and elver nets are used to catch eels in tidal or still waters. Net Limitation Orders are applied by the EA to estuarine salmon and sea trout fisheries. These limit the number of nets allowed to fish a particular area. Net Limitation Orders are in place for the following estuaries in the region: Camel, Lyn, Severn, Wye and Usk. The use of nets (apart from those used to catch eels) is not permitted in any other estuaries. The number of nets licensed for the listed estuaries in 1993 is shown in Table 9.1.7. All licences issued by the EA are subject to seasonal and weekly closure times.

Maitland & Campbell (1992) summarise the possible effects of various issues of relevance to freshwater fish. The movement of salmonids into and from tributaries is restricted by adverse water quality, low flows and artificial barriers such as weirs and tidal exclusion barrages. A decline over the last fifteen years (which follows the pattern throughout Europe) in the number of elvers entering the Severn has been noted. It has been attributed to unknown factors acting on the oceanic phase of the eel lifecycle, such as changes in the North Atlantic current system (White & Knights 1994). These, together with historic pollution problems and a decrease in the extent of wetlands, ponds and ditches, have probably contributed to a decline in adult eel populations. There is some indication that juvenile recruitment is starting to recover. However, once the elvers have entered the Severn, weirs have a major impact on the speed and extent to which eels can penetrate through the system. In addition, eels are caught as a bycatch in the salmon putchers (see section 9.1.2) in the upper part of the Severn Estuary (EA pers. comm.).

MAFF/SO/WO (1996) concludes that the predator species likely to have the most widespread effects on salmon fisheries and populations in GB are cormorants, sawbill ducks, otters and seals. It concludes that more information is needed on the numbers, distribution and diet of all these predators and of their impact on salmon.

5.8.4 Information sources used

The Environment Agency publishes catch statistics (which before April 1996 were published by the National Rivers Authority) for the rivers shown in Map 5.8.1 (see also section 9.1). Tributaries and minor rivers with a shared estuary are included under the main river and any remaining rivers are recorded separately in the 'others' category. There are therefore diadromous fish present in other rivers and streams that are not shown on Map 5.8.1. Rivers in the region are shown on the maps in National Rivers Authority (1994a) and the distribution of Atlantic salmon in England and Wales is presented in Russell (1989).

The Institute of Freshwater Ecology (part of the Natural Environment Research Council) conducts a programme of research into freshwater habitats and species. Their 'fish counters' yield information on various species of fish, and other studies involve sampling salmon, sea trout and eels from rivers in the UK.

5.8.5 Acknowledgements

The authors thank the following for their comments on draft text: Mike Camplin (Devon Wildlife Trust), A.S. Churchward (Environment Agency Midlands Region), Mike Pawson (MAFF Directorate of Fisheries Research, Lowestoft), Stephanie Tyler (Gwent Wildlife Trust), Alan Winstone (Environment Agency Welsh Region), E.J. Derriman (Cornwall Sea Fisheries Committee) and Mask Tasker (JNCC).

5.8.6 Further sources of information

A. *References cited*

Jones, J.W. 1959. *The salmon.* London, Collins.

MAFF/SO. 1991. *Salmon net fisheries: report of a review of salmon net fishing in the areas of the Yorkshire and Northumbria regions of the National Rivers Authority and the salmon fishery districts from the River Tweed to the River Ugie.* London, HMSO.

MAFF/SO/WO. 1996. *The effects of predation on salmon fisheries.* London, MAFF. (Report to the Salmon Advisory Committee.)

Maitland, P.S., & Campbell, R.N. 1992. *Freshwater fishes of the British Isles.* London, Harper Collins. (New Naturalist series.)

Mills, D.H. 1971. *Salmon and trout: a resource, its ecology, conservation and management.* Edinburgh, Oliver and Boyd.

Mills, D.H. 1989. *Ecology and management of Atlantic salmon.* London, Chapman and Hall.

Moriarty, C. 1978. *Eels.* Newton Abbot, David and Charles.

National Rivers Authority. 1994a. *The quality of rivers and canals in England and Wales (1990 to 1992).* Bristol, National Rivers Authority. (Water Quality Series No. 19.)

National Rivers Authority. 1994b. *The NRA National Fisheries Classification Scheme: a guide for users.* Bristol, National Rivers Authority. (R & D Note 206).

National Rivers Authority. 1996. *A strategy for management of salmon in England and Wales.* Bristol, National Rivers Authority.

Russell, I.C. 1989. *A map of the distribution of Atlantic salmon* (Salmo salar L.) *in England and Wales.* Lowestoft, MAFF Directorate of Fisheries Research.

Shearer, W.M. 1992. *The Atlantic salmon: natural history, exploitation and future management.* Oxford, Blackwell Scientific.

Sinha, V.R.P., & Jones, J.W. 1975. *The European freshwater eel.* Liverpool, University of Liverpool Press.

Tesch, F.W. 1977. *The eel: biology and management of Anguillid eels.* London, Chapman and Hall.

White, E.M., & Knights, B. 1994. *Elver and eel stock assessment in the Severn and Avon.* Bristol, National Rivers Authority. (R & D Project Record 256/13/ST.)

B. *Further reading*

Davidson, N.C., Laffoley, D.d'A., Doody, J.P., Way, L.S., Gordon, J., Key, R., Drake, C.M., Pienkowski, M.W., Mitchell, R., & Duff, K.L. 1991. *Nature conservation and estuaries in Great Britain.* Peterborough, Nature Conservancy Council.

National Rivers Authority. 1992. *Sea trout in England and Wales.* Bristol, National Rivers Authority. (Fisheries Technical Report, No. 1.)

National Rivers Authority. 1992. *Sea trout literature review.* Bristol, National Rivers Authority. (Fisheries Technical Report, No. 3.)

National Rivers Authority. 1992. *The feasibility of developing and utilising gene banks for sea trout* (Salmo trutta) *conservation.* Bristol, National Rivers Authority. (Fisheries Technical Report, No. 4.)

National Rivers Authority. 1994. *Salmonid and freshwater fisheries statistics for England and Wales, 1993.* London, HMSO & NRA.

North Atlantic Salmon Conservation Organisation. 1995. *Ten year review of the activities of the North Atlantic Salmon Conservation Organisation 1984 - 1994.* Edinburgh, North Atlantic Salmon Conservation Organisation.

Solomon, D.J. 1992. *Diversion and entrapment of fish at water intakes and outfalls.* London, HMSO and NRA.

C. Contact names and addresses

Type of information	Contact address and telephone no.
Regional scientific information and advice	*Regional Fisheries Officer, Environment Agency South West Region, Exeter, tel: 01392 444000
Regional scientific information and advice	*Regional Fisheries Officer, Environment Agency Midlands Region, Solihull, tel: 0121 711 2324
Regional scientific information and advice	*Regional Fisheries Officer, Environment Agency Welsh Region, Cardiff, tel: 01222 770088
Scientific advice and policy; Fisheries Classification Scheme	*Head of Department, Environment Agency - Fisheries Department, Bristol, tel: 01454 624400
General enquiries	*Public Relations Officer, Environment Agency - Public Relations Department, Bristol, tel: 01454 624400
Research programme into freshwater habitats and species	Director, Institute of Freshwater Ecology - Head Office, Windermere Laboratory, Far Sawrey, Ambleside, Cumbria LA21 0LP, tel: 015394 42468
Local inshore fisheries information and advice - Cornwall	Chief Fishery Officer, Cornwall Sea Fisheries Committee, The Old Bonded Warehouse, Quay Street, Penzance, Cornwall TR18 4BD, tel: 01736 69817
Local inshore fisheries information and advice - Isles of Scilly	Assistant Chief Executive, Isles of Scilly Sea Fisheries Committee, Town Hall, St. Mary's, Isles of Scilly TR1 0LW, tel: 01720 422536
Local inshore fisheries information and advice - Devon	Deputy Clerk & Chief Fishery Officer, Devon Sea Fisheries Committee, Forde House, Newton Abbot, Devon TQ12 3XX, tel: 01803 854648 / 882004
Local inshore fisheries information and advice - South Wales	Director, South Wales Sea Fisheries Committee, Queens Buildings, Cambrian Place, Swansea, West Glamorgan SA1 1TW, tel: 01792 654466
Conservation of wild salmon; salmonid research	Director, The Atlantic Salmon Trust, Moulin, Pitlochry PH16 5JQ, tel: 01796 473439

*Starred contact addresses are given in full in the Appendix.

In spring and early summer, basking sharks are often seen in coastal waters off the region. Despite their rarity in UK waters generally, they are unprotected (except close to the Isle of Man). They were until recently caught for the oil their livers yield, formerly used in aviation engineering. Drawing: Ian Reach, JNCC.

5.9 Fish: other species

Dr G.W. Potts & S.E. Swaby

5.9.1 Introduction

The estuaries and coastal waters of this region contain a diverse range of fish species. There are 111 species of exploited and unexploited fish recorded for the Severn Estuary (Potts & Swaby 1993b) (out of a national total of 336), comprising two lampreys (Agnatha), nine sharks or rays (elasmobranchs) and 100 bony fish (teleosts). In addition other fish are caught in the wider area beyond the Isles of Scilly, including southern species on the edge of their distribution and vagrants brought in by oceanic currents.

This region has confirmed records of all seven British marine and estuarine species protected under national, European and international legislation (Table 5.9.1). These include lampern *Lampetra fluviatilis* and sea lamprey *Petromyzon marinus*, sturgeon *Acipenser sturio*, allis shad *Alosa alosa* and twaite shad *Alosa fallax*. These species are considered threatened in UK and European waters (Potts & Swaby pers. comm.) (the sand goby *Pomatoschistus minutus* and common goby *P. microps* are both very abundant in UK). The Bristol Channel and Severn Estuary contain the only known viable populations of allis and twaite shad in the UK (Map 5.9.1), as well as some significant populations of lamperns and sea lampreys (Map 5.9.2) (Potts & Swaby 1993c). For this reason the region is of national importance.

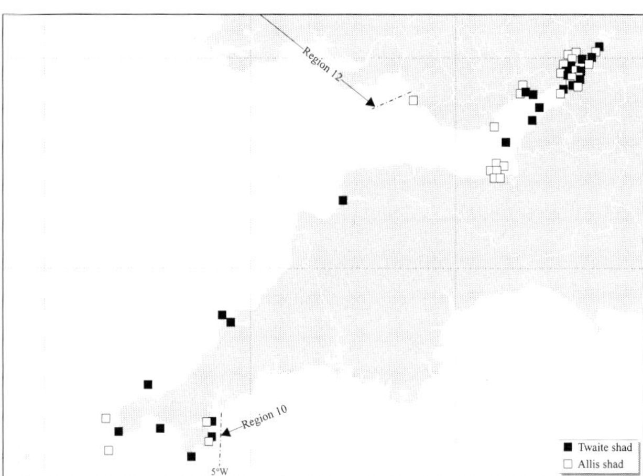

Map 5.9.1 Distribution records on the British Marine Fishes Database of allis shad and twaite shad. Source: after Potts & Swaby (1993c).

Map 5.9.2 Distribution records on the British Marine Fishes Database of lampern and sea lamprey. Source: after Potts & Swaby (1993c).

5.9.2 Important locations and species

Map 5.9.2 shows the recorded distribution of sea lamprey and lampern in the region. Early references to the lampern report them as common in the rivers of eastern Cornwall in spring (Cunningham 1906), but concern was expressed by Lloyd (1941) about diminishing stocks, although large numbers were still being taken from the Severn Estuary. There are recent reports of lamperns being taken in large numbers on power station intake screens (Claridge *et al.* 1986). Lampern spawning occurs between March and April and peak abundance is reported between October and January (Potter *et al.* 1986). The sea lamprey has been recorded as common in the south-west, with two records from St. Ives (Cunningham 1906), but is uncommon off Ilfracombe (Palmer 1946). Most records come from the Severn Estuary, from the extensive power station intake screen data (Henderson & Holmes 1985). Other sightings are of sea lampreys as parasites on other species.

The associations of fish with habitats are given in Potts & Swaby (1993a). Major marine habitat types have been identified and divided into a series of 'ecotypes', including estuarine, littoral, sublittoral, offshore and specialist habitats (symbiotic and other relationships). These are further refined with reference to substrate type (mud, sand, gravel and particulate substrate, bedrock or boulders (reef) and

Table 5.9.1 Scheduled species and protected status

Species	*Wildlife and Countryside Act (Schedule)*	*EC Habitats & Species Directive (Annex)*	*Bern Convention (Appendix)*	*CITES (Appendix)*
Lampern		IIa, Va	III	
Sea lamprey		IIa	III	
Sturgeon	5	IIa, Va	III	I
Allis shad	5	IIa, Va	III	
Twaite shad		IIa, Va	III	
Common goby			III	
Sand goby			III	

Source: after Potts & Swaby (1993, pers. comm.).

water column, where appropriate). This classification provides a structure for identifying and classifying fish/habitat associations. However, many fish have complex life-styles and habitat requirements and may occupy several habitats during different phases of their life-cycles.

Sturgeon records reflect no clear pattern and are scattered in time and location throughout the region. The sturgeon was once considered relatively common in the Bristol Channel (Matthews 1933). Although they were formerly considered rare in Cornwall (Cunningham 1906; Palmer 1946), they were considered fairly frequent along the south coast and in the south-west, with individual records from Porthleven in 1900 and Newlyn in 1902 (Clark 1907). More recent records from the region are listed in Table 5.9.2.

Table 5.9.2 Records of sturgeon from the region

Location	*Dates and numbers recorded (in brackets)*
Cornish coast	1953 (1), 1956 (1), 1959 (3), 1971 (3), 1972 (2)
Bristol Channel	1957 (1)
Newlyn	1958 (1)
Barnstaple Bay	1970 (1)
Newlyn	1971 (1)
Sennen Cove	1971 (1)

Source: British Marine Fishes Database

Both allis and twaite shad records are spread across the region (Map 5.9.1), with the greatest concentration in the Severn Estuary, where large numbers congregate while on spawning migrations upstream. The peak spawning period is from May to June, with peak abundance between August to September. Both species of shad were reported as caught in 'considerable numbers' in the Severn at the turn of the century. In the Severn Estuary, twaite shad are now more abundant than the allis. The River Wye SSSI is believed to be an important breeding site for allis and twaite shad (C. Pagendam, English Nature, pers. comm.).

Giltheads *Sparus auratus* and triggerfish *Balistes carolinensis*, which in this region are towards the northern edge of their distribution, are not uncommon. Increasing numbers of triggerfish are reported by fishermen who catch them removing bait from shellfish pots. In the spring and early summer, basking sharks *Cetorhinus maximus* and sunfish *Mola mola* are often seen in coastal waters of the region.

5.9.3 Human activities

Human activities affecting estuaries and adjacent coasts in the region are summarised in Buck (1993); they also affect the abundance and distribution of fish. Nationally, estuaries are used by up to 180 fish species for migration, spawning, feeding and as nursery grounds (Potts & Swaby 1993c). Of the estuaries in the region, the Severn Estuary is subject to the largest number of human impacts, including industrial, agricultural and urban waste disposal. Discharges of trade effluent containing heavy metals (see also section 9.6) have had damaging effects on fish in the estuaries of the Severn (Hardisty *et al.* 1974) and Fal (Bryan & Gibbs 1983). Also in the Severn Estuary, the operation of a major power station at Hinckley Point influences fish abundance and diversity (Henderson & Holmes 1985), with large numbers of fish (including twaite and allis shads) caught on the power station water intake screens. In the estuary of the River Taw pesticides have been found to affect fish populations (Hamilton 1985). The discharge of treated and untreated sewage (see also section 9.6) creates special problems, which may result in low dissolved oxygen levels. Fish are known to leave areas where oxygen levels are low (Potts & Swaby 1993c). Large numbers of twaite shad are caught as a by-catch in the fixed salmon putcher ranks (see section 9.1.2) in the upper part of the Severn Estuary (Churchward, Environment Agency, pers. comm.). The possible effects of fisheries on species is discussed in sections 5.7 and 9.1. Sea angling occurs in many places throughout the region (Orton 1996) (see section 9.1.2).

5.9.4 Information sources used

The estuaries and coastal waters of the approaches to the Bristol Channel and the Severn Estuary have been the subject of numerous studies by research and educational institutes and are monitored by the Ministry of Agriculture, Fisheries and Food (MAFF). The MAFF Fisheries Laboratory at Lowestoft has records of species, including non-exploited species, taken during sampling programmes in the Bristol Channel and Western Approaches. Newlyn fish market is also a good source of records of rare and unusual fish landed by fishing boats. Studies have also been carried out in this region on accumulations of heavy metals in fish and of populations of fish taken from the intake screens of power stations. Surveys in this region are carried out by the Environment Agency (EA), universities and other research institutes. The Bristol Channel Federation of Sea Anglers keeps records of fish caught in the Channel. Fish lists are available for the major estuaries in the area (Potts & Swaby 1993c). The Welsh part of this region is covered by a monitoring programme, supported by the Countryside Council for Wales, to identify the impact of environmental change on fish distribution (Potts & Swaby 1993a, 1994). The review of estuarine fish in selected English estuaries (Potts & Swaby 1993c), carried out by the Marine Biological Association for English Nature, is included in the British Marine Fishes Database, which covers fish in the UK and individual records for this region. Information is being gathered from a variety of sources, including the EA, the Sea Fisheries Committees, anglers and fishermen. The data include published literature, unpublished reports and personal communications from fish biologists. The information obtained from all these and other sources has been collated on the British Marine Fishes Database.

5.9.5 Acknowledgements

The authors wish to thank staff at the Cornwall Biological Records Unit, Redruth, for help in preparing this section and Charlotte Pagendham, English Nature, for information about allis and twaite shad breeding areas.

5.9.6 Further sources of information

A. References cited

Bryan, G.W., & Gibbs, P.E. 1983. *Heavy metals in the Fal Estuary, Cornwall. A study of long-term contamination by mining waste and its effects on estuarine organisms.* Plymouth, Marine Biological Association. (Occasional Publications of the Marine Biological Association, No. 2.)

Buck, A.L. 1993. *An inventory of UK estuaries. Volume 2: South-west Britain.* Peterborough, Joint Nature Conservation Committee.

Claridge, P.N., Potter, I.C., & Hardisty, M.W. 1986. Seasonal changes in movements, abundance, size composition and diversity of the fish fauna of the Severn Estuary. *Journal of the Marine Biological Association of the United Kingdom, 66:* 229-258.

Clark, J. 1907. An annotated list of Cornish fishes. *Zoologist, 4*(11): 415-427.

Cunningham, M.J.T. 1906. Fishes. *In: The Victoria county history of the county of Cornwall. Vol. 1,* ed. by W. Page, 291-306. London, James Street.

Hamilton, R.M. 1985. Discharges of pesticides to the rivers Mole and Taw, their accumulation in fish flesh and possible effects on fish stocks. *Journal of Fish Biology, 27* (Supplement A): 139-147.

Hardisty, M.W., Huggins, R.J., Kartar, S., & Sainsbury, M. 1974. Ecological implications of heavy metal in fish from the Severn Estuary. *Marine Pollution Bulletin, 5*: 12-15.

Henderson, P.A., & Holmes, R.H.A. 1985. *The effect on fish populations of impingement on the screens of Hinkley point 'A' and 'B' cooling water intakes.* Fawley, Central Electricity Research Laboratories. (Laboratory Note No. TPRD/L/2911/N85.)

Lloyd, A.J. 1941. Studies on the biology of the Bristol Channel. Part V: The marine fish fauna of the southern shores of the Bristol Channel. *Proceedings of the Bristol Naturalists Society, IX*(2): 202-230.

Matthews, L.H. 1933. The seafish and fisheries of the Bristol district. *Proceedings of the Bristol Naturalists' Society, 7:* 442-462.

Orton, D.A., *ed.* 1996. *Where to fish 1996 - 1997.* 85th ed. Beaminster, Thomas Harmsworth.

Palmer, M.G., *ed.* 1946. *The fauna and flora of the Ilfracombe district of North Devon.* Exeter, Ilfracombe Field Club.

Potter, I.C., Claridge, P.N., & Warwick, R.M. 1986. Consistency of seasonal changes in an estuarine fish assemblage. *Marine Ecology Progress Series, 32:* 217-228.

Potts, G.W., & Swaby, S.E. 1993a. *Marine and estuarine fishes of Wales. The development of the British marine fishes database and monitoring programme for Wales.* Bangor, Countryside Council for Wales.

Potts, G.W., & Swaby, S.E. 1993b. *Marine fishes on the EC Habitats and Species Directive.* Peterborough, Joint Nature Conservation Committee. (Confidential report.)

Potts, G.W., & Swaby, S.E. 1993c. *Review of the status of estuarine fishes.* Peterborough, English Nature. (English Nature Research Reports, No. 34.)

Potts, G.W., & Swaby, S.E. 1994. *Marine and estuarine fishes of Wales. Fact sheets.* 2nd ed. Bangor, Countryside Council for Wales.

B. Further reading

Aprahamian, M.W., & Aprahamian, C.D. 1990. Status of the genus *Alosa* in the British Isles, past and present. *Journal of Fish Biology, 37* (Supplement A): 257-258.

Davidson, N.C., Laffoley, D.d'A., Doody, J.P., Way, L.S., Gordon, J., Key, R., Drake, C.M., Pienkowski, M.W., Mitchell, R., & Duff, K.L. 1991. *Nature conservation and estuaries in Great Britain.* Peterborough, Nature Conservancy Council.

Gill, C., & Mercer, T. 1989. *Surveys of harbours, rias and estuaries in southern Britain: Volume I. Camel Estuary.* Peterborough, Nature Conservancy Council.

Hardisty, M.W., & Huggins, R.J. 1973. Lamprey growth as a possible indication of biological conditions in the Bristol Channel. *Nature, London, 243:* 229-231.

Helford Voluntary Marine Conservation Area. 1995. *The Helford River fish.* Truro, Cornwall County Council/WWF/English Nature.

Henderson, P.A., Holmes, R.H.A., & Bamber, R.N. 1984. *The species of fish and arthropods captured during cooling-water extraction by power stations in the Bristol Channel and Severn Estuary 1980-1984.* Fawley, Central Electricity Research Laboratories. (Laboratory Note No. TRPD/L/2694/N84.)

Holbrook, A. 1991. *The Severn barrage: a bibliography 1909-1990.* University of Bath.

Isles of Scilly Museum. Undated. *Fish around the Isles of Scilly.* Isles of Scilly Museum Publication, No. 1.

Little, A. 1989. *Surveys of harbours, rias and estuaries in Southern Britain: Volume I. Taw and Torridge Estuary.* Peterborough, Nature Conservancy Council.

Miller, P.J., & El-Tawil, M.Y. 1974. A multidisciplinary approach to a new species of Gobius (Teleosti: Gobiidae) from Southern Cornwall. *Journal of Zoology, London, 174:* 539-574.

National Rivers Authority. 1994. *Status of rare fish: a literature review of freshwater fish in the UK.* Bristol, National Rivers Authority. (R & D Report, No. 18.)

Pullin, R.S.V. 1977. The marine fauna of Lundy (Pisces: Fishes). *Report of the Lundy Field Society, 28:* 45-54.

Turnpenny, A.W.H., & Nedwell, J.R. 1994. *The effects on marine fish, diving mammals and birds of underwater sound generated by seismic surveys.* Southampton, Fawley Aquatic Research Laboratories Ltd.

C. Contact names and addresses

Type of information	Contact address and telephone no.
British Marine Fishes Database	Dr G.W. Potts/S.E. Swaby, Marine Biological Association UK, Citadel Hill, Plymouth PL1 2PB, tel: 01752 633100
Fisheries - England & Wales	*Director, MAFF Directorate of Fisheries Research, Lowestoft, tel: 01502 562244
Maintenance, improvement and development of salmon, sea trout and eel fisheries - England and Wales	*Head of Department, Environment Agency (EA) Fisheries Department, Bristol, tel: 01454 624400
Fish conservation - UK	*Fisheries Officer, JNCC Peterborough, tel: 01733 62626
Fish conservation - England	*Marine Fisheries Officer, EN HQ, Peterborough, tel: 01733 340345
Fish conservation - Wales	*Marine and Coastal Section, CCW HQ, Bangor, tel: 01248 370444

*Starred contact addresses are given in full in the Appendix.

5.10 Seabirds

M.L. Tasker

5.10.1 Introduction

This section deals with seabirds both at their colonies on land and while at sea. It covers not only those species usually regarded as seabirds (listed in Table 5.10.1), but also seaducks, cormorant, divers and grebes: species that are reliant for an important part of their life on the marine environment. (Section 5.12.2 includes information on these waterfowl species, where they occur close inshore, especially within estuaries.) Scientific names of all species are given in the tables.

This region is internationally important for seabirds. Six colonies are of importance in a national context and three in the international context. All but one of these are located in the Isles of Scilly. More than 1% of the European populations of six species (cormorant, shag, lesser and great black-backed gull, roseate tern and razorbill) breed in the region, with a further two (herring gull and common tern) present in nationally important numbers (more than 1% of the GB population). Table 5.10.1 summarises the importance of the region for breeding seabirds.

Table 5.10.1 Overall importance of seabirds breeding in the region

Species	*Total*	*% GB*	*% Europe*
Fulmar *Fulmarus glacialis*	2,214	<1.0	<1.0
Manx shearwater *Puffinus puffinus*	?	?	?
Storm petrel *Hydrobates pelagicus*	1,000+	?	?
Cormorant *Phalacrocorax carbo*	211	3.1	1.6
Shag *Phalacrocorax aristotelis*	1,727	4.7	3.3
Lesser black-backed gull *Larus fuscus*	6,402	7.8	5.5
Herring gull *Larus argentatus*	5,690	3.8	<1.0
Great black-backed gull *Larus marinus*	1,397	7.6	5.7
Kittiwake *Rissa tridactyla*	3,461	<1.0	<1.0
Sandwich tern *Sterna sandvicensis*	20	<1.0	0
Roseate tern *Sterna dougallii*	<10	12.5	1.4
Common tern *Sterna hirundo*	171	1.3	<1.0
Guillemot *Uria aalge*	4,037	<1.0	<1.0
Razorbill *Alca torda*	2,140	1.4	1.2
Puffin *Fratercula arctica*	282	<1.0	<1.0

Sources: figures for Great Britain from Walsh *et al.* (1995) and for Europe from Lloyd *et al.* (1991). Notes: counts are of pairs, except for guillemots, razorbills and puffins, which are counted individually. Regional totals are compiled from the most recent available good-quality counts up to 1994. Key: ? = unknown.

Numbers of birds at sea off the region are generally low compared with those in more northern waters of the United Kingdom. The greatest concentrations of seabirds at sea occur in this region following the breeding period, when concentrations of gannets and herring gulls occur offshore. There is an influx of razorbills to waters off north Cornwall in late winter. During the breeding season, waters far to the west of the region are used by relatively high numbers of Manx shearwater and gannet. Waters off Hartland Point are of national importance for red-throated divers in winter.

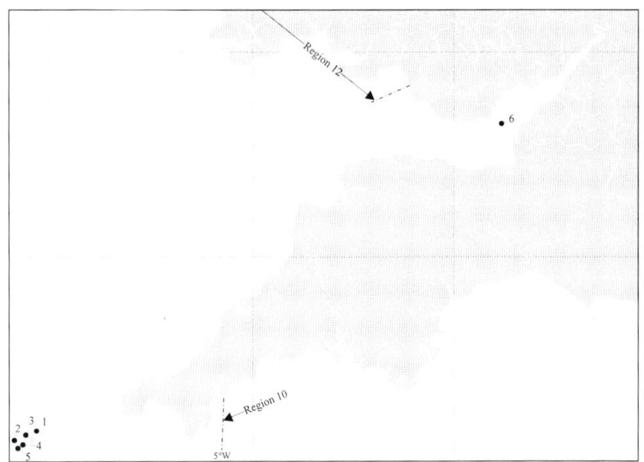

Map 5.10.1 Colonies holding at least 1% of the GB population of any seabird species. Numbers are those listed in Table 5.10.3. Source: JNCC Seabird Colony Register.

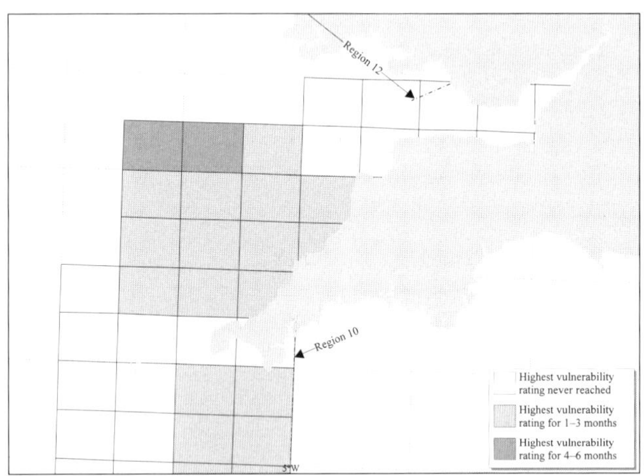

Map 5.10.2 Relative importance of region and adjacent seas for seabirds. The grid is of 15'N x 30'W rectangles; see text for explanation of vulnerability ratings. Source: JNCC Seabirds at Sea Team.

5.10.2 Important locations and species

Breeding seabirds require habitat that is free from predatory mammals, so all colonies in this region are on offshore islands or cliffs. The Isles of Scilly are the most important location for seabirds in the region. Four colonies, all in the Isles of Scilly, are important at the European level, with a further two colonies in the region important at the Great Britain level (Table 5.10.2; Map 5.10.1). Several other colonies are within SSSIs and hold regionally important numbers of birds. Manx shearwaters breed in unknown (but small) numbers on Lundy.

At sea, seabird food ranges from zooplankton to small fish and waste from fishing fleets. Habitats that concentrate any of these foods are preferred. Zooplankton can be concentrated in zones where water masses meet or where tides converge around headlands or over some sea-bed features. Both lesser and great black-backed gulls feed offshore, with lesser black-backed gulls in particular feeding on fishery wastes. Of the other species present in

Table 5.10.2 Recent counts of seabird colonies in the region holding more than 1% of the EU or 1% of the Great Britain total for particular species

*Site no.**	*Colony*	*Grid ref.*	*Species*	*Year*	*Count*	*>1% EU/GB*	*Protected status*
	Isles of Scilly						
1	Eastern Isles	SV945145	Great black-backed gull	1987	481	EU	SSSI
2	Isles of Scilly	SV81	Common tern	1992	197	GB	AONB, Heritage
			Storm petrel		2,000+	EU	Coast, SMA, VMNR, possible SAC
3	Samson	SV877127	Lesser black-backed gull	1993	1,132	EU	SSSI
4	Annet	SV863086	Lesser black-backed gull	1994	935	GB	SSSI
5	Western Rocks	SV835065	Shag	1987	529	EU	SSSI
	South Glamorgan						
6	Flat Holm	ST220650	Lesser black-backed gull	1989	1,200	GB	SSSI, LNR

Source: JNCC/Seabird Group Seabird Colony Register. Key: *site number refers to Map 5.10.1. GB = nationally important; SSSI = Site of Special Scientific Interest; AONB = Area of Outstanding Natural Beauty; SMA = Sensitive Marine Area; VMNR = Voluntary Marine Nature Reserve; SAC = Special Area of Conservation; LNR = Local Nature Reserve; EU = internationally important; GB = nationally important. Notes: counts are of pairs; for most species the most recent available good-quality count is presented; for terns (whose numbers may fluctuate markedly from year to year, reflecting inter-colony movements) the highest count from 1992 is presented.

internationally important numbers, cormorants, shags, roseate and common terns and razorbills all feed comparatively close inshore near their colonies. Offshore waters far to the west of the region are of importance to gannets and Manx shearwaters in summer; these birds probably originate in the large colonies off south-west Wales. Three nearshore sites are of importance to wintering waterfowl (Table 5.10.3), of which the most significant is the probably the poorly-known concentration of red-throated divers off Hartland Point. Areas of sea holding the most vulnerable concentrations of seabirds during parts of the year are shown on Map 5.10.2. These derive from the database supporting Webb *et al.* (1995).

Table 5.10.3 Important locations in the region for marine-wintering waterfowl*

Species	*Peak numbers*	*1% GB*	*1% NW Europe*
Camel Estuary			
Red-throated diver *Gavia stellata*	55	50	750
Slavonian grebe *Podiceps auritus*	11	50	50
Kelsey Head - Towan Head			
Red-throated diver *Gavia stellata*	86	50	750
Hartland Point			
Red-throated diver *Gavia stellata*	320	50	750
Black-throated diver *Gavia arctica*	126	50	1,200

Sources: peak numbers from Lock & Robins (1994), Slade (1996); 1% GB from Waters & Cranswick (1993), 1% NW Europe from Rose & Scott (1994). Key: *seaducks, divers, grebes and cormorant.

5.10.3 Human activities

The vulnerability of seabirds at sea to the effects of human activities is calculated from the abundance of birds in the rectangles shown on Map 5.10.2 and a factor derived from the amount of time spent on the water, the overall population size and the rate at which the species recruits new individuals to the population. For a discussion of vulnerability see Carter *et al.* (1993), Williams *et al.* (1994) or Webb *et al.* (1995).

Seabirds can be particularly affected by marine oil pollution. Spills near the main colonies during the breeding season could be catastrophic. The risk of accidents from tankers passing through the region was highlighted by the infamous wreck of the Torrey Canyon in 1967. This tanker, *en route* to Milford Haven, hit the Seven Stones rocks between the Isles of Scilly and Land's End. The resultant pollution affected much of the north Cornish coastline as well as moving southwards across the Channel and dramatically raised the profile of oil spills and their consequences. The effects on bird numbers were unclear, as too little was known of them prior to the spill. One consequence of the spill was the first complete census of Britain and Ireland's seabirds. Spills can also occur from non-tanker shipping movements. Sheens of very thin oil were seen in waters off the region following the *Sea Empress* oil spill in February 1996. The major shipping routes in the English Channel pass south of the region and a traffic separation scheme is in force around Land's End and the Isles of Scilly to reduce the risk of collision. Some birds may become entangled in fishing nets in the region, but the scale at which this occurs is not believed to be great overall.

5.10.4 Information sources used

All seabird colonies in the region were counted or reappraised between 1984 and 1987. These counts, and all those made since 1979, are held on the JNCC/Seabird Group Seabird Colony Register. Numbers and breeding performance of several species are evaluated annually at sites on the Isles of Scilly, on Lundy and at Woody Bay, north Devon. Surveys of birds at sea off this coast have been carried out by JNCC's Seabirds at Sea Team (SAST). Survey effort from ships by SAST has been greatest off Land's End and to the west of the region; there have been fewer surveys close to the north Cornish coast and in the Bristol Channel. Waters at 2 km and 5 km from the shore have been surveyed from the air by SAST on a bi-monthly basis over one year. Coverage, from the land, of most nearshore waters in the region has been patchy. Insufficient counts have been carried out to determine how peak numbers of seabirds wintering at sea in the region relate to average numbers using each area.

5.10.5 Further sources of information

A. References cited

Carter, I.C., Williams, J.M., Webb, A., & Tasker, M.L. 1993. *Seabird concentrations in the North Sea: an atlas of vulnerability to surface pollutants.* Aberdeen, Joint Nature Conservation Committee.

Lloyd, C.S., Tasker, M.L., & Partridge, K. 1991. *The status of seabirds in Britain and Ireland.* London, Poyser.

Lock, L., & Robins, M. 1994. *Wintering divers, grebes and seaduck in inshore coastal waters in south-west England.* Exeter, Royal Society for the Protection of Birds.

Rose, P.M., & Scott, D.A. 1994. *Waterfowl population estimates.* Slimbridge, International Waterfowl and Wetlands Research Bureau. (IWRB publication No. 29.)

Slade, G. 1996. *Nearshore winter seabird survey of south-west England.* Exeter, Royal Society for the Protection of Birds.

Walsh, P.M., Brindley, E., & Heubeck, M. 1995. *Seabird numbers and breeding success in Britain and Ireland, 1994.* Peterborough, Joint Nature Conservation Committee. (UK Nature Conservation, No. 18.)

Waters, R.J., & Cranswick, P.A. 1993. *The wetland bird survey 1992-93: wildfowl and wader counts.* Slimbridge, British Trust for Ornithology / Wildfowl and Wetlands Trust / Royal Society for the Protection of Birds / Joint Nature Conservation Committee.

Webb, A., Stronach, A., Stone, C.S., & Tasker, M.L. 1995. *Vulnerable concentrations of birds to the south and west of Britain.* Peterborough, Joint Nature Conservation Committee.

Williams, J.M., Tasker, M.L., Carter, I.C., & Webb, A. 1994. A method of assessing seabird vulnerability to surface pollutants. *Ibis, 137:* S14-S152.

B. Further reading

Kirby, J.S., Evans, R.J., & Fox, A.D. 1993. Wintering seaducks in Britain and Ireland: populations, threats, conservation and research priorities. *Aquatic Conservation: Marine and Freshwater Ecosystems, 3:* 105-137.

Owen, M., Atkinson-Willes, G.L., & Salmon, D.G. 1986. *Wildfowl in Great Britain,* 2nd ed. Cambridge, Cambridge University Press.

Prater, A.J. 1981. *Estuary birds of Britain and Ireland.* Calton, Poyser.

Skov, H., Durinck, J., Leopold, M.F., & Tasker, M.L. 1995. *Important bird areas for seabirds in the North Sea including the Channel and the Kattegat.* Cambridge, BirdLife International.

Stone, C.J., Webb, A., Barton, C., Ratcliffe, N., Reed, T.C., Tasker, M.L., & Pienkowski, M.W. 1995. *An atlas of seabird distribution in north-west European waters.* Peterborough, Joint Nature Conservation Committee.

C. Contact names and addresses

Type of information	*Contact address and telephone no.*
Seabird colonies	*Coordinator, Seabird Colony Register, JNCC, Aberdeen, tel: 01224 655703
Seabirds at sea	*Seabirds at Sea Team, JNCC, Aberdeen, tel: 01224 655702
Birds database	*Vertebrate Ecology and Conservation Branch, JNCC, Peterborough, tel: 01733 62626
Nearshore waterfowl	*Wildfowl and Wetlands Trust, Slimbridge, tel: 01453 890333

*Starred contact addresses are given in full in the Appendix.

5.11 Other breeding birds

D.M. Craddock & D.A. Stroud

5.11.1 Introduction

This section outlines the importance of the region to breeding birds other than seabirds. Because of their distinctive ecology and mixed-species breeding colonies, seabirds are described separately in section 5.10.

The physical nature of this coastline is varied and this determines the distribution of the different breeding bird assemblages occurring. As well as extensive stretches of cliff, there are several small estuaries in the region and a major estuarine system (the Severn Estuary), holding extensive areas of saltmarsh and associated wet grassland, especially on the Somerset and Gwent Levels. Wide expanses of intertidal sand and mud flats are backed in places by large vegetated sand dune systems and reed beds.

Map 5.11.1 shows the incidence of confirmed breeding in coastal 10 km squares of selected species characteristic of wet grassland (teal *Anas crecca*, lapwing *Vanellus vanellus*, redshank *Tringa totanus*, snipe *Gallinago gallinago* and pintail *Anas acuta*). The Somerset Levels are one of the most important sites in the region for wet-grassland breeding waders; one of the largest assemblages of breeding waders on lowland grassland in England and Wales occurs here. The population of snipe alone is 4-8% of the estimated total breeding population on wet grassland in England and Wales (Green & Robins 1993). The British breeding population of redshank is strongly coastal in distribution and the majority of the population breeds on saltmarsh sites (Green 1991). Redshank are known to breed in the region in areas such as the Gwent Levels between Rumney and Chepstow (Griffin *et al.* 1991). A recent survey found that 10% of the Welsh population of redshank breed in Gwent (although this includes non-coastal sites). Outside the main sites, there are only a few other lowland wet grasslands in England and Wales with comparable numbers of breeding redshank.

Map 5.11.2 shows the incidence of confirmed breeding in coastal 10 km squares of selected species characteristic of shingle, sand dune and other dry grassland (ringed plover *Charadrius hiaticula*, oystercatcher *Haematopus ostralegus* and shelduck *Tadorna tadorna*). The region is nationally important for the number of breeding shelduck that occur here. The Severn Estuary one of the most important sites in Great Britain for this species (WWT pers. comm.). The Isles of Scilly are important for other breeding birds of dry grassland, notably ringed plover and oystercatcher (Map 5.11.2).

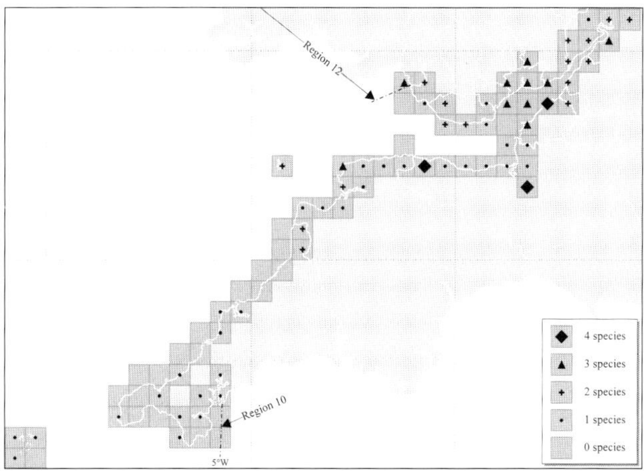

Map 5.11.1 Number of confirmed breeding species characteristic of wet grassland (redshank, snipe, lapwing, pintail and teal) in coastal 10 km squares. Source: based on Gibbons *et al.* (1993).

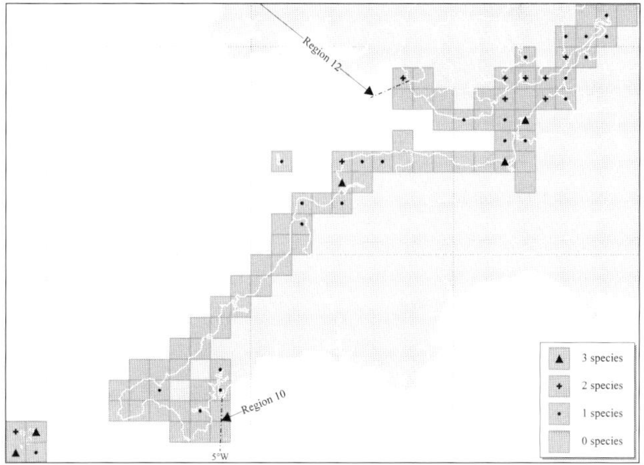

Map 5.11.2 Number of confirmed breeding species characteristic of shingle, sand dunes and other dry grasslands (ringed plover, oystercatcher and shelduck) in coastal 10 km squares. Source: based on Gibbons *et al.* (1993).

5.11.2 Important locations and species

The Isles of Scilly are mainly important for their breeding seabirds (see also section 5.10); other species breeding on these islands include shelduck and mallard *Anas platyrhynchos*. Oystercatchers are widespread, breeding on rocky stacks such as Scilly Rock and Mincarlo, as well as in more varied habitats such as at Gweal and Samson and the less populous inhabited islands (Allen 1974). Low numbers of ringed plover breed on Tean and St. Helens (Allen 1974).

A national shelduck survey in 1992 by WWT found that several estuaries within the region support at least 45 birds (Table 5.11.1). The most important breeding area for shelduck on the Severn is probably Flatholm Island, from where it is likely that ducklings are led to the Taff/Ely Estuary to mature (Fox & Salmon 1994). Other key parts of the estuary serve as important nesting areas, characterised by suitable feeding grounds for females both during pre-breeding and incubation periods. Particularly important areas include the Peterstone-Wentlooge shore, Uskmouth-Collister Pill, Oldbury-Littleton, and Purton-Frampton sections. These areas hold most of the ducklings reared in the Severn Estuary (Fox & Salmon 1994). Bridgwater Bay also supports nationally important numbers of breeding shelduck (Green 1991).

In Gwent the coast is the stronghold of the redshank population, where breeding occurs mainly on the extensive saltings but also behind the sea walls on the damper pastures of the levels (Tyler *et al.* 1987). In South Glamorgan breeding redshank are now confined to small concentrations in the Rhymney Estuary and Kenfig Burrows (Griffin *et al.* 1991). Other important areas include the Somerset Levels and the water meadows of the Usk Valley. In a 1983 survey the Somerset Levels were important in the context of lowland England and Wales for numbers of four additional species (lapwing, curlew *Numenius arquata*, redshank and black-tailed godwit *Limosa limosa*), in addition to the nationally important numbers of breeding snipe (Green & Cadbury 1987). Table 5.11.2 shows the densities of three species of breeding waders (oystercatcher, lapwing and redshank) from a 1985 survey on a sample of saltmarshes in the region.

Table 5.11.3 shows the numbers of pairs of territorial (presumed breeding) ringed plovers in counties of the region in 1994, in relation to numbers nationally. Because there is relatively little of the birds' breeding habitat (dry grassland) in the region, relatively few ringed plovers breed here, other than in Mid Glamorgan and the Isles of Scilly.

Although not recorded as supporting particularly high concentrations of breeding waterfowl species overall, the region does support notable concentrations of several species, e.g. little grebe *Tachybaptus ruficollis*, great crested grebe *Podiceps cristatus*, grey heron *Ardea cinerea*, mute swan *Cygnus olor*, water rail *Rallus aquaticus* and spotted crake *Porzana porzana* (Gibbons *et al.* 1993). In addition, the region is one of the few where cirl bunting *Emberiza cirlus*, Dartford warbler *Sylvia undata* and Cetti's warbler *Cettia cetti* breed (Gibbons *et al.* 1993). Bearded tit *Panurus biarmicus* has also been recorded breeding. This region is also one of the few southern regions to support breeding eider *Somateria mollissima*. The region has notable concentrations of rock pipits *Anthus petrosus* breeding along its coast (Gibbons *et al.* 1993).

Raptor species that have been known to breed in the region include peregrine falcon *Falco peregrinus*, goshawk *Accipiter gentilis*, sparrowhawk *Accipiter nisus*, buzzard *Buteo buteo*, kestrel *Falco tinnunculus*, marsh harrier *Circus aeruginosus*, merlin *Falco columbarius*, hobby *F. subbuteo* and Montagu's harrier *Circus pygargus* (unusually for a southern region, in the case of the latter). Breeding owls include long-eared owl *Asio otus*, short-eared owl *A. flammeus* and barn owl *Tyto alba*.

5.11.3 Human activities

In England and Wales improvements to land drainage systems since the 1920s have led to a substantial reduction in lowland wet grassland (Williams & Bowers 1987). Although limited in extent, wet grassland along parts of the region's coastline contains small but significant numbers of breeding waders. Appropriate management of these areas is of crucial importance for the continued well-being of these wader populations (see papers in Hötker (1991)), which depend on the maintenance of a winter flooding regime, with a high but controlled water table in summer, to protect nests from flooding during the breeding season (Green *et al.* 1987), together with low-intensity agricultural management (Green 1991). Green & Cadbury (1987) drew attention to the redshank's requirements for the water table to be maintained 2-3 cm below the surface during the breeding season, conditions which are now scarce in the region owing to land drainage.

Table 5.11.1 Sites supporting at least 45 shelduck

Site name	*Total*	*Males*	*Pairs*	*Non-breeding*
Severn Estuary	1,592	76	423	670
Fal Estuary	407	7	100	54
Taw-Torridge Estuary	134	8	15	10
Camel Estuary	68	10	9	40
Hayle Estuary	64	0	6	49

Source: WWT national shelduck survey, 1992. Note: for some larger sites double counting may have occurred.

Table 5.11.2 Densities of breeding waders on a sample of saltmarshes surveyed in 1985

Site	*Oystercatcher (pairs/ km²)*	*Lapwing (pairs/ km²)*	*Redshank peak nests/ km²*	*Total waders pairs/ km²*
Gwent				
Caldicot	n/a	3	n /a	4?
St. Brides, Wentlooge	n/a	26	24	50
Peterstone - Wentlooge	n/a	24	45	69
South Glamorgan				
Rhymney	n/a	n/a	n/a	10?
Lamby	3	n/a	21	24

Source: Allport *et al.* 1986. Key: n/a = not available; ? = estimated figure. Note that other saltmarshes in the region were not surveyed, so this is not a comprehensive listing.

Table 5.11.3 Numbers of pairs of territorial (presumed breeding) ringed plovers in 1984

	Pairs (coastal) counted in survey	*% GB total counted in survey*
Cornwall	0	0
Isles of Scilly	40*	
Devon	5	<1
Somerset	0	0
Avon	4	<1
Gloucestershire	0	0
Gwent	0	0
Mid Glamorgan	29	
South Glamorgan	11	
Region 11	***89***	
England	1,984	27.5
Wales	221	
GB	7,207	100

Source: Prater (1989). Key: *estimated total; only 20 birds counted. Note: survey coverage varied between counties.

The importance of managing water levels for the wader populations of the Somerset Levels has been shown by the correlation of the birds' distribution with that of damp, unimproved grassland (Green & Robins 1993). Numbers of all species of breeding waders surveyed on the Somerset Levels declined between 1977 to 1987. The largest declines were for snipe (68.5% decline) and lapwing (54.3% decline) (Green & Robins 1993). Williams & Bowers (1987) noted that the contraction of breeding snipe and redshank distribution has been accompanied by accelerated drainage improvement on agricultural land since the 1960s. A marked decline in the numbers of breeding redshank has also been recorded on the Gwent Levels, where numbers fell by 73% between 1985 and 1991. Possible reasons for declining redshank numbers in Gwent include overgrazing and land-claim for industrial development. Different grazing regimes on saltmarshes can also significantly alter the density and nesting success of breeding waders through effects on vegetation composition and structure (Cadbury *et al.* 1987).

Another species that is particularly prone to changes in water levels is the water rail (Gibbons *et al.* 1993). The British range of the yellow wagtail *Motacilla flava* appears to have contracted in the last two decades, and areas of loss include South Glamorgan and the Gwent Levels. Possible reasons may include drainage and the intensification of agriculture (Gibbons *et al.* 1993).

Incremental land claim along the soft coasts of estuarine and sand dune systems has the potential to affect breeding waterfowl populations through loss of nesting and feeding habitat. Major barrage proposals would greatly alter the environment of the region for waterfowl. Tidal barrages have been proposed across the mouth of the Severn, at Cardiff Bay where the Rivers Taff and Ely discharge (now proceeding) and across the River Usk (now dropped). The proposed Severn tidal barrage would permanently remove an area of intertidal habitat containing almost half that used by birds at low-tide in the area studied by Fox & Salmon (1994), and submerge large feeding areas where many waterfowl, including breeding birds, obtain part of their daily food requirements.

Conservation priorities may be furthered through site designations and agricultural support programmes. The RSPB own and manage several areas of this coastline, including Isley Marsh, part of the Hayle Estuary and Marazion Marsh. At Slimbridge The Wildfowl & Wetlands Trust owns and manages a large reserve for captive and wild birds. The Severn Estuary is designated as both a Special Protection Area (SPA) (under the EC Directive 79/409 on the Conservation of Wild Birds) and a Ramsar site under the Ramsar Convention (see also Chapter 7). The site includes both the Upper Severn and Bridgwater Bay, both also designated as internationally important in their own right.

Human disturbance during the breeding season may have significant effects on birds' breeding success (Pienkowski 1992), although there are few good assessments of the scale of the problem for this region's breeding birds other than seabirds.

Oil and heavy metal pollution are serious potential threats to wintering waterfowl in areas where high densities of birds occur. In 1996 the stranded tanker *Sea Empress* discharged thousands of tonnes of crude oil into the sea with serious implications for the wildlife in the region, especially around the Bristol Channel, on Lundy Island and along the north Devon coast. Heavy metal pollution is thought to be a potential threat in the Fal Estuary (see also section 9.6).

5.11.4 Information sources used

The most recent and comprehensive overview of the status of breeding birds throughout Britain and Ireland is provided by Gibbons *et al.* (1993). This summarises the results of a national breeding bird census undertaken between 1988 and 1991 and compares distributions at the 10 x 10 km square level with those recorded in the first breeding bird atlas of 1968-1972 (Sharrock 1976). Whilst the data are one of the best sources for comparisons at county, regional or national scales, care should be taken with their use to assess individual sites or 10 km squares. This is because the coverage of each 10 km square was not always equally thorough, and since the atlas survey period (1988-1991) distributions of some breeding species may have changed. Between- and within-region comparisons of precise distributions and densities based on coastal 10 x 10 km should be undertaken with caution as there may be greatly varying amounts of land within each square.

Extensive survey work by volunteers has also been undertaken for a number of species. Usually these surveys are organised as part of wider British surveys, e.g. that in 1991 by the Wildfowl & Wetlands Trust for shelduck.

5.11.5 Acknowledgements

We would like to thank George Boobyer and Dr Dave Cole (JNCC), Simon Delany (WWT) and Dr Rob Fuller (BTO) for their assistance. We are also grateful to Mark Robins and Stephanie Tyler (RSPB), Steve Moon (Countryside Commission), Dr H. Prosser (Welsh Office) and Peter Cranswick (WWT) for their useful comments.

5.11.6 Further sources of information

A. References cited

Allen, R. 1974. *Gulls and other sea-birds in the Isles of Scilly, April to August, 1974.* London, Nature Conservancy.

Allport, G., O'Brien, M., & Cadbury, C.J. 1986. Survey of redshank and other breeding birds on saltmarshes in Britain 1985. *Nature Conservancy Council, CSD Report,* No. 649.

Cadbury, C.J., Green, R.E., & Allport, G. 1987. Redshanks and other breeding waders of British saltmarshes. *RSPB Conservation Review, 1:* 37-40.

Fox, A.D., & Salmon, D.G. 1994. Breeding and moulting shelduck (*Tadorna tadorna*) of the Severn Estuary. *Biological Journal of the Linnean Society, 51:* 237-245.

Gibbons, D.W., Reid, J.B., & Chapman, R. 1993. *The new atlas of breeding birds in Britain and Ireland 1988-1991.* London, T. & A.D. Poyser.

Green, R.E. 1991. Breeding waders of lowland grasslands in England and Wales. *In: Birds and pastoral agriculture in Europe,* ed. by D.J. Curtis, E.M. Bignal & M.A. Curtis, 32-34. Paisley, Scottish Chough Study Group.

Green, R.E., & Cadbury, C.J. 1987. Breeding waders of lowland wet grasslands. *RSPB Conservation Review, 1:* 10-13.

Green, R.E., Cadbury, C.J., & Williams, G. 1987. Floods threaten black-tailed godwits breeding at the Ouse Washes. *RSPB Conservation Review, 1:* 14-16.

Green, R.E., & Robins, M. 1993. The decline of the ornithological importance of the Somerset Levels and Moors, England, and changes in the management of water levels. *Biological Conservation, 66:* 95-106.

Griffin, B., Saxton, N., & Williams, I. 1991. *Breeding redshank in Wales 1991.* Newtown, RSPB.

Hötker, H., *ed.* 1991. Waders breeding in wet grassland. *Wader Study Group Bulletin, 61:* Supplement.

Pienkowski, M.W. 1992. The impact of tourism on coastal breeding waders in western and southern Europe: an overview. *Wader Study Group Bulletin, 68:* 92-96.

Prater, A.J. 1989. Ringed plover *Charadrius hiaticula* breeding population of the United Kingdom in 1984. *Bird Study, 36:* 154-159.
Sharrock, J.T.R., *ed.* 1976. *The atlas of breeding birds in Britain and Ireland.* Calton, T. & A.D. Poyser.
Tyler, S., Lewis, J., Venables, A., & Walton, J. 1987. *The Gwent atlas of breeding birds.* Newport, Gwent Ornithological Society.
Williams, G., & Bowers, J.K. 1987. Land drainage and birds in England and Wales. *RSPB Conservation Review, 1:* 25-30.

B. Further reading

Davidson, N.C. 1991. Breeding waders on British estuarine wet grasslands. *Wader Study Group Bulletin, 61,* Supplement: 36-41.
Davidson, N.C., Laffoley, D.d'A., Doody, J.P., Way, L.S., Gordon, J., Key, R., Drake, C.M., Pienkowski, M.W., Mitchell, R., & Duff, K.L. 1991. *Nature conservation and estuaries in Great Britain.* Peterborough, Nature Conservancy Council.
Everett, M.J. 1989. Reedbeds - a scarce habitat. *RSPB Conservation Review, 3:* 14-19.
Hurford, C., & Lansdown, P. 1995. *Birds of Glamorgan.* Glamorgan, D. Brown & Sons Ltd.
Lovegrove, R., Williams, G., & Williams, I. 1994. *Birds in Wales.* Calton, T. & A.D. Poyser.
Pritchard, D.E., Housden, S.D., Mudge, G.P., Galbraith, C.A., & Pienkowski, M.W. 1992. *Important bird areas in the United Kingdom including the Channel Islands and the Isle of Man.* Sandy, RSPB/JNCC.
Ratcliffe, D.A. 1995. *The peregrine falcon.* 2nd ed. Calton, T. & A.D. Poyser.

C. Contact names and address

Type of information	*Contact address and telephone no.*
Breeding atlas data and breeding wader data	*Development Unit, British Trust for Ornithology, Thetford, tel: 01842 750050
Breeding bird surveys; coastal habitat management	*RSPB HQ, Sandy, tel: 01767 680551
Coastal breeding wildfowl data	*Wildfowl & Wetlands Trust, Slimbridge, tel: 01453 890333
Site designations - England	*EN HQ, Peterborough tel: 01733 340345
Site designations - Wales	*CCW HQ, Bangor, tel: 01248 370444

*Starred contact address is given in full in the Appendix.

5.12 Migrant and wintering waterfowl

D.M. Craddock & D.A. Stroud

5.12.1 Introduction

This section describes the importance of the region to waterfowl, defined as waders and wildfowl (divers, grebes, ducks, geese and swans together with coot *Fulica atra*), during their non-breeding period. The section also notes the occurrence of marine-wintering waterfowl and cormorant *Phalacrocorax carbo* where they occur close inshore, especially within estuaries; their overall regional distribution, including the importance of offshore areas, is covered in section 5.10.

The region is an important area of coastal Britain for wintering waterfowl. Table 5.12.1 gives the total January 1993 waterfowl count for the region as a proportion of the coastal totals for England, Wales and Great Britain. Such comparisons can give only a rough approximation of relative importance, since some areas are better counted than others and the data are not corrected to compensate for this.

According to the WeBS national survey of wetland sites (see section 5.12.4), six coastal wetland sites in the region support nationally important numbers of overwintering waterfowl species, some of which occur in internationally important numbers. The relative importance of the regularly counted wetlands (estuaries and adjacent marshes) in the region is shown on Map 5.12.1.

The estuaries of the region are also of major importance for migrant waterfowl in spring and autumn. The region lies on the major migratory flyway of the east Atlantic and many birds moving to and from wintering areas on the African, Mediterranean and south-west European coasts to Arctic breeding grounds pass through and stage on the coast here. The region can increase in importance in periods of severe cold weather further east in Britain or Europe.

Habitats of high importance for wintering birds in the region include the very large intertidal areas in the Severn Estuary, extensive saltmarshes in the Taw-Torridge and Severn (including Bridgwater Bay) Estuaries and the lowland wet grasslands of the Somerset and Gwent Levels. The species compositions of assemblages of estuarine and non-estuarine migrant and wintering waterfowl in the region are shown in Figure 5.12.1. Species assemblages vary greatly with the exposure of the coast and the type of substrate (Moser & Summers 1987). On estuarine shores the main component species of the assemblage are dunlin *Calidris alpina*, lapwing *Vanellus vanellus*, wigeon *Anas*

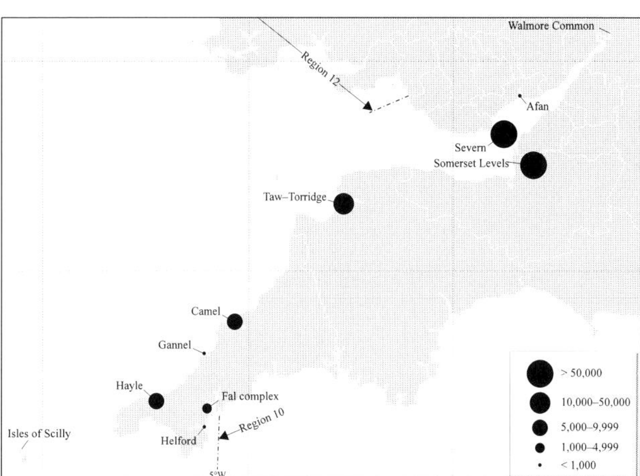

Map 5.12.1. Distribution of main concentrations of wintering intertidal waterfowl. Size of circle proportional to five-year mean of waterfowl numbers, from Waters & Cranswick (1993).

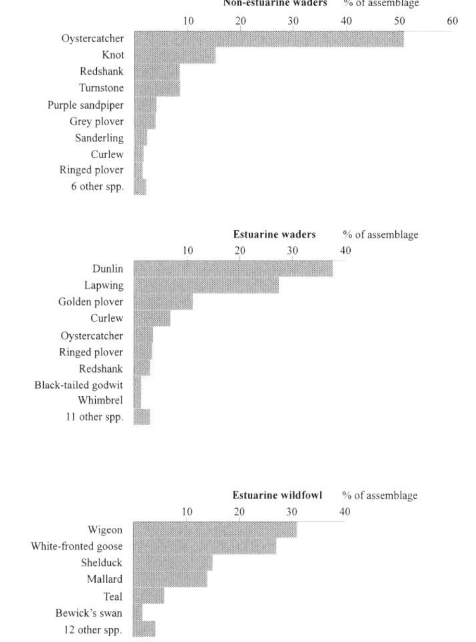

Figure 5.12.1 Relative species composition of non-breeding waterfowl assemblages on coastal areas of the region. Sources: estuarine waterfowl data from Prater (1981), non-estuarine wader data from Moser & Summers (1987).

Table 5.12.1 Waterfowl count in Region 11, England, Wales and GB in January 1993

	Total waterfowl count in January 1993	*Number of sites counted*	*% of count in Region 11*
Region 11 English sites	33,308	22	-
Region 11 Welsh sites	52,589	6	-
Region 11 total	***85,897***	**28**	-
All counted English coastal sites	1,577,388	106	5.4
All counted Welsh coastal sites	131,642	33	39.9
All counted British coastal sites	2,060,961	214	4.2

Sources: Waters & Cranswick (1993), Rose & Taylor (1993). Note: care should be taken in interpretation as count coverage varies from country to country and the data have not been corrected.

penelope and European white-fronted goose *Anser albifrons albifrons*. Although not all sections have been regularly monitored, the rocky (non-estuarine) shoreline of the region is known to be of importance for several wintering wader species, by far the most proportionately numerous of which is oystercatcher *Haematopus ostralegus*. Outside the inner Severn Estuary densities of non-estuarine waders are relatively low (Table 5.12.2) compared with densities occurring on the North Sea coast (Regions 5 and 6).

5.12.2 Important locations and species

Sites of major importance within the region include the Somerset Levels and the Severn Estuary (including Bridgwater Bay). The Fal Estuary, the Isles of Scilly and Walmore Common also hold species in nationally or internationally important numbers. Twenty-two species winter in nationally important numbers on wetlands in the region, of which nine (turnstone *Arenaria interpres*, teal *Anas crecca*, Bewick's swan *Cygnus columbianus bewickii*, shelduck *Tadorna tadorna*, gadwall *Anas strepera*, dunlin, curlew *Numenius arquata*, lapwing and redshank *Tringa totanus*) achieve internationally important numbers. Table 5.12.3 shows numbers of wintering waterfowl on wetland sites in the region, during the winters of 1990/1 to 1994/5.

The Severn Estuary is of particular note for holding fifteen waterfowl populations at levels of national importance, six of them attaining international importance. The site also qualifies as internationally important by virtue of its assemblage of significantly over 20,000 waterfowl, of which dunlin was the most abundant species recorded between 1990 and 1995. The Severn Estuary was also the most important site in Britain for European white-fronted goose during this period. Ringed plovers were recorded in large numbers in May 1984 on only four west coast estuaries, one of which was the Severn Estuary (Moser *et al.* 1985). The lowland wet grasslands of the Somerset Levels are also of major importance, in the winter of 1994/5 supporting a peak number of over 101,000 waterfowl.

This region is of major importance for its numbers of wintering Bewick's swans. Between 1990/1 and 1994/5 the fifth largest flock in Britain was supported here, constituting a significant proportion of the international population. The

Table 5.12.2 Overall densities of wintering waders on non-estuarine coasts

	Number of wader species recorded	*Total number non-estuarine waders*	*Extent of non-cliff, non-estuarine coast in county (km)*	*Extent of coast surveyed (km)*	*Overall wader density (approx. nos. of birds/km coast)*
Devon (whole county coast)	14	2,110	242.6	217.4	10
Cornwall (whole county coast, including Isles of Scilly)	16	6,483	272.2	261.3	24
Somerset	11	1,167	39.0	39.0	30
Glamorgan	13	6,505	106.4	106.4	61

Source: Winter Shorebird Count (Moser & Summers 1987).

Table 5.12.3 Wintering waterfowl numbers on WeBS-surveyed wetlands in the region

	Ramsar/ SPA	*Five year mean waterfowl nos. (1990/1-1994/5)*	*1994/5 peak waterfowl nos.*	*1994/5 peak wildfowl nos.*	*1994/5 peak wader nos.*	*Species occurring at levels of national/international* importance*
Fal complex		4,556	3,421	1,604	1,817	Black-tailed godwit
Helford		206	149	82	67	
Isles of Scilly		n/a	n/a	n/a	n/a	Turnstone*, ringed plover, sanderling
Hayle Estuary		5,116	3,396	1,898	1,498	
Gannel Estuary		541	387	170	217	
Camel Estuary		9,028	11,924	1,010	10,914	
Taw-Torridge Estuary		11,524	12,969	3,274	9,695	
Somerset Levels	Ramsar/SPA	82,348	101,043	40,093	60,950	Teal*, Bewick's swan*, lapwing*, wigeon, mute swan, shoveler, gadwall
Severn Estuary (including Bridgwater Bay)	Severn Estuary Ramsar/SPA (includes Bridgwater Bay Ramsar); Upper Severn Estuary Ramsar/SPA	85,308	100,667	24,152	76,515	Bewick's swan*, shelduck*, gadwall*, dunlin*, redshank*, curlew*, mallard, pochard, tufted duck, European white-fronted goose, wigeon, grey plover, golden plover, pintail, teal
Walmore Common[a]	SPA, Ramsar					Bewick's swan
Afan Estuary		592	902	152	750	

Sources: WeBS data from Waters *et al.* (1996), except [a] which is from 1993/4 WeBS data; Isles of Scilly data from Kirby (1990). The winter season used by WeBS is November to March for waders and September to March for wildfowl. WeBS data include divers, grebes, cormorant and grey heron. See Waters & Cranswick (1993) for further detail on interpretation of counts and limitations of data. Key: n/a = not available; *species occurring at levels of international importance; SPA = Special Protection Area; Ramsar = internationally important wetland under the Ramsar Convention.

Severn Estuary and the Somerset Levels are internationally important and Walmore Common is nationally important for this species. Studies of ringed birds have shown much interchange between all these sites. Other herbivorous wildfowl such as wigeon occur in nationally important numbers on the Somerset Levels and the Severn Estuary (Waters *et al.* 1996). The Somerset Levels and the Taw-Torridge Estuary both hold large numbers of grey heron *Ardea cinerea* (Cranswick *et al.* 1995) in winter.

At the time of the Winter Shorebird Survey in 1984/85, the Isles of Scilly supported turnstone in internationally important numbers and sanderling *Calidris alba* and ringed plover in nationally important numbers; these three species, plus oystercatcher, were the most abundant recorded there. Tresco and St. Mary's supported the most waders, while Samson held the highest densities (Kirby 1990).

Some sites are important because they hold important concentrations of a particular species or because they are the only sites in the area to provide suitable habitat for certain species. The Taw-Torridge was one of the few British sites where more than 20 greenshank *Tringa nebularia* were counted in 1992/93. The Hayle Estuary and the Taw-Torridge Estuary support little egret *Egretta gazetta*, a species with a restricted, although increasing, winter distribution in Britain (Cranswick *et al.* 1995).

There are several important roost sites in the region. These include the River Parrett for black-tailed godwit *Limosa limosa*, the Welsh shore of the Severn Estuary and Bridgwater Bay for whimbrel, and the Caldicot Levels and Taff/Ely for knot (Clark & Prŷs-Jones 1994). Known roost sites for Bewick's swan include the upper Severn and Slimbridge (Fox & Salmon 1994b). Lapwing and dunlin are known to roost at Rodley (Clark & Prŷs-Jones 1994).

In addition to the importance of the region's shores for non-breeding waterfowl, the inshore waters of the region are important for some wintering seaduck, divers and grebe species. Around Carrick Roads/Falmouth Bay nationally important numbers of black-throated diver *Gavia arctica*, red-necked grebe *Podiceps grisegena*, black-necked grebe *P. nigricollis* and Slavonian grebe *P. auritus* are recorded. Red necked grebes and Slavonian grebes are also found in nationally important numbers around Mount's Bay and St. Ives Bay and the latter species at Sennen Cove. Internationally important numbers of red-throated diver *G. stellata*, black-throated diver and great northern diver *G. immer* occur off Hartland Point. Around Windbury Point/Westward Ho! numbers of common scoter *Melanitta fusca* are nationally important (Lock & Robins 1994). All of these diver species and Slavonian grebe are Annex I species of the EC Birds Directive.

Some sites in the region are particularly important during the autumn and spring migration periods. Important migratory feeding areas for whimbrel are found in the Severn Estuary and the Somerset and Gwent Levels. During late April and early May about 2,000 whimbrel gather in the estuary complex comprising the Severn Estuary and Bridgwater Bay, using this as a final staging area before continuing their migration (Ferns *et al.* 1979). Birds of the *schinzii* race of dunlin, which breed in northern Britain and Iceland, pass through the Severn Estuary and Taw-Torridge Estuary in autumn and spring (Davidson *et al.* 1991; Clark & Prŷs-Jones 1994). The Severn Estuary is one of the most important sites in Britain for migrating ringed plover and common sandpiper. Bridgwater Bay is one of the most important sites for moulting shelduck outside the Wadden Sea and probably supports all the Severn Estuary's moulting birds (Fox & Salmon 1994a).

Many species demonstrate complex patterns of interchange between sites during the course of a winter, which means that individual sites cannot be considered in isolation: grey plover *Pluvialis squatarola*, for example, are known to move from moulting areas in The Wash to the Severn and the Taw-Torridge Estuaries (Davidson *et al.* 1991). For other species, the sudden appearance of large wintering flocks on the Severn Estuary suggests that it may constitute an overflow site, accommodating birds displaced from elsewhere (Ferns 1994). Shelduck increase in numbers on the Severn Estuary after the turn of the year, probably as a result of a post-moult influx of birds from elsewhere (Clark & Prŷs-Jones 1994). There is regular interchange of Bewick's swans between Slimbridge and Walmore Common (Cranswick pers. comm.).

In addition, the region can increase in importance for waterfowl in periods of severe weather further east. Under these conditions there may be major influxes of waterfowl such as wigeon and teal from other coastal regions or inland areas (Ridgill & Fox 1990). Locally some sites also act as cold weather refuges where parts of estuarine system freeze more slowly than other coastal and inland wetlands, and thus provide open-water feeding when other sites are unavailable (Owen *et al.* 1986). In severe weather in 1981/82 populations increased substantially on estuaries throughout Britain, including the Severn (Davidson *et al.* 1991). Caldicot is known to have influxes of grey plover that may be linked to severe weather in continental Europe (Ferns 1980, 1983). The Welsh shore at Wentlooge and the Rhymney Estuary is also important for shelduck in severe winters (Fox & Salmon 1994b). Tufted duck *Aythya fuligula* and pochard *A. ferina* move onto the Severn Estuary in cold spells and there is evidence of them establishing a pattern of wintering on the estuary even in mild winters (Fox & Salmon 1994b).

5.12.3 Human activities

Wintering waterfowl are potentially affected, either directly or indirectly, by a wide range of human activities. Incremental land claim, including barrage schemes, has the potential to affect waterfowl populations through loss of feeding habitat, although at important sites conservation designations, including SSSI, can sometimes allow limitation of such activities. Two major development proposals could greatly alter the environment of the Severn Estuary for waterfowl conservation. These are the potential tidal barrage across the mouth of the Severn itself and the barrage under construction across Cardiff Bay where the Taff/Ely discharges (Fox & Salmon 1994b).

The proposed Severn tidal barrage would permanently remove an intertidal area containing almost half the low tide bird usage in the study by Clark & Prŷs-Jones (1994). It would therefore submerge large feeding areas where many of the waterfowl populations on the Severn collect at least part of their daily food requirements. It is estimated that the proposed Severn Estuary tidal barrage would eliminate intertidal areas accounting for between 40% (for shelduck and curlew) and 80% (for redshank) of the current total low tide usage by the internationally important populations present (Clark & Prŷs-Jones 1994).

The Cardiff Bay barrage will result in the impounding of freshwater in Cardiff Bay, thereby permanently inundating the estuarine mudfalts and saltmarshes of the Taff-Ely SSSI (Nugent 1991), with consequent loss of feeding and roosting areas for intertidal waterfowl. The development was opposed by conservation organisations, but following Parliamentary review, the scheme was approved in 1991. Mitigation measures, including the creation of artificial roosting sites, are proposed, and the development is subject to detailed monitoring to assess long-term impacts (Donald & Clark 1991).

Conservation designations can result in land management that favours the conservation of waterfowl. For instance, the RSPB own and manage several areas of this coastline, including Isley Marsh, part of the Hayle Estuary and Marazion Marsh. At Slimbridge the Wildfowl & Wetlands Trust own and manage a 303 ha reserve for captive and wild birds.

Land that is intensively managed for agriculture can also provide important habitat for wintering and migrant waterfowl: species such as Bewick's swan, shelduck, curlew, lapwing and golden plover feed on the agricultural land near the region's estuaries (Clark & Prŷs-Jones 1994). However, drainage of wetlands and their conversion to arable, or inappropriate management of water levels, can have major effects on waterfowl populations. Detailed studies on the Severn in recent years, such as those by Ferns (1994) and Fox & Salmon (1994a, b), show that several changes have occurred in the distribution of birds since the 1970s. Many birds appear to have been displaced from Bridgwater Bay, where all of the significant population changes have been declines in numbers. The Usk to Wye section has also shown reductions in the numbers of several wader species. A similar pattern of change has occurred in the Severn Bridge to Portishead section on the opposite side of the estuary (Ferns 1994). Whilst Bridgwater Bay remains the most important site in the Severn Estuary for waders, declines in numbers of so many wader species is cause for concern. One possible cause is the drainage of parts of the Somerset Levels, where many of the Bridgwater Bay birds feed, coupled with an encroachment of common cord-grass *Spartina anglica* in the bay, reducing the birds' feeding areas (Owen *et al.* 1986). A regular flock of 500-700 Greenland white-fronted geese *Anser albifrons flavirostris* roosting at Bridgwater Bay and feeding on the Somerset Levels declined from the late 1950s and has now disappeared (Fox & Salmon 1994b). There has also been a decline in the number of golden plover using the Taw-Torridge Estuary in recent years.

Conversely, a significant positive change has been the recent emergence of the Rhymney to Usk section of the Severn Estuary as important for waterfowl. A remarkably high density and diversity of mud-dwelling invertebrates has been found there in recent years (C. Mettam and N.A Clark pers. comm), with a possible link to the reduction of industrial effluent input to the River Rhymney (Ferns 1994). Previously, effluent from a local steel works was discharged into the River Rhymney and it seems possible that this may have suppressed invertebrate, and hence bird, populations (Clark & Prŷs-Jones 1994). Ferns (1994) also noted the potential for parallels between the Rhymney area and the Clyde Estuary (Furness *et at.* 1986), where huge improvements in water quality in the post-war period in terms of its organic content led to reductions in invertebrate food supplies and consequently a decline in the numbers of waders.

Wildfowling occurs especially in estuaries, although it is generally subject to good regulation (see also section 9.7). The impacts and regulation of wildfowling have been reviewed on National Nature Reserves (NNRs) by Owen (1992). Permit systems generally operate and there is close liaison in the regulation of wildfowling between local shooting clubs, the British Association for Shooting and Conservation (BASC) and English Nature/Countryside Council for Wales local staff. Owen (1992) made a number of recommendations for improving the operation of existing schemes to regulate shooting on NNRs. Shooting has been strictly controlled on the Slimbridge New Grounds for centuries. A small, but crucial, no shooting area was established at Peterstone on the Wentlooge Levels (part of the Severn Estuary) in 1979. In the more populous parts of the region disturbance to waterfowl as a result of recreational activities can also have significant effects.

The digging of fishing bait and the collection of shellfish from intertidal sediments, and other recreational disturbances, may deny waterfowl access to feeding areas (see also section 9.1). The significance of these activities varies not only from site to site (in relation to intensity and size/topography of site) but also with the time of year. Disturbance may be a particular problem if it occurs in cold periods when wintering waterfowl need to feed almost continuously in order to survive (Davidson & Rothwell (1993) and papers therein).

Oil pollution is well known as a serious potential threat to wintering waterfowl in areas where high densities of birds occur. During winter 1996 the stranded tanker *Sea Empress* discharged thousands of tonnes of crude oil, with serious implications for the wildlife in the region especially around the Bristol Channel, on Lundy Island and along the North Devon coast (SEEEC 1996).

Coastal wind farm developments (see section 8.3.2) have the potential to be highly disruptive to wintering waterfowl (as reviewed by Crockford 1992).

5.12.4 Information sources used

As with other areas of the UK, migrant and wintering waterfowl are well surveyed by the Wetland Bird Survey (WeBS - organised by the British Trust for Ornithology, The Wildfowl & Wetlands Trust, The Royal Society for the Protection of Birds and the Joint Nature Conservation Committee). This volunteer-based survey collates monthly counts from coastal and inland wetlands through the UK. Coastal coverage is generally good for estuaries, although the open coast is not thoroughly surveyed on an annual basis (Waters & Cranswick 1993). The WeBS waterfowl count scheme publishes an extensive annual summary report, the most recent being Cranswick *et al.* (1995) covering the winter season 1992/93. This report summarises species trends, based on counts at wetlands throughout the UK. It also tabulates counts of total waterfowl numbers at all counted estuaries, as well as inland sites. It is the primary source of information on wintering and migrant waterfowl in the UK. Copies are available from the WeBS National Organisers listed in section 5.12.6C. The annual report can only summarise what are very detailed data, and in summary form such counts may be subject to misinterpretation for a number of reasons. Detailed count data for sites can be provided by WeBS and inspection of these data is recommended for any planning-related activity. The WeBS waterfowl counts are generally undertaken at high-tide when waterfowl gather in high densities on traditional roosting areas. To complement this information, at selected estuaries WeBS organises low-tide counts to give information on the feeding distributions of waterfowl during the intertidal period. Sites in the region at which such information are already available include the Taw-Torridge, Gannel, Camel and Severn estuaries.

The whole British coastline was surveyed for wintering waders during the wintering shorebird survey of 1984/85 (Moser & Summers 1987), and there are current WeBS plans for a repeat national survey. Such information on the wintering waterfowl of the non-estuarine coast is important to place annual estuaries counts into a wider perspective.

There have been a number of more detailed studies of the wintering waterfowl of the Severn Estuary. In particular, proposed developments on the Severn have generated recent detailed studies on the importance of each section of the estuary (Warbrick *et al.* 1991; Clark & Prŷs-Jones 1994; Fox & Salmon 1994a, b). The occurrence of rare birds on the Isles of Scilly is well documented; however, there is relatively little published information on the commoner bird communities of the islands, especially outside the breeding season. During the 1984/85 winter, the shoreline of the Isles of Scilly was surveyed for the national Winter Shorebird Count (Kirby 1990).

Although the data are now becoming slightly dated, Owen *et al.* (1986) give a thorough and comprehensive account of the wildfowl and wetlands of the region, summarising data available up to the mid-1980s. The volume is an invaluable source of initial information on sites and species, although those data presented should now be supplemented by more recent count information, available as indicated elsewhere in this section. Prater (1981) gives useful descriptive accounts of the birds of British estuaries, as well as placing these in a wider national and international context, using data from the period 1969-1975. As in Owen *et al.* (1986), much of the numerical information is dated, and the site accounts should be supplemented by the more recent reviews of Davidson *et al.* (1991).

For sites of international importance (either proposed or designated), *Important bird areas in the UK*, published jointly by RSPB and the country agencies (Pritchard *et al.* 1992), provides further information. Data on the important bird populations of each site are summarised, together with information on location and habitats. Further details of other important sites in the region can be found in recent studies by Fox & Salmon (1994a, b), Ferns (1994) and Clark & Prŷs-Jones (1994).

5.12.5 Acknowledgements

We would like to thank Simon Delany at WWT for his assistance and Nick George (English Nature), Jon Stewart (English Nature), Mark Robins (RSPB) and Peter Cranswick (WWT) for their comments.

5.12.6 Further sources of information

A. References cited

Clark, N.A., & Prŷs-Jones, R.P. 1994. Low tide distribution of wintering waders and shelduck on the Severn Estuary in relation to the proposed tidal barrage. *Biological Journal of the Linnean Society, 51:* 199-217.

Cranswick, P.A., Waters, R.J., Evans, J., & Pollitt, M.S. 1995. *The wetland bird survey 1993-1994: wildfowl and wader counts.* Slimbridge, British Trust for Ornithology/Wildfowl and Wetlands Trust/Royal Society for the Protection of Birds/Joint Nature Conservation Committee.

Crockford, N.J. 1992. A review of the possible impacts of wind farms on birds and other wildlife. *JNCC Report,* No. 27.

Davidson, N.C., Laffoley, D.d'A., Doody, J.P., Way, L.S., Gordon, J., Key, R., Drake, C.M., Pienkowski, M.W., Mitchell, R., & Duff, K.L. 1991. *Nature conservation and estuaries in Great Britain.* Peterborough, Nature Conservancy Council.

Davidson, N.C., & Rothwell, P.I. 1993. Disturbance to waterfowl on estuaries: the conservation and coastal management implications of current knowledge. *Wader Study Group Bulletin, 68:* 97-105.

Donald, P.F., & Clark, N.A. 1991. *The effect of the Cardiff Bay barrage on waterfowl populations. 2. Distribution and movement studies, July 1990 - May 1991.* Thetford, British Trust for Ornithology. (Research Report, No. 83.)

Ferns, P.N. 1980. *Intertidal feeding area of seven species of shorebirds at seven sites in the Severn Estuary.* University College, Cardiff, report to the United Kingdom Atomic Energy Authority.

Ferns, P.N. 1983. Sediment mobility of the Severn Estuary and its effect upon the distribution of shorebirds. *Canadian Journal of Fisheries and Aquatic Sciences, 40* (supplement 1): 331-340.

Ferns, P.N. 1994. The Severn Estuary's changing wader populations during the last two decades. *Biological Journal of the Linnean Society, 51:* 219-227.

Ferns, P.N., Green, G.H., & Round, P.D. 1979. Significance of the Somerset and Gwent Levels in Britain as feeding areas for migrant whimbrels *Numenius phaeopus. Biological Conservation, 16:* 7-22.

Fox, A.D., & Salmon, D.G. 1994a. Breeding and moulting shelduck *Tadorna tadorna* of the Severn Estuary. *Biological Journal of the Linnean Society, 51:* 237-245.

Fox, A.D., & Salmon, D.G. 1994b. Changes in the wildfowl populations wintering on the Severn Estuary. *Biological Journal of the Linnean Society, 51:* 229-236.

Furness, R.W., Galbraith, H., Gibson, I.P., & Metcalfe, N.B. 1986. Recent changes in numbers of waders on the Clyde Estuary, and their significance for conservation. *Proceedings of the Royal Society of Edinburgh, 90B:* 171-184.

Kirby, J.S. 1990. Numbers, distribution and habitat preferences of waders wintering on the Isles of Scilly. *Wader Study Group Bulletin, 57:* 47-52.

Lock, L., & Robins, M. 1994. *Wintering divers, grebes and seaduck in inshore coastal waters in south west England.* Exeter, Royal Society for the Protection of Birds.

Moser, M., Ferns, P., & Baillie, S. 1985. BTO/WSG west coast spring passage project: a progress report. *Wader Study Group Bulletin, 43:* 9-13.

Moser, M., & Summers, R.W. 1987. Wader populations on the non-estuarine coasts of Britain and Northern Ireland: results of the 1984-85 Winter Shorebird Count. *Bird Study, 34:* 71-81.

Nugent, M.J. 1991. Cardiff Bay Barrage Bill - Severn Estuary proposed Ramsar site and SPA. *In: Britain's birds in 1989-90: the conservatioin and monitoring review,* ed. by D.A. Stroud & D. Glue, 11-12. Thetford, British Trust for Ornithology/Nature Conservancy Council.

Owen, M. 1992. An analysis of permit systems and bag records on NNRs. *JNCC Report,* No. 68.

Owen, M., Atkinson-Willes, G.L., & Salmon, D.G. 1986. *Wildfowl in Great Britain.* 2nd ed. Cambridge, Cambridge University Press.

Prater, A.J. 1981. *Estuary birds in Britain and Ireland.* Calton, Poyser.

Pritchard, D.E., Housden, S.D., Mudge, G.P., Galbraith, C.A., & Pienkowski, M.W., *eds.* 1992. *Important bird areas in the UK including the Channel Islands and the Isle of Man.* Sandy, RSPB.

Ridgill, S.C., & Fox, A.D. 1990. *Cold weather movements of waterfowl in western Europe.* IWRB, Slimbridge. (IWRB Special Publication No. 13.)

Rose, P.M., & Taylor, V. 1993. *Western Palearctic and south west Asia waterfowl census 1993. Mid-winter waterfowl counts, January 1993.* Slimbridge, International Waterfowl and Wetlands Research Bureau.

SEEEC. 1996. *Sea Empress Environmental Evaluation Committee. Initial Report.* Cardiff, SEEEC.

Warbrick, S., Clark, N.A., & Donald, P.F. 1991. *Distribution studies of waders and shelduck on the Severn Estuary with reference to sediment mobility.* Thetford, British Trust for Ornithology. (Research Report, No. 78.)

Waters, R.J., Cranswick, P.A., Evans, J., & Pollitt, M.S. 1996. *The Wetland Bird Survey 1994-1995: wildfowl and wader counts.* Slimbridge, British Trust for Ornithology / Wildfowl and Wetlands Trust / Royal Society for the Protection of Birds / Joint Nature Conservation Committee.

B. Further reading

Buck, A.L. 1993. *An inventory of UK estuaries. Volume 2, South-west Britain.* Peterborough, JNCC.

Clark, N.A. 1983. The ecology of dunlin (*Calidris alpina L.*) wintering on the Severn Estuary. Unpublished PhD thesis, University of Edinburgh.

Eltringham, S.K., & Boyd, H. 1960. The shelduck population in the Bridgwater Bay moulting area. *Wildfowl Trust Annual Report, 11:* 107-117.

Eltringham, S.K., & Boyd, H. 1963. The moult migration of the shelduck to Bridgwater Bay. *British Birds, 54:* 145-160.

Goss-Custard, J.D., Kay, D.G., & Blundell, R.M. 1977. The density of migratory and over wintering redshanks *Tringa totanus (L.)* and curlew *Numenius arquata (L.)* in relation to the density of their prey in south-east England. *Estuarine, Coastal and Marine Science, 5:* 497-510.

Green, R.E., & Robins, M. 1993. The decline of the ornithological importance of the Somerset Levels and Moors, England and changes in the management of water levels. *Biological Conservation, 66:* 95-106.

Hurford, C., & Lansdown, P. 1995. *Birds of Glamorgan.* Glamorgan, D. Brown & Sons Ltd.

Kirby, J.S., Evans, R.J., & Fox, A.D. 1993. Wintering seaducks in Britain and Ireland: populations, threats, conservation and research priorities. *Aquatic conservation: marine and freshwater ecosystems, 3:* 105-137.

Patterson, I.J. 1982. *The shelduck.* Cambridge, Cambridge University Press.

Prater, A.J. 1989. Ringed plover *Charadrius hiaticula* breeding population of the United Kingdom in 1984. *Bird Study, 36:* 154-159.

Warwick, R.N., Goss-Custard, J.D., Kirby, R., George, C.L., Pope, N.D., Rowden, A.A. 1991. Static and dynamic environmental factors determining the community structure of estuarine macrobenthos in south-west Britain: why is the Severn Estuary different? *Journal of Applied Ecology, 28:* 329-345.

Worrall, D.H. 1984. Diet of the dunlin *Calidris alpina* in the Severn Estuary. *Bird Study, 31:* 203-212.

C. Contact names and address

Type of information	*Contact address and telephone no.*
High tide and low tide counts of wintering and migrant wildfowl (WeBS)	*WeBS National Organiser (Wildfowl), The Wildfowl & Wetlands Trust, Slimbridge, tel: 01453 890333
High tide counts of wintering and migrant waders (WeBS)	*WeBS National Organiser (Waders), The British Trust for Ornithology, Thetford, tel: 01842 750050
Low tide counts of wintering and migrant waders (WeBS)	*WeBS National Organiser (Low Tide Counts), The British Trust for Ornithology, Thetford, tel: 01842 750050
Site designations (Wales)	*CCW South Area Office, Cardiff, tel: 01222 772400
Site designations (England)	*EN HQ, Peterborough, tel: 01733 340345

*Starred contact addresses are given in full in the Appendix.

5.13 Land mammals

Dr C.E. Turtle & K. Meakin

5.13.1 Introduction

This section covers mammals that occur in the coastal 10 km squares in the region, concentrating on those that are truly coastal, such as otters, and those that occur on the coast for reasons of shelter and foraging, such as the greater horseshoe bat *Rhinolophus ferrumequinum*. Other mammals - common and widespread throughout Britain, feral or recently introduced - have not been considered.

The region is important for some nationally important mammal species, most of which are vulnerable and declining (Morris 1993). The region includes the Isles of Scilly, which are of note as one of the few sites for the lesser white-toothed shrew *Crocidura suaveolens*. Thirteen of the fourteen species of British bat are recorded for this region (Arnold 1993), of which the greater horseshoe *Rhinolophus ferrumequinum*, the lesser horseshoe *R. hipposideros* and the grey long-eared *Plecotus austriacus* are the most important, owing to their limited national distribution and declining numbers. The population of greater horseshoe bat in the region is of national importance and the lesser horseshoe bat is restricted in Britain to the south-west. Both species are classified as endangered (Stebbings & Griffith 1986) and in this region are at the northern edge of their European range (Arnold 1993). The dormouse *Muscardinus avellanarius* is also found in the region. In Britain it is on the western edge of its range in Europe (Corbett & Harris 1991). Otters *Lutra lutra* are also present here; they are classed as endangered and are absent from many areas of England and Wales.

All species of bat are protected under Schedule 5 of the Wildlife & Countryside Act 1981 and under Schedule 2 of the Conservation (Natural Habitats etc.) Regulations 1994. Other species recorded from the region and protected under these schedules are the dormouse and the otter. All British bats are listed under Appendix II of the Bern Convention, whereas the dormouse is listed under Appendix III.

5.13.2 Important locations and species

Table 5.13.1 summarises the recorded distribution of protected mammals in the region.

The otter is the terrestrial mammal that uses the coast most frequently (Arnold 1993). The South-West Peninsula is regarded as a stronghold for otters but there are no positive records from the 1984-86 otter survey of England (Strachan *et al.* 1990) or from the areas of the south Wales coast covered by the 1991 otter survey of Wales (Andrews *et al.* 1993). Bad weather conditions during the otter surveys may account for a lack of records from this region. On the basis of anecdotal evidence, otter populations are thought to be recovering along the north coast of Cornwall, especially on the Land's End peninsula (T. Edwards pers. comm.), and are spreading into Avon along the Somerset coast (J. Martin pers. comm.). Otters are also recolonising several river catchments in the north of the region, especially the River Taff (Mid Glamorgan). Otter populations are now well established on the lower sections of the River Wye SSSI (C. Pagendam pers. comm.).

Map 5.13.1 shows the recorded distribution of greater and lesser horseshoe bats in the region. The greater horseshoe bat is normally associated with semi-natural areas, particularly pastureland; they have been observed foraging along the coast (J. Page pers. comm.). The national bat habitat survey shows that other species of bat also use the coast for foraging (Walsh & Harris 1996). Disused mines on the coast are widely used by both greater and lesser horseshoe bats as hibernation sites, some of the most important sites being along the north Cornish coast between St. Ives and Morwenstow. The extent to which these mines are also used as nursery roosts is uncertain, but there is one known nursery roost in a mine near Kilkhampton (J. Page pers. comm.). The lesser horseshoe bat is associated with areas of semi-natural habitat and particularly ancient

Table 5.13.1 Records of protected species distribution

Species	*Estimate of importance in region*
Greater horseshoe bat *Rhinolophus ferrumequinum*	Rare: Cornwall, Devon, Somerset, Avon, Gloucestershire
Lesser horseshoe bat *R. hipposideros*	Occasional (absent South Glamorgan)
Brandt's bat *Myotis brandtii*	Rare: Cornwall, Devon, Gloucestershire
Whiskered bat *Myotis mystacinus*	Rare: Avon
Natterer's bat *M. nattereri*	Occasional: Cornwall, Devon, Somerset, Avon
Daubenton's bat *M. daubentonii*	Rare: Cornwall, Somerset, Avon
Serotine bat *Eptesicus serotinus*	Rare: Devon and Cornwall
Noctule bat *Nyctalus noctula*	Rare: Cornwall, Avon, Gloucestershire
Leisler's bat *N. leisleri*	Rare: Cornwall and Gloucestershire
Pipistrelle bat *Pipistrellus pipistrellus*	Frequent
Barbastelle bat *Barbastella barbastellus*	Rare: Cornwall
Brown long-eared bat *Plecotus auritus*	Rare: Cornwall, Devon, Avon, Gloucestershire
Grey long-eared bat *P. austriacus*	Rare: Devon
Dormouse *Muscardinus avellanarius*	Occasional: Cornwall, Devon, Somerset, Avon, Gloucestershire, Mid Glamorgan
Otter *Lutra lutra*	Frequent: Cornwall, Devon, Somerset, Avon, S. Glamorgan
Polecat *Mustela putorius*	Rare: Gloucestershire, Gwent

Source: Arnold (1993); various pers comm.

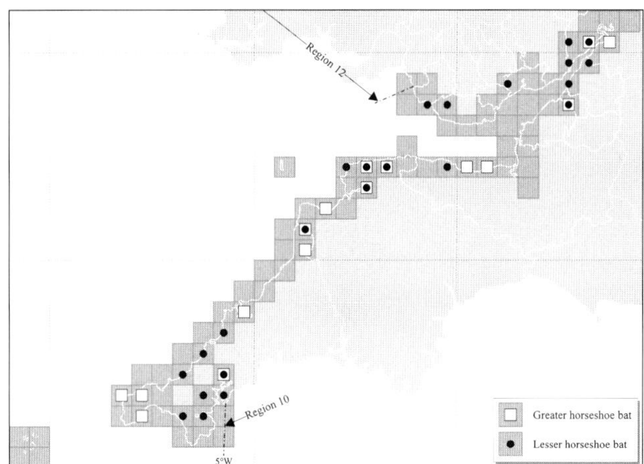

Map 5.13.1 Recorded distribution of greater and lesser horseshoe bats in coastal 10 km squares. Records from 1975 onwards. Source: Arnold (1993).

woodlands. Linear features such as hedgerows, tree lines and rivers are important to this and other bat species for foraging and flight lines. The lesser horseshoe bat is more common in the region than the greater horseshoe and a number of nursery sites are known. It appears that lesser horseshoes may be less restricted in their choice of roost site than greater horseshoes, as their smaller size allows them to use sites with smaller entrances (J. Page pers. comm.).

Dormice are associated with ancient semi-natural woodland and edge habitats, such as broadleaved trees on the edge of forestry plantations or mature, diverse hedgerows and scrub. Isolated areas of suitable habitat are unlikely to hold viable populations if they are less than 20 ha in extent (Bright *et al.* 1994). The preliminary findings of the Great Nut Hunt (Morris *et al.* in press) show that dormice occur along the north Devon and Somerset coast. The distribution of dormice in Cornwall is not well known, but they are recorded from woods near the Helford River and the coastal coombe valley woodland at Marsland Valley. There is potential dormouse habitat in other coombe valley woodlands along the north Cornwall coast (G. Pilkington pers. comm.). There are recent records of dormice from two sites in Mid Glamorgan.

Polecats are recorded from a variety of habitats, particularly farmland that is not intensively managed. They are known to use the coastal dunes and strips of remnant habitat between farmland and the coast. There are three records of polecats from the region (Arnold 1993). One record is from the Slimbridge area (Gloucestershire) and two are from the Welsh coast around Newport. Polecats are widely distributed in south Wales and it is likely that they occur elsewhere on the lowland farmland on the north side of the Severn Estuary (J. Birks pers. comm.).

5.13.3 Human activities

Areas of the region's coastline are under heavy pressure from the tourism and leisure industry. Disturbance is mainly concentrated in tourist 'honey pot' areas, but this, combined with habitat degredation, may deter otters from breeding in these areas. Use of the Severn Estuary by otters may be hampered by the loss of wetlands to industrial developments around the Severn Bridge and second Severn crossing and redevelopment schemes in south Wales, such as at Cardiff Bay (J. Martin & N. Ajax-Lewis pers. comm.). Otters may also be locally affected by out-wash from disused mines in parts of Cornwall and south Wales and nitrate and pesticide pollution from farming and sewage outfalls (T. Edwards pers. comm.).

Intensification of farming and especially pesticide use have had an adverse effect on all species of bat. Removing hedgerows and woodland destroys bat roosting and foraging sites as well as reducing shelter: indeed, the loss of any semi-natural habitat will reduce the quality of the environment for most species of bat. The loss of mature hedgerows, particularly those that connect with other woodlands, will also have a severe effect on the dormouse population, as will destruction, fragmentation and inappropriate management of ancient woodlands, including hazel coppice. However, habitat loss over much the region's coastline has been reduced over the last decade, owing to a decline in agriculture and the introduction of more wildlife-friendly land management practices under initiatives such as the Countryside Stewardship scheme and complementary schemes in Wales (T. Edwards, F. Rush & N. Ajax-Lewis pers. comm.).

5.13.4 Information sources used

There are no reliable estimates of the numbers of mammals in the region that could be used to quantify the resource. Using data from Arnold (1993) - although the records are incidental rather than comprehensive - an estimate has been made of their occurrence in the region. As a general observation (Morris 1993), mammal surveys are not recorded with the same intensity as botanical ones, and the occurrence of mammals within 10 km squares is not enough to establish the status of species.

There have been no specifically coastal mammal surveys within this region and even the nationally comprehensive surveys, such as for otters, have their limitations when assessing the importance of the coast. There have been no comprehensive surveys for any of the bats, although there are recent records for all species (BRC data). The BRC data for bats demonstrate the bias that can occur for rarer species, as the commoner bats are clearly under-recorded. The information from the English Nature Bat Sites Register (Mitchell-Jones in press) may confirm further records. The known roost sites for bats in Britain are recorded on the Bat Sites Register.

5.13.5 Acknowledgements

Thanks go to J. Martin, The Wildlife Trust for Bristol, Bath & Avon, T. Edwards, Cornwall Wildlife Trust, F. Rush, Devon Wildlife Trust, N. Ajax-Lewis, Glamorgan Wildlife Trust, J. Winder, Gwent Wildlife Trust, Gary Pilkington, Warden, Marsland Valley, J. Birks, Vincent Wildlife Trust, and J. Page, Cornwall Bat Group, for their valuable information and their time. The Biological Records Centre, Monks Wood, provided recent data for the region.

5.13.6 Further sources of information

A. References cited

Andrews, E., Howell P., & Johnson K. 1993. *Otter survey of Wales 1991.* London, The Vincent Wildlife Trust.

Arnold, H.R. 1993. *Atlas of mammals in Britain.* London, HMSO. (ITE Research Publication, No. 6.)

Bright, P.W., Mitchell, P., & Morris, P.A. 1994. Dormouse distribution: survey techniques, insular ecology and selection of sites for conservation. *Journal of Applied Ecology, 31:* 329-339.

Corbett, G.B., & Harris, S.H., *eds.* 1991. *The handbook of British mammals.* 3rd ed. Oxford, Blackwell Scientific Publications.

Mitchell-Jones, A.J. 1995. The status and conservation of horseshoe bats in Britain. *Myotis, 32-33:* 271-284.

Morris, P.A. 1993. *A red data book for British mammals.* London, Mammal Society.

Morris, P.A., Bright, P.W., & Mitchell-Jones, A.J. In press. *The great nut hunt.* Peterborough, English Nature. (1993 dormouse survey, England and Wales.)

Stebbings, R.E., & Griffith, F. 1986. *Distribution and status of bats in Europe.* Huntingdon, Institute of Terrestrial Ecology, Monks Wood.

Strachan, R., Birks, J.D.S., Chanin, P.R.F., & Jefferies, D.J. 1990. *Otter survey of England 1984-1986.* Peterborough, Nature Conservancy Council.

Walsh A., & Harris, S. 1996. Foraging habitat preferences of vespertilionid bats in Britain. *Journal of Applied Ecology, 33:* 508-518.

B. Further reading

Chanin, P.R.F. 1985. *The natural history of otters.* London, Croom Helm.

Hurrell, E., & McIntosh, G. 1984. Mammal Society dormouse survey, January 1975 - April 1979. *Mammal Review, 14:* 1-18.

Kenwood, R.E., Hodder, K.H., & Rose, R.J. 1994. *Conservation of red squirrels. Final report.* Institute of Terrestrial Ecology, contract report to Pedigree Pet Foods through WWF, BP Exploration, The Rutland Group of Companies.

MacDonald, S.M. 1983. The status of the otter *Lutra lutra* in the British Isles. *Mammal Review, 13:* 11-23.

MacDonald, S.M., & Mason, C.F. 1983. Some factors influencing the distribution of otters *Lutra lutra. Mammal Review, 13:* 1-10.

National Rivers Authority. 1933. *Otters and river management.* Bristol, NRA. (Conservation Technical Handbook, No. 3.)

Schober, W., & Grimmberger, E. 1987. *A guide to bats of Britain and Europe.* London, Hamlyn.

Stebbings, R.E. 1988. *Conservation of European bats.* London, Christopher Helm.

Walsh A., & Harris, S. 1996. Factors determining the abundance of vespertilionid bats in Britain: geographic, land class and local habitat relationships. *Journal of Applied Ecology, 33:* 519-529.

Whitten, A.J. 1990. *Recovery: a proposed programme for Britain's protected species.* Peterborough, Nature Conservancy Council.

C. Contact names and addresses

Type of information	*Contact address and telephone no.*
Local site and species information - Cornwall	*T. Edwards, Cornwall Wildlife Trust, Truro, tel: 01872 73939
Local site and species information - Devon	*F. Rush, Devon Wildlife Trust, Exeter, tel: 01392 79244
Local site and species information - Avon & Somerset	*J. Martin, The Wildlife Trust for Bristol, Bath & Avon, Bristol, tel: 0117 926 8018
Local site and species information - Somerset	B. Butcher, Somerset Environmental Records Centre, Pickney, Kingston St. Mary, Taunton, Somerset TA2 8AS, tel: 01823 451778
Local site and species information - Gloucestershire	*Conservation Officer, Gloucester Wildlife Trust, Gloucester, tel: 01452 383333
Local site and species information - Gwent	*J. Winder, Gwent Wildlife Trust, Monmouth, tel: 01600 715501
Local site and species information - Glamorgan	*N. Ajax-Lewis, Glamorgan Wildlife Trust, Bridgend, tel: 01656 724100
Bats in Cornwall	John Page, Cornwall Bat Group, 3 Belgravia Place, Sheffield, Penzance TR19 6UJ, tel: 01736 732037, or Rowena Varley, Cornwall Bat Group, Bat Lodge, Trenowth, Grampound Road, Truro TR2 4EH, tel: 01726 883323
Bats in Devon	George Bemment, Devon Bat Group, 19 Fore Street, Kings Kerswell, Newton Abbot TQ12 5HT, tel: 01803 874028
Bats in Somerset & Avon	*C. Hosey, EN Somerset & Avon Team, Taunton, tel. 01823 283211
Dormice	Gary Pilkington, Chapel Cottage, Gooseham Mill, Morwenstow, Cornwall EX23 9PQ, tel: 01288 331266
Otters	Hilary Marshall, Devon & Cornwall Otter Recorder, Meadowside, Virginstow, Beaworthy, Devon EX21 5DZ
Polecats	J. Birks, 3 Knell Cottages, Harcourt Road, Mathon, Nr Malvern, Worcs WR13 5PG, tel: 01684 575876
National site and species information: England	*Mammal Ecologist, EN HQ, Peterborough, tel 01733 340345
National site and species information: Wales	*Mammal Ecologist, CCW HQ, Bangor, tel 01248 370444
General mammal information	The Mammal Society, Unit 15, Cloisters House, Cloisters Business Centre, 8 Battersea Park Road, London SW8 4BG, tel: 0171 498 4358
National recording schemes and collated biological data from throughout UK	*Biological Records Centre, ITE Monks Wood, Huntingdon, tel: 01487 773381

*Starred contact addresses are given in full in the Appendix.

5.14 Seals

C.D. Duck

5.14.1 Introduction

There are no reliable recent records of common seals *Phoca vitulina* in the region. A haul-out site in the Severn Estuary off Newport has not been used in recent years and there have been no recent confirmed sightings from this area. Grey seals *Halichoerus grypus,* although not abundant, may be seen throughout the region. Here, their breeding season is early and protracted in comparison with breeding sites in Scotland and on the east coast of England: pups are born from July to November and occasionally as late as March. The region produces approximately 0.5% of the grey seal pups born in Great Britain (Table 5.14.1). Outside the breeding season, numbers of grey seals at haul-out sites are unpredictable and can vary greatly from day to day. For comparability with regions elsewhere in GB, this section therefore refers mainly to grey seal numbers and distribution during the breeding season.

Table 5.14.1 Grey seal pup production and population size for the region in relation to the rest of GB

Location	*Pup production*[1]	*Associated total population >=1 year old*	*% of GB population*
Cornwall (west and north)	64	217	0.2
Isles of Scilly	80	272	0.2
Devon (north)	20	68	0.1
Somerset	0	0	0
Avon	0	0	0
Gloucestershire	0	0	0
Gwent	0	0	0
South Glamorgan	0	0	0
Mid Glamorgan	0	0	0
Region 11	***164***	***557***	***0.5***
South-west Britain (Regions 10 - 12)	1,650	5,650	4.9
GB total	33,850	115,000	-

Sources: S. Westcott, Isles of Scilly Environment Trust, Sea Mammal Research Unit, Dyfed Wildlife Trust, Lundy Warden. Key: [1]pup production figures are estimates based mostly on single surveys of breeding sites at variable dates during the 1991 to 1994 breeding seasons.

5.14.2 Important locations

Grey seals breed and haul-out at the rear of sea-caves, on remote islands and on beaches on isolated stretches of the coast. The main grey seal breeding sites in the region are on the Eastern Isles, the Norrard and Western Rocks in the Isles of Scilly (41% of pups born in the region), around Boscastle (20%) and on Lundy (10%) with smaller sites round Lizard Point, Land's End and along the north Cornwall coast (Clark 1977; Willcox 1986, 1987). These and important non-breeding haul-out sites are shown on Map 5.14.1 (Table 5.14.2). There are no breeding sites in Somerset, Avon, Gloucestershire, Gwent, South or Mid Glamorgan. The rugged nature of the coast throughout the region and the

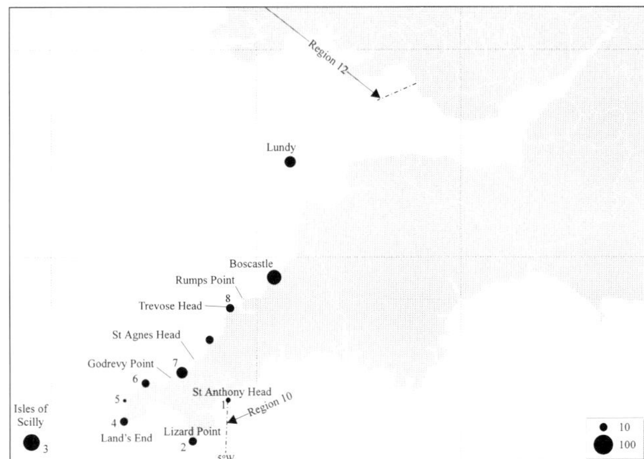

Map 5.14.1 Grey seal pup production. Circles represent the number of pups born along sections of the coast. Figures refer to important haul-out sites in Table 5.14.2. Sources: see Table 5.14.2.

remoteness of sites used by seals makes regular and systematic surveying extremely difficult; there may therefore be other, smaller breeding sites that remain as yet undiscovered. Breeding sites are frequently inundated by water at high tide and/or during storms, and pups regularly have to swim within a few days of birth. As well as further complicating estimation of total pup production (Table 5.14.2), this may result in high pup mortality in stormy breeding seasons (Bonner 1970; Summers 1974; Prime 1985). Results from an aerial survey of the Isles of Scilly in 1982 suggested that four consecutive days of gales severely reduced the numbers of pups on the breeding sites (Prime 1985).

A lone female sea lion has been hauling-out on The Brisons, north of Land's End, for six to twelve years. This animal has not been definitely identified and may have escaped from a collection. It is thought to be a Steller's sea lion *Eumetopias jubatus*.

5.14.3 Human activities

Despite the small numbers of seals in the region, they attract considerable local interest. Tour boats take visitors to view seals in the Isles of Scilly, with trips continuing into the breeding season. Tour boats also operate out of St. Ives. There is no local regulation of tour boat activity and its effects on seals are unknown. Mother-pup pairs are particularly vulnerable to disturbance during the breeding season. The National Seal Sanctuary at Gweek rehabilitates between fifteen and 35 pups each year. Several of the seal breeding and haul-out sites in the region are managed at least partly for their wildlife interest.

The region supports a thriving fishing industry, with Newlyn one of the most important ports in England (see also sections 9.1 and 9.2). Seals are occasionally caught in nets around Devon and Cornwall, but there is no quantitative information on the numbers of animals involved. Some seals at haul-out sites can be seen with

Table 5.14.2 Estimated grey seal breeding figures (1990-94) and locations of important haul-out sites in the region

*Site no.**	*Location*	*Grid ref.*	*Estimated no. of pups born in the breeding season*	*% of region total*
	Breeding sites			
	St. Anthony Head	SW848310	3	1.5
	Lizard Point	SW721140-SW673136	12	6
	Isles of Scilly	SV870120	80	40
	Land's End	SW360227-SW512410	21**	10.5
	Godrevy to St. Agnes	SW580434-SW700515	15	7.5
	St. Agnes to Trevose Head	SW700515-SW860767	5	2.5
	Trevose to Rumps Point	SW860767-SW935812	5	2.5
	Boscastle area	SS100910-SS120935	40	20
	Lundy	SS140450	20	10
	Main haul-out sites			
1	Black Rock	SW833316	-	-
2	Lizard Point	SW702109	-	-
3	Isles of Scilly	SV850145	-	-
4	Longships	SW321252	-	-
5	The Brisons	SW340311	-	-
6	The Carracks	SW467409	-	-
7	Godrevy Island	SW576435	-	-
8	Islands off Padstow Bay	SW900800	-	-

Sources: Emma Parkes (Lundy Island) and Andrew Gibson (Isles of Scilly Environmental Trust), pers. comms. Data for all other sites supplied by Stephen Westcott, Cornwall Wildlife Trust. Key: *site numbers (haul-out sites only) are as shown on Map 5.14.1. Breeding sites in the region are named on the map. **Actual number of pups born in 1994.

fishing net caught round their necks. A number of amenity and power generation barrage proposals have either been approved or are still pending in the region (see also sections 9.7 and 8.3). These could have considerable impacts, not only by causing habitat loss and change, but also by increasing levels of water use and disturbance in the area. Seals are vulnerable to contamination and pollution of coastal waters by toxic substances, which can accumulate in waters that are only partially flushed by the tide, as in some estuaries and behind barrages. Lead and mercury are of particular concern (Law *et al.* 1991, 1992). In September 1994, during a period of unusually calm sea conditions, seventeen out of a sample of 25 pups from one breeding site in west Cornwall were fouled by oil, especially on their bellies (S. Westcott pers. comm.). In late February 1996 oil from the tanker *Sea Empress* spread across the Bristol Channel. Fortunately the spill occurred after the most vulnerable category of seals, young pups, had left the breeding beaches. Although grey seals contaminated with oil were seen along the south Pembrokeshire coast and on Lundy Island, they are unlikely to have been seriously affected. The long-term effects on any seals of swimming in the newly-formed slick and inhaling volatile hydrocarbons are unknown but it is unlikely that many animals would have been affected.

5.14.4 Information sources used

The information presented here is derived from counts of seals made by Stephen Westcott, Cornwall Wildlife Trust, between 1990 and 1994. Prior to this, there had been a number of attempts to survey grey seals in the region (Davies 1956; Summers 1974; Prime 1985). These surveys were largely single visits to sites in late September and early October; total pup production figures may have been underestimated as they were based on the assumption that breeding occurs only between September and early November. Current survey techniques include observations from cliff-tops and from boats, swimming into caves using sub-aqua equipment and paddling the coast on a wave-ski.

5.14.5 Acknowledgements

I am grateful to Stephen Westcott for making available the information he has painstakingly accumulated since 1990. Rebecca Wright (CCW), Emma Parkes (Lundy Island), Andrew Gibson and Will Wagstaffe (Isles of Scilly Environmental Trust) and James Barnett (National Seal Sanctuary) also kindly provided information.

5.14.6 Further sources of information

A. References cited

Bonner, W.N. 1970. *Seal deaths in Cornwall, autumn 1969*. London, HMSO. (NERC Publication Series, No. 1.)

Clark, N.A. 1977. Composition and behaviour of the grey seal colony of Lundy. *Report of the Lundy Field Society, 28:* 32-42.

Davies, J.L. 1956. The grey seal at the Isles of Scilly. *Proceedings of the Zoological Society of London, 127:* 161-166.

Law, R.J., Fileman, C.F., Hopkins, A.D., Baker, J.R., Harwood, J., Jackson, D.B., Kennedy, S., Martin, A.R., & Morris, R.J. 1991. Concentrations of trace metals in the livers of marine mammals (seals, porpoises and dolphins) from waters around the British Isles. *Marine Pollution Bulletin, 22:* 183-191.

Law, R.J., Jones, B.R., Baker, J.R., Kennedy, S., Milne, R., & Morris, R.J. 1992. Trace metals in the livers of marine mammals from the Welsh coast and Irish Sea. *Marine Pollution Bulletin, 24:* 296-304.

Prime, J.H. 1985. The current status of the grey seal *Halichoerus grypus* in Cornwall, England. *Biological Conservation, 33:* 81-87.

Summers, C.F. 1974. The grey seal (*Halichoerus grypus*) in Cornwall and the Isles of Scilly. *Biological Conservation, 6:* 285-291.

Willcox, N. 1986. A review of grey seal (*Halichoerus grypus*) pupping on Lundy, and some new observations. *Report of the Lundy Field Society, 37:* 32-34.

Willcox, N. 1987. Grey seal pupping on Lundy in 1987. *Report of the Lundy Field Society, 38:* 47.

B. Further reading

Gubbay, S. 1988. *A coastal directory for marine nature conservation.* Ross-on-Wye, Marine Conservation Society.

McGillivray, D. 1995. Seal conservation legislation in the UK: past, present and future. *International Journal of Marine and Coastal Law, 10:* 19-52.

Richardson, W.J., Hickie, J.P., Davis, R.A., & Thomson, D.H. 1989. *Effects of offshore petroleum operations on cold water marine mammals: a literature review.* American Petroleum Institute Publication, No. 4,485.

Steven, G.A. 1936. Seals (*Halichoerus grypus*) of Cornwall coasts. *Journal of the Marine Biological Association 20:* 1-14.

Turnpenny, A.W.H., & Nedwell, J.R. 1994. *The effects on marine fish, diving mammals and birds of underwater sound generated by seismic surveys.* Southampton, Fawley Aquatic Research Laboratories Ltd.

C. Contact names and addresses

Type of information	*Contact address and telephone no.*
Seals in Cornwall	*Stephen Westcott, c/o Cornwall Wildlife Trust, Truro, tel: 01872 73939
Seals in Cornwall	Cornish Biological Records Unit, Trevithick Building, Trevenson Road, Pool, Redruth, Cornwall TR15 3PL, tel: 01209 710424
Seals in Cornwall and Devon	*English Nature Devon and Cornwall Team, Truro, tel: 01872 262550
Seals in Devon	*Devon Wildlife Trust, Exeter, tel: 01392 79244
Seals on Lundy	The Warden, Lundy Island, Bristol Channel, Devon EX39 2LY, tel: 01237 431831
Seals in Somerset	*Somerset Wildlife Trust, Bridgwater, tel: 01823 451587
Seals in south Wales	*Countryside Council for Wales, Cardiff, tel: 01222 772400
Seal rehabilitation	National Seal Sanctuary, Gweek, Helston, Cornwall TR12 6UG, tel: 01326 221361
Seal numbers and distribution around GB	Callan Duck, Sea Mammal Research Unit, Gatty Marine Laboratory, University of St. Andrews, Fife KY16 8LB, tel: 01334 476161

*Starred contact addresses are given in full in the Appendix.

The south-west approaches to the English Channel are richer in cetaceans (whales, dolphins and porpoises) than the waters of any other part of southern Britain. Close to the region's shore, the harbour porpoise is the most frequently seen cetacean. Uncommon in Europe, it is listed in the EC Habitats & Species Directive as a species whose conservation requires the designation of Special Areas of Conservation, although delimiting areas for this wide-ranging species has proved difficult. Drawing: Ian Reach, JNCC.

5.15 Whales, dolphins and porpoises

Dr P.G.H. Evans

5.15.1 Introduction

The south-west approaches to the English Channel are richer in cetaceans (whales, dolphins and porpoises) than the waters of any other part of southern Britain. Seventeen species of cetaceans have been recorded along the coasts or in nearshore waters (within 60 km of the coast) of the region since 1980. Of these, nine species (33% of the 27 UK species) are either present throughout the year or recorded annually as seasonal visitors to the region (Table 5.15.1). As one moves east into the Bristol Channel, cetacean species-richness and abundance declines markedly. The most common offshore species are the common dolphin *Delphinus delphis* and the long-finned pilot whale *Globicephala melas*, while nearer to shore the bottlenose dolphin *Tursiops truncatus,* harbour porpoise *Phocoena phocoena* and Risso's dolphin *Grampus griseus* are the most frequently seen.

The harbour porpoise and bottlenose dolphin are listed in Annex II of the EC Habitats & Species Directive as species whose conservation requires the designation of Special Areas of Conservation.

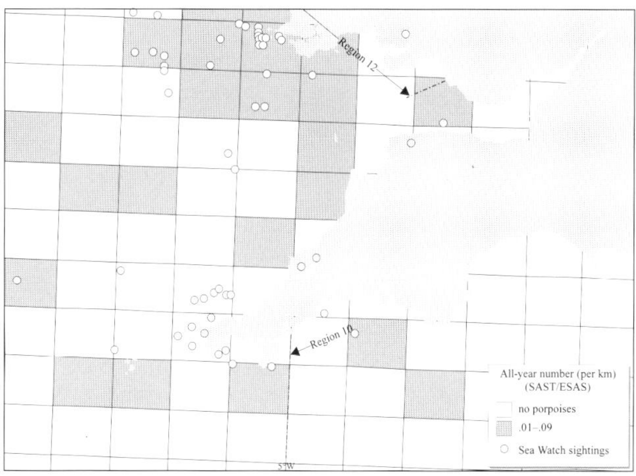

Map 5.15.1 Harbour porpoise: all-year numbers sighted per kilometre of Seabirds at Sea survey (source: JNCC SAST / ESAS); and sightings reported to the Sea Watch sighting system (source: Evans (1992)).

5.15.2 Important locations and species

Prominent headlands and bays are the most favoured localities for cetaceans in coastal waters. The commonest species in nearshore waters are the harbour porpoise (Map 5.15.1), common dolphin (Map 5.15.2), long-finned pilot whale (Map 5.15.3) and bottlenose dolphin (Map 5.15.4), with Risso's dolphin, striped dolphin and killer whale recorded occasionally. Since 1990, bottlenose dolphins have been reported nearshore in every month, with most sightings records coming from Penzance Bay, the Land's End peninsula and St. Ives Bay. Small numbers of harbour porpoises are reported between September and December, mainly along the west Cornish coast (for example Cape Cornwall) and north Devon coast.

In offshore waters, common dolphin and long-finned

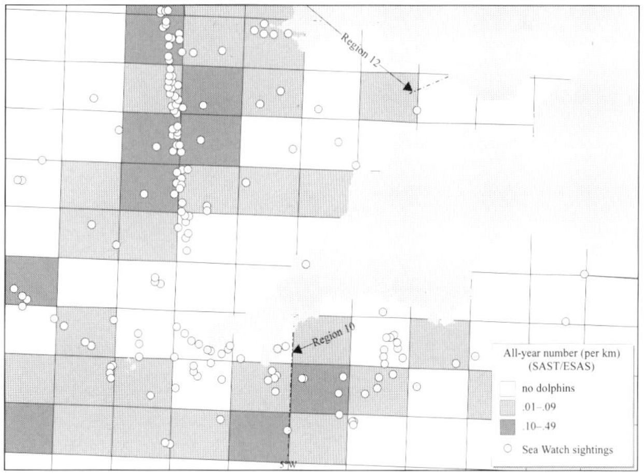

Map 5.15.2 Common dolphin: all-year numbers sighted per kilometre of Seabirds at Sea survey (source: JNCC SAST / ESAS); and sightings reported to the Sea Watch sighting system (source: Evans (1992)).

Table 5.15.1 Cetacean species regularly recorded in the region

Species	*Status, distribution & seasonal occurrence*
Fin whale *Balaenoptera physalus*	Rare visitor to offshore waters, where it is recorded mainly along continental shelf edge at depths of 500-3,000 m between June and December
Sperm whale *Physeter macrocephalus*	Rare visitor to offshore waters, where it is recorded mainly along the continental shelf edge at depths of 1,000-3,000 m between October and December
Harbour porpoise *Phocoena phocoena*	Uncommon, occurring in small numbers in nearshore waters, mainly between December and March
Bottlenose dolphin *Tursiops truncatus*	Recorded regularly only since 1990, but now the most frequently observed dolphin in nearshore waters, though generally in groups numbering 5-20 individuals. Recorded in every month of the year, but since 1990 mainly between January and April
Common dolphin *Delphinus delphis*	The commonest dolphin in the region, but occurring mainly offshore. Peak numbers and frequency of sightings between August and January.
Striped dolphin *Stenella coeruleoalba*	Rare, but recorded annually in the western English Channel in very small numbers, mainly between September and February
Risso's dolphin *Grampus griseus*	Uncommon, occurring in nearshore waters mainly in the months of March-April and August-September
Long-finned pilot whale *Globicephala melas*	Present throughout the year mainly offshore, sometimes in large numbers, particularly in November and December
Killer whale *Orcinus orca*	Rare, occurring mainly between August and November

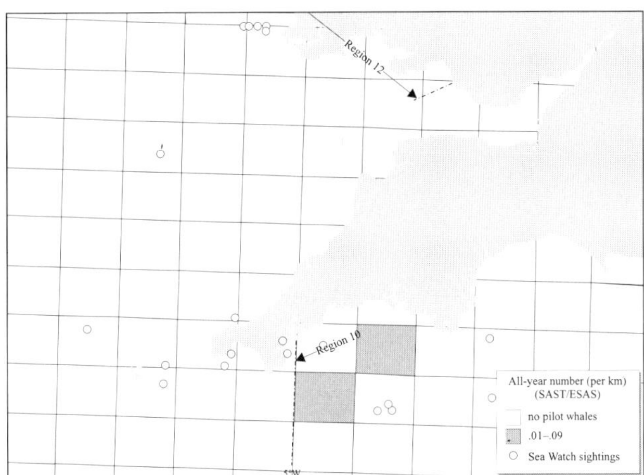

Map 5.15.3 Long-finned pilot whale: all-year numbers sighted per kilometre of Seabirds at Sea survey (source: JNCC SAST/ESAS); and sightings reported to the Sea Watch sighting system (source: Evans (1992)).

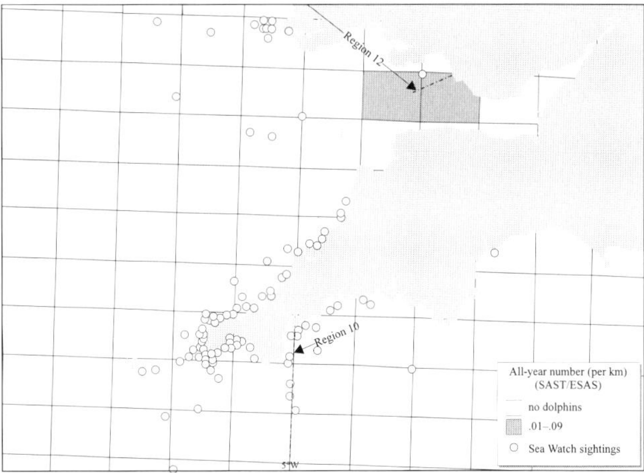

Map 5.15.4 Bottlenose dolphin: all-year numbers sighted per kilometre of Seabirds at Sea survey (source: JNCC SAST/ESAS); and sightings reported to the Sea Watch sighting system (source: Evans (1992)).

pilot whale are the most abundant species; both appear to be wide-ranging, with no specific location favoured nearshore, as they are more concentrated along the continental shelf edge in the south-west approaches. Fin whale and sperm whale are also recorded occasionally, mainly offshore. Other cetacean species recorded in the region include minke whale *Balaenoptera acutorostrata*, humpback whale *Megaptera novaeangliae*, Cuvier's beaked whale *Ziphius cavirostris*, Sowerby's beaked whale *Mesoplodon bidens*, northern bottlenose whale *Hyperoodon ampullatus*, white-beaked dolphin *Lagenorhynchus albirostris*, white-sided dolphin *Lagenorhynchus acutus* and false killer whale *Pseudorca crassidens*.

5.15.3 Human activities

Cetaceans in the region face three potential pressures from human activities: conflicts with fisheries (either by competition for a common food resource, or accidental capture in fishing gear), habitat degradation (mainly by pollution), and disturbance (from underwater sounds, e.g. ships' propellers, seismic survey).

There have been several reports from the western English Channel of small cetaceans (mainly common dolphins and long-finned pilot whales in autumn and winter) being killed accidentally in fishing gear, primarily involving gill nets bottom set around wrecks, although bottom trawls and beam trawls may bring up already dead animals. Between January and March 1992, 118 dolphin carcasses (of which 54 were positively identified as common dolphins) were found stranded on the coast of Cornwall and Devon. Of 38 dolphins examined for cause of death, thirty showed signs associated with incidental capture in fishing gear (Kuiken *et al.* 1994b). Skin lesions characteristic of capture in a small-meshed net and the predominance of recently ingested Atlantic mackerel *Scomber scombrus* and pilchard *Sardina pilchardus* in the stomachs of the dolphins suggested that they had been caught in the trawl or purse seine nets used for these fish. The geographic location of capture is not known but there is an intense multi-national fishery for these two species of fish in the south-west approaches to the English Channel. There is little fishing along the north Devon and Somerset coasts from Ilfracombe to Avonmouth, but some salmon drift netting occurs around Newport, and static gill nets are set in Swansea Bay and Scarweather Sands, West Glamorgan (Northridge 1988; Thomas 1992).

Contaminant levels in cetaceans from the region are low, though generally higher than in other regions of the UK. Mean total PCB (25 congeners) levels of nine harbour porpoises sampled from the south coast of England (Sussex to Cornwall), 1988-92, amounted to 31 ppm (Kuiken *et al.* 1994a). Only one (bycaught) harbour porpoise has been sampled for contaminants in the region between Devon and Glamorgan. Total PCB (25 congeners) levels amounted to 9 ppm (Kuiken *et al.* 1994a). Eight common dolphins sampled in 1990-91 and eleven in 1992 along the Devon and Cornwall coasts (including part of Region 10) gave mean values of 50 ppm and 31 ppm total PCBs respectively (Kuiken *et al.* 1994a). Trace metal contaminant levels of five common dolphins from the same area in 1992 were generally low, only zinc (at 46 ppm) having a mean value exceeding 5 ppm.

Underwater sounds from seismic activities (as part of oil and gas exploration in the English Channel) involve low frequencies and therefore are most likely to affect baleen whales (not a resident of or frequent visitor to this region), which communicate primarily at these frequencies (20-500 Hz). Nevertheless recent studies indicate that other cetaceans may also be disturbed by seismic surveying, as they are sighted less frequently, either acoustically or visually, during seismic surveys (Goold 1996). It is possible that porpoises are also affected by seismic activities (Baines 1993), perhaps indirectly by changing the distribution of their fish prey (Evans 1996). Heavy shipping may also disturb cetaceans. Most of the sound produced by vessels with large engines is at frequencies below 1 kHz, thus also overlapping more with baleen whales than with dolphins and porpoises (Evans 1987). Supertankers typically produce sound levels which from studies elsewhere are known to cause negative responses by baleen whales at distances of c. 0.5-5.0 km (Evans 1996). However, particularly if their propellors are damaged, even those vessels can also generate high frequency (>1 kHz) sound overlapping the frequencies used by small cetaceans (i.e. 1-150 kHz). Negative responses (vessel avoidance and increased dive times) by both bottlenose dolphins and harbour porpoises to such sounds have been reported by Evans *et al.* (1992, 1994).

Recreational activities (speedboats, jet skis etc.) around such resorts as Penzance, Mount's Bay and Ilfracombe and to a lesser extent areas such as St. Ives, Newquay, Minehead and Weston-super-Mare pose threats of direct physical damage from collisions as well as disturbance from the high frequency (>1 kHz) noise generated by these vessels (Evans *et al.* 1992). A code of conduct for boat users has been produced by Sea Watch Foundation and distributed around yacht clubs and marinas (Sea Watch Foundation & UK Mammal Society 1992).

5.15.4 Information sources used

For geographical comparisons of sightings rates for various cetacean species in UK waters, see Evans (1990, 1992) and Northridge *et al.* (1995). Strandings and sightings data, while helpful in providing some indications of the current status of populations, their distribution and migration patterns, do not as yet allow any definite statements to be made about any species. The information presented here on cetacean status and distribution comes primarily from the national sightings database (1973-present) maintained by the Sea Watch Foundation (SWF) (Evans 1992) and the strandings scheme organised by the Natural History Museum in London (1913-present) (Sheldrick *et al.* 1994). Systematic land-based watches have been carried out at Cape Cornwall on the Land's End Peninsula, at Trevose/Park Head and at Hartland and Morte Points on the north Devon coast. Sea-based coverage is generally better in nearshore waters than offshore, although that situation is changing following emphasis upon greater all-round coverage of the English Channel using observers aboard fishing vessels. Opportunistic sightings effort has been greatest between the months of April and September, when sea conditions are also usually best, although this has not prevented several species from being seen most often in late autumn or early winter.

A major international collaborative programme, the Small Cetacean Abundance in the North Sea (SCANS) project, has aimed to provide a baseline assessment of abundance from intensive survey work in July 1994 (Hammond *et al.* 1995). Coverage has extended into the Celtic Shelf and the English Channel.

5.15.5 Acknowledgements

Thanks are due to I. Grant and J. Heimlich-Boran for help in the preparation of the maps and to all those who contributed valuable sightings data, particularly the systematic observations provided by R. Dennis, N. Fletcher, D. Jenkins, J. and L. Hingley, K. Kempinski, R.J. Law, L. Peters, J. Ramster, H.P.K. Robinson, C. Speedie, M.L. Tasker, N. Tregenza and A. Webb.

5.15.6 Further sources of information

A. References cited

Baines, M.E. 1993. *Marine mammal monitoring during the seismic exploration of block 107/21 in Cardigan Bay, Autumn 1993.* Haverfordwest, Dyfed Wildlife Trust.

Evans, P.G.H. 1987. *The natural history of whales and dolphins.* London, Christopher Helm.

Evans, P.G.H. 1990. Whales, dolphins and porpoises. The order Cetacea. *In: Handbook of British mammals*, ed. by G.B. Corbet & S. Harris, 299-350. Oxford, Blackwell.

Evans, P.G.H. 1992. *Status review of cetaceans in British and Irish waters.* Oxford, Sea Watch Foundation. (Report to DoE.)

Evans, P.G.H. 1996. Human disturbance of cetaceans. *In: Exploitation of mammals*, ed. by N. Dunstone & V. Taylor, 376-394. London, Chapman & Hall.

Evans, P.G.H., Canwell, P.J., & Lewis, E.J. 1992. An experimental study of the effects of pleasure craft noise upon bottle-nosed dolphins in Cardigan Bay, West Wales. *In: European research on cetaceans - 6*, ed. by P.G.H. Evans, 43-46. Cambridge, European Cetacean Society.

Evans, P.G.H., Carson, Q., Fisher, P., Jordan, W., Limer, R., & Rees, I. 1994. A study of the reactions of harbour porpoises to various boats in the coastal waters of SE Shetland. *In: European research on cetaceans - 8*, ed. by P.G.H. Evans, 60-64. Cambridge, European Cetacean Society.

Goold, J.C. 1996. Acoustic assessment of populations of common dolphins *Delphinus delphis* in conjunction with seismic surveying. *Journal of the Marine Biological Association of the UK, 16:* 811-820.

Hammond, P.S., Benke, H., Berggren, P., Borchers, D.L., Buckland, S.T., Collet, A., Heide Jørgensen, M.P., Heimlich-Boran, S., Hiby, A.R., Leopold, M.F., & Øien, N. 1995. *Distribution and abundance of the harbour porpoise and other small cetaceans in the North Sea and adjacent waters.* Unpublished final report. (LIFE 90-2/UK/027.)

Kuiken, T., Bennett, P.M., Allchin, C.R., Kirkwood, J.K., Baker, J.R., Lockyer, C.H., Walton, M.J., & Sheldrick, M.C. 1994a. PCBs, cause of death and body condition in harbour porpoises *Phocoena phocoena* from British Waters. *Aquatic Toxicology, 28:* 13-28.

Kuiken, T., Simpson, V.R., Allchin, C.R., Bennett, P.M., Codd, G.A., Harris, E.A., Howes, G.J., Kennedy, S., Kirkwood, J.K., Law, R.J., Merrett, N.R., & Phillips, S. 1994b. Mass mortality of common dolphins *Delphinus delphis* in south-west England due to incidental capture in fishing gear. *Veterinary Record, 134:* 81-89.

Northridge, S. 1988. *Marine mammals and fisheries.* London, Wildlife Link (unpublished report).

Northridge, S., Tasker, M.L., Webb, A., & Williams, J.M. 1995. Seasonal distribution and relative abundance of harbour porpoises *Phocoena phocoena* (L.), white-beaked dolphins *Lagenorhynchus albirostris* (Gray) and minke whales *Balaenoptera acutorostrata* (Lacepède) in the waters around the British Isles. *ICES Journal of Marine Science, 52(1):* 55-66.

Sea Watch Foundation & UK Mammal Society. 1992. *Dolphin code of conduct.* Oxford, Sea Watch Foundation & UK Mammal Society.

Sheldrick, M.C., Chimonides, P.J., Muir, A.I., George, J.D., Reid, R.J., Kuiken, T., Iskjaer-Ackley, C., & Kitchener, A. 1994. Stranded cetacean records for England, Scotland and Wales, 1987-1992. *Investigations on Cetacea, 25:* 259-283.

Thomas, D. 1992. *Marine wildlife and net fisheries around Wales.* Newtown, Royal Society for the Protection of Birds, & Bangor, Countryside Council for Wales.

B. Further reading

Evans, P.G.H. 1990. European cetaceans and seabirds in an oceanographic context. *Lutra, 33:* 95-125.

Natural History Museum. 1990-1994. *Annual reports.* London, Natural History Museum.

Simpson, J.H. 1981. The shelf-sea fronts: implications of their existence and behaviour. *Philosophical Transactions of the Royal Society of London, A302:* 532-546.

Tregenza, N. 1992. Fifty years of cetacean sightings from the Cornish coast, SW England. *Biological Conservation, 59:* 65-70.

Turnpenny, A.W.H., & Nedwell, J.R. 1994. *The effects on marine fish, diving mammals and birds of underwater sound generated by seismic surveys.* Southampton, Fawley Aquatic Research Laboratories Ltd.

C. Contact names and addresses

Type of information	Contact address and telephone no.
Cetacean strandings	Dr D. George & A. Muir, Natural History Museum, Cromwell Road, London SW7 5BD, tel: 0171 938 8861
Cetacean sightings & surveys	Dr P.G.H. Evans, Sea Watch Foundation, c/o Dept. of Zoology, University of Oxford, South Parks Road, Oxford OX1 3PS, tel: 01865 727984
Cetacean sightings & surveys	*Seabirds & Cetaceans Team, JNCC, Aberdeen, tel: 01224 655700
Cetacean land-based watches	C. Speedie, Sea Trident Ltd, 4 Carlton Place, Teignmouth, Devon TQ14 8AB, tel: 01841 521162
Cetacean sightings and bycatches	Dr N. Tregenza, Beach Cottage, Long Rock, Penzance, Cornwall TR20 8JE, tel: 01736 711783
SCANS Project	*European Wildlife Division, Department of the Environment, Bristol, tel: 0117 987 8000
Cetacean organochlorine & heavy metal levels	*Dr R.J. Law, MAFF Directorate of Fisheries Research, Burnham-on-Crouch, tel: 01621 782658
Cetacean pathology	Dr J.R. Baker, Veterinary Field Station, 'Leahurst', Neston, Wirral, Cheshire L64 7TE, tel: 0151 794 6120

*Starred contact addresses are given in full in the Appendix.

Chapter 6 History and archaeology

A. Gale & V. Fenwick

6.1 Introduction

The physical remains of the human past - archaeological evidence - are an integral and irreplaceable part of the coastal resource. Archaeological sites, whether discrete or part of wider landscapes, are fragile, and those not yet located can be unwittingly destroyed. The distribution of known sites is biased by the uneven spread of survey work, and the discovery and scientific investigation of new sites is vital to developing a full picture of the past. This chapter provides an introduction to the archaeology of the region, gives information on the provisions for safeguarding known and unknown sites, and describes the extent of survey work and how to report new discoveries. Map 6.1.1 shows archaeological locations mentioned in the text; these are listed in Table 6.1.1.

This region contains two strongly contrasting coastal environments: in the south-west there are rocky cliffs open to Atlantic storms, in the east there are sheltered estuaries such as the Taw-Torridge, Avon and Severn. Sea communication is the link between human activities in this area. The settlements on the English and Welsh sides of the Bristol Channel have been characterised by trade since prehistory; their contact with the rest of England was inland via the river valleys and with the wider world via the Irish Sea and the Atlantic. Long-term recording on the Somerset Levels has produced a remarkable array of organic structures and artefacts chronicling human use of the wetlands in prehistory. Current work shows that a similar wealth of material is constantly being revealed, and destroyed, in the intertidal area. Survey in the Severn Estuary is demonstrating the importance of interpreting discrete sites within the framework of a changing coast, especially where shoreline retreat is caused by rising sea level and shoreline extension is caused by land claim, often capitalising on natural accumulation of sediment. There is a high potential for the discovery of waterlogged deposits from coastal sites, especially evidence of palaeo-environments - the landscapes of history and prehistory. These have been preserved beneath sand dunes, as at Gwithian, Mawgan Porth, St. Enodoc, Merthyr Mawr and Kenfig, and as waterlogged peat and forest remains in the intertidal and subtidal zones. A recent survey listed 39 submerged forest sites between Falmouth and Cardiff (M. Bell pers. comm.) - 23 from Cornwall alone (Johnson & David 1982). In addition, the intertidal zone of the Isles of Scilly has standing remains in the form of field walls and burial cists (stone chambers).

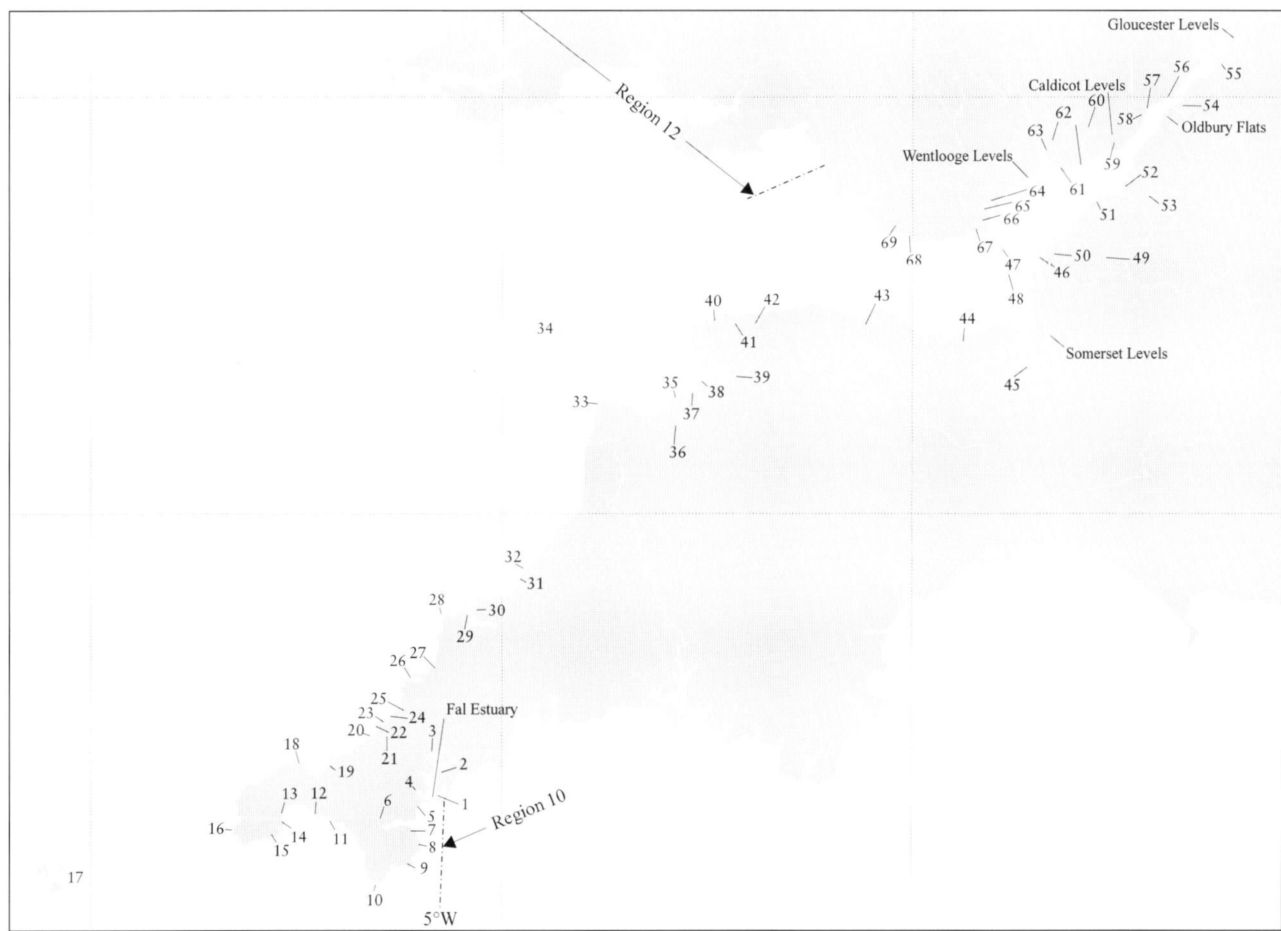

Map 6.1.1 Archaeology: locations mentioned in the text.

Table 6.1.1 Key to numbered locations on Map 6.1.1

No. on Map 6.1.1	*Location*[a]	*No. on Map 6.1.1*	*Location*[a]
1	St. Mawes	36	Bideford
2	St. Just	37	Appledore
3	Truro	38	Yelland
4	Falmouth	39	Barnstaple
5	Pendennis	40	Ilfracombe
6	Helston	41	Coombe Martin
7	Gillan	42	Martinhoe
8	Porthoustock	43	Porlock
9	St. Keverne	44	Doniford
10	Lizard	45	Bridgwater
11	Perran Sands	46	Brean Down
12	St. Michael's Mount	47	Flat Holm
13	Newlyn	48	Steep Holm
14	Mousehole	49	Westbury sub Mendip
15	Lamorna		
16	Land's End	50	Weston-super-Mare
17	Tean, Scilly	51	Clevedon
18	St. Ives	52	Avonmouth
19	Gwithian	53	Bristol
20	Portreath	54	Sharpness
21	Carn Brea	55	Gloucester
22	Porthtowan	56	Lydney
23	St. Agnes	57	Woolaston
24	Gear Sands	58	Chepstow
25	Penhale	59	Caldicot
26	Newquay	60	Magor
27	Mawgan Porth	61	Goldcliff
28	Trevose Head	62	Caerleon
29	Padstow	63	Newport
30	St. Enodoc	64	Cardiff
31	Trebarwith	65	Llandough
32	Tintagel	66	Dinas Powys
33	Hartland Point	67	Barry
34	Lundy	68	Llantwit
35	Westward Ho!	69	St. Donat's

Key: [a]large sites are named on the map.

The region is rich in post-Medieval industrial remains linked to maritime activity. These include lighthouses, seamarks and lifeboat stations; protective piers, slipways, limekilns and pilchard cellars in the small harbours of Cornwall; dock complexes such as those of Avonmouth, Bristol, Sharpness, Gloucester, Newport, Cardiff and Barry; and piers and promenades of towns such as Weston-super-Mare. Some elements of the diverse shipping that served this region can be observed among the hulks of abandoned vessels in the intertidal areas of estuaries and rivers. The Caldicot plank fragment and Mawgor Pill boat show that remains of Medieval and earlier maritime structures can be discovered in locations that were not favoured by the builders of later harbours.

In the sub-tidal zone shipwrecks are expected to be the most numerous site type. Most located shipwrecks around Britain are metal ships that sank in this century. They usually stand proud of the sea bed and can be located by remote sensing equipment. It is difficult to estimate the number of surviving wrecks, but the number of recorded losses of ships suggests that only a very small proportion have been discovered. Records of losses are comprehensive for the 19th century, relatively complete for the 18th, and patchy for the 14th to 17th centuries. For earlier periods it is necessary to examine written evidence for sea-borne trade and extrapolate the opportunities for ship losses by considering hazards to navigation. This process can be extended into the prehistoric period by looking at inland sites for archaeological evidence for trade and seafaring.

6.2 History and archaeology of the region

6.2.1 Hunters, gatherers and early farmers (Palaeolithic, Mesolithic and Neolithic)

Early humans first visited Britain about 450,000 years ago. In a few caves, undisturbed for millennia, their flint hand-axes have been found with the bones of the animals that they hunted. One such cave on the edge of the Somerset Levels at Westbury sub Mendip contains both human and ancient animal bones, but it is not certain that they were contemporaneous. Apart from cave sites, so little evidence survives from this Palaeolithic period that great importance is attached to discoveries of worked flints. Recently, for example, on the foreshore of the Caldicot Levels, the first flints from a non-cave site in Wales were found. Other flints eroded from gravel cliffs at Doniford also hint at occupation of open land as well as caves.

From *c.* 15,000 BC the last Ice Age was in retreat. By *c.* 10,000 BC, the warming climate enabled plants to recolonise the region, and grazing herds moved northwards across the European land mass, to which Britain was still joined. Estuaries offered diverse, all-year-round food sources for the hunter-gatherers of this Mesolithic period. The lower sea level meant that a greater area of coastal plain was available than today, and the Bristol Channel was only a river flowing through lowlands. Sites now on the foreshore suggest that others may survive on the sea bed beyond. A Mesolithic midden (rubbish tip) at Westward Ho! contained marine shells, bone and flint tools and waterlogged biological evidence, which was used to build a picture of the environment of about 7,000 years ago. Elsewhere dunes and beaches of sand or gravel have built up over the old land surface at, for example, Penhale Sands and Porlock. Use of high ground is indicated by scatters of flints on cliff tops, such as at Trevose Head, Dinas Head (Cornwall) and Hartland Point.

By about 6,000 BC rising sea level severed Britain from Europe and dramatically changed this region, drowning the coast and river valleys and inundating low-lying areas such as the Somerset and Gloucester Levels. Hunter-gatherers continued to use the region; scatters of their tools have been found on the rock knolls of the Somerset Levels, which were once islands in the marshy landscape. Mesolithic flints found on Lundy are indirect evidence of more widespread water transport.

From about 4,000-3,500 BC a more settled life-style becomes apparent with the adoption of cultivation and animal husbandry. The Somerset Levels had become a freshwater area with a developing fenland environment. Using higher ground for settlement, crops and grazing, Neolithic farmers exploited the rich resources of the Levels. Peat beds have sealed and preserved remarkable evidence of their lives: long trackways, constructed of stakes and planks, crossing marshy areas; wooden tools; and even a long bow. Not found on conventional 'dry' sites, such artefacts give a direct insight into the technology of the time, while analysis of the timber reveals how woodlands were managed at the time. The erosion of foreshores is revealing intertidal deposits of submerged peat and forest, especially on the Severn Levels, and could potentially yield similarly dramatic discoveries of international significance.

Neolithic tools are dominated by highly polished stone axes, which were essential for clearing forest ready for cultivation. Axes manufactured from the igneous rocks of this region have been found across Britain. In addition to this extensive communication system, the more complex structure of society is seen in the construction of communal stone burial monuments. Away from the rich archaeology of the Levels, for example in Cornwall, these long cairns are the most common structures surviving from Neolithic activity.

6.2.2 Metal-working peoples (Bronze Age and Iron Age)

Cultural development in the 2nd millennium BC is signified by a change in burial monument style, favouring round barrows in place of long cairns. At this time, new metal-working technology was providing tools and weapons of copper and tin alloy. Cornwall and Devon were among the few north European sources of tin.

Plank fragments, found at Caldicot Castle (Parry & McGrail 1991) and Goldcliff (Bell 1992b), provide rare proof of the wide use of boats, evident from the land-based spread of Bronze Age artefacts. Sections of hulls and wreck cargo, discovered only outside the region, at Dover (Region 7) and Salcombe (Region 10), indicate that similar sea-going craft traded with the continent.

In Cornwall, excavation at Gwithian, Trevisker and Trethellan has revealed lowland settlements contemporary with the finely preserved Bronze-Age landscapes on Dartmoor and Bodmin. On the Isles of Scilly, comparable sites are now intertidal, while in those eroding from the cliffs the use of marine resources is indicated by shellfish and the bones of fish, marine mammals and seabirds. On the mainland, submergence of the contemporary coastal plain is evident from the position of stone rows at Yelland, burials at Brean Down and pottery at Blackstone Rocks.

The exceptionally well preserved remains within the Somerset Levels demonstrate the continued use of the wetland environment throughout the Bronze Age and the ensuing Iron Age. Field systems on the cliffs of Penwith show a continuing reliance on agriculture in the Iron Age. The period is, however, characterised by a technological move to iron-making, associated with a cultural change in which large social groups occupied hilltops or promontories, such as Embury Beacon, Hartland Point. The defended promontories - cliff castles - are particularly numerous in Cornwall. Excavation within the enclosed areas, for example at Carn Brea, has revealed round huts interpreted as houses. Whereas on dry land these often survive only as post holes, on the intertidal area at Goldcliff contemporary rectangular huts have been discovered with the remains of upright poles and flooring material. Such preservation demonstrates the potential of the intertidal area to continue furnishing vital new information.

6.2.3 The Roman province

The formal Roman conquest of Devon and Cornwall is not well recorded historically or, as yet, archaeologically. An increasing number of forts are now being identified in Devon. It is also clear that control was rapidly exerted over this region, with the 2nd Legion deploying from Exeter and Gloucester before moving to its permanent base at Caerleon in AD 74. Strategy was closely allied to sea communications. Smaller fortlets or signal stations at Martinhoe, Old Burrow, Sea Mills and on Steep Holm seem to have been designed as the 'eyes' of the fleet overlooking the Bristol Channel and Severn Estuary (Frere 1973). Military supplies, building materials and luxury imports were transported by sea and port installations have been found at Sea Mills and Caerleon.

Towns were established, and this period is seen as one of high activity on land fringing the estuaries, with land claim of part of what is now the Severn Levels. Many of the claimed areas lie outside the current sea defences. Investigation of these eroding intertidal sites, such as Oldbury Flats, is yielding information on the intensity of activities such as metalworking (Allen & Fulford 1992). Saltworking is also known from abundant evidence at Burtle. Cornwall and Scilly, largely beyond the Romanising influences, remained rural. From the 2nd century the population developed a unique form of settlement - courtyard houses - which were an arrangement of oval dwellings and farm buildings around a central court or farmyard.

Land claim and silting in pills (small streams flowing into tidal waters) has resulted in the sealing of maritime structures within coastal land. At Magor a quay structure, dating from the 4th century AD, was found with a 9.5 m portion of a boat alongside (Lawler & Nayling 1993). This is seen as an important further example of Romano-Celtic boatbuilding, paralleled by two earlier discoveries outside the region: the Blackfriar's ship, London, and the St. Peterport (Guernsey) wreck.

6.2.4 Roman departure to Norman conquest

The Roman occupation appears to have had little long-term effect on the more remote parts of this region, and continuity of maritime trade is apparent. Pottery from the 5th - 7th centuries shows that Tintagel and Dinas Powys, a fortified strategic site, were the destinations for imports from the eastern Mediterranean and Africa. A local resource, such as tin at Tintagel, may have enabled such sites to act as a focus for trade. Local redistribution might account for the discovery of small amounts of Mediterranean pottery around the Bristol Channel at sites including Gwithian and Perran Sands and on the Isles of Scilly.

The region was subject to external influences and pressures during this period. The spread of Christianity is marked by the establishment of small monasteries such as St. Germans at Padstow and others at Tintagel, Lundy and Llantwit. Chapels were also built in remote locations including the Gear Sands and Tean Island. Inscribed memorial stones, which are known across Cornwall, in Devon and on Lundy, are a further clue to early Christianity, which may have persisted since Roman times in places such as Llandough (British Archaeology 1995). In contrast to religious and high status sites, much-needed evidence of everyday lifestyles has come from Mawgan Porth.

From the 7th century, Devon and Cornwall were being drawn under the control of Saxon Wessex. The end of the struggle for an independent kingdom in Cornwall was marked by a battle in 838. In the latter half of the 9th century, however, Viking raids targeted the region. Scandinavian place-names such as Flat Holm and Steep Holm are evidence of the impact of these sea-borne invaders and immigrants.

6.2.5 Medieval period

From the arrival of the Normans to the reign of the Tudor dynasty, castle building developed from a means of subjugating the local population to a system of defending the realm. Throughout this transition their sites, such as Tintagel, Bude, Chepstow, Caldicot, St. Donat and the later St. Mawes and Pendennis, were chosen with an understanding of the importance of supply by sea and control of ports. The documents that survive from this period show a number of towns growing in wealth and influence as a result of maritime trade: Truro traded in tin from the 12th century; Gillan in tin from the 16th century; Helston was a coinage town for Edward I; Bude had a mint by the 10th century; Ilfracombe supplied ships to Edward III; and Coombe Martin exported silver and lead from 1293 on. Many of these towns subsequently lost their prominent positions because their rivers or harbours silted and became unnavigable.

Nationally, few examples of Medieval ships have been discovered. During the Victorian construction of Alexandra Dock, Newport, a portion of a clinker-built boat was found (Hutchinson 1984). This has since been dated to the 10th century. The decline of early trading centres means that boats and harbour facilities can be discovered away from modern ports. At Woolaston Pill a 12-13th century quay has been found; and from Magor Pill the bottom of a 13th century boat has been recovered.

Documents show that fishing emerged as a commercial activity in the newly formed Duchy of Cornwall from 1377, with Mousehole noted as the prime pilchard port. Fishing was of sufficient value to necessitate harbour works: Mousehole required a quay in 1392; Newlyn constructed a pier in 1435; and a pier at Newquay was repaired in 1439. Within the Severn Estuary the use of fish traps called 'putts' is documented from 956. Rows of stakes, understood to be the remains of fishtraps, have been dated to the 9th - 13th centuries, and similar structures have been recorded along the coasts of Cornwall, Devon, Somerset, Avon, Gloucester and Gwent.

6.2.6 Post-medieval and modern times

By the 17th century patterns of trade were emerging based on ports whose activity continued into the present century. They fall into two groups. The pier ports, so-called after the protective piers which provide shelter on relatively inhospitable stretches of coast, had no true hinterland, but were built either for a sole export such as granite, slate or metal ores, or purely as a haven for a fishing fleet. Their location and scale afforded no chance of diversification if their primary function became obsolete. Examples include Porthoustock (serving quarries), Lamorna (exporting granite), and Portreath, Porthtowan and St. Agnes (exporting copper). In contrast, river ports such as Falmouth, Padstow, Bridgwater, Bideford, Barnstaple, Bristol, Gloucester and Newport imported for their own hinterlands and maintained a coastwise trade distributing goods from these areas.

In the 18th century the region's trade was largely in raw materials. Coal from south Wales was carried across the Bristol Channel for domestic use and to power steam engines, which pumped copper and tin mines dry, and to burn lime (often as limestone brought from the Gower Peninsula) for mortar and agriculture. The latter activity was based on lime kilns in the small ports of Devon and Cornwall. From Cornwall copper was taken to the foundries sited on the south Wales coal field. Manufactured goods were also sent from the south-western counties: from the late 17th century the Bideford and Barnstaple area was a major exporter of pottery to south Wales, Ireland and the New World, and cider and cloth were distributed coastally.

Many raw materials and goods produced within the region were shipped to Bristol and then redistributed along the coast. Kelp burning was a major industry on Scilly, with the soda ash being shipped to Bristol (Ratcliffe 1992). Being close to the mouths of the Frome, Avon and Severn, this port also received goods brought down-river to be shipped along the coast or for export. Thus, Gloucester enjoyed a symbiotic relationship with Bristol. Goods coming down the Severn were transhipped at Gloucester onto vessels suited to the estuary trip to Bristol, where they were again reshipped for coastal or foreign voyages. Goods destined inland went through the reverse process.

Bristol also flourished as an entrepot for foreign imports from the Mediterranean, the Newfoundland fisheries and the American sugar and tobacco plantations. Smaller ports also engaged in foreign trade. Bideford, for example, was a major 18th century importer of tobacco. The renowned shipbuilding industry of Appledore was founded on the construction of schooners for the Mediterranean fruit trade.

Cardiff owed its early prosperity to iron ore, which was exported via the Glamorganshire Canal, built in 1798. However, it was the opening of the West Bute Dock (1839) and Taff Railway (1840) that precipitated the rapid expansion of the port as a coal exporter. By the end of the century, massive docks had been constructed at Newport and Barry solely for the coal trade. The shipping industry was supported by a variety of activities, from which surviving buildings such as lighthouses and seamarks, coastguard and lifeboat stations are now features of the coast.

Upriver ports such as Bristol were inaccessible for the larger vessels that were introduced with the advent of steel hulls and steam propulsion. The pilchard fishery collapsed in 1870, leaving many small harbours redundant. Coal exports peaked in 1913, since when the south Wales ports have suffered from the decline of the mining industry. The local trade maintained by small sailing coastal and river vessels, the traditional boats of this region, was lost to road transport in the 20th century. Holiday resorts have arisen in many places. The earliest include Weston-super-Mare and Clevedon, with their long piers a reminder of the age of paddle steamer travel. Many once thriving ports are now redeveloped as tourist areas; examples include Gloucester, which has a focus on inland waterways, Bristol, home of Brunel's *Great Britain*; and Cardiff, with its soon-to-be constructed tidal barrage.

The strategic importance of the region is reflected in surviving coastal installations. The Isles of Scilly have a wide range, from Elizabethan defensive walls to 1939-1945 seaplane bases.

6.3 Human activities

6.3.1 Integrated management

Today's intensive use of this region has led to the growth of many organisations with an interest in integrated management. Archaeological interests are represented in many local management plans and initiatives (see also Chapter 10). The impact of certain activities on archaeology has given rise to new organisations which direct or coordinate research activities.

6.3.2 Activities and processes affecting the archaeological resource

The region's archaeological resource does not consist entirely of discrete sites such as intact wrecks. Many sites are scattered. Some sites, including palaeo-environments, are extensive and straddle the terrestrial, intertidal and sub-tidal zones; wrecks can be broken, with some of their parts left in deep water while other parts are cast onto the shore; and harbour facilities can relate to inland industrial sites. The potential effects of development in the terrestrial zone are recognised (see section 6.3.5).

Cliff-top sites, such as Embury Beacon (Devon County Council 1995), and cliff-face sites, such as on Scilly, can suffer both natural and visitor erosion. Low-lying sites are vulnerable to natural erosion and inundation; for example, an archaeological evaluation of Porlock Marsh was necessitated by the threat of the sea breaking through its protective natural pebble ridge. Such sites are also at risk from projects to control inundation and erosion; for example, the raising of sea defences along the Gwent Levels has necessitated an archaeological appraisal. Drainage, which alters the water table and causes shrinking of the land surface, will also have an effect: extraction of materials, such as peat cutting on the Somerset Levels, has totally destroyed some sites.

The area around the Severn faces potentially the greatest changes as a result of the new Severn crossing, which has inspired a rush of development proposals including retail, industrial and business premises, new link roads and an international airport (Bell 1993). It is important to note that measures to mitigate the impact of developments on the natural environment will have implications for the archaeological resource. Examples of mitigation measures in this region include the creation of alternative bird feeding grounds to replace intertidal areas to be lost to the Cardiff Bay Barrage (Rippon & Turner 1993) and the rehabilitation of wetlands in the Somerset Levels after peat extraction (Cox & Rackham 1993).

In the intertidal zone, natural erosion threatens sites on both open beaches and estuarine shores. These processes present the greatest challenge to archaeological recording in areas such as the Severn Estuary. Landscapes of Romano-British and earlier date are being eroded by storms stripping protective sediments from large areas containing many archaeological features (Bell 1992a). In the Taw-Torridge Estuary the changing course of rivers has similarly cut into palaeo-environmental and man-made sites on the foreshore (McDonnell 1993). This area is also subject to extraction of sand from the intertidal area (Devon County Council 1995).

The influence of human activities on the subtidal resource is poorly understood because so little survey work has been done. The precise effects of, for example, changes in the chemical composition of the environment due to sewage outfall (Larn *et al.* 1974) are as yet unknown. It is clear, however, that some activities, for example dredging for aggregates, salvage diving and fishing with gear that is in contact with the sea bed, can directly damage or destroy sites.

The Lundy Marine Nature Reserve includes the Historic Wrecks *Iona II* and the Gull Rock Wreck, presenting the first opportunity to explore the opportunities for management of wrecks as archaeological sites within a framework of wider controls.

6.3.3 Protection of sites, monuments and wrecks

In England and Wales three statutory designations are intended to protect *in situ* remains of archaeological or historic importance. The Ancient Monuments & Archaeological Areas Act 1979 provides for Scheduled Ancient Monuments (SAMs). The Act's definition of monument includes sites both on land and in UK territorial waters, including remains of vehicles, vessels and aircraft. In practice, however, scheduling has been applied only above low water mark in England and Wales (Firth 1993). There is a presumption against the destruction of SAMs and prior consent is necessary for any works that will destroy, damage, repair or remove such a monument. There is a published list of criteria for determining the national importance of a monument (DoE 1990; Welsh Office 1991). Scheduled sites in the region range from Iron Age hillforts to Medieval fortifications. In 1990, Cornwall had the greatest number of scheduled sites of any English county (Johnson & Rose 1990). The number of scheduled sites is being increased as a result of a review - the Monuments Protection Programme. Table 6.3.1 shows the numbers of coastal SAMs in this region.

The Town & Country Planning (Listed Buildings and Conservation Areas) Act 1990 provides for Listed Buildings - buildings considered of special architectural or historic importance. There is now a presumption in favour of the preservation of Listed Buildings and their settings, and consent is required prior to any demolition, alteration or extension (DoE 1994). Listed buildings in this region include maritime structures such as warehouses, docks and lighthouses.

The Protection of Wreck Act 1973 provides for the designation of shipwrecks of national importance for their artistic, archaeological or historical value. There are no standard criteria for designation but Cadw and the Department of National Heritage (DNH) receive guidance from the Advisory Committee on Historic Wreck. Archaeological investigation is only permitted under licence from DNH. Designation usually applies to an area of sea bed in which the wreck is considered to lie. Within the designated area it is illegal to tamper with or remove material, to use diving or salvage equipment or to deposit anything that may damage or obliterate the wreck

Table 6.3.1 Numbers of Scheduled Ancient Monuments (SAMs) in coastal 10 km squares in the region

Location	*No. of SAMs*	*Location*	*No. of SAMs*
Cornwall	**492**	**Gloucestershire**	**76**
Penwith	244	Stroud	5
Kerrier	124	Gloucester	26
Carrick	26	Tewkesbury	5
Restormel	15	Forest of Dean	40
North Cornwall	83	**Gwent**	**75**
Devon	**99**	Monmouth	27
Torridge	22	Newport	46
North Devon	67	Torfaen	2
Somerset	**80**	**South Glamorgan**	**71**
West Somerset	67	Cardiff	8
Sedgemoor	13	Vale of Glamorgan	63
Avon	**56**	**Mid Glamorgan**	**47**
Woodspring	23	Ogwr	47
Bristol	30	***Region 11***	***996***
Northavon	3		

Source: English Heritage (1994): Cornwall, Devon, Somerset, Avon, Gloucestershire; Cadw (1993): Gwent, South and Mid Glamorgan.

(Archaeological Diving Unit 1994). There are eight Historic Wrecks designated in the region (Table 6.3.2). However, as fewer than 45 wrecks have been designated for the whole of Britain, their distribution cannot be accepted as a reasonable guide to the total sea bed resource (see section 6.4). Sites may be visited on behalf of Cadw or DNH by the Archaeological Diving Unit, which is contracted by DNH to provide field inspection.

6.3.4 Key organisations and their responsibilites

English Heritage and Cadw have responsibility, in England and Wales respectively, for Scheduled Monuments. They schedule and inspect sites, assist owners by drawing up management agreements supported by grants, and directly manage those monuments in Guardianship. They also fund elements of rescue archaeology. The Department of National Heritage (DNH) is responsible for sites protected under the Protection of Wrecks Act (1973). In Wales this responsibility is exercised by Cadw.

The Royal Commission on the Historical Monuments of England (RCHME) and its Welsh counterpart the Royal Commission on the Ancient and Historical Monuments of Wales (RCAHMW) have responsibility for survey and inventory of archaeological sites. They maintain databases of archaeological sites known as National Monuments Records (NMR). In 1992 new Royal Warrants extended their remit to the territorial seas. RCHME has since added a Maritime Section to the NMR, and RCAHMW is developing a comparable facility. The two Commissions are the lead agencies responsible for overseeing data standards in local archaeological databases, the Sites and Mounments Records (SMRs).

The role of SMRs as a source of information for planning authorities was recently confirmed (DoE 1990; Welsh Office 1991). In this region the English County Councils for Devon, Cornwall, Somerset and Gloucestershire and the Unitary Authorities of the former county of Avon maintain SMRs. Cornwall's SMR includes the Isles of Scilly. In Wales the region is covered by the SMR maintained by the Glamorgan Gwent Archaeological Trust. Exmoor National Park has the responsibilities of a local Planning Authority, and the Park Archaeologist uses the SMRs of Cornwall and Devon for development control purposes. The Cornwall SMR includes a number of intertidal and submerged sites for this region, particularly from the Isles of Scilly. The Devon SMR is being extended to include shipwreck sites on the sea bed, in addition to intertidal sites. Reference to published sources has permitted the entry of about 100 known sites for the whole county. The other SMRs have not undertaken recording programmes to extend their records to shipwrecks as a site type, but include incidental entries for the foreshore and estuary.

The increased use of the region's wetlands, whether for peat cutting or development, has revealed both their rich archaeological content and the fragility of the resource. In response, rescue and research activity has intensified and has given rise to a number of organisations. In 1973, following earlier excavations, the Somerset Levels Project was established to provide full-time monitoring of peat cutting. In 1985 the Severn Estuary Levels Research Committee (SELRC) was formed. It aims to coordinate the activities of the many archaeological organisations active in the estuary and to disseminate information about their work.

In recent years closer liaison has been pursued between archaeological and environmental concerns within the

Table 6.3.2 Historic wrecks designated in the region

Site name	*Location*	*Grid ref.*	*Description*	*Designation order*
Tearing Ledge Wreck	Bishop Rock, Isles of Scilly	SV809061	Probably remains of a vessel from Sir Cloudisley Shovell's fleet; wrecked 22/23 October 1707	1975 No. 1 1975/174
Rill Cove Wreck	Rill Cove, Lizard	SW676134	Wreck known from cannon and coins; tentative date 1616	1976 No. 1 1976/203
Bartholemew Ledge Wreck	St. Mary's Sound, Isles of Scilly	SV891095	Unidentified late 16th century wreck	1980 No. 4 1980/1456
St. Anthony	Loe Bar, Mount's Bay	SW649226	Portugese carrack lost 1527	1982 No. 1 1982/47
Schiedam	Gunwalloe Cove	SW654206	Dutch fluyt lost 1684	1982 No. 1 1982/47
Iona II	Lundy	SS150461	Paddle steamer built 1863, lost 1864	1989 No. 2 1989/2294
Gull Rock Wreck	Lundy	SS143463	Unidentified; artefacts from 15th/16th century	1990 No. 1 1990/234
Royal Anne	Stag Rocks, Lizard	SW693114	5th rate warship lost 1721. Last oared fighting ship built for the Royal Navy.	1993 No. 2 1993/2526

Source: Department of Natural Heritage; grid references: RCHME.

wetlands. For example, Somerset County Council has established a Levels and Moors Project, employing both an archaeologist and an ecologist to achieve "a more comprehensive approach to local wetland management" (Cox 1992). On the Welsh side, for example, Cadw and the Countryside Council for Wales are working on a *Historic landscape study of the Gwent Levels*, aimed at assessing their historical importance, ecological value and visual interest, as the basis for formulating a management methodology.

County Archaeological Officers also contribute to integrated management. In Cornwall, for example, information and survey have played a part in initiatives such as the St. Keverne Historic Landscape Countryside Stewardship project, the South West Coastal Path, and the Land's End to Lizard Point Strategic Coastline Study. A specific management plan has been prepared for the archaeology of the Isles of Scilly (Ratcliffe 1990).

6.3.5 Development control

To landward of mean low water mark archaeology is considered within the unified system of development control provided by the planning system. Planning Policy Guidance Note 16 (DoE 1990) explains the regard that should be accorded to archaeological remains. In essence there is a presumption in favour of preservation *in situ,* because "the desirability of preserving an ancient monument and its setting is a material consideration in determining planning applications, whether that monument is scheduled or unscheduled." Stress is laid on early consultation between planning authorities and developers, with information and advice from the SMR, in order to reconcile the needs of archaeology and development. Where preservation *in situ* is not justified, planning authorities may require the developer to make "appropriate and satisfactory provision for excavation and recording of remains." The presumption in favour of preservation *in situ* has been extended to Listed Buildings and their settings (DoE 1994).

Planning decisions should take into account the more detailed policies related to archaeology and historic landscapes contained in Development Plans. For example, the Gwent County Structure Plan has recognised the national importance of the Gwent Levels by designating them 'Special Landscape Areas' (Rippon & Turner 1993). Local Plans of the constituent districts also contain policies. Current research has enabled authorities such as Newport, Northavon and Bristol to include information on the archaeological potential of their areas (Bell 1993). For certain types of development (listed in Schedules 1 and 2 to the Town & Country Planning (Assessment of Environmental Effects) Regulations 1988), formal Environmental Assessments are necessary. The Environmental Assessment should include information on any effects on the cultural heritage, including archaeology. Archaeology is integral to the landscape; a review of the Devon landscape has identified the characteristic features (including archaeological sites and historic settlements) of particular zones, thirteen of which are coastal (Devon County Council 1994).

To seaward of low water mark there is a sectoral approach to development control (DoE 1993). Regulation, including requirement for Environmental Assessment, is divided between a range of government departments and agencies. Until recently, the lack of information on the extent of the resource and the absence of a management structure for archaeology in the subtidal zone had precluded its consideration by many local authorities. However, growing awareness of marine archaeology is leading to voluntary consideration of the archaeological resource. Such practice is encouraged by a new *Code of practice for seabed developers* (Joint Nautical Archaeology Policy Committee 1995).

6.3.6 Reporting archaeological information

The Royal Commission on the Historical Monuments of England (RCHME), the Royal Commission on the Ancient and Historical Monuments of Wales (RCAHMW) and the Sites and Monuments Records (SMRs) are the accepted reporting points for new archaeological information. There is a legal requirement to report archaeological and historical artefacts only when the objects fall within the laws on either Treasure Trove or Salvage. The law of Treasure Trove is used to secure important treasures for the nation (Longworth 1993). Objects of gold or silver found on land must be reported to the police, the coroner, the British Museum (in England) or the National Museum of Wales (in Wales). Should a coroner's inquest then declare the objects Treasure Trove, the British Museum or National Museum of Wales may retain them and, in return, make an *ex gratia* payment to the finder. These museums may waive their rights in favour of another museum.

The Merchant Shipping Act 1894 requires any recovered wreck to be reported to the Receiver of Wreck. Wreck is now defined as any ship, aircraft, hovercraft or parts of these, their cargo, or equipment, found in or on the shores of the sea, or any tidal water. The Receiver provides advice and supplies forms for reporting recovered wreck. These include a form which finders may use to volunteer to the RCHME or the RCAHMW information on the identity and condition of wreck sites. The Receiver advertises reported wreck, regardless of age, in order that owners may claim their property. After one year, unclaimed wreck becomes the property of the Crown and is disposed of in order to pay the expenses of the Receiver and any salvage awards. During the statutory year, such items may be lodged with an appropriate museum or conservation facility with suitable storage conditions. There is a policy of offering unclaimed wreck of historic, archaeological or artistic interest to registered museums. Finders are often allowed to keep unclaimed wreck in lieu of a salvage award. The responsibility of the Receiver to the finder, with regard to salvage awards, remains regardless of the historic character of the wreck.

Information and enquiries concerning either Designated Historic Wrecks or Scheduled Monuments and Listed Buldings should be directed in Wales to Cadw and in England to DNH or English Heritage.

6.4 Information sources

6.4.1 Information gathering and collation

English Heritage and RCHME have commissioned a project, *England's coastal heritage*, which will inform the development of a strategic approach to survey, recording and management. Under the project the Aerial Photographic Unit of RCHME is investigating the feasibility of using aerial photographs for intertidal survey, and Reading University is producing a synthesis of information within the National Monuments Records (NMRs), SMRs and published sources.

Survey in Somerset, Avon, Gloucester and Gwent has been drawn together by the Severn Estuary Levels Research Committee (SELRC), and information is available from their annual reports. The work, which has focused primarily on assessments related to development proposals, has demonstrated that a previous lack of field survey meant that the SMRs contained few sites for areas bordering the estuaries, and the SMRs were, therefore, limited in their ability to truly represent the potential of these locations (Bell 1992a).

On the coast of Devon, recent work at the mouth of the River Parret has highlighted the potential resource, resulting in funding of survey by RCHME (McDonnell 1993).

The Cornwall Archaeological Unit (CAU) have undertaken a number of coastal or partially coastal projects, including surveys of National Trust properties of west Penwith; slate quarries between Trebarwith and Tintagel; the mining district of St. Just; rapid identification for RCHME in the Stratton area; and a historic survey of the Fal Estuary. The Exmoor National Park have undertaken limited survey in some coastal areas, notably an archaeological/ palaeoenvironmental assessment of Porlock Marsh including the intertidal zone. Cornwall Archaeological Unit and English Heritage have undertaken a programme of recording and sampling intertidal peat in the Isles of Scilly.

Intertidal work within the Severn Estuary has focused on Oldbury, Caldicot, Wentlooge and the Gwent Levels. Information is available from SELRC annual reports. Several projects have investigated individual post-Medieval vessels in the intertidal zone. These include the *Louisa* in the Taff at Cardiff and a presumed Severn trow at Lydney (Barker 1992; Williams & Clark undated).

The initial compilation of records for the National Monuments Record - Maritime Section (NMR-MS) was completed by RCHME in 1995. The records have been compiled primarily from the Hydrographic Department Wreck Index, which lists mainly 20th century shipwrecks and unidentified sea-bed obstructions. RCHME has also drawn on lists of shipwrecks compiled by private researchers (Gale 1995). Table 6.4.1 lists records entered in the NMR-MS in October 1994.

Reports by the Cornwall Archaeological Unit from 1989-1994 entitled *Fieldwork in Scilly* (e.g. Ratcliffe & Straker 1996) include descriptions of cliff-face and intertidal recording and sampling. The Silver Jubilee volume of *Cornish Archaeology* (No. 25 1985) contains period-by-period summaries of the current state of knowledge.

Table 6.4.1 Records entered in the National Monuments Record - Maritime Section

County	*Known wrecks*[1]	*Documented casualties*[2]	*Unidentified obstructions*[3]
Cornwall (south coast)	27	303	39
Isles of Scilly	51	559	23
Devon (north coast, inc. Lundy)	77	766	48
Somerset	52	No records	39
Avon	20	No records	36
Bristol Channel	36	No records	7
Gloucestershire	No records	No records	No records

Source: RCHME (October 1994). Key: [1]primarily sites recorded on the Hydrographic Wreck Index; [2]historic records of ship losses; [3]net fasteners etc.

6.4.2 Acknowledgements

Thanks are due to the individuals named and the staff of all the organisations mentioned in the text who gave their time to provide information. The authors are also indebted to Jane Tyson of Reading University, who made available information from the England's Coastal Heritage project.

6.4.3 Further sources of information

A. *References cited*

Allen, J., & Fulford, M. 1992. Roman British and later geoarchaeology at Oldbury Flats: reclamation and settlement on the changeable coast of the Severn Estuary. *Archaeological Journal, 149:* 82-123.

Archaeological Diving Unit. 1994. *Guide to historic wrecks designated under the Protection of Wrecks Act 1973.* St. Andrews, University of St. Andrews.

Barker, R. 1992. A probable clinker-built Severn River trow at Lydney. *International Journal of Nautical Archaeology, 21*(3): 205-208.

Bell, M., *ed.* 1992a. *Annual report of the Severn Estuary Levels Research Committee.* Lampeter, Severn Estuary Levels Research Committee.

Bell, M. 1992b. Field survey and excavation at Goldcliff 1992. *In: Annual report of the Severn Estuary Levels Research Committee,* ed. by M. Bell, 15-29. Lampeter, Severn Estuary Levels Research Committee.

Bell, M., *ed.* 1993. *Annual report of the Severn Estuary Levels Research Committee.* Lampeter, Severn Estuary Levels Research Committee.

British Archaeology. 1995. Welsh monastery found to have Roman origins. *British Archaeology, March 1995,* No. 2. York, Council for British Archaeology.

Cadw. 1993. *Schedule of Ancient Monuments of National Importance in Wales.* Cardiff, Cadw.

Cox, M. 1992. Archaeology in the Somerset Levels and Moors. *In: Annual report of the Severn Estuary Levels Research Committee,* ed. by M. Bell, 63-68. Lampeter, Severn Estuary Levels Research Committee.

Cox, M., & Rackham, J. 1993. Survey of derelict industrial landscape at Shapwick Heath, Somerset. *In: Annual report of the Severn Estuary Levels Research Committee,* ed. by M. Bell, 57-64. Lampeter, Severn Estuary Levels Research Committee.

Department of the Environment. 1990. *Planning Policy Guidance Note (PPG) 16: archaeology and planning.* London, HMSO.

Department of the Environment. 1993. *Development below low water mark. A review of regulations in England and Wales.* London, HMSO.

Department of the Environment. 1994. *Plannning Policy Guidance Note (PPG) 15: planning and the historic environment.* London, HMSO.

Devon County Council. 1994. *Devon landscape: a draft strategy for consultation.* Exeter, Devon County Council.

Devon County Council. 1995. *Devon coastal statement a report for discussion of the principal issues that affect the Devon coastline.* Exeter, Devon County Council.

English Heritage. 1994. *County lists of Scheduled Monuments.* London, English Heritage.

Firth, A. 1993. The management of underwater archaeology. *In: Archaeological resource management in the UK: an introduction,* ed. by J. Hunter & I. Ralston, 65-76. Stroud, Alan Sutton.

Frere, S. 1973. *Britannia.* London, Book Club Associates (by arrangement with Routledge, Kegan Paul).

Gale, A. 1995. A review of *Shipwreck index of the British Isles: Volume I. Isles of Scilly, Cornwall, Devon, Dorset,* by R. & B. Larn. *International Journal of Nautical Archaeology, 24*(3): 237-239.

Hutchinson, G. 1984. A plank fragment from a boat-find from the River Usk at Newport. *International Journal of Nautical Archaeology, 13*(1): 27-32.

Johnson, N., & David, A. 1982. A mesolithic site on Trevose Head and contemporary geography. *Cornish Archaeology, 21:* 67-103.

Johnson, N., & Rose, P. 1990. *Cornwall's archaeological heritage.* Truro, Cornwall Archaeological Unit.

Joint Nautical Archaeology Policy Committee. 1995. *A code of practice for seabed developers.* Swindon, Joint Nautical Archaeology Policy Committee.

Larn, R., McBride, P., & Davis, R. 1974. The mid-17th century merchant ship found near Mullion Cove, Cornwall. *International Journal of Nautical Archaeology, 3*(1): 67-80.

Lawler, M., & Nayling, N. 1993. Investigation at Barland's Farm, Magor, 1993. *In: Annual report of the Severn Estuary Levels Research Committee,* ed. by M. Bell, 109-112. Lampeter, Severn Estuary Levels Research Committee.

Longworth, I. 1993. Portable antiquities. *In: Archaeological resource management in the UK an introduction,* ed. by J. Hunter & I. Ralston, 56-64. Stroud, Alan Sutton.

McDonnell, R. 1993. Preliminary archaeological assessment in Bridgwater Bay: Gore Sand and Stert Flats. *In: Annual report of the Severn Estuary Levels Research Committee,* ed. by M. Bell, 41-46. Lampeter, Severn Estuary Levels Research Committee.

Parry, S., & McGrail, S. 1991. A prehistoric plank boat fragment and a hard from Caldicot Castle lake, Gwent, Wales. *International Journal of Nautical Archaeology, 20*(4): 321-324.

Ratcliffe, J. 1990. *The archaeology of Scilly. Management plan.* Truro, Cornish Archaeological Unit.

Ratcliffe, J. 1992. *Scilly's archaeological heritage.* Truro, Cornish Archaeological Unit.

Ratcliffe, J., & Straker, V. 1996. *The early environment of Scilly: palaeoenvironmental assessment of cliff face and intertidal deposits 1989-1993.* Truro, Cornish Archaeological Unit.

Rippon, S., & Turner, R. 1993. The Gwent Levels Historic Landscape Study. *In: Annual report of the Severn Estuary Levels Research Committee,* ed. by M. Bell, 113-117. Lampeter, Severn Estuary Levels Research Committee.

Welsh Office. 1991. *Planning Policy Guidance Note (PPG) 16: archaeology and planning.* Cardiff, Welsh Office.

Williams, A., & Clark, C. Undated. *A River Severn trow at Lydney, Gloucestershire.* Unpublished report to English Heritage. (Ironbridge Archaeological Series No. 27).

B. Further reading

Breeze, D.J. 1993. Ancient monuments legislation. *In: Archaeology resource management in the UK - an introduction,* ed. by J. Hunter & I. Ralston, 56-65. Stroud, Alan Sutton.

Chaddock, P.T., & Hook, D.R. 1987. Ingots from the sea: the British Museum collection of ingots. *International Journal of Nautical Archaeology, 16*(3): 201-206.

English Heritage/Royal Commission on the Historical Monuments of England. 1996. *England's coastal heritage.* London.

Higgins, L.S. 1993. An investigation into the problems of sand dune areas of the south Wales coast. *Archaeologia Cambrensis, 88:* 26-67.

Shipwrecks are likely to be the most common type of archaeological site in the region, although there are relatively few designated wreck sites. Most known wrecks are of modern vessels, such as this broken hulk at Hartland Point, Devon. Photo: Pat Doody, JNCC.

C. Contact names and addresses

Type of information	*Contact address and telephone no.*
Reporting of recovered wreck	Receiver of Wreck, Coastguard Agency, Spring Place, 105 Commercial Road, Southampton S015 1EG, tel: 01703 329474
England: Scheduled Ancient Monuments; Listed Buildings; designated wreck sites; rescue archaeology; management of monuments in care	Chief Archaeologist, English Heritage, 23 Savile Row, London W1X 2HE, tel: 0171 9733000
England: maritime archaeological sites; code of practice for sea bed developers (published by the Joint Nautical Archaeology Policy)	Head of Recording (Maritime), Royal Commission on the Historical Monuments of England, National Monuments Record Centre, Kemble Drive, Swindon SN2 2GZ, tel: 01793 414600
England: historic wreck sites	The Secretary, The Advisory Committee on Historic Wreck Sites, Department of National Heritage, Room 306, 2-4 Cockspur Street, London SW1Y 5DH, tel: 0171 211 6369 or 6367
England: archaeological sites (general)	National Monuments Record, Royal Commission on the Historical Monuments of England, National Monuments Record Centre, Kemble Drive, Swindon SN2 2GZ, tel: 01793 414600
England: reporting of Treasure Trove	The British Musem, Bloomsbury, London W1 3DG, tel: 0171 323 8629 (Medieval to Present), or 0171 323 8454 (Prehistoric to Romano-British)
Sites & Monuments Record (SMR), Cornwall (including Isles of Scilly)	SMR Officer, Cornwall Archaeological Unit, Cornwall County Council, Old County Hall, Station Road, Truro TR1 3AY, tel: 01872 323603
Sites & Monuments Record (SMR), Devon (including Lundy)	SMR Officer, Environment Department, Devon County Council, County Hall, Exeter EX2 4QW, tel: 01392 382266
Sites & Monuments Record (SMR), Somerset	SMR Officer, Planning Department, Somerset County Council, County Hall, Taunton TA1 4DY, tel: 01823 333451
Sites & Monuments Record (SMR), North Somerset	SMR Officer, Town Hall, Weston-super-Mare, North Somerset BS23 1UJ, tel: 01934 631701
Sites & Monuments Record (SMR), Bristol	City Archaeologist, Urban Design Department, Bristol City Council, Brunel House, Bristol, tel: 0117 922 3044
Sites & Monuments Record (SMR), South Gloucestershire	SMR Officer, c/o Civic Centre, High Street, Kingswood, Bristol, BS15 2TR, tel: 01454 863649
Sites & Monuments Record (SMR), Gloucester	SMR Officer, Environment Department, Gloucestershire County Council, Shire Hall, Gloucester GL1 2TN, tel: 01452 425705/425683
Exmoor National Park archaeology	Archaeologist, Exmoor National Park, Exmoor House, Dulverton, Somerset TA22 9HL, tel: 01398 323665
Archaeological research and survey in the Somerset Levels	Archaeologist, Somerset Levels and Moors Project, Environment Department, Somerset County Council, County Hall, Taunton TA1 4DY, tel: 01823 333451
Archaeological research and survey in the Severn Estuary	Secretary, Severn Estuary Research Committee, c/o Glamorgan-Gwent Archaeological Trust, Ferryside Warehouse, Bath Lane, Swansea, West Glamorgan SA1 1RD, tel: 01792 655208
Wales: statutory body responsible for archaeological conservation; funding of rescue archaeology and survey; designated historic wrecks	Inspector of Ancient Monuments, CADW, Brunel House, 2 Fitzalan Road, Cardiff CF2 1UY, tel: 01222 500200
Wales: National Monuments Enquiry Service, Scheduled Monuments, Listed Buildings	National Monuments Record Archive & Library, Royal Commission on the Historic & Ancient Monuments of Wales, Crown Building, Plas Crug, Aberystwyth, Dyfed SY23 1NJ, tel: 01970 621200
Wales: advice on finds; reporting point for Treasure Trove	National Museum of Wales, Department of Archaeology and Numismatics, Cathays Park, Cardiff CF1 3NP, tel: 01222 397951
Sites & Monuments Record (SMR), Gwent and Glamorgan	SMR Officer, Glamorgan-Gwent Archaeological Trust Ltd, Ferryside Warehouse, Bath Lane, Swansea, West Glamorgan SA1 1RD, tel: 01792 655208

*Starred contact addresses are given in full in the Appendix.

The glorious scenery and the staggering variety of rare plants and animals on the Isle of Scilly have earned them a plethora of conservation designations, including possible Special Area of Conservation (Europe's top protection listing) and Area of Outstanding Natural Beauty. Pictured is a carpet of thrift at Annet Island SSSI. Photo: Peter Wakely, English Nature.

Chapter 7 Coastal protected sites

R.G. Keddie

7.1 Introduction

7.1.1 Chapter structure

This chapter incorporates statutory and non-statutory site protection mechanisms operating at international, national and local level, including those administered by voluntary bodies and other organisations who own land. It covers only the various types of site protection mechanisms currently found within this region, giving a brief explanation for each category. For the purposes of this chapter, any site that is wholly or partly intertidal, and any terrestrial site at least partly within 1 km of the Mean High Water Mark, or any tidal channel as depicted on 1:50,000 Ordnance Survey maps, is included as 'coastal'. Where a site straddles the boundary between two Coastal Directories Project regions and there is no easy way of calculating the percentage of the site lying in each, the site area has been halved, one half being included in each region. National data included in this section have been collated since 1994 and are as up to date as practicable; regional data are correct as at September 1996, unless otherwise stated.

Statutory protected sites are those notified, designated or authorised under European Directives and/or implemented through British legislation (most notably the Wildlife and Countryside Act 1981) by a statutory body, thereby having recognised legal protection. 'Non-statutory sites' include a wide variety of sites not directly protected by legislation but which are recognised by statutory bodies or owned, managed or both by non-statutory organisations for their nature conservation or aesthetic value. Note that the categories of conservation protection (e.g. National Nature Reserve, RSPB Reserve) are not mutually exclusive. In many localities several different types of protected site overlap, since they have been identified for different wildlife and landscape conservation purposes. Patterns of overlap are often complex, since site boundaries for different categories of site are not always the same.

Further explanation of the various site protection mechanisms can be found in Davidson *et al.* (1991). Planning Policy Guidance Note (PPG) 9 - Nature Conservation (DoE 1994) gives useful summaries of existing site protection mechanisms. It also includes copies of the Ramsar Convention, the Birds Directive and the EC Habitats & Species Directive (including lists of important species and habitat types).

The following types of protected site have not been included in this chapter:

- archaeological designations and protected sites (covered in Chapter 6);
- 'Sites of Importance for Nature Conservation' (SINCs): a general term for the variously-named non-statutory sites identified by local authorities and wildlife trusts as having special local value for nature conservation but not currently managed for nature conservation; the most common are Sites of Nature Conservation Importance. For more information, see Collis & Tyldesley (1993);
- sites designated for fisheries purposes, e.g. areas covered by Several Orders and Regulating Orders, which are summarised in Table 7.1.1 and covered in more detail in sections 5.7, 9.1 and 9.2.

Non-site based measures contained in conventions and directives aimed at broad species and habitat protection, such as the Bonn Convention, the Convention on International Trade in Endangered Species of Wild Fauna and Flora (CITES), parts of the EC Birds Directive and parts of the EC Habitats Directive, are also not covered. For further information, see references in section 7.1.3.

This chapter is divided into five sections. A regional summary of all categories of site is given in Table 7.1.1. Section 7.2 covers those site-based protection measures falling under international conventions or European directives. Sites identified under national statute are discussed in section 7.3, whereas section 7.4 covers sites without statutory protection but which are identified, owned or managed by statutory bodies; and finally, other types of site (i.e. those identified, owned or managed by charities, trusts etc.) are described in section 7.5. For each category of protected site, a list of coastal sites is given (clockwise around the coast), showing their type, area/length and location, with an accompanying map. Each section concludes with further information sources and contact points relevant to the region.

7.1.2 Importance of the region

The region contains a large proportion of the coastal Biogenetic Reserves and National Trust-owned coast of Britain – 34.4% and 22.4% respectively by area, 20% and 31.8% by number. Within the region a considerable length of coast is designated as Heritage Coasts (27%), and there is also one of only two designated Marine Nature Reserves in Britain. Table 7.1.1 summarises site protection in the region, showing the numbers and areas of each type of site and comparing these with West Coast and Great Britain coast totals.

Table 7.1.1 Summary of site protection in Region 11

	Number					*Area covered by site protection*				
	Region	*West Coast*	*% of West Coast total in region*	*GB coast*	*% of GB coast total in region*	*Region (ha)*	*West Coast (ha)*	*% of West Coast area in region*	*GB coast (ha)*	*% of GB area in region*
Biosphere Reserves	1	7	14.3	8	12.5	604	21,746	2.8	27,243	2.2
Ramsar sites	4	23	17.4	58	6.9	27,412	114,618	23.9	290,359	9.4
Special Protection Areas	3	39	7.7	93	3.2	24,709	123,243	20.1	306,711	8.1
Possible Special Areas of Conservation	12	63	19.0	112	10.7	n/a[b]	n/a[b]	n/a[b]	n/a[b]	n/a[b]
Environmentally Sensitive Areas	2	10	20.0	17	11.8	87,900	1,118,067	7.9	1,397,545	6.3
Biogenetic Reserves	1	1	100.0	5	20.0	1,300	1,300	100.0	3,777	34.4
National Nature Reserves	4	37	10.8	80	5.0	4,802	51,548	9.32	86,617	5.5
Sites of Special Scientific Interest	157	646	24.3	1,198	13.1	56,005	373,454	15.0	703,844	8.0
Local Nature Reserves	9	25	36.0	94	9.6	693	4,569	15.1	13,300	5.2
Marine Nature Reserve	1	2	50.0	2	50.0	1,390	2,890	48.1	2,890	48.1
Areas of Special Protection	2	9	22.2	23	8.7	n/a[b]	n/a[b]	n/a[b]	n/a[b]	n/a[b]
Areas of Outstanding Natural Beauty	4.5	9.5	47.4	24	18.8	109,100	185,100	58.9	899,900	12.1
National Parks	1	4	25.0	6	16.7	69,300	571,100	12.1	745,000	9.3
Country Parks	4	14	28.6	34	11.8	292.5	1,498	19.6	4,441	6.6
Geological Conservation Review sites	145	510	28.4	1,000	14.5	n/a[a]	n/a[a]	n/a[a]	n/a[a]	n/a[a]
Heritage Coasts	13.5	27.5	49.1	45	30.0	412[c]	890[c]	46.3	1,539[c]	26.8
Sensitive Marine Areas	6.5	10.5	61.9	27	24.1	n/a[b]	n/a[b]	n/a[b]	n/a[b]	n/a[b]
Voluntary Marine Nature Reserves	5	5	100.0	14	38.5	n/a[b]	n/a[b]	n/a[b]	n/a[b]	n/a[b]
National Trust & National Trust for Scotland sites	149	262	56.9	452	33.0	14,363	45,517	31.6	62,974	22.8
Royal Society for the Protection of Birds	3	29	10.3	82	3.7	235	14,125	1.7	38,680	0.6
Wildfowl and Wetlands Trust reserves	1	3	33.3	6	16.7	305	1,113	27.4	1,585	19.2
The Wildlife Trusts reserves	20	95	21.1	217	9.2	227	13,108	1.7	23,420	1.0
Ministry of Defence	7	45	15.6	110	6.4	1,463	18,961	7.7	53,410	2.7
Woodland Trust	10	29	34.5	64	15.6	81.5	363	22.3	1,458	5.6

Source: JNCC. Key: n/a[a] = not applicable; n/a[b] = not available; [c]Heritage Coast data in these columns refer to lengths in kilometres; *some sites lie partly within Region 11; half the area has been included in the total. Notes: site types not currently found in the region: World Heritage (Natural) Sites. In this table any site that is wholly or partly intertidal, and any terrestrial site at least partly within 1 km of the Mean High Water Mark, or any tidal channel as depicted on 1:50,000 Ordnance Survey maps, is included as 'coastal'.

7.1.3 Further sources of information

A. References cited

Collis, I., & Tyldesley, M. 1993. *Natural assets: non-statutory sites of importance for nature conservation.* Newbury, Local Government Nature Conservation Initiative.

Davidson, N.C., Laffoley, D.d'A., Doody, J.P., Way, L.S., Gordon, J., Key, R., Drake, C.M., Pienkowski, M.W., Mitchell, R., & Duff, K.L. 1991. *Nature conservation and estuaries in Great Britain.* Peterborough, Nature Conservancy Council.

Department of the Environment. 1994. *Planning Policy Guidance Note 9 - nature conservation.* London, HMSO.

B. Further reading

Countryside Council for Wales. 1995. *The European Habitats Directive: information booklet.* Bangor, Countryside Council for Wales.

Countryside Council for Wales. 1995. *The European Habitats Directive: Marine Special Areas of Conservation.* Bangor, Countryside Council for Wales.

Doody, J.P., Johnston, C., & Smith, B. 1993. *The directory of the North Sea coastal margin.* Peterborough, Joint Nature Conservation Committee.

English Nature. 1994. *Natura 2000 - European Habitats Directive. European wildlife sites in England.* Peterborough, English Nature.

Gubbay, S. 1988. *A coastal directory for marine conservation.* Ross-on-Wye, Marine Conservation Society.

Hatton, C. 1992. *The Habitats Directive: time for action.* Godalming, WWF-UK (World Wide Fund for Nature).

Hywell-Davies, J., & Thom, V. 1984. *Macmillan's guide to Britain's Nature Reserves.* London, Macmillan.

Marren, P.R. 1994. *England's National Nature Reserves.* Newton Abbott, David & Charles.

7.2 Sites designated under international conventions and directives

This section describes those types of site designated under international conventions to which the UK is a contracting party and sites designated under UK statute to implement EC Directives concerning wildlife and landscape conservation. Sites protected by domestic legislation only are covered in section 7.3.

7.2.1 Biosphere Reserves

Biosphere Reserves are non-statutory protected areas representing significant examples of biomes - terrestrial and coastal environments, throughout the world - protected for conservation purposes. They have particular value as benchmarks or standards for the measurement of long-term changes in the biosphere as a whole. They were devised by UNESCO as Project No. 8 of their Man and the Biosphere (MAB) ecological programme and were launched in 1970. Criteria and guidelines for selection of sites were produced by a UNESCO task force in 1974. All British sites except Braunton Burrows are also National Nature Reserves (section 7.3.1). There is one coastal Biosphere Reserve (604 ha) in Region 11, at Braunton Burrows (Table 7.2.1; Map 7.2.1).

Table 7.2.1 Biosphere Reserves

Site name	*No. of sites*	*Grid ref.*	*Area (ha)*	*Date designated*
Devon				
Braunton Burrows		SS455340	604	1976
Region 11	***1***		***604***	
West Coast	7		21,746	
GB coast	8		27,243	
GB whole country	13		44,258	

Source: JNCC. Note: in this table any site that is wholly or partly intertidal, and any terrestrial site at least partly within 1 km of the Mean High Water Mark, or any tidal channel as depicted on 1:50,000 Ordnance Survey maps, is included as coastal.

7.2.2 Wetlands of international importance (Ramsar sites)

Ramsar sites are statutory areas designated by the UK government on the advice of the conservation agencies under the Ramsar Convention (the Convention on wetlands of international importance especially as waterfowl habitat). Contracting parties (of which the UK is one) are required to designate wetlands of international importance and to promote their conservation and 'wise use'. Ramsar sites are thus designated for their waterfowl populations, their important plant and animal assemblages, their wetland interest or a combination of these. All Ramsar sites have first to be designated as Sites of Special Scientific Interest (SSSIs) (see section 7.3.2). There are four coastal Ramsar sites (27,412 ha) in Region 11 (Table 7.2.2; Map 7.2.1). Table 7.2.2 summarises the interest for which the site has been designated, and sections 5.10, 5.11 and 5.12 describe the importance of these sites for the region's birds. The

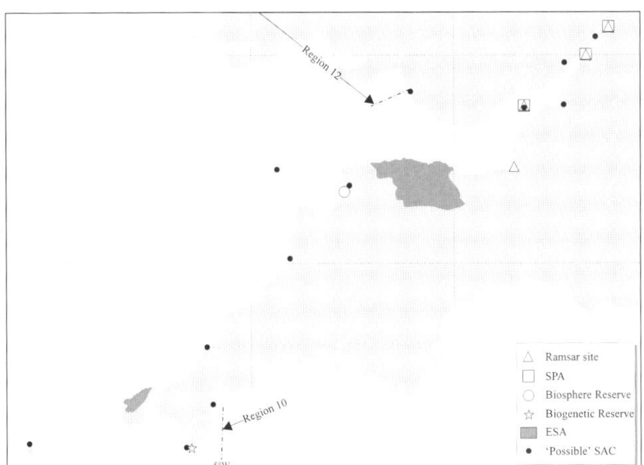

Map 7.2.1 Coastal Biosphere Reserve, Ramsar sites, Special Protection Areas, Environmentally Sensitive Areas, Biogenetic Reserves and 'possible' Special Areas of Conservation. Source: JNCC.

Somerset Levels and Moors, a Ramsar site of particular note, is not 'coastal' by the definition used in this chapter and is therefore excluded from this section.

7.2.3 Special Protection Areas

The 1979 EC Directive on the Conservation of Wild Birds (the Birds Directive) requires member states to take conservation measures particularly for certain rare or vulnerable species and for regularly occurring migratory species of birds. In part this is achieved through the designation of statutory Special Protection Areas (SPAs) by the UK government on the advice of the statutory conservation agencies. This designation is implemented through the Wildlife & Countryside Act 1981; all SPAs have first to be notified as SSSIs. There are three coastal SPAs (24,709 ha) in Region 11 (Table 7.2.3; Map 7.2.1). Table 7.2.3 summarises the interest of these sites, and sections 5.10, 5.11 and 5.12 describe the importance of these sites for the region's birds. The Somerset Levels and Moors, an SPA of particular note, is not 'coastal' by the definition used in this chapter and is therefore excluded from this section.

7.2.4 Special Areas of Conservation

The designation of Special Areas of Conservation (SACs) is one of the main mechanisms by which the EC Habitats & Species Directive 1992 will be implemented. SACs are areas identified as outstanding examples of selected habitat types or areas important for the continued well-being or survival of selected non-bird species. The protection measures are based around a series of six annexes: Annexes I and II list the habitats and species that require the designation of SACs; Annex IV prohibits the taking of certain species; Annex V requires the taking of certain species to be monitored; and Annex VI prohibits some means of capture or killing of mammals and fish. In the UK the Directive will be implemented through the Conservation (Natural

Table 7.2.2 Ramsar sites

Site name	*No. of sites*	*Grid ref.*	*Area (ha)*	*Date designated*	*Qualifying interest*
Somerset	1				
Bridgwater Bay*		ST290480	2,703	1976	1% of a waterfowl species population
Somerset/Avon/Gloucestershire/South Glamorgan/Mid Glamorgan/Gwent	1				
Severn Estuary		ST480830	23,301	1995	Representative wetland; 1% of a waterfowl species population
Gloucestershire	2				
Upper Severn Estuary*		SO7106	1,357	1988	Representative wetland; 1% of a waterfowl species population
Walmore Common		SO745150	51	1991	1% of a waterfowl species population
Region 11	4		***27,412****		
West Coast	23		114,618**		
GB coast	58		290,359**		
GB whole country	99		304,527**		

Sources: JNCC, English Nature. Key: *lies entirely within Severn Estuary Ramsar Site, but retains its separate designation; **includes areas of all Ramsar designations, whether or not they relate to discrete areas. Note: in this table any site that is wholly or partly intertidal, and any terrestrial site at least partly within 1 km of the Mean High Water Mark, or any tidal channel as depicted on 1:50,000 Ordnance Survey maps, is included as 'coastal'.

Table 7.2.3 Special Protection Areas (SPAs)

Site name	*No. of sites*	*Grid ref.*	*Area (ha)*	*Date designated*	*Qualifying interest*
Somerset/Avon/Gloucestershire/South Glamorgan/Mid Glamorgan/Gwent	1				
Severn Estuary		ST480830	23,301	1995	Internationally or nationally important numbers of sixteen species of wintering and migrating waterfowl; nationally important numbers of breeding shelduck *Tadorna tadorna* and lesser black-backed gull *Larus fuscus*; regularly supports over 20,000 waterfowl
Gloucestershire	2				
Upper Severn Estuary*		SO7106	1,357	1988	Internationally or nationally important numbers of sixteen species of wintering and migrating waterfowl; nationally important numbers of breeding shelduck and lesser black-backed gull; regularly supports over 20,000 waterfowl
Walmore Common		SO745150	51	1991	Internationally important numbers of wintering Bewick's swan *Cygnus columbianus bewickii*
Region 11	3		***24,709****		
West Coast	39		123,243**		
GB coast	93		306,711**		
GB whole country	124		439,663**		

Sources: JNCC, English Nature. Key: *lies entirely within Severn Estuary SPA, but retains its separate designation; **includes areas of all SPA designations, whether or not they relate to discrete areas. Note: in this table any site that is wholly or partly intertidal, and any terrestrial site at least partly within 1 km of the Mean High Water Mark, or any tidal channel as depicted on 1:50,000 Ordnance Survey maps, is included as coastal.

Habitats etc.) Regulations 1994. A list of 'possible' SACs was announced by the Government on 31 March 1995. There are twelve 'possible' SACs proposed for Region 11 (Table 7.2.4; Map 7.2.1) (see JNCC (1995) for more information).

7.2.5 Environmentally Sensitive Areas

European Community authorisation for Environmentally Sensitive Areas (ESAs) is derived from Article 19 of Council Regulation (EEC) No. 797/85 - National Aid in Environmentally Sensitive Areas. ESAs are statutory areas in which the Government seeks to encourage environmentally sensitive farming practices, prevent damage that might result from certain types of agricultural intensification, and restore traditional landscapes, for which member states are allowed to make payments to farmers. There are two ESAs (87,900 ha) that include land in Region 11 (Table 7.2.5; Map 7.2.1).

7.2.6 Biogenetic Reserves

In 1973 the European Ministerial Conference on the Environment recommended that a European network of reserves to conserve representative examples of European

Table 7.2.4 Possible Special Areas of Conservation (SACs) in Region 11

Site name	*No. of sites*	*Qualifying interest*
Isles of Scilly	1	
Isles of Scilly Complex		Shore dock *Rumex rupestris;* mudflats and sandflats not covered by seawater at low tide; sandbanks which are slightly covered by sea water all the time
Cornwall	3	
Fal and Helford		Shore dock; Atlantic salt meadows (Glauco-Puccinellietalia); large shallow inlets and bays; mudflats and sandflats not covered by seawater at low tide; sandbanks which are slightly covered by sea water all the time
The Lizard		Shore dock; dry coastal heaths with Cornish heath *Erica vagans* and gorse *Ulex maritimus*; hard oligo-mesotrophic waters with benthic vegetation of stoneworts *Chara* spp. formations; Mediterranean temporary ponds; Northern Atlantic wet heaths with cross-leaved heath *Erica tetralix;* vegetated sea cliffs of the Atlantic and Baltic coasts
Penhale Dunes		Petalwort *Petalophyllum ralfsii;* shore dock; dunes with woolly willow *Salix arenaria;* embryonic shifting dunes; fixed dunes with herbaceous vegetation (grey dunes)
Cornwall/Devon	1	
Tintagel-Marsland-Clovelly Coast		Vegetated sea cliffs of the Atlantic and Baltic coasts
Devon	2	
Lundy		Reefs
Braunton Burrows		Petalwort; dunes with woolly willow; embryonic shifting dunes; fixed dunes with herbaceous vegetation (grey dunes); humid dune slacks; shifting dunes along the shoreline with marram *Ammophila arenaria* (white dunes)
Somerset/Avon/Gloucestershire/ Gwent/South Glamorgan	1	
Severn Estuary / Mor Hafren		Sandbanks which are slightly covered by sea water all the time; Atlantic salt meadows; estuaries; mudflats and sandflats not covered by seawater at low tide
Avon	1	
Avon Gorge Woodlands		Tilio-Acerion ravine forests
Gloucestershire/Gwent	2	
Wye Valley and Forest of Dean Bat Sites / Safleoe dd Ystlumod Dyffryn Gwy a Fforest Ddena		Greater horseshoe bat *Rhinolophus ferrumequinum*, lesser horseshoe bat *R. hipposideros*
Wye Valley Woodlands / Coetiroedd Dyffryn Gwy		Asperulo-Fagetum beech forests; yew *Taxus baccata* woods; Tilio-Acerion ravine forests
Mid Glamorgan	1	
Kenfig / Cynffig		Fen orchid *Liparis loeselii*; petalwort; dunes with woolly willow; fixed dunes with herbaceous vegetation (grey dunes); humid dune slacks
Region 11	**12**	
West Coast	63	
GB	112	

Source: JNCC. Note: in this table any site that is wholly or partly intertidal, and any terrestrial site at least partly within 1 km of the Mean High Water Mark, or any tidal channel as depicted on 1:50,000 Ordnance Survey maps, is included as coastal.

Table 7.2.5 Environmentally Sensitive Areas

Site name	*No. of sites*	*Area (ha)*	*Date designated*	*Interest*
Cornwall	1			
West Penwith		7,200	1987	Historic intricate arrangement of stone-hedged fields and stone-walled homesteads; prehistoric settlements; small fields, maritime grassland, cliffs and heathland
Cornwall/Devon	1			
Exmoor		80,700	1993	Open heath and grass moor provide habitat for rare birds and red deer. Steep-sided wooded river valleys bisect moor; also enclosed grassland fields, coastal heath, high beech hedges. 19th century archaeological interest.
Region 11	2	***87,900***		
West Coast	10	1,118,067		
GB coast	17	1,397,545		

Sources: JNCC, English Nature. Note: in this table any site that is wholly or partly intertidal, and any terrestrial site at least partly within 1 km of the Mean High Water Mark, or any tidal channel as depicted on 1:50,000 Ordnance Survey maps, is included as coastal.

flora, fauna and natural areas be established. All sites in the UK are existing Sites of Special Scientific Interest (SSSIs), and most are also National Nature Reserves (NNRs). All five of the coastal Biogenetic Reserves in Britain are designated for their heathland interest. There is one Biogenetic Reserve (1,300 ha) in Region 11, at The Lizard (Table 7.2.6; Map 7.2.1). In 1992 there were eighteen sites declared in Europe (DoE 1992): eleven heathland and seven dry grassland reserves (data provided by International Branch, JNCC).

Table 7.2.6 Biogenetic Reserves

Site name	*No. of sites*	*Grid ref.*	*Area (ha)*	*Date designated*
Cornwall	1			
The Lizard		SW7012	1,300	1992
Region 11	*1*		***1,300***	
West Coast	1		1,300	
GB coast	5		3,777	

Sources: JNCC, English Nature. Note: in this table any site that is wholly or partly intertidal, and any terrestrial site at least partly within 1 km of the Mean High Water Mark, or any tidal channel as depicted on 1:50,000 Ordnance Survey maps, is included as coastal.

7.2.7 Acknowledgements

Thanks are due to Alan Law (JNCC), Biotopes and International Policy Branches (JNCC), Siâron Hooper (English Nature), WOAD and the Ministry of Agriculture, Fisheries and Food (MAFF) for information used in this section. Thanks also go to R. Aston, Forest of Dean District Council, and Charlotte Pagendam, English Nature, for their helpful comments.

7.2.8 Further sources of information

A. References cited

Joint Nature Conservation Committee. 1995. *Council Directive on the Conservation of natural habitats and wild fauna and flora (92/43/EEC) - the Habitats Directive: a list of possible Special Areas of Conservation in the UK. List for consultation (31 March 1995).* Peterborough (unpublished report to the Department of the Environment).

B. Further reading

Countryside Council for Wales. 1994. *Marine Special Areas of Conservation in Wales.* Bangor, Countryside Council for Wales.

Department of the Environment. 1995. *The Habitats Directive: how it will apply in Great Britain.* London, Department of Environment, Scottish Office and the Joint Nature Conservation Committee.

Department of the Environment. 1996. *European marine sites in England and Wales. A guide to the Conservation (Natural Habitats &C.) Regulations 1994 and to the preparation and application of management schemes.* London, Department of Environment and The Welsh Office. (Draft for consultation.)

English Nature. 1994. *Marine Special Areas of Conservation.* Peterborough, English Nature.

Goodier, R., & Mayne, S. 1988. United Kingdom Biosphere Reserves: opportunities and limitations. *Ecos, 9:* 33-39.

Gubbay, S. 1988. *A coastal directory for marine conservation.* Ross-on-Wye, Marine Conservation Society.

IUCN. 1979. *The Biosphere Reserve and its relationship with other protected areas.* Morges, International Union for the Conservation of Nature and Natural Resources.

L'Hyver-Yésou, M.-A. 1993. Biogenetic Reserves. *Naturopa, 71:* 22-23.

Ministry of Agriculture, Fisheries and Food. 1989. *Environmentally Sensitive Areas.* London, HMSO.

Nature Conservancy Council. 1988. *Internationally important wetlands and Special Protection Areas for birds.* Peterborough, Nature Conservancy Council.

Pritchard, D.E., Housden, S.D., Mudge, G.P., Galbraith, C.A., & Pienkowski, M.W., *eds.* 1992. *Important bird areas in the UK including the Channel Islands and the Isle of Man.* Sandy, Royal Society for the Protection of Birds.

Stroud, D.A., Mudge, G.P., & Pienkowski, M.W. 1990. *Protecting internationally important bird sites. A review of the EEC Special Protection Area network in Great Britain.* Peterborough, Nature Conservancy Council.

Von Droste, B., & Gregg, W.P. 1985. Biosphere Reserves: demonstrating the value of conservation in sustaining society. *Parks, 10:* 2-5.

C. Contact names and addresses

Type of information	*Contact address and telephone no.*
Biosphere Reserve, Environmentally Sensitive Areas (Devon)	*Conservation Officer, English Nature Devon and Cornwall Local Team, Okehampton, tel: 01837 55045
Special Areas of Conservation, Biogenetic Reserves, Environmentally Sensitive Areas (Cornwall, Isles of Scilly)	*Conservation Officer, English Nature Devon and Cornwall Local Team, Truro, tel: 01872 262550
Ramsar site, SPAs, Special Areas of Conservation (Avon, Somerset)	*Conservation Officer, English Nature Somerset and Avon Local Team, Taunton, tel: 01823 283211
Ramsar sites, SPAs, Special Areas of Conservation (Gloucestershire)	*Conservation Officer, English Nature Three Counties Local Team, Worcestershire, tel: 01684 560616
Ramsar sites, SPAs, Special Areas of Conservation (South Glamorgan, Mid Glamorgan, Gwent)	*Senior Officer, CCW, South Wales Area Office, Cardiff, tel: 01222 772400
Ramsar sites, SPAs (Somerset)	*Regional Officer, RSPB, South-West England Office, Exeter, tel: 01392 432691
Ramsar sites, SPAs (Gloucestershire)	*Regional Officer, RSPB, Central Office, Banbury, tel: 01295 253330
Environmentally Sensitive Areas	MAFF / ADAS Land Service, Ministry of Agriculture, Fisheries and Food, Whitehall Place, London SW1A 2HH, tel: 0171 270 3000
Special Areas of Conservation	*European Wildlife Division, DoE, Bristol, tel: 0117 987 8000

*Starred contact addresses are given in full in the Appendix.

7.3 Sites established under national statute

Included in this section are the types of site identification made under national legislation relating to wildlife, landscape and amenity value. Identifications are made by the statutory conservation agencies (in this region English Nature and the Countryside Council for Wales), local authorities or the government acting on advice from these bodies.

7.3.1 National Nature Reserves

National Nature Reserves (NNRs) contain examples of some of the most important natural and semi-natural ecosystems in Great Britain. They are managed to conserve their habitats, providing special opportunities for scientific study of the habitats, communities and species represented within them (Marren 1994). They are declared by the country agencies under section 19 of the National Parks and Access to the Countryside Act 1949 or section 35 of the Wildlife and Countryside Act 1981. All NNRs are also Sites of Special Scientific Interest (SSSIs). There are four coastal NNRs (5,406 ha) in Region 11 (Table 7.3.1; Map 7.3.1).

7.3.2 Sites of Special Scientific Interest

Sites of Special Scientific Interest (SSSIs) are notified under the Wildlife & Countryside Act 1981. They are intended to form a national network of areas, representing in total the parts of Britain in which the natural features, especially those of greatest value to wildlife conservation, are most highly concentrated or of highest quality. Each SSSI represents a significant fragment of the much-depleted resource of wild nature remaining in Britain. Within the area of an SSSI the provisions of the Wildlife & Countryside Act 1981 and its 1985 amendments aim to limit or prevent operations that are potentially damaging to the wildlife interest of the area. There are 157 coastal SSSIs (56,005 ha) in Region 11 (Table 7.3.2; Map 7.3.1). 8.2% of the total land mass of Britain is SSSI, as at March 1995.

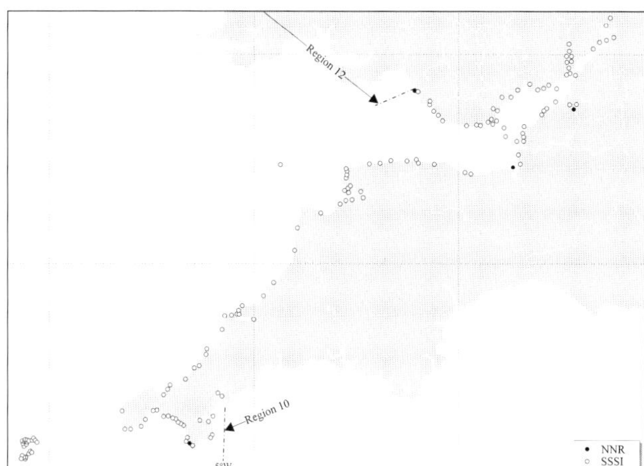

Map 7.3.1 Coastal National Nature Reserves and Sites of Special Scientific Interest. Source: English Nature, CCW, JNCC. Note: a single symbol may represent more than one site in close proximity.

Of the 157 coastal SSSIs in the region, over half (52.8%) include intertidal land to mean low water mark, while around one quarter (24.2%) are purely terrestrial. Nearly three-quarters were selected at least partly for their biological interest and over one half at least partly for their geological or geomorphological interest. Of the total, almost one quarter have both biological and earth science interest. Examples of a very wide range of habitats and species occur within the SSSIs in this region, the most frequently occurring habitats being sand dunes, hard sea cliffs, dry grassland, maritime heath and woodland, these habitats occurring in 17-45% of sites. SSSIs in the region include many sites of interest for their rare higher and lower plants, terrestrial invertebrates and breeding seabirds. Further details of SSSIs may be found in the coastal and marine UKDMAP datasets module disseminated by JNCC Coastal Conservation Branch (BODC 1992; Barne *et al.* 1994).

Table 7.3.1 National Nature Reserves

Site name	*No. of sites*	*Grid ref.*	*Area (ha)*	*Date last declared/ extended*	*Habitats*
Cornwall	1				
Lizard		SW715218	1,662	1994	Serpentine heath, coastal grassland and cliffs
Somerset	1				
Bridgwater Bay		ST267475	2,559	1974	Mudflats, saltmarsh, grazing marsh, islands
Avon	1				
Avon Gorge		ST560738	63	1970	Mature woodland, scrub, limestone grassland and crags
Mid Glamorgan	1				
Kenfig Pools and Dunes		SS780820	518	1989	Open, vegetated and wooded dunes, dune slacks, reed fringed pool, marsh and wet woodland
Region 11	*4*		***4,802***		
West Coast	37		51,548		
GB coast	80		86,617		
GB whole country	289		195,440		

Sources: English Nature, Countryside Council for Wales, JNCC. Note: in this table any site that is wholly or partly intertidal, and any terrestrial site at least partly within 1 km of the Mean High Water Mark, or any tidal channel as depicted on 1:50,000 Ordnance Survey maps, is included as coastal.

Table 7.3.2 SSSIs in Region 11

Site name	No. of sites	Grid ref.	Area (ha)	Date last notified
Cornwall	**30**			
Upper Fal Estuary & Woods		SW850410	603	1996
Malpas Estuary		SW835430	73	1986
Rosemullion		SW795281	21	1990
Merthen Wood		SW730263	72	1986
Meneage coastal section		SW777261	80	1994
Main Dale		SW785200	32	1987
Coverack to Porthoustock		SW785189-SW808218	159	1993
Coverack Cove & Dolor Point		SW783185-SW785181	6	1992
Kennack to Coverack		SW733164-SW783178	266	1993
Caerthillian to Kennack		SW695124-SW732164	141	1993
Kynance Cove		SW690130	30	1986
West Lizard		SW685174	777	1995
Mullion Cliff to Predannack Cliff		SW660164	65	1986
Baulk Head to Mullion		SW654223	152	1995
Loe Pool		SW647250	129	1986
Porthleven Cliffs East		SW634250	17	1990
Wheal Penrose		SW634252	1	1993
Porthleven Cliffs		SW623257	9	1986
Tremearne Par		SW610266	15	1992
Porthcew		SW593270	10	1990
Folly Rocks		SW573280	2	1990
Cudden Point to Prussia Cove		SW553278	16	1991
St. Michael's Mount		SW515298	3	1995
Marazion Marsh		SW515318	60	1985
Penlee Point		SW473269	2	1990
Tater-Du		SW440231	5	1992
Treen Cliff		SW395224	49	1986
Porthgwarra to Pordenack Point		SW371217	158	1986
Cape Cornwall to Clodgy Point		SW353313	343	1968
Aire Point to Carrick Du		SW360279	705	1995
Isles of Scilly	**23**			
White Island		SV925176	17	1989
Plains & Great Bay		SV924163	15	1986
Chapel Down		SV942159	35	1986
Eastern Isles		SV947144	84	1986
Porth Seal		SV918166	7	1989
Tean		SV909166	121	1986
Great Pool		SV894146	17	1986
Pool of Bryher & Popplestone Bank		SV875148	6	1986
Rushy Bay & Heathy Hill		SV874142	12	1986
Samson		SV878125	39	1986
Norrand Rocks		SV860135	36	1986
Shipman Head & Shipman Down		SV877158	41	1986
Castle Down		SV885160	58	1986
St. Helens (Northwethel & Men-A-Vaur)		SV900170	27	1986
Pentle Bay, Merrick & Round Islands		SV901141	43	1995
Higher Moors & Porth Hellick Pool		SV924108	16	1987
Lower Moors		SV912106	10	1986
Peninnis Head		SV911094	16	1989
Gugh		SV890083	38	1986
Wingletang Down		SV884075	29	1986
Big Pool & Browarth Point		SV879087	10	1986
Annet		SV862088	120	1986
Western Rocks		SV850070	63	1986
Cornwall	**22**			
Hayle Estuary & Carrack Gladden		SW550370	166	1984
Gwithian to Mexico Towans		SW570395	371	1987
Godrevy Head to St. Agnes		SW582423	627	1989
Nance Wood		SW665450	10	1984
St. Agnes Beacon Pits		SW705510	8	1986
Trevaunance Cove		SW723517	7	1993
Cligga Head		SW725521	111	1986
Penhale Dunes		SW771572	10,704	1986
Kelsey Head		SW775600	228	1986
Bedruthan Steps & Park Head		SW850700	81	1986
Trevose Head & Constantine Bay		SW858753	159	1986
Trevone Bay		SW889763	9	1990
Stepper Point		SW915783	2	1990
Harbour Cove		SW915768	29	1988
Rock Dunes		SW926765	68	1986
Amble Marshes		SW994746	57	1986
Trebetherick Point		SW925780	21	1986
Pentire Peninsula		SW934798	114	1986
Tintagel Cliffs		SX042857	222	1988
Boscastle to Widemouth		SX092916	639	1990
Bude Coast		SS200069	93	1987
Steeple Point to Marsland Mouth		SS212174	343	1987
Devon	**19**			
Marsland to Clovelly Coast		SS212175-SS315254	952	1993
Hobby to Peppercombe		SS320242	241	1986
Lundy		SS135460	345	1987
Westward Ho! Cliffs		SS420291	33	1985
Northam Burrows		SS445305	423	1988
Taw-Torridge Estuary		SS470310	1,337	1988
Fremington Claypits		SS530315	4	1985
Fremington Quay Cliffs		SS517340	11	1988
Braunton Burrows		SS430350	1,357	1986
Greenways & Freshwater Marsh		SS464353	14	1988
Braunton Swanpool		SS471368	12	1988
Saunton to Baggy Point Coast		SS447408	153	1986
Mill Rock		SS455431	0.2	1989
Barricane Beach		SS453443	8	1989
Morte Point		SS450455	99	1986
Napps Cave		SS563475	12	1986
West Exmoor Coast & Woods		SS665495	710	1986
Watersmeet		SS745487	349	1986
Glenthorne		SS794499	13	1989
Somerset	**11**			
Exmoor Coastal Heaths		SS620480; SS750500; SS800485; SS920480	1,758	1994
Porlock Marsh		SS880479	165	1990
Blue Anchor to Lilstock Coast		ST033435	743	1986
Cleeve Hill		ST056428	15	1989
North Moor		ST325305	676	1986
Curry & Hay Moors		ST323273	473	1992
Southlake Moor		ST370300	196	1985
Langmead & Weston Level		ST353330 & ST365335	169	1991
Bridgwater Bay		ST290480	1,594	1989
Brean Down		ST290590	65	1984
Berrow Dunes		ST293520	200	1986

Table 7.3.2 SSSIs in Region 11 (continued)

Site name	*No. of sites*	*Grid ref.*	*Area (ha)*	*Date last notified*
Avon	12			
Steep Holm		ST228607	26	1983
Uphill Cliff		ST318583	20	1984
Ellenborough Park West		ST319608	2	1989
Spring Cove Cliffs		ST310625	2	1986
Middle Hope		ST322659	95	1986
Clevedon Shore		ST402719	0	1991
Holly Lane		ST418727	1	1990
Walton Common		ST428738	26	1991
Portishead Pier to Black Nore		ST474778	72	1986
Ham Green		ST539758	1	1990
Avon Gorge		ST560743	155	1988
Aust Cliff		ST565894	5	1986
Somerset/Avon/ Gloucestershire/Gwent/ South Glamorgan	1			
Severn Estuary		ST480830	15,950	1989
Gloucestershire	13			
Purton Passage		SO687045	5	1986
Upper Severn Estuary		SO720060	1,437	1987
Frampton Pools		SO753073	60	1984
Walmore Common		SO740162	58	1984
Garden Cliff		SO718128	5	1986
Lydney Cliff		SO654020	8	1990
Caerwood, Tidenham		ST547965	0.1	1991
Shorn Cliff & Caswell Woods		SO540005	69	1986
Lower Wye Gorge		ST548983	29	1987
The Hudnalls		SO540042	94	1987
Pennsylvania Fields		ST542929	27	1985
Sylvan Barn		SO534023	0.01	1995
River Wye		ST542900	*	1978
Gwent	8			
Pierce, Alcove & Piercefield Woods		ST530958	177	1983
Gwent (continued)				
Blackcliff-Wyndcliff		ST531979	119	1983
Bushy Close		ST510889	4	1982
Gwent Levels: Magor & Undy		ST440860	587	1989
Gwent Levels: Redwick & Llandevenny		ST410855	940	1989
Gwent Levels: Whitson		ST390840	937	1988
Gwent Levels: Nash & Goldcliff		ST350850	954	1987
Gwent Levels: St. Brides		ST290825	1,322	1991
South Glamorgan	14			
Gwent Levels: Rhymney & Peterstone		ST250800	486	1993
Rhymney River Section		ST209789	2	1983
Flat Holm		ST220649	24	1983
Taf/Ely Estuary		ST185735	165	1983
Cwm Cydfin, Leckwith		ST165739	6	1983
Penarth Coast		ST189681	93	1983
Cosmeston Park		ST173693	46	1985
Sully Island		ST167670	12	1986
Hayes Point to Bendrick Rock		ST138671	30	1996
Barry Island		ST110662	16	1990
Cliff Wood - Golden Stairs		ST091670	13	1986
East Aberthaw Coast		ST042658	68	1983
Nash Lighthouse Meadow		SS920680	2	1982
Monknash Coast		SS903705	131	1983
Mid Glamorgan	4			
Southerndown Coast		SS884731	62	1983
Sutton Flats		SS860756	32	1990
Merthyr Mawr Warren		SS861768	344	1983
Kenfig Pool & Dunes		SS790820	627	1983
Region 11	157		56,005	
West Coast	646		373,454	
GB coast	1,198		703,844	
GB whole country	6,097		1,941,833	

Sources: English Nature, JNCC. Key: *no area available: river length 416 km. Note: in this table any site that is wholly or partly intertidal, and any terrestrial site at least partly within 1 km of the Mean High Water Mark, or any tidal channel as depicted on 1:50,000 Ordnance Survey maps, is included as coastal.

7.3.3 Local Nature Reserves

Local Nature Reserves (LNRs) are designated by local authorities, under section 21 of the National Parks and Access to the Countryside Act 1949, for the same purposes as NNRs, but because of the local rather than the national interest of the site and its wildlife. Under this Act local authorities have the power to issue bylaws to protect the LNR. There are nine LNRs (693 ha) in Region 11 (Table 7.3.3; Map 7.3.2).

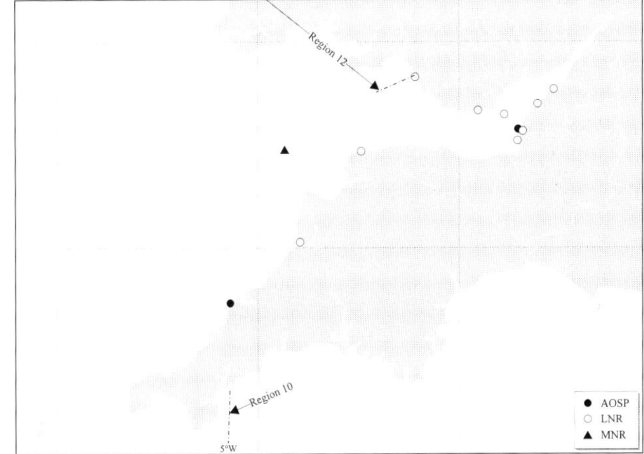

Map 7.3.2 Coastal Local Nature Reserves, Areas of Special Protection and Marine Nature Reserves. Source: English Nature, CCW, DOE.

7.3.4 Marine Nature Reserves

Marine Nature Reserves (MNRs) are created by statute (under the Wildlife & Countryside Act 1981) to conserve marine flora and fauna and geological or physiographical features of special interest, while providing opportunities for study of the systems involved. MNRs may be established within 3 nautical miles of the coast under the Territorial Seas Act 1987 or, by an Order in Council, to the limits of UK territorial waters; they include both the sea and the sea bed. MNRs can be protected by bylaws. There is one Marine Nature Reserve in Region 11 – Lundy (1,390 ha), off the north Devon coast (Table 7.3.4; Map 7.3.2).

Table 7.3.3 Local Nature Reserves

Site name	*No. of sites*	*Grid ref.*	*Area (ha)*	*Date of declaration*
Cornwall	1			
Bude Marshes		SS208056	6	1983
Devon	1			
Hillsborough		SS533478	17	1993
Somerset	1			
Berrow Dunes		ST293538	14	1993
Avon	3			
Uphill Down & Quarry		ST317583	17	1988
Poet's Walk, Clevedon		ST393708	9	1993
Eastwood & Battery Point, Portishead		ST470777	12	1993
South Glamorgan	2			
Flat Holm Island		ST220649	38	1977
Cliff Wood		ST091670	5	1970
Mid Glamorgan	1			
Kenfig Pool and Dunes		SS790820	575	1978
Region 11	*9*		*693*	
West Coast	25		4,569	
GB coast	94		13,300	
GB whole country	396		21,513	

Sources: English Nature, Countryside Council for Wales. Note: in this table any site that is wholly or partly intertidal, and any terrestrial site at least partly within 1 km of the Mean High Water Mark, or any tidal channel as depicted on 1:50,000 Ordnance Survey maps, is included as coastal.

Table 7.3.4 Lundy Marine Nature Reserve (MNR)

Site name	*No. of sites*	*Grid ref.*	*Area (ha)*	*Date designated*
Devon	1			
Lundy		SS135460	1,390	1986
Region 11	*1*		*1,390*	
West Coast	2		2,890	
GB coast	2		2,890	

Source: English Nature. Note: in this table any site that is wholly or partly intertidal, and any terrestrial site at least partly within 1 km of the Mean High Water Mark, or any tidal channel as depicted on 1:50,000 Ordnance Survey maps, is included as coastal.

Table 7.3.5 Areas of Special Protection (AoSPs)

Site name	*No. of sites*	*Date designated*
Cornwall	1	
Trethias Island (No. 2144)		1960
Somerset	1	
Brean Down (No. 562)		1968
Region 11	*2*	
West Coast	9	
GB coast	23	
GB whole country	38	

Source: DOE European Wildlife Division. Note: in this table any site that is wholly or partly intertidal, and any terrestrial site at least partly within 1 km of the Mean High Water Mark, or any tidal channel as depicted on 1:50,000 Ordnance Survey maps, is included as coastal.

7.3.5 Areas of Special Protection

'Area of Special Protection' (AoSP) is a designation replacing Bird Sanctuary Orders made under the 1954 to 1967 Protection of Birds Acts, which were repealed and amended under the Wildlife & Countryside Act 1981. Designation aims to prevent the disturbance and destruction of the birds for which the area is identified, by making it unlawful to damage or destroy either the birds or their nests and in some cases by prohibiting or restricting access to the site. There are two AoSPs in Region 11 (Table 7.3.5; Map 7.3.2).

7.3.6 Areas of Outstanding Natural Beauty

The primary purpose of the Area of Outstanding Natural Beauty (AONB) designation is to conserve natural beauty, but account is taken of the need to safeguard agriculture, forestry and other rural industries, and of the economic and social needs of local communities (Countryside Commission 1994). AONBs are designated, in England by the Countryside Commission and in Wales by the Countryside Commission for Wales, under the National Parks and Access to the Countryside Act 1949. There are four whole and part of one other AONB (109,100 ha) in Region 11 (Table 7.3.6; Map 7.3.3). In 1995 the total area covered by AONBs was just over 14% of the countryside of England and Wales.

7.3.7 National Parks

The purpose of National Parks is to preserve and enhance the most beautiful, dramatic and spectacular expanses of countryside in England and Wales (Countryside Commission 1993), while promoting public enjoyment of them, and having regard for the social and economic well-being of those living within them. National Parks in England and Wales were designated by the National Parks Commission and confirmed by the Government between 1951 and 1957, and one area with similar status, The Broads, was established in 1989. The Countryside Commission (England) and the Countryside Council for Wales advise government on National Parks, each of which is administered by a Park Authority. There is one National Park (69,300 ha) in Region 11 (Table 7.3.7; Map 7.3.3).

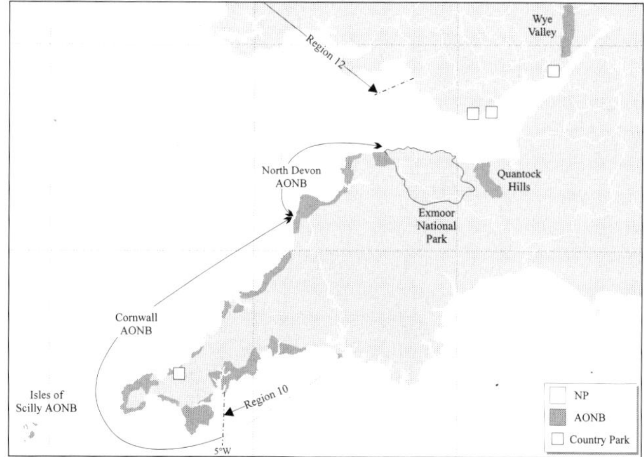

Map 7.3.3 Coastal Areas of Outstanding Natural Beauty, National Parks and Country Parks. Source: Countryside Commission.

Table 7.3.6 Areas of Outstanding Natural Beauty (AONBs)

Site name	*No. of sites*	*Area (ha)*	*Date designated*
Cornwall	**0.5***		
Cornwall*		47,900*	1983
Isles of Scilly	**1**		
Isles of Scilly		1,600	1976
Devon	**1**		
North Devon		17,100	1960
Somerset	**1**		
Quantock Hills		9,900	1957
Gloucestershire/Gwent	**1**		
Wye Valley		32,600	1971
Region 11	*4.5**	***109,100****	
West Coast	9.5	185,100	
GB coast	24	899,900	
GB whole country		2,123,700	

Source: Countryside Commission. Key: *Cornwall AONB lies partly within Region 10 - half of its area has been included in the total. Note: in this table any site that is wholly or partly intertidal, and any terrestrial site at least partly within 1 km of the Mean High Water Mark, or any tidal channel as depicted on 1:50,000 Ordnance Survey maps, is included as coastal.

Table 7.3.7 National Parks

Site name	*No. of sites*	*Area (ha)*	*Date designated*
Devon/Somerset	**1**		
Exmoor		69,300	1954
Region 11	*1*	***69,300***	
West Coast	4	571,100	
GB coast	6	745,000	

Source: Countryside Commission. Note: in this table any site that is wholly or partly intertidal, and any terrestrial site at least partly within 1 km of the Mean High Water Mark, or any tidal channel as depicted on 1:50,000 Ordnance Survey maps, is included as coastal.

Table 7.3.8 Country Parks

Site name	*No. of sites*	*Grid ref.*	*Area (ha)*	*Date designated/ opened*
Cornwall	**1**			
Tehidy Woods		SW645435	93	1983
Gwent	**1**			
Caldicot Castle		ST486884	21.5	1978
South Glamorgan	**2**			
Cosmeston Lakes		ST174693	89	1978
Porthkerry Park		ST092672	89	1972
Region 11	***4***		***292.5***	
West Coast	14		1,498	
GB coast	34		4,441	
GB whole country	281		35,150	

Sources: Countryside Commission, English Nature. Note: in this table any site that is wholly or partly intertidal, and any terrestrial site at least partly within 1 km of the Mean High Water Mark, or any tidal channel as depicted on 1:50,000 Ordnance Survey maps, is included as coastal.

7.3.8 Country Parks

Country Parks are primarily intended for recreation and leisure opportunities close to population centres and do not necessarily have any nature conservation interest. Nevertheless, many are in areas of semi-natural habitat and so form a valuable network of locations at which informal recreation and the natural environment co-exist. They are declared and managed by local authorities under section 7 of the Countryside Act 1968. There are four coastal Country Parks (292.5 ha) in Region 11 (Table 7.3.8; Map 7.3.3).

7.3.9 Acknowledgements

Thanks are due, in particular, to Ray Woolmore (Countryside Commission), and also to Roger Bolt (JNCC), English Nature and Countryside Council for Wales regional office staff, Site Safeguards Team (Countryside Council for Wales), Neale Oliver (DoE), and Paul Johnson (Countryside Commission).

7.3.10 Further sources of information

A. *References cited*

Barne, J., Davidson, N.C., Hill, T.O., & Jones, M. 1994. *Coastal and marine UKDMAP datasets: a user manual.* Peterborough, Joint Nature Conservation Committee.

British Oceanographic Data Centre. 1992. *UKDMAP (United Kingdom digital marine atlas).* Birkenhead, BODC. (Computer software.)

Countryside Commission. 1993. *The National Park Authority - purposes, powers and administration: a guide for members of National Park Authorities.* Cheltenham, Countryside Commission and Countryside Council for Wales.

Countryside Commission. 1994. *Areas of Outstanding National Beauty in England and Wales.* Rev. ed. Cheltenham, Countryside Commission (leaflet CCP276).

Marren, P.R. 1994. *England's National Nature Reserves.* Newton Abbott, David & Charles.

B. *Further information*

Countryside Commission. 1992. *Directory of Areas of Outstanding Natural Beauty.* Cheltenham, Countryside Commission.

Countryside Commission. 1992. *National Parks in England and Wales.* Rev. ed. Cheltenham, Countryside Commission (leaflet CCP208).

Countryside Commission. 1994. *Areas of Outstanding Natural Beauty - a guide for members of Joint Advisory Committees.* Cheltenham, Countryside Commission (leaflet CCP246).

Countryside Commission. 1994. *Countryside planning file.* Cheltenham, Countryside Commission.

Countryside Commission. 1994. *United Kingdom protected environment map.* Southampton, Ordnance Survey.

Hodgetts, N.G. 1992. *Guidelines for selection of biological SSSIs: non-vascular plants.* Peterborough, Joint Nature Conservation Committee.

Joint Nature Conservation Committee. 1996. *Guidelines for selection of biological SSSIs: intertidal marine habitats and saline lagoons.* Peterborough, Joint Nature Conservation Committee.

Nature Conservancy Council. 1984. *Nature conservation in Great Britain.* Peterborough, Nature Conservancy Council.

Nature Conservancy Council. 1989. *Guidelines for selection of biological SSSIs.* Peterborough, Nature Conservancy Council.

Nature Conservancy Council. 1989. *Local Nature Reserves.* Peterborough, Nature Conservancy Council. (Library information sheet No. 6.)

C. Contact names and addresses

Type of information	*Contact address and telephone no.*
NNR, SSSIs, LNR, Areas of Special Protection (Cornwall)	*Conservation Officer, English Nature Devon and Cornwall Local Team, Truro, tel: 01872 262550
NNR, SSSIs, LNR, MNR (Devon)	*Conservation Officer, English Nature Devon and Cornwall Local Team, Okehampton, tel: 01837 55045
NNRs, SSSIs, LNR, Areas of Special Protection (Somerset & Avon)	*Conservation Officer, English Nature Somerset and Avon Local Team, Taunton, tel: 01823 283211
SSSIs (Gloucestershire)	*Conservation Officer, English Nature Three Counties Local Team, Malvern Wells, tel: 01684 560616
NNRs, SSSIs, LNR (Mid Glamorgan, South Glamorgan & Gwent)	*South Wales Area Office, CCW, Cardiff, tel: 01222 772400
Areas of Special Protection	*European Wildlife Division, DoE, Bristol, tel: 0117 987 8000
Exmoor National Park	Exmoor National Park, Exmoor House, Dulverton, Somerset TA22 9HL, tel: 01398 23665
AONB, Country Park, Exmoor National Park (England)	*Countryside Commission, South West Region, Bristol, tel: 0117 973 9966
Country Park, AONB (Wales)	*Senior Officer, CCW South Wales Area Office, Cardiff, tel: 01222 772400

*Starred contact addresses are given in full in the Appendix.

The region holds nearly a third of all the UK's coastal Geological Conservation Review sites - localities of national or international importance for earth science. Three occur in the Blue Anchor Bay to Lilstock Coast SSSI, Somerset, where inclined beds of Lower Jurassic/Upper Triassic mudstones and limestones are dramatically exposed on the foreshore. Photo: Peter Wakely, English Nature.

7.4 Sites identified by statutory agencies

This section covers sites which, although not protected by statute, have been identified by statutory agencies as being of nature conservation or landscape importance.

7.4.1 Nature Conservation Review sites

Nature Conservation Review (NCR) sites are non-statutory sites that are the best representative examples of wildlife habitat; for some coastal sites, for example estuaries, all sites that were above a critical standard of nature conservation importance were selected. Ratcliffe (1977) related this particularly to migrant and wintering waterfowl populations and breeding bird assemblages. The NCR helps to identify sites that may qualify for declaration as National Nature Reserves. There are 953 NCR sites (approximately 1,500,000 ha) in Britain. 149 of them (approximately 360,000 ha) are coastal as defined by Ratcliffe (1977), but his definition of 'coastal' differed from that adopted in this chapter.

7.4.2 Geological Conservation Review sites

Geological Conservation Review (GCR) sites are non-statutory sites identified as having national or international importance for earth science. The GCR selection process describes and assesses key sites in the context of their geology, palaeontology, mineralogy or geomorphology; GCR sites are the earth science equivalent of NCRs (see section 7.4.1). There are 167 coastal GCR Single Interest Locations (SILs) in Region 11 (Table 7.4.1; Map 7.4.1). Detailed scientific accounts of 519 (coastal and inland) GCR SILs have been published or are in preparation in nine volumes of a planned 42-volume *Geological Conservation Review* series (Ellis *et al.* 1995).

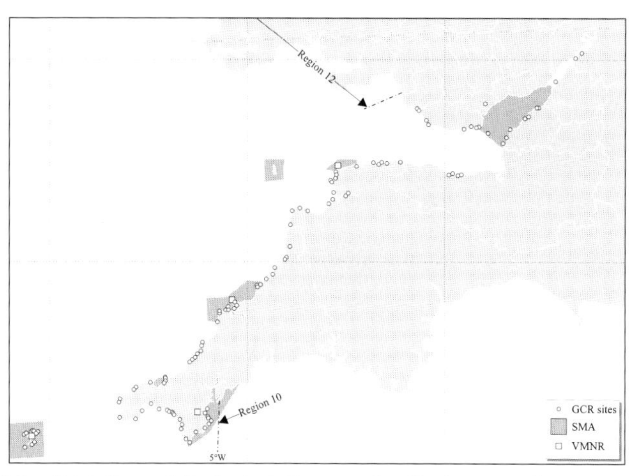

Map 7.4.1 Coastal Geological Conservation Review sites, Sensitive Marine Areas and Voluntary Marine Nature Reserves. Source: English Nature, JNCC. Note: a single symbol may represent more than one site in close proximity.

Table 7.4.1 GCR Single Interest Localities (SILs)

Site name	*No. of sites*
Cornwall	75
Rosemullion Head	
Little Dennis - Gillian Harbour - Nare Head - Porthallow	
Meneage Coastal Section	
Porthallow Cove to Porthkerris Cove	
Porthoustock Point	
Dean Quarry	
Coverack	
Kennack Sands	
Lizard Point	
Kynance Cove	
Mullion Island (2 SILs)	
Poldhu Cove - Polurrian Cove	
Baulk Head - Gunwalloe Church	
Wheal Penrose	
Porthleven (3 SILs)	
Loe Bar*	
Trenearne Par	
Megiliggar Rocks	
Porthcew	
Folly Rocks	
Cudden Point to Prussia Cove	
St. Michael's Mount	
Penlee Point	
Tater-Du	
Nanjizal Cove	
Porth Nanven	
Cape Cornwall	
Priest's Cove	
Cornwall (continued)	
Botallack Mine and Wheal Owles	
Botallack Head to Porth Ledden	
Godrevy	
Porthmeor Cove	
Godrevy Point	
Gurnard's Head	
Carrick Du to Clodgy Point	
Upton and Gwithian Towans*	
Godrevy Point and Straps Rocks	
Cameron Quarry (2 SILs)	
Wheal Coates	
St. Agnes Beacon	
Trevaunance Cove	
Cligga Head Mine	
Cligga Head	
Cotty's Point, Perranporth	
Gravel Hill Mine	
Perran Beach to Holywell Bay	
Bedruthan Steps (2 SILs)	
Booby's Bay to Trevose Head	
Dinas Head to Trevose Head	
Pentonwarra Point	
Trevone Bay	
Marble Cliff	
Porthmissen Bridge	
Stepper Point	
Harbour Cove	
Daymer Bay	

Table 7.4.1 GCR Single Interest Localities (SILs) (continued)

Site name	*No. of sites*
Cornwall (continued)	
Trebetherick Point	
Pentire Head	
Polzeath to Pentire Point	
Pentire Point to Rumps Point	
Trebarwith Strand	
Tintagel*	
Smith's Cliff to Tintagel Island	
Tintagel Head to Bossiney Haven	
Boscastle	
Rusey Cliff to Buckator	
Widemouth to Crackington	
Millook to Foxhole Point	
Widemouth to Saltstone Strand	
Bude Coast	
Isles of Scilly	**10**
Chad Girt	
Bread and Cheese Cove	
Northward Bright	
Porth Seal	
Isles of Scilly*	
Castle Porth	
Battery (Castle Down)	
Higher Moors	
Peninnis Head	
Old Man	
Devon	**22**
Welcombe Mouth	
Hartland Quarry*	
Hartland Point	
Clovelly to Mouth Mill	
Westward Ho!	
Westward Ho! Cobble Ridge*	
Braunton Burrows*	
Downend	
Croyde - Saunton Coast	
Baggy Point	
Mill Rock	
Barricane Beach	
Fremington Quay	
Fremington Quay	
Fremington Quay (South)	
Napps Cave	
Coombe Martin Beach	
Hollowbrook	
Crack Point	
Devon (continued)	
Valley of Rocks (2 SILs)	
Myrtleberry Cleave	
Devon/Somerset	**1**
Glenthorne	
Somerset	**5**
Blue Anchor Point	
Blue Anchor - Lilstock Coast	
Blue Anchor - Watchet - Lilstock*	
Doniford	
St. Audries Bay	
Avon	**16**
Brean Down (2 SILs)	
Spring Cove (2 SILs)	
Middle Hope (2 SILs)	
Clevedon Shore	
Holly Lane	
Portishead (2 SILs)	
Portishead Point	
Portishead Pier Section	
Aust	
Aust Cliff (3 SILs)	
Gloucestershire	**3**
Lyndney	
Tites Point (2 SILs)	
South Glamorgan	**10**
Flat Holm	
Lavernock - St. Mary's Well Bay	
River Rhymney	
Lavernack - Penarth	
Sully Island	
Hayes Point - Bendrick Rock	
Barry Island	
Nash Point	
Cwm Nash (2 SILs)	
Mid Glamorgan	**3**
Pant y Slade - Witches Point	
Ogmore	
Sutton Flats	
Region 11	***145***
West Coast	510
GB coast	1,000
GB whole country	3,002

Sources: English Nature, JNCC. Key: *sites selected wholly or partly for their coastal geomorphological interest (all other sites geological). Notes: site names that occur more than once refer to SILs at different grid reference points but with the same name. In this table any site that is wholly or partly intertidal, and any terrestrial site at least partly within 1 km of the Mean High Water Mark, or any tidal channel as depicted on 1:50,000 Ordnance Survey maps, is included as coastal.

7.4.3 Heritage Coasts

A Heritage Coast is an area selected for having a coastline of exceptionally fine scenic quality exceeding 1 mile in length, substantially undeveloped and containing features of special significance and interest. This non-statutory protection is agreed between local authorities and the Countryside Commission (in England) or the Countryside Commission for Wales (in Wales), as an aid to local authorities in planning and managing their coastlines. There are thirteen whole and part of one other Heritage Coasts (412 km) in Region 11 (Table 7.4.2; Map 7.4.2). Of the English coastline encompassed by Heritage Coasts, 39.5% is protected by the National Trust (Heritage Coast Forum 1993).

7.4.4 Sensitive Marine Areas

Sensitive Marine Areas (SMAs) are non-statutory marine areas in England that are nationally important and notable for their marine animal and plant communities or which provide ecological support to adjacent statutory sites. They are identified by English Nature with the aim of raising awareness and disseminating information to be taken into

Table 7.4.2 Heritage Coasts

Site name	*No. of sites*	*Grid ref.*	*Length (km)*	*Date designated*
Isles of Scilly	1			
Isles of Scilly		SV820020	64	1974
Cornwall	7.5*			
The Roseland*		SW843395-SX016441	26	1986
The Lizard		SW633250-SW729149	27	1976
Penwith		SW512410-SW469260	54	1976
Godrevy - Portreath		SW648458-SW579433	9	1976
St. Agnes		SW747540-SW691484	11	1976
Trevose Head		SW860764-SW957754	4	1976
Pentire Point - Widemouth		SS194011-SW933796	52	1976
Hartland (Cornwall)		SS206086-SS211174	11	1976
Devon	3			
Hartland (Devon)		SS212174-SS423292	37	1990
Lundy		SS120490	14	1990
North Devon		SS574476-SS467318	32	1992
Devon/Somerset	1			
Exmoor		SS575475-SS963478	45	1991
Mid Glamorgan/South Glamorgan	1			
Glamorgan		SS838769-SS020663	26	1973
Region 11	*13.5**		*412*	
West Coast	27.5*		890	
England & Wales	45		1,539	

Source: Countryside Commission. Key: *part of site in Region 10 and therefore partly also on the North Sea Coast. Note: all Heritage Coasts are completely defined (i.e. also have defined landward boundaries).

Map 7.4.2 Heritage Coasts. Source: Countryside Commission.

account in estuarine and coastal management planning. These areas rely on the co-operation of users and local communities for sustainable management, with the help of grant aid. SMA is the term used for areas described in previous technical documents (eg. English Nature 1994a) as 'Important Areas for Marine Wildlife' under English Nature's initiative '*Managing England's marine wildlife*' (English Nature 1994b). The whole of six and part of one other Sensitive Marine Areas are in Region 11 (Table 7.4.3; Map 7.4.1): all were identified in 1994.

Table 7.4.3 Sensitive Marine Areas

Site name	*No. of sites*
Cornwall	**0.5***
Dodman Point to the Lizard*	
Isles of Scilly	1
The Isles of Scilly	
Cornwall	2
St. Ives Bay	
North Cornwall	
Devon	2
Lundy	
North Devon	
Devon/Somerset/Avon/Gloucestershire/ Gwent/S. Glamorgan	1
Severn Estuary	
Region 11	*6.5**
West Coast	10.5
GB coast	27

Source: English Nature (1994a). Key: *site partly within Region 10.

7.4.5 Voluntary Marine Nature Reserves

Voluntary Marine Nature Reserves (VMNRs) (also called voluntary marine conservation areas or voluntary marine wildlife areas) may be set up by representatives of the users of a subtidal area or an area of shore in order to initiate management of that area. Management may have a variety of purposes, from conservation of a marine biologically important area, to use for educational purposes. These reserves or conservation areas usually have a management committee or steering group composed of users of the area, interested members of the public, fishermen, harbour authorities and local Wildlife Trusts. There are five Voluntary Marine Nature Reserves in Region 11 (Table 7.4.4; Map 7.4.1).

Table 7.4.4 Voluntary Marine Nature Reserves

Site name	*No. of sites*	*Date established*
Cornwall	2	
Roseland (Fal)*		1982
Helford (VMCA)		1987
Isles of Scilly	1	
Isles of Scilly Marine Park		1989
Cornwall	1	
Polzeath (VMWA)		1995
Devon	1	
North Devon		1994
Region 11	5	
West Coast	5	
GB coast	14	

Source: English Nature. Key: *currently inactive (September 1996); VMCA = Voluntary Marine Conservation Area; VMWA = Voluntary Marine Wildlife Area.

7.4.6 Acknowledgements

Thanks are due to Ray Woolmore and Paul Johnson (Countryside Commission), Roger Bolt and Earth Sciences Branch (JNCC), Phillip Biss, Paul Gilliland and Des Gallagher (English Nature) and Site Safeguards Team (Countryside Council for Wales).

7.4.7 Further sources of information

A. References cited

Ellis, N.V. (*ed.*), Bowen, D.Q., Campbell, S., Knill, J.L., McKirdy, A.P., Prosser, C.D., Vincent, M.A., & Wilson, R.C.L. 1995. *An introduction to the Geological Conservation Review.* Peterborough, Joint Nature Conservation Committee. (Geological Conservation Review series, No. 1.)

English Nature. 1994a. *Important areas for marine wildlife around England.* Peterborough, English Nature.

English Nature. 1994b. *Managing England's marine wildlife.* Peterborough, English Nature.

Heritage Coast Forum. 1993. *Heritage Coasts in England and Wales; a gazetteer.* Manchester, Heritage Coast Forum.

Ratcliffe, D.A., *ed.* 1977. *A nature conservation review.* Cambridge, Cambridge University Press.

B. Further reading

Cleal, C.J., & Thomas, B.A. 1995. *Palaeozoic palaeobotany of Great Britain.* London, Chapman & Hall. (Geological Conservation Review series.)

Cleal, C.J., & Thomas, B.A. In prep. *British Upper Carboniferous stratigraphy.* London, Chapman & Hall. (Geological Conservation Review series.)

Countryside Commission. 1992. *Heritage Coasts in England: policies and priorities.* Cheltenham, Countryside Commission.

Countryside Commission. 1993. *Heritage Coasts in England and Wales.* Rev. ed. Cheltenham, Countryside Commission (leaflet CCP252).

Gregory, K.J., *ed.* In prep. *Fluvial geomorphology of Great Britain.* London, Chapman and Hall. (Geological Conservation Review series.)

Smith, D.B. In press. *Marine Permian of England.* London, Chapman & Hall. (Geological Conservation Review series.)

C. Contact names and addresses

Type of information	*Contact address and telephone no.*
NCR sites, GCR sites, SMAs, VMNRs (Cornwall, Isles of Scilly)	*Conservation Officer, English Nature Devon and Cornwall Local Team, Truro, tel: 01872 262550
NCR sites, GCR sites, SMAs (Devon)	*Conservation Officer, English Nature Devon and Cornwall Local Team, Okehampton, tel: 01837 55045
NCR sites, GCR sites, SMAs (Somerset and Avon)	*Conservation Officer, English Nature Somerset and Avon Local Team, Taunton, tel: 01823 283211
NCR sites, GCR sites, SMAs (Gloucestershire)	*Conservation Officer, English Nature Three Counties Local Team, Malvern Wells, tel: 01684 560616
NCR sites, GCR sites (Wales)	*Senior Officer, CCW South Wales Area Office, Cardiff, tel: 01222 772400
Heritage Coasts (England)	*Countryside Commission, South West Region, Bristol, tel: 0117 973 9966
Heritage Coasts (Wales)	*Arfordir Officer, Headquarters, CCW Bangor, tel: 01248 370734
VMNRs and SMAs	*Maritime Team, English Nature, Peterborough, tel: 01733 340345
Helford Voluntary Marine Conservation Area	Mrs P. Tompsett, Cornish Biological Records Unit, Trevithick Centre, Pool, Cornwall TR15 3PL, tel: 01209 710424
Isles of Scilly Marine Park (VNMR)	Andrew Gibson, Director, Isles of Scilly Environment Trust, Corn Thomas, Hugh Town, St. Mary's, Isles of Scilly TR21 0PT, tel: 01720 422153
Polzeath Voluntary Marine Wildlife Area	North Cornwall Heritage Coast Service, 3/5 Barn Lane, Bodmin, Cornwall PL31 1LZ, tel: 01208 74121
North Devon VMNR	North Devon Heritage Coast Service, Council Offices, Northfield Road, Ilfracombe EX34 8AL, tel: 01271 867496

*Starred contact addresses are given in full in the Appendix.

7.5 Other types of protected site

7.5.1 The National Trust

The National Trust is an independent charity that is currently the largest private landowner in Britain. The National Trust owns about 230,000 ha of land in England, Wales and Northern Ireland, and over 200 buildings of outstanding importance. It has also accepted or bought covenants that protect against development for a further 31,600 ha of land and buildings. Many of the tenanted properties have individual intrinsic value; together they protect large areas of unique landscape and countryside. The National Trust has statutory powers to protect its properties, under an Act of Parliament (1907) which declares its holdings of land and buildings inalienable; these properties cannot be sold or mortgaged. In addition, National Trust properties can be protected by bylaws. In 1985 the National Trust relaunched its 1965 campaign 'Enterprise Neptune' to raise funds for the purchase of coastal areas. A total of 850 km of coast are now owned or managed by the National Trust (National Trust 1993). There are 147 National Trust sites (14,322 ha) in Region 11 (Table 7.5.1; Map 7.5.1).

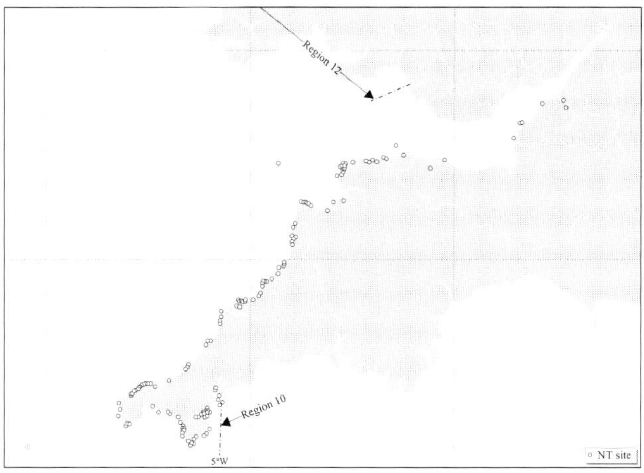

Map 7.5.1 Coastal National Trust sites. Source: National Trust. Note: a single symbol may represent more than one site in close proximity.

Table 7.5.1 National Trust sites

Site name	*No. of sites*	*Grid ref.*	*Area (ha)*	*Date acquired*	*Landform*
Cornwall	**107**				
St. Anthony-in-Roseland[a]		SW865325	88	1958-60	Cliffs, headland, beaches, estuary, farmland
St. Anthony Head (including Zone Point)[a]		SW846312	14	1959-85	Headland
Trelonk		SW885413	9	1966	Foreshore
Ardevora		SW875405	24	1964	Foreshore
Newton Farm		SW845334	38	1988	Coastal farmland
St. Mawes		SW841335	16	1974-75	Foreshore, cliff, meadow and farmland
St. Just-in-Roseland		SW848353	48	1977-85	Foreshore and farmland
Trelissick		SW837396	158	1955-87	Estuarine woods, farmland and parkland
Pill Farm		SW830386	71	1994	Coastal farm and woodland
Maenporth		SW790296	5	1989	Cliffs and fields
Nansidwell		SW790283	23	1986	Valley
Rosemullion Head		SW797278	22	1939	Headland
Mawnan Glebe		SW787272	18	1963	Farmland and wooded cliff
Carwinion and Chenhalls		SW780280	44	1969	Coastal woodland
Bosloe		SW775275	66	1980	Beach and farmland
Glendurgan		SW772277	16	1962	Beach, property and gardens
Penarvon Cove and Pengwedhen		SW756264	15	1969-71	Cove, farm and woodland
Tremayne Woods		SW728257	20	1978	Mixed woodland
Frenchman's Creek		SW748258	15	1946-87	Wooded creek
Gillan Creek		SW775251	6	1976-89	Wooded creek and farmland
Trewarnevas & Coneysburrow Cove		SW790252	2	1935-65	Cliffs
Lowland Point		SW803196	23	1956	Cliff and farmland
Chynhalls Cliff		SW780170	21	1983	Cliff and farmland
Beagles Point		SW768166	30	1966	Cliff and farmland
Poltesco and Carleon Cove		SW726157	66	1974-90	Foreshore, cliffs, farm and woodland
Kildown Point and Enys Head		SW727146	20	1981	Cliff and fields
Inglewidden		SW717143	22	1966	Cliff and farmland
Parn Voose Cove and the Balk		SW713130	11	1976	Cliffs and quarry
Bass Point		SW716119	4	1967-92	Cliff
Tregullas & Tregominion Farms, Lizard		SW708120	49	1994	Coastal farm
Lizard Point		SW698115	54	1987-93	Cliff, cave, meadow
Kynance Cove and Lizard Downs		SW690133	53	1935-92	Cliff and fields
Predannack		SW665158	273	1968	Cliff, heath and farmland
Predannack Wartha		SW660169	3	1937	Headlands

Table 7.5.1 National Trust sites (continued)

Site name	*No. of sites*	*Grid ref.*	*Area (ha)*	*Date acquired*	*Landform*
Cornwall (continued)					
Mullion Cove and Island		SW666179	7	1945-82	Cliff, harbour, island, rocky shores
Polurrian Cove		SW668184	2	1959-61	Cliff
Marconi Memorial		SW664193	23	1937-65	Cliff with memorial
Poldhu Cove		SW665199	4	1984	Beach and undercliff
Gunwalloe Church Cove		SW661204	103	1956-74	Cliffs, beach, cove, farmland, golf course
Chymder Farm		SW667211	17	1994	Coastal farmland
Gunwalloe Fishing Cove		SW654224	20	1979-81	Beach and farmland
The Loe and Penrose		SW645250	629	1974-82	Shingle beach, foreshore, freshwater lake, woods and farmland
Rinsey Cliff		SW594269	13	1969	Cliffs
Lesceave Cliff		SW587275	6	1965	Cliff
Cudden Point		SW548275	6	1979	Headland
St. Michael's Mount		SW515298	41	1954	Island, foreshore, castle and mainland fields
Penberth Cove and Treen Cliff		SW397223	80	1933-61	Headland, cliffs, cove and fort
Porthcurno		SW387224	12	1994	Beach and coastland
St. Leven Cliffs		SW384218	4	1966	Cliffs and headland
Mayon and Trevescan Cliffs		SW349259	23	1935-64	Cliff and castle
Bollowal Common and Carn Gloose		SW356311	24	1992	Cliff and coastal land
Hendra Cliff and Boscregan Farm		SW358296	28	1983	Cliff and farmland
Cape Cornwall		SW351319	32	1987	Cliff and foreshore
Nanjulian Farm		SW360290	37	1993	Cliff and farmland
Watchcroft		SW420358	67	1990-92	Cliffs and heath
Rosemergy and Trevean Cliffs		SW415365	104	1958-87	Cliff and farmland
Porthmeor		SW431372	31	1986-87	Coastal farmland
Bosigran and Carn Galver		SW425367	202	1978-82	Cliffs and farmland
Gurnard's Head		SW432386	13	1982	Headland
Zennor Head		SW450396	25	1954-68	Cliff, moor and farmland
Boswednack		SW440383	54	1980-92	Cliff and farmland
Tregerthen Cliff		SW462399	10	1962	Cliff and farmland
Treveal		SW470403	69	1983	Cliff and farmland
Trevaga		SW474407	14	1983-86	Cliff and farmland
Carn Naun Point		SW477407	48	1994	Cliff and farmland
Pen Enys Point		SW491410	15	1984	Cliffs
Hor Point and Hellesveor Cliff		SW498411	10	1957	Rocky coast
Porthminster Point		SW525395	5	1961	Cliffs and fields
Godvrey to Portreath		SW600431	325	1939-91	Cliffs, beaches, coves, headland, farmland
Chapel Porth		SW697496	145	1956-80	Cliff and moorland
St. Agnes Beacon		SW710504	25	1956	Hill and barrows
Newdowns Head		SW708518	9	1980	Headland
The Kelseys and Cubert Common		SW770600	185	1951-72	Cliff, beach, islands, field & common
West Pentire Farm		SW774610	41	1960	Cliff and farm
The Gannel, Newquay		SW787609	39	1956-64	Saltings, sandhills, farmland
Cainewas		SW849692	25	1930-75	Clifftop
Park Head, St. Eval		SW845710	78	1966	Headland
Porthcothan		SW857722	12	1967-92	Inlet and beach
Booby's Bay*		SW857752	6	1986	Cliff and foreshore
Fishing Cove Field		SW927777	3	1964-68	Cliff fields
Trenain Farm		SW937774	29	1963	Coastal farm
Pentire Farm		SW935803	147	1936-39	Headland and farm
Pentireglaze Farm		SW943798	74	1969-73	Farmland
Carnweather Point		SW950802	13	1953	Headland
Lundy Bay		SW958798	39	1937-82	Cliffs and farmland
Trevan Cliffs		SW962802	5	1984	Cliffs
Doyden and Port Quin		SW968805	16	1956	Cliff, harbour and farmland
Port Gaverne		SX003808	7	1958-59	Beach and foreshore
Dannonchapel Farm		SX032825	80	1991	Coastal farmland
Tregardock Beach		SX040840	27	1968	Cliffs and beach
Trebarwith Strand		SX050866	14	1929-62	Cliffs
Higher and Lower Penhallic Point		SX046877	7	1953-86	Cliffs
Glebe Cliff		SX049882	29	1928-59	Cliff and pasture
Barras Nose		SX054893	6	1897	Headland
Willapark		SX063898	25	1976	Headland
Boscastle		SX095915	47	1955-82	Harbour and cliffs
Rusey Cliff		SX127938	98	1968-85	Cliff and farmland

Table 7.5.1 National Trust sites (continued)

Site name	*No. of sites*	*Grid ref.*	*Area (ha)*	*Date acquired*	*Landform*
Cornwall (continued)					
Cambeak		SX130967	156	1959	Cliff and beach
St. Gennys		SX150972	76	1959-81	Cliff and farmland
Lower Tresmorn Farm		SX159978	89	1989	Coastal farm
The Dizzard		SX160987	58	1968-77	Cliffs and pasture
Maer Cliff, Bude		SS200077	47	1975	Clifftop pastures
Northcott Mouth		SS202085	11	1981	Foreshore and grassland
Houndapit Cliffs		SS202100	44	1970	Cliff and farmland
Coombe		SS201118	78	1960-85	Cliff and farmland
Stowe Barton		SS210114	161	1988	Cliff and farmland
Morwenstow		SS205153	96	1959-85	Cliff and farmland
Devon	**34**				
East Titchberry Farm		SS244270	49	1988	Cliff and farmland
Westward Ho!		SS423289	7	1938	Coastal hill
Welcombe & Marsland Mouths		SS220175	187	1963-69	Foreshore, cliffs, wooded valleys
Lundy		SS135455	424	1969	Island
Gawlish		SS258274	12	1980	Cliffs
Fatacott Cliff		SS265273	67	1972-80	Cliff and farmland
Exmansworthy Cliff		SS275273	16	1988	Coastland
Beckland Cliffs		SS284265	57	1976	Cliff and farmland
The Brownshams		SS285260	120	1969	Coastal farm and woodland
Portledge Estate		SS375243	311	1988	Cliff, beaches, foreshore and farmland
Abbotsham		SS410277	7	1982	Coastal farmland
Burrough Farm		SS457288	18	1966-67	Cove, wooded cliffs, estuary and farmland
Baggy Point		SS420415	131	1939-90	Cliff and farmland
Vention		SS451411	8	1964-85	Coastal scrub and ruins
Woolacombe Warren		SS455424	41	1951	Sand dunes
Potters Hill		SS458430	12	1935	Coastal hill
Combegate Beach		SS455444	3	1950	Beach
Woolacombe Barton		SS460445	221	1951	Coastland
Town Farm		SS457451	47	1951-90	Coastal farmland
Morte Fields		SS451451	12	1937	Coastal fields
Morte Point		SS443456	68	1909-81	Headland
Woolacombe and Mortehoe		SS456466	10	1984	Coast
Bull Point		SS461469	74	1973	Headland
Damage Cliffs		SS470465	46	1968-69	Hillocky cliffs
Ilfracombe		SS500471	106	1942-67	Cliffs and coastland
Golden Cove, Berrynarbor		SS565477	4	1966	Wooded cliff
West Challacombe Farm		SS585476	38	1991	Coastal farmland
The Great & Little Hangman		SS601480	160	1972-91	Cliffs and moorland
Holdstone Down		SS620475	30	1967-80	Cliff and moorland
Heddon Valley		SS6549	381	1963-85	Coastal woodland and moorland
Highveer Point		SS660495	76	1989	Cliffland
Woody Bay		SS675487	49	1965-77	Cliff, moorland and woodland
Lynmouth		SS740555	734	1934-93	Cliffs, headland, estuary, wooded valleys and earthworks
Holden Head		SS759497	45	1990	Coastal moorland and woodland
Somerset	**3**				
Holnicote Estate, Dunkery etc.		SS8844	5,036	1932-78	Coastal estate
Greenaleigh Point, Minehead		SS955483	19	1985-86	Coast
Brean Down		ST290590	65	1954	Headland
Avon	**5**				
Sand Point, Kewstoke		ST325660	13	1964	Coastal headland
Middle Hope		ST335665	77	1968-91	Coast and farmland
Redcliffe Bay		ST440762	1	1966	Coastal belt
Leigh Woods		ST560734	65	1909-53	Woodland
Shirehampton Park		ST545768	40	1922	Part golf course
Region 11	***149***		***14,363***		
West Coast*	262		45,517		
GB whole coast*	452		62,974		

Source: National Trust. Key: [a]part of each of these sites is in Region 10; half of the area has been included in the total; *includes National Trust for Scotland sites. Note: in this table any site that is wholly or partly intertidal, and any terrestrial site at least partly within 1 km of the Mean High Water Mark, or any tidal channel as depicted on 1:50,000 Ordnance Survey maps, is included as coastal.

7.5.2 The Royal Society for the Protection of Birds

The Royal Society for the Protection of Birds (RSPB) has substantial non-statutory reserve holdings and currently manages over 130 reserves (84,000 ha) in Britain (RSPB 1993). Wherever possible, reserves are purchased, so that the level of safeguard for the wildlife and their habitats is high. Where reserves are leased, the RSPB aims to acquire long leases (longer than 21 years) with appropriate management rights. There are three RSPB reserves (235 ha) in Region 11 (Table 7.5.2; Map 7.5.2).

7.5.3 The Wildfowl & Wetlands Trust

As well as their wildfowl collections, used extensively for education, The Wildfowl & Wetlands Trust (WWT - formerly the Wildfowl Trust) has established non-statutory reserves in a number of key wintering areas for migrant wildfowl. The level of protection afforded to such sites is high, since the land is either owned or held on long leases. There is one WWT site (305 ha) in Region 11 (Table 7.5.3; Map 7.5.2).

7.5.4 The Wildlife Trusts

The Wildlife Trusts were established to promote non-statutory nature conservation at a local level. They own, lease and manage, by agreement with owners, over 1,800 nature reserves (more than 52,000 ha). There is usually one trust covering a whole county or group of counties. The Trusts with coastal sites in the region are the Cornwall Wildlife Trust, Gloucestershire Wildlife Trust, The Wildlife Trust for Bristol, Bath and Avon, Gwent Wildlife Trust and Glamorgan Wildlife Trust. There are twenty coastal Wildlife Trusts sites (227 ha) in Region 11 (Table 7.5.4; Map 7.5.2).

7.5.5 The Ministry of Defence

As at August 1994, the Ministry of Defence (MoD) owned, leased or used under licence landholdings covering some

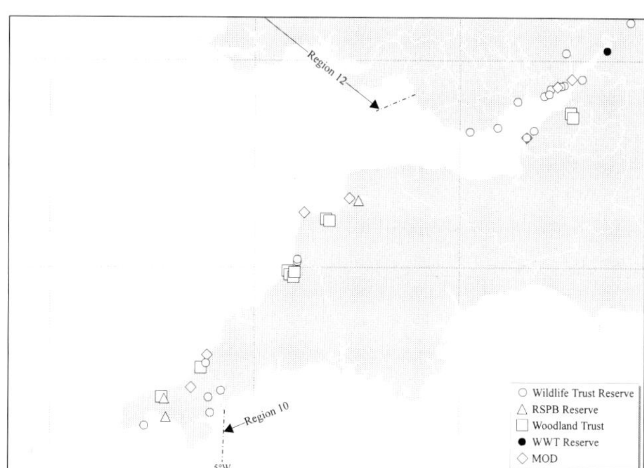

Map 7.5.2 Other voluntary and private sites. Source: Ministry of Defence (MOD), Wildlife Trusts, RSPB, Wildfowl & Wetlands Trust (WWT), Woodland Trust. Note: a single symbol may represent more than one site in close proximity.

320 km of coastline around the UK, not all of it significant for its nature conservation value. The MoD gives high priority to nature conservation on the Defence Estate, subject to the overriding importance of military training. The restrictions to public access on some sites mean that they can be amongst the most pristine areas of wildlife habitat in the region. There are seven MoD sites (1,463 ha) in Region 11 (Table 7.5.5; Map 7.5.2).

Table 7.5.3 Wildfowl & Wetlands Trust sites

Site name	*No. of sites*	*Grid ref.*	*Area (ha)*	*Date acquired*
Gloucestershire	1			
Slimbridge		SO725055	305	1946
Region 11	*1*		***305***	
West Coast	3		1,113	
GB coast	6		1,585	

Source: WWT. Note: in this table any site that is wholly or partly intertidal, and any terrestrial site at least partly within 1 km of the Mean High Water Mark, or any tidal channel as depicted on 1:50,000 Ordnance Survey maps, is included as coastal.

Table 7.5.2 Royal Society for the Protection of Birds reserves

Site name	*No. of sites*	*Grid ref.*	*Area (ha)*	*Date acquired*	*Interest*
Cornwall	2				
Marazion Marsh		SW513311	52	1991	Marsh, shallow pools, reeds and scrub, breeding reedbirds and waterfowl, waders
Hayle Estuary		SW546364	144	1990	Intertidal mudflats, saltmarsh, sand dunes and beach, wintering wildfowl and waders, raptors and seabirds
Devon	1				
Isley Marsh		SS492328	39	1990	Tidal saltmarsh with cord grass *Spartina* spp., mud and shingle, wintering and roosting waterfowl, including redshank *Tringa totanus*
Region 11	3		**235**		
West Coast	29		14,125		
GB coast	82		38,680		

Source: RSPB *in litt.* Note: in this table any site that is wholly or partly intertidal, and any terrestrial site at least partly within 1 km of the Mean High Water Mark, or any tidal channel as depicted on 1:50,000 Ordnance Survey maps, is included as coastal.

Table 7.5.4 Wildlife Trusts sites

Site name	*No. of sites*	*Grid ref.*	*Area (ha)*	*Date acquired*
Cornwall Wildlife Trust	7			
Fal Ruan Estuary		SW890405	101	1966
Perran Meadows		SW774386	3	1986
Swan Vale		SW800317	1	1986
Kemyel Crease		SW460244	3	1974
Nansmellyn Marsh		SW762543	3	1986
Phillip's Point		SS199043	2	1983
Upton Meadow		SS207044	1	1987
The Wildlife Trust for Bristol, Bath and Avon	3			
Middle Hope		ST348666	16	1981
Blakes's Pool		ST373664	4	1984
Littleton Brick Pits		ST591913	2	1981
Gloucestershire Wildlife Trust	1			
Over Ponds		SO820193	4	1968
Gwent Wildlife Trust	7			
Cleddon Shoots		SO523041	8	1980s
Sudbrook Bee Orchid Site		ST495876	1	1982
Caldicot Bee Orchid Site		ST487877	1	1982
Magor Marsh		ST448854	23	1960
Magor Pill		ST435845	9	1982
Cold Harbour Pill		ST410833	2	1981
Peterstone Wentlooge		ST278807	1	1966
Glamorgan Wildlife Trust	2			
Lavernock Point		ST182680	6	1966
Aberthaw Saltmarsh		ST043659	36	1980
Region 11	***20***		***227***	
West Coast	95		13,108	
GB coast	217		23,420	

Source: Wildlife Trusts (1990 data). Note: in this table any site that is wholly or partly intertidal, and any terrestrial site at least partly within 1 km of the Mean High Water Mark, or any tidal channel as depicted on 1:50,000 Ordnance Survey maps, is included as coastal.

Table 7.5.5 MoD sites

Site name	*No. of sites*	*Area (ha)**	*Habitats*	*Protected status*
Cornwall	2			
Portreath		350	Cliff	SSSI
Penhale		383	Cliff, sand dune	SSSI
Devon	2			
Hartland Point		6	Cliff	SSSI, AONB
Braunton Burrows		583	Sand dune	SSSI, AONB
Avon	1			
Weston-super-Mare		26	Cliffs, rocks, mudflats	SSSI
Gloucestershire	1			
Chepstow		88	Mudflats	SSSI
Gwent	1			
Caldicot		27	Mudflats	SSSI
Region 11	***7***	***1,463***		
West Coast	45	18,961		
GB coast	110	53,410		

Source: Ministry of Defence. Key: *all areas are approximate and include land leased or used under licence; SSSI = Site of Special Scientific Interest; AONB = Area of Outstanding Natural Beauty. Note: in this table any site that is wholly or partly intertidal, and any terrestrial site at least partly within 1 km of the Mean High Water Mark, or any tidal channel as depicted on 1:50,000 Ordnance Survey maps, is included as coastal.

7.5.6 The Woodland Trust

The Woodland Trust was established in 1972 with the aim of conserving, restoring and re-establishing trees (particularly broad-leaved) and woodland plants and wildlife in the United Kingdom. There are ten Woodland Trust sites (81 ha) in Region 11 (Table 7.5.6; Map 7.5.2).

Table 7.5.6 The Woodland Trust sites

Site name	*No. of sites*	*Grid ref.*	*Area (ha)*
Cornwall	6		
Ann's Wood		SW547372	1.0
Shute Wood		SW742522	0.2
Trengayor Copse & Crannow Combe		SX180981	17.0
Tamps & Landy Wood		SX175988	17.0
Lundy Wood		SX182995	4.0
Trebarfoote Wood		SX184994	22.0
Devon	2		
Barton Wood (part)		SS344235	3.0
Buck's & Keivill's Wood		SS355234	14.0
Avon	2		
Bishops Knoll extension, Bristol		ST555751	0.3
Bishops Knoll, Bristol		ST553754	3.0
Region 11	***10***		***81.5***
West Coast	29		363
GB coast	64		1,458

Source: Woodland Trust (1993). Note: in this table any site that is wholly or partly intertidal, and any terrestrial site at least partly within 1 km of the Mean High Water Mark, or any tidal channel as depicted on 1:50,000 Ordnance Survey maps, is included as coastal.

7.5.7 Acknowledgements

Thanks go to Andrea Firth (MoD), Jo Burgon, Richard Offen and David Wilkinson (The National Trust), Bob Scott (RSPB), Mark Pollitt (Wildfowl & Wetlands Trust) and Sarah Hawkswell (The Wildlife Trusts) for providing information.

7.5.8 Further sources of information

A. *References cited*

National Trust. 1993. Enterprise Neptune - saving our unspoiled coastline. *Coastline 1993,* No. 2, 1-11.

Royal Society for the Protection of Birds. 1993. *Nature reserves - information for visitors.* Sandy, Royal Society for the Protection of Birds.

Woodland Trust. 1993. *Directory of Woodland Trust properties 1993.* The Woodland Trust.

B. *Further reading*

Davidson, N.C., Laffoley, D.d'A., Doody, J.P., Way, L.S., Gordon, J., Key, R., Drake, C.M., Pienkowski, M.W., Mitchell, R., & Duff, K.L. 1991. *Nature conservation and estuaries in Great Britain.* Peterborough, Nature Conservancy Council.

National Trust. 1995. *Properties of the National Trust.* Reading, The National Trust.

C. Contact names and addresses

Type of information	*Contact address and telephone no.*
National Trust sites - England and Wales	*Coast and Countryside Adviser, The National Trust, Cirencester, tel: 01285 651818
National Trust sites - Devon	*Regional Land Agent, The National Trust, Killerton House, Broadclyst, Exeter EX5 3LE, tel: 01392 881691
National Trust sites - Cornwall	*Regional Land Agent, The National Trust, Lanhydrock, Bodmin, PL30 4DE, tel: 01208 742481-4
National Trust sites - Wales	Area Manager, The National Trust, The King's Head, Bridge Street, Llandeilo, Dyfed SA19 6BB, tel: 01558 822800
RSPB reserves	*Regional Officer, RSPB, South - West England Office, Exeter, tel: 01392 432691
The Wildfowl and Wetlands Trust reserve (Slimbridge)	Curator, The Wildfowl and Wetlands Trust, Slimbridge, Gloucester GL2 7BT, tel: 01453 890333
Devon Wildlife Trust sites	*Conservation Officer, Devon Wildlife Trust, Exeter, tel: 01392 79244
Cornwall Wildlife Trust sites	*Conservation Officer, Cornwall Wildlife Trust, Truro, tel: 01872 273939
The Wildlife Trust for Bristol, Bath and Avon sites	*Conservation Officer, The Wildlife Trust for Bristol, Bath and Avon, Bristol, tel: 01272 268018/265490
Gloucestershire Wildlife Trust sites	*Conservation Officer, Gloucestershire Wildlife Trust, Gloucester, tel: 01452 383333
Gwent Wildlife Trust sites	*Conservation Officer, Gwent Wildlife Trust, Monmouth, tel: 01600 715501
Glamorgan Wildlife Trust sites	*Conservation Officer, Glamorgan Wildlife Trust, Mid Glamorgan, tel: 01656 724100
The Woodland Trust sites	The Woodland Trust, Autumn Park, Dysart Road, Grantham, Lincolnshire NG31 6LL, tel: 01476 74297
MoD sites	Conservation Officer, MoD Conservation Office, B2/3, Government Buildings, Leatherhead Road, Chessington, Surrey KT9 2LU, tel: 0181 391 3028/9

*Starred contact addresses are given in full in the Appendix.

Chapter 8 Land use, infrastructure and coastal defence

S.L. Fowler, M.J. Dunbar, C.A. Crumpton & M.J. Goodwin

8.1 Introduction

This chapter is divided into three sections: (rural) land use, covering agriculture (especially as it affects important coastal wildlife habitats) and woodland; infrastructure, covering population distribution, industry, ports, harbours, ferries and power generation; and coastal defence, including sea defence and coast protection.

Land use in this region is predominantly agricultural. A significant amount of the coastline is characterised by semi-natural habitats, often used for livestock grazing, with arable land being concentrated around the estuaries. Some important coastal woodlands occur in the region. After agriculture, tourism and recreation are the second most important land use (see also section 9.7). Overall, industrial activity is low, although there is a major industrial site at Avonmouth stretching along several kilometres of shore, and there are several industrial parks on the south Wales coast, where Newport and Cardiff are the main centres. Avonmouth and Cardiff are major UK ports. There are several minor ports, although activity has declined significantly from the last century when the region handled much of the UK's international trade. Fishing is still important, although this activity has also declined: Newlyn is a major fishing base, and there are many smaller fishing harbours (see section 9.1). Today, many of these harbours serve mainly recreational craft and perhaps only a small inshore fishing fleet. Only a small amount of the region's coastline is protected against coastal erosion, but there are very extensive lengths of sea defence against flooding.

Region 11 is ideally situated to expoit renewable sources of energy for power generation, because much of the coast is exposed to the prevailing south-westerly winds and the tidal range in the Severn Estuary is the second largest in the world. Although the proposal to build a tidal power barrage across the Severn is not currently being pursued, there are two operating wind farms in the region, this one at Goonhilly Downs, on the Lizard, and another at Delabole, north Cornwall. Photo: Peter Wakely, English Nature.

8.2 Land use

S.L. Fowler & M.J. Dunbar

8.2.1 Introduction

Land use in this region is predominantly agricultural. Much of the coastline in the south of the region is characterised by semi-natural habitats, mostly grassland, managed either as rough grazing or for more intensive agricultural use. Changes in agricultural practice mean that grazing is becoming less common on areas of semi-natural cliff-top vegetation, with much coastal semi-natural grassland and coastal heath being ploughed for arable crops (Doody undated). Further north, dairy and beef cattle are raised on the grasslands of the Somerset and Gwent Levels, and on the low-lying shores of the Severn Estuary between Bristol and Gloucester, where orchards are also widespread. Cultivation of spring bulbs is an important industry in the mild south-west, especially on the Isles of Scilly.

Grazing is the oldest form of saltmarsh management. There are approximately 44,000 ha of saltmarsh in Great Britain (Burd 1989), of which about 31,600 ha are grazed, with major concentrations in the south-east and north-west of England. Doody's (1988) study of saltmarsh management identified stocking densities around the UK ranging from one to six animals per hectare, with grazing usually only taking place from May to September. In the region there are approximately 1,625 ha of saltmarsh on which some grazing takes place. This accounts for 87% of the region's total saltmarsh and represents approximately 5% of grazed saltmarsh in Great Britain.

Dune vegetation in England and Wales has been modified by agriculture for centuries (Dargie 1994). The characteristic semi-natural vegetation of most stable dunes is grass or heath, developed through the grazing of sheep, cattle and rabbits. Many of the dune areas found on the region's coast are not grazed commercially but retain the characteristics of grazed dunes owing to the prevalence of rabbits.

8.2.2 Locations and land uses

Maps 8.2.1, 8.2.2 and 8.2.3 show the distributions in the region of, respectively, tilled land, intensively managed mown/grazed turf and lightly managed meadow/semi-natural grassland. Arable land is concentrated around major estuaries such as those of the Taw-Torridge and the Parrett, as well as the Severn Estuary, which has a long history of land-claim for agriculture. The proportion of intensively-managed grassland increases from west to east across the region (Map 8.2.2).

The majority of agricultural land in this region is MAFF land grades 3 and 4, with the upland areas (which extend inland) being mainly grade 5. The latter is most significant between Ilfracombe and Minehead, where the upland area of Exmoor abuts the coast for some 50 km. However, there are pockets of higher quality land, mostly grade 2, around some of the major rias and smaller river valleys, notably around the Fal Estuary, the lowland area between Penzance and Hayle, the head of the Camel Estuary and in small pockets between Minehead and Watchet. There is also a

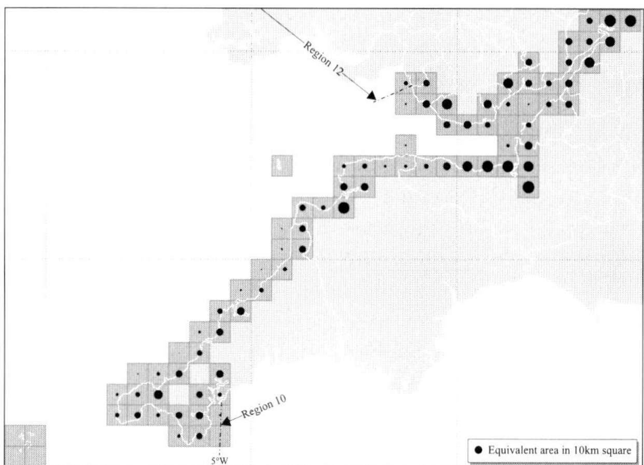

Map 8.2.1 Tilled land. Note: area of circle indicates the area of this land cover type in the 10 km square. Source: Countryside Survey (1990), ITE Monks Wood.

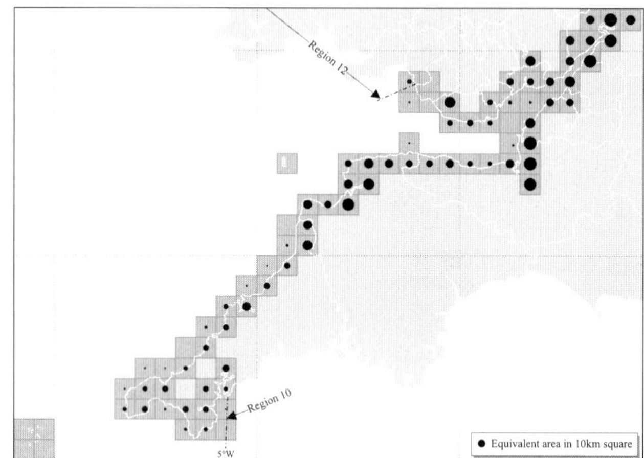

Map 8.2.2 Pastures and amenity swards, mown or grazed to maintain a short turf throughout the year. Note: area of circle indicates the area of this land cover type in the 10 km square. Source: Countryside Survey (1990), ITE Monks Wood.

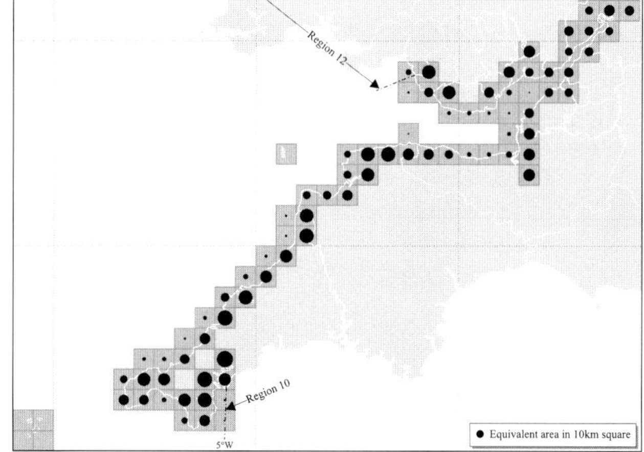

Map 8.2.3 Meadows, verges and low intensity amenity grasslands and semi-natural cropped swards, not maintained as short turf. Note: area of circle indicates the area of this land cover type in the 10 km square. Source: Countryside Survey (1990), ITE Monks Wood.

large area of grade 2 land extending for some 30 km along the coastal plain between Barry and Kenfig. The rocky headlands of south-west Cornwall are not in agricultural use and are therefore not graded (MAFF 1979).

The Somerset Levels and the Gwent Levels have been used for agriculture since the Roman occupation, often on land claimed from the intertidal zone. Much of the Somerset Levels remains as unimproved pasture, but the Gwent Levels have experienced considerable agricultural improvement. In some parts of the Somerset Levels the ditches are regularly inundated by seasonal or daily high tides. Improved drainage and the use of fertilisers have resulted in the ecological impoverishment of many of the ditches in the Gwent and Somerset Levels. In the Somerset Moors and the Gordano Levels (Avon), further inland, the wet grassland overlies peat, which is still being extracted on a commercial basis. Water level management schemes are being developed for wet grasslands throughout the region (see also section 3.5.3).

Doody (undated) compares 1:10,000 maps from 1889 and 1963 and summarises the changes in agricultural land use on the Cornwall and north Devon coasts. During the period there was a reduction of 21% in the area of 'rough pasture' or 'scrub'. Where grazing has declined on cliff-top habitats, grassland is tending to scrub over; the loss of the Cornish chough has been attributed to this habitat change (Bignal & Curtis 1989).

The two main recent overviews relating to dune grazing in the region are Radley's (1994) study of English dunes and Dargie's (1994) study of Welsh dunes. The distribution of grazed sites identified in the surveys is shown on Map 8.2.4. The Cornwall and Devon section of the region's coastline showed some of the highest concentrations of dune grazing in the country, comparable with levels in northern England. This corresponds with the stronger tradition of livestock grazing in these areas generally, compared with southern and eastern England, where agriculture on sand dunes has largely been displaced by recreational use. In the north-eastern part of the region dune grazing is uncommon.

Map 8.2.4 also shows the distribution of grazed saltmarsh in the region. Sheep are grazed on the marshes of the Severn Estuary and Ogmore. In addition, the extensive grassy lawns found on saltmarshes are often of particular value for grazing wildfowl (see also section 5.12).

The west of the region is notable for its extensive areas of coastal broadleaved woodlands, much of which is ancient semi-natural woodland (Spencer & Kirby 1992). Table 8.2.1 lists the major coastal woodlands in the region, including the larger (>5 ha) ancient semi-natural woodlands listed in English Nature's and the Countryside Council for Wales's Ancient Woodland Inventories (Map 8.2.5).

8.2.3 Information sources used

The main source of information on agricultural land was the Countryside Survey 1990 (ITE 1993), which is based primarily on high resolution satellite images. These images show the dominant land cover for each 25 m x 25 m area of Great Britain. Land cover is classified into seventeen key types (including tilled land and managed grassland) and field surveys of randomly selected areas were used to check the results. Maps 8.2.1, 8.2.2 and 8.2.3 are derived from these data from the DoE Countryside Information System.

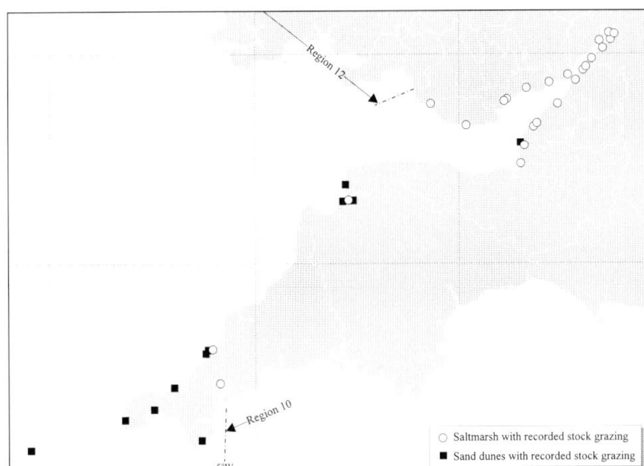

Map 8.2.4 Saltmarshes and sand dunes with recorded grazing. See Maps 3.6.1 and 3.2.1 for distribution of saltmarsh and sand dune sites respectively. Source: JNCC Coastal Database.

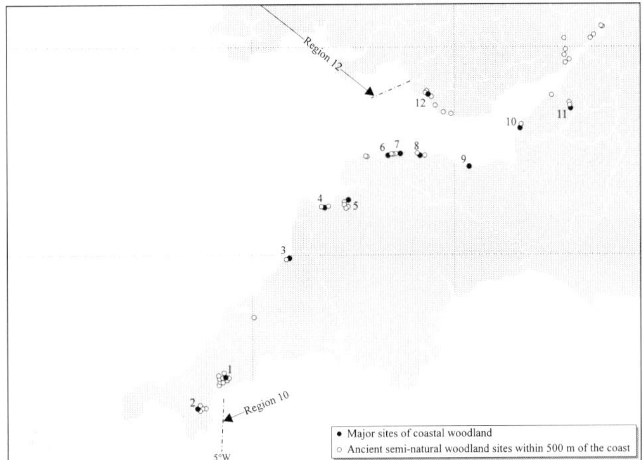

Map 8.2.5 Coastal woodland. Numbers refer to Table 8.2.1. Source: English Nature Ancient Woodland Inventory, Countryside Council for Wales Ancient Woodland Inventory, Ordnance Survey Landranger maps (© Crown copyright).

The main limitations of the data derive from errors in classifying areas covered by a mixture of land types and from the form of presentation used in the maps. The Countryside Information System can provide data on a 1 km square framework. More detailed information on agricultural land use and grades (for example, information on set-aside targets) is available from ADAS, Heritage Coast plans and local plans. Sand dune and saltmarsh grazing information for Map 8.2.4 comes from the JNCC's Coastal Database, and from cited references. Woodland information (Map 8.2.5) was obtained from the 1:50,000 scale Ordnance Survey Landranger maps and the Inventory of Ancient Woodlands (see Spencer & Kirby 1992), available from English Nature local teams and Countryside Council for Wales offices.

8.2.4 Acknowledgements

Thanks to Chris Reid, English Nature, and Jim Latham, Countryside Council for Wales, for assistance with Ancient Woodland Inventory data.

Table 8.2.1 Areas of significant woodland within 500 m of the coast (centre grid ref.)

Site no.	*Site name*	*Grid ref.*	*Area of wood (ha)*	*Area of ancient semi-natural woodland (ha)*	*Notes*
	Cornwall				
1	River Fal and Tresillian River (banks of ria), including:	SW83, SW84	350	?	Woodland in discontinuous blocks along the arms of this ria; the majority is ancient semi-natural, with a small proportion of replanted woodland and more recent plantation
	'Ruan Lanihorne Wood'	SW891424	11	11	AWI
	Lamorran Wood	SW882423	34	34	AWI
	Penkevil Wood	SW872413	28	26	AWI
	Penhale Wood	SW857439	36	36	AWI
	Kea Wood	SW846424	6	6	AWI
	'Truro River Wood'	SW853420	25	25	AWI
	Polgerran/Borlase/+ Woods	SW860402	59	52	AWI
	Chapel/Cododden Woods	SW844394	21	21	AWI
	'Tolcarne Wood'	SW843387	7	7	AWI
2	Helford River, including:	SW72, SW71	100	?	Mostly along north bank, upriver. Some is ancient woodland.
	Calamansack Wood	SW753271	11	11	AWI
	'Helford Wood'	SW751265	5	5	AWI
	Merthen Wood	SW731262	63	63	AWI
	Bonallack Wood	SW716261	9	9	AWI
	Treraven/Derry's Woods	SX002707	13	6	AWI
3	Dizzard Point, including:	SX1699	75	?	Oak-dominated broadleaved woodland on cliffs; trees dwarfed due to exposure; important for lichens
	Dizzard Woodland	SX168992	39	39	AWI
	Devon				
4	Windbury Point to Peppercombe, including:	SS2630-SS2438	350	?	Long stand of broadleaved woodland along 10 km of coast
	Barton/Buck's/+Woods	SS333237	119	85	AWI
	Worthygate/Sloo Woods	SS368238	39	39	AWI
5	River Torridge above Bideford, including:	SS4723	50	?	Broadleaved woods on both banks just below tidal limit
	Upcott Wood	SS450250	8	8	AWI
	Ford House Wood	SS450257	5	5	AWI
	Pillmouth Wood	SS464238	9	9	AWI
	Pixey Copse/+	SS474242	35	35	AWI
	Northfield Wood	SS555477	18	18	AWI
	Bamant's Wood	SS560476	6	6	AWI
6	Woody Bay	SS6849	125	?	Broadleaved
	West Woodybay Wood	SS672492	12	12	AWI
	Woody Bay/The Pines	SS678488	19	19	AWI
	Six Acre/+ Woods	SS696490	36	25	AWI
7	Lynton	SS7149	25	?	Mixed
	Somerset				
	Stag's Head Wood/+	SS801493	5	5	AWI
8	Foreland Point to Porlock Bay	SS7949-SS8648	300	?	8 km stand of broadleaved woodland, continuing inland at the eastern end
	Yearnor/Worthy/+ Woods	SS845484	290	247	AWI
9	Watchet	ST0443 & ST1043	25	?	Several small stands of mixed and broadleaved woodland
	Avon				
10	Weston-super-Mare (Weston Woods), including:	ST3162-ST3262	125	?	Broadleaved woods abutting sea and north edge of town
	Weston Woods	ST325627	23	23	AWI
	East Wood	ST471775	11	11	AWI
11	Avon Gorge, including:	ST5474-ST5673	250	?	Large area of mixed woodland on west bank of River Avon
	Rownham Wood	ST563728	5	5	AWI
	Clifton Down Wood	ST563745	10	10	AWI

Table 8.2.1 Areas of significant woodland within 500 m of the coast (centre grid ref.) (continued)

Site no.	*Site name*	*Grid ref.*	*Area of wood (ha)*	*Area of ancient semi-natural woodland (ha)*	*Notes*
	Gloucestershire				
	Smith's Wood	SO725095	5	5	AWI
	Gatcombe Wood	SO680055	9	9	AWI
	Warren Grove	SO656033	19	19	AWI
	Cumberland / Baker's Woods	ST560940	18	18	AWI
	Chapelhouse Wood	ST537953	16	15	AWI
	Caswell Wood / James' Thorns	ST540985	233	175	AWI
	Lord's / Victual's Groves	SO533039	94	94	AWI
	Gwent				
	Bulwark*	ST542922	5	5	AWI
	South Glamorgan				AWI
	Porthkerry*	ST086669	5	5	AWI
	Tresilian*	SS948679	5	5	AWI
	Cwm Nash*	SS906701	5	5	AWI
	Mid Glamorgan				
12	Candleston Woods, Ogmore River	SS8777	50	?	Broadleaved woodland bordering dunes on western river bank
	Cwm Mawr*	SS895723	5	5	AWI
	Dunraven Bay*	SS886734	5	5	AWI
	Ewenny Down*	SS903763	10	10	AWI

Sources: English Nature & Countryside Council for Wales Ancient Woodland Inventories; OS Landranger 1:50,000 series maps. Key: / + several small sites grouped together; *name of wood not available: adjacent place name given and approximate area; AWI = Ancient Woodland Inventory site; ? = not known. Note: site numbers refer to Map 8.2.5.

8.2.5 Further sources of information

A. References cited

Bignal, E.M., & Curtis, D.J., *eds*. 1989. *Choughs and land use in Europe.* Paisley, Scottish Chough Study Group.

Burd, F. 1989. *The saltmarsh survey of Great Britain.* Peterborough, Nature Conservancy Council. (Research & survey in nature conservation, No. 17.)

Dargie, T.C.D. 1994. *Sand dune vegetation of Great Britain. Part 3. Wales.* Peterborough, Joint Nature Conservation Committee.

Doody, J.P. 1988. *The management of saltmarshes.* Peterborough, Nature Conservancy Council. (Coastal habitat network, No. 2. April, 32.)

Doody, J.P. Undated. *Coastal habitat change - a historical review of man's impact on the coastline of Great Britain.* Peterborough, Nature Conservancy Council (unpublished draft).

Institute of Terrestrial Ecology. 1993. *Countryside survey 1990: main report.* London, Department of the Environment.

Ministry of Agriculture, Fisheries and Food and Welsh Office Environment Department. 1979. *Agricultural land classification of England and Wales (Map).* Pinner, Ministry of Agriculture, Fisheries and Food and Welsh Office Environment Department.

Radley, G.P. 1994. *Sand dune vegetation of Great Britain. Part 1. England.* Peterborough, Joint Nature Conservation Committee.

Spencer, J.W., & Kirby, K.J. 1992. An inventory of ancient woodland for England and Wales. *Biological Conservation, 62:* 77-93.

B. Further reading

Beeftink, W.G. 1977. Saltmarshes. *In: The coastline.* London, John Wiley and Sons.

Davidson, N.C., Laffoley, D.d'A., Doody, J.P., Way, L.S., Gordon, J., Key, R., Drake, C.M., Pienkowski, M.W., Mitchell, R., & Duff, K.L. 1991. *Nature conservation and estuaries in Great Britain.* Peterborough, Nature Conservancy Council.

Devon County Council. 1995. *Devon Coastal Statement.* Exeter, Devon County Council.

Doody, J.P. 1987. *Botanical and entomological implications of saltmarsh management in intertidal areas.* Sandy, Royal Society for the Protection of Birds. (RSPB Symposium.)

Eno, N.C., *ed.* 1991. *Marine conservation handbook.* 2nd ed. Peterborough, English Nature.

Nature Conservancy Council. 1986a. *Cornwall inventory of ancient woodland.* Peterborough, Nature Conservancy Council (provisional).

Nature Conservancy Council. 1986b. *Devon inventory of ancient woodland.* Peterborough, Nature Conservancy Council (provisional).

Rothwell, P. 1989. Saving our saltmarsh. *Shooting and Countryside Times, July/Aug.*

Thomas, R.C. *Ancient woodland inventory: database documentation.* Peterborough, English Nature. (English Nature Reseach Report, No. 131.)

Welsh Office. 1993. *Environmental digest for Wales No. 8, 1994.* Cardiff, Welsh Office.

Whitbread, A.M., & Kirby, K.J. 1992. *Summary of NVC woodland descriptions.* Peterborough, JNCC. UK Nature Conservation Series, No. 4.

C. Contact names and addresses

Type of information	Contact address & telephone no.
Agriculture policy, England	MAFF, Whitehall Place, London SW1A 2HH, tel: 0171 270 3000
Land use, agricultural land grades, set-aside (MAFF/ ADAS Land Service) - England	ADAS, Oxford Spire Business Park, The Boulevard, Kidlington, Oxford OX5 1NZ, tel: 01865 842742
Agriculture policy, land use, agricultural land grades, set-aside, Wales	*Welsh Office Agriculture Department, Cardiff, tel: 01222 825111
ITE Countryside Survey 1990	*Department of Rural Affairs, DoE, Bristol, tel: 0117 921 8811
ITE Countryside Survey 1990	*Land Use Group, ITE, Merlewood, tel: 01539 532264
ITE Countryside Survey 1990	*Environmental Information Centre, ITE, Monks Wood, tel: 01487 773381
Agriculture - Devon	MAFF Regional Service Centre, Government Buildings, Alphington Road, Exeter, Devon EX2 8NQ, tel: 01392 77951
Agriculture - Cornwall	MAFF Regional Service Centre, Pydar House, Pydar Street, Truro, Cornwall TR1 2XD, tel: 01872 265 400
Ancient semi-natural woodland - Devon & Cornwall	*EN Devon & Cornwall Local Team, Okehampton, tel: 01837 55045
Ancient semi-natural woodland - Somerset & Avon	*EN Somerset & Avon Local Team, Taunton, tel: 01823 283211
Ancient semi-natural woodland - Gloucestershire	*EN Three Counties Local Team, Malvern Wells, tel: 01684 560616
Ancient semi-natural woodland - Monmouth, Newport, Cardiff, Vale of Glamorgan and Bridgend	*CCW South Area, Cardiff, tel: 01222 772400
Distribution, ownership and management of woodlands - England	West Country Conservancy, Forestry Authority, The West Country, The Castle, Mamhead, Exeter, Devon EX6 8HD, tel: 01626 890666
Distribution, ownership and management of woodlands - Wales	South Wales Conservancy, Forestry Authority, Cantref Court, Brecon Road, Abergavenny, Gwent NP7 7AX, tel: 01873 850060
Soil surveys in England and Wales	John Hazelden, Soil Survey and Land Research Centre, Cranfield University, Silsoe, Bedford MK45 4DT, tel: 01525 863000

*Starred contact addresses are given in full in the Appendix.

8.3 Infrastructure

S.L. Fowler, M.J. Dunbar, C.A. Crumpton & M.J. Goodwin

8.3.1 Introduction

This section summarises the infrastructure of the region, including population distribution, industry, ports, harbours, communications and power generation. Oil and gas exploration and development are covered in section 9.5.

The coastline from Falmouth to Portishead in the Severn Estuary is very sparsely populated, with few large towns, while further north the region is more populous: Bristol, Newport and Cardiff are major population centres, with good rail and road communications. However, average coastal population density is low compared with the south coast of England, and the area in the region occupied by industrial and domestic developments is relatively small. Avonmouth (Bristol) is the main centre of industrial activity, with other industrial centres at Newport and Cardiff. There are no large oil refineries. The region has many non-industrial developments under way on its estuaries, including housing, car parks and marinas, and there are many plans for further developments of this kind (Buck 1993). Cardiff Bay is undergoing major development for recreation and business, especially related to the recently-approved tidal barrage. The open coast is generally unmodified by industrial or urban use.

Competition in the electricity generating industry has been intense since privatisation in 1990. This has stimulated some diversification, which has been further encouraged by guidelines such as the government's Non Fossil Fuel Obligation (NFFO) and the EC's 1988 Directive on Large Combustion Plant. Power is produced on the region's coast by conventional, nuclear and renewable processes. Although the number of power producers has increased since privatisation, conventional power production is still largely controlled by two companies, PowerGen and National Power. UK power stations owned by National Power and PowerGen have a combined capacity of 36,500 MW: approximately 90% of conventional power production in the UK (40,555 MW) (PowerGen pers. comm.). The remainder is produced by a number of smaller companies.

There are significant renewable energy developments in the region. The south-west of England and south Wales are particularly suitable for wind power generation because much of the coast is exposed to the prevailing south-westerly winds. In the Non Fossil Fuel Obligation (NFFO) Third Renewables Order, 141 projects were awarded contracts in England and Wales, with a combined output capacity of 630 MW. Of these, five (all wind farms) are in this region. The output of the region's two existing wind farms represents 6% of the 160.5 MW UK total wind power capacity (including that of wind farms under construction) (British Wind Energy Association 1994 pers. comm.). Including inland wind farms, south-west England and Wales account for two-thirds of the total British capacity for wind power generation.

8.3.2 Important locations

Residential development

Population levels in the west of the region are low, with Truro, Falmouth, Penzance, Newquay and Barnstaple the main residential centres. Further north-east there are more large population centres, but extensive sections of coast still remain relatively unpopulated: many towns and cities, such as Bridgwater, Bristol, Gloucester, Chepstow and Newport, are located on inner tidal stretches of rivers, away from the open coast. Others, such as Weston-super-Mare, Cardiff and Barry, are on the coast itself. Ilfracombe, Minehead, Burnham-on-Sea, Weston-super-Mare, Clevedon, Penarth, Barry and Porthcawl receive large numbers of holiday visitors in the summer (see section 9.7). Map 8.3.1 shows the coastal centres of population; the main towns and cities are listed in Table 8.3.1.

Industry

Large port facilities in the region were originally associated with major industrial developments and the proximity of sources of raw materials, such as (formerly) metals in Cornwall and coal, iron ore and limestone in south Wales. At Appledore there is a large ship and boatbuilding yard but it suffers from the restriction that ship launches are only possible at equinoctial high tides, owing to the presence of a sand bar across the mouth of the Taw-Torridge Estuary. In the north-east, the major port and industrial complex at Avonmouth dominates the industry of the Severn Estuary. Here there are chemical and refining works, industrial estates and associated docks and storage facilities. The

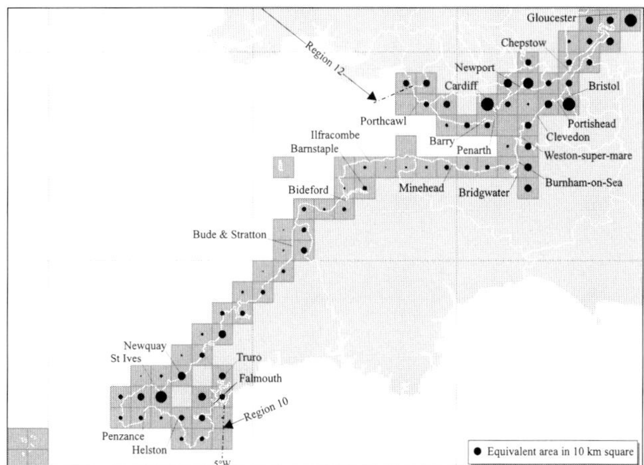

Map 8.3.1 Distribution of areas of residential development, major towns and cities. Note: area of circle indicates the area of this land cover type in the 10 km square. Source: Countryside Survey (1990); ITE Monks Wood; OS Landranger maps.

Table 8.3.1 Main towns and cities in Region 11

Town/City	*Population*
Truro	16,300
Falmouth	18,500
Helston	10,700
Penzance	19,500
St. Ives	11,000
Newquay	16,000
Bude & Stratton	6,800
Bideford	12,200
Barnstaple	19,000
Ilfracombe	10,100
Minehead	11,200
Bridgwater	26,100
Burnham-on-Sea	15,000
Weston-super-Mare	58,000
Clevedon	18,000
Portishead	11,300
Bristol	392,000
Gloucester	104,000
Chepstow	9,300
Newport	135,000
Cardiff	290,000
Penarth	24,000
Barry	41,600
Porthcawl	15,600

Source: Cook (1993). See Map 8.3.1.

industrial areas of south Wales, which arose from coal mining and heavy industries that have now declined, are diversifying into other activities such as electronics. Newport and Cardiff are still important industrial centres. Industrial infrastructure in the region is detailed in Table 8.3.2; important locations are named on Map 8.3.2.

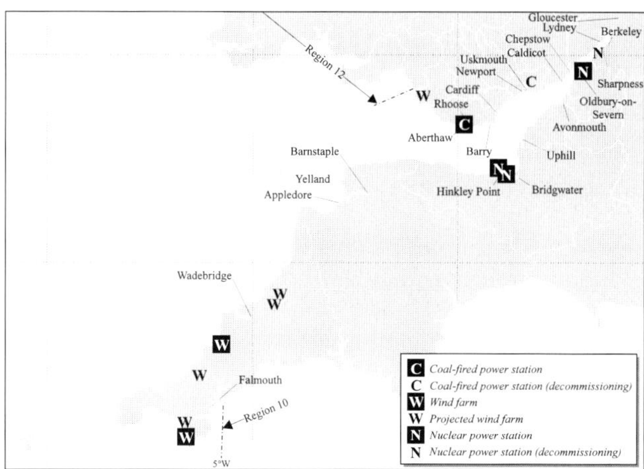

Map 8.3.2 Major centres of industrial activity. Source: OS Landranger maps.

Ports and harbours

Table 8.3.3 lists ports and harbours in the region (Map 8.3.3). The tin and copper boom of the 18th and 19th centuries made Cornwall's ports some of the busiest in the country. Similarly, the south Wales ports were major exporters of coal and steel products. In parallel with the decline in the metallurgical industries, many of these ports have declined in national importance and some currently serve only leisure boating. Today, the largest ports in the region are Avonmouth (Port of Bristol), Newport, Cardiff and Barry Port; Newlyn is the largest fishing port in England (Penwith District Council 1994), with landings in 1992 worth £21 million (see also section 9.1). Docks and significant berthing facilities are also located at Falmouth, Truro, on the Helford River, at Hayle, Padstow, Bideford, Bridgewater and Sharpness. Some of the smaller ports, such as Bideford,

Table 8.3.2 Major areas of coastal industrial development

Location	*Grid ref.*	*Details*
Falmouth	SW8332	30 ha shipyards
Wadebridge	SW9973	Boat building
Appledore	SS4629	10 ha shipyard
Yelland	SS4832	Disused power station; boatyards
Barnstaple	SS5433	30 ha industrial estate
Bridgwater	ST3038	Factory
	ST3041	Dunball wharf: warehouses
Avonmouth	ST5078-ST5483	900 ha; major port and industrial area along 6 km of coastline, including fuel depots, industrial estates, smelting works, chemical works and various other works
Sharpness	SO6702	Industry associated with docks, development land allocated
Gloucester	SO8015	15 ha works; docks area undergoing redevelopment
Lydney	SO6401	70 ha industrial estate, paper mills
Chepstow	ST5391	Newhouse Development Park
Caldicot	ST5087	Sudbrook paper mill (10 ha); works
Newport	ST3586-ST3986	500 ha steel works, 3 km from coast
Uskmouth	ST3284-ST3385	150 ha works, intermingled with dock facilities
Newport	ST3185-ST3285	>200 ha chemical works; large areas of industry
Cardiff	ST1973-ST2179	300 ha various industry, much of which is closely associated with docks. Includes Gulf Oil, Spillers Milling, Allied Steel and Wire. Barrage currently under development.
Barry	ST1368	70 ha chemical works; trading estate to east of harbour
	ST1167	40 ha; various works intermingled with docks
Rhoose	ST0665	10 ha works
Aberthaw	ST0366	20 ha; most of estuary claimed for industry (now much declined except for two power stations); cement works at north of site

Source: Ordnance Survey Landranger 1:50,000; Buck (1993; in prep.). See Map 8.3.2.

Table 8.3.3 Ports and harbours

Name	*Details*
St. Mawes	Small harbour on east side of Fal Estuary
Falmouth Harbour	Very large natural, sheltered, deep-water harbour owned by Falmouth Harbour Comissioners, operated by A & P Appledore, Falmouth Docks. Yacht marina and leisure harbour.
Falmouth Docks	Port Authority: Falmouth; operated by A & P Falmouth Ltd; container facilities; three dry docks and five quays; associated leisure boatbuilding facilities; 10,000 sq m open storage, 10,000 sq m covered storage. Principal traffic & facilities: dry bulks, general cargo, project cargo (heavy lift), fish.
Falmouth Yacht Marina	280 berths plus 80 visitors berths
Mylor Yacht Harbour	Small wharf and harbour at entrance to Mylor Creek
Truro Harbour	Busy commercial port; owned and operated by Carrick District Council; harbour and approaches have to be dredged annually. Four berths, total length: 330 m; 40-50,000 tonnes per year; dry bulks, grain / feedstuffs, forest products, project cargo (heavy lift). Export cargoes include calcified seaweed, scrap steel, boat hulls and specialist cargoes such as generators. Import cargoes include coal, steel, coils, animal feed, fertiliser and palletised timber. Shiprepair / graving docks, lay up berths and yacht marina.
Penryn Harbour	Fishing and leisure port
Helford River	Three quays on north bank at Merthan, Constantine and Gweek (latter is a small fishing port with proposals to extend its commercial wharf); three on south bank at Tremayne Quay, Witham Quay, quay and slip at Helford
Mullion Cove Harbour	Small fishing port owned and operated by the National Trust; ten moorings only
Porthleven	Small harbour
Penzance Harbour	Five berths (310 m); 20,000 tonnes per year; much of cargo handled is for the Isles of Scilly; passenger and cargo ferries to Scilly. Dry bulks, general and project cargo (heavy lift). Ship repair / graving docks, lay-up berths & yacht marina.
Newlyn Harbour	Owned and operated by Newlyn Pier and Harbour Commissioners. Largest fishing port in England (150 vessels); little other commercial traffic.
Mousehole	Small harbour
Isles of Scilly: St. Mary's	Small port operated by the Duchy of Cornwall. The principal port for import of goods and supplies from the mainland. Passenger ferry from Penzance (more frequent and very busy between May-September).
St. Ives	Small harbour
Hayle	Owner / operator: Hayle Harbour Co Ltd; three berths: 200 m length; 70,000 tonnes pa; open storage: 3,000 sq m. Handles dry bulks, general cargo, fish. Commercial vessel building and repair.
Newquay	Fishing port owned and operated by Restormel Borough Council
Padstow Harbour	Fishing fleet (also fishing from Wadebridge), and leisure harbour, some commercial traffic. Main cargoes are fertilisers, rock, stone and sand from Camel Estuary.
Bude	Small harbour owned and operated by North Cornwall District Council
Lundy Island	Landing point only. Regular tourist trips from Bideford. Island owned by the Landmark Trust.
Appledore	Free port (small harbour)
Bideford Harbour	Small port owned by Torridge District Council; two berths: 164 m total length; occasional commercial traffic; 60,000 tonnes pa; dry bulks; tourist trips to Lundy Island
Instow, Barnstaple	Quays and berthing
Ilfracombe	Harbour
Watermouth	Small harbour
Porlock Weir	Small harbour
Minehead	Harbour
Watchet Harbour	Presently used by light commercial traffic
Bridgwater	Port owned by North Somerset Council and operated by Watts Shipping, ARC and Nuclear Electric. Proposals for expansion of facilities at Combwich and Hinkley Point. Facilities at Dunball wharf: 200 m of berthing; 80,000 tonnes pa; 11,000 sq m open storage; 5,500 sq m covered storage; principal cargoes dry bulks, grain / feedstuffs, forest products. Ro-ro (roll on, roll off) capacity at Nuclear Electric Combwich berth for own cargoes.
Burnham-on-Sea	Jetty
Weston-super-Mare	Harbour, pier
Bristol City	Owned and operated by Bristol City Council; docks and yacht marina; accepts vessels up to 14.9 m beam
Port of Bristol	Owned and operated by The Bristol Port Company; includes Royal Edward Dock, Avonmouth Dock (on north bank of Avon) and Royal Portbury Dock (south bank), all at Avonmouth; 18 berths, 3,935 m total length; 7,500,000 tonnes pa; principal traffic & facilities: lo-lo (crane load on and off), vehicles / wheeled cargoes, passengers, dry bulks, grain / feedstuffs, hazardous cargoes, forest products, oil / petroleum, other liquid bulk, general cargo, project cargo (heavy lift)
Sharpness Docks	Owned and operated by British Waterways. 12 berths, 3,650 total length; 45,000 sq m open storage, 35,000 sq m covered storage; dry bulks, grain / feedstuffs, hazardous cargoes, forest products, general cargo, project cargo (heavy lift); ship repair / graving docks, yacht marina, lay up berths, leisure craft moorings
Gloucester Docks	Gloucester Harbour Trustees. No longer operating as a commercial dock. Subject to major dockland redevelopment for leisure and commerce during 1980s.
Lydney	Harbour
Newport Docks	Associated British Ports. 23,000 sq m open storage. 73,760 sq m covered storage. 5,569 m length of berths. Lo-lo, ro-ro, dry bulks, grain / feedstuffs, fruit / vegetables, forest products (major port for timber, over 500,000 tonnes handled per year), general cargo, project cargo (heavy lift). Shiprepair / graving docks and lay up berths.

Table 8.3.3 Ports and harbours (continued).

Name	*Details*
Cardiff Port	Associated British Ports. Major general port; five berths, 5,589 total length; 2,500,000 tonnes pa; particular facilities for coal, perishables, grain, sand, liquids, scrap metal; lo-lo, ro-ro, passengers, dry bulks, grain/feedstuffs, fruit/vegetables, refrigerated products, hazardous cargoes, forest products, oil/petroleum, other liquid bulk, general cargo, fish, livestock, project cargo (heavy lift); freeport area; rail terminal; open storage; covered storage: 55,000 sq m
Barry Port	Port administered from Cardiff; owned and operated by Associated British Ports; 8 berths: 5,743 m total length; 500,000 tonnes pa; dry bulks, grain/feedstuffs, fruit/vegetables, hazardous cargoes, forest products, oil/petroleum & other liquid bulk, general cargo, project cargo (heavy lift). Three docks. Dockland regeneration scheme. Large storage areas, wide range of liquids facilities (one of largest storage facilities in Britain). Open storage; 20,000 sq m covered storage. Rail terminal.

Sources: Walker (1996), D'Olivera & Featherstone (1993) and Ordnance Survey Landranger 1:50,000 maps. Note: refer to Table 9.7.3 for further details of recreational harbours and associated facilities.

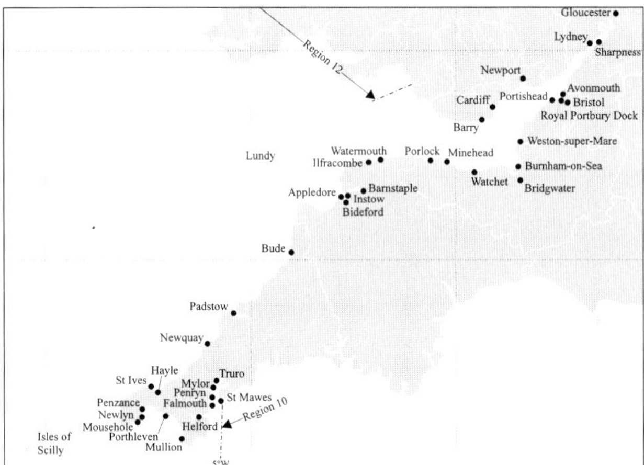

Map 8.3.3 Ports and harbours. Source: OS Landranger maps.

Hayle and Padstow, take infrequent commercial traffic, and the ports of Penzance and St. Mary's (Isles of Scilly) ply an important supply and passenger trade between the Cornish mainland and the Isles of Scilly. There are also numerous small harbours and landing beaches on the Cornish coast, which take recreational boating traffic as well as being traditional fishing ports or landing places. Some of the estuaries and coastal towns also have substantial marinas and recreational boating facilities (see also section 9.7).

Power generation

Map 8.3.2 shows all the region's power installations, listed in Table 8.3.4. The operational coal-fired power station at Aberthaw produces 4% of the UK's conventionally-produced power. Another coal-fired power station (Uskmouth) is now being decommissioned. Approximately one-fifth of UK electricity is currently produced by nuclear power. This is produced by thirteen power stations (eleven owned by Nuclear Electric plc and two by British Nuclear Fuels Ltd.), of which three, with a combined output of 2,090 MW, are located in the region, at Hinkley Point (two) and Oldbury-on-Severn. A fourth, Berkeley, is currently being decommissioned. The eleven operating stations owned by Nuclear Electric in England and Wales produce 8,639 MW, estimated to be around one sixth of present electricity requirements (Nuclear Electric 1994 pers. comm.). The nuclear power stations in this region, with a combined output of 2,090 MW, account for approximately one quarter of this total.

Table 8.3.5 lists proposed renewable energy installations in the region that have received contracts under the NFFO Third Renewables Order.

The Severn Estuary has the second largest tidal range in the world. Four years of research into the environmental and technical implications of a proposed tidal barrage have recently been completed by a group of public and private organisations. With an installed capacity of 8,640 MW the barrage would have the capacity to produce 6% of the UK's electricity needs (DTI 1994). However, the economic and environmental implications of constructing such a barrage have brought the project to an indefinite standstill (ETSU pers. comm.).

Road, rail, air and sea communications

General access to the coastal population centres is good, with the M4, M5 and A30 roads carrying large volumes of business and recreational traffic. Roads serving the South Wales area are particularly good, having initially developed to serve the large populations working in the coal mining, steel and associated industries. In contrast, parts of the north Cornwall and Devon coast are still relatively inaccessible by road or rail. The Severn Bridge has recently been augmented by the Second Severn Crossing, opened in 1996. There is a rail tunnel 4 km south of the original suspension bridge. Cardiff has an international airport, situated at Rhoose, and there are several other airfields and smaller airports (Table 8.3.6).

There is a traffic separation scheme for shipping off Land's End and routeing recommendations exist to the south and west of the Isles of Scilly. Vessels of more than 10,000 Gross Registered Tonnage (GRT) should not use the traffic separation scheme between Land's End and the Isles of Scilly in poor weather. There are several regionally important ferries in the region, including the main communication link to the Isles of Scilly, and smaller ferries across estuaries and inlets.

8.3.3 Information sources used

The information on population statistics comes from Cook (1993), which uses data from population censuses from a number of dates, including the 1991 census; some figures may therefore be somewhat out of date. Map 8.3.1 is adapted from the ITE (1993) Countryside Survey database, which is derived from 1990 satellite imagery. Areas

Table 8.3.4 Coastal power generating installations in Region 11

Name of project	*Method of production*	*Power producing capacity (MW)*
Goonhilly Downs	Wind	5.6 (14 x 400 KW turbines)
Delabole	Wind	4.0 (10 x 400 KW turbines)
Hinkley Point A	Nuclear (Magnox)	470.0
Hinkley Point B	Nuclear (Advanced Gas Cooled Reactor)	1,170.0
Oldbury-on-Severn	Nuclear (Magnox)	450.0
Berkeley	Nuclear (Magnox)	Decommissioning
Uskmouth	Coal	20.0 (decommissioning)
Aberthaw	Coal	1,700.0
Total		***3,819.6***

Source: DTI pers. comm., Nuclear Electric pers. comm., National Power pers. comm.

Table 8.3.5 Schemes awarded contracts under the NFFO Third Renewables Order

Site name	*Location*	*Proposer*	*Technology*	*Proposed power output (MW)*
Trannack Downs	Helston	Windfarms Ltd	Wind	0.380
Greenlane Farm	Porthtowan	Atlantic Energy Ltd	Wind	0.508
Greylake Barton	Camelford	Greylake Barton Ltd	Wind	3.371
Davidstow	Camelford	Davidstow Windfarm Ltd	Wind	3.371
New Werfa	Ogmore	Zond UK Ltd	Wind	5.226
Total				***12.856***

Source: DTI (pers. comm.)

represent land cover types 'urban' and 'suburban/rural development'. Information on industrial development was taken from Buck (1993, and in prep.), Cook (1993) and Ordnance Survey Landranger 1:50,000 maps.

Areas of coastal industrial developments in Table 8.3.2 and Map 8.3.2 are as shown on OS 1:50,000 Landranger maps; further information may be obtained from local councils or Chambers of Commerce. Most of the information on ports was derived from Walker (1996).

Lord Donaldson (1994) records that there is virtually no clear information available on where ships go within UK waters. The Department of Transport, UK Offshore Operators Association and the Health and Safety Executive have addressed this issue by jointly funding a project to produce a computer assisted ship traffic database (COAST), which provides details of 3,500 shipping routes across the UK continental shelf, giving the number of vessels and their distribution by ship type, age and flag. Lord Donaldson also records that no records are kept of how many ships use UK port facilities. Under MARPOL (the United Nations' International Convention on the Prevention of Pollution from Ships), the UK must provide port facilities that are "adequate to meet the needs of ships using them and do not cause undue delay to ships". These facilities should prevent ships from discharging oil and other wastes into the sea. However, Lord Donaldson (1994) describes UK facilities as "inadequate". A survey of the quality of UK port reception facilities for the disposal of ship's wastes was carried out by WRC (1995). The Marine Safety Agency also carry out a regular quantification of port reception facilities for the International Maritime Organisation.

8.3.5 Acknowledgements

Thanks go to Sam Davis, English Nature, for information used in this section.

8.3.6 Further sources of information

A. References cited

Buck, A.L. 1993. *An inventory of UK estuaries. Volume 2. South-west Britain*. Peterborough, Joint Nature Conservation Committee.

Buck, A.L. In prep. *An inventory of UK estuaries. 6. Southern England*. Peterborough, Joint Nature Conservation Committee.

Cook, C. 1993. *Pears cyclopaedia 1993-1994*. London, Penguin.

Department of Trade and Industry. 1994. *Technology status report No. 3: tidal power*. London, Department of Trade and Industry.

D'Olivera, B., & Featherstone, N.L. 1993. *The Macmillan and Silk Cut nautical almanac 1994*. Basingstoke, Macmillan.

Donaldson, J.F., Lord. 1994. *Safer seas, cleaner ships. Report of Lord Donaldson's inquiry into the prevention of pollution from merchant shipping*. London, HMSO. (CM2560.)

Institute of Terrestrial Ecology. 1993. *Countryside survey 1990: main report*. London, Department of the Environment.

Walker, N., *ed.* 1996. *Compass UK Ports Directory 1996/97*. King's Lynn, Compass Publications.

WRC. 1995. *The survey of UK reception facilities for oil and garbage*. Southampton, Marine Safety Agency Report No. 352.

B. Further reading

Brady, P. 1995. *Fishing vessels of Britain & Ireland 1995*. 3rd ed. London, Emap Business Communications.

British Marine Industries Federation. Undated. *Steering a balanced course: the boating industry and the marine environment*. Egham, British Marine Industries Federation.

British Oceanographic Data Centre. 1992. *UKDMAP (United Kingdom digital marine atlas)*. Birkenhead, BODC. (Computer software.)

British Ports Association. 1994. *British Ports Association 1994*. King's Lynn, Charter International.

British Ports Federation. Undated. *UK member ports directory*. London, British Ports Federation.

Davidson, N.C., Laffoley, D.d'A., Doody, J.P., Way, L.S., Gordon, J., Key, R., Drake, C.M., Pienkowski, M.W., Mitchell, R., & Duff, K.L. 1991. *Nature conservation and estuaries in Great Britain*. Peterborough, Nature Conservancy Council.

Department of the Environment. 1992. *Enterprise Zones*. London, Department of the Environment.
Department of Trade and Industry. 1994. *Digest of UK energy statistics 1994*. London, HMSO.
Department of Trade and Industry. 1994. The non-fossil fuel obligation. London, Department of Trade and Industry. *REview: the magazine of renewable energy, 22* (supplement).
Department of Transport. 1991. *Port statistics 1990*. London, Department of Transport & British Ports Federation.
Doody, J.P. Undated. *Coastal habitat change - an historical review of man's impact on the coastline of Great Britain*. Peterborough, Nature Conservancy Council (unpublished draft).
ENDS. 1994. Cleaner combustion technology - a revolution waiting to happen. *ENDS Report, No. 230, March 1994*. Environmental Data Services Ltd.
National Power plc. 1994. *Annual review 1994*. Swindon, National Power plc.
Office of Population Censuses & Surveys. 1994. *Mid-1993 population estimates for England and Wales*. London, OPCS. (OPCS Monitor PP1 94/2, 26 July 1994.)
Penwith District Council. 1994. *West Cornwall*. Penzance.
Sutton, G., *ed*. 1989. *ABP '89, a guide to the ports and shipping services of Associated British Ports Holdings plc*. King's Lynn, Charter International Publications.
Technica. 1985. *Shipping routes in the area of the United Kingdom continental shelf*. Prepared by Technica for the Department of Energy. London, HMSO.

C. Contact names and addresses

Type of information	*Contact address & telephone no.*
Planning developments: English and Welsh councils	
Bridgend	*Bridgend County Borough Council, Bridgend, tel: 01656 643643
City and County of Bristol	*Bristol City Council, Bristol, tel: 0117 922 2000
Cardiff	*Cardiff Council, Cardiff, tel: 01222 872000
Carrick	*Carrick District Council, Truro, tel: 01872 278131
Cornwall	*Cornwall County Council, Truro, tel: 01872 322000
Devon	*Devon County Council, Exeter, tel: 01392 382000
Forest of Dean	*Forest of Dean District Council, Coleford, tel: 01594 810000
Gloucestershire	*Gloucestershire County Council, Gloucester, tel: 01452 425000
Kerrier	*Kerrier District Council, Camborne, tel: 01209 712941
Monmouthshire	*Monmouthshire County Council, Pontypool, tel: 01495 762311
Newport	*Newport County Borough Council, Newport, tel: 01633 244491
North Cornwall	*North Cornwall District Council, Wadebridge, tel: 01208 812255
North Devon	*North Devon District Council, Barnstaple, tel: 01271 327711
North Somerset	*North Somerset District Council, Weston-super-Mare, tel: 01934 631701
Penwith	*Penwith District Council, Penzance, tel: 01736 62341
Restormel	*Restormel District Council, St. Austell, tel: 01726 74466
Sedgemoor	*Sedgemoor District Council, Bridgwater, tel: 01278 435435
Somerset	*Somerset County Council, Taunton, tel: 01823 333451

Type of information	*Contact address & telephone no.*
Planning developments: English and Welsh councils (continued)	
South Gloucestershire	*South Gloucestershire District Council, Bristol, tel: 01454 416262
Stroud	*Stroud District Council, Stroud, tel: 01453 766321
Torridge	*Torridge District Council, Bideford, tel: 01237 476711
Vale of Glamorgan	*Vale of Glamorgan Council, Barry, tel: 01466 700111
West Somerset	*West Somerset District Council, Taunton, tel: 01984 632291
Power generation	
Energy production general	Department of Energy, 1 Palace Street, London SW1E 5HE, tel: 0171 238 3000
Energy production general	Secretary, Institute of Energy, 18 Devonshire Street, London W1N 2AU, tel: 0171 580 7124
Conventional power production, further details of power stations	Corporate Communications Officer, PowerGen plc, Westwood Way, Westwood Business Park, Coventry, CV4 8LG, tel: 01203 424000
Conventional power production, further details of power stations	Public Information Officer, National Power plc., Senator House, 85 Queen Victoria Street, London EC4V 4DP, tel: 0171 454 9494
Renewable energy	Secretary, Energy Technology Support Unit (ETSU), Renewable Energy Enquiries Bureau, Harwell, Oxfordshire OX11 0RA, tel: 01235 432450
Wave and hydro power	Project Director, Energy Systems Group, Coventry Polytechnic, Dept of Electrical, Electronic and Systems Engineering, Priory Street, Coventry CV1 5FB, tel: 01203 838861
Wind energy	British Wind Energy Association, 42 Kingsway, London WC2B 6EX, tel: 0171 404 3433

C. Contact names and addresses (continued)

Type of information	Contact address & telephone no.
Power generation (continued)	
Nuclear power production	Public Information Officer, Nuclear Electric plc., Barnett Way, Barnwood, Gloucester GL4 7RS, tel: 01452 652776
Nuclear issues - general	Secretary-General, British Nuclear Forum, 22 Buckingham Gate, London SW1E 6LB, tel: 0171 828 0166
Radioactive monitoring reports	*MAFF - DFR, Fisheries Laboratory, Lowestoft, tel: 01502 562244
Radioactive discharges	Information Officer, National Radiological Protection Board (NRPB), Chilton, Didcot, Oxfordshire OX11 0RQ, tel: 01235 831600
Ports and harbours	
British Ports Association	Africa House, 64-78 Kingsway, London WC2B 6AH, tel: 0171 242 1200
The UK Major Ports Group Ltd	150 Holborn, London EC1N 2LR, tel: 0171 404 2008
Port reception facilities	Marine Safety Agency, Spring Place, 105 Commercial Road, Southampton SO15 1EG, tel: 01703 329100
Barry Port	*Associated British Ports, tel: 01222 471311
Bideford Harbour	*Torridge District Council, tel: 01237 276711
Ports and harbours (continued)	
Bristol Port	*Port of Bristol Authority, tel: 0117 982 0000
Cardiff Port	*Associated British Ports, tel: 01222 471311
Falmouth Docks	*A&P Appledore (Falmouth) Ltd., tel: 01326 212100
Falmouth Harbour	*Falmouth Harbour Commissioners, tel: 01326 211376 (commercial), 314379/312285 (leisure)
Gloucester Harbour	*Gloucester Harbour Trustees, tel: 01452 25524
Newlyn Harbour	*Newlyn Pier and Harbour Commissioners, tel: 01736 62523
Newport Docks	*Associated British Ports, tel: 01633 244411
Newport Harbour	*Newport Harbour Commissioners, tel: 01633 265702
Padstow Harbour	*Padstow Harbour Commissioners, tel: 01841 532239
Penryn Harbour	*Carrick District Council, tel: 01872 278131
Penzance Harbour	*Penwith District Council, tel: 01736 62341
Sharpness Docks	*British Waterways Board, tel: 01453 811644
Truro Harbour	*Carrick District Council, tel: 01872 278131 (Harbour Office: tel: 01872 72130)

*Starred contact addresses are given in full in the Appendix.

8.4 Coastal defence

S.L. Fowler

8.4.1 Introduction

Coastal defence covers two types of works: coast protection and sea (or flood) defence. Coast protection works prevent or slow the erosion of land and encroachment by the sea. Sea defences protect low-lying land from flooding by the sea or rivers, especially to preserve human life and property in coastal settlements and industrial areas; many lengths were built in the past to protect low-lying agricultural land from flooding by the sea and to allow agricultural improvement and drainage. It is sometimes difficult to differentiate between the two different categories of coastal works, particularly where they protect against both erosion and flooding, or are owned and maintained privately or by bodies that are not usually responsible for coastal defences, for example the Ministry of Defence (MoD).

Coast protection works in Britain are most widely distributed along eroding coasts formed from relatively soft geological formations, and along urban and industrial coastlines, although some may border farmland. The Ministry of Agriculture, Fisheries and Food (MAFF) has recently published a detailed assessment of the extent and state of repair of coast protection works on the English coast (MAFF 1994). According to this report, more coastal works are found on the coasts of south and east England (which are gradually sinking following the end of the ice age) than occur anywhere else in England. Long stretches of these coasts are also heavily developed and/or eroding. There are relatively few eroding coasts or urban and industrial areas in south-west England, and this region has the lowest percentage of coast protection works recorded in England. Table 8.4.1 shows that less than 6% of the region's coast is protected against erosion. Coast protection works in Region 11 were mainly built to protect coastal settlements, industrial areas or historic sites; some are also located alongside bridges or road and rail embankments. Mechanisms include simple wooden groynes installed on beaches to control coastal sediment movement, soft engineering options such as the beach dewatering used to protect Newquay beach, through to major concrete engineering works (berms and seawalls). Some of these forms of coastal defence can provide vital 'toe' support to the base of coastal cliffs. Coastal works in the region are most extensive in the Severn Estuary (Map 8.4.1).

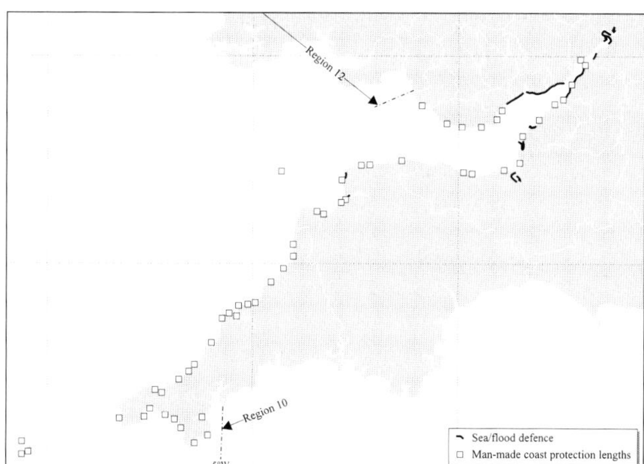

Map 8.4.1 Locations of coastal defence works. Man-made structures such as docks are included as coast protection. Source: MAFF (1994); OS Landranger maps.

Table 8.4.1 Coast protection in Region 11 and England

Coastline	*Total length (km)*	*Undeveloped length (km)*	*Coast protection length (km)*	*% protected*
Region 11 (English part only)	648	611	378	6
England	*2,925*	*2,065*	*860*	*29*
% English coast	24	32	4	-

Source: MAFF 1994 database. Note: lengths exclude estuary and harbour shorelines and are given to the nearest km.

Table 8.4.2 indicates the condition of coastal works in the region as identified in the MAFF survey and the degree of erosion that they are experiencing. According to that survey, there is significant erosion over only about 3 km (2%) of the region's English coast, rather less than the average on the coast of England as a whole (4%). About 17% of the coastal defences in the south-west of England require moderate or significant work, much less than on the coast of England as a whole (35%). The full results of the 1995 coastal defence survey by the Welsh Office were not available at the time of writing, but will provide an up-to-date overview of the scale and condition of works in Wales

Table 8.4.2 Condition of coast protection works and state of coastal erosion

Survey area	*Total length of coast** (km)*	*Length of coast defended (km)*	*Length of coast suffering significant erosion (km)*	*Proportion of coast defended (%)*	*Proportion of defences requiring work: Significant work (%)*	*Proportion of defences requiring work: Moderate work (%)*	*Proportion of coast suffering significant erosion (%)*
Taunton Area (Dorset to Wales)*	1,479	146	3	9.9	2	15	2.3
England	*3,763*	*860*	*134*	*23*	*6*	*29*	*4*

Source: MAFF (1994). Key: *this area includes most of Region 11; figures for Region 11 alone were not available; **estimated whole coast length to nearest km, including estuaries and harbours; see also section 8.4.4.

when published. According to that survey, 52% of the coasts of Gwent, South Glamorgan and Mid Glamorgan have coastal works of some kind in place.

Flood defences are particularly common on the British coast (and also in the region) where areas of former intertidal land (including saltmarsh) have been claimed from the sea for agricultural or industrial use, particularly in estuarine areas such as the Severn. They often take the form of artificial embankments bordering areas of land-claim. Storm surges, particularly when combined with high spring tides and/or heavy rain causing peak river flows, are the major flooding threat to this type of area. Rising sea levels and increasing frequency of storm conditions in the Atlantic and North Sea as a result of climate change are also increasing the future potential for coastal flooding and erosion on the coast and decreasing the expected useful life of coastal works in many regions (Irish Sea Forum 1992). National Rivers Authority (now the Environment Agency) (undated) maps suggest that nearly 300 km of the more than 400 km of sea defences in the three relevant NRA Sea Defence survey regions fall within Region 11 (Table 8.4.3). Virtually all estuaries in the region have been to some extent altered as a result of flood defence works. Major flood defence works are generally confined to the larger estuaries, most notably the Severn.

Table 8.4.3 England: ownership of sea defences in Region 11

Environment Agency Region	*Environment Agency (km)*	*Local authority (km)*	*Private/ other (km)*	*Total defended coast (km)*
South West	23	33	24	80
Wessex	43	30	24	98
Welsh	112	73	55	240
English parts of region	*178*	136	*103*	*418*
England	*805*	*242*	*212*	*1,259*

Source: NRA (1992). Notes: at the time of the survey, Region 11 comprised parts of the NRA South West, Wessex and Welsh Regions; figures for the region alone were not available. Thames Region was omitted from the survey as, being inland, it has no sea defences. Lengths are given to nearest km.

8.4.2 Important locations

Sea defences in the region are mainly built in low-lying estuaries and inlets, such as the Taw-Torridge Estuary, Bridgwater Bay and the Severn Estuary. Most of these defences are maintained by the Environment Agency. There are only a few sea defences in the south of the region.

Table 8.4.4 details the length of coast protection works on the south-west coast of England that were covered by the MAFF coast protection survey (MAFF 1994). These, in contrast to sea defence works, are concentrated along exposed (and thus eroding) coastlines.

Being low-lying, a high proportion of the coast of the former county of Gwent has sea defences, while about half of the South Glamorgan coast has either coast protection or sea defence works; the coast of Mid Glamorgan is largely natural (Table 8.4.5).

8.4.3 Management

Departmental responsibility for coast protection and sea defence in England and Wales lies with MAFF. Operational responsibility for coast protection works is generally the responsibility of local authorities under the Coast Protection Act (1949), although other bodies may maintain some stretches of coast protection. For example Railtrack (formerly British Rail) maintains some stretches of coastal works alongside railway lines, to prevent erosion or flooding. Flood or sea defences are generally the responsibility of the Environment Agency under the Water Resources Act 1991 and the Land Drainage Act 1994, although Internal Drainage Boards and local authorities are also empowered to undertake flood defence works.

MAFF set up an English Coastal Groups Forum in 1991 to promote the formation of coastal groups, to further co-operation between parties responsible for coastal defences, to identify research needs and to promote strategic planning of coastal defences. The forum meets twice a year and includes representatives of the Environment Agency and the regional coastal groups, which coordinate the work of adjacent coastal defence agencies (see section 10.2). The similar Welsh Coastal Groups Forum also meets twice a year.

Table 8.4.4 Lengths* of coastal protection (against erosion) on the English coast of Region 11 (to the Forest of Dean)

Local authority	*Total length of coast (km)*	*Length of coast protected (km)*	*Unprotected coast length (km)*	*Proportion of coast protected (%)*
Isles of Scilly	45	4	41	8.5
Penwith	147	10	137	6.8
Kerrier	88	1	87	1.5
Carrick (North)	25	<1	25	0.4
Restormel (North)	0	1	29	3.8
North Cornwall	117	4	114	3.1
Torridge	64	23	61	4.3
North Devon	79	2	77	2.3
West Somerset	28	3	26	10.4
Sedgemoor	13	<0	12	3.0
Woodspring	16	1	15	7.1
Bristol	16	5	12	28.1
Northavon	4	<0	4	2.2
Stroud	3	1	2	42.5
Forest of Dean	13	2	11	14.1

Source: MAFF 1994 database. Key: *to the nearest whole km.

Table 8.4.5 Wales: lengths* of coast with and without coastal works in Gwent, South Glamorgan and Mid Glamorgan

Local authority	*Coast protection* (km)	*Sea defence* (km)	*Unprotected 'soft' coast* (km)	*Unprotected 'hard' coast* (km)	*Total length of coastal works* (km)	*Total length of unprotected coast* (km)	*Total coast length* (km)	*Proportion protected/ defended* (%)
Gwent	1	35	<1	2	37	3	40	93
South Glamorgan	16	12	4	33	28	37	65	43
Mid Glamorgan	3	<1	6	16	3	22	25	11
Region 11 (Welsh counties)	20	47	11	52	67	63	130	52

Source: Welsh Office 1995 survey. Key: *rounded to the nearest whole km.

Five non-statutory regional coastal groups (sometimes known as coastal engineering groups), all based on coastal sediment cells (see section 2.4), have been established to promote coordination and liaison between coastal defence agencies in the region (see also section 10.3.2). The Cornwall Coast Protection Advisory Group covers the whole of this county, and extends into Region 10. The Devon Coast Protection Advisory Group and the Somerset and South Avon Group are also based on administrative boundaries, but the Severn Estuary Group includes representatives from England and Wales. The remit of the Swansea Bay Group (see Region 12) includes part of Region 11. The main aims of these groups are to seek a coordinated approach to all coastal engineering works by member authorities, to reduce the risk of works adversely affecting the neighbouring coastline and improve their understanding of coastal processes.

8.4.4 Information sources used

MAFF (1994) have recently published a detailed assessment of the extent and state of repair of coast protection works on the English coast and defence requirements to the end of the century. The survey also identified lengths of unprotected coast that were significantly eroding and where works might be necessary during the ten years following the survey. These detailed data are held by the contractors (Sir William Halcrow & Partners) and MAFF on a Geographic Information System (GIS), from which the information in Tables 8.4.1, 8.4.2 and 8.4.4 and on Map 8.4.1 was extracted. In these tables it is important to distinguish between whole-coast lengths and figures that refer only to coastal lengths included in the survey.

The National Rivers Authority carried out its Sea Defence Survey in 1991 (NRA 1992). The results are held mainly in a proprietary database cross-referenced to maps, and may be viewed at regional Environment Agency offices by prior arrangement. No detailed information from the database was available at the time of writing, so Table 8.4.3, drawn from the published survey, is general in scope. However this is a very accurate and detailed source of information, although now due for updating (by the time of publication, most of the defences classified as in need of significant or moderate works may have been improved or be included in a medium term capital programme).

The Welsh Office coastal defence survey provides an up-to-date overview of the scale and condition of works in Wales.

Summaries of the extent of coast protection and sea defence works in estuaries are available for those sites covered by English Nature's Estuaries Initiative coastal processes reports (Coastal Research Group 1994; Institute of Estuarine and Coastal Studies 1995).

8.4.5 Acknowledgements

Thanks are due to officers of the County Councils, MAFF, the Environment Agency, DoE and staff of English Nature and Countryside Council for Wales. Huw Payne of the Welsh Office kindly provided coastal defence data.

8.4.6 Further sources of information

A. References cited

Coastal Research Group, Glasgow University Department of Geography and Topographic Science. 1994. *Coastal processes and conservation. Taw Torridge.* Peterborough, unpublished report to English Nature.

Institute of Estuarine and Coastal Studies, University of Hull. 1995. *Coastal processes and conservation: the Fal.* Peterborough, unpublished report to English Nature.

Irish Sea Forum. 1992. *Global warming and climatic change.* Liverpool, University Press. (Seminar Report, University of Liverpool, April 1992.)

Ministry of Agriculture, Fisheries and Food. 1994. *Coast protection survey of England. Volume 1, summary report.* London, HMSO.

National Rivers Authority. 1992. *Sea defence survey.* Bristol, NRA.

B. Further reading

Boorman, L., & Hazelden, J. 1995. Saltmarsh creation and management for coastal defence. *In: Directions in European coastal management*, ed. by M.G. Healy and J.P. Doody, 175-183. Cardigan, Samara Publishing Ltd.

Buck, A.L. 1993. *An inventory of UK estuaries. Volume 2. South-west Britain.* Peterborough, Joint Nature Conservation Committee.

CIRIA. 1996. *Beach management manual.* London, Construction Industry Research and Information Association.

Green, C. 1984. *Saltings and sea defences on the Gwent Levels.* Cranfield, Conference of River Engineers.

House of Commons Environment Select Committee. 1992. *Report on coastal zone protection and planning.* London, HMSO. (HC17/1991/92.)

Hydraulics Research Ltd. 1991. A summary guide to the selection of coast protection works for geological Sites of Special Scientific Interest. *Nature Conservancy Council, CSD Report,* No. 1,245.

Lee, E.M. 1995. Coastal cliff recession in Great Britain: the significance for sustainable coastal management. *In: Directions in European coastal management*, ed. by M.G. Healy and J.P. Doody, 185-193. Cardigan, Samara Publishing Ltd.

Ministry of Agriculture, Fisheries and Food. 1993. *Coastal defence and the environment: a guide to good practice.* London, MAFF.

Ministry of Agriculture, Fisheries and Food. 1993. *Coastal defence and the environment: a strategic guide for managers and decision makers in the National Rivers Authority, local authorities and other bodies with coastal responsibilities.* London, MAFF.

Ministry of Agriculture, Fisheries and Food. 1993. *Flood and coastal defence project appraisal guidance note.* London, MAFF.

Ministry of Agriculture, Fisheries and Food & Welsh Office. 1993. *Strategy for flood and coastal defence in England and Wales.* London, MAFF/WO.

Ministry of Agriculture, Fisheries and Food. 1994/95. *Shoreline management plans. A procedural guide for operating authorities.* London, MAFF.

Ministry of Agriculture, Fisheries and Food. 1995. *Shoreline management plans. A guide for coastal defence authorities.* London, MAFF (PB2197).

Ministry of Agriculture, Fisheries and Food. 1995. *The EC Habitats Directive: implications for flood and coastal defence.* London, MAFF.

National Rivers Authority. 1993. *NRA flood defence strategy.* Bristol, NRA.

Swash, A.R.H., Leafe, R.N., & Radley, G.P. 1995. Shoreline management plans and environmental considerations. *In: Directions in European coastal management*, ed. by M.G. Healy and J.P. Doody, 161-167. Cardigan, Samara Publishing Ltd.

C. Contact names and addresses

Type of information	*Contact address and telephone no.*
Coast protection survey database for Wales (1994/95)	*Huw Payne, Welsh Office Environment Division, Cardiff, tel: 01222 823176
Departmental responsibility for flood defence and coast protection policy, provision of grants towards capital expenditure by the responsible bodies. Coast Protection Survey of England.	*Ministry of Agriculture, Fisheries and Food (MAFF), Flood and Coastal Defence Division, London, tel: 0171 238 6660
Coast protection and prevention of the flooding of non-agricultural land - England and Wales	*Local authorities
Storm Tide Warning Service	Meteorological Office, Johnstone House, London Road, Bracknell, Berkshire RG12 2SZ, tel: 01344 420242
Flood defence - general	*Environment Agency HQ, Bristol, tel: 01454 624400
Flood defence - Wales; sea defence survey 1991 regional database	*Environment Agency Welsh Region, Rivers House, Cardiff, tel: 01222 770088
Flood defence - England; sea defence survey 1991 regional database	*Environment Agency South West Region, Exeter, tel: 01392 444000
Co-operation between parties responsible for coastal defences, identification of research needs and promotion of strategic planning of coastal defences - England	*English Coastal Groups Forum, MAFF Flood and Coastal Defence Division, tel: 0171 238 6660
Co-operation between parties responsible for coastal defences, identification of research needs and promotion of strategic planning of coastal defences - Wales	*Huw Payne, Welsh Coastal Groups Forum, Welsh Office Environment Division, Cardiff, tel: 01222 823176
Coordination and liaison between agencies undertaking coastal works - Cornwall	Cornwall and Isles of Scilly Coast Protection Group, J. V. Calvert, Kerrier District Council, Council Offices, Dolcoath Avenue, Camborne, Cornwall TR14 8RY, tel: 01209 712941
Coordination and liaison between agencies undertaking coastal works - north Devon, Somerset and South Avon	*D. Rodwell, North Devon, Somerset and South Avon Coastal Group, Environmental Services Department, Sedgemoor District Council, Bridgwater, tel: 01278 435235
Coordination and liaison between agencies undertaking coastal works - Severn Estuary	J. Mackay, Severn Estuary Coastal Cell Group, Cardiff County Council, Hodge House, St. Mary Street, Cardiff CF1 1JT, tel: 01222 822376
Coordination and liaison between agencies undertaking coastal works - Swansea Bay	Chief Technical Officer, Swansea Bay Coastal Group, Bridgend County Borough Council Civic Buildings, PO Box 4, Angel St., Bridgend CF31 1LX, tel: 01656 643643, or H.R. Richards, Neath and Port Talbot County Borough Council, Port Talbot Civic Centre, Port Talbot SA13 1PJ, tel: 01639 763333
Coastal Engineering Advisory Panel	Anne-Marie Ferguson, Institute of Civil Engineers, Great George Street, London SW1P 3AA, tel: 0171 222 7722
Coastal Engineering Research Advisory Committee	International Council for the Exploration of the Sea, Palægade 2-4, DK-1261, Copenhagen K, Denmark

*Starred contact addresses are given in full in the Appendix.

The abandoned tin mines of Cornwall are striking features of the landscape, often perched on the very cliff's edge, as here at Cape Cornwall. Their spoil heaps are sometimes colonised by rare and specialised lower plants, such as liverworts. The Cornish tin mining industry may be reactivated in future. Photo: Peter Wakely, English Nature.

Chapter 9 Human activities

9.1 Fisheries

C.F. Robson

9.1.1 Introduction

This section gives an overview of the main fishing activities in the coastal waters and rivers of the region. There are fisheries for pelagic and demersal fish and several marine shellfish species (demersal fish live on or near the sea bed; pelagic fish tend to be found in midwater) and diadromous species - in this section salmon, sea trout and eels - which spend part of their lives in fresh water and part at sea. The section also covers sea angling and bait collection. For more information about the species concerned, including their scientific names, see sections 5.5, 5.7 and 5.8.

Falmouth and Newlyn are the two 'major' fishing ports (as defined by MAFF) in the region. These and other MAFF-defined ports where fish and shellfish are landed and recorded in the region are shown on Map 9.1.1. Newlyn, where the majority of offshore boats in Cornwall are based, is one of the largest fishing ports in England and Wales. The boats land their catches into the daily fish market, which regularly includes landings from visiting boats from Brixham (Region 10) and the Channel Islands. Newquay and Padstow are the most important ports on the north coast of Cornwall. However, the fishing opportunities available on the north coast of the region are not as diverse or as productive as those on the south coast. Anchorage on the north coast is limited by strong prevailing winds, a large tidal range and shallow estuaries, and much of the region's coastline is fully exposed to Atlantic weather fronts. A large sand bar at the entrance to the Taw-Torridge Estuary makes it difficult to navigate and only at certain states of the tide is entry or exit by fishing boats possible. St. Mary's, where 60% of the islands' fishermen are based, is the main centre for fishing in the Isles of Scilly (Atlantic Consultants 1995). Most of the fish and shellfish from the Isles of Scilly is exported to France and Spain, via Newlyn. Local purchasers also buy a small amount of shellfish such as crab and lobster (Council of the Isles of Scilly 1995).

In 1992, 2.2% of all recorded landings of fish and shellfish species in Britain and the Isle of Man were made in this region (Table 9.1.1), which is below the average of all regions of 5.9%. The total tonnages of pelagic, demersal and shellfish species landed in the region in 1992 represent 0.3%, 4.0% and 2.1% respectively of the British and Isle of Man totals. The total tonnage of demersal species is the highest for all species groups in the region and, although only 4.0% of the British and Isle of Man total, represents 13.6% of the England and Wales total. The tonnage of conger eel landed in the region represents 45.5% of the British and Isle of Man total and there are also significant landings of megrim (31.8%), hake (31.6%), pollack (31.5%), gurnards (19.0%) and Dover sole (15.5%).

The majority of all fish landed in the region in 1992 was landed to the ports of Falmouth and Newlyn. Table 9.1.2 summarises landings to these major ports in the four years from 1991 to 1994, showing trends in landings in relation to 1992, the year on which the more detailed landings data analysis in Table 9.1.1 was based.

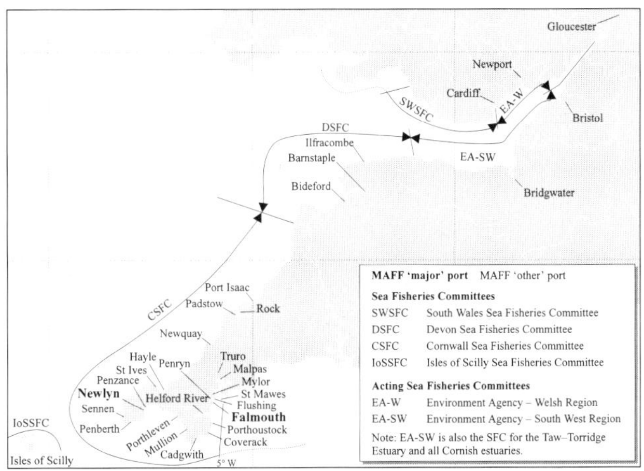

Map 9.1.1 MAFF-defined fisheries landing ports, Sea Fisheries Committees and acting Sea Fisheries Committees. © Crown copyright.

Table 9.1.1 Species group landings in 1992 (tonnes)

Species group	*Region 11*	*West Coast (including Isle of Man*	*England & Wales*	*Britain and Isle of Man*	*% of West Coast total landed in region*	*% of combined British and Isle of Man total landed in region*
Pelagic	684	68,026	23,809	252,335	1.0	0.3
Demersal	11,059	47,404	81,237	275,460	23.3	4.0
Shellfish	2,246	42,984	55,360	104,917	5.2	2.1
All groups	***13,989***	***158,414***	***160,406***	***632,712***	***8.8***	***2.2***

Sources: Ministry of Agriculture, Fisheries and Food (1994); Scottish Office Agriculture and Fisheries Department (1993); Isle of Man Department of Agriculture, Fisheries & Forestry (pers. comm.). Notes: amounts landed are rounded up to the next whole tonne. Calculating the figures in this table was a complex process: refer to section 9.1.4.

Table 9.1.2 Landings[a] of all fish species to selected Region 11 ports 1991 - 1994 (thousands of tonnes)

	1991	*1992*	*1993*	*1994*
Falmouth	1.7	1.7	0.9	1.2
Newlyn	10.0	9.4	10.1	11.1
Region 11 selected ports	***11.7***	***11.1***	***11.0***	***12.3***
England & Wales	169.0	160.6	165.5	178.7
% of England & Wales total landed in Region 11 selected ports	6.9	6.9	6.6	6.9

Sources: Ministry of Agriculture, Fisheries and Food (1995c). Key: [a]landings totals relate to 'nominal live weight', i.e. weight of the whole fish. Note: calculating the figures in this table was a complex process: refer to section 9.1.4.

Three diadromous species - salmon, sea trout and eel - support important licensed fisheries in the region. As well as rod and line, many types of net are used in rivers and in the Bristol Channel (see section 9.1.2). The main rivers of interest for salmon (and grilse, which are young salmon that have spent not more than one winter at sea before maturing) and sea trout are the Severn, Wye and Usk. As shown in Table 9.1.3, a relatively small percentage of the salmon and grilse recorded as caught in Great Britain are from this region, and the percentage is lower still for sea trout. Adult eels are targeted using fyke nets, and the elver fishery in the Severn is extremely important.

Table 9.1.3 Average catch (numbers of fish) of salmon and grilse and sea trout 1989-1993

	Salmon and grilse	*Sea trout*
Region 11	7,702	1,868
West Coast	58,582	37,024
England & Wales	67,347	76,337
GB	***254,829***	***141,813***
% of West Coast total in region	12.9	5.1
% of GB total in region	3.0	1.4

Sources: Scottish Office Department of Agriculture and Fisheries (1990), National Rivers Authority (1991, 1992, 1993, 1994a, b), Scottish Office (1991, 1992, 1993, 1994). Note: calculating the figures in this table was a complex process: refer to section 9.1.4.

9.1.2 The fisheries

Pelagic species

Table 9.1.4 gives the quantities of various pelagic species landed in 1992 in the region, compared with landings nationally. Several boats from Newlyn pair up to trawl for pelagic fish such as mackerel during the winter. Other boats use longlines and handlines to target mackerel in Mount's Bay from autumn onwards. A handline fishery involves some boats based in ports from Falmouth to Appledore and Bideford. They target mackerel as they appear in early spring, until they move offshore in the autumn. Low market prices can deter effort, but the fishery is equally important to the tourism industry, through chartered sea-angling trips. The inshore fleet based in Newlyn sets gill nets for a variety of fish. Boats from small ports on the North Devon coast (Clovelly, Appledore and Bideford) use drift nets to catch herring, usually from October to the end of December. Boats from Newlyn and elsewhere, mainly abroad, trawl for pilchards during the winter. A few boats from St. Mawes and Falmouth occasionally pair up to trawl for sprats in the autumn. There are no landings of pelagic fish into the Isles of Scilly on a commercial basis (Atlantic Consultants 1995).

Demersal species

Table 9.1.5 gives the quantities of various demersal species landed in 1992 in the region, compared with landings nationally. Boats based in Newlyn, Falmouth, Appledore, Bideford and the Isles of Scilly use otter trawls throughout the year and land principally whiting, cod, lemon sole and plaice during the winter. During the summer the catch also includes rays, and flatfish such as plaice, Dover sole, lemon sole, turbot and brill. During early spring, up to 20 visiting trawlers arrive in Padstow to join the brief fishery for Dover sole. Beam trawlers from Newlyn fish offshore for monkfish (angler), megrim, Dover sole and lemon sole. Red mullet and sea bream are targeted more in the summer. Larger gill netting boats from Falmouth, Newlyn and Padstow target hake and monkfish far offshore in summer. Many small boats fish for red mullet, bass and grey mullet. Nets are set

Table 9.1.4 Pelagic species landings for 1992 (tonnes)

Species group	*Region 11*	*West Coast (including Isle of Man)*	*England & Wales*	*Britain and Isle of Man*	*% of West Coast total landed in region*	*% of British and Isle of Man total landed in region*
Herring	1	10,944	915	85,650	0	0
Horse mackerel	19	125	1,026	1,499	15.2	1.3
Mackerel	664	55,360	9,142	150,726	1.2	0.4
Pilchard	P	P	4,244	4,244	-	-
Sprat	0	1,554	8,478	10,032	0	0
Whitebait	0	0	1	1	0	0
Others	0	43	3	183	0	0
Total	***684***	***68,026***	***23,809***	***252,335***	***1.0***	***0.3***

Sources: Ministry of Agriculture, Fisheries and Food (1994), Scottish Office Agriculture and Fisheries Department (1993), Isle of Man Department of Agriculture, Fisheries & Forestry (pers. comm.). Key: P = species landed in the region in small quantities (here <0.5 tonnes); - = % not calculated. Notes: amounts landed are rounded up to the next whole tonne. Calculating the figures in this table was a complex process: refer to section 9.1.4.

Table 9.1.5 Demersal species landings in 1992 (tonnes)

Species group	*Region 11*	*West Coast (including Isle of Man)*	*England & Wales*	*Britain and Isle of Man*	*% of West Coast total landed in region*	*% of British and Isle of Man total landed in region*
Elasmobranchs						
Dogfish	274	5,899	3,625	13,348	4.6	2.1
Skates and rays	915	4,011	4,142	7,827	22.8	11.7
Gadoids						
Cod	825	6,084	23,530	59,524	13.6	1.4
Haddock	146	4,365	3,706	53,586	3.3	0.3
Hake	1,144	3,031	1,621	3,620	37.7	31.6
Ling	798	1,433	1,708	6,027	55.7	13.2
Pollack (lythe)	952	1,102	1,734	3,023	86.4	31.5
Saithe	435	1,570	2,284	12,602	27.7	3.5
Whiting	455	4,322	5,088	41,055	10.5	1.1
Whiting, blue	0	0	P	6,531	0	0
Flatfish						
Brill	47	126	392	443	37.3	10.6
Dab	13	198	456	1,215	6.6	1.1
Dover sole	446	855	2,812	2,876	52.2	15.5
Flounder	1	106	269	273	0.9	0.4
Halibut	0	28	80	194	0	0
Halibut, Greenland	0	18	117	137	0	0
Lemon sole	323	569	3,000	5,573	56.8	5.8
Megrim	1,285	2,658	1,471	4,037	48.3	31.8
Plaice	459	3,138	15,970	23,887	14.6	1.9
Turbot	97	181	545	742	53.6	13.1
Other species						
Catfish	0	39	557	1,935	0	0
Conger eel	232	411	403	510	56.4	45.5
Gurnard	119	259	589	627	45.9	19.0
Monkfish/angler	1,638	4,865	3,102	14,678	33.7	11.2
Redfish	P	56	581	774	-	-
Sand eels	0	0	P	4,152	0	0
Torsk (tusk)	0	42	13	207	0	0
Witch	73	576	192	1,981	12.7	3.7
Others	375	1,414	3,151	3,833	26.5	9.8
Fish roes	7	48	99	243	14.6	2.9
Total	***11,059***	***47,404***	***81,237***	***275,460***	**23.3**	**4.0**

Sources: Ministry of Agriculture, Fisheries and Food (1994), Scottish Office Agriculture and Fisheries Department (1993), Isle of Man Department of Agriculture, Fisheries & Forestry (pers. comm.). Key: P = species landed in the region in small quantities (here <0.5 tonnes); - = % not calculated. Notes: amounts landed are rounded up to the next whole tonne. Calculating the figures in this table was a complex process: refer to section 9.1.4.

over wrecks or on hard, rough ground, inaccessible to trawlers, off the north Cornwall and Devon coast, to catch pollack, ling, turbot, monkfish (angler), conger eels and rays. Monkfish (angler), lemon sole, elasmobranchs (sharks, skates and rays) and gadoids (members of the cod family) are also taken from rough ground using 'rock hopper' gear.

Trawlers based at Cardiff, Barry, Porthcawl and Port Talbot catch plaice, turbot, whiting and rays from sandbanks in the Bristol Channel from spring onwards. Elsewhere longlines, each having up to 1,000 hooks, are used to target conger eel, ling, pollack, monkfish (angler), dogfish and rays. Drift lines may be set for blue shark and porbeagle and handlines are used to target pollack and bass. For example, around the Manacles from spring through to autumn, boats from Porthallow and Porthoustock catch bass using handlines. A restricted gill net fishery targets bass. Tangle nets are used for turbot, rays, monkfish/angler and brill and there is a small seine-net fishery for sand eel on the River Camel.

Shellfish species

Table 9.1.6 gives the quantities of various shellfish species landed in 1992 in the region, compared with landings nationally.

Potting, using inkwell or parlour pots, provides the mainstay of many small fishing ports in the region, with edible crabs, lobsters, spider crabs, crawfish and velvet crabs being landed. Edible crabs make up the bulk of shellfish landings in the region and are targeted in spring and early summer and again in the autumn before they spawn. In the Isles of Scilly shellfish accounted for two-thirds of the total landings by value in 1994; edible crabs, lobster and crawfish make up the majority (Atlantic Consultants 1995). Larger boats set up to 1,000 pots up to 30 miles offshore all around the region and as far into the Bristol Channel as Burnham-on-Sea, principally targeting edible crab. To keep this fishery economically viable, fishermen have steadily increased the number of pots set

Table 9.1.6 Shellfish* landings in 1992 (tonnes)

Species group	*Region 11*	*West Coast (including Isle of Man)*	*England & Wales*	*Britain and Isle of Man*	*% of West Coast total landed in region*	*% of British and Isle of Man total landed in region*
Cockles	0	5,848	29,501	32,047	0	0
Crabs	1,238	7,853	9,453	16,970	15.8	7.3
Lobsters	63	447	504	1,069	14.1	5.9
Mussels	7	1,690	3,488	6,555	0.4	0.1
Nephrops	14	11,271	1,918	19,639	0.1	0.1
Periwinkles	0	1,592	70	1,907	0	0
Queen scallops	0	9,066	2,989	11,273	0	0
Scallops	661	3,771	2,589	8,290	17.5	8.0
Shrimps	0	128	563	743	0	0
Squids	158	623	919	2,005	25.4	7.9
Whelks	0	488	1,535	2,393	0	0
Others	105	207	1,831	2,026	50.7	5.2
Total*	***2,246***	***42,984***	***55,360***	***104,917***	***5.2***	***2.1***

Sources: Ministry of Agriculture, Fisheries and Food (1994), Scottish Office Agriculture and Fisheries Department (1993), Isle of Man Department of Agriculture, Fisheries & Forestry (pers. comm.). Key: *excluding landings of farmed shellfish - see section 9.2. Notes: amounts landed are rounded up to the next whole tonne. Calculating the figures in this table was a complex process: refer to section 9.1.4.

per boat, as catch rates and market prices have fallen. Smaller boats work closer inshore; in addition to edible crab, they also land lobster, crawfish, spider crab and velvet crab. Lobster landings peak during May and again at the end of the summer. In the winter months velvet crabs and lobsters are caught in pots set in sheltered waters close to the shore. The fishery for spider crab, caught in both pots and tangle nets, peaks in spring and autumn. Tangle nets are also used to target crustacea, especially crawfish and lobster. During the summer season a significant quantity of these shellfish species landed are sold to local hotels and restaurants, and the opening of markets abroad (particularly in France and Spain) has greatly expanded the inshore potting industry. Lorries equipped with vivier tanks (sea water tanks that keep the catch alive) transport the shellfish to the continent, and there are many shellfish storage facilities on quaysides, such as at Hayle.

Scallop dredgers from St. Mawes, Flushing and Falmouth dredge within 12 miles of the coast around the Lizard. Dredgers from Penryn fish mainly for scallops (and a few queen scallops) within 20 miles of the coast for most of the year. Sometimes the beam and otter trawlers from Newlyn switch to scallop dredging, especially during the summer, with the majority fishing within 12 miles of the coast.

In this region, all oysters are harvested by dredges in rowed or sail-powered vessels, with no mechanical power used. The historic oyster fisheries of the Helford and Fal are described in Masters (1994). The Helford River used to have a natural spat settlement good enough to sustain the fishery. However, young oyster stock is now imported from the Fal, grown for a while on trays then relaid on grounds upriver of Pedn Billy Point as far as Bishop's Quay. There they are left to grow and fatten until they reach marketable size. Approximately 200,000 are dredged each year between early September to April (Masters 1994) (see also section 9.2.2). Between 300,000 and 400,000 native oysters a year were dredged from the Fal between 1992 and 1995. This fishery is doing very well and it is estimated that for the 1996 season the total will be nearer 500,000 (Cornwall Sea Fisheries Committee pers. comm.). In 1992 approximately 14 tonnes of native oysters were fished off Porthcawl, but since then this has been an occasional fishery.

Mussels in the Fal Estuary/Helford River are harvested on an irregular basis and there is no large commercial interest. The mussels in the Taw-Torridge are no longer exploited, owing to poor water quality. Mussels are occasionally dredged from off Porthcawl, and whelks are targeted using specially designed pots. In some areas whelks have begun to attract commercial interest. On Stert Flats, east of Hinkley Point, there are ranks of about 100 fixed stowe nets (also called stake nets), primarily to catch brown shrimp.

Cuttlefish and squid have become more important in summer as traditionally targeted demersal fish have become either scarce or subject to quota restrictions (see section 9.1.3). The local fish merchants and processors have become more dependent on these species as the increasingly nomadic offshore demersal fleet often work away from their home ports during the summer. The landing figures for cuttlefish are included in the 'Others' category in Table 9.1.6.

Diadromous species

The distribution of diadromous fish species in rivers in the region is discussed in section 5.9. Salmon and sea trout in the region support net fisheries. Another method, characteristic of the region, is the use of ranks of 'putchers'. Traditionally, the conical-shaped traps of the putchers, which are fixed to a frame to form the ranks, were made from willow and hazel; metal is now commonly used. Fish swimming with the current become trapped and are collected when the tide recedes. Putcher ranks may fish the ebb and/or flood tide, depending on their position. Putchers are licensed for the Rivers Parrett and Usk. Within the Parrett Estuary two short ranks are worked, each with approximately 100 baskets. The ones licensed for the Usk are situated in the Severn Estuary, off the Usk headland (at Gold Cliff), and they also catch fish on their way to other rivers, for example the Wye, Severn and Taff. The fixed engine at Lynmouth is a weir designed to trap salmonids on a falling tide as they congregate at the mouth of the River Lyn.

Table 9.1.7 shows the average numbers of salmon and grilse and sea trout caught in the region's rivers in the five years between 1989 and 1993, the methods used to catch them, and the numbers of net licences issued in 1993.

Table 9.1.7 Salmon and grilse and sea trout five-year (1989 - 1993) average catch (as numbers of fish reported), catch methods used and number of net licences issued in 1993

	Salmon & grilse	*Sea trout*	*Method used/net licences issued*
Camel*	302	565	Rod, drift nets (7)
Torridge	73	168	Rod
Taw	205	329	Rod
Taw-Torridge**	182	140	Rod
Lyn	220	137	Rod, fixed engine (1)
Parrett	70	1	Dip nets (4), putcher ranks (1)
Severn	3,091	0	Rod, fixed engines (14), nets: seine (6), lave (40)
Wye	1,394	20	Rod, lave nets (9)
Usk***	2,109	127	Rod, putcher rank (1), drift nets (8)
Rhymney	0	10	Rod
Taff	33	68	Rod
Ogmore	22	304	Rod
Region 11	*7,702*	*1,868*	*91*

Sources: National Rivers Authority (1991, 1992, 1993, 1994a, b).
Key: *1992 and 1993 data only; **includes data for seine nets, used in 1989 only; ***Usk licences are based in the Severn Estuary, outside the Usk headland (at Gold Cliff). Notes: 'sea trout' here includes all migratory trout. 'Nets' are defined as instruments other than rod and line. Rivers with very small recorded catches have been excluded from this table, so the distribution of rod and line fishing may be more widespread than appears here.
Map 5.8.1 shows the locations of rivers in this table.

In the Taw-Torridge Estuary the fourteen seine net licences were fully revoked from the 1990 season until the 1996 season (all but four were revoked in 1989). The salmonid netsmen were compensated as part of a salmon and sea trout rehabilitation scheme. In theory the licensed netsmen were to be able to fish their nets in the 1996 season, within the closure times. However, further proposals have been submitted to MAFF by the Environment Agency (EA) for a Net Limitation Order and associated bylaws, to reduce the netting time allowed to the last eight weeks of the season for a period of five years. This is to allow the further escape of salmon and sea trout to their spawning grounds. The salmonid fishery on the Camel Estuary was closed from 1989 to 1991 (inclusive) as part of a rehabilitation scheme following a pollution incident in the River Camel in 1988. Eel fyke nets are set in the Camel and other estuaries to catch adult eels (silver eels). The elver fishery in the Severn is extremely important, with annual catches of between 10 and 80 tonnes a year. Peak catches are made in April and early May, but the fishery lasts from February to June. Most fishing is during spring tides at night when river temperatures are greater than 6°C. Elver dip nets are used in the River Parrett to catch juvenile eels when they begin their immigration during the winter and early spring. Greatest catches are taken on spring tides close to the river bank, where elver fishermen are able to scoop the elvers out of the water with their dip nets.

Sea angling

Sea angling is a popular sport practised by over two million people in Great Britain (Fowler 1992). The governing body in England is the National Federation of Sea Anglers, which has approximately 570 affiliated clubs with some 33,000 individual members. Sea angling is distinguished from two other types of sport fishing: game fishing for salmon, sea trout, brown and rainbow trout (the first two are covered here) and coarse fishing, which is for freshwater fish species and so is not covered here. Sea angling has three main forms: angling from the shore, inshore fishing within about 5 km of the shore and deep sea fishing. Boats in places such as Falmouth, St. Ives, Boscastle, Appledore, Bideford, Ilfracombe, Minehead, Barry, Cardiff, Newport and Porthcawl are chartered for angling trips, especially for mackerel and sometimes shark in the warmer months. Sea fishing is carried out in the Fal Estuary and further offshore. Mount's Bay is good for bass, which are caught from Porthleven, Penzance and Mousehole. Mackerel, bream, pollack, conger and whiting may also be taken. The Isles of Scilly yield big catches of cod, ling, conger and pollack, but bass are rare. Surf fishing for bass is popular at St. Ives. A wide range of species are caught between Newquay and Ilfracombe, and Lynmouth is good for boat fishing, with tope, skate and conger caught in Lynmouth Bay. Minehead, Watchet and Weston-super-Mare yield conger, sole, bass, skate, eel, whiting and flounder. From autumn to spring cod fishing in the Bristol Channel is popular with boats operating from Cardiff, Newport and Barry. Spearfishing is a popular activity in the south-west, and bass are frequently caught in this way. Orton (1994) also lists further sea fishing stations, the facilities available and potential catch species.

Bait collection

Bait collection for sea angling occurs in many areas in the region, although some areas are more prolific than others and may attract commercial collectors. Anglers often collect their own bait locally, while commercial collectors travel in teams to suitable shores (Fowler 1992). Many species are collected in the region, including ragworm, lugworm, peeler crabs (moulting shore crabs), mussels, cockles, limpets and razor shells (see also section 5.5). Different bait species are targeted according to the species of fish being caught as well as the location and time of year. The main collecting techniques are digging and boulder turning. Bait digging, especially for lugworms, is carried out over the lower part of muddy and sandy shores around the time of low water. Fowler (1992) identified that the exploitation of bait species was taking place at many locations in the region. Areas such as Falmouth, Helford, Hayle Estuary, Padstow and Newton Beach experience larger numbers of diggers and some problems have been encountered in National Nature Reserves such as Bridgwater Bay and at Sites of Special Scientific Interest such as Braunton Burrows, Caldicot/ Sudbrook, Magor Pill and Gold Cliff Point and Redwich (see also section 5.5).

9.1.3 Management and issues

Responsibility for the management of fisheries in coastal waters rests with the Commission for the European Union (EU), who delegate it to member states under the Common

Fisheries Policy (CFP). European Council regulations are implemented through UK law (see Gray (1995) for a brief description), usually by means of statutory instruments, which define limits and restrictions and set down powers of enforcement and penalties. All national regulation measures, including local sea fisheries bylaws, must conform with requirements of the CFP.

The CFP seeks to manage stocks of fish in EU waters on a biological basis, principally by implementing catch quota management measures, by setting agreed annual Total Allowable Catches (TACs) for particular stocks. The policy came into effect in 1983 and was subject to a mid-term review in 1993, with a full review planned for 2002. The CFP is described in Coffey (1995), which sets out the basic elements of the policy and contributes to the debate on fisheries and the environment. A central principle of the policy is the rule of 'equal access' - that all member states of the EU have equal access to all community waters and all fishing resources. However, this rule is subject to the principle of 'relative stability', which takes account of established practice, and consequently a number of exceptions have been adopted, based on various precedents and historic fishing patterns. Between 6 and 12 nautical miles from baseline (low water mark) other member states with historic rights also have access, and beyond 12 nautical miles (the limit of the British Territorial Seas) access to vessels from the other member states is limited based on historic fishing rights and to vessels from non-member countries by reciprocal agreements within the European Union.

For the purpose of stock assessment, the UK coastal waters have been designated by the International Council for the Exploration of the Sea (ICES) into statistical areas. The coastal seas around this region are part of two 'divisions': Division VIIf (Bristol Channel) and, offshore from South Cornwall, Division VIIe (English Channel, West). ICES provides scientific advice on the management of all the important commercial species of fin fish and some shellfish stocks in all areas of the north-east Atlantic. This work is summarised in the annual report of the Advisory Committee for Fisheries Management, which is responsible for providing scientific advice on TACs and other conservation measures to the international fisheries commissions, including the EU. The TAC is a fishery management tool which may, amongst other management needs, take account of the maximum level of exploitation that a given stock can sustain. Precautionary TACs are applied to important stocks where there are not enough scientific data to make an analytical assessment. Once the TACs are set for each stock they are divided between member states in the form of catch quotas. European Council Regulation No. 3074/95 (European Council 1995) fixes, for 1996, details of the national catch quotas for fish and shellfish species for all European countries and certain conditions under which the species may be fished. The annual TACs, UK quotas and 'uptake' for each species in the two ICES statistical divisions in the region are given in Ministry of Agriculture, Fisheries and Food (1994, 1995b, c, 1996b). European Council Regulation No. 3760/92 (European Council 1992) summarises the CFP, including the proportions by which TACs are allocated as national quotas. Minimum landing sizes and whether an annual quota applies in the region for the important pelagic and demersal species are listed in Table 5.7.1.

The Sea Fisheries Committees (SFC) in this region are the Cornwall SFC, the Isles of Scilly SFC, the Devon SFC and the South Wales SFC, which manage the inshore fisheries from the high water mark out to 6 nautical miles from UK baselines (as defined by the Territorial Water Order in Council 1964, as amended). There is no SFC east of the Devon SFC boundary to the England/Wales border in the Severn Estuary; the Environment Agency (EA)'s South West Region undertakes SFC functions in this area. The EA (Welsh Region) also undertakes SFC functions east of Cardiff (from Beachly) to the mouth of the River Rhymney (see Map 9.1.1). Local MAFF fishery officers deal with quota management, enforcement of UK and EC legislation and licensing of fishing vessels. Fisheries managers have been given environmental responsibilities under the Environment Act 1995 and the Conservation (Natural Habitats etc.) Regulations 1994.

The EA's South West, Midlands and Welsh Regions have responsibility in the region to regulate, protect and monitor salmon, sea trout and eel fisheries from rivers to coastal waters out to the 6 nautical mile limit. The EA South West Region are also the Sea Fisheries Committee for the Taw-Torridge Estuary and all Cornish estuaries including the Fal. The SFCs also have powers to support the conservation of salmonid fisheries whilst exercising their responsibilities towards the regulation of sea fisheries. All licences issued by the EA are subject to seasonal and weekly closure times. The Duchy of Cornwall owns the rights to fish all parts of the Helford River and leases this right to a local family.

In England and Wales, MAFF's Sea Fisheries Inspectorate is responsible for collecting and the Directorate of Fisheries Research (DFR) Laboratory at Lowestoft for collating information on fish stocks exploited by UK vessels. The MAFF DFR Fisheries Laboratory at Conwy is the Directorate's centre for assessing the implications of non-fisheries activities and coastal zone usage on fish stocks and fisheries. MAFF DFR databases are described in Flatman (1993).

Regulating Orders are granted in England by MAFF to a responsible body to enable it to regulate the fishery for particular wild stocks of molluscan shellfish species. The specified shellfish stock may only be fished in accordance with the terms of the order and any regulations made under it. There is one Regulating Order in this region (Table 9.1.8), out of nine in Britain covering a total of approximately 215,889 ha (as at July 1995).

Table 9.1.8 Regulating Order in the region

Title	*Species*	*Location*	*Grid ref.*	*Grantee*	*Approx area (ha)*	*Expiry date*
Truro Port Fishery Order 1936	Oysters, mussels	Between Truro and Falmouth (Cornwall)	SX830370	Carrick District Council Harbour Office	1,101	2014

Source: Ministry of Agriculture, Fisheries and Food (1995a). Note: Several Orders are listed in Table 9.2.2.

Issues relating to the fisheries for pelagic, demersal and shellfish species and sea angling and bait collection are closely linked to wildlife conservation in several ways; for instance, factors such as over-fishing, pollution and development are thought to have been responsible for seriously reducing the eel fishery in the region. Issues include the effects of fisheries on target species as major components in marine ecosystems, the changed availability of food for predators, the effects on non-target species, and effects on species and habitats of nature conservation interest. These issues are under consideration by the 'Marine Fisheries Task Group', an inter-agency team of the statutory nature conservation organisations (the Countryside Council for Wales, English Nature, Scottish Natural Heritage and the Department of the Environment for Northern Ireland, together with the JNCC). A consultation paper prepared by the group, entitled *Developing an action programme for sea fisheries and wildlife* (Marine Fisheries Task Group 1994), identifies the main areas where marine fisheries (broadly defined to encompass the exploitation of all living marine resources) affect wildlife and identifies any action needed. Further information on issues concerning fisheries can be found in references such as Commission of the European Communities (1995), and concerning the species targeted in references given in sections 5.5, 5.7 and 5.8.

9.1.4 Information sources used

The coastal fisheries of England and Wales (Gray 1995) has been used in compiling this section. It describes the different types of fishing gear used inshore to catch specific species. Its 'Regional' section gives details of the numbers of boats operating from ports in the region, the amount of fishing effort involved by various methods and which species or species groups are targeted during the different seasons. Shellfish News (Ministry of Agriculture, Fisheries and Food 1996a) includes information on shellfish harvesting (and figures on the total shellfish landings in the UK in 1994) and is published twice yearly. Brady (1995) lists details of all fishing vessels, their base ports and main fishing methods. The key GB statutes relating to fisheries are described in Eno & Hiscock (1995).

Figures given in Tables 9.1.1 - 9.1.7 come from various sources: MAFF, National Rivers Authority (now the Environment Agency), the Scottish Office Agriculture, Environment and Fisheries Department (SOAEFD) and the Isle of Man Department of Agriculture Fisheries & Forestry (IoM DAFF); their interpretation is described below.

Pelagic, demersal and shellfish species

Statistics given here are for landings recorded in the region, as distinct from fish catches made. Some fish caught in the region may not be landed in the region's ports or even in the UK; other fish are landed in the region but are caught outside it; and until 1993, boats under 10 m were not obliged to register their landings. Vessels are not required to report landings of non-quota species, so the figures for these species may be underestimates. The EA and SFCs should be consulted for clarification. The data presented give an indication of the economic importance of the species that were landed in the region in 1992 (used as a reference year), compared with the rest of Britain and the Isle of Man. Data for 1993, 1994 and 1995 for England and Wales have also been published in Ministry of Agriculture, Fisheries and Food (1995b, c, 1996b).

The tonnages of various pelagic, demersal and shellfish species (fresh and frozen) landed by UK vessels at the major ports in England and Wales come from *UK sea fisheries statistics for 1991 and 1992* (Ministry of Agriculture, Fisheries and Food 1994): this applies to Newlyn and Falmouth, the two 'major' ports in the region. A total for the 'other', smaller, ports was provided by the MAFF Fisheries Statistics Unit. These data have been combined to give the figures in the 'Region 11' column for Tables 9.1.1 and 9.1.4 - 9.1.6.

The figures in the 'West Coast' column in Tables 9.1.1 and 9.1.4 - 9.1.6 were calculated by adding together all the landings data for the six regions on the west coast of Great Britain, as defined in section 1.1.

The figures in the 'England & Wales' column were obtained by adding together all of the MAFF data for England and Wales, and those in the 'Britain and Isle of Man' column were obtained by combining MAFF, SOAEFD and IoM DAFF data. Because these organisations do not use the same categories, landings in some of their categories have been added to the 'Others' rows in the tables in this section. Also, SOAEFD publish the weight of fish as 'standard landed weight' (gutted fish with head on), whereas MAFF and IoM DAFF publish them as 'nominal live weight' (whole fish). These two are the same for pelagic and shellfish species, but converted data from SOAEFD were used for all demersal species, apart from sandeels (which are not gutted), so that all the data are presented as 'nominal live weight'.

Diadromous species

National Rivers Authority (now the Environment Agency (EA)) reported catches for salmon, grilse and sea trout vary in accuracy from year to year, as they represent only declared catches by individuals with a net or rod-and-line licence; in addition, catches themselves fluctuate, and so the relationship between catch and stock is not straightforward. Further, in 1992, the introduction of changes to the catch recording system may have resulted in a temporarily reduced level of recording. Therefore the figures given in Tables 9.1.3 and 9.1.7 should be used only as an indication of the pattern of the catch in the region. The annual publication *Salmonid and freshwater statistics for England and Wales* (National Rivers Authority 1991, 1992, 1993, 1994a, b) contains more detailed information.

Sea angling

In the 84th edition of *Where to fish*, Orton (1994) lists much useful information relating to angling, including the locations from which various species of fish can be caught.

Bait collection

Bait collection is discussed by Fowler (1992), who presents results from a survey around the coast of Britain in 1985.

9.1.5 Acknowledgements

The author thanks the following for their contributions and comments on drafts, which enabled the production of this section: Stephen Lockwood and Mike Pawson (MAFF DFR), Miran Aprahamian (Environment Agency (EA) North-West Region), Bill Cook (North Wales & North Western Sea Fisheries Committee (SFC)), Phil Coates (South Wales SFC), Russell Bradley (Association of SFCs), Neil Downes (Devon SFC), Paul Knapman (English Nature), Blaise Bullimore (Countryside Council for Wales), Indrani Lutchman (WWF-UK), and Clare Eno and Mark Tasker (JNCC). The author also thanks the following for their comments on drafts of the text: R.C.A. Bannister (Shellfish Resource Group, MAFF DFR), A.S. Churchward (EA Midlands Region), Steve Watt (Isles of Scilly SFC), Alan Winstone (EA Welsh Region), E.J. Derriman and R.G. Teague (Cornwall SFC) and Stuart Bray (EA South-West Region).

9.1.6 Further sources of information

A. References cited

Atlantic Consultants. 1995. *Sustainable economic development strategy: research report for the Council of the Isles of Scilly*. Truro, Atlantic Consultants.

Brady, P. 1995. *Fishing vessels of Britain & Ireland 1995*. 3rd ed. London, Emap Business Communications.

Coffey, C. 1995. *Introduction to the Common Fisheries Policy: an environmental perspective*. London, Institute for European Environmental Policy. (IEEP London Background Briefing No. 2.)

Commission of the European Communities. 1995. *Evaluation of the biological impact of fisheries*. Brussels, Commission of the European Communities. (5.5.95, COM (95) 40.)

Council of the Isles of Scilly. 1995. *Sustainable economic development strategy: 1995 and beyond*. St. Mary's, Council of the Isles of Scilly

Eno, N.C., & Hiscock, K. 1995. *Key statutes, Directives and Conventions for marine wildlife conservation in Great Britain*. Peterborough, Joint Nature Conservation Committee. (Marine Information Notes, No. 3 (edition 1, June 1995).)

European Council. 1992. EC Regulation No. 3760/92. *Official Journal of the European Communities, L 389* (35).

European Council. 1995. EC Regulation No. 3074/95. *Official Journal of the European Communities, L 330* (38).

Flatman, S. 1993. MAFF fisheries databases. *In: The Irish Sea Forum. Marine & coastal databases,* 50-58. Liverpool, Liverpool University Press for Irish Sea Forum. (Irish Sea Forum 3rd Seminar Report.)

Fowler, S.L. 1992. Survey of bait collection in Britain. *JNCC Report,* No.17.

Gray, M.J. 1995. *The coastal fisheries of England and Wales. Part III: a review of their status 1992-1994*. Lowestoft, MAFF Directorate of Fisheries Research. (Fisheries Research Technical Report, No. 100.)

Marine Fisheries Task Group. 1994. *Developing an action programme for sea fisheries and wildlife*. Peterborough, JNCC. (Consultation paper by the Marine Fisheries Task Group.)

Masters, J. 1994. *The Helford oysterage with notes on the River Fal*. Truro, Cornwall County Council. (A report to the Helford Voluntary Marine Conservation Area Advisory Group.)

Ministry of Agriculture, Fisheries and Food. 1994. *UK sea fisheries statistics 1991 and 1992*. London, HMSO.

Ministry of Agriculture, Fisheries and Food. 1995a. *List of Fishery Orders in England, Scotland and Wales*. MAFF (unpublished).

Ministry of Agriculture, Fisheries and Food. 1995b. *UK sea fisheries statistics 1993*. London, HMSO.

Ministry of Agriculture, Fisheries and Food. 1995c. *UK sea fisheries statistics 1994*. London, HMSO.

Ministry of Agriculture, Fisheries and Food. 1996a. *Shellfish news. No. 1*. Lowestoft, MAFF.

Ministry of Agriculture, Fisheries and Food. 1996b. *UK sea fisheries statistics 1995*. London, HMSO.

National Rivers Authority. 1991. *Salmonid and freshwater fisheries statistics for England and Wales, 1989*. Almondsbury, NRA.

National Rivers Authority. 1992. *Salmonid and freshwater fisheries statistics for England and Wales, 1990*. Almondsbury, NRA.

National Rivers Authority. 1993. *Salmonid and freshwater fisheries statistics for England and Wales, 1991*. Almondsbury, NRA.

National Rivers Authority. 1994a. *Salmonid and freshwater fisheries statistics for England and Wales, 1992*. London, HMSO & NRA.

National Rivers Authority. 1994b. *Salmonid and freshwater fisheries statistics for England and Wales, 1993*. London, HMSO & NRA.

Orton, D.A., *ed*. 1994. *Where to fish 1994 - 1995*. 84th ed. Beaminster, Thomas Harmsworth.

Scottish Office. 1991. *Scottish salmon and sea trout catches: 1990*. Edinburgh, Scottish Office. (Scottish Office Statistical Bulletin, Fisheries Series.)

Scottish Office. 1992. *Scottish salmon and sea trout catches: 1991*. Edinburgh, Scottish Office. (Scottish Office Statistical Bulletin, Fisheries Series No. Fis/1992/1.)

Scottish Office. 1993. *Scottish salmon and sea trout catches: 1992*. Edinburgh, Scottish Office. (Scottish Office Statistical Bulletin, Fisheries Series No. Fis/1993/1.)

Scottish Office. 1994. *Scottish salmon and sea trout catches: 1993*. Edinburgh, Scottish Office. (Scottish Office Statistical Bulletin, Fisheries Series No. Fis/1994/1.)

Scottish Office Agriculture and Fisheries Department. 1993. *Scottish sea fisheries statistical tables 1992*. Edinburgh, Scottish Office.

Scottish Office Department of Agriculture and Fisheries. 1990. *Scottish salmon and sea trout catches: 1989*. Edinburgh, Scottish Office. (DAFS Statistical Bulletin 1/90.)

B. Further reading

Bergman, M.J.N, Fonds, M., Hup, W., & Uyl, D. den. 1990. Direct effects of beam trawling fishing on benthic fauna. *In: Effects of beam trawl fishery on the bottom fauna in the North Sea. Beleidgericht Ecologisch Onderzoek Norddzee - Wadenzee. Rapport, 8:* 33 - 57.

Boon, M.J. 1992. *Landings into England and Wales from the UK demersal fisheries of the Irish Sea and Western Approaches, 1979 - 1990*. Lowestoft, MAFF Directorate of Fisheries Research. (Fisheries Research Data Report No. 26.)

Dunn, E., & Harrison, N. 1995. *RSPB's vision for sustainable fisheries*. Sandy, RSPB.

Evans, E. 1995. *Traditional fishing in Wales*. Llanrwst, Gwasg Carreg Gwalch. (Welsh Heritage Series, No. 5.)

Fowler, S.L. 1989. *Nature conservation implications of damage to the seabed by commercial fishing operations*. Peterborough, Nature Conservancy Council (unpublished report).

Franklin, A., Pickett, G.D., & Connor, P.M. 1980. *The scallop and its fishery in England and Wales*. Lowestoft, MAFF Directorate of Fisheries Research. (MAFF Laboratory Leaflet, No. 51.)

Gray, M.J. 1994. *Inshore fisheries review of England, Scotland and Wales, 1992/1993*. Godalming, World Wide Fund for Nature.

Helford Voluntary Marine Conservation Area. 1995. *The Helford River fishing*. Truro, Cornwall County Council/WWF/English Nature.

Helford Voluntary Marine Conservation Area. 1995. *The Helford River oysters*. Truro, Cornwall County Council/WWF/English Nature.

Horwood, J. 1993. The Bristol Channel sole (*Solea solea*): a fisheries case study. *Advances in Marine Biology, 29:* 215-367.

Huggett, D. 1992. *Foreshore fishing for shellfish and bait*. Sandy, Royal Society for the Protection of Birds.

Kaiser, M.J., & Spencer, B.E. 1993. *A preliminary assessment of the immediate effects of beam trawling on a benthic community in the Irish Sea.* Copenhagen, Denmark, International Council for the Exploration of the Sea (ICES).

Lucas, M.C., Diack, I., & Laird, L. 1991. *Interactions between fisheries and the environment. Proceedings of the Institute of Fisheries Management 22nd Annual study course, 10-12th September 1991.* Aberdeen, University of Aberdeen.

Lutchman, I. 1992. *A general overview of European and UK fisheries.* Godalming, WWF International.

Mason, J. 1987. *Scallop and queen fisheries in the British Isles.* Farnham, Fishing News Books for Buckland Foundation.

Ministry of Agriculture, Fisheries and Food. 1992. *Directorate of Fisheries Research, Fisheries Laboratory, Conwy: Handout 4.* Lowestoft, MAFF.

Pawson, M.G., & Rogers, S.I. 1989. *The coastal fisheries of England and Wales. Part ii: a review of their status in 1988.* Lowestoft, MAFF Directorate of Fisheries Research. (Internal Report No.19.)

South Wales Sea Fisheries Committee. 1996. *SWSFC News, January 1996.* (Newsletter of the South Wales Sea Fisheries Committee.)

Southward, A.J., Boalch, G.T., & Maddock, L. 1988. Climatic change and fluctuation in the herring and pilchard fisheries of Devon and Cornwall. *Exeter Maritime Studies, 3:* 33 - 57.

Southward, A.J., Boalch, G.T., & Maddock, L. 1988. Fluctuations in the herring and pilchard fisheries of Devon and Cornwall linked to change in climate since the 16th C. *Journal of Marine Biological Assessment of the UK, 68:* 423 - 445.

Vas, P. 1995. The status and conservation of sharks in Britain. *Aquatic Conservation: Marine and freshwater ecosystems, 5*: 67-79.

Wildlife & Countryside Link Seals Group. 1995. *Seals and fisheries: the facts.* East Grinstead, Wildlife & Countryside Link Seals Group.

C. Contact names and addresses

Type of information	*Contact address and telephone no.*
Scientific aspects of managing important fish and shellfish stocks	General Secretary, International Council for the Exploration of the Sea, Palaegade 2 - 4, DK-1261 Copenhagen K, Denmark, tel: 00 45 33157092
Central contact for the local SFCs; general policy issues	Chief Executive, Association of Sea Fisheries Committees, Buckrose House, Commercial Street, Norton, Malton, North Yorkshire YO17 9HX, tel: 01653 698219
Local inshore fisheries information and advice on bylaws, national and EC legislation - Cornwall	Chief Fishery Officer, Cornwall Sea Fisheries Committee, The Old Bonded Warehouse, Quay Street, Penzance, Cornwall TR18 4BD, tel: 01736 69817
Local inshore fisheries information and advice on bylaws, national and EC legislation - Isles of Scilly	Assistant Chief Executive, Isles of Scilly Sea Fisheries Committee, Town Hall, St. Mary's, Isles of Scilly TR1 0LW, tel: 01720 422536
Local inshore fisheries information and advice on bylaws, national and EC legislation - Devon	Deputy Clerk & Chief Fishery Officer,Devon Sea Fisheries Committee, Forde House, Newton Abbot, Devon TQ12 3XX, tel: 01803 854648 / 882004
Local inshore fisheries information and advice on bylaws, national and EC legislation - South Wales	Director, South Wales Sea Fisheries Committee, Queens Buildings, Cambrian Place, Swansea, West Glamorgan SA1 1TW, tel: 01792654466
Assessment of implications of non-fisheries activities and coast usage on fish stocks and fisheries; advice to assist with management and policy decisions for the coastal zone. Interaction between fisheries and non-fisheries conservation issues.	*Head of Laboratory, MAFF Directorate of Fisheries Research, Fisheries Laboratory (Conwy), tel: 01492 593883
Assessment and advice on the conservation of fish stocks exploited by UK vessels. Seals and fisheries.	*Director, MAFF Directorate of Fisheries Research, Fisheries Laboratory (Lowestoft), tel: 01502 562244
Shellfish hygiene and fish diseases	Director, MAFF Fish Diseases Laboratory, Barrack Road, The Nothe, Weymouth, Dorset DT4 8UB, tel: 01305 206600
Additional statistics other than those in publications (available from HMSO)	MAFF Fisheries Statistics Unit, Nobel House, 17 Smith Square, London SW1P 3JR, tel: 0171 238 6000
Local fisheries, quota management, licensing of fishing vessels and enforcement, UK and EC legislation, from Fowey to North Bude	District Inspector, MAFF Sea Fisheries Inspectorate, West District Fisheries Office, 46 Fore Street, Newlyn, Penzance, Cornwall TR18 5JR, tel: 0173662805
Local fisheries, quota management, licensing of fishing vessels and enforcement, UK and EC legislation, in South Wales	District Inspector, MAFF Sea Fisheries Inspectorate, South Wales District Fisheries Office, Hamilton Terrace, Milford Haven, Dyfed SA73 2AL, tel: 01646 693412
Administration of fisheries and mariculture in Wales	Welsh Office Agriculture Department, Fisheries Department, Division 2B, New Crown Buildings, Cathays Park, Cardiff CF1 3NQ, tel: 01222 823567
National Environment Agency fisheries policy and projects; salmonid and freshwater statistics for England and Wales	*Head of Department, Fisheries Department, EA Head Office, Bristol, tel: 01454 624400
Regional information and advice on diadromous fisheries; salmonid and freshwater statistics. Acting SFC for Cornish estuaries and Taw-Torridge Estuary.	*Regional Fisheries Officer, EA SouthWest Region, Exeter, tel: 01392 444000

C. Contact names and addresses (continued)

Type of information	Contact address and telephone no.
Regional information and advice on diadromous fisheries; salmonid and freshwater statistics	*Regional Fisheries Officer, EA Midlands Region, Solihull, tel: 0121 7112324
Regional information and advice on diadromous fisheries; salmonid and freshwater statistics	*Regional Fisheries Officer, EA Welsh Region, Cardiff, tel: 01222770088
Research and development, marketing and training for the fishing industry	Technical Director, Sea Fish Industry Authority, Seafish Technology Division, Sea Fish House, St. Andrew's Dock, Hull HU3 4QE, tel: 01482 27837
UKDMAP software; mapped fishing areas of selected species, ICES Statistical Division boundaries etc.	*Project Manager, BODC, Birkenhead, tel: 0151 652 3950
National representation of fishermen's and boat owners' interests in the fishing industry	Honorary Secretary, National Federation of Fishermen's Organisations, Marsden Road, Fish Docks, Grimsby DN31 3SG, tel: 01472 352141
Shellfish production (commercial)	Director, Shellfish Association of the UK, Fishmongers' Hall, London Bridge, London EC4R 9EL, tel: 0171 626 3531
Affiliated angling clubs	Secretary, National Federation of Sea Anglers, 51a Queens Street, Newton Abbot, Devon TQ12 2QJ, tel: 01626 331330
Game fishing	Director, Salmon and Trout Association, Fishmongers' Hall, London Bridge, London EC4R 9EL, tel: 0171 2835838
Interaction between fisheries and non-fisheries conservation issues in England	*Fisheries Liaison Officer, English Nature HQ, Peterborough, tel: 01733 340345
Interaction between fisheries and non-fisheries conservation issues in Wales	*Marine and Coastal Section, CCW HQ, Bangor, tel: 01248 370444
Marine Fisheries Task Group paper; interaction between fisheries and non-fisheries conservation issues	*Fisheries Officer, JNCC Peterborough, tel: 01733 62626
Interaction between fisheries and non-fisheries conservation issues	*Marine Policy Officer, RSPB HQ, Sandy, tel: 01767 680551
Interaction between fisheries and non-fisheries conservation issues	*Fisheries Officer, WWF-UK, Godalming, tel: 01483 426444
Interaction between fisheries and non-fisheries conservation issues	*Conservation Officer, Marine Conservation Society, Ross-on-Wye, tel: 01989 566017
Interaction between fisheries and non-fisheries conservation issues	Honorary Secretary, The Marine Forum for Environmental Issues, c/o University College Scarborough, Filey Road, Scarborough YO11 3AZ, tel: 01723 362392
Information and advice on marine conservation issues - Cornwall	*Cornwall Wildlife Trust, Truro, tel: 01872 273939
Information and advice on marine conservation issues - Devon	*Devon Wildlife Trust, Exeter, tel: 01392 79244
Information and advice on marine conservation issues - Somerset	*Somerset Wildlife Trust, Bridgwater, tel: 01823 451587
Information and advice on marine conservation issues - Gloucestershire	*Gloucestershire Wildlife Trust, Gloucester, tel: 01452 383333
Information and advice on marine conservation issues - Gwent	*Gwent Wildlife Trust, Monmouth, tel: 01600 715501
Information and advice on marine conservation issues - Glamorgan	*Glamorgan Wildlife Trust, Tondu, tel: 01656 724100
Seals and fisheries	Sea Mammal Research Unit (SMRU), University of St. Andrew's, School of Biochemical and Medical Sciences, St. Andrew's, Fife KY16 8LB, tel: 01334 463472
Seals and fisheries	Susan Joy, Co-ordinator, Wildlife & Countryside Link Seals Group, 15 Park Road, East Grinstead, West Sussex RH19 1DW, tel: 01342 315400

*Starred contact addresses are given in full in the Appendix.

9.2 Mariculture

C.F. Robson

9.2.1 Introduction

Mariculture is the cultivation of marine species. In this region shellfish farming is concentrated in the estuaries of Cornwall.

9.2.2 Locations and species

Map 9.2.1 shows the location of commercial mariculture areas and the species that are cultivated in the region. Table 9.2.1 lists the main species that are under commercial cultivation in the region and in Great Britain and the Isle of Man. There is currently no cultivation of salmonid fish, non-salmonid fish or polychaetes in this region.

Table 9.2.1 Main species cultivated in the region and in Great Britain and the Isle of Man

Species	*Species status*	*Cultivated in region?*
Salmonids		
Atlantic salmon *Salmo salar*	Native	
Sea trout *Salmo trutta*	Native	
Non-salmonids		
Turbot *Psetta maxima*	Native	
Halibut *Hippoglossus hippoglossus*	Native	
Shellfish: bivalve molluscs		
Common mussel *Mytilus edulis*	Native	✔
Native oyster *Ostrea edulis*	Native	✔
Pacific oyster *Crassostrea gigas*	Un-established introduction	✔
Hard-shelled clam *Mercenaria mercenaria*	Non-native	
Manila clam *Tapes philippinarum*	Un-established introduction	
Palourde *Tapes decussatus*	Native	
Scallop *Pecten maximus*	Native	
Queen scallop *Aequipecten opercularis*	Native	
Polychaetes		
King ragworm *Neanthes virens*	Native	

Sources: Ministry of Agriculture, Fisheries and Food, The Crown Estate, La Tene Maps (1995). Note: for the JNCC's Marine Nature Conservation Review (MNCR), non-native species are those introduced species that are established in the wild; other introduced species are described as un-established introductions.

Mussels are being cultivated from natural spat settlement on ropes from pontoons in the King Harry Passage area of the Fal Estuary. Historically native oysters, and to a lesser extent extent Pacific oysters, have been cultivated in the Fal, based in the Penryn River, but these farms are currently non-operational.

The Helford River used to have natural native oyster spat settlement good enough to sustain the fishery. However young oyster stock is now imported from the Fal, grown for a while on trays then relaid on grounds upriver of Pedn Billy Point as far as Bishop's Quay. There they are left to grow and fatten until they reach marketable size.

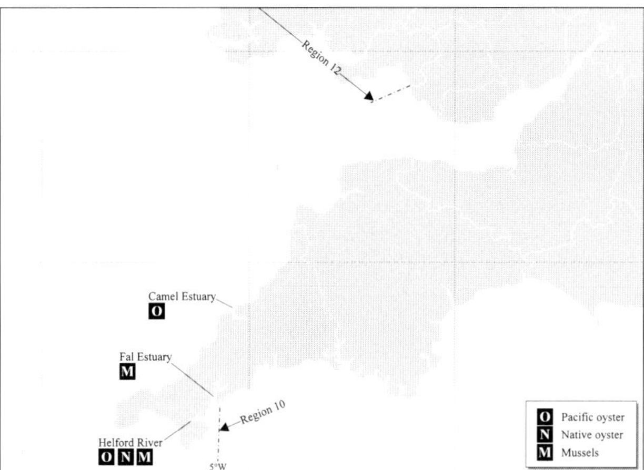

Map 9.2.1 General location of mariculture areas and species in culture. Sources: MAFF, The Crown Estate, La Tene Maps © Crown copyright.

Approximately 200,000 are dredged a year between early September to April (Masters 1994). In addition to the native oyster fishery the Duchy of Cornwall oyster farm, which is run by a local family, also cultivates Pacific oysters and mussels at Port Navas. The mussels are grown directly on the sea bed and some naturally-occurring mussels collected from the Camel Estuary are re-laid in the Helford River. The Pacific oysters are grown from hatchery-reared 'seed' (3-4 mm long oysters). These are initially grown in sacks on trays, and once they are at a size that is more resistant to predation they are moved to ground lays in the Helford River.

Pacific oysters are cultivated on racks on the foreshore of the Camel Estuary. Because of the poor water quality the oysters are re-laid in the Helford River before consumption.

The cultivation of Pacific oysters used to occur on St. Mary's Island and between Bryher and Tresco. However, mariculture is not currently regarded as a viable proposition in the Isles of Scilly, owing to the impact of severe weather conditions due to the lack of suitably sheltered sites (Atlantic Consultants 1995; Council of the Isles of Scilly 1995).

Shellfish News (Ministry of Agriculture, Fisheries and Food 1996) includes information on shellfish cultivation (and figures on the total shellfish production in the UK in 1994) and is published twice yearly.

9.2.3 Management and issues

The Food Safety (Live Bivalve Molluscs) Regulations (which implement European Council Directives) require that all waters from which bivalve molluscs are taken for human consumption are classified by MAFF, following sampling carried out by the Port Health Authority or local authority. Samples of live shellfish are submitted to the Public Health Laboratory Service for bacteriological examination and, depending on the resulting category (A - D), restrictions and further treatment may apply before human consumption is permitted. Samples are taken regularly and the classification can change. Shellfish must also meet the 'End Product Standard', with which all live bivalves intended for immediate consumption must comply. A database of the current hygiene status of shellfish harvesting areas is maintained by MAFF (Fisheries Division, Nobel House, and DFR Fish Diseases Laboratory, Weymouth).

The introduction of non-native shellfish species for cultivation has caused concern over their potential to establish self-sustaining populations, which may affect marine ecosystems. Since January 1993 there have been new requirements for the control of shellfish disease in Great Britain and for the importation and 'deposit' of molluscan shellfish and lobsters, under the EC Fish Health Directive (Directive 91/67). The Directive lists diseases on which national authorities will take action and those animals that are susceptible to notifiable diseases. The lists may be amended with changing circumstances. In Great Britain two shellfish diseases are now notifiable: *Bonamia* and *Marteilia*, both of which are of serious economic importance and are present in one or more EU member states. The agents of the diseases, *Bonamia ostreae* and *Marteilia refringens*, are parasites that cause high mortalities in susceptible species, notably the native oyster. Movements of species susceptible to these diseases can be made only from areas of equal or better health status, and imports of Pacific oysters are subject to screening for species contamination. Importation from non-EU countries is permitted only under licence, and imports must enter through designated border inspection posts. Shellfish and fish farms have to be registered with MAFF under the Fish Farming and Shellfish Farming Business Order 1985. Registration is designed to assist MAFF in dealing with any outbreaks of pests and diseases.

The consent of the owners or managers of the sea bed is required and a lease may be needed before structures for mariculture can be erected on the sea bed. In many areas a lease must be sought from the Crown Estate, since it owns or manages 55% of the foreshore and the same proportion of the beds of tidal rivers between mean high and low water in GB, together with virtually the entire territorial sea bed. Of the remainder of the foreshore in this region, the majority is owned by the Duchy of Cornwall. If intended new mariculture structures are potentially hazardous to navigation the Department of Transport must also issue a consent. If they are to be above mean low water mark planning permission must be sought from the local authority. In this region much of the coast, including the locations of existing maricultural operations, is protected by national and international designations, including Site of Special Scientific Interest (SSSI), Heritage Coast and AONB (Area of Outstanding Natural Beauty), as well as local and voluntary conservation measures, so nature conservation and landscape considerations also apply.

Several Orders are granted under section 1 of the Sea Fisheries (Shellfish Act) 1967 and are administered in England by MAFF. They are granted to an individual, a co-operative or a responsible body to enable the cultivation of the sea bed within a designated area of water and to conserve and develop named molluscan species of shellfish. Sea Fisheries Committees (SFCs) may sub-let the rights of a several fishery, subject to the consent of MAFF. There is one Several Order in this region (Table 9.2.2), out of 22 in Britain covering a total of approximately 3,299 ha (as at July 1995). The existence of a Several Order does not necessarily mean that mariculture is actively occurring at the location covered. The Taw mussel fishery is closed because the water quality is too poor, although the Taw-Torridge Estuary is currently showing signs of improvement. South-West Water has taken over the Several Order from the original grantee of the Taw Fishery Order, who retains lease rights to other beds near the site of the (now defunct) Yelland Power Station.

Mariculture and its effects are limited in this region compared with some other parts of Britain. However, issues relating to the cultivation of marine species are closely linked to marine nature conservation interests, particularly the possible effects on species and habitats of nature conservation interest. These issues for mariculture in general are under consideration by the 'Marine Fisheries Task Group', an inter-agency team of the statutory nature conservation organisations (the Countryside Council for Wales, English Nature, Scottish Natural Heritage and the Department of the Environment for Northern Ireland, together with the JNCC). A consultation paper prepared by the group, entitled *Developing an action programme for sea fisheries and wildlife* (Marine Fisheries Task Group 1994), identifies the main areas where marine fisheries (broadly defined to encompass the exploitation of all living marine resources and therefore including mariculture) affect wildlife and identifies any action needed.

9.2.4 Acknowledgements

Thanks are due to the following members of the Fisheries Working Group for their contributions and comments: Bill Cook (North Wales & North Western Sea Fisheries Committee (SFC)), Phil Coates (South Wales SFC), Brian Spencer (MAFF DFR Conwy), Neil Downes (Devon SFC), Dr P.D. McGovern (The Crown Estate, Scotland), Paul Knapman (English Nature), Blaise Bullimore (Countryside Council for Wales), Indrani Lutchman (WWF-UK), Clare Eno and Mark Tasker (JNCC) and Nancy Harrison (RSPB). The author also thanks the following for their comments on draft text and for additional information: Stephanie Tyler (Gwent Wildlife Trust), Alan Winstone (EA Welsh Region), E.J. Derriman and R.G. Teague (Cornwall SFC), Stuart Bray (EA South-West Region), Peter Hill (Padstow Harbour Commissioners), Sam Davis (English Nature) Steve Watt (Isles of Scilly SFC) and A. Herbert and A. Panayi (The Crown Estate).

Table 9.2.2 Several Orders in the region

Title	*Species covered*	*Grid ref.*	*Location*	*Grantee*	*Approx. area (ha)*	*Year of expiry*
River Taw Mussel Fishery Order 1962	Mussels	SS492338	River Taw, near Barnstaple, Devon	B. Hill	22	2022

Source: Ministry of Agriculture, Fisheries and Food (1995). Note: Regulating Orders are summarised in Table 9.1.8.

9.2.5 Further sources of information

A. References cited

Atlantic Consultants. 1995. *Sustainable economic development strategy: research report for the Council of the Isles of Scilly*. Truro, Atlantic Consultants.

Council of the Isles of Scilly. 1995. *Sustainable economic development strategy: 1995 and beyond*. St. Mary's, Council of the Isles of Scilly.

La Tene Maps. 1995. *Aquaculture of England and Wales*. Dublin, La Tene Maps.

Marine Fisheries Task Group. 1994. *Developing an action programme for sea fisheries and wildlife*. Peterborough, JNCC. (Consultation paper by the Marine Fisheries Task Group.)

Masters, J. 1994. *The Helford oysterage with notes on the River Fal*. Truro, Cornwall County Council. (A report to the Helford Voluntary Marine Conservation Area Advisory Group.)

Ministry of Agriculture, Fisheries and Food. 1995. *List of Orders in England, Wales and Scotland*. London, MAFF. (Unpublished.)

Ministry of Agriculture, Fisheries and Food. 1996. *Shellfish news. No. 1*. Lowestoft, MAFF.

B. Further reading

Cobham Resource Consultants. 1987. *An environmental assessment of fish farms*. Final report to Countryside Commission for Scotland, Crown Estate Commissioners, Highlands and Islands Development Board and Scottish Salmon Growers Association.

Dixon, F. 1986. *Development of the bottom culture mussel industry in the UK*. Sea Fish Authority Industrial Development Unit. (Internal Report, No. 1271.)

Frid, C.L.J., & Mercer, T.S. 1989. Environmental monitoring of caged fish farming in macrotidal environments. *Marine Pollution Bulletin, 20*: 379-383.

Helford Voluntary Marine Conservation Area. 1995. *The Helford River oysters*. Truro, Cornwall County Council/WWF/English Nature.

Ministry of Agriculture, Fisheries and Food. 1982. Bonamia, *a new threat to the native oyster fishery*. Lowestoft, MAFF. (Directorate of Fisheries Research Fisheries Notices, No. 71.)

Ministry of Agriculture, Fisheries and Food, Welsh Office and Scottish Office Agriculture and Fisheries Department. 1994. *A guide to importing fish*. Lowestoft, MAFF.

Ministry of Agriculture, Fisheries and Food, Welsh Office and Scottish Office Agriculture and Fisheries Department. 1994. *A guide to shellfish health controls*. Lowestoft, MAFF.

Nature Conservancy Council. 1989. *Fish farming in the UK*. Memorandum to the House of Commons Agriculture Committee. Peterborough, Nature Conservancy Council.

Pawson, M.G., & Rogers, S.I. 1989. *The coastal fisheries of England and Wales. Part ii: a review of their status in 1988*. Lowestoft, MAFF. (Directorate of Fisheries Research Internal Report, No. 19.) (Being updated.)

Ross, A. 1988. Fish farms and wildlife: are they really compatible? *Marine Conservation*, summer 1988.

Spencer, B.E. 1990. *Cultivation of Pacific oysters*. Lowestoft, MAFF. (Directorate of Fisheries Research Laboratory Leaflet, No. 63.)

Spencer, B.E., Edwards, D.B., & Millican, P.F. 1991. *Cultivation of Manila clams*. Lowestoft, MAFF. (Directorate of Fisheries Research Laboratory Leaflet, No. 65.)

Wildlife & Countryside Link Seals Group. 1995. *Seals and fisheries: the facts*. East Grinstead, Wildlife & Countryside Link Seals Group.

C. Contact names and addresses

Type of information	*Contact address and telephone no.*
Central contact for the local SFCs; general SFCs policies	Chief Executive, Association of Sea Fisheries Committees, Buckrose House, Commercial Street, Norton, Malton, North Yorkshire YO17 9HX, tel: 01653 698219
Shellfish reports etc.; Several Orders; mariculture activities and local bylaws - Cornwall	Chief Fishery Officer, Cornwall Sea Fisheries Committee, The Old Bonded Warehouse, Quay Street, Penzance, Cornwall TR18 4BD, tel: 01736 69817
Shellfish reports etc.; Several Orders; mariculture activities and local bylaws - Isles of Scilly	Assistant Chief Executive, Isles of Scilly Sea Fisheries Committee, Town Hall, St. Mary's, Isles of Scilly TR1 0LW, tel: 01720 422536
Shellfish reports etc.; Several Orders; mariculture activities and local bylaws - Devon	Deputy Clerk & Chief Fishery Officer, Devon Sea Fisheries Committee, Forde House, Newton Abbot, Devon TQ12 3XX, tel: 01803 854648/882004
Shellfish reports etc.; Several Orders; mariculture activities and local bylaws - South Wales	Director, South Wales Sea Fisheries Committee, Queens Buildings, Cambrian Place, Swansea, West Glamorgan SA1 1TW, tel: 01792 654466
Scientific advice: marine fish and shellfish cultivation; advice on management and policy issues for the coastal zone. Mariculture and marine nature conservation issues. Seals and mariculture.	*Head of Laboratory, MAFF Directorate of Fisheries Research, Fisheries Laboratory (Conwy), tel: 01492 593883
Bivalve mollusc production areas; classification of shellfish waters and shellfish diseases	Head of Laboratory, MAFF Directorate of Fisheries Research, Fish Diseases Laboratory, Barrack Road, The Nothe, Weymouth, Dorset DT4 8UB, tel: 01305 206600
Fisheries and mariculture in England, including Several Orders; seals and mariculture	Director, MAFF (Aquaculture Division), Nobel House, 17 Smith Square, London SW1P 3JR, tel: 0171 238 5940
Fisheries and mariculture in Wales, including Several Orders; seals and mariculture	Welsh Office Agriculture Department, Fisheries Department, Division 2B, New Crown Buildings, Cathays Park, Cardiff CF1 3NQ, tel: 01222 823567
Technical advice on shellfish purification (depuration)	Sea Fish Industry Authority, Sea Fish House, St. Andrews Dock, Hull HU3 4QE, tel: 01482 27837
Leases	The Crown Estate, Marine Estates, 16 Carlton House Terrace, London SW1Y 5AH, tel: 0171 210 4377
Leases	The Duchy of Cornwall Office, Station Road, Liskeard, Cornwall PL14 4EE, tel: 01579 343149
Salmon farming	Director, Scottish Salmon Growers Association, Drummond House, Scott Street, Perth PH1 5EJ, Scotland, tel: 01738 635420
Commercial advice on shellfish	Director, Shellfish Association of the UK, Fishmongers Hall, London Bridge, London EC4R 9EL, tel: 0171 6263531
Interaction between mariculture activities and marine nature conservation issues in England	*Fisheries Liaison Officer, EN HQ, Peterborough, tel: 01733 340345
Interaction between mariculture activities and marine nature conservation issues in Wales	*Marine and Coastal Section, CCW HQ, Bangor, tel: 01248 370444
Marine Fisheries Task Group paper; interaction between mariculture activities and marine nature conservation issues	*Fisheries Officer, JNCC Peterborough, tel: 01733 62626
Interaction between mariculture activities and marine nature conservation issues	*Coastal Policy Officer, RSPB HQ, Sandy, Beds., tel: 01767 680551
Interaction between mariculture activities and marine nature conservation issues	*Fisheries Officer, WWF-UK, Godalming, tel: 01483 426444
Interaction between mariculture activities and marine nature conservation issues	*Conservation Officer, Marine Conservation Society, Ross-on-Wye, tel: 01989 566017
Interaction between mariculture activities and marine nature conservation issues	*County Wildlife Trusts
Interaction between mariculture activities and marine nature conservation issues	Honorary Secretary, The Marine Forum for Environmental Issues, c/o University College Scarborough, Filey Road, Scarborough YO11 3AZ, tel: 01723 362392
Seals and mariculture	Sea Mammal Research Unit (SMRU), Gatty Marine Laboratory, University of St. Andrews, Fife KY16 8LB, tel: 01334 463472/476161
Seals and mariculture	Co-ordinator, Wildlife & Countryside Link Seals Group, 15 Park Road, East Grinstead, West Sussex RH19 1DW, tel: 01342 315400

*Starred contact addresses are given in full in the Appendix.

9.3 Quarrying and landfilling

C.A. Crumpton & M.J. Goodwin

9.3.1 Introduction

In this section, quarries are classified as coastal if they are less than 2 km inland and landfill sites if they are in a coastal 10 km square. A wide range of minerals are mined along the region's coastline, reflecting the diversity of rock types occurring there (see also section 2.1). The minerals quarried along the coast include igneous rock, used mainly for roadstone and other construction; sand and gravel for concrete mix and fill; slate for roofing; sandstone for roadstone and other constructional uses; limestone for roadstone and industrial purposes such as steelmaking, concrete aggregate and other construction; and finally, common clay and shale for bricks, pipes, tiles and cement.

There is a long history of tin mining in Cornwall, and by the 19th century, both tin and copper were mined in great quantities. With the collapse of the tin market in 1985 the industry almost ceased, although there are numerous disused mines scattered along the coastline, particularly at St. Just and St. Agnes. Some are operated as tourist attractions, and Cornish mining could possibly restart in the future.

Table 9.3.1 shows the whole-county production levels of the minerals extracted in the region's coastal quarries, compared with national and British levels.

Table 9.3.2 shows the numbers of mineral workings on the region's coast by type of mineral, compared with British totals.

The 86 coastal landfill sites in this region represent approximately 0.6% of the British whole country total of approximately 15,000.

9.3.2 Important locations

In this region there are 31 coastal workings (at 20 sites) extracting one or more minerals (Table 9.3.3; Map 9.3.1).

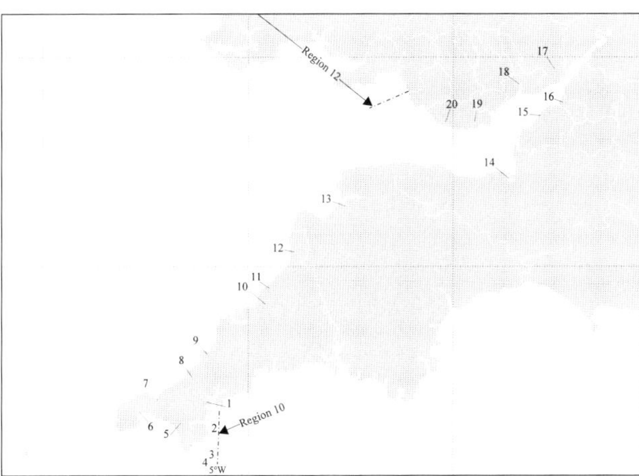

Map 9.3.1 Coastal quarries. Numbers refer to Table 9.3.3. Source: BGS (1994). © Crown copyright.

Table 9.3.2 Numbers of coastal workings in the region compared with British totals (including inland workings) by mineral type

Type of working	*No. on region's coast*	*No. in Britain (including inland)*
Sandstone	2	276
Igneous	12	236
Slate	6	42
Limestone	6	339
Silica sand	1	46
Common clay and shale	1	176
Serpentinite	1	1
Sand and gravel	3	896
Totals	*31*	*2,012*

Source: British Geological Survey 1994

Table 9.3.1 Minerals production[a] in Region 11 (1993)

	Limestone		*Sandstone*		*Igneous rock*		*Common clay and shale*		*Sand and gravel*	
	Tonnes[a]	*% of GB total*	*Tonnes[a]*	*% of GB total*	*Tonnes[a]*	*% of GB total*	*Tonnes[a]*	*% of GB total*	*Tonnes[a]*	*% of GB total*
Cornwall	0	0	47	<1.0	1,922	3.9	0	0	738	.8
Devon	3,022	2.9			763	1.6	n/a	n/a	1,642**	1.8
Somerset	14,913	14.1	810†	6.7†	646	1.3	0	0	n/a	n/a
Avon	5,857	5.5			0	0	n/a	n/a	n/a	n/a
Gwent	1,914	1.8	0	0	n/a	n/a	0	0	n/a	n/a
South Glamorgan	1,725	1.6	0	0	0	0	0	0	449**	.5
Mid Glamorgan	5,780	5.5	n/a	n/a	0	0	0	0	0	0
Region 11	***33,211***	***31.4***	***857***	***7.1***	***3,331***	***6.8***	***651****	***6.0***	***7,038*****	***7.9***
England	84,123	80.0	9,003	74.4	24,783	50.4	9,883	90.7	74,833	83.6
Wales	20,330	19.2	1,381	11.4	3,621	7.4	386	3.5	1,701	1.9
Great Britain	105,885	100	12,100	100	49,209	100	10,891	100	89,470	100

Source: Central Statistical Office 1994. Key: n/a = not available; [a]thousands of tonnes, rounded up to the next whole thousand tonnes; *includes Wiltshire; **includes marine dredged material; ***includes Powys; †combined total for Devon, Somerset and Avon.

By far the majority of the region's coastal quarries are in Cornwall. The county produces mainly igneous rock; it also has the only coastal quarries for slate, serpentinite and silica sand in the region. That for serpentinite is the only such quarry in Britain. Other counties in the region have few or no coastal quarries. All China clay produced in Britain (2.8 million tonnes in 1993) comes from Devon and Cornwall, although none of the quarries lies on the coast in this region (see Region 10 for further information). A substantial proportion of the national limestone production comes from the counties of this region, especially from Somerset (where there are many quarries in the Carboniferous Limestone around the Mendips) and south Wales.

Map 9.3.2 shows the location of the region's currently used coastal landfill sites, according to Aspinwall's Sitefile Digest (Aspinwall & Co. 1994); the status codes are defined in Table 9.3.4. Landfill sites in the region are relatively evenly distributed along the coast, apart from around the conurbations of Bristol and Cardiff, where greater concentrations occur, especially of sites that deal with 'difficult wastes'.

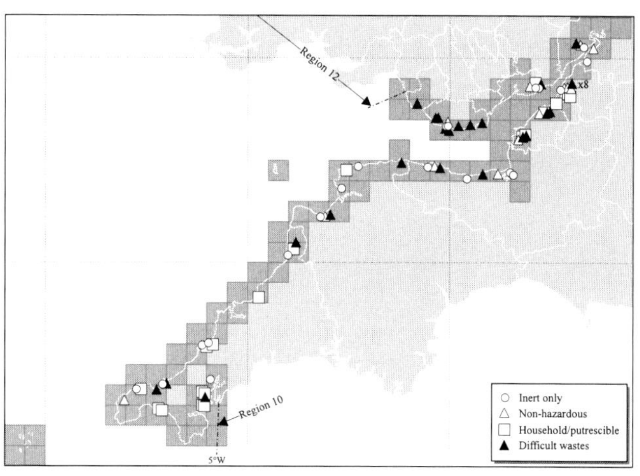

Map 9.3.2 Coastal landfill sites. Note: a single symbol may represent more than one site in close proximity. Source: Aspinwall & Co. (1994).

Table 9.3.3 Coastal quarries

Site no.	*Location*	*Operator*	*Mineral*
	Cornwall		
1	Penryn	C. Lawer	Igneous
2	Falmouth	W. & J. Andrews	Igneous
2	Falmouth	ECC Quarries	Igneous
2	Falmouth	International Quarry Consultants	Igneous
2	Falmouth	S. Knowles Ltd.	Igneous
2	Falmouth	Trevone Quarries	Igneous
3	St. Keverne	Redland Aggregates	Igneous
4	Lizard	R. Hendy	Serpentinite
5	Helston	Redland Aggregates	Igneous
5	Helston	Cornish Roadstone Ltd.	Igneous
6	Penzance	ARC - Southwestern	Igneous
6	Penzance	ARC - Southwestern	Igneous
7	Hayle	ARC - Southwestern	Igneous
7	Hayle	DGW Sand Co.	Sand and gravel
8	St. Agnes	W. Doble	Silica sand
9	Camel Estuary	DGW Sand Co.	Sand and gravel
10	Delabole	S. Boundy	Slate
10	Delabole	Delabole Slate Ltd.	Slate
10	Delabole	M. Dungey	Slate
10	Delabole	Hillson Bros.	Slate
11	Tintagel	Mill Hill Quarry (Tavistock) Ltd.	Slate
11	Tintagel	Realstone Ltd.	Slate
12	Bude	Penhill Quarry and Haulage Ltd.	Sandstone
	Devon		
13	Taw-Torridge Estuary	T.E. Grace	Sand and gravel
	Somerset		
14	Cannington	Castle Hill Quarry Co. Ltd.	Limestone
	Avon		
15	Clevedon	Bristol Pennant Stone	Sandstone
16	Avonmouth	Tarmac Bricks and Tiles	Common clay and shale
	Gwent		
17	Tintern	ARC South Wales	Limestone
18	Rogiet, Newport	ARC South Wales	Limestone
	South Glamorgan		
19	Aberthaw	Blue Circle	Limestone
19	Barry	Croxton & Garry Ltd.	Limestone
20	St. Athan	Lliswerry	Limestone

Source: British Geological Survey (1994). Note: site numbers refer to Map 9.3.1.

Table 9.3.4 Status of the region's landfill sites

Status code	*Definition*	*No. in region*
1 Inert only	Uncontaminated excavated natural earth materials, and uncontaminated brick rubble and concrete with similar properties to natural earth materials.	21
2 Non-hazardous	Mainly uncontaminated and industrial wastes such as packaging materials, wood and plastic. Some of these wastes are biodegradable but not rapidly so.	14
3 Household/putrescible	Typical contents of a household dustbin and similar wastes of industrial origin e.g. food processing wastes.	20
4 Difficult wastes	Any wastes which require particular handling techniques at the disposal site, e.g. vehicle tyres, dry feathers, animal carcasses. They are not the same as Special Wastes, which are toxic and require pre-notification of disposal to the Waste Regulation Authority.	31
Total		*86*

Source: Aspinwall & Co. (1994). See Map 9.3.2.

9.3.3 Management

Minerals Planning Guidance 6 (DoE 1994) estimated future demand for aggregates in England and advocated change in the sources of aggregates used, in line with the aims of sustainable development. It is recognised that a major proportion of aggregate demand will be met from traditional supplies of crushed rock and sand and gravel, but there is a desire to increase the contribution from alternative sources, e.g. marine dredged aggregates (see also section 9.4), coastal superquarries and secondary aggregates. Marine dredged aggregates already make a significant contribution to the aggregates supply in south Wales. The supply from secondary/recycled sources, including power station ash, metallurgical slag and slate waste, is expected to provide between 20% and 25% of consumption up to 2006. The principle of sustainable development is reflected in the 1995 Cornwall Minerals Local Plan, in which heavy emphasis is placed on the use of minerals waste as an aggregate.

Although DoE's superquarry study (DoE 1992) identified potential areas of hard quarriable rock in this region, no superquarries are planned. The granite at Land's End is located in an area that is too exposed for safe shipping access, and quarrying there has been ruled out on technical grounds. Suitable areas exist on the Avon coast, but they are already substantially exploited.

The demand for aggregate from quarries in Devon has fallen in the last two to three years because of the absence of major new road construction in the county and the County Council's policy of using recycled and secondary materials for highway maintenance and construction. A working party has been set up to develop a highway maintenance recycling policy; it will monitor national developments.

The construction of the Second Severn Crossing approach roads experienced some problems in 1993 and 1994, owing to the use of some unsuitable aggregate sources, including an inactive colliery spoil tip, which was used primarily because of a lack of other locally available constructional fill (South West Regional Aggregates Working Party 1994).

Landfill regulation, including landfill site licensing, now falls within the remit of the Environment Agency under the 1995 Environment Act. The new agency integrates the functions of Her Majesty's Inspectorate of Pollution (HMIP), the local Waste Regulation Authorities (WRAs) and the National Rivers Authority (NRA). In general terms the agency's regional boundaries follow local authority or national administrative boundaries, to facilitate local accountability. The activities of the new agency are grouped under two broad headings: pollution prevention and control, including waste regulation, the work of HMIP and the NRA's work on water quality; and water management, covering the NRA's other functions. Also within the Environment Act 1995 is the requirement for mine operators to give the agency at least six months' notice of their intention to abandon a mine, in order that steps can be taken to avoid pollution from minewater. Provisions relating to producer responsibility for waste will provide a mechanism to ensure that business initiatives on re-using, recovering and recycling waste are not undermined by operators seeking to avoid their obligations. Waste management licences were introduced by the 1990 Environmental Protection Act to replace the disposal site licences previously required by the 1974 Control of Pollution Act.

9.3.4 Information sources used

Data on quarrying were obtained from the British Geological Survey's *Directory of mines and quarries* (1994) and are the most up to date and comprehensive available. Nevertheless these data may be up to three years old and may therefore include information on some operations that have now ceased. In a very small number of cases, exact addresses of quarries were not listed and therefore it was not known if they were coastal. Local mineral plans are available through the local authorities listed in section 9.3.6 C.

The data for landfilling were obtained from the Aspinwall & Co. *Sitefile digest* (1994), which represents the most comprehensive and up to date record of publicly available waste management statistics in Great Britain.

9.3.5 Acknowledgements

Thanks go to Dr Ron Moore and Susan Morley (Aspinwall and Co.) for providing information from the Sitefile Digest.

9.3.6 Further sources of information

A. References cited

Aspinwall & Co. 1994. *Sitefile digest. A digest of authorised waste treatment and disposal sites in Great Britain.* Shrewsbury, Environment Press.

British Geological Survey. 1994. *Directory of mines and quarries 1994.* 4th ed. Keyworth, Nottingham, British Geological Survey.

Central Statistical Office. 1994. *Business monitor 1993, PA1007 - minerals.* Cardiff, HMSO.

Department of the Environment. 1992. *Coastal superquarries to supply south-east England aggregate requirements.* London, HMSO.

Department of the Environment. 1994. *Minerals Planning Guidance Note 6: guidelines for aggregate provision in England.* London, HMSO.

South West Regional Aggregates Working Party. 1994. *South West Regional Aggregates Working Party combined annual report for 1993 and 1994.* Bristol, Avon County Council.

B. Further reading

British Geological Survey. 1995. *United Kingdom minerals yearbook 1994.* Keyworth, Nottingham, British Geological Survey.

Eno, N.C., *ed.* 1991. *Marine conservation handbook.* 2nd ed. Peterborough, English Nature.

C. Contact names and addresses

Type of information	*Contact address and telephone no.*
Mines and quarries (British Directory of Mines and Quarries)	Director, British Geological Survey, Keyworth, Nottingham NG12 5GG, tel: 01602 363393
Details of disused collieries	Coal Authority, Bretby Business Park, Ashby Road, Burton-on-Trent, Staffs. DE15 0QD, tel: 01283 553291
Landfill sites (Sitefile Digest)	Dr. Ron Moore or Dr. Phil Marsh (senior consultants), Aspinwall & Co., Walford Manor, Baschurch, Shrewsbury SY4 2HH, tel: 01939 262200
Waste regulation	Environment Agency South West Region, Exeter, tel: 01392 444000
Local minerals plans - Cornwall	Minerals Planning Officer, Cornwall County Council, Minerals Planning Dept., Western Divisional Group Centre, Radnor Road, Scorrier, Redruth TR16 5EH, tel: 01209 820611
Local minerals plans - Devon	Minerals Planning Officer, Devon County Council, County Hall, Exeter EX2 4QW, tel: 01392 383380
Local minerals plans - North Somerset	*P. Hale, Team Manager, Development Control, Minerals and Waste, North Somerset District Council, Town Hall, Weston-super-Mare BS23 1UJ, tel: 01934 888888 ext. 8731
Local minerals plans - Somerset	*Minerals Planning Officer, Somerset County Council, Taunton, tel: 01823 333451
Local minerals plans - Bristol	Sarah Tucker, Minerals Officer, Directorate of Planning, Transport and Development, Bristol City Council, Brunel House, St. George's Road, Bristol BS1 5UY, tel: 0117 922 3769
Local minerals plans - Gloucestershire	Gloucestershire County Council, Oxleaze Wing, Shire Hall, Bearland, Gloucester, GL1 2TH, tel: 01452 425835
Local minerals plans - Gwent	Monmouthshire County Council, County Hall, Cwmbran, Gwent, tel: 01633 832128
Local minerals plans - South Glamorgan	Cardiff Council, County Hall, Atlantic Wharf, Cardiff CF1 5VW, tel: 01222 872000
Local minerals plans including Mineral Local Plan for limestone quarrying in Mid Glamorgan	Newport Council, Planning Department, Greyfriars Road, Cardiff, South Glamorgan CF1 3LG, tel: 01222 820820

*Starred contact addresses are given in full in the Appendix.

9.4 Marine aggregate extraction, dredging and solid waste disposal at sea

C.A. Crumpton & M.J. Goodwin

9.4.1 Introduction

Sand and gravel on the sea bed are important sources of industrial aggregate for concrete production, beach replenishment and beach protection. The main market is in the south-east of England, although a large proportion of material dredged from the region's waters is used to meet local demand. The national demand for aggregate from all sources increased steadily during the 1980s. Aggregates from terrestrial sources are insufficient to meet the rising demand (Doody *et al.* 1993) and marine aggregates satisfy an increasing proportion of the national requirement - 15% in 1992 (Crown Estate 1995).

Marine sand and gravel are extracted by commercial mineral companies under licence from the Crown Estate. Marine aggregates extracted in England and Wales reached a peak of 28 million tonnes in 1989, but amounts have since fallen steadily. In 1995, a total of 26,122,758 tonnes of aggregate were landed under licence from the Crown Estate Commissioners from the bed of the Territorial Sea and Continental Shelf (Table 9.4.1). This figure includes approximately 7 million tonnes of aggregate that were dredged in Great Britain but exported to landing ports abroad. The marine dredged aggregates landed at the ports in the region (1,541,519 tonnes) represent 5.9% of the total landed in England and Wales under licence from the Crown Estate (Crown Estate 1996).

Navigational dredging is of two types: capital dredging and maintenance dredging. Capital dredging refers to the one-off removal of sediment, chiefly when deepening shipping channels and during the construction of new dock facilities. Thereafter, maintenance dredging is the regular dredging of existing ports and their approaches to maintain safe navigation. The majority of dredged material, which can range in composition from silts to boulder clay and rock, is disposed of at sea. Some dredged material is also used for land claim and increasingly for 'soft' coastal defences such as beach recharge. During the NCC's Estuaries Review surveys, carried out in 1989, out of a total of 155 estuaries around Great Britain, capital dredging was taking place in fifteen and maintenance dredging in 72 - 9.7% and 46.5% respectively of the estuaries surveyed (Davidson *et al.* 1991). Dredged material was being disposed of in ten of the estuaries surveyed.

The amount of dredged material deposited in the region in 1993 (2,956,767 tonnes) constituted 9.9% of the total deposited around the UK as a whole (Table 9.4.2) (MAFF 1995). This compares with a figure of 12.0% for 1992, when 3,489,035 tonnes were deposited in the region and 29,161,946 tonnes were deposited around the UK as a whole (MAFF 1994). From 1989 to 1993, a yearly average of 33,000,000 tonnes (wet weight) of dredged material was deposited at sea in England and Wales. Amounts varied between 40,810,718 tonnes (wet weight) in 1989 and 26,086,503 tonnes in 1993 (MAFF 1995).

Other solid materials deposited in British waters under licence from MAFF include sewage sludge. Some sewage sludges are principally of domestic origin and contain only low levels of metals and other persistent components. Others include industrial inputs, resulting in higher concentrations of contaminants. In terms of sewage disposal, the UK produces some 1.1 million tonnes dry solids (tds) of sewage sludge annually and currently disposes of approximately 300,000 tds to sea, although disposal at sea is to be phased out by 1998, under the Urban Waste Water Treatment Directive (91/271/EEC). It will have to be replaced by disposal on land, by tipping or incineration. UK sewage sludge production is set to increase dramatically over the next decade, to a predicted 3.3 million tds in 2006. No sewage sludge has been deposited in the region's waters since 1994.

Table 9.4.1 Marine dredged aggregates and contract fill/beach nourishment material licensed, extracted and landed in the region and Great Britain in 1995 (tonnes)

	Aggregates		*Contract fill/beach nourishment*	*Total aggregates and fill/beach nourishment*
	licensed	*extracted*	*extracted*	*landed*
South West Coast*	4,843,200	2,285,899	1,559,836	3,845,735
England and Wales*	***42,068,599***	***20,953,623***	***5,169,136***	***26,122,758***

Source: Crown Estate (1996). Key: *includes part of Region 12 as far as Pembroke; **no marine aggregates are dredged off Scotland.

Table 9.4.2 Dredged material licensed and disposed of at sea in 1993

	Licences issued	*Sites under licence*	*Sites used*	*Tonnes licensed*	*Wet tonnage deposited*
Region 11	**10**	**8**	**7**	**12,358,500**	2,956,767*
England and Wales	110	89	67	66,074,966	26,086,503
UK	***143***	***146***	***110***	***70,245,516***	***29,866,256***

Source: MAFF (1995). Note: licences may commence at any time and generally last for one year. Key: *includes Swansea Bay (Region 12).

9.4.2 Important locations

Marine aggregates dredging

Much of the Bristol Channel and Cornish coast has been subject to marine aggregate extraction licence applications, but production licences in the region are currently limited to the inner Bristol Channel, where coarse gritty sand is worked. In 1994 planning permission was issued by Avon County Council to dredge approximately 3 million tonnes of sand fill from the Bristol Channel, for use in the construction of the Cardiff Bay barrage. Map 9.4.1 shows the areas licensed for the dredging of marine aggregates in 1994. Table 9.4.3 shows the total amounts of marine dredged aggregates landed to ports in the region in 1995.

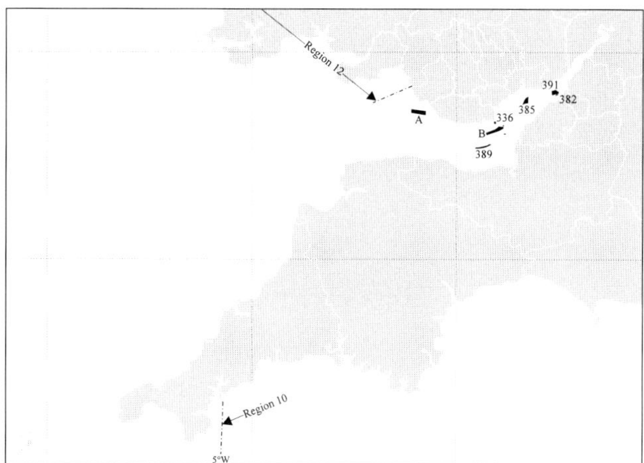

Map 9.4.1 Licensed marine aggregate dredging areas (1994). Source: Crown Estate (1995).

Navigational dredging

Capital dredging has occurred at a number of locations in the region in the last few years, including dredging for taking equipment to the new Hinkley Point C power station and for several marina/housing developments, e.g. on the Taff at Cardiff. Cardiff Bay is the only location in the region where significant amounts of maintenance dredging occur, although the construction of the Cardiff Bay barrage is reported to have reduced the need for dredging in the Cardiff Bay area since work commenced in 1994, such that no dredging has taken place since then (Cardiff Harbour Authority pers. comm.). The barrage is due to be completed in 1997 and it is envisaged by the Harbour Authority that the level of dredging required will fall by at least two thirds of its original levels (around 2 million tonnes per annum), due to the resultant change in the strength and direction of currents. Elsewhere, approximately 5,000 tonnes of material is dredged from Truro Harbour each year (Truro Harbour Authority pers. comm.); this represents a reduction of around 2,000 tonnes per year from previous years, as a result of the high cost involved.

Table 9.4.3 Marine dredged aggregates landed in the region in 1995 (tonnes)

Landing port	*Tonnes landed*
Appledore, Devon	19,042
Bridgwater, Somerset	52,928
Avonmouth, Avon	501,229
Newport, Gwent	436,331
Cardiff, South Glamorgan	447,814
Barry, South Glamorgan	84,175
Total	*1,541,519*

Source: Crown Estate (1996)

Map 9.4.2 shows the main marine disposal sites licensed in 1993 for the disposal of dredged material in the region (Table 9.4.4). The dominant inputs are from the maintenance dredging of the ports of Cardiff and Swansea.

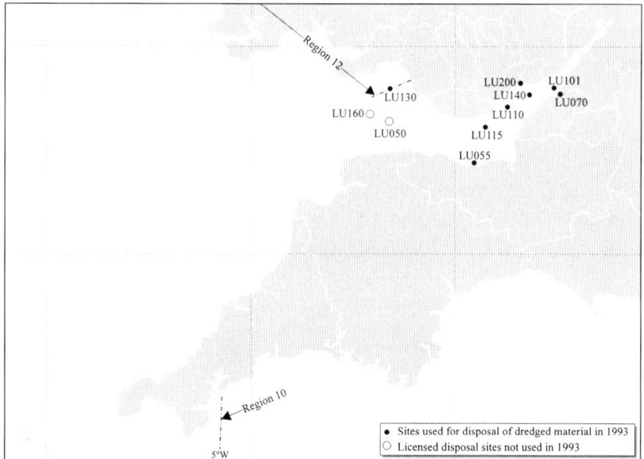

Map 9.4.2 Sites licensed for the disposal of dredged materials at sea (1993) (Table 9.4.3). Source: MAFF (1995). © Crown copyright.

9.4.3 Management and issues

All dredging activities have short-term, localised effects, such as the removal of material and organisms, but long-term effects on, say, fish stocks or morphology are much more difficult to assess, owing to the difficulty of determining which effects are the result of dredging and which the result of the many other factors operating (Doody *et al.* 1993). In response to increased national demand for aggregate during the 1980s, the aggregate industry invested in new ships, which allowed the more efficient exploitation of licence areas and the dredging of new, deeper waters (Kenny & Rees 1994). These factors expand the area of sea bed affected by aggregate dredging and potentially intensify the effects. A study was carried out in 1990 (Bullen Consultants 1990) on behalf of a group of eight private and public organisations in the region of the present and predicted future effects of dredging and other activities and processes along the coastline. The study covered a 115 km length of coastline stretching from Penarth Head to Worms Head (Region 12).

A joint Welsh Office and Department of the Environment project entitled *Bristol Channel marine aggregate: resources and constraints* will catalogue marine aggregate resources in the area and report on the constraints on their exploitation, for example the availability of aggregates, the water depth, likely environmental impacts on sea-bed species, fish populations and water turbidity and potential erosive effects on the coastline.

Table 9.4.4 Dredged material disposed of at licensed sites in the region in 1992 and 1993

Site name	*MAFF code (on Map 9.4.2)*	*Dredging waste type*	*Depth (m)*	*Tonnage disposed 1992*	*1993*
Watchet Harbour	LU055	Maintenance	Within harbour limits below high tide level	16,940	12,000
Portishead	LU070	Capital	0-10	25,980	167,785
New Denny Island	LU101	Capital	0.5	26,360	88,600
Cardiff Grounds	LU110	Capital Maintenance	5-10	0	0
				1,078,748	786,675
Merkour Buoy	LU115	Maintenance	5	0	28,860
Swansea Bay (Outer)	LU130	Capital	20	0	0
		Maintenance		1,632,692	1,401,365
Newport	LU140	Maintenance	0-10	601,595	373,058
Uskmouth (on River Usk near power station)	LU200	Maintenance	n/a	106,720	98,424
Total				*3,489,035*	*2,956,767*

Source: MAFF pers. comm.

Marine aggregates dredging

Marine sand and gravel are extracted by commercial mineral companies under licence from the Crown Estate. Government policy for the provision of aggregates, formulated in 1982 and 1989, has encouraged marine extraction of sand and gravel: Minerals Planning Guidance Note 6 states that "it has a very important role to play in maintaining supplies of aggregate and, as far as possible, its use is to be encouraged" (Crown Estate 1992). The government has announced its intention (as at November 1995) to change the system whereby approval is given for the issuing of licences for aggregate extraction. The current system involves obtaining a favourable 'Government View', through a non-statutory analysis and consultation process co-ordinated by the Department of the Environment. The government intends that, in future, applications for marine aggregate extraction licences should be subject to the same type of process as terrestrial planning applications under the Town and Country Planning Acts, regardless of the ownership of the sea bed. The interim position is described in Department of the Environment (1995), which recommends that "the dredging industry will find it helpful to produce a formal Environmental Statement to support most applications for a production licence".

The government promotes environmentally sustainable coastal defences, and, as a result, the use of marine-dredged sand and gravel for beach recharge is predicted to grow substantially (NERC undated; see also section 8.4).

Aggregate extraction from the sea bed commonly involves using either suction pipes or hoppers. The former method creates long shallow tracks or large round holes several metres deep, depending on whether the pipe is trailed or fixed. The latter method results in localised depressions, the size of which depends on the capacity of the hopper. The biological implications of extraction depend upon the characteristics of the individual area concerned and are potentially far reaching. If an area is used by fish for spawning, for which a stable bed is required, egg laying can be disrupted. Short- or long-term changes in sediment deposition can result, as well as inevitable changes in the topography of the bed. Disturbance of muddy material in order to access underlying aggregate can destroy feeding grounds for flatfish through the displacement of muddy sand fauna. Where aggregate is overlain by clean sand, it is thought unlikely that long-term damage to benthic fauna will occur (Irish Sea Study Group 1990).

Navigational dredging

Navigational dredging is the responsibility of individual harbour authorities, although a licence from MAFF is required for disposal of the dredged material offshore.

Dredged material disposal at sea

The primary legislation in force to control the disposal of dredged material at sea in the UK is the Food and Environmental Protection Act (1985) (deposition at sea and in intertidal areas). Also, the Oslo Convention for the Prevention of Marine Pollution by Dumping from Ships and Aircraft, and the London Convention on the Dumping of Wastes at Sea, include within their scope disposal of dredged material at sea. In this region, licences to deposit dredged material are issued by MAFF. Each licence is subject to conditions, which have become more stringent in the last few years. Illegal dumping of material may occur: for instance, in 1986 and 1987 six and three cases respectively of alleged illegal dumping were investigated in England and Wales (MAFF 1989).

Blanketing of the sea bed is the main impact of the disposal of dredged material. If the input rate is significantly greater than the natural sedimentation rate, benthic flora and fauna may be killed through the prevention of respiration and feeding. Other impacts include the localised elevation of levels of metals originating in industrial waste and effluent discharged into the rivers from which the material was dredged. Localised increases in water column turbidity, which are often caused by dredged material disposal, may interfere with fish migration for as long as the increase lasts. Changes in sediment particle size can result in changes in benthic flora and fauna which, whilst not damaging *per se*, may affect the distribution of higher animals by altering the food chain. Shallows over banks of sediment may also be created, which could be a navigational hazard (Irish Sea Study Group 1990).

9.4.4 Information sources used

The statistics on marine aggregate extraction relate to 1995 royalty returns to the Crown Estate, as managers of the foreshore and sea bed. The regional landing port totals do not equate to the amount dredged from each region, owing to the presence of the export market and movement of aggregate to meet differing home market demands. It is not always possible to state definitively where the aggregate landed at specific ports was dredged, owing to the movement of aggregate to different markets within Britain. Generally however, the material is supplied from the adjacent dredging areas. Information on navigational dredging was obtained from the Nature Conservancy Council's 1991 Estuaries Review (Davidson *et al.* 1991) and from personal communication with Harbour Commissioners.

The information on the disposal of dredged material and sewage sludge is derived from licences granted by MAFF. Further information on sewage sludge disposal grounds is available from MAFF.

9.4.5 Acknowledgements

Thanks are due to the Crown Estate Commissioners for information on marine aggregate extraction in the region, Dr C. Vivian of MAFF Fisheries Laboratory, Burnham-on-Crouch, for providing information on solid waste disposal at sea, and to Ian Cromie of the British Marine Aggregate Producers Association for his useful comments.

9.4.6 Further sources of information

A. References cited

Bullen Consultants. 1990. *The south Wales coastline response study.* Bridgend, Bullen Consultants.

Crown Estate. 1992. *Marine aggregate extraction and the Government view procedure.* London, Crown Estate.

Crown Estate. 1995. *Marine aggregates - Crown Estate licences - summary of statistics 1994.* London, Crown Estate.

Crown Estate. 1996. *Marine aggregates - Crown Estate licences - summary of statistics 1995.* London, Crown Estate.

Davidson, N.C., Laffoley, D.d'A., Doody, J.P., Way, L.S., Gordon, J., Key, R., Drake, C.M., Pienkowski, M.W., Mitchell, R., & Duff, K.L. 1991. *Nature conservation and estuaries in Great Britain.* Peterborough, Nature Conservancy Council.

Department of the Environment. 1995. *Policy guidelines for the coast.* London, HMSO.

Doody, J.P., Johnston, C., & Smith B. 1993. *Directory of the North Sea coastal margin.* Peterborough, Joint Nature Conservation Committee.

Irish Sea Study Group. 1990. *The Irish Sea; an environmental review. Part 2; waste inputs and pollution.* Liverpool, Liverpool University Press.

Kenny, A.J., & Rees, H.L. 1994. The effects of marine gravel extraction on the macrobenthos: early post-dredging recolonisation. *Marine Pollution Bulletin, 7:* 442-447.

Ministry of Agriculture, Fisheries and Food (Department of Agriculture and Fisheries for Scotland). 1989. *Report on the disposal of waste at sea, 1986 and 1987.* London, MAFF.

Ministry of Agriculture, Fisheries and Food (Directorate of Fisheries Research). 1994. *Monitoring and surveillance of non-radioactive contaminants in the aquatic environment and activities regulating the disposal of wastes at sea, 1992.* Lowestoft, MAFF. (Aquatic Monitoring Report, No. 40.)

Ministry of Agriculture, Fisheries and Food (Directorate of Fisheries Research). 1995. *Monitoring and surveillance of non-radioactive contaminants in the aquatic environment and activities regulating the disposal of wastes at sea, 1993.* Lowestoft, MAFF. (Aquatic Monitoring Report, No. 44.)

NERC. Undated. *Marine sand and gravel: resources and exploitation.* London, NERC.

B. Further reading

Anon. 1987. Shift on sewage sludge disposal methods. *Marine Pollution Bulletin, 18*(12): 619.

Anon. 1989. Sewage sludge statistics. *Marine Pollution Bulletin, 20*(2): 54.

Baker, B. 1993. The burning issue. *Surveyor,* 2/12/93: 18-19.

British Marine Aggregate Producers Association. 1994. *Aggregates from the sea: why dredge?* London, British Marine Aggregate Producers Association (BMAPA).

British Oceanographic Data Centre. 1992. *United Kingdom digital marine atlas. User guide. Version 2.0.* Birkenhead, Natural Environment Research Council, British Oceanographic Data Centre.

Campbell, J.A. 1991. The disposal of capital dredging - the role of the licensing authority. *In: Capital dredging,* ed. by the Institution of Civil Engineers, 111-123. London, Thomas Telford.

Campbell, J.A. 1993. *Guidelines for assessing marine aggregate extraction.* Lowestoft, MAFF. (DFR Laboratory Leaflet, No. 73.)

Construction Industry Research and Information Association. 1996. *The beach management manual.* London, Construction Industry Research and Information Association.

ICES. 1978. Input of pollutants to the Oslo Commission area. *International Council for the Exploration of the Seas, Cooperative Research Report, 77:* 57.

Irish Sea Study Group. 1990. *The Irish Sea; an environmental review. Part 1; nature conservation.* Liverpool, Liverpool University Press.

Ministry of Agriculture, Fisheries and Food. 1989. *Coastal defence and the environment: a strategic guide for managers and decision makers in the National Rivers Authority, Local Authorities and other bodies with coastal responsibilities.* London, HMSO.

Nunney, R.S., & Chillingworth, P.C.H. 1986. *Marine dredging for sand and gravel.* London, HMSO, for Department of the Environment Minerals Division. (Minerals Planning Research Project, No. PECD 7/1/163 - 99/84.)

Parker, M.M. 1987. The future for the disposal of dredged material in the UK. *Maintenance dredging.* London, Thomas Telford.

Parker, M.M., & McIntyre, A.D. 1987. Sewage sludge disposal at sea - options and management. *In: Marine treatment of sewage and sludge,* ed. by the Institution of Civil Engineers, 123-136. London, Thomas Telford. (Proceedings of the conference organized by the Institution of Civil Engineers and held in Brighton on 29-30 April 1987.)

Posford Duvivier Environment. 1992. *Capital and maintenance dredging: a pilot case study to review the potential benefits for nature conservation.* Peterborough, English Nature. (Unpublished report to English Nature & Poole Harbour Commissioners.)

Pullen, S. Undated. *Dumping of dredged spoils from ports: contamination, pollution control.* Godalming, World Wide Fund for Nature.

C. Contact names and addresses

Type of information	Contact address and telephone no.
Marine sand and gravel extraction in the UK (BMAPA & BACMI)	British Marine Aggregate Producers Association / British Aggregate Construction Materials Industries, 156 Buckingham Palace Road, London SW1 9TR, tel: 0171 730 8194
Marine resource management (managing agents offshore for the Crown Estate)	Technical Manager, Posford Duvivier, Eastchester House, Harlands Road, Haywards Heath, West Sussex RH16 1PG, tel: 01444 458551
Marine aggregate extraction licensing	Business Manager, Marine Estates (Offshore), Crown Estate, 16 Carlton House Terrace, London SW1Y 5AH, tel: 0171 210 4377
Minerals extraction: the Government view procedure	Mrs T. Piccolo, Room C15/17, DoE Minerals Division, 2 Marsham St., London, tel: 0171 276 4472
Bristol Channel marine aggregates study	*Welsh Office Planning Department, Cardiff, tel: 01222 825111
Sand and gravel extraction	Sand and Gravel Association (SAGA), 1 Bramber Court, 2 Bramber Road, London W14 9PB, tel: 0171 381 8778
Offshore geoscience data including 1:250,000 maps of geology of coastline	Director, British Geological Survey, Keyworth, Nottingham NG12 5GG, tel: 01602 363100
Disposal of dredge spoil at sea	The Oslo and Paris Commissions, New Court, 48 Carey Street, London WC2A 2JE, tel: 0171 242 9927
Database of licensed disposal operations at sea	*Dr C. Vivian, Marine Environmental Protection Division, Ministry of Agriculture, Fisheries and Food, Fisheries Laboratory, Burnham-on-Crouch, tel: 01621 782658
Disposal of dredged material at sea - international	London Convention Secretariat, International Maritime Organisation (IMO), 4 Albert Embankment, London SE1 7SR, tel: 0171 735 7611

*Starred contact addresses are given in full in the Appendix.

9.5 Oil and gas developments

M.J. Goodwin & C.A. Crumpton

9.5.1 Introduction

This section describes oil and gas exploration and related development in the region; oil and gas infrastructure is described in section 8.3.

The coastal shelf around the west of the British Isles is of increasing interest to the oil and gas industry. In the 16th Offshore Licensing Round, the results of which were announced in June 1995, many companies gave high priority to blocks in the Irish Sea and Cardigan Bay to the north-west of this region (in Region 12). However, no blocks were offered for licensing in this region and none are currently under licence. The 17th Round was started in November 1995 and is currently underway. In July 1995 the 7th Landward Round for oil and gas exploration was announced, under which applications were invited for licences covering both land and certain inshore 'watery areas', including the inner Severn Estuary (although no application was made in respect of this area). Results were announced in March 1996, when 74 blocks were awarded, none of them in this region. Map 9.5.1 shows the location of areas previously licensed at sea and on land in the region.

Map 9.5.2 shows the UK continental shelf (UKCS) sedimentary basins and structural 'highs', which determine the distribution of oil and gas deposits. A narrow sedimentary basin extends from the Celtic Sea up the Bristol Channel, with the most promising areas being located some 50 km offshore.

Total UK Continental Shelf (UKCS) oil production in 1993 was a record 100.1 million tonnes from 85 fields, including fifteen new ones. Gas production was a record 65.5 billion cubic metres from 50 fields, including thirteen new ones. Total UK oil consumption in 1993, including imports, was 84.6 million tonnes. The Gross National Product arising within the UK oil and gas production sector was £7,700 million in 1993 (1.4% total UK GNP). Estimated 'undiscovered recoverable reserves' in the Irish Sea (Regions 12 and 13), the Southern Basin of the North Sea (Regions 5, 6 and 7) and the Celtic Sea (Regions 11 and 12) combined are 0-70 million tonnes for oil and 245-890 billion cubic metres for gas (DTI 1996).

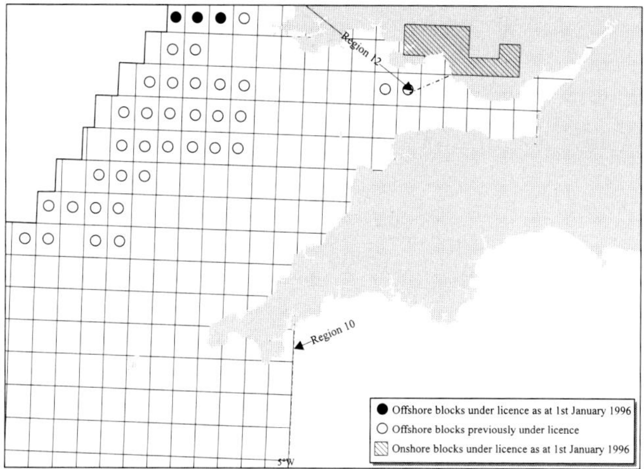

Map 9.5.1 Oil and gas fields previously licensed in the region. Source: DTI. © Crown copyright.

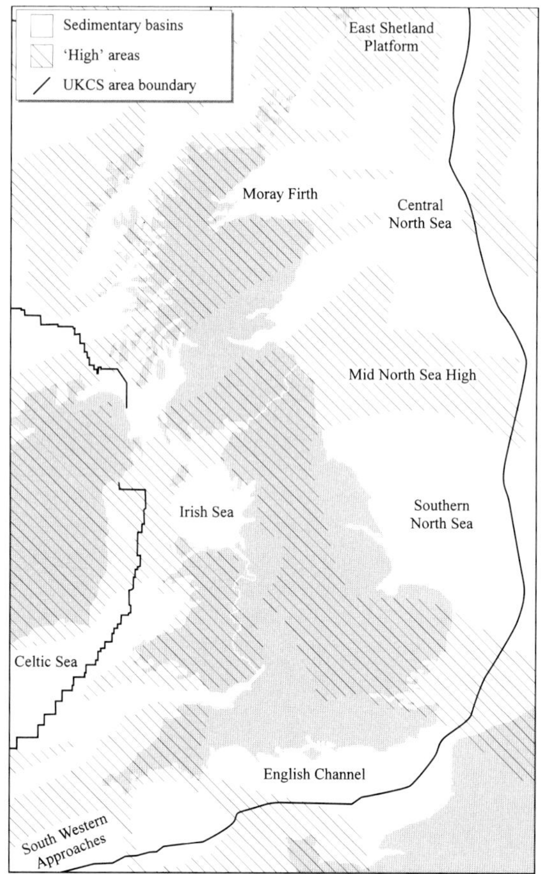

Map 9.5.2 UK Continental Shelf (UKCS) sedimentary basins and structural 'highs'. Source: DTI. © Crown copyright.

9.5.2 Important locations

There is no oil or gas exploration or development current in the region.

9.5.3 Management

Licences are awarded by the Department of Trade and Industry, in consultation with a wide range of organisations, including government departments, environmental agencies, local groups, local authorities, fishermen's federations and other non-governmental organisations. A range of conditions may be applied, linked to the environmental sensitivity of the block (see Davies & Wilson 1995 for conditions applied to the 16th round). For more recent sets of conditions consult the DTI.

The range of potential issues for nature conservation is wide. The potential for oil spills to harm birds and marine and coastal wildlife is well known, especially in sheltered embayments and estuaries (see also sections 5.10, 5.11 and 5.12). Spills may result from exploration and production procedures or from oil transportation, such as that caused by the stranding of the tanker *Sea Empress* in 1996, from which oil was carried from Milford Haven into the waters of this region. Concern has been expressed particularly about the potential risk to seals and dolphins if oil-related developments were to occur in the region (see also sections 5.14.3 and 5.15.3). There is a very small risk of injury to seals in the immediate vicinity of a vessel conducting seismic surveys. The air-gun arrays used in seismic surveys generate high levels of low frequency sound, most of which is outside the known hearing range of seals and is unlikely to disturb them. In the case of cetaceans, results obtained during seismic surveys by Marathon Oil UK Ltd and BHP Petroleum Ltd in the Irish Sea were inconclusive, and experimental evidence for disturbance arising from seismic activities remains lacking (Evans *et al.* 1993). Nevertheless recent studies indicate that cetaceans may be disturbed by seismic surveying, as they are sighted less frequently, either acoustically or visually, during seismic surveys (Goold 1996). Best practice environmental management guidance for carrying out seismic surveys in areas where marine mammals occur is among environmental issues considered in UKOOA's *Environmental guidelines for exploration operations in near-shore and sensitive areas* (UKOOA 1994).

9.5.4 Information source used

Many of the data used here come from the DTI's 'Brown Book' (DTI 1995), which should be referred to for further explanation.

9.5.5 Acknowledgements

Thanks are due to Colin Macduff-Duncan, Esso, and Mark Tasker, JNCC, for assistance with this section.

9.5.6 Further sources of information

A. References cited

Davies, G.J., & Wilson, J.L.J. 1995. *Wildlife sensitivity criteria for oil and gas developments in Great Britain.* Peterborough, Joint Nature Conservation Committee. (Consultation report prepared by Environment and Resource Technology Ltd.)

Department of Trade and Industry. 1996. *The energy report 2: oil and gas resources of the UK - 1996.* London, HMSO.

Evans, P.G.H., Lewis, E.J., & Fisher, P. 1993. *A study of the possible effects of seismic testing upon cetaceans in the Irish Sea.* Oxford, Sea Watch Foundation. (Report to Marathon Oil UK.)

Goold, J.C. 1996. Acoustic assessment of populations of common dolphins *Delphinus delphis* in conjunction with seismic surveying. *Journal of the Marine Biological Association of the UK, 16:* 811-820.

UKOOA. 1994. *Environmental guidelines for exploration operations in near-shore and sensitive areas.* London, United Kingdom Offshore Operators Association.

B. Further reading

Advisory Committee on the Pollution of the Sea. 1990. Surveys of oil pollution around the coasts of the United Kingdom. *In: ACOPS year book 1990,* 158-163. Oxford, Permagon Press.

Baines, M.E. 1993. *Marine mammal monitoring during the seismic exploration of block 107/21 in Cardigan Bay, Autumn 1993.* Haverfordwest, Dyfed Wildlife Trust.

British Gas. 1994. *Transportation and storage.* Solihull, British Gas Transto.

Hailey, N. 1995. *Likely impacts of oil and gas activities on the marine environment and integration of environmental considerations in licensing policy.* Peterborough, English Nature. (English Nature Research Reports, No. 145.)

Institute of Petroleum Information Service. 1993. *Know more about oil: the North Sea.* London, Institute of Petroleum.

Institute of Petroleum Information Service. 1993. *Know more about oil: the UK refining industry.* London, Institute of Petroleum.

Institute of Petroleum Information Service. 1993. *UK petroleum industry statistics: consumption and refinery production for 1991 and 1992.* London, Institute of Petroleum.

Turnpenny, A.W.H., & Nedwell, J.R. 1994. *The effects on marine fish, diving mammals and birds of underwater sound generated by seismic surveys.* Southampton, Fawley Aquatic Research Laboratories Ltd.

C. Contact names and addresses

Type of information	Contact address and telephone no.
Oil and gas developments	Public Relations Officer, Department of Trade and Industry, 1 Palace Street, London SW1E 5HE, tel: 0171 215 5000
Oil and gas industry issues	Public Relations Officer, UK Offshore Operators Association, 3 Hans Crescent, London SW1X 0LN, tel: 0171 589 5255
Oil transportation and terminals	Technical Adviser, Oil Companies International Marine Forum (OCIMF), 15th Floor, 96 Victoria Street, London SW1E 5JW, tel: 0171 828 7966
General information on the oil industry	Librarian, Institute of Petroleum Library and Information Service, 61 New Cavendish Street, London W1M 8AR, tel: 0171 467 7100
Gas industry	Director and Secretary, Society of British Gas Industries, 36 Holly Walk, Leamington Spa, Warwickshire CV32 4LY, tel: 01926 334357
Oil spillages: government body carrying out pollution control at sea	Marine Pollution Control Unit, Spring Place, 105 Commercial Road, Southampton SO15 1EG, tel: 01703 329484
Response (privately-funded) to oil spills worldwide	Oil Spill Response, Oil Spill Service Centre, Lower William St., Northam, Southampton SO14 5QE, tel: 01703 331551
Research into oil pollution	Oil Pollution Research Unit, Fort Popton, Angle, Pembroke, Dyfed SA71 5AD, tel: 01646 641404
Advice on oil pollution strategies worldwide	International Tanker Owner's Pollution Federation Ltd, Staple Hall, Stonehouse Court, 87-90 Houndsditch, London EC3A 7AX, tel: 0171 621 1255
Advice on oil spill control equipment	British Oil Spill Control Association (BOSCA), 4th Floor, 30 Great Guildford Street, London SE1 0HS, tel: 0171 928 9199
Licensing of drilling muds and oil spill dispersants	MAFF Marine Environment Protection Division, Nobel House, 17 Smith Square, London SW1P 3JR, tel: 0171 238 6000
Toxicological assessment of drilling muds and oil spill dispersants	*Head of Laboratory, MAFF DFR, Burnham-on-Crouch, tel: 01621 782658
Local information on the environmental effects of exploration and production - Cornwall	*Cornwall Wildlife Trust, Truro, tel: 01872 273939
Local information on the environmental effects of exploration and production - Devon	*Devon Wildlife Trust, Exeter, tel: 01392 79244
Local information on the environmental effects of exploration and production - Somerset	*Somerset Wildlife Trust, Bridgwater, tel: 01823 451587
Local information on the environmental effects of exploration and production - Avon	*Wildlife Trust for Bristol, Bath & Avon, Bristol, tel: 0117 926 8018
Local information on the environmental effects of exploration and production - Gloucestershire	*Gloucestershire Wildlife Trust, Gloucester, tel: 01452 383333
Local information on the environmental effects of exploration and production - Gwent	*Gwent Wildlife Trust, Monmouth, tel: 01600 715501
Local information on the environmental effects of exploration and production - Glamorgan	*Glamorgan Wildlife Trust, Tondu, tel: 01656 724100
Information on the environmental effects of exploration and production	*WWF - UK, Godalming, tel: 01483 426444

*Starred contact addresses are given in full in the Appendix.

9.6 Water quality and effluent discharges

C.A. Crumpton & M.J. Goodwin

9.6.1 Introduction

This section summarises information about water quality and effluent discharge from a number of sources. Sewage sludge disposal is covered in section 9.4. Full interpretation of the information base on pollutants and water quality is complex and beyond the scope of this book.

Waste products and effluents containing contaminants reach the region's coastal environment principally from rivers and direct pipe discharges into coastal and estuarine areas. Contaminants can also reach the sea by airborne means, for example aerosols and rain. Industrial pollutants can enter the marine environment when there is an accidental or intentional release. Discharges occurring outside the region may also have an effect. In Region 11, coastal industrial development and its associated effluent discharges and potential for contamination are concentrated around the Severn Estuary, in particular around Avonmouth, Cardiff and Newport. This area supports a variety of industry, including power production; it also contains a large proportion of the region's resident population. Table 9.6.1 summarises the distribution of the major sources of trade and domestic effluent in the region.

There are 81 EC Identified Bathing Waters in Region 11, with a high concentration around Devon and Cornwall. 89% of these bathing waters reached the mandatory standards in 1995 (Map 9.6.1), a marked improvement over the previous year when only 68% passed (Table 9.6.2). On this measure, water quality in the region corresponds to the UK average. The 1995 data for the UK as a whole, assessed by the Department of the Environment (DoE) in accordance with the EC Bathing Water Directive, show a slight increase in compliance with the mandatory standards since 1994: 89% compared with 82%. The Environment Agency (EA) expects a further increase in compliance after the majority of capital schemes being undertaken by the water service companies are completed in 1995. Trend data show that although the percentage of bathing waters consistently complying with the mandatory standards has remained at around 64%, the number consistently failing has reduced. Analysis of median faecal coliform values suggests that the improvement in water quality has been maintained over the last four years.

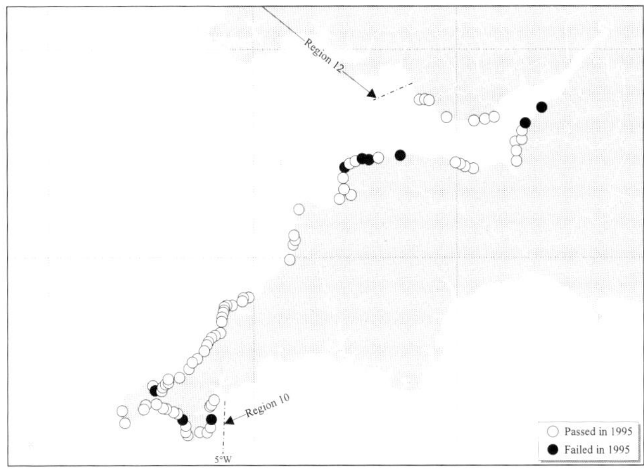

Map 9.6.1 Bathing water quality. Results of 1995 sampling of EC-identified bathing waters. Source: NRA (pers. comm.). Adapted with permission.

In the 1993 Beachwatch survey (MCS 1994), twelve beaches in the region were rated as of high quality, a further eleven beaches were listed in the best category, 39 passed EC standards but were not recommended by the Marine Conservation Society (MCS), and 29 were not tested. There are three Blue Flag beaches in the region, representing 17.6% of the UK total of 17 for 1994. The 18 Tidy Britain Group Seaside Award beaches in the region in 1996 represent 8.9% of the UK total of 203.

Table 9.6.1 Numbers of trade and sewage outfalls with maximum consented daily flows >6,000 m^3

	Sewage	*Trade*	*Total*
Cornwall	3	1	4
Devon	5	1	6
Somerset	3	0	3
Avon	5	0	5
Gloucestershire	2	0	2
Gwent	4	2	6
Mid Glamorgan	6	2	8
South Glamorgan	1	0	1
Region 11	***29***	***6***	***35***

Sources: MAFF, Environment Agency

9.6.2 Important locations

Map 9.6.2 shows the region's sewage and trade effluent outfalls with consented flows greater than 6,000 m^3 per day. Table 9.6.3 summarises discharge data from the 29 largest sewage outfalls to tidal waters in the region, i.e. those with permitted dry-weather discharges >6,000 m^3 per day,

Table 9.6.2 Bathing waters survey: 1994, 1995

	Pass (numbers)		*Fail (numbers)*		*Total (numbers)*	
	1994	***1995***	***1994***	***1995***	***1994***	***1995***
Region 11	***55***	***72***	***16***	***9***	***71***	***81***
England & Wales	347	380	72	45	419	425
Scotland	16	19	7	4	23	23
N. Ireland	15	15	1	1	16	16
UK	376	413	81	51	458	464

Source: DoE (pers. comm.). Note: pass denotes compliance with Bathing Water Directive (76/160/EEC): Coliform standards.

Table 9.6.3 Coastal sewage outfalls in the region with maximum permitted discharges >6,000 m^3 per day

Outfall name	*Location*	*Grid ref.*	*Maximum consented daily dry-weather sewage flow (m^3)*					
			Untreated	*Primary treated*	*Secondary treated*	*Other*	*County total from these outfalls*	*Notes*
Cornwall							**29,070**	
Newham Sewage Treatment Works	Truro	SW834432			10,000			
The Stones Outfall	Hayle Gwithian	SW559432		12,240				
Bude Long Sea Outfall	Bude	SS189063				6,830		Fine screened
Devon							**55,100**	
Rock Nose Sea Outfall	Westward Ho!	SS419291	7,521					
Ashford Sewage Treatment Works	Barnstaple	SS532344		7,500				
Woolacombe Esplanade Sea Outfall	Woolacombe	SS451441			13,144			Tertiary treated
Ilfracombe Sewage Treatment Works, Larkstone Lane	Ilfracombe	SS522481				12,040		UV treated
Cheyne Beach Outfall	Ilfracombe	SS522481	14,895					
Somerset							**34,100**	
Minehead Outfall	Minehead	SS994469				12,600		Disinfected
Bridgwater Chilton Trinity Sewage Treatment Works	Bridgwater	ST303388				8,000		Disinfected
West Huntspill Sewage Treatment Works Disinfected Effluent	Burnham-on-Sea, West Huntspill	ST294468				13,500		Disinfected
Avon							**217,600**	
Weston-super-Mare Sewage Treatment Works	Weston-super-Mare	ST311570				20,000		Fine screened disinfected
Kingston Seymour Sewage Treatment Works	Kingston Seymour	ST380685				13,600		Screened (6 mm)
Kingston Seymour Sewage Treatment Works	Kingston Seymour	ST384686				13,600		Disinfected
Portbury Sewage Treatment Works	Portishead Portbury	ST485781				10,400		Fine screened
Avonmouth Sewage Treatment Works	Avonmouth	ST519807		160,000				
Gloucestershire							**52,200**	
Netheridge Sewage Treatment Works	Gloucester	SO807160			42,800			
Lydney Water Reclamation Works	Lydney	SO636005		9,400				
Gwent							**251,817**	
Nash Sewage Treatment Works	Nash	ST335841			19,318			
Newport Liswerry Outfall	Newport	ST327869	69,954					
Newport Coronation Park Outfall	Newport	ST319860	22,545					
Western Valley Trunk Sewer Outfall	Newport	ST294803	140,000					
Mid Glamorgan							**484,973**	
Cardiff Eastern District Pumping Station	Cardiff	ST225750				60,335		Macerated / comminuted
Cardiff Central Outfall	Cardiff	ST209750		11,725				
Western District Pumping Station	Cardiff	ST190679	48,162					

Table 9.6.3 Coastal sewage outfalls in the region with maximum permitted discharges >6,000 m³ per day (continued)

Outfall name	*Location*	*Grid ref.*	*Maximum consented daily dry-weather sewage flow (m³)*					
			Untreated	*Primary treated*	*Secondary treated*	*Other*	*County total from these outfalls*	*Notes*
Mid Glamorgan								
Lavernock Long Sea Outfall Cog Mors Sewage Treatment Works	Lavernock Point	ST194673				345,600		Fine screened
Bendricks New Outfall	Barry	ST131671	6,244					
Barry West Existing Town Outfall (Temporary)	Barry	ST103659				12,907		Fine screened
South Glamorgan							**23,000**	
Penybont Sewage Treatment Works	Penybont	SS878768			23,000			
Region 11	***29 outfalls***		***309,321***	***200,865***	***108,262***	***529,412***	***1,147,860***	

Source: MAFF

indicating their locations and the type of discharge. The great majority of sewage discharged from these larger outfalls in the region (938,733 m³ daily - 82%) is either untreated or has had less than primary treatment (screened or comminuted sewage). Only 108,262 m³ daily from such outfalls has had secondary treatment. The largest sewage treatment works in the region, at Avonmouth, discharges 160,000 m³ daily of sewage that has had only primary treatment. Nearly a quarter of a million cubic metres of untreated sewage is discharged daily from large outfalls around Newport, south Wales. During the MAFF sea-bed litter survey of 1992/93, the site in Bristol Channel (no longer used for sewage sludge disposal - see also section 9.4) produced only a small quantity of litter items, but a large proportion (70%) of those items were fragments of sanitary materials and therefore sewage-derived (MAFF 1995). The sewage sludges were principally of domestic origin and contained low levels of metals and other persistent components.

Table 9.6.4 lists major sources of trade effluent (outfalls with a consented daily flow >6,000 m³ per day) in the region, with their maximum consented output (Map 9.6.2). From these larger outfalls, all discharged effluent has had some treatment, except that from the Appledore shipyard. The total quantity of effluent discharged from these outfalls in the region (110,710 m³ per day) is very low, compared with amounts from similar discharges in more actively

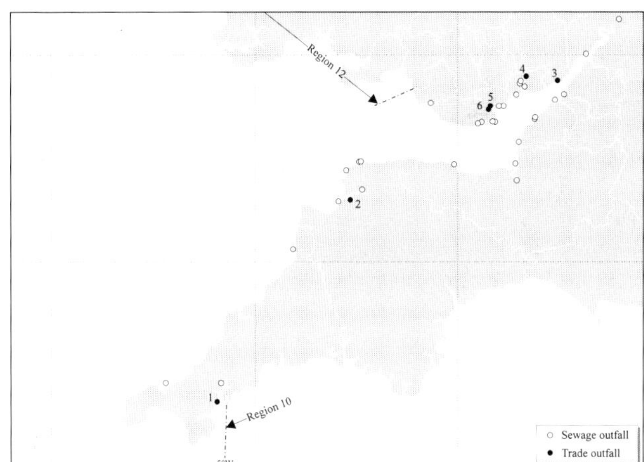

Map 9.6.2 Sewage and trade effluent outfalls with consented flows greater than 6,000 m³ per day. Sources: MAFF (sewage outfalls), NRA (trade effluent outfalls).

Table 9.6.4 Trade effluent outfalls with a consented daily flow >6,000 m³

No. on Map 9.6.2	*Outfall name*	*Location*	*Grid ref.*	*Maximum consented daily dry-weather flow (m³)*			
				Untreated	*Treated*	*Cooling water*	*Total*
	Cornwall						
1	Falmouth Docks and Engineering Co.	Falmouth	SW819326		10,000		10,000
	Devon						
2	Appledore Ferguson Shipbuilders	Appledore	SS464294	8,710			8,710
	Gwent						
3	Sudbrook Mill	Sudbrook	ST501870		50,000		50,000
4	ORB Works	Newport	ST321863		20,000		20,000
	Mid Glamorgan						
5	Idem Mill	Cardiff	ST151763			2,000	2,000
6	Ely Paper Mill	Cardiff	ST149766		20,000		20,000
	Region 11	***6 outfalls***		***8,170***	***100,000***	***2,000***	***110,710***

Source: Environment Agency

industrial regions, such as Region 13 (Northern Irish Sea) (>5.5 million m^3 per day) or Region 9 (including the Solent waterway) (>6 million m^3 per day). This reflects the region's predominantly rural land use and relatively small resident coastal population (see also Chapter 8).

A variety of artificial radionuclides are discharged directly into the Severn Estuary. Their sources include the nuclear power stations at Berkeley (now decommissioning), Oldbury and Hinkley Point, the Amersham International and Atomic Weapons Establishment sites at Cardiff and local hospitals around the estuary. The levels of radioactivity in the estuary are monitored through surveys of various environmental media (sediment, seaweed and seafood) by the site operators and the Ministry of Agriculture, Fisheries and Food (MAFF). These data are published annually by the MAFF Fisheries Radiological Inspectorate (e.g. MAFF 1995).

The Severn received the largest input of cadmium - from the metal smelting industry on Severnside - of any major estuary in Britain in the period 1990-1993, but levels are now decreasing. In the same period total nitrogen input, mainly from agricultural run-off but also from sewage and trade effluent, was found to be second only to the River Trent (Region 6) (NRA 1995c).

Further impacts on water quality arising from industrial land use include pollution by water from disused tin mines, which has occurred in certain Cornish rivers. In 1991 contaminated water from the Wheal Jane tin mine spilled into the Carnon River and the Fal Estuary: a variety of techniques are now in place to reduce the input of heavy metals, for example copper, to the water. There has been a recorded loss of species richness in part of the Fal, attributed to locally high nutrient levels and very elevated concentrations of metals from mining activity, particularly from drainage water from disused tin mines (English Nature pers. comm.). Turbidity due to china clay inputs into the River Fal has reduced in recent years (Environment Agency South Western Region pers. comm.). Pollution of the River Camel with aluminium from a water purification plant in 1988 closed the salmon fishery in the river from 1989 - 1991 and also affected drinking water supplies. Pollution from port and harbour operations, including antifouling paint containing tributyl tin (TBT) from ships in yards (Langston *et al.* 1990; Waite *et al.* 1991), has also been a problem. TBT is known to affect the growth of benthic organisms, and in 1986 legislation was introduced to control its use.

The Tidy Britain Group Seaside Award beaches are located at Sennen Cove, Porthmeor, St. Merryn (Treyarnon), St. Merryn (Constantine Bay), St. Merryn (Harlyn Bay), Polzeath, Bude (Widemouth Sand), Bude (Crooklets), Bude (Sandymouth), Weston-super-Mare, Burnham-on-sea, Woolacombe, Porthminster, Newport (North), Newport (South), Southerndown and St. Bride's Haven. The three Blue Flag beaches are located at Sennen Cove, Porthmeor and Woolacombe. These, with beaches at St. Merryn (Treyarnon), St. Merryn (Constantine Bay), Polzeath, Bude (Widemouth Sand), Bude (Sandymouth) and Woolacombe, are also the Tidy Britain Group Premier Seaside Award beaches.

The Coastwatch survey results from 1994 show an overall deterioration in the quality of the region's beaches compared with the previous year's survey (Table 9.6.5). Results from Devon and Cornwall were generally better than the national average, although the overall quality of beaches in these counties was worse than in the previous year. In Somerset radioactivity posed a significantly higher threat to water quality than elsewhere in the UK - 12% of surveyed sites were affected, compared with only 2% nationwide. Results in Avon, Gwent and South and Mid Glamorgan were below the national average, with Mid Glamorgan having very high counts of both cans and plastic bottles.

The 1993 Beachwatch survey rated the following beaches as of high quality: Woolacombe Sand and Putsborough Beach (Woolacombe), Widemouth Sand, Constantine Bay (Treyarnon), Treyarnon Bay (Padstow), The Towans (Hayle), Porthmeor (St. Ives), Whitesand Bay (Sennen), Praa Sands (Ashton), Gunwalloe Cove, Polpeor (The Lizard), and Kennack Sands, Kuggar.

9.6.3 Management and issues

In April 1996, the new Environment Agency (EA) became operational. It integrates the functions of Her Majesty's Inspectorate of Pollution, the local Waste Regulatory Authorities and the National Rivers Authority (NRA). Its activities are grouped under two broad headings: pollution prevention and control, including waste regulation, the work of HMIP and the NRA's work on water quality; and water management, covering the NRA's other functions. However, a strong link is maintained between pollution

Table 9.6.5 Beach quality in the region* compared with national standards in 1994

Area	*% of beaches rated as*					
	Excellent		*Moderate*		*Polluted*	
	1993	*1994*	*1993*	*1994*	*1993*	*1994*
Cornwall	30	18	43	39	27	43
Devon	18	13	45	49	37	38
Somerset	12	5	49	42	39	53
Avon	14	11	53	48	33	41
Gwent	0	0	50	10	50	90
South Glamorgan	0	2	36	47	64	51
Mid Glamorgan	0	0	10	36	90	64
Region 11	***7***	***5***	***41***	***39***	***52***	***56***
England	10	6	44	50	46	44
Wales	7	7	39	39	54	54
Scotland	7	10	37	41	56	49
Great Britain	8	8	42	43	50	49

Source: Coastwatch UK (1993, 1994). Key: *includes parts of the coasts of Devon and Cornwall lying in Region 10.

prevention and control and water management, to ensure continuing integrity of estuarine and coastal management.

A range of legislation is in force to control discharges to the aquatic environment. In England and Wales the primary statute is the Water Resources Act 1991. The Environment Agency has overall responsibility for the control of discharges and the maintenance of water quality, both on land and at sea. The EA authorises sewage discharges to the sea by issuing 'consents', with MAFF as a statutory consultee to safeguard fishery interests. Trade effluent involving scheduled (hazardous) substances must be authorised by Her Majesty's Inspector of Pollution under the Environmental Protection Act 1990, with the EA as a statutory consultee. The substances are listed in the Trade Effluents (Prescribed Substances and Processes) Regulations 1989, 1990 and 1992. Environmental Quality Standards (EQSs) are set for many of the substances in the Surface Water (Dangerous Substances) (Classification) Regulations 1989 and 1992. The EQSs may be set nationally (DoE Circular 7/89, March 1989) or by the EC (under the Dangerous Substances Directive 76/464/EEC and Framework Directive 86/280/EEC). The NRA's booklet on *Discharge consents and compliance* (NRA 1994) contains details of national and European discharge regulations. Sewage disposal on land is also controlled by the EA (see section 9.3).

In 1988 all licensed disposal of liquid industrial waste at sea in UK waters ceased. In common with other parts of the UK coast, coastal waters in the region receive sewage and trade effluent directly from both large and small outfalls. In addition other outfalls, both large and small, discharge into rivers a short distance from the coast. Cumulatively, these discharges are capable of affecting the maritime environment, both in this region and beyond. Under the Urban Waste Water Treatment Directive (91/271/EEC), except in 'high natural dispersion areas', all significant sewage discharges (thus including all those in Table 9.6.3) to coastal waters, where the outfalls serve populations >10,000 (roughly equivalent to 1,800 m^3 per day), and to estuaries, where they serve populations >2,000 (roughly 360 m^3 per day), will require at least secondary treatment, to be phased in by 2005. However, some outfalls will be permitted to discharge sewage with a minimum of primary treatment, provided that comprehensive studies, currently being carried out by the relevant water companies, show that there will be no adverse effects on the environment. In this region these outfalls, all discharging into 'high natural dispersion areas', are at St. Ives/Camborne/Redruth, Perranporth, Newquay, Bude, Bideford, Minehead/Watchet, Kingston Seymour, Portishead/Avonmouth, and Aberthaw/Llantwit Major.

A new management tool, the General Quality Assessment (GQA) classification scheme for estuaries and coastal areas, is to be introduced by the EA. This scheme is intended to enable a consistent and quantitative comparison of water quality to be made, both over time and between geographic areas. The proposed components to be used in this classification are basic water chemistry (estuaries only), nutrient levels, and aesthetic, sediment and biological quality. The basic chemistry, nutrient and aesthetic components will be implemented and tested in 1996, although further research is required to determine appropriate criteria to establish sediment and biological quality (NRA 1996).

There are currently several schemes (statutory and non-statutory) for assessing the quality of beaches and their waters in relation to waste disposal. First, there is the EC Bathing Water Directive (76/160/EEC), with its associated monitoring of identified bathing waters for levels of coliforms (bacteria that indicate sewage presence). Monitoring is carried out by the EA, and beaches are tested regularly to assess whether they have met the 'mandatory' or more stringent 'guideline' standards. Any measures required to improve the quality of the waters are a matter for the dischargers of industrial effluent or the sewerage authorities. Under the terms of the Environmental Protection Act 1990, the quality of bathing beaches is the responsibility of district councils. Secondly, there is the European Blue Flag Award Scheme for beaches that meet the EC guideline standards of beach and water quality, as well as certain land-based criteria. Thirdly, there is the Tidy Britain Group Seaside Award Scheme, designed to complement the Blue Flag scheme, for beaches that meet minimum standards of beach and water cleanliness and selected land-based criteria but not the Blue Flag standard. Finally there are the annual litter surveys of Coastwatch UK and Beachwatch, both of which employ volunteers to survey lengths of coastline for litter and other signs of pollution. Coastwatch UK is organised by Farnborough College of Technology and Beachwatch by Reader's Digest and the Marine Conservation Society.

9.6.4 Information sources used

Monitoring of water quality in the region is carried out by EA and MAFF, with EA concerned mainly with point sources of contamination from outfalls in the nearshore environment. The interests of MAFF lie in the disposal of sewage sludge and dredge spoil further offshore, and their possible effects on fisheries; and they carry out a wide range of sampling work associated with this. EA and MAFF contribute to the National Marine Monitoring Plan, which monitors a wide range of listed chemicals in water, biota and sediments, at a range of frequencies that decrease from the estuarine to the offshore environment.

Helicopter surveys of the Severn Estuary have been undertaken on a regular basis since 1975, but little has been published. Owens (1984) appraised the situation up to that time but his results are too complex to summarise here; more recent findings are to be included in a document for the Severn Estuary Strategy (see also section 10.3).

The Department of the Environment (DoE) Environmental Protection Statistics Division publishes an annual *Digest of environmental protection and water statistics* (DoE 1995), which provides detailed national statistics on aspects of environmental protection, including coastal and marine waters, radioactivity, waste and recycling, and wildlife.

Schemes such as the Tidy Britain Group Seaside Award and the European Blue Flag monitor beaches during the year previous to the publication of their results. Monitoring of the EC Bathing Waters and other beaches under schemes such as Coastwatch UK and Beachwatch take place over one or two days. The results may therefore be skewed by heavy rain or localised effects at the time of survey. Coastwatch UK and Beachwatch do not sample the whole coastline in their region, owing to a shortage of volunteers. The results may therefore be unrepresentative because of the small sample size.

Other information sources available include the NRA's Water Quality Series reports (e.g. NRA 1995a, c), and its quarterly ship- and air-borne National Coastal Baseline Survey, which monitors a large number of water quality parameters in coastal waters, including metals, nutrients and turbidity (Boxall *et al.* 1993). Further information on sewage and trade discharges can be obtained from the local offices of the Environment Agency, who issue discharge consents and authorisations. MAFF (Burnham-on-Crouch) maintains a database of consented sewage outfalls in England and Wales.

9.6.5 Acknowledgements

Thanks are due to Mrs F.L. Franklin of MAFF Fisheries Laboratory, Burnham-on-Crouch, for sewage outfalls data, and to Chris Moore of the EA South Western Region and R.A. Fisher of the EA Southern Region for providing information on trade and domestic outfalls in their regions.

9.6.6 Further sources of information

A. References cited

Boxall, S.R., Chaddock, S.E., Matthews, A., & Holden, N. 1993. *Airborne remote sensing of coastal waters*. Southampton, Department of Oceanography. (R & D Report No. 4, prepared for NRA.)

Coastwatch UK. 1993. *1993 survey report.* Farnborough, Farnborough College of Technology.

Coastwatch UK. 1994. *1994 survey report.* Farnborough, Farnborough College of Technology.

Department of the Environment. 1995. *Digest of environmental protection and water statistics.* London, HMSO.

Langston, W.J., Bryan, G.W., Burt, G.R., & Gibbs, P.E. 1990. Assessing the impact of tin and TBT in estuaries and coastal regions. *Functional Ecology, 4:* 433-443.

Marine Conservation Society. 1994. *The Reader's Digest good beach guide.* Newton Abbot, David & Charles.

Ministry of Agriculture Fisheries and Food. 1995. *Monitoring and surveillance of non-radioactive contaminants in the aquatic environment and activities regulating the disposal of wastes at sea, 1993.* Lowestoft, MAFF Directorate of Fisheries Research. (Aquatic Environment Monitoring Report, No. 44.)

National Rivers Authority. 1994. *Discharge consents and compliance: the NRA's approach to control of discharges to water.* Bristol, National Rivers Authority.

National Rivers Authority. 1995a. *Bathing water quality in England and Wales - 1994.* London, HMSO and National Rivers Authority. (Water Quality Series, No. 22.)

National Rivers Authority. 1995c. *Contaminants entering the sea.* London, HMSO and National Rivers Authority. (Water Quality Series, No. 24.)

National Rivers Authority. 1996. *Development and testing of General Quality Assessment scheme.* London, HMSO and National Rivers Authority. (R & D Report, No. 27.)

Owens, M. 1984. Severn Estuary - an appraisal of water quality. *Marine Pollution Bulletin, 15*(2): 41-47.

Waite, M.E., Waldock, M.J., Thain, J.E., Smith, D.J., & Milton, S.M. 1991. Reductions in TBT concentrations in UK estuaries following legislation in 1986 and 1987. *Marine Environmental Research, 32:* 89-111.

B. Further reading

Anon. 1993. Lies, damned lies and statistics in the great water debate. *ENDS Report.* No. 227, 12/93, 16-19.

Baker, B. 1993. The burning issue. *Surveyor,* 2/12/93: 18-19.

Bryan, G.W., & Gibbs, P.E. 1993. *Heavy metals in the Fal Estuary, Cornwall: a study of long-term contamination by mining waste and its effects on estuarine organisms.* Plymouth, Marine Biological Association of the UK.

Earll, R., *ed.* 1995. *Coastal and riverine litter: problems and effective solutions.* Kempley, Marine Environmental Management and Training.

Eno, N.C., *ed.* 1991. *Marine conservation handbook.* 2nd ed. Peterborough, English Nature.

HMIP. 1994. *UK national monitoring plan.* London, HMIP. (Marine Pollution Monitoring Management Group - Monitoring Co-ordination Subgroup.)

Irving, R. 1993. *Too much of a good thing: nutrient enrichment in the UK's coastal waters.* A report to the World Wide Fund for Nature (WWF). London, WWF.

Kay, D., & Wyer, M. 1994. Making waves: recreational water quality. *Biologist, 41*(1): 17-20.

Kennedy, V.H., Horrill, A.D., & Livens, F.R. 1990. *Radioactivity and wildlife.* Peterborough, Nature Conservancy Council. (Focus on nature conservation, No. 24.)

Knap, A.H., Le B. Williams, P.J., & Tyler, I. 1979. Contribution of volatile petroleum hydrocarbons to the organic carbon budget of an estuary. *Nature (London), 279:* 517-519.

McGilvray, F. 1994. *Beachwatch 1993.* Ross-on-Wye, Marine Conservation Society & Readers' Digest.

Ministry of Agriculture Fisheries and Food. 1994. *Radioactivity in surface and coastal waters of the British Isles, 1993.* Lowestoft, MAFF Directorate of Fisheries Research. (Aquatic Environment Monitoring Report, No. 42.)

National Rivers Authority. 1991. *The quality of rivers, canals and estuaries in England and Wales.* Bristol, National Rivers Authority. (Water Quality Series, No. 4.)

National Rivers Authority. 1994. *The quality of rivers and canals in England and Wales (1990 to 1992).* London, HMSO and National Rivers Authority.

National Rivers Authority. 1995b. *Bathing water quality reports.* South Western Region, Exeter.

C. Contact names and addresses

Type of information	*Contact address and telephone no.*
Discharge consents and coastal water quality	*Environment Agency South Western Region, Exeter, tel: 01392 444000
Water quality and sewage treatment	South West Water Services Ltd, Peninsula House, Rydon Lane, Exeter EX2 7HR, tel: 01392 219666
Beachwatch	*Marine Conservation Society, Ross-on-Wye, tel: 01989 66017
Coastwatch UK	Project Officer, Coastwatch UK, Farnborough College of Technology, Boundary Road, Farnborough, Hampshire GU14 6SB, tel: 01252 377503
Tidy Britain Group Seaside Award and European Blue Flag beaches	Tidy Britain Group, Lion House, 26 Muspole St., Norwich NR3 1DJ, tel: 01603 762888
Radioactive monitoring reports	*MAFF - DFR, Fisheries Laboratory, Lowestoft, tel: 01502 562244
Aquatic environmental research and monitoring related to water quality and waste disposal at sea; consented outfalls database	*Head of Laboratory, MAFF Directorate of Fisheries Research, Fisheries Laboratory, Burnham-on-Crouch, tel: 01621 782658

*Starred contact addresses are given in full in the Appendix.

9.7 Leisure and tourism

M.J. Dunbar & S.L. Fowler

9.7.1 Introduction

The region's coast holds many of the most popular tourist and leisure destinations in the southern half of Britain, because of its fine scenery, warm climate, good beaches and rocky shores and clear, relatively warm water. The region's larger tourism areas and holiday resorts include the Mount's Bay area, the Isles of Scilly, St. Ives, Newquay, Padstow, Bude, Ilfracombe, Minehead, Watchet, Burnham-on-Sea, Weston-super-Mare, Penarth, Barry and Porthcawl, and there are numerous smaller towns and villages that depend upon the tourism industry. Cornwall and Devon in particular have long coastlines visited by a large tourist influx during the summer months, which places coastal resources and recreational facilities under considerable pressure. Tourism is also one of the main sources of income for the Somerset and south Avon coast. In south Wales, seaside resorts serve the cities and large towns of the coast and hinterland.

Access to most of the region's main holiday centres from large centres of population within and outside the region is good, although much of the western coast remains relatively inaccessible. There is a growing tourism industry away from the traditional seaside holiday centres, offering, for example, water sports activities and walking/nature holidays. The South West Coast Path, a a long-distance trail, runs through the western part of the region as far east as Minehead. The Tarka Trail follows the River Torridge and in south Wales the Heritage Coast walk extends for 18 miles from near Penarth to Porthcawl.

All kinds of land- and water-based leisure activity take place around the coast, ranging from traditional seaside and beach holidays to more specialised pursuits such as sand yachting or surfing. Land-based tourist infrastructure includes golf courses, caravan parks and campsites, holiday camps, rural car parks (which provide the access points necessary for most land- and water-based leisure activities), leisure centres and amusement/theme parks. The region's long coastline has the greatest density of caravan and camp sites in the UK: a total of 217 caravan parks and/or campsites, seven holiday camps and 38 golf courses have been identified on the coast of the region (Maps 9.7.1 and 9.7.2). Wildfowling is a traditional coastal activity in the region and targets coastal species including ducks, geese and waders such as the golden plover *Pluvialis apricaria*. Shooting on some coastal sites involves both local wildfowlers and those from further afield.

Recreation involving water craft generally makes use of some kind of land-based infrastructure: quays, marinas or pontoons for larger craft, moorings or slipways for smaller boats. There are five marinas in the region (Table 9.7.2) and about 40 Royal Yachting Association-affiliated yacht clubs are listed in RYA (1992). Most of these are centred on sheltered inlets; limited facilities (primarily recreational craft moorings) are also found in most of the small fishing ports and harbours around the coastline. Boat trips are an important coastal activity in some areas during the main tourist season, and sea angling trips are available from almost all of the region's harbours. There are boatyards for storage, boat-building and repair.

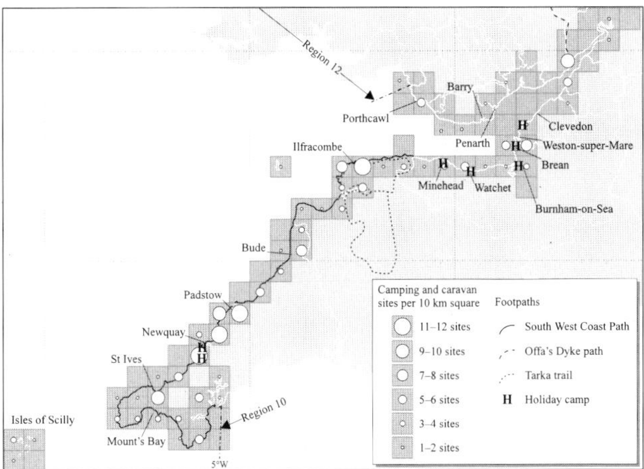

Map 9.7.1 Distribution of land-based leisure and tourism facilities. Sources: tourist brochures, Ordnance Survey Landranger maps and Field Studies Council Research Centre (1992).

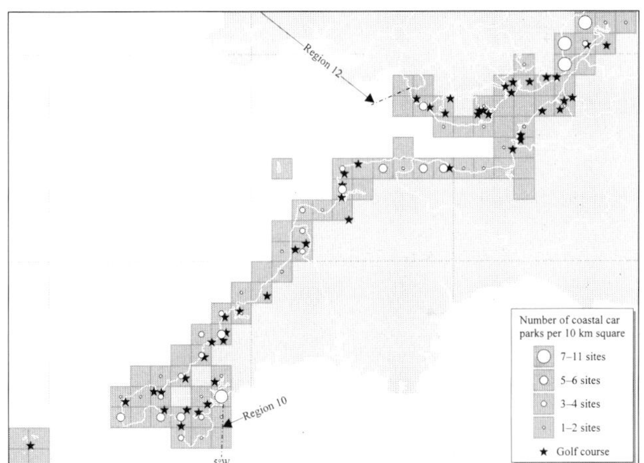

Map 9.7.2 Distribution of coastal car parks and golf courses. Sources: tourist brochures and Ordnance Survey Landranger maps.

9.7.2 Important locations

Important locations for land-based leisure and tourism are marked on Maps 9.7.1 and 9.7.2 and listed in Table 9.7.1; important locations for water-based leisure are shown on Map 9.7.3 and described in Table 9.7.2.

The spectacular coastline of north Cornwall attracts large numbers of staying visitors, particularly those visiting for the scenery. There are numerous picturesque villages, such as Clovelly, which is so popular that access has to be restricted at peak times. St. Ives, Newquay and Padstow are popular for beach recreation. The sheltered areas of the south Cornish coast, such as Carrick Roads and Mount's Bay, are popular for watersports such as sailing, water-skiing, canoeing and powerboating. The exposed beaches on the west side of the Lizard are popular for surfing. The coves and cliffs of the Cornish coast are widely used for shore angling and there are thriving sea angling clubs at Helford and Mount's Bay. The cliffs at Land's End are an

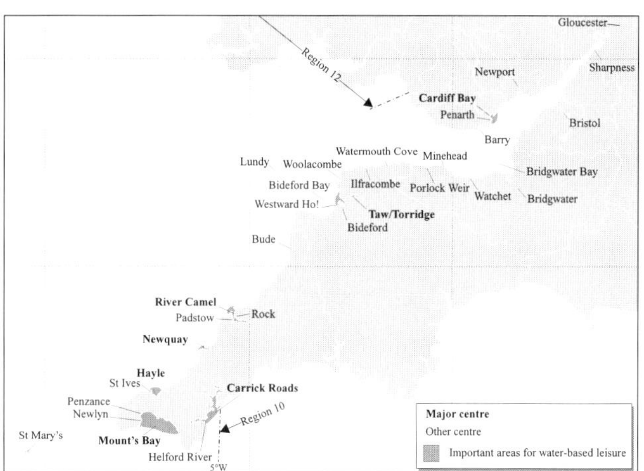

Map 9.7.3 Important locations for water-based leisure and tourism. Sources: tourist brochures, Ordnance Survey Landranger maps and South West Council for Sport and Recreation (1990)

Table 9.7.1 Important locations for land-based leisure and tourism

Location	Infrastructure
Mount's Bay	Golf courses, camping and caravan sites, St. Michael's Mount
Isles of Scilly	Camp sites, Tresco Gardens, golf course, pier (St. Mary's)
St. Ives	Large caravan park (The Towans), golf course
Newquay	Two holiday camps (Gear Sands and Penhale), leisure park, golf courses, many camping and caravan sites
Padstow	Golf course (Rock), campsites, caravan parks
Bude	Golf course, many camping and caravan sites
Ilfracombe	Golf course
Minehead	Holiday camp, golf course
Watchet	Holiday camp, camping sites, caravan parks
Burnham-on-Sea	Holiday camp, pier, golf course
Brean	Holiday camp, many campsites and caravan parks
Weston-super-Mare	Holiday camp at Sand Bay, golf courses, swimming pool, piers, caravan parks
Clevedon	Pier, golf course, boating lake
Penarth	Pier, golf course
Barry	Country park
Porthcawl	Large caravan site, golf course

Sources: various.

Table 9.7.2 Water-based leisure and tourism facilities

Site	*Facilities (see footnote)*	*Notes*
St. Mawes	624 moorings (buoy)	
Truro	1,200 moorings (buoy)	
Mylor	Harbour; marina; buoy; 20 pontoon berths, 112 moorings	
Penryn	300 marina berths, 350 moorings (buoy)	
Falmouth	60 pontoons, 70 marina berths, harbour: 867 moorings; 200 private berths in estuary	Swanpool marine lake
Helford River	460 moorings (buoy)	
Portscatho	Small harbour	
Coverack	Small harbour	
Cadgwith	Small harbour	
Mullion Cove	Small harbour	
Porthleven	Small harbour	
St. Michael's Mount	Small harbour	
Penzance	Harbour; buoy; 300 moorings	
Newlyn	Harbour	
Mousehole	Small harbour	
St Mary's	Small harbour	
St. Ives	Small harbour	
Hayle	Small harbour	Partially enclosed lagoons
Bude	Small harbour	
Newquay	62 moorings (buoy)	Boating lake
Padstow	65 moorings (buoy)	
Taw-Torridge	190 moorings (buoy)	
Ilfracombe	Harbour; buoy; 120 moorings	Harbour developments
Watermouth Cove	120 moorings (buoy)	
Lundy	Anchorage in bay	
Porlock Weir	Small harbour	
Watchet	Small harbour	
Burnham-on-Sea	Harbour	Several boating lakes
Weston-super-Mare	80 moorings (buoy)	Marine lake
Bristol	Marina: 80 berths; harbour: 400 moorings; buoy	
Sharpness	Harbour: 130 moorings	
Cardiff/Penarth	Harbour; marina: 400 berths	Barrage under construction
Barry	Harbour: 130 moorings	
Porthcawl	Harbour: 35 moorings	

Sources: D'Olivera & Featherstone (1993), BPA (1994), Willis (1995). Key: buoy = buoy or pontoon moorings in river; harbour = buoy or quay moorings in harbour.

internationally renowned rock climbing site. West Cornwall is nationally important for sub-aqua activities, owing to the large number of wrecks, the clear waters, and the marine life, which is unique in the UK (see sections 4.2 and 5.4). Premier dive areas include the Lizard Peninsula, Land's End and the Isles of Scilly. The north Cornish coast is quite inhospitable for small craft, although there are sailing clubs at St. Ives and Rock, which are also popular water-skiing locations. This stretch of coast is the premier UK location for surfing, surf life-saving and surf canoeing. There are around 50 surfing sites near Newquay alone and the National Surfing Centre is at Fistral Beach. Almost every beach is used for surfing on an informal basis at some time and there are beach facilities at the most popular sites. Surf life-saving is also popular as a sport and there are eighteen clubs in North Cornwall. Perranporth is an important location for sand yachting.

Ilfracombe is the major resort and sailing centre on the eastern part of the north Devon coast, although sailing activity is limited by the exposed and rocky nature of the coast. There is a thriving sea angling club at Bideford. The Taw-Torridge Estuary provides sheltered waters which afford a wide variety of leisure opportunities, especially watersports. Some rowing takes place on the Taw-Torridge and Camel Estuaries. The Exmoor coast is relatively undeveloped and is a popular walking destination for visitors. Hang gliding is practised from Hurlstone Point. Lundy Island is popular with divers.

The southern Severn Estuary coastline provides an important recreation resource for the population of the towns and cities in the inner estuary area. The Somerset and south Avon coast mostly caters for beach holidays, with major resorts at Minehead, Burnham-on-Sea, Weston-super-Mare and Clevedon. There are several holiday camps along this coastline. The beaches are popular for casual watersports such as windsurfing and the use of personal watercraft (jet skis), and in some places sand flats are used for trial biking and four-wheel drive recreation. The extensive sand flats around the Severn Estuary provide a nationally important location for sand yachting, with a national club at Brean Sand. Shore angling is popular at Minehead, Weston-super-Mare, Clevedon, Portishead and on the upper Severn Estuary. A wide variety of fish are found in the Severn, and there are 20 angling clubs. Brean Down is popular for rock climbing, as are some of the cliffs in the Avon Gorge.

The main centres for sailing along this coast are Burnham-on-Sea, Portishead and Bristol. Water-based recreation is limited within the estuary by the high tidal range, strong currents and exposure to westerly winds; however, there has been an expansion in the numbers of cruising craft in the Severn Estuary as the facilities for yachtsmen on the northern side of the estuary have improved. Sailing is also popular at non-tidal locations, such as in Bristol Docks, where water-skiing is also zoned. The sheltered parts of the upper Severn Estuary are popular for rowing.

Table 9.7.3 shows a breakdown of land- and water-based sites within Gwent, South Glamorgan and Mid Glamorgan, by local authority.

Table 9.7.3 Land- and water-based recreation sites within 10 km of the south Wales coast

District	*Land-based sites*	*Water-based sites*
Gwent	**35**	**18**
Monmouth	15	5
Newport	20	12
Torfaen	0	1
South Glamorgan	**25**	**57**
Cardiff	11	22
Vale of Glamorgan	14	35
Mid Glamorgan	**12**	**26**
Ogwr	10	26
Rhymney Valley	2	0
Region 11 Welsh districts	***72***	***101***
Wales	549	619

Source: Welsh Natural Facilities Database (Sports Council for Wales/CCW). Notes: sites may be important for land- and/or water-based leisure; the figures are not exclusive; 'land-based sites' include those listed in the database as 'air-based'.

Construction of the Cardiff Bay barrage, which is part of a programme of urban renewal involving recreational facilities, is now under way. The Cardiff Bay area is the major centre for watersports on the south Wales coast, but there are informal watersports on many of the beaches to the west. Organised surfing and surf life-saving occur at Llantwit Major and a variety of watersports take place around Porthcawl. Some trial biking has taken place in the Ogmore area.

Table 9.7.4 shows the distribution of known accommodation in coastal districts of Gwent, South Glamorgan and Mid Glamorgan in 1991; the original document (Wales Tourist Board 1991) should be referred to for an explanation of the assumptions and constraints in using the data. It is not known how much of this accommodation is on or near the coast, but in many areas it is probably a large proportion.

Table 9.7.4 Known bedspaces in tourist accommodation in Gwent, South Glamorgan and Mid Glamorgan

District	*Serviced*	*Self-catering*	*Caravan/camping*
Monmouth	282,100	470	1,975
Newport	1,663	317	255
Cardiff	4,824	281	129
Vale of Glamorgan	1,013	5,266	1,055
Ogwr	1,638	189	2,350
Total	***291,238***	***6,523***	***5,764***

Source: Wales Tourist Board (1991)

In this region there are 1,819 members belonging to 56 British Association for Shooting and Conservation (the BASC) affiliated clubs, representing 28% of the UK total of affiliated clubs. Not all the region's clubs shoot on the coast, and not all engage in wildfowling. The figures include members who shoot on the south coast of Devon (Region 10) or the area of the Cornish coastline that falls within Region 10, as well as those who shoot inland. Relative proportions of coastal- and inland-shooting members are not known. A 1989 study of night shooting of wildfowl in Great Britain revealed that night shooting took place at 54% of the estuarine/coastal sites surveyed, compared with only 10% of inland sites (Mudge 1989). Table 9.7.5 lists BASC-affiliated clubs in the region and their membership numbers.

9.7.3 Management and issues

Many land-based leisure developments, for example campsites and golf course developments, have had significant effects on coastal habitats and have reduced the area of semi-natural vegetation at these locations. Even low-key visitor activities, such as walking, climbing and bird-watching, have caused conflicts with other uses of the coast in the region, either because of the numbers of people involved in the activity or because of the sensitivity of the areas involved. Major issues include erosion of footpaths and fragile coastal habitats (particularly on the north Cornwall coast), loss of habitat to car parks, damaging use of trial bikes, four-wheel drive vehicles and personal watercraft, unsympathetic developments, and general visitor pressure, especially where there is only limited access to the coast (for example much of the Cornish and north-west Devon coast between the Camel and Westward Ho!). For safety reasons, unskippered boats cannot be hired on the exposed north coast.

Because of the importance of the region for leisure and tourism, all the local authorities are concerned over tourism developments and consider them within their structure and local plans. On much of the Cornish, Devon and Exmoor

Table 9.7.5 BASC affiliated clubs in the region

Club name	No. of clubs	No. of members
Cornwall	**3**	
Cornwall Association for Shooting and Conservation		139
City Clay Pigeon Club		17
Culdrose Sporting Club		22
Devon	**10**	
Woodbury Shoot		14
HMS Heron Sporting Gun Club		26
Taw and Torridge Wildfowling Club		85
West Dartmoor Shooting Club		19
South Hams Fox Control Society		18
Kingsbridge and District Pigeon Shoot Club		101
Killerton Shoot		20
Devon Wildfowlers' Association		127
Tamar Valley Association for Shooting and Conservation		112
Westward Sporting Gun Club		35
Somerset	**2**	
Bridgwater Bay Wildfowlers' Association		51
Highbridge, Huntspill and Burnham District Wildfowling Association		44
Avon	**9**	
Shorditch Clay Busters		5
Rath Muzzle and Historic Breech Loaders Association		38
Wessex Smooth Bore Club		8
Chipping Sodbury Shotgun Club		14
Churchill Gun Club		21
Clevedon and District Gun and Wildfowling Club		63
Weston Sporting Club		20
Stockwood Vale Gun Club		17
Bristol Twelve Bore Club		48
Gloucestershire	**5**	
Three Counties Wood Pigeon Shooting Association		10
Ashcroft Shoot		10
Gloucestershire Wildfowlers' Association		121
Lydney Clay Pigeon Shooting Club		16
Upton and District Woodpigeon Club		17
Gwent	**14**	
Newport Woodpigeon and Pest Control Shooting Club		23
Rhymney and District Gun and Wildfowling Club		20
Treetops Shooting Club		8
Newport Wildfowling and Gun Club		26
West Monmouthshire Gun Club		12
Severn Wildfowlers' Association		35
Cwmbran Gun Club		30
Vale of Usk Gun Club		17
Monmouth Gun Club		16
Llanbradach Field Sportsman Club		47
Spencer Works Rough and Clay Shooting Club		20
Talywain Gun Club		35
Gockett Gun Club		13
The Borders Gun Club		26
South Glamorgan	**6**	
Crowhill Field Sports Club		10
Barry and District Wood Pigeon Club		11
Glamorganshire Wild Pigeon Shooting Club		22
Wentloog Wildfowlers		35
Pen y Duffryn Wildfowling and Rough Shooting Club		11
Llandaff City Clay Shooting Club		31
Mid Glamorgan	**7**	
St. Gwynno Sporting Club		10
Troedrhiwfuwch Gun and Sporting Club		21
Caerphilly and District Wildfowling and Gun Club		12
Aberkenfig and District Clay Shooting Club		17
Trethomas Clay Shooting Club		10
Garw Valley Field Sports Society		10
The Kenfig and District Wildfowling and Conservation Association		53
Total	*56*	*1,819*

Source: BASC pers. comm.

coast, local councils control all kinds of development very strictly. Much of the western coastline is designated as Tourism Protection Areas (TPAs) and the undeveloped coast is sedulously guarded by local councils. In recent years there has been presumption against development that would adversely affect the landscape or nature conservation value of the coastline. Most of the north coast of Cornwall and Devon is designated an Area of Outstanding Natural Beauty (AONB) and there are three stretches of Heritage Coast; suitable new sites for water sports infrastructure are extremely limited. Conservation designations have precluded even low-key development in some areas. There is now evidence of a shift from the traditional holidays to more 'green' tourism, including the expansion of farm businesses to include holiday accommodation and other attractions.

There is significant demand for more watersports facilities on the northern coast of the South West Peninsula, although there are few places where development can take place, either for planning or geomorphological reasons. There is unlikely to be any expansion of activities at Rock, because of the shifting bar at the entrance to the estuary, although there are continuing proposals for further developments in the lower reaches of the Taw-Torridge. The Taw-Torridge Estuary is a major regional centre for watersports, and zoning is being piloted, using a code of practice devised by local user groups to ease congestion and conflict. Falmouth is earmarked for further sailing facility development. Other areas likely to see further development include Hayle, Ilfracombe and possibly Watchet Harbour. At Brean Sand, sand yachting is restricted in summer to avoid conflict with other beach users. Water-skiing is zoned at Bristol Docks. At Portishead the decline in commercial use of the harbour may increase opportunities for leisure development. The British Water Ski Federation wishes to see an expansion of facilities at Burnham-on-Sea, where conditions are ideal for the sport (South Western Council for Sport and Recreation 1990).

The economic boom of the 1980s stimulated a vast number of speculative developments associated with leisure and tourism. Amenity barrages became particularly popular in the UK; their popularity is often associated with the perception that the new developments will provide new employment opportunities for local people and boost the local economy. Amenity barrages are constructed in marine inlets and estuaries to impound a lake of water upstream, which can then be used for recreational activities at all stages of the tide or may be considered to improve the appearance of waterside developments. Barrages may form sills to prevent complete drainage of the impounded area at low tide, or incorporate locks to allow small boats to travel through. Some amenity barrages used for recreation during the summer season may be designed to restore a normal tidal flow during the winter months, when wintering birds require mud-flats exposed at low tide for feeding. Others are intended to replace 'unsightly' mud-flats with a more attractive permanent artificial lake. Some amenity barrage proposals are still under consideration in this region. Leisure barrages have been suggested for the Hayle and Camel; and the proposed Severn Barrage would offer a significant expansion in opportunities for water-based leisure in the estuary: a study by Leisure Consultants (1989) suggested a potential increase in the number of boats of between 50% and 70% (9-16,000 more boats). Without the barrage development, development of water-based leisure would be significantly constrained, by both nature conservation considerations and the physical characteristics of the estuary (see also section 5.12). The Cardiff Bay barrage, now under construction, will result in the impounding of freshwater in Cardiff Bay (see also section 5.12).

The representative body for sport shooting in the UK is the British Association for Shooting and Conservation (the BASC). Targeted wildfowling species and shooting seasons (the open season for coastal wildfowling in England and Wales is 1 September to 20 February) are regulated through the Wildlife and Countryside Act 1981. As elsewhere in Britain, much of the wildfowling in Region 11 is operated and managed through wildfowling clubs and syndicates. Much takes place on areas covered by national and international site protection, including on several National Nature Reserves (NNRs), where it is mostly managed through permit systems; around 90% of land used for wildfowl shooting in England is designated as Sites of Special Scientific Interest (SSSIs). Wildfowling on NNRs is reviewed by Owen (1992).

During periods of severe winter weather, disturbance to waterfowl (including non-targeted species) from shooting threatens the birds' survival; at these times national statutory wildfowling bans can be imposed after fourteen days of freezing conditions (voluntary restraint is called for after seven days). Bans are important in this region since it is used by some species as a refuge when weather further east in continental Europe is severe (Ridgill & Fox 1990). Further information on the history and operation of cold-weather shooting bans is given in Stroud (1992).

9.7.4 Information sources used

Most of the above information is derived from materials received from Tourist Information Centres (up to date, but of varying detail within the region), from Ordnance Survey 1:50,000 Land Ranger maps and Admiralty Charts, from a nautical almanac (D'Olivera & Featherstone 1993) and from the Sports Council (South Western Council for Sport and Recreation 1990). It is not possible to gauge the scale of some facilities, other than in Wales, where the Sports Council for Wales Natural Facilities database is the source. This GIS database has logged more than 2,200 sites used for recreation in Wales (Sports Council for Wales 1992). Equivalent detailed information is not readily available for England. The maps and tables are therefore only indicative of the distribution of leisure and tourism in the region.

A comprehensive listing of contact addresses for leisure activities in the region may be found in *Sport in the South West* (Sports Council 1995).

9.7.5 Acknowledgements

Thanks go to Paula Lloyd Jones (Rural Surveys Research Unit) for providing data from the Natural Facilities Database, and to John Harrison (Sports Council for Wales), Andrew Bell (Taw-Torridge Estuary Manager) and Teresa Mackie (Wales Tourist Board) for their helpful comments.

9.7.6 Further sources of information

A. References cited

British Ports Association. 1994. *British Ports Association 1994.* King's Lynn, Charter International.

D'Olivera, B., & Featherstone, N.L. 1993. *The Macmillan and Silk Cut nautical almanac 1994.* Basingstoke, Macmillan.

Leisure Consultants. 1989. *Tourism and recreation. Assessment of additional activity arising from the proposed Severn barrage.* Sudbury, Leisure Consultants.

Mudge, G.P. 1989. Night shooting of wildfowl in Great Britain: an assessment of its prevalance, intensity and disturbance impact. *Nature Conservancy Council, CSD Report,* No. 987.

Owen, M. 1992. An analysis of permit systems and bag records on NNRs. *JNCC Report,* No. 68.

Ridgill, S.C., & Fox., A.D. 1990. *Cold weather movements of waterfowl in western Europe.* Slimbridge, International Waterfowl & Wetlands Research Bureau. (IWRB Special Publication No. 13.)

Royal Yachting Association (RYA). 1992. *RYA affiliated organisations.* Romsey, RYA. (G25/92.)

South Western Council for Sports and Recreation. 1990. *Regional strategy for sport and recreation in south-west England - subject report: a strategy for coastal recreation.* Crewkerne, South Western Council for Sport and Recreation.

Sports Council. 1995. *Sport in the South West 95/96.* Crewkerne, Sports Council.

Sports Council for Wales. 1992. *Sport, recreation and protected areas in Wales.* Cardiff, Sports Council.

Stroud, J.M. 1992. Statutory suspension of wildfowling in severe weather: review of past winter weather and actions. *Joint Nature Conservation Committee Report,* No. 75.

Wales Tourist Board. 1991. *Compendium of statistical information on tourist accommodation.* Cardiff.

Willis, T. 1995. *Yachting Monthly British mooring and marina guide 1995.* London, IPC Magazines.

B. Further reading

Bell, D.V., & Fox, P.J.A. 1991. Shooting disturbance: an assessment of its impact and effects on overwintering waterfowl populations and their distribution in the UK. *Nature Conservancy Council, CSD Report,* No. 1,242.

British Marine Industries Federation. 1992. *A guide to boating and the environment.* Egham, The British Marine Industries Federation. (BMIF Environment Initiative.)

British Marine Industries Federation. Undated. *Steering a balanced course: the boating industry and the marine environment.* Egham, British Marine Industries Federation.

British Tourist Authority. 1989. *Walking in Britain.* London, British Tourist Authority.

Buck, A.L. 1993. *An inventory of UK estuaries. Volume 2 South-west Britain.* Peterborough, Joint Nature Conservation Committee.

Cornwall Tourist Board. 1994. *Golf in Cornwall.* Truro.

Davidson, N.C., Laffoley, D.d'A., Doody, J.P., Way, L.S., Gordon, J., Key, R., Drake, C.M., Pienkowski, M.W., Mitchell, R.M., & Duff, K.L. 1991. *Nature conservation and estuaries in Great Britain.* Peterborough, Nature Conservancy Council.

Doody J.P. Undated. *Coastal habitat change - a historical review of man's impact on the coastline of Great Britain.* Peterborough, Joint Nature Conservation Committee. (Unpublished draft.)

Eno, N.C., *ed.* 1991. *Marine conservation handbook.* 2nd ed. Peterborough, English Nature.

Evans, D.M., & Thomason, H. 1990. Tourism and recreational developments. *In: The Irish Sea: an environmental review. Part 4. Planning, development and management,* ed. by H.D. Smith & A.J. Geffen. Liverpool, Liverpool University Press. (Irish Sea Study Group.)

Kerr, A.J. 1974. The permit issue and control scheme. *In: Caerlaverock. Conservation and wildfowling in action,* ed. by J. Harrison, 33-43. Sevenoaks, Wildfowlers' Association of Great Britain & Ireland.

Kerr, A.J. 1974. Wildfowl, wildfowlers and their bag. *In: Caerlaverock. Conservation and wildfowling in action,* ed. by J. Harrison, 43-63. Sevenoaks, Wildfowlers' Association of Great Britain & Ireland.

Macadam, J. Undated. *South West Coast Path: Padstow to Falmouth.* Northampton, Countryside Commission.

Marine Conservation Society. 1994. *The Reader's Digest good beach guide.* Newton Abbot, David & Charles.

National Rivers Authority. 1993. *Navigation function strategy document.* Exeter, South Western Region.

National Rivers Authority. 1993. *Recreation function strategy document.* Exeter, South Western Region.

North Devon Tourism. 1994. *Devonia beaches and watersports.* Barnstaple.

Pain, D. 1990. Lead poisoning of wildfowl: the waste of a natural resource. *IWRB News,* No. 4, July.

Ratcliffe, T. 1989. *The management of coastal water sports in South Wales.* PhD thesis, University of Wales.

Rusbridge, B.J. 1992. *Municipal Year Book, Vol. 2.* London, Municipal Journal Ltd.

Sidaway, R. 1988. *Sport, recreation and nature conservation.* London, Sports Council. (Study No. 32.)

Sidaway, R. 1991. *A review of marina developments in Southern England.* Report to the RSPB and WWF-UK.

Sports Council. 1992. *Heritage Coasts: good practice in the planning, management and sustainable development of sport and active recreation.* London, Sports Council.

Sports Council. 1992. *Planning and managing watersports on the coast: lessons from Canada and the USA.* London, Sports Council. (Factfile 3: Countryside and water recreation.)

Sports Council. 1993. *Water skiing and the environment.* London, Sports Council.

Sports Council for Wales. 1991. *Sport and recreation in the natural environment: a digest for Wales.* Cardiff, Sports Council.

Tarr, R. Undated. *South West Coast Path: Minehead to Padstow.* Northampton, Countryside Commission.

Wales Tourist Board. 1988. *Tourism in Wales. Developing the potential.* Cardiff.

Wales Tourist Board. 1994. *Tourism 2000 - a strategy for Wales.* Cardiff.

C. Contact names and addresses

Type of information	*Contact address and telephone no.*
Tourism information service - Britain	Commercial Information Library, British Tourist Authority / English Tourist Board, Thames Tower, Black's Road, Hammersmith, London W6 9EL, tel: 0181 846 9000 x 3011 / 3015
Tourist facilities - Wales	Wales Tourist Board, Brunel House, 2 Fitzalan Road, Cardiff CG2 1UY, tel: 01222 499909, or 34 Piccadilly, London W1, tel: 0171 409 0969
Tourist Information Centres	
Falmouth	28 Killigrew Street, Falmouth TR11 3PN, tel: 01326 312300
Penzance	Station Road, Penzance TR18 2NF, tel: 01736 62207
St. Ives	The Guildhall, Street-an-Pol, St. Ives TR26 2DS, tel: 01736 796297
Newquay	Municipal Buildings, Marcus Hill, Newquay TR7 1BD, tel: 01637 871345
Bude	Bude Visitor Centre, The Crescent, Bude EX23 8LE, tel: 01288 354240
Bideford	Victoria Park, The Quay, Bideford EX39 2QQ, tel: 01237 477676
Barnstaple	North Devon Library, Tuly Street, Barnstaple EX31 1TY, tel: 01271 388583
Ilfracombe	The Promenade, Ilfracombe EX34 9BX, tel: 01271 863001
Lynton	Town Hall, Lee Road, Lynton EX35 6BT, tel: 01598 752225
Minehead	17 Friday Street, Minehead TA24 5UB, tel: 01643 702624
Burnham-on-Sea	South Esplanade, Burnham-on-Sea TA8 1BB, tel: 01278 787852
Weston-super-Mare	Beach Lawns, Weston-super-Mare BS23 1AT, tel: 01934 626838
Bristol	St. Nicholas Church, St. Nicholas Street, Bristol BS1 1UE, tel: 0117 926 0767

C. Contact names and addresses (continued)

Type of information	Contact address and telephone no.
Newport	Newport Museum & Art Gallery, John Frost Square, Newport, Gwent NP9 1HZ, tel: 01633 842962
Cardiff	Central Station, Cardiff South Glamorgan CF1 1QY, tel: 01222 227281
Penarth (seasonal)	The Esplanade, Penarth Pier, South Glamorgan CF64 3AU, tel: 01222 708849
Barry Island (seasonal)	The Triangle, Paget Road, South Glamorgan CF62 5TG, tel: 01446 747171
Porthcawl	The Old Police Station, John Street, Mid Glamorgan CF36 3DT, tel: 01656 786639
Funding for tourism-related developments - Wales	Welsh Development Agency, Pearl House, Greyfriars Road, Cardiff CF1 3XX, tel: 01222 222666
Funding for tourism-related developments - Wales	Wales Tourist Board, Brunel House, 2 Fitzalan Road, Cardiff CF2 1UY, tel: 01222 499909 or 34 Piccadilly, London W1, tel: 0171 409 0969
Sports - Wales	Senior Planning Officer, The Sports Council for Wales, Sophia Gardens, Cardiff, South Glamorgan CF1 9SW, tel: 01222 397571
Sports - England	Sports Council Headquarters, 16 Upper Woburn Place, London WC1H 0QP, tel: 071 388 1277
Natural facilities GIS database (Sports)	Rural Surveys Research Unit, Institute of Earth Studies, University of Wales, Aberystwyth, Dyfed SY23 3DB, tel: 01970 622585
Sport and recreation	The Sports Council, Headquarters: 16 Upper Woburn Place, London WC1H 0QP, tel: 0171 388 1277, or South West Region, Ashlands House, Ashlands, Crewkerne, Somerset TA18 7LQ, tel: 01460 73491
Water quality of bathing beaches - UK	Marine Conservation Society, 9 Gloucester Road, Ross-on-Wye, Herefordshire HR9 5BU, tel: 01989 566017
Marine industries	British Marine Industries Federation, Meadlake Place, Thorpe Lea Road, Egham, Surrey TW20 8HE, tel: 01784 473377
Coastal recreation, particularly related to planning policy	*County and District Councils

Type of information	Contact address and telephone no.
Small boat movements and safety	Coastguard, Falmouth and Swansea: HM Coastguard, MRCC Swansea, Tutt Head, Mumbles, Swansea SA3 4EX, tel: 01792 366534 HM Coastguard, MRCC Falmouth, Pendennis Point, Castle Drive, Falmouth TR11 4WZ, tel: 01326 317575
Windsurfing	British Windsurfing Association, 86, Sinah Lane, Hayling Island, Hants. PO11 9JX, tel: 01705 468182
Yachting, windsurfing and power-boating	Royal Yachting Association, RYA House, Romsey Road, Eastleigh, Hants. SO5O 9YA, tel: 01703 627400
Board sailing	UK Board Sailing Association, Mason's Road, Stratford-Upon-Avon, Warwickshire CV37 9NZ, tel: 01789 299574
Harbour Masters	See Appendix
Canoeing	British Canoe Union, Adbolton Lane, West Bridgford, Nottingham NG2 5AS, tel: 0115 982 1100
Diving	British Sub Aqua Club, Telford Quay, Elsmere Port, Cheshire L65 4FY, tel: 0151 357 1951
Water skiing	British Water Ski Federation, 390 City Road, London EC1V 2QA, tel: 0171 833 2855
Wildfowling (general, including information on affiliated clubs)	Information Officer, The British Association for Shooting and Conservation, Marford Mill, Rossett, Wrexham LL12 0HL, tel: 01244 573000
Wildfowl and wetlands (conservation)	*Publicity Officer, Wildfowl and Wetlands Trust, Slimbridge, tel: 01453 890333
Wildfowling (general information on wildfowl, habitats and conservation)	*Enquiry Officer, RSPB, Sandy, tel: 01767 680551
Wildfowling (the sport)	Press and Information Officer, British Field Sports Society, 59 Kennington Road, London SE1 7PZ, tel: 0171 928 4742
Severe weather wildfowling bans - England	*Licensing Officer, English Nature HQ, Peterborough, tel: 01733 340345
Severe weather wildfowling bans - Wales	*Licensing Officer, CCW HQ, Bangor, tel: 01248 370444

*Starred contact addresses are given in full in the Appendix.

The Severn Estuary is the second largest estuary in the UK and overwhelmingly the largest in the region. In addition to its 55,000 hectares of estuarine habitats, it is the setting for the majority of the region's towns and cities, human activities and associated infrastructure. The salmon fishery, which uses ranks of putchers, as shown here, is an element of this complex environment. Management of the estuary involves a huge range of organisations and individuals in fora such as the Severn Estuary Coastal Group, the Standing Conference of Severnside Local Authorities and the Severn Estuary Strategy Group. Photo: Pat Doody, JNCC.

Chapter 10 Coastal management

S.L. Fowler

10.1 Introduction

This chapter describes national (section 10.2) and local and regional (section 10.3) coastal management initiatives taking place wholly or partly within Region 11. GB and UK national initiatives without a specific regional focus, notably those led by non-governmental agencies and user groups, are outside the scope of this chapter. However, as the whole chapter concludes with a list of contacts with a wider involvement or interest in coastal management (section 10.3.5 C), contact points for some of these organisations are included there. In addition, names and addresses of many contacts are given within the relevant section.

10.1.1 Coastal management in the UK

This section outlines the direction of national policy-making, within which many of the regional initiatives operate. Many, frequently competing, issues and activities affect the coastal environment and inshore waters, making the task of coastal planning and management a very complex one, particularly as numerous different authorities are responsible for particular statutory duties. Coastal management promotes an integrated, inter-disciplinary approach to multiple use and conflict resolution between interest groups, "to ensure the long-term future of the resources of the coastal zone through environmentally sensitive programmes, based on the principle of balanced, sustainable use" (Gubbay 1990). Coastal management ensures that all land and sea use issues are co-ordinated, including development, conservation, waste disposal, fisheries, transport, and coast protection and flood defence. The advantages of this have been recognised by coastal planners in many areas, and several local authorities and other bodies now promote coastal management. However, approaches differ from area to area, with overlap in some places and patchy coverage elsewhere (Earll 1994; King & Bridge 1994).

The House of Commons Environment Committee Second Report (House of Commons 1992), although limited in scope to England and the estuaries it shares with Wales and Scotland, made recommendations for the planning and implementation of coastal management that have had policy and practical implications throughout the UK. Among the recommendations were:

- the endorsement of an integrated approach to coastal management, incorporating maritime land, sea and intertidal areas;
- a review of existing legislation;
- the need for international (EU-wide) policy initiatives;
- clearer responsibilities for planning and action in the coastal zone, based on a national strategic framework;
- appropriate funding for accountable bodies with responsibilities;
- research into the physical functioning of the coastal zone and associated protection and conservation measures;
- a review of planning mechanisms to allow effective safeguard of the coastal resource;
- monitoring and environmental assessment of coastal activities to assess their impacts;
- the involvement of local communities in coastal management planning;
- the integration of responsibility for coast protection and sea defence under one body;
- better statutory protection for sites of nature conservation importance;
- better provisions for control of marine pollution;
- the need for fisheries activities to take account of marine conservation issues.

Later in 1992, the Department of the Environment and the Welsh Office issued *Planning Policy Guidance: Coastal Planning* (PPG 20), which made clearer the requirement for planning decisions to take account of environmental and conservation issues.

The Environment Select Committee's recommendations were followed up, in 1993, by the publication of *Development below low water mark: a review of regulation in England and Wales* (Department of the Environment/Welsh Office 1993a), in parallel with the discussion paper *Managing the coast: a review of coastal management plans in England and Wales and the powers supporting them* (Department of the Environment/Welsh Office 1993b). That same year, The Ministry of Agriculture, Fisheries and Food (MAFF) and the Welsh Office brought out their *Strategy for flood and coastal defence in England and Wales* (MAFF/WO 1993). In this their policy is spelled out: ". . . reducing the risks to people and the developed and natural environment from flooding and coastal erosion by encouraging the provision of technically, environmentally and economically sound and sustainable defence measures."

In December 1994 the Department of the Environment launched a standing forum on coastal management for England (the Coastal Forum); it meets twice a year (see section 10.2.2). In 1995 the Department of the Environment published national policy guidelines for the coast (DoE 1995). These guidelines do not replace existing documents but provide a concise digest, pointing out common themes and principles. Public and private bodies are asked to have close regard to them in taking forward their coastal management functions. In 1994 the Department also undertook to highlight good practice in coastal management plans, clarify the interaction of the different elements of coastal management and review relevant bylaw powers. This *Best practice guide* is being prepared by Nicholas Pearson Associates and is due for publication in 1996. It will set out the basic principles and objectives relating to coastal management plans, helping to define the respective roles of key players, taking account of the diverse uses of the coastal zone and giving examples of best practice in helping to resolve competing pressures on the coast, and help make clearer how the different elements of coastal management interact, including relationships with other strategies. The *Review of bylaw-making powers for the coast* is examining the bylaw powers available to bodies with responsibilities for the coast and aims to assess whether they meet modern needs. It is also considering the broader relationship between the voluntary principle and other regulatory mechanisms. A final statement on the outcome of the review is expected in 1996.

The UK government published a Rural White Paper in October 1995, which was to have included a statement on coastal policy, although in the event only sea fishing was addressed. For Wales, a comprehensive PPG draft is at consultation stage at the time of writing.

The European Commission was asked by the Council of the EU to propose a strategy for the whole of the Community coast before the end of 1994. The initial response was to adopt the *Communication on integrated management of coastal zones* (COM/511/95), which sets out proposals for EU funding for demonstration programmes of coastal management. The strategy is to be based on the principles of sustainability and sound ecological and environmental practice, but will have no legal standing.

In 1994, the UK Government published its Regulations to implement the EC Habitats & Species Directive (Department of the Environment/Welsh Office 1994). As they relate to the coast, these regulations provide for single management groups to be set up for whole sites, making the production of unified management plans a practical proposition. Where these sites are of European importance for their nature conservation interest, the conservation of that interest must be the primary consideration of the management plan. For this, the regulations require all relevant authorities to exercise a general duty of care for their long-term conservation. At the time of writing, discussions are continuing on how these requirements will work in practice (see also section 10.2.9).

In 1995 guidance was forthcoming from the Local Government Management Board on the implementation of local sustainable coastal development strategies, i.e. Local Agenda 21 initiatives (Local Government Management Board 1995).

10.2 National coastal initiatives with regional elements

10.2.1 Introduction

Partly as a result of developments at a UK and international level, many national bodies are now becoming involved in the promotion of coastal management initiatives, including several with no direct management role through a statutory remit or ownership of coastal land. These include the National Coasts and Estuaries Advisory Group (NCEAG), which advises local authorities and speaks on their behalf, and non-governmental organisations with a particular interest in the conservation of the coastal zone: the Marine Conservation Society, World Wide Fund for Nature - UK, and the Royal Society for the Protection of Birds (RSPB) (see section 10.2.6). Only national initiatives that have distinct local elements in the region are described here. Many other diverse interest groups and organisations now have national policies with regard to coastal management and estuaries management, for example the British Association for Shooting and Conservation and the Royal Yachting Association, and their representatives are involved in most local or regional groups or fora, listed in Table 10.3.1. For further information on regionally-led coastal management initiatives, see section 10.3.

10.2.2 National coastal fora

The Coastal Forum (for England)

The Coastal Forum was launched in December 1994; it is chaired and serviced by the Department of the Environment and meets twice yearly. It brings together key bodies with interests in the coast, from commerce and industry to leisure and environmental bodies, and includes representatives of central and local government. It provides for an exchange, by a wide range of interested bodies, of views on issues related to the coastal zone in England. In particular, it seeks to promote understanding of coastal zone initiatives; build on existing liaison arrangements at regional and local level; assist evaluation of action to implement coastal zone initiatives and monitor preparation of a guide to good practice; complement the work of other bodies with interests in coastal issues; and liaise with other relevant initiatives elsewhere in the United Kingdom. Forum proceedings are reported to government ministers. The Forum intends to produce a *Good practice guide* in 1996.

English Coastal Groups Forum

Established in 1991, the English Coastal Groups Forum has a remit to promote the formation of coastal groups, including bodies with responsibilities for coastal defence and management and the strategic and local planning functions that would influence coastal defence; to further co-operation between those bodies; to act as a link between centrally-based organisations and coastal groups; to facilitate the development of a coastal zone appraisal and management approach, ensuring that the most environmentally consistent practice is adopted in relation to physical development in the coastal zone; to promote common standards of approach; and to identify policy, administrative and research requirements. Forum members include one representative from each coastal group (see section 10.3.2), the Environment Agency, Local Authority Associations, English Nature, Railtrack and Department of the Environment. The English Coastal Groups Forum met three times in 1995.

Welsh Coastal Groups Forum

Like the English Coastal Groups Forum, this was established in 1991, to coordinate the work of the Welsh Coastal Groups. Members include one representative from each coastal group in Wales (see section 10.3.2), the Tidal Dee Users Group, the Severn Estuary Coastal Group, the Environment Agency, the Assembly of Welsh Counties, the Council of Welsh Districts, the Countryside Council for Wales, Railtrack, the Welsh Office Planning Division and the Welsh Office Environment Division. The Forum meets twice a year.

The Coastal Heritage Network (CoastNET)

The Coastal Heritage Network (CoastNET) (formerly the Heritage Coast Forum) is funded by the Countryside Commission, English Nature and Scottish Natural Heritage and provides contact between those individuals and groups concerned with the management of coasts in England (the Arfordir Group fulfills a similar role in Wales); proposals have been put forward to broaden this forum to the whole of the UK.

10.2.3 Countryside Council for Wales

The Countryside Council for Wales's marine and coastal zone policy was launched at the Prince of Wales Lecture in December 1995 (CCW 1995). It commits the Council to striving for the integrated, holistic management of the marine and coastal environment, and includes specific policies to achieve this. A review of coastal management of three test areas in Wales (Swansea Bay, part of which falls within this region, Ceredigion coast and the Menai Strait) has been carried out by the University of Wales Department of Maritime Studies. CCW has issued a document: *Seas, shores and coastal areas* (CCW 1996), which aims to guide coastal policy.

10.2.4 English Nature

English Nature organises or participates in a number of national coastal zone management initiatives, as detailed below (see also section 10.2.9).

Estuaries Initiative

The Estuaries Initiative for achieving the sustainable management of estuaries is described in *Caring for England's estuaries: an agenda for action* (English Nature 1992); estuary projects are listed in Grabrovaz (1995). Out of a total of 35 projects underway or proposed in England, four areas within the region have been targeted under this initiative: Falmouth Bay and Estuaries, the Camel Estuary, the Taw-Torridge Estuary and the Severn Estuary. English Nature's involvement in these projects may vary from full participation in the management committee through membership of a Topic Group to responding to consultation drafts.

Sensitive Marine Areas

English Nature's Sensitive Marine Areas (SMA) initiative is set out in *Managing England's marine wildlife* (English Nature 1994) (see also section 7.4.4). Under the initiative, which is modelled on the Estuaries Initiative, English Nature and the managers and users of the marine environment are, with joint funding, developing ways of managing areas of marine wildlife importance, based on voluntary measures used in conjunction with existing regulatory controls. SMAs within the region are Dodman Point to the Lizard, the Isles of Scilly, St. Ives Bay, North Cornwall coast, Lundy, North Devon coast and the Severn Estuary.

Maritime Natural Areas

English Nature has, through consultation, identified 23 proposed Maritime Natural Areas around the coast of England (described in *Conserving England's maritime heritage - a strategy* (EN 1993)). These non-statutory areas represent coherent maritime wildlife systems based on major sediment cells and other coastal features. The seaward boundary of each is the 12 mile limit, and the landward boundary the limit of coastal habitats. The Natural Areas approach is being tried out at one Maritime Natural Area (Lyme Bay, in Regions 9 and 10). The trial includes a review of the coastline, adjacent areas, the mechanisms by which the area is regulated and how these may be applied in future, and development of a framework to decide what the management objectives for the area are and how they may be achieved. A strategy will be derived from this review, including the management objectives for the Maritime Natural Area and an action plan for their implementation. Future projects should extend this approach to the five main Maritime Natural Areas within Region 11: Porthallow to Trevose Head, Isles of Scilly, Trevose Head to Morte Point, Morte Point to Brean Down, and the Severn Estuary. A sixth area (Start Point to Porthallow) lies mainly within Region 10.

10.2.5 Arfordir Group

The Arfordir group is the local authority coastal officers' forum in Wales. It aims to promote integrated coastal management and best management practice for the whole of the Welsh coast, and to achieve Wales-wide representation after local government re-organisation. Membership is open to all maritime local authorities.

10.2.6 Royal Society for the Protection of Birds

In 1990, the Royal Society for the Protection of Birds (RSPB) launched a national campaign to promote the importance of estuaries in the UK and the need for coordinated management (Rothwell & Housden 1990). The campaign ran for three years. The RSPB Estuaries Inventory project compiled mapped and numerical information on land use and selected human activities for 57 major UK estuaries, including in this region the Fal, Camel, Taw-Torridge and Severn Estuaries. In 1994, the RSPB launched its 'Marine Life' campaign, which aims to increase awareness of the problems facing the marine environment and its wildlife, including pollution, fisheries and shipping safety. It has recently published a *Review of coastal zone management powers* (RSPB 1995).

10.2.7 Shoreline management plans

Shoreline Management Plans (SMPs) set out a strategy for coastal defence for a specified length of coast, taking account of natural processes and human and other environmental influences and needs (MAFF *et al.* 1994).

They are based on coastal sub-cells and are compiled in accordance with government guidelines on assessing the environmental impacts of proposals, including soft defence and 'do nothing' options, to be produced in association with and grant aided by MAFF (Table 10.2.1). Each is managed by a Shoreline Management Group, which comprises the lead authority, other local authority partners within the coastal sub-cell, the Environment Agency, English Nature, MAFF and any other important maritime local organisations. Such groups are also known as Coastal Engineering Groups.

The Lizard Point to Land's End SMP, one of the first to get underway, is engineering-led, seeking to address sea defence and coastal protection at a strategic scale; English Nature has let an additional contract to collate nature conservation information and draft nature conservation objectives for the study area.

10.2.8 Local Environment Action Plans

River catchments, including estuaries and coastal waters, are the Environment Agency's basic water management unit. The Environment Agency is building on the success of the former NRA Catchment Management Plans to provide integrated plans covering all the agency's functions - Local Environment Action Plans (LEAPs). These deal with a wide range of environmental issues, environmental protection and enhancement of water, land and air. A LEAP is an agreed strategy to realise the environmental potential of the catchment, within prevailing economic and political constraints. River catchments are shown on Map 10.2.1. Table 10.2.2 gives the Environment Agency's Welsh, South-western and Midlands Regions' programmes for the completion of consultation reports for LEAPs in Region 11 (NRA 1994). LEAPs are prepared by the Environment Agency for each catchment once consultation has been completed.

10.2.9 Designated sites

Site designations are discussed in detail in Chapter 7. However, several statutory and non-statutory designations are also relevant here because they provide a degree of coastal management through their area or site management plans. These often tend to focus strongly on the conservation of landscapes, buildings and/or habitats and species, rather than on wider and more integrated coastal issues, although in management planning for some sites a focus on visitor use and community involvement is

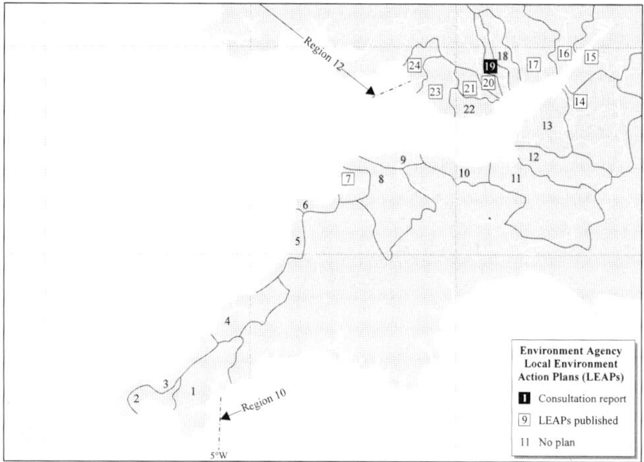

Map 10.2.1 River catchment areas for Local Environment Action Plans. Source: Environment Agency; reproduced by kind permission.

important. Designated sites include reserves managed by English Nature, CCW, wildlife trusts, local authorities, the RSPB or other bodies for nature conservation objectives, Heritage Coasts (see below) and proposed marine Special Areas for Conservation (see also section 7.1).

Heritage Coasts

The defined areas of Heritage Coasts include only the finest sections of undeveloped coast (section 7.4.3). Most Heritage Coast Services (management teams working from within local authorities) are producing or implementing management plans through their respective local authorities and associated Steering Groups (see also section 10.2.2). There are twelve Heritage Coasts in the region (see Table 10.3.1).

The National Trust

The National Trust, which has extensive coastal land holdings in the region (see section 7.5.1), has recently been carrying out a complete review of its Coastal Strategy Plans and has a review ongoing of coastal site management plans. It has produced a *Coastal strategy for Wales* (National Trust 1995), which provides guidance for the acquisition of coastal sites under Enterprise Neptune and for responses to coastal issues.

Marine Special Areas of Conservation (SACs)

Under the EC Habitats & Species Directive 1992, a list of marine Special Areas of Conservation (SACs) to be designated in the UK must be agreed by the UK

Table 10.2.1 State of progress of Shoreline Management Plans in the region

Coastal cell	*Cell no.*	*Status of SMP*	*Lead authority*
Rame Head to Lizard Point	6d	In progress	EA and Caradon Council
Lizard Point to Land's End	6e	Complete	EA and Penwith Council
Land's End to Trevose Head	7a	In progress	EA and Caradon Council
Trevose Head to Hartland Point	7b	In progress	EA and Caradon Council
Hartland Point to Morte Point	7c	In progress	EA and West Somerset Council
Morte Point to Sand Bay	7d	In progress	EA and West Somerset Council
Sand Bay to Sharpness	7e	In progress	EA and Cardiff Council
Wellhouse to Lavernock Point	8a	In progress	EA and Cardiff Council
Lavernock Point to Worms Head	8b	In progress	Ogwr Council

Source: MAFF

10.2.2 Local Environment Action Plans timetable

No. on Map 10.2.1	*Catchment area*	*Current status of LEAP*	*Contact*
1	Fal	In preparation	EA South western Region
2	Cober & South Cornwall	In preparation	EA South western Region
3	Hayle & Red River	In preparation	EA South western Region
4	Gannel & Camel	In preparation	EA South western Region
5	North Cornwall Coast, Strat & Neet	In preparation	EA South western Region
6	Abbey River & Clovelly Stream	In preparation	EA South western Region
7	Taw-Torridge Estuary	LEAP available	EA South western Region
8	Taw	In preparation	EA South western Region
9	North Devon coastal & Lyn	In preparation	EA South western Region
10	West Somerset Rivers	In preparation	EA South western Region
11	Isle, Yeo, Cary & Parrett	In preparation	EA South western Region
12	Brue, Sheppey & Hartlake	In preparation	EA South western Region
13	North Somerset Rivers	In preparation	EA South western Region
14	Lower Bristol Avon	LEAP available	EA South western Region
15	Severnside	LEAP available	EA Midlands Region
16	Lower Wye	LEAP available	EA Wales Region
17	Usk	LEAP available	EA Wales Region
18	Ebbw	In preparation	EA Wales Region
19	Rhymney	Consultation report available	EA Wales Region
20	Taff	LEAP available	EA Wales Region
21	Ely	LEAP available	EA Wales Region
22	Thaw	In preparation	EA Wales Region
23	Ogmore	LEAP available	EA Wales Region
24	Afan & Kenfig	LEAP available	EA Wales Region

Government and the European Commission by 1998 (see section 7.2.4). Marine SACs may include intertidal areas and/or subtidal areas; terrestrial SACs may include important coastal maritime habitats such as lagoons, saltmarshes or sand dunes. A list of 280 possible marine and terrestrial sites was published in March 1995; of these 112 were coastal and 37 were selected, in whole or in part, for their marine habitats and/or species. Consultations are being carried out for all possible sites; meanwhile, all sites on the published list should be managed, on a voluntary basis, as though they were already designated. Under the Directive, marine and terrestrial SACs will have to be managed in a way that secures their 'favourable conservation status'. A range of bodies and individuals will be involved, including all 'relevant and competent authorities', e.g. local authorities, the Environment Agency, ports and harbour authorities, Sea Fisheries Committees, English Nature and the Countryside Council for Wales, as well as owners and occupiers of foreshore land and representatives of those who rely on marine areas for their livelihood or for recreation. Management will be coordinated through an agreed management scheme, backed by existing statutory measures, as appropriate. The Department of the Environment have prepared draft guidelines for the preparation and application of management schemes for marine SACs, which were published in March 1996 for consultation (DoE 1996). At the instigation of the Scottish Office, the four country nature conservation agencies are preparing a generic management model for marine SACs, giving an overview of how schemes of management should develop.

10.2.10 Esturiales

Esturiales is a European Association of elected local authority representatives (municipal or regional), together with experts or non-elected officials. It aims to achieve sustainable development in estuaries by upgrading the environment, facilitating port economy and restructuring historic ports, and assisting the implementation and development of EU objectives as specified in the environmental programme and/or coastal zone management proposals. Actions and studies are undertaken jointly. The economy and environment of the Severn Estuary was the subject of one of the original case studies carried out in 1991. A Forum and strategic framework for integrated management have arisen from this study.

10.3 Regional coastal management groups and initiatives

10.3.1 Introduction

There are currently numerous regional coastal management initiatives arising around the coastline under the leadership of local planning, harbour and port authorities. Other locally-based coastal management initiatives, although not strictly integrated as defined in section 10.1.1, are also under way. These include Coastal Engineering Groups (see section 10.3.2), which are primarily concerned with promoting coordination and liaison between organisations undertaking coastal works (see section 8.4). In some places wider coastal fora have developed from a range of coastal designations and various management initiatives. The great value of such fora is that they bring all interest and user groups together and enable issues of concern to be examined from all points of view.

Table 10.3.1 lists regional coastal management initiatives, in many of which local authorities are involved or take a leading role.

Table 10.3.1 Regional coastal management initiatives

Initiative name	*Scope/aims*	*Organisations involved*	*Contact address*
South West Regional Planning Conference	Regional planning guidance published 1994; joint action required by all local planning authorities and agencies to adopt an agreed vision and set priorities; maintain and enhance coastal features; and prevent development on undeveloped parts of coast	South West County Councils (Dorset, Devon, Cornwall, Wilts., Somerset, Avon & Glos.) and District Councils	*Devon County Council, Exeter, tel: 01392 382000
Cornwall and Isles of Scilly Coast Protection Group	Aims to improve coordination and liaison between agencies undertaking coastal works	Cornwall County Council, Caradon, Kerrier, North Cornwall, Penwith and Restormel District Councils	*Kerrier District Council, Camborne, tel: 01209 712941
Towards 2000, Cornwall's Coast & Countryside	Strategy in preparation; five year and annual programmes; integrated management through a network of area countryside services and initiatives	Cornwall County Council, partner local authorities and agencies	*Brian Shipman, Cornwall County Council, Truro, tel: 01872 322000
Dodman-Fal Estuary Countryside Service	Area Management Strategy in preparation; rolling programme of environmental, interpretative and recreation management; aims for sustainable management of the coast through public and private sector partnerships, community involvement; conservation and interpretation of historic sites	Cornwall County Council, Countryside Commission, Carrick District Council, Restormel Borough Council, National Trust, landowners, relevant local interests	Jeremy Williams, Dodman-Fal Estuary Countryside Service, Lander Building, Daniell Road, Truro, Cornwall TR1 2DA, tel: 01872 322000 ext. 3608
Falmouth Bay and Estuaries Initiative	Three year project from November 1993 (part of EN's Estuaries Initiative). Strategic Guidelines and nature conservation overview in preparation.	Cornwall County Council, Carrick District Council, English Nature, South West Water, National Trust; Ports of Truro and Penryn	Sam Davis, Coastal Officer, Cornwall County Council, Lander Building, Daniell Road, Truro, Cornwall TR1 2DA, tel: 01872 322000 ext. 3607
Lizard Peninsula Countryside Service	Rolling programme of environmental, interpretative and recreation management; *Area Management Strategy* in preparation	Cornwall County Council and Countryside Commission, with Advisory Group of agencies, National Trust, landowners and local interests	Lizard Peninsula Countryside Service, The Yard, Trelowarren, Helston, Cornwall TR12 6AF, tel: 01326 221708
Shoreline Management Plans, Cornwall	Study to establish clear strategic guidelines for sustainable and effective management of the coastline, with due regard for natural processes, land use etc.	Kerrier and Penwith District Councils, English Nature, Environment Agency, Cornwall County Council; MAFF grant aiding study; LG Mouchell & Partners, contractors	*John Calvert, Kerrier District Council, Camborne, tel: 01209 712941
The Lizard Heritage Coast	No formal management plan. Work guided by Steering Group of local authorities and other interested parties. Management Service covers the whole of the Lizard Peninsula.	Run by Lizard Peninsula Projects, managed by Cornwall County Council, funded by Cornwall County Council and Countryside Commission	Lizard Peninsula Projects, Trelowarren, Mawgan, Helston, Cornwall TR12 6AF, tel: 01326 22708

Table 10.3.1 Regional coastal management initiatives (continued)

Initiative name	*Scope/aims*	*Organisations involved*	*Contact address*
Penwith Heritage Coast	No formal management plan; three sponsoring agencies carry out planning; Management Service covers whole of Penwith District	Managed by Penwith Peninsula Project, a partnership between Cornwall County Council, Penwith District Council and Countryside Commission	Penwith Peninsula Project, The Old Booking Hall, Station Road, Penzance, Cornwall TR18 2LL, tel: 01736 332211
Isles of Scilly Heritage Coast	Isles of Scilly Environmental Management Plan 1989 in use	Managed by Isles of Scilly Environmental Trust, which is responsible for all uninhabited land in the islands and has a Board of Trustees	Isles of Scilly Environmental Trust, Hamewith, The Parade, St. Mary's, Isles of Scilly TR21 0LP, tel: 01720 22153
Tehidy-Hayle Countryside Service (covers Godrevy-Portreath Heritage Coast)	Rolling programme of environmental, interpretative and recreation management	Cornwall County Council, Countryside Commission, with Advisory Group of agencies, local councils, NT, landowners & local interests	Tehidy-Hayle Countryside Service, Tehidy Country Park, Camborne, Cornwall TR14 0HA, tel: 01209 714494
St. Agnes - Newquay Countryside Service (covers St. Agnes Heritage Coast)	Rolling programme of environmental, interpretative and recreation management	Cornwall County Council, Countryside Commission, with Advisory Group of agencies, local councils, National Trust, landowners & local interests	St. Agnes - Newquay Countryside Service, Municipal Offices, Room 22, Marcus Hill, Newquay TR7 1AF, tel: 01637 851889
Droskyn Head to the Gannel Coastal Management Plan 1995	Programme of improvements to ensure future management of tourism, recreation, conservation and access	Carrick District Council, Countryside Commission, Cornwall County Council, English Nature; Steering Group includes Parish Councils	*Planning Department, Carrick District Council, Truro, tel: 01872 278131
Camel Estuary Initiative	Discussion Document (1994) considers major coastal issues in estuary and foreshore: recreation & tourism, interpretation, sand extraction, fishing and port development, water quality, community involvement, sustainable management	Cornwall County Council, English Nature, Countryside Commission, Duchy of Cornwall, North Cornwall District Council; Steering Group of sponsoring agencies and key users	Camel Valley Countryside Service, 3/5 Barn Lane, Bodmin, Cornwall PL3 1LP, tel: 01208 788087, or *Project Manager, English Nature, Truro, tel: 01872 262550
North Cornwall Heritage Coast (Trevose Head, Pentire Point - Widemouth, and Hartland Heritage Coasts) and Countryside Service	Rolling programme of environmental, interpretative and recreation management; Management Service covers the whole of the North Cornwall District coast	North Cornwall District Council, Countryside Commission	North Cornwall District Council, Council Offices, 3/5 Bath Lane, Bodmin, Cornwall PL3 1LP, tel: 01208 74121 ext. 239
Devon Coast Protection Advisory Group	Aims to improve coordination and liaison between agencies undertaking coastal works	Forum of local authority coastal engineers	South Hams District Council, Follaton House, Totnes, Devon TQ9 5NE, tel: 01803 861234
Devon Coastal Statement	Coastal fora established for Lyme Bay and North Devon; Devon Coastal Statement sets the scene, identifies issues, sets out policies and responsibilities and provides guidance for local coastal management plans	Devon County Council coordinates contributions from all agencies, organisations and local authorities in area	*Aidan Winder, Devon County Council, Exeter, tel: 01392 383019
Hartland Heritage Coast Service	Heritage Coast Service covers seven coastal parishes in addition to Hartland and Lundy Heritage Coasts; Management Plan due for completion 1996	Devon County Council, Torridge District Council, Countryside Commission; work guided by Steering Group	Heritage Coast Service, Bideford Station, East-the-Water, Bideford, Devon EX39 4BB, tel: 01237 423612
Taw-Torridge Estuary Management Plan	Draft summary report (1993) considers recreation conflicts, conservation, water quality, development pressures, erosion and water table; recommends policies for sustainable use, management zoning by agreement and negotiation; appointment of an Estuary Manager to implement plan	Torridge and North Devon District Councils, Devon County Council, English Nature, South West Water; consultants W.S. Atkins	*Planning and Technical Services, Torridge District Council, tel: 01237 476711, or Estuary Manager, Bideford Station, Railway Terrace, East-the-Water, Bideford, Devon EX39 4BB, tel: 01237 423655

Table 10.3.1 Regional coastal management initiatives (continued)

Initiative name	*Scope/aims*	*Organisations involved*	*Contact address*
Managing Lundy's wildlife	Lundy Marine Nature Reserve and SSSI Management Plan also covers Lundy Heritage Coast; recommends management for the benefit of wildlife, sustainable use of resources and promotes use for education and enjoyment of marine conservation	Island Warden, English Nature, Landmark Trust, Devon Sea Fisheries Committee, National Trust	The Warden, Lundy Island, Bristol Channel, Devon EX39 2LY, tel: 01237 431831, or *English Nature, Okehampton, tel: 01837 55045
North Devon Heritage Coast	No formal management plan; responsibilities of the Management Service extend to wider countryside beyond Heritage Coast boundary	Managed by Devon County Council Countryside Management Service, guided by a Steering Group	North Devon Heritage Coast Service, Council Offices, Northfield Road, Ilfracombe, Devon, tel: 01271 867496
Exmoor Heritage Coast and National Park	Operates as part of the National Park, with Management Service covering whole Park; draft Heritage Coast Management Plan and Exmoor National Park Plan	Exmoor National Park Authority manages the Heritage Coast	Management Planning Officer, Exmoor National Park Authority, Dulverton, Somerset TA22 9HL, tel: 01398 23665
North Devon and Somerset Coastal Group	Aims to improve coordination and liaison between agencies undertaking coastal works	Devon and Somerset County Councils, District Councils, English Nature, Environment Agency	*D.C. Rodwell, Sedgemoor District Council, Bridgwater, tel: 01278 435235
Severn Estuary Coastal Group	Aims to improve coordination and liaison between agencies undertaking coastal works	Glos. and Gwent County Councils, Unitary Authorities (of former Avon), City / Borough / District Councils, English Nature, CCW, Internal Drainage Boards, Environment Agency	*J. Mackay, City of Cardiff, tel: 01222 822376
Standing Conference of Severnside Local Authorities (SCOSLA)	Co-operation in the Severn Estuary, particularly in connection with the proposed Tidal Barrage and its impacts; proposed Strategic Framework Plan; possible Estuary Management Authority	Seven County and ten District Councils around the Estuary; special reports and studies funded by Government and Severn Tidal Power Group (a private consortium)	Severnside Consortium of Local Authorities, Chief Executive's Department, Woodspring District Council, Town Hall, Weston-super-Mare BS23 1UJ, tel: 01934 631701
Severn Estuary Strategy	Aims to develop a strategic management framework for the Severn Estuary and associated coastal zone; Estuary Management Plan. Business Plan published December 1995.	Partners including local authorities (five County Councils), Environment Agency (three regions), ports and harbours, and representatives of industry, commerce, conservation, recreation, archaeology and coastal defence	Project Manager, Severn Estuary Strategy, c/o Environment Agency, Hadnock Road, Monmouth NP5 3NQ, tel: 01600 772102
Forest of Dean District Local Plan 1993	Comprehensive consideration of coastal issues, including estuary conservation and access; support for Estuary Management Plan	Forest of Dean District Council	*Planning & Leisure Services, Forest of Dean District Council, tel: 01594 810000
Standing Conference on Regional Policy in South Wales	High-level planning issues for south Wales	Members of the Severn Estuary Strategy	P. Slater, Blaenau Gwent Business Advice Centre, Enterprise House, Rassau Industrial Estate, Ebbw Vale, Newport NP3 5SD, tel: 01495 306770
Glamorgan Heritage Coast	Management Plan covers ten-year period to 1998	Vale of Glamorgan Council, CCW	Glamorgan Heritage Coast Centre, Dunraven Park, Southerndown CF32 0RF, tel: 01656 880157
Swansea Bay Coastal Group	Aims to improve coordination and liaison between agencies undertaking coastal works; covers Lavernock Point (nr. Penarth) to Worm's Head (SW Gower); produced Swansea Bay Coastal Response Study (1993)	Swansea City Council, Ogwr, Neath, Port Talbot and Vale of Glamorgan Borough Councils, Environment Agency, British Steel, Countryside Council for Wales, Welsh Office (observer)	*Port Talbot Borough Council, Port Talbot, tel: 01656 643643

*Starred contact addresses are given in full in the Appendix.

10.3.2 Coastal (Engineering) Groups

Five non-statutory coastal groups (sometimes known as coastal engineering groups) have been established within the region to improve coordination and liaison between agencies undertaking coastal works (Table 10.3.1) (see also section 8.4). The main aim of all these groups is to seek a coordinated approach to all coastal engineering works by member authorities; reduce the risk of works adversely affecting the neighbouring coastline; and improve members' understanding of coastal processes. The geographical coverage of the Cornwall and Isles of Scilly Coast Protection Group, the Devon Coast Protection Advisory Group and the North Devon and Somerset Coastal Group is based on administrative boundaries rather than natural coastal sediment cells. The Severn Estuary Coastal Group includes representatives from both England and Wales, and the area covered by the Swansea Bay Coastal Group falls partly in Region 12.

10.3.3 Local planning authority and ports/harbours initiatives

The maritime local planning authorities are involved in most, if not all, of the major coastal zone management initiatives described above. Their own planning documents (County Structure Plans and Local Plans) usually pay particular attention to coastal matters, particularly when produced following PPG20 (DoE/WO 1992) (see also section 10.1). In Wales the Welsh Office invited the Assembly of Welsh Counties, in liaison with the District Councils, to draw up proposals for Strategic Planning Guidance, the equivalent of Regional Guidance in England. As part of this process a number of topic groups were formed, including a Coastal Strategy Working Party. Local authority planning departments hold details of county structure plans, local plans and accompanying documentation.

An important local authority initiative, at county level, is SWRPCON (South West Regional Planning Conference), which covers Devon, Gloucestershire, Somerset and Cornwall (Table 10.3.1). SWRPCON produced a regional strategy document in 1994 which set out guidelines to assist the local planning authorities in the preparation of strategic plans and policies. The report highlighted three topics of major significance in the south-west: the landscape, historic environment and the coast (SWRPCON 1994).

Port and Harbour Authorities also have a statutory remit to control activities within their areas of authority, which may include coastal waters, and will have additional responsibilities in the management of marine Special Areas of Conservation, under the EC Habitats & Species Directive (see section 10.2.1).

10.3.4 Acknowledgements

Thanks are due to Graham King (NCEAG), Sarah Soffe for information on Wales, Andrew Bell, Taw-Torridge Estuary Manager, and English Nature's Maritime Team for their helpful comments.

10.3.5 Further sources of information

A. References cited

Bown, D.P. 1992. *Strategic planning guidance for coastal Wales.* Carmarthen, Carmarthen County Planning Department (Coastal Strategy Topic Group).
Countryside Council for Wales. 1995. *CCW's maritime Agenda 21 - a policy framework.* Bangor, Countryside Council for Wales.
Countryside Council for Wales. 1996. *Seas, shores and coastal areas.* Bangor, Countryside Council for Wales.
Department of the Environment. 1995. *Policy guidelines for the coast.* London, HMSO.
Department of the Environment. 1996. *European marine sites in England and Wales. A guide to the Conservation (Natural Habitats &c.) Regulations 1994 and to the preparation and application of management schemes.* London, Department of Environment and The Welsh Office. (Draft for consultation.)
Department of the Environment/Welsh Office. 1992. *Planning policy guidance - coastal planning.* London, HMSO (PPG 20).
Department of the Environment/Welsh Office. 1993a. *Development below low water mark: a review of regulation in England and Wales.* London, HMSO.
Department of the Environment/Welsh Office. 1993b. *Managing the coast: a review of coastal management plans in England and Wales and the powers supporting them.* London, HMSO.
Department of the Environment/Welsh Office. 1994. *The Conservation (Natural Habitats &c.) Regulations.* London, HMSO (SI 2716).
Earll, R.C., *ed.* 1994. *Statutory and non-statutory plans in the estuarine and coastal environment. Overlapping plans - is this an issue?* Unpublished report of a meeting in July 1994.
English Nature. 1992. *Caring for England's estuaries: an agenda for action.* Peterborough, English Nature.
English Nature. 1993. *Conserving England's maritime heritage - a strategy.* Peterborough, English Nature.
English Nature. 1994. *Managing England's marine wildlife.* Peterborough, English Nature.
Grabrovaz, M. 1995. *Review of estuary projects.* Peterborough, English Nature.
Gubbay, S. 1990. *A future for the coast? Proposals for a UK coastal zone management plan.* Ross-on Wye, a report to the World Wide Fund For Nature from the Marine Conservation Society (unpublished).
House of Commons. 1992. *Coastal zone protection and planning.* London, HMSO. (Environment Committee Second Report.)
King, G., & Bridge, L. 1994. *Directory of coastal planning and management initiatives in England.* Maidstone, National Coasts and Estuaries Advisory Group.
Local Government Management Board. 1995. *Local agenda 21 roundtable guidance: action on the coast.* Luton, Local Government Management Board.
Ministry of Agriculture, Fisheries and Food/Welsh Office. 1993. *Strategy for flood and coastal defence in England and Wales.* London, MAFF.
Ministry of Agriculture, Fisheries and Food, Welsh Office, Association of District Councils, English Nature & National Rivers Authority. 1994. *Shoreline management plans: a guide for coastal defence authorities.* London, MAFF (PB2197).
National Rivers Authority. 1994. *Corporate Plan 1994/95.* Bristol, National Rivers Authority.
National Trust. 1995. *Coastal strategy for Wales.* Llandudno. (Internal report.)
Rothwell, P.I.Y., & Housden, S.D. 1990. *Turning the tide, a future for estuaries.* Sandy, Royal Society for the Protection of Birds.
Royal Society for the Protection of Birds. 1995. *Review of coastal zone management powers.* Sandy, RSPB.
SWRPCON. 1994. *South West Regional Planning Conference: regional strategy. The landscape, coast and historic environment of the south west.* Somerset, South West Regional Planning Conference.

B. Further reading

Ballinger, R.C. 1995. *Review of coastal management in Wales.* Cardiff, University of Wales. (Report to the Countryside Council for Wales. CCW Science Report, No. 153.)

Bown, D. 1988. *Coastal development: a planner's view.* Paper presented to CPRW Annual Study Conference (unpublished).

Coastal Heritage Forum. 1995. *Heritage Coasts: a guide for councillors and officers.* Manchester.

English Nature. 1994. *Environmental objective setting for shoreline management plans.* Peterborough, English Nature. (Marine Guidance Note.)

Gubbay, S. 1994. *Seas: the opportunity. Working together to protect our marine life.* Sandy, Royal Society for the Protection of Birds.

Halliday, J.E. 1987. Coastal planning and management in England and Wales. The contribution of district councils. *Town Planning Review, 58*(3): 317-329.

Halliday, J.E. 1988. Coastal planning and management: the role of the county councils in England and Wales. *Ocean and Shoreline Management, 11:* 211-230.

Heritage Coasts Forum. 1993. *Heritage Coasts in England and Wales - a gazetteer.* Manchester, Heritage Coasts Forum.

Jones, R. 1993. Coastal cell studies - a basis for coastal zone management. *Earth Science Conservation, 32:* 12-15.

National Coasts and Estuaries Advisory Group. 1993. *Coastal planning and management: a good practice guide.* Maidstone, National Coasts and Estuaries Advisory Group.

Nature Conservancy Council. 1990. *Marine Consultation Areas.* Edinburgh, Nature Conservancy Council.

Rendel Geotechnics. 1994. *Coastal planning and management: a review.* London, HMSO. (Report for the Department of the Environment.)

Royal Society for the Protection of Birds. 1992. *A shore future. RSPB vision for the coast.* Sandy, Royal Society for the Protection of Birds.

Williams, R. 1989. *A coastal strategy for Wales: pre-prints symposium and workshop: planning and management of the coastal heritage 10-12 October.* RTPI North West Update and Sefton Metropolitan Borough Council.

World Wide Fund For Nature UK. 1994. *Coastal management plans.* Godalming, World Wide Fund For Nature UK. (Marine Update No. 18.)

World Wide Fund For Nature UK. 1994. *International commitments to integrated coastal zone management.* Godalming, World Wide Fund For Nature UK. (Marine Update No. 17.)

World Wide Fund For Nature UK. 1995. *Integrated coastal zone management: UK and European initiatives.* Godalming, World Wide Fund for Nature. (Marine Update No. 19.)

Newsletters

Many national statutory, non-governmental and scientific bodies are now producing publications or newsletters on the subject of coastal management. These provide either information on particular local or national initiatives (such as the statutory or non-governmental organisations' estuaries and firths initiatives) or general information on a range of coastal news (for example the newsletters of Eurocoast UK and the European Union for Coastal Conservation). Some of these publications are listed below. Addresses of those publishing the newsletters are given in section 10.3.5 C.

Coastline UK. Newsletter of the National Coasts and Estuaries Advisory group (NCEAG). Aimed at local authority planners. Published by NCEAG.

Coastline. Quarterly magazine of the European Union for Coastal Conservation (EUCC). Intended to establish a pan-European forum on coastal issues, including coastal management. Published by EUCC.

Coastline. The bulletin of the Parliamentary All Party Coastal Group. Provides information summaries for MPs. Published by the All Party Coastal Group.

CoastNET. The bulletin of the Coastal Heritage Network. A quarterly publication on all matters concerned with coastal management in the UK. Published by the Coastal Heritage Network.

CZM News. Occasional newsletter of Eurocoast UK, reporting on projects and developments in the field of coastal zone management. Published by Eurocoast UK.

SWSFC News. Occasional newsletter of the South Wales Sea Fisheries Committee, by whom it is published.

Wavelength. The Coastal Forum newsletter. Reports the work of the Forum to a wider audience. Published by the Department of the Environment.

National planning/management publications

DoE/Welsh Office. 1992. *Planning policy guidance - coastal planning.* PPG 20. London, HMSO. (Recognises the need to define a coastal zone incorporating areas affected by natural near-shore processes. Advises local authorities to consider the impacts of off-shore and on-shore developments within the full coastal zone. Endorses the precautionary approach.)

DoE/Welsh Office. 1993. *Development below Low Water Mark - a review of regulation in England and Wales.* London, HMSO. (Rejects the 1992 Environment Committee's recommendations for the extension of development controls off-shore. Seeks to strengthen existing arrangements to overcome limitations and drawbacks in the present land-use planning system.)

DoE/Welsh Office. 1993. *Managing the coast: a review of coastal management plans in England and Wales and the powers supporting them.* London, HMSO. (Includes proposals for coastal management plans to be based on a voluntary, multi-agency approach, generally led by local authorities.)

Department of the Environment. 1995. *Policy guidelines for the coast.* London, HMSO. (Highlights government coastal policy and summarises essential guidance.)

House of Commons Environment Committee. 1992. *Second report - coastal zone protection and planning.* London, HMSO. (Recommended that coastal zone management be adopted as the framework for all coastal zone planning and management practice in the United Kingdom. Called for a national coastal strategy, a review of the many organisations responsible for the coast, the extension of planning controls offshore, and the establishment of a Coastal Zone Unit in The Department of the Environment.)

MAFF. 1994. *Shoreline management plans.* London, MAFF. (A procedural guide for operating authorities. 4th draft, July 1994.)

C. Contact names and addresses

(See also Tables 10.2.1 and 10.3.1.)

Organisation/group	Activities	Contact address and telephone no.
Arfordir Group	Local authorities coastal officers' forum in Wales	*Sarah Soffe, Assistant Maritime Policy Officer, CCW HQ, Bangor, tel: 01248 370444
Coastal Forum	Launched in 1994 by the DoE, the Coastal Forum provides for an exchange of views on issues related to the coastal zone in England by a wide range of interested bodies, including central and local government, and conservation, commercial and recreation organisations. Forum proceedings are reported to government ministers.	*Secretariat: Department of the Environment, Room 912, Bristol, tel: 0117 987 8003
CoastNET (Coastal Heritage Network)	An independent Charitable Trust and membership organisation. Established in 1995 by the Countryside Commission, English Nature and Scottish Natural Heritage with a part-time secretariat. Links individuals and organisations working for the sustainable management of the coastal and marine environment.	CoastNET, The Manchester Metropolitan University, St. Augustines, Lower Chatham Street, Manchester M15 6BY, tel: 0161 247 1067
Coastal Technical Officers Group	The coastal group of the statutory conservation agencies (English Nature, Scottish Natural Heritage, Countryside Council for Wales, Department of the Environment for Northern Ireland, Joint Nature Conservation Committee and the Countryside Commission)	*Coastal Technical Officers Group: English Nature, Maritime Team, Peterborough, tel: 01733 340345 (secretariat)
Countryside Council for Wales	Coastal management of designated sites	*Mike Gash, Maritime Policy Officer, CCW HQ, Bangor, tel: 01248 370444
English Coastal Groups Forum	Established by MAFF in 1991. Coordinates the work of the English Coastal Groups (see section 10.1.3); promotes the formation of coastal groups; acts as a link between centrally-based organisations and coastal groups; promotes sustainable coastal management and common standards. Forum members include one representative from each coastal group, the Environment Agency, Local Authority Associations, English Nature, Railtrack and Department of the Environment.	*R. Hathaway, Head of Flood and Coastal Defence Division, MAFF, London, tel: 0171 238 6660
English Nature	Management of designated coastal sites; nature conservation and development planning, Estuaries Initiative, Sensitive Marine Areas, Maritime Natural Areas	*English Nature HQ, Peterborough, tel: 01733 340345
Environment Agency	Local Environmental Action Plans, sea defences	*Flood Defence Section, Environment Agency HQ, Bristol, tel. 01454 624400, or *Welsh Region, Plas-yr-Afon, Cardiff, tel: 01222 770088, or *South Western Region, Exeter, tel: 01392 444000, or *Severn-Trent Region, Solihull, tel: 0121 711 2324
Eurocoast UK	The Eurocoast Association aims to improve the basis for protection, development and management of the coastal zone. Primarily a communication network.	Eurocoast UK, Burderop Park, Swindon, Wiltshire SN4 0QD, tel: 01793 812479
European Union for Coastal Conservation (EUCC)	International grouping of organisations and individuals with an interest in coastal nature conservation matters, including coastal management.	European Union for Coastal Conservation (EUCC) Secretariat, PO Box 11059, NL-2301 EB Leiden, tel: +31 71 122900/123952
Joint Nature Conservation Committee - Geology / Coastal Advisor	Advice and information on coastal conservation in Great Britain as a whole and internationally	*JNCC, Peterborough, tel: 01733 62626
JNCC Coastal Directories Team	Project to produce a series of publications *(Coasts and seas of the United Kingdom)* giving baseline coastal and marine environmental, management and human use information on a regional basis	*JNCC, Peterborough, tel: 01733 62626
Joint Nature Conservation Committee - Marine Advisor	Advice and information on marine nature conservation in Great Britain as a whole and internationally	*JNCC, Peterborough, tel: 01733 62626

C. Contact names and addresses (continued)

(See also Tables 10.2.1 and 10.3.1.)

Organisation/group	Activities	Contact address and telephone no.
JNCC Marine Nature Conservation Review	Project to extend knowledge of benthic marine habitats, communities and species in Great Britain and identify sites and species of nature conservation importance; producing a series of 15 reports *(Coasts and seas of the United Kingdom. MNCR series.)* on a coastal sector basis, as well as more detailed area summaries.	*JNCC, Peterborough, tel: 01733 62626
Les Esturiales Environmental Study Group	International programme for co-operation, the exchange of experience on estuarine management and personal contacts between local authority practitioners in Europe.	Esturiales Environmental Study Group, Prof. Graham King, CZM Associates, 2 Newton Villas, Newton, Swansea SA3 4SS, tel: 01792 367552
Marine Conservation Society	Provides advice and supports local coastal management initiatives: runs grant-aided coastal management workshops and courses for coastal managers; promotes the establishment of voluntary coastal groups.	*Marine Conservation Society, Ross-on-Wye, tel: 01989 566017
Marine Forum	National network provides forum for discussion of marine issues relating to the seas around UK. Members include governmental and non-governmental organisations and individuals. Occasional seminars are held, covering a range of topics including coastal management.	Honorary Secretary, The Marine Forum for Environmental Issues, c/o University College Scarborough, Filey Road, Scarborough YO11 3AZ, tel: 01723 362392
Ministry of Agriculture, Fisheries and Food (MAFF) Flood & Coastal Defence Division	Shoreline Management Plans	*MAFF, Flood and Coastal Defence Division, Eastbury House, London, tel: 0171 238 3000
MAFF, Marine Environment Protection Division	Policy advice on marine environmental management	MAFF, Marine Environment Protection Division, Nobel House, 17 Smith Square, London SW1P 3HX, tel: 0171 238 6433
MAFF, Directorate of Fisheries Research	Scientific advice on marine environment and living resources management	*Head of Laboratory, MAFF Directorate of Fisheries Research, Fisheries Laboratory, Conwy, tel: 01492 593883
National Coasts and Estuaries Advisory Group (NCEAG)	On behalf of local authorities, provides advice on sustainable management of coastal and estuarine environments; published guide to good practice (NCEAG 1993)	Environment Programme Manager, National Coasts and Estuaries Advisory Group (NCEAG), Environment Programme, Kent County Council, Springfield, Maidstone ME14 2LX, tel: 01622 696180
National Trust	Has extensive coastal land holdings in the region (see section 7.5.1). Recently carried out a complete review of its Coastal Strategy Plans; has an ongoing review of coastal site management plans.	*National Trust, Cirencester, tel: 01285 651818, or *NT Cornwall Office, Bodmin, Cornwall PL30 4DE, tel: 01208 74281, or *NT Devon Office, Exeter, Devon EX5 3LE, tel: 01392 881691, or *NT Wessex Office (includes Somerset and Avon), Warminster, Wilts BA12 9HW, tel: 01985 843600, or *NT Severn Office (includes Gloucestershire), Tewkesbury, tel: 01684 850051, or *NT South Wales Office, Llandeilo, Dyfed SA19 6BB, tel: 01558 822800
Royal Society for the Protection of Birds	Launched national campaign in 1990 to promote the importance of estuaries in the UK. Monitors the development of coastal zone initiatives around the UK. In 1994, launched Marine Life campaign, to increase awareness and to promote integrated coastal and marine management. Manages some coastal nature reserves. Produced a regional strategy.	*D. Huggett, Coastal Policy Officer, RSPB HQ, Sandy, tel: 01767 68055

C. Contact names and addresses (continued)

(See also Tables 10.2.1 and 10.3.1.)

Organisation/group	*Activities*	*Contact address and telephone no.*
Welsh Coastal Groups Forum	Coordinates the work of the Welsh coastal groups	*Hugh Payne, Welsh Coastal Groups Forum, Environment Division, Welsh Office, Cardiff, tel: 01222 823176
The Wildlife Trusts	Have extensive coastal land holdings throughout the UK. Actively involved in coastal zone initiatives in this region. Manage some voluntary conservation areas. Have extensive experience of coastal interpretation, marine survey and policy work.	Joan Edwards, Marine Conservation Officer, The Wildlife Trusts, The Green, Witham Park, Waterside South, Lincoln LN5 7JR, tel: 01522 544400
World Wide Fund for Nature - UK	Provides funding for research, local voluntary policy development and local initiatives, and publications on integrated coastal management. Draws on considerable international experience with coastal management initiatives.	*World Wide Fund for Nature - UK, Godalming, tel: 01483 426444

Addresses and telephone numbers of local planning authorities are given in full in the Appendix, as are *starred contact addresses.

Leisure and tourism are very important to this region, where every outdoor leisure activity imaginable is catered for. Here at Cotty's Point, Perranporth, paragliding off the cliff is the chosen - heartstopping - pursuit. Photo: Bill Sanderson, JNCC.

Appendix

A1 Frequently cited contact names and addresses

Name	Contact address and telephone no.
Statutory bodies	
British Oceanographic Data Centre - NERC (BODC), Proudman Oceanographic Laboratory	Bidston Observatory, Birkenhead, Merseyside L43 7RA, tel: 0151 652 3950
Countryside Commission (CC), HQ	John Dower House, Crescent Place, Cheltenham, Gloucestershire GL50 3RA, tel: 01242 521381
CC, South Western Region	Bridge House, Sion Place, Clifton Down, Bristol BS8 4AS, tel: 0117 973 9966
Countryside Council for Wales (CCW) HQ	Plas Penrhos, Fford Penrhos, Bangor, Gwynedd LL57 2LQ, tel: 01248 370444
CCW South Wales Area Office	Unit 4, Castleton Court, Fortran Road, St. Mellons, Cardiff CF3 0LT, tel: 01222 772400
CCW Abergavenny Sub-Office	Unit 13B, Mill Street Industrial Estate, Abergavenny, Gwent NP7 5HE, tel: 01873 857938
Department of the Environment (DoE), European Wildlife Division / Department of Rural Affairs	DoE, Tollgate House, Houlton Street, Bristol BS2 9DJ, tel: 0117 987 8000
DoE, Water Resources and Marine	Romney House, 43 Marsham Street, London SW1P 3PY, tel: 0171 276 0900
English Nature (EN) HQ	Northminster House, Peterborough PE1 1UA, tel: 01733 340345
EN Cornwall Office	Trevint House, Strangways Villas, Truro, Cornwall TR1 2PA, tel: 01872 262550
EN Devon Office	The Old Mill House, 37 North Street, Okehampton, Devon EX20 1AR, tel: 01837 55045
EN Somerset Local Team	Roughmoor, Bishop's Hull, Taunton, Somerset TA1 5AA, tel: 01823 283211
EN Three Counties Team (serves Gloucestershire)	Masefield House, Wells Road, Malvern Wells, Worcestershire WR14 4PA, tel: 01684 560616
Environment Agency (EA) HQ	Rio House, Waterside Drive, Aztec West, Almondsbury, Bristol BS12 4UD, tel: 01454 624400
EA South West Region	Manley House, Kestrel Way, Exeter EX2 7LQ, tel: 01392 444000
EA Midlands Region	Sapphire East, 550 Streetsbrook Road, Solihull B91 1QT, tel: 0121 711 2324

Name	Contact address and telephone no.
Statutory bodies (continued)	
EA Welsh Region	Plas-yr-Afon, St. Mellons Business Park, St. Mellons, Cardiff CF3 0LT, tel: 01222 770088
Institute of Terrestrial Ecology (ITE), Monks Wood	Abbots Ripton, Huntingdon, Cambridgeshire PE17 2LS, tel: 01487 773381
Joint Nature Conservation Committee (JNCC), HQ	Monkstone House, City Road, Peterborough, Cambs. PE1 1JY, tel: 01733 62626
JNCC Seabirds and Cetaceans Project	Seabirds and Cetaceans Project, Joint Nature Conservation Committee, Dunnet House, 7 Thistle Place, Aberdeen AB1 1UZ, tel: 01224 655700
Ministry of Agriculture, Fisheries and Food (MAFF) Directorate of Fisheries Research (DFR) Fisheries Laboratory, Conwy	Benarth Road, Conwy, Gwynedd LL32 8UB, tel: 01492 593883
MAFF DFR, Fisheries Laboratory, Lowestoft	Pakefield Road, Lowestoft, Suffolk NR33 OHT, tel: 01502 562244
MAFF DFR, Fisheries Laboratory, Burnham-on-Crouch	Remembrance Avenue, Burnham-on-Crouch, Essex CM0 8HA, tel: 01621 787 200
MAFF Flood and Coastal Defence Division	Eastbury House, 30/34 Albert Embankment, London SE1 7TL, tel: 0171 238 3000
Welsh Office (Y Swyddfa Gymreig), Environment Division; Agriculture Department	Parc Cathays, Cardiff CF1 3NQ, tel: 01222 825111
Coastal fora	
Marine Forum for Environmental Issues	Honorary Secretary, The Marine Forum for Environmental Issues, c/o University College Scarborough, Filey Road, Scarborough YO11 3AZ, tel: 01723 362392
National voluntary bodies	
British Trust for Ornithology	The Nunnery, Nunnery Place, Thetford, Norfolk IP24 2PU, tel: 01842 750050
Marine Conservation Society	9 Gloucester Road, Ross-on-Wye, Herefordshire HR9 5BU, tel: 01989 566017
National Trust (NT) Coast and Countryside Adviser	33 Sheep Street, Cirencester, Gloucestershire GL7 1RQ, tel: 01285 651818
NT Cornwall Office	Lanhydrock, Bodmin, Cornwall PL30 4DE, tel: 01208 74281

Name	Contact address and telephone no.
National voluntary bodies (continued)	
NT Devon Office	Killerton House, Broadclyft, Exeter, Devon EX5 3LE, tel: 01392 881691
NT Wessex Office (includes Somerset and Avon)	Eastleigh Court, Bishopstrow, Warminster, Wilts BA12 9HW, tel: 01985 843600
NT Severn Office (includes Gloucestershire)	Mythe End House, Tewkesbury, Gloucestershire GL20 6EB, tel: 01684 850051
NT South Wales Office	The Kings Head, Bridge Street, Llandeilo, Dyfed SA19 6BB, tel: 01558 822800
Royal Society for the Protection of Birds (RSPB) HQ	The Lodge, Sandy, Bedfordshire SG19 2DL, tel: 01767 680551
RSPB South West England Regional Office	10 Richmond Road, Exeter, Devon EX4 4JA, tel: 01392 432691
RSPB Central England Office (includes Gloucestershire)	46 The Green, South Bar, Banbury, Oxon OX16 9AB, tel: 01295 253330
RSPB Wales Office	Bryn Adern, The Bank, Newtown, Powys SY16 2AB, tel: 01686 626678
Wildfowl & Wetlands Trust (WWT), HQ	Slimbridge, Gloucestershire GL2 7BX, tel: 01453 890333

Name	Contact address and telephone no.
National voluntary bodies (continued)	
Worldwide Fund For Nature - UK	Panda House, Weyside Park, Cattershall Lane, Godalming, Surrey GU7 1XR, tel: 01483 426444
County Wildlife Trusts	
Cornwall Wildlife Trust	Five Acres, Allet, Truro TR4 9DJ, tel: 01872 273939
Devon Wildlife Trust	Shirehampton House, 35-37 St. David's Hill, Exeter, Devon EX4 4DA, tel: 01392 79244
Somerset Wildlife Trust	Fyne Court, Broomfield, Bridgwater TA5 2EQ, tel: 01823 451587
The Wildlife Trust for Bristol, Bath & Avon	The Wildlife Centre, 32 Jacob's Wells Road, Bristol BS8 1DR, tel: 0117 926 8018
Gloucestershire Wildlife Trust	The Dulverton Building, Robins Wood Hill Country Park, Reservoir Road, Gloucester GL4 6SX, tel: 01452 383333
Gwent Wildlife Trust	16 White Swan Court, Monmouth NP5 3NY, tel: 01600 715501
Glamorgan Wildlife Trust	Nature Centre, Fountain Road, Tondu, Bridgend CF32 0EH, tel: 01656 724100

A.2 Local planning authorities; port and harbour authorities

Authority	Address and telephone no.
Bridgend	Bridgend County Borough Council, Civic Buildings, PO Box 4, Angel Street, Bridgend CF31 1LX, tel: 01656 643643
Bristol	Bristol City Council, The Council House, College Green, Bristol BS1 5TR, tel: 0117 922 2000
Cardiff	Cardiff County Council, City Hall, Cardiff CF1 3ND, tel: 01222 872000
Carrick	Carrick District Council Carrick House, Pydar Street, Truro TR1 1EB, tel: 01872 278131
Cornwall	Cornwall County Council, County Hall, Truro, Cornwall TR1 3AY, tel: 01872 322000
Devon	Devon County Council, County Hall, Exeter EX2 4QD, tel: 01392 382000
Forest of Dean	Forest of Dean District Council, Council Offices, High Street, Coleford GL16 8HG, tel: 01594 810000
Gloucestershire	Gloucestershire County Council, Shire Hall, Gloucester GL1 2TG, tel: 01452 425000
Isles of Scilly	The Council of the Isles of Scilly, Town Hall, St. Mary's TR21 0LW, tel: 01720 422537

Authority	Address and telephone no.
Kerrier	Kerrier District Council, Council Offices, Dolcoath Avenue, Camborne TR14 8RY, tel: 01209 712941
Monmouthshire	Monmouthshire County Council, Mamhilad House, Mamhilad Park Estate, Pontypool NP4 0YL, tel: 01495 762311
Newport	County Borough of Newport, Civic Centre, Newport NP9 4UR, tel: 01633 244491
North Cornwall	North Cornwall District Council, Council Offices, Higher Trenant Road, Wadebridge PL27 6TW, tel: 01208 812255
North Devon	North Devon District Council, Civic Centre, North Walk, Barnstaple EX31 1EA, tel: 01271 327711
North Somerset	North Somerset District Council, Town Hall, Weston-super-Mare BS23 1UJ, tel: 01934 631701
Penwith	Penwith District Council, Council Offices, St. Clare, Penzance TR18 3QW, tel: 01736 62341
Restormel	Restormel District Council, Borough Offices, 39 Penwinnick Road, St. Austell PL25 5DR, tel: 01726 74466

Authority	Address and telephone no.
Sedgemoor	Sedgemoor District Council, Bridgwater House, King Square, Bridgwater TA6 3AR, tel: 01278 435435
Somerset	Somerset County Council, County Hall, Taunton TA1 4DY, tel: 01823 333451
South Gloucestershire	South Gloucestershire Council, Council Offices, Castle Street, Thornbury, Bristol BS12 1HF, tel: 01454 416262
Stroud	Stroud District Council, Ebley Mill, Westward Road, Stroud GL5 4UB, tel: 01453 766321
Torridge	Torridge District Council, Riverbank House, Bideford EX39 2QG, tel: 01237 476711
Vale of Glamorgan	Vale of Glamorgan County Borough Council, Civic Offices, Holton Road, Barry CF6 6RU, tel: 01466 700111
West Somerset	West Somerset District Council, Council Offices, 20 Fore Street, Williton, Taunton TA4 4QA, tel: 01984 632291
Port and Harbour Authorities:	
Barry (Associated British Ports)	Pierhead Building, Bute Docks, Cardiff CF1 5TH, tel: 01222 471311
Bideford Harbour (Torridge District Council)	The Town Hall, Bideford, Devon EX39 2HS, tel: 01237 476711
Bristol (Bristol Port Company)	St. Andrews Road, Avonmouth, Bristol BS11 9DQ, tel: 0117 982 0000
Port and Harbour Authorities (continued):	
Cardiff (Associated British Ports)	Pierhead Building, Bute Docks, Cardiff CF1 5TH, tel: 01222 471311
Falmouth Harbour Commissioners	44 Arwenack Street, Falmouth, Cornwall TR11 3JQ tel: 01326 312285 & 314379 (leisure); 211376 (commercial)
Falmouth Docks	A&P Ltd., The Docks, Falmouth, Cornwall TR11 4NR, tel: 01326 212100
Gloucester Harbour Trustees	Llanthony Warehouse, The Docks, Gloucester GL1 2EJ, tel: 01452 25524
Newlyn Pier and Harbour Commissioners	Harbour Office, Newlyn, Penzance, Cornwall TR18 5HW, tel: 01736 62523
Newport Docks (Associated British Ports)	Alexandra Dock, Newport, Gwent NP9 2UW, tel: 01633 244411
Newport Harbour Commissioners	25 Lower Dock Street, Newport, Gwent NP9 1EG, tel: 01633 265702
Padstow Harbour Commissioners	Harbour Office, South Quay, Padstow, Cornwall PL28 8AQ, tel: 01841 532239
Penryn Harbour (Carrick District Council)	Carrick House, Pydar Street, Truro, Cornwall TR1 1EB, tel: 01872 278131
Penzance Harbour (Penwith District Council)	The Council Offices, St. Clare, Penzance, Cornwall TR18 3QW, tel: 01736 62341
Sharpness Docks (British Waterways Board)	Dock Office, The Docks, Sharpness, Berkeley, Gloucester GL13 9UX, tel: 01453 811644
Truro Harbour (Carrick District Council)	Carrick House, Pydar Street, Truro, Cornwall TR1 1EB, tel: 01872 278131

A.3 Core reading list

There are a number of important publications that either provide information on a variety of topics covered in these regional reports (and so are frequently referred to) or give a good overview of regional and national information on coasts and seas. They are listed below.

Barne, J., Davidson, N.C., Hill, T.O., & Jones, M. 1994. *Coastal and marine UKDMAP datasets: a user manual.* Peterborough, Joint Nature Conservation Committee.

British Oceanographic Data Centre. 1992. *United Kingdom digital marine atlas (UKDMAP). User guide. Version 2.0.* Birkenhead, Natural Environment Research Council, British Oceanographic Data Centre.

Brown, A. 1992. *The UK environment.* London, HMSO

Buck, A.L. 1993. *An inventory of UK estuaries. 2. South-west Britain.* Peterborough, Joint Nature Conservation Committee.

Buck, A.L. In prep. *An inventory of UK estuaries. 6. Southern England.* Peterborough, Joint Nature Conservation Committee.

Cordrey, L. 1996. *The biodiversity of the south-west: an audit of the south-west biological resource.* A report prepared by RSPB, the County Wildlife Trusts and the South West Regional Planning Conference.

Davidson, N.C., Laffoley, D.d'A., Doody, J.P., Way, L.S., Gordon, J., Key, R., Drake, C.M., Pienkowski, M.W., Mitchell, R., & Duff, K.L. 1991. *Nature conservation and estuaries in Great Britain.* Peterborough, Nature Conservancy Council.

Department of the Environment. 1995. *Policy guidelines for the coast.* London, HMSO.

Devon County Council. 1995. *Devon coastal statement.* Exeter, Devon County Council.

Eno, N.C., *ed.* 1991. *Marine conservation handbook.* 2nd ed. Peterborough, English Nature.

Environment Agency. 1996. *The environment of England and Wales: a snapshot.* Bristol, Environment Agency

Gubbay, S. 1988. *A coastal directory for marine conservation.* Ross-on-Wye, Marine Conservation Society.

Lee, A.J., & Ramster, J.W. 1981. *Atlas of the seas around the British Isles.* Lowestoft, MAFF.

Robinson, A., & Millward, R. 1983. *The Shell book of the British coast.* Newton Abbot, David and Charles.

Steers, J.A. 1964. *The coastline of England and Wales.* 2nd ed., 112-183 (Geology and geomorphology). Cambridge, Cambridge University Press.

SWRPCON. 1994. *South West Regional Planning Conference: regional strategy. The landscape, coast and historic environment of the south west.* Somerset, South West Regional Planning Conference.

A.4 Contributing authors

Author	Address
Dr M. Aprahamian	Environment Agency - North West Region, Fisheries Department, PO Box 12, Richard Fairclough House, Knutsford Road, Warrington WA4 1HG
Dr R.N. Bamber	Fawley Aquatic Research Laboratories Ltd, Marine and Freshwater Biology Unit, Fawley, Southampton, Hants. SO4 1TW
Dr R.S.K. Barnes	Department of Zoology, Downing Street, Cambridge CB2 3EJ
British Geological Survey	Coastal Geology Group, BGS, Keyworth, Nottingham NG12 5GG
D.M. Craddock	JNCC, Monkstone House, City Road, Peterborough PE1 1JY
C.A. Crumpton	RSK Environment, 47 West Street, Dorking, Surrey RH4 1BU
Dr T.C.D. Dargie	Loch Fleet View, Skelbo Street, Dornoch, Scotland IV25 3QQ
Dr N.C. Davidson	JNCC, Monkstone House, City Road, Peterborough PE1 1JY
Dr J.P. Doody	JNCC, Monkstone House, City Road, Peterborough PE1 1JY
C.D. Duck	NERC Sea Mammal Research Unit (SMRU), University of St. Andrews, School of Biochemical and Medical Sciences, St. Andrews, Fife KY16 8LB
M.J. Dunbar	Nature Conservation Bureau, 36 Kingfisher Court, Hambridge Road, Newbury, Berkshire RG1 5SJ
M. Edwards	Sir Alister Hardy Foundation for Ocean Science, c/o Plymouth Marine Laboratory, Citadel Hill, Plymouth, Devon PL1 2PB
Dr P.G.H. Evans	Seawatch Foundation, Dept of Zoology, University of Oxford, South Parks Road, Oxford OX1 3PS
S.J. Everett	Nature Conservation Bureau, 36 Kingfisher Court, Hambridge Road, Newbury, Berkshire RG14 5SJ
V. Fenwick	Riverbank House, River Road, Taplow, Maidenhead SL6 0BG
A.P. Foster	23 The Dawneys, Crudwell, Malmesbury, Wiltshire SN16 9HE
S.L. Fowler	Nature Conservation Bureau, 36 Kingfisher Court, Hambridge Road, Newbury, Berkshire RG14 5SJ
A. Gale	Riverbank House, River Road, Taplow, Maidenhead SL6 0BG

Author	Address
Dr H.T. Gee	SGS Environment, Yorkshire House, Chapel St., Liverpool L3 9AG
M.J. Goodwin	RSK Environment, 47 West Street, Dorking, Surrey RH4 1BU
Dr M.I. Hill	SGS Environment, Yorkshire House, Chapel St., Liverpool L3 9AG
N.G. Hodgetts	JNCC, Monkstone House, City Road, Peterborough PE1 1JY
R.A. Irving	14 Brookland Way, Coldwaltham, Pulborough, W. Sussex RH20 1LT
A.W.G. John	Sir Alister Hardy Foundation for Ocean Science, c/o Plymouth Marine Laboratory, Citadel Hill, Plymouth, Devon PL1 2PB
R.G. Keddie	JNCC, Monkstone House, City Road, Peterborough PE1 1JY
K. Meakin	SGS Environment, Units 15 & 16, Pebble Close, Amington, Tamworth, Staffs. B77 4RD
V.M. Morgan	2 Flaxen Walk, Warboys, Huntingdon PE17 2TR
M.S. Parsons	3 Stanton Road, Raynes Park, London SW20 8RL
Dr M.G. Pawson	Ministry of Agriculture, Fisheries and Food, Directorate of Fisheries Research, Fisheries Laboratory, Pakefield Road, Lowestoft, Suffolk NR33 OHT
Dr G.W. Potts	The Marine Biological Association of the UK, The Laboratory, Citadel Hill, Plymouth PL1 2PB
Dr R.E. Randall	Girton College, Huntingdon Road, Cambridge CB3 0JG
C.F. Robson	JNCC, Monkstone House, City Road, Peterborough PE1 1JY
Dr W.G. Sanderson	JNCC, Monkstone House, City Road, Peterborough PE1 1JY
D.A. Stroud	JNCC, Monkstone House, City Road, Peterborough PE1 1JY
S.E. Swaby	The Marine Biological Association of the UK, The Laboratory, Citadel Hill, Plymouth PL1 2PB
Dr M.J.S. Swan	19 St. Judith's Lane, Sawtry, Huntingdon, Cambs. PE17 5XE
M.L. Tasker	JNCC, Thistle House, 7 Thistle Place, Aberdeen AB1 1UZ
Dr C.E. Turtle	SGS Environment, Units 15 & 16, Pebble Close, Amington, Tamworth, Staffs. B77 4RD